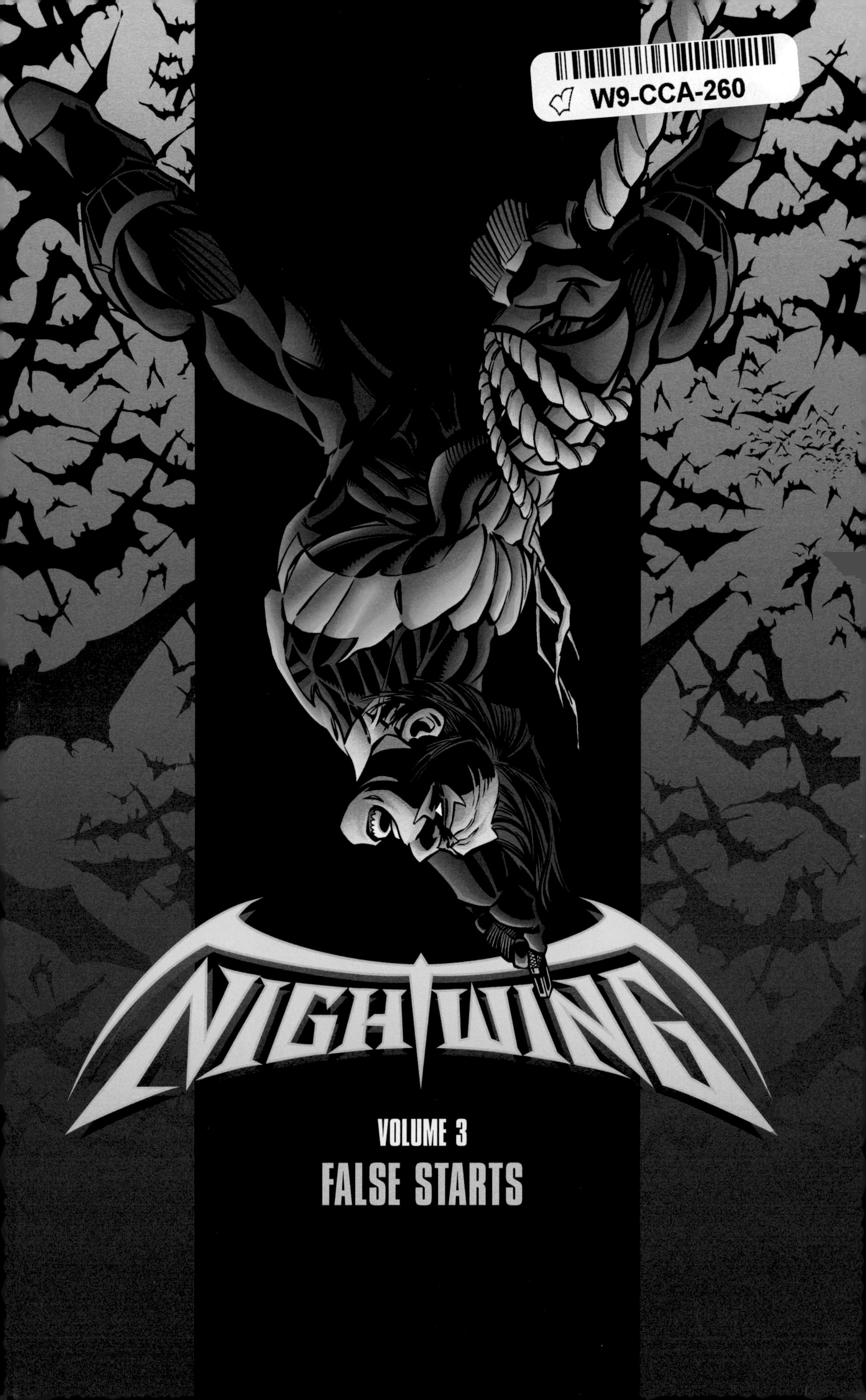
NIGHTWING
VOLUME 3
FALSE STARTS

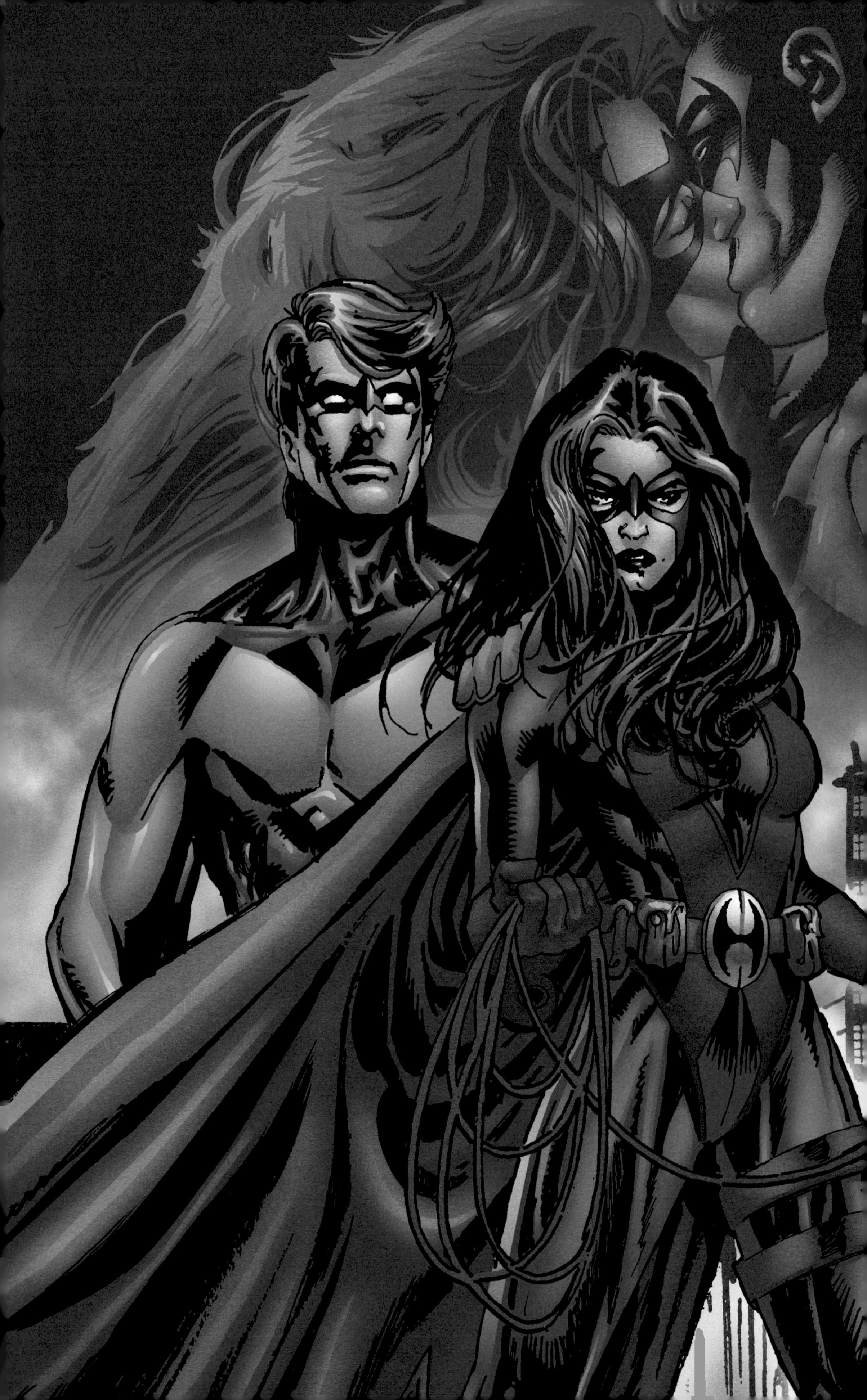

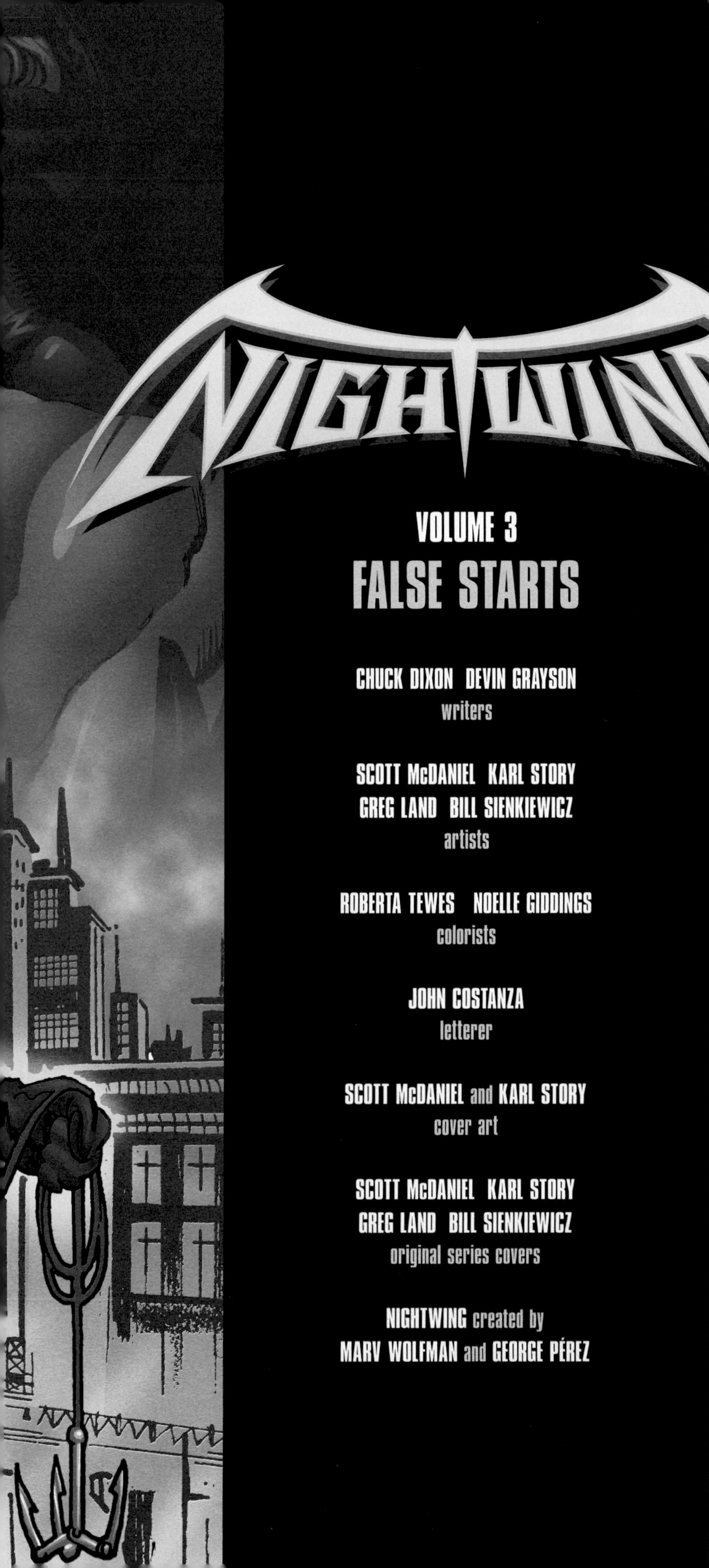

NIGHTWING

VOLUME 3
FALSE STARTS

CHUCK DIXON DEVIN GRAYSON
writers

SCOTT McDANIEL KARL STORY
GREG LAND BILL SIENKIEWICZ
artists

ROBERTA TEWES NOELLE GIDDINGS
colorists

JOHN COSTANZA
letterer

SCOTT McDANIEL and KARL STORY
cover art

SCOTT McDANIEL KARL STORY
GREG LAND BILL SIENKIEWICZ
original series covers

NIGHTWING created by
MARV WOLFMAN and GEORGE PÉREZ

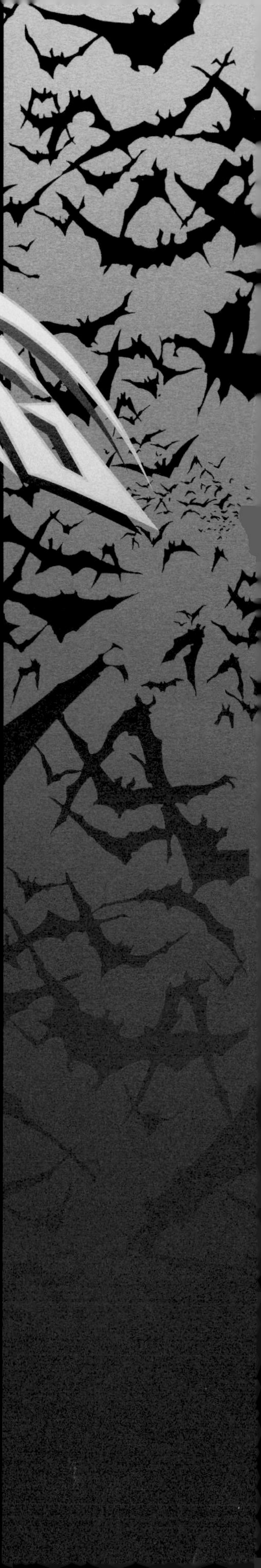

TABLE OF CONTENTS

Scott Peterson Editor – Original Series   Darren Vincenzo Associate Editor – Original Series
Jeb Woodard Group Editor – Collected Editions   Paul Santos Editor – Collected Edition
Sarabeth Kett Publication Design

Bob Harras Senior VP – Editor-in-Chief, DC Comics

Diane Nelson President
Dan DiDio and Jim Lee Co-Publishers
Geoff Johns Chief Creative Officer
Amit Desai Senior VP – Marketing & Global Franchise Management
Nairi Gardiner Senior VP – Finance
Sam Ades VP – Digital Marketing
Bobbie Chase VP – Talent Development
Mark Chiarello Senior VP – Art, Design & Collected Editions
John Cunningham VP – Content Strategy
Anne DePies VP – Strategy Planning & Reporting
Don Falletti VP – Manufacturing Operations
Lawrence Ganem VP – Editorial Administration & Talent Relations
Alison Gill Senior VP – Manufacturing & Operations
Hank Kanalz Senior VP – Editorial Strategy & Administration
Jay Kogan VP – Legal Affairs
Derek Maddalena Senior VP – Sales & Business Development
Jack Mahan VP – Business Affairs
Dan Miron VP – Sales Planning & Trade Development
Nick Napolitano VP – Manufacturing Administration
Carol Roeder VP – Marketing
Eddie Scannell VP – Mass Account & Digital Sales
Courtney Simmons Senior VP – Publicity & Communications
Jim (Ski) Sokolowski VP – Comic Book Specialty & Newsstand Sales
Sandy Yi Senior VP – Global Franchise Management

NIGHTWING VOL. 3: FALSE STARTS

Published by DC Comics. Compilation Copyright © 2015 DC Comics. All Rights Reserved.

Originally published in single magazine form in NIGHTWING 19-25; NIGHTWING/HUNTRESS 1-4;
NIGHTWING 1/2. Copyright © 1996, 1998 DC Comics. All Rights Reserved. All characters, their
distinctive likenesses and related elements featured in this publication are trademarks of DC Comics.
The stories, characters and incidents featured in this publication are entirely fictional.
DC Comics does not read or accept unsolicited submissions of ideas, stories or artwork.

DC Comics, 2900 West Alameda Avenue, Burbank, CA 91505
Printed by RR Donnelley, Salem, VA, USA. 11/27/15. First printing.
ISBN: 978-1-4012-5855-9

Dixon, Chuck, 1954-
  Nightwing. Volume 3 / Chuck Dixon, writer ; Scott McDaniel, Karl Story, artists.
      pages cm
  ISBN 978-1-4012-5855-9 (paperback)
  1. Graphic novels. I. McDaniel, Scott, illustrator. II. Story, Karl C., illustrator. III. Title.
  PN6728.N55D55 2016
  741.5'973–dc23
                            2015034659

PEFC Certified

Printed on paper from
sustainably managed
forests and controlled
sources

PEFC/29-31-75   www.pefc.org

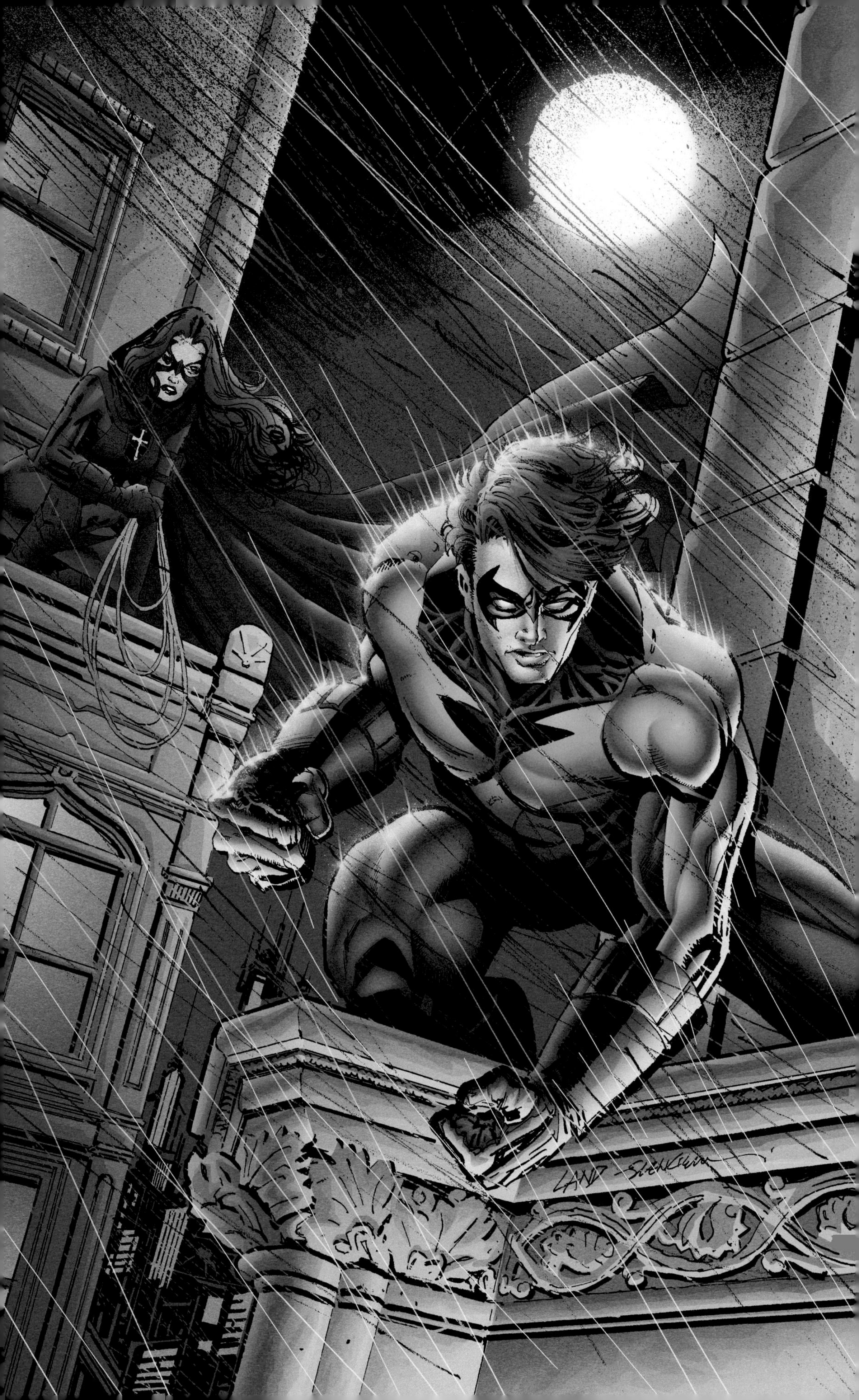

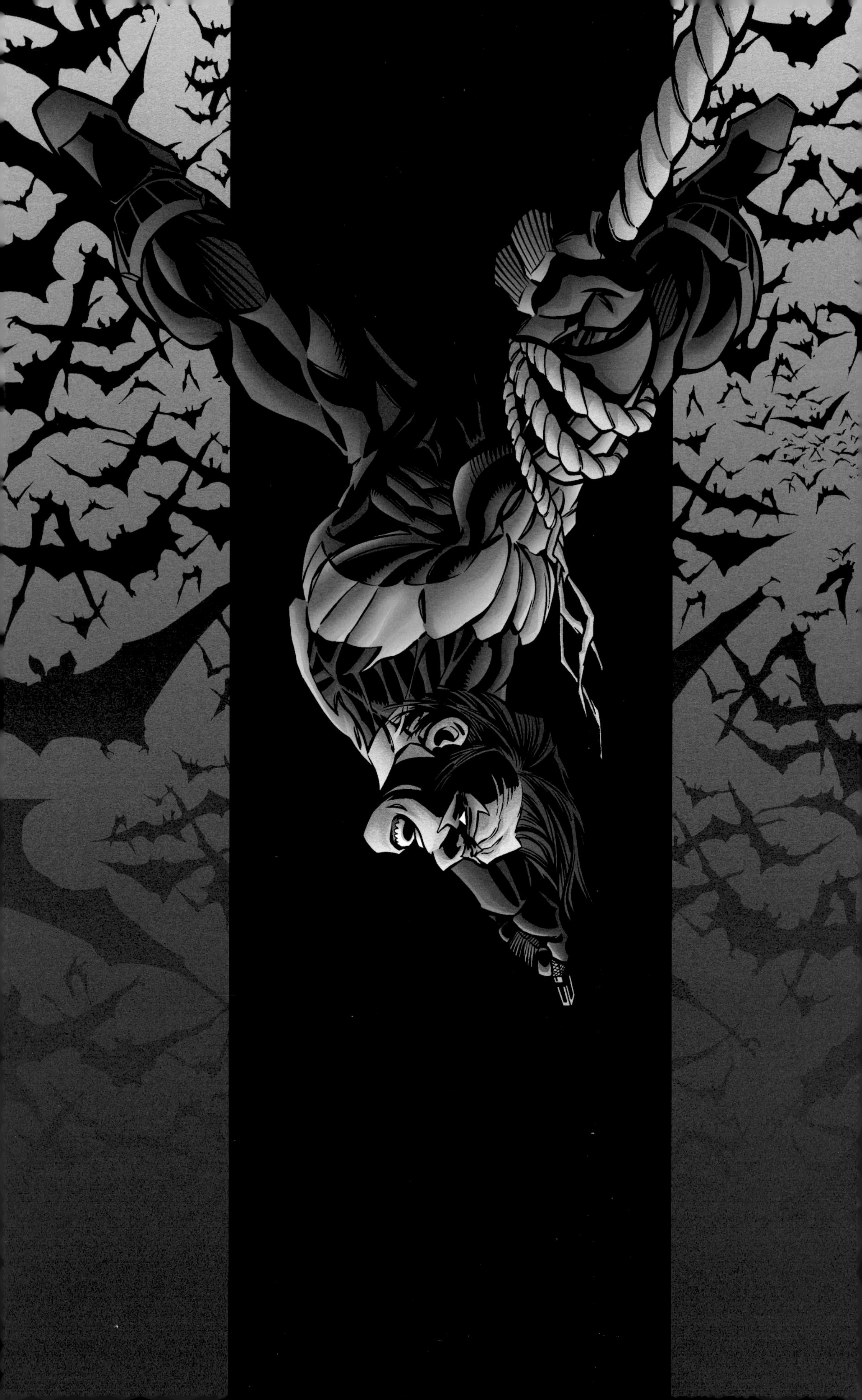

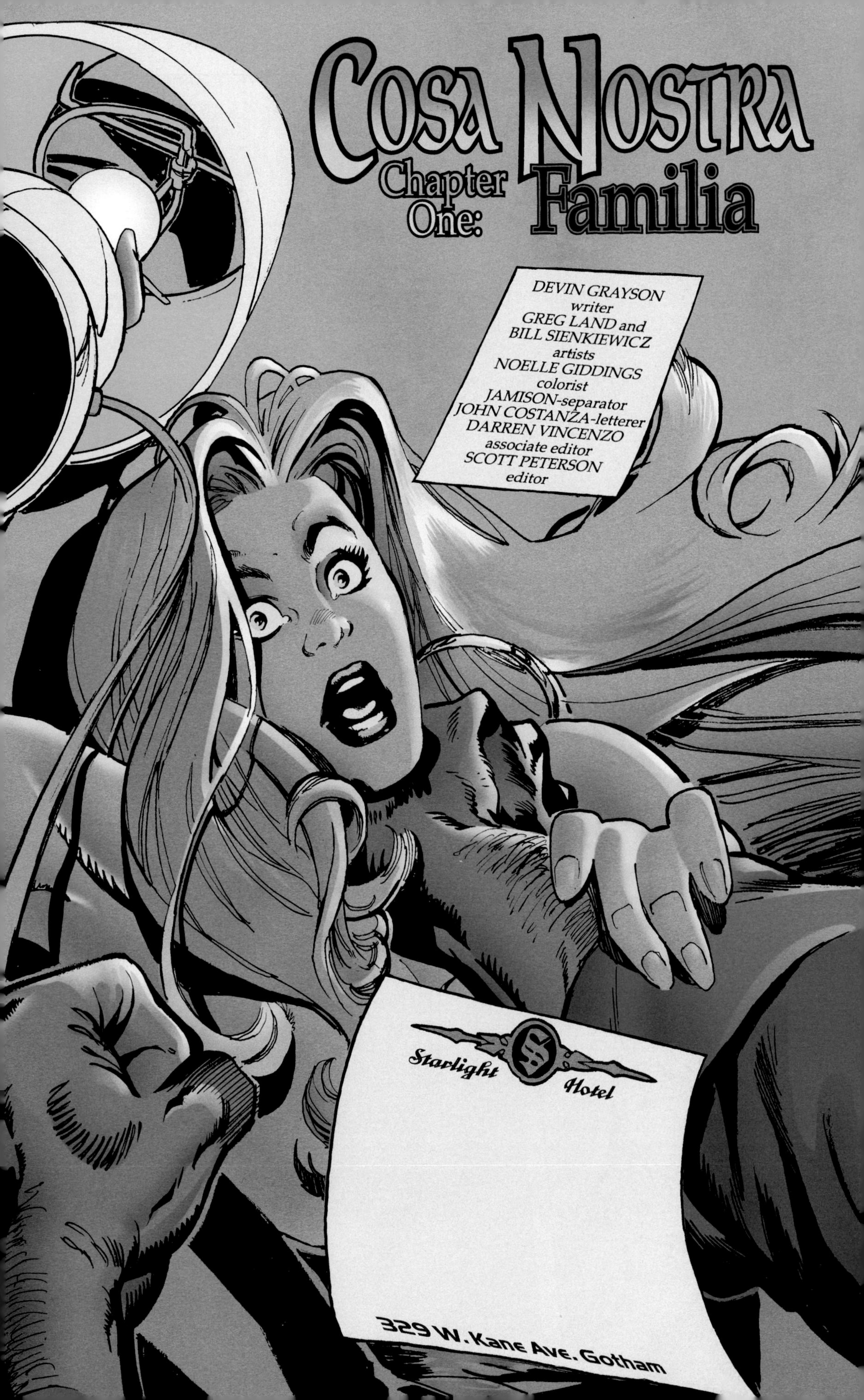

COSA NOSTRA
Chapter One: Familia
DEVIN GRAYSON writer
GREG LAND and BILL SIENKIEWICZ artists
NOELLE GIDDINGS colorist
JAMISON-separator
JOHN COSTANZA-letterer
DARREN VINCENZO associate editor
SCOTT PETERSON editor
Starlight Hotel
329 W. Kane Ave. Gotham

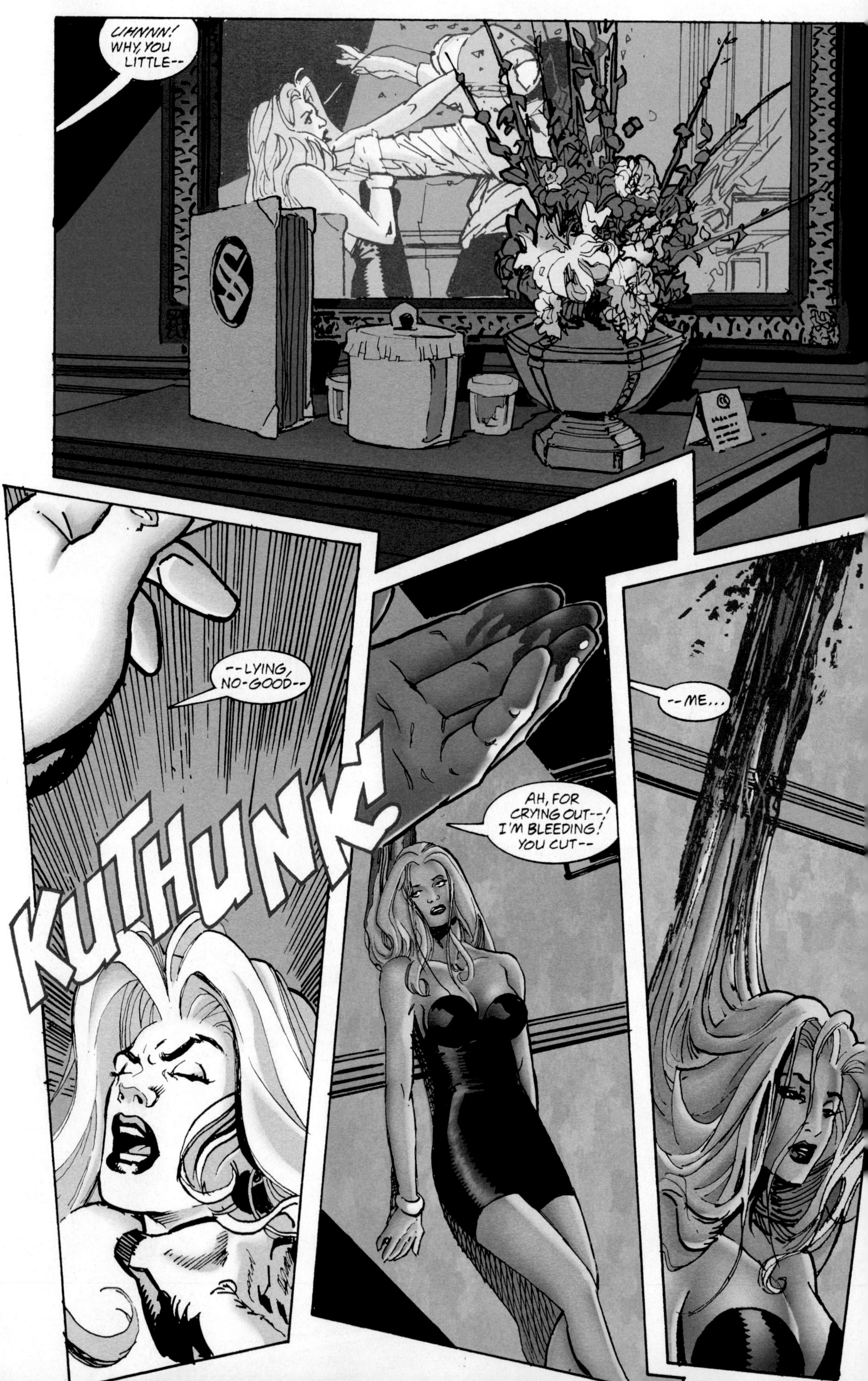
UHNNN! WHY, YOU LITTLE--
--LYING, NO-GOOD--
KUTHUNK
AH, FOR CRYING OUT--! I'M BLEEDING! YOU CUT--
--ME...

OH, MAN, OH, MAN!

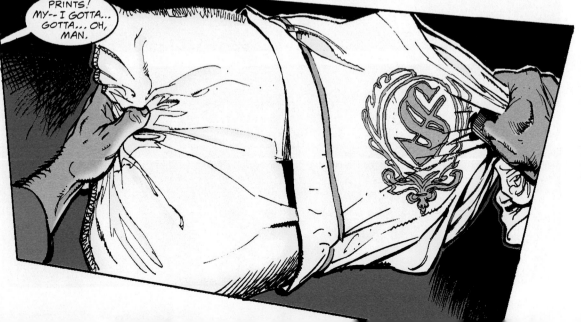

PRINTS! MY-- I GOTTA... GOTTA... OH, MAN.

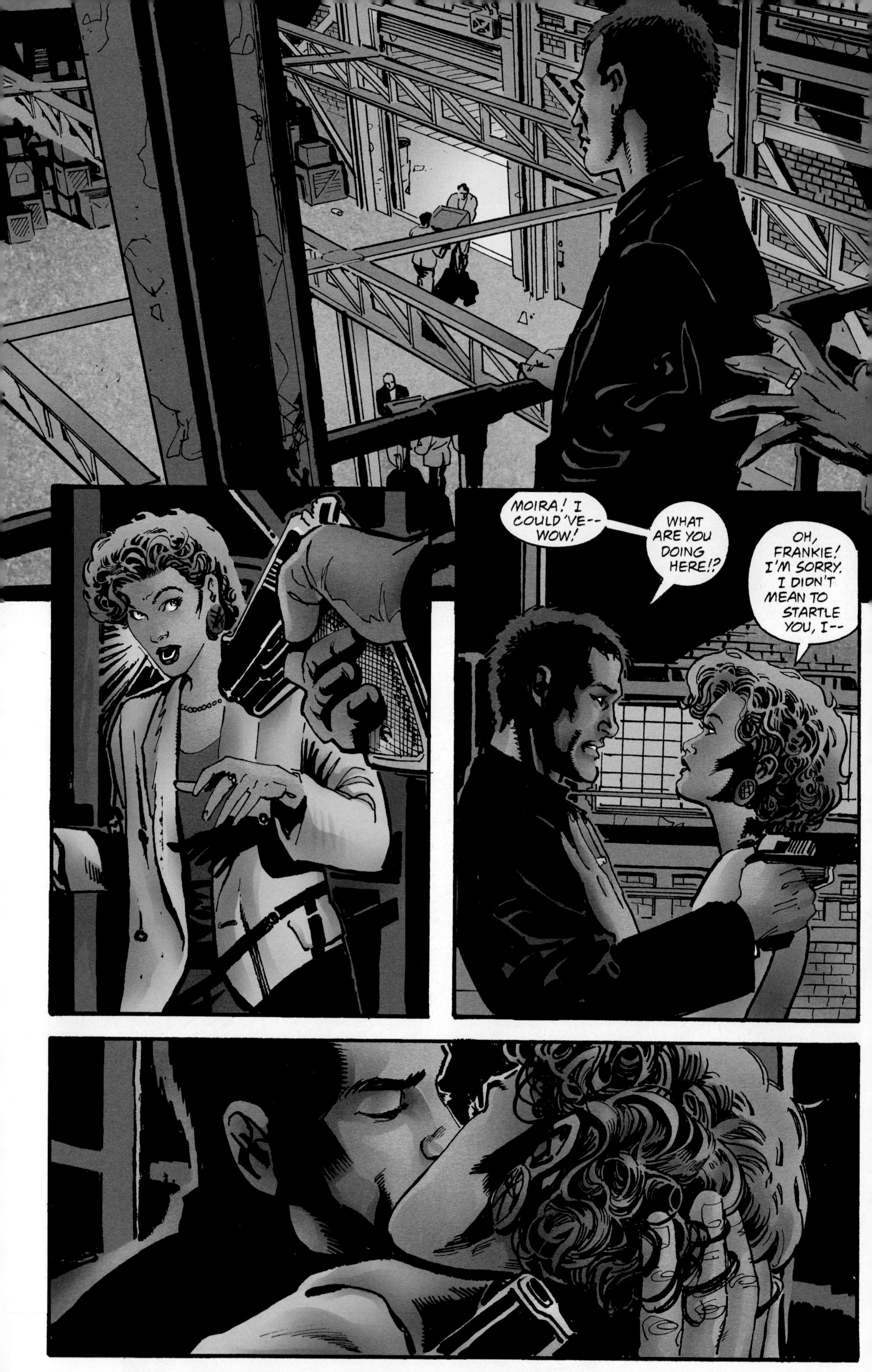
MOIRA! I COULD'VE--WOW!
WHAT ARE YOU DOING HERE!?
OH, FRANKIE! I'M SORRY. I DIDN'T MEAN TO STARTLE YOU, I--

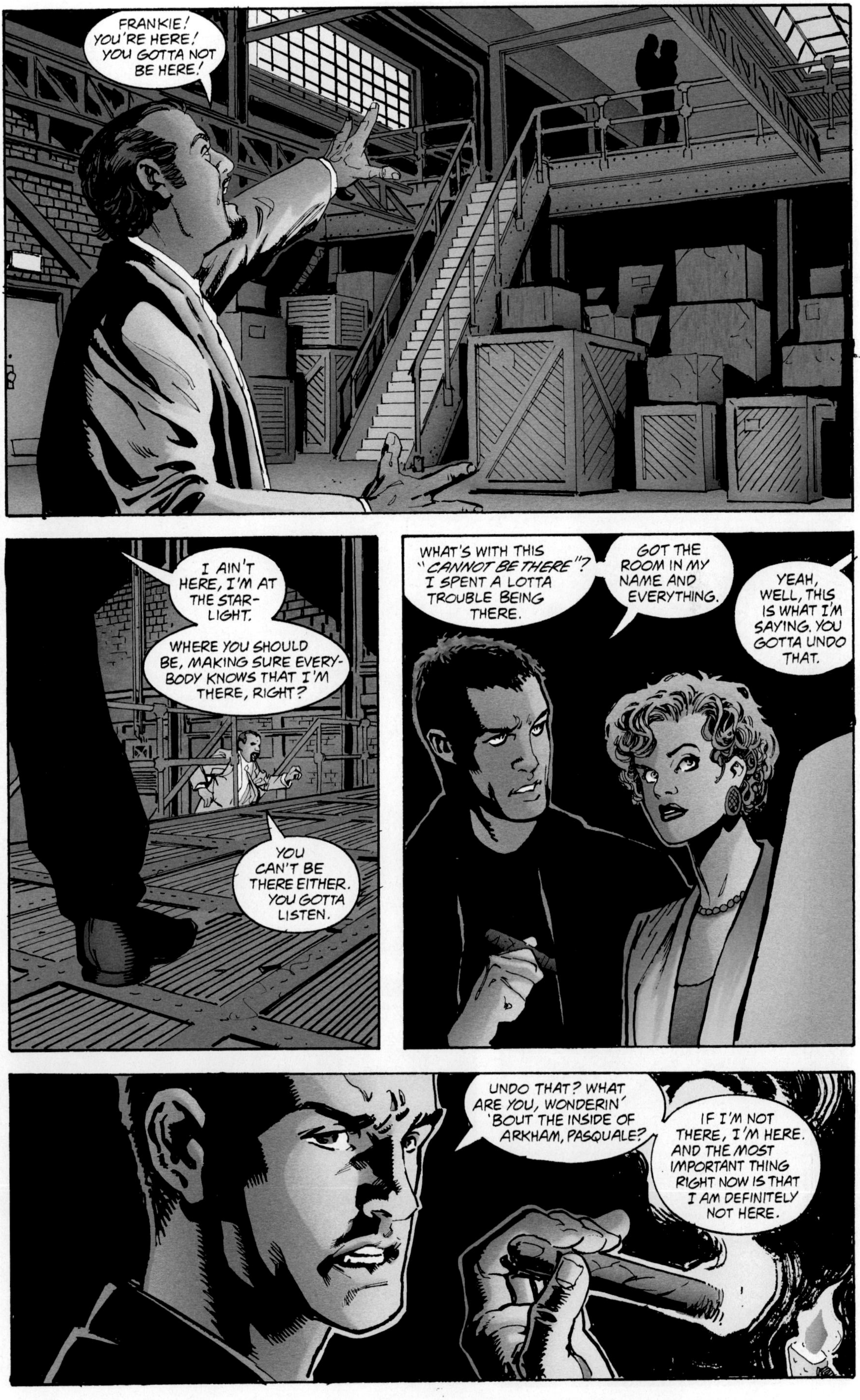
FRANKIE! YOU'RE HERE! YOU GOTTA NOT BE HERE!
I AIN'T HERE, I'M AT THE STAR-LIGHT.
WHERE YOU SHOULD BE, MAKING SURE EVERY-BODY KNOWS THAT I'M THERE, RIGHT?
YOU CAN'T BE THERE EITHER. YOU GOTTA LISTEN.
WHAT'S WITH THIS "CANNOT BE THERE"? I SPENT A LOTTA TROUBLE BEING THERE.
GOT THE ROOM IN MY NAME AND EVERYTHING.
YEAH, WELL, THIS IS WHAT I'M SAYING. YOU GOTTA UNDO THAT.
UNDO THAT? WHAT ARE YOU, WONDERIN' 'BOUT THE INSIDE OF ARKHAM, PASQUALE?
IF I'M NOT THERE, I'M HERE. AND THE MOST IMPORTANT THING RIGHT NOW IS THAT I AM DEFINITELY NOT HERE.

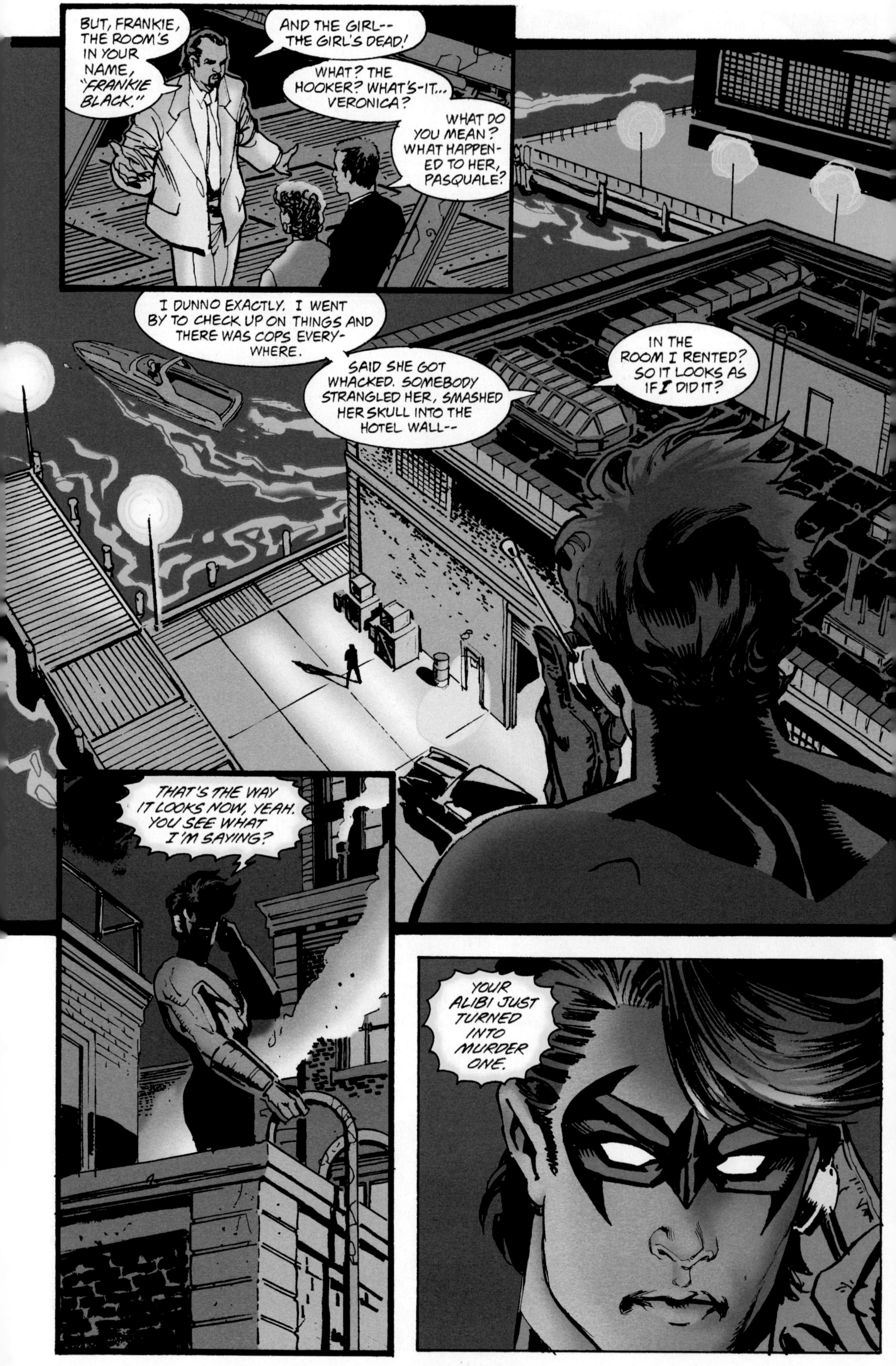

BUT, FRANKIE, THE ROOM'S IN YOUR NAME, "FRANKIE BLACK."
AND THE GIRL-- THE GIRL'S DEAD!
WHAT? THE HOOKER? WHAT'S-IT... VERONICA?
WHAT DO YOU MEAN? WHAT HAPPEN-ED TO HER, PASQUALE?
I DUNNO EXACTLY. I WENT BY TO CHECK UP ON THINGS AND THERE WAS COPS EVERY-WHERE.
SAID SHE GOT WHACKED. SOMEBODY STRANGLED HER, SMASHED HER SKULL INTO THE HOTEL WALL--
IN THE ROOM I RENTED? SO IT LOOKS AS IF I DID IT?
THAT'S THE WAY IT LOOKS NOW, YEAH. YOU SEE WHAT I'M SAYING?
YOUR ALIBI JUST TURNED INTO MURDER ONE.

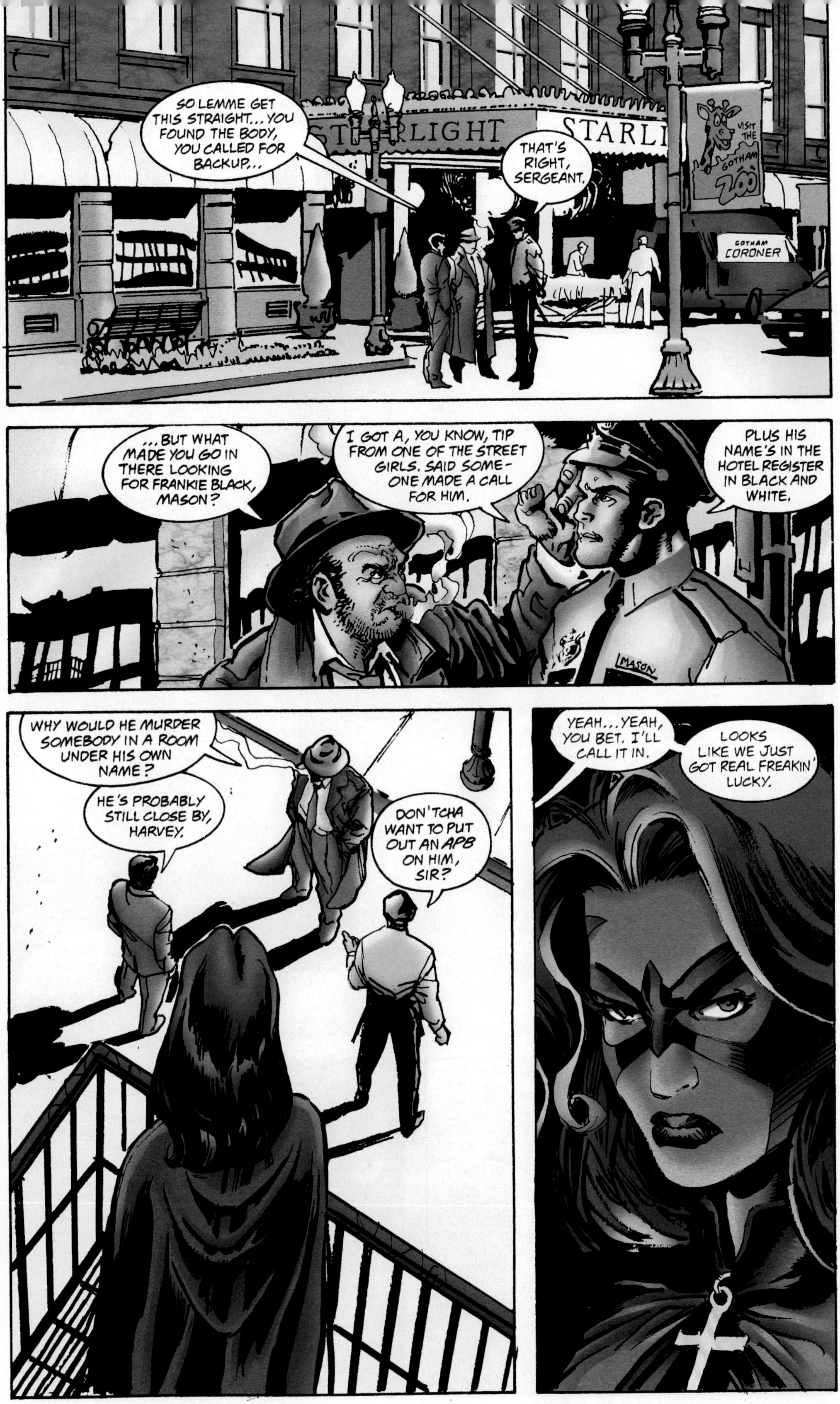
SO LEMME GET THIS STRAIGHT... YOU FOUND THE BODY, YOU CALLED FOR BACKUP...
THAT'S RIGHT, SERGEANT.
STARLIGHT
STARLI
VISIT THE GOTHAM ZOO
GOTHAM CORONER
...BUT WHAT MADE YOU GO IN THERE LOOKING FOR FRANKIE BLACK, MASON?
I GOT A, YOU KNOW, TIP FROM ONE OF THE STREET GIRLS. SAID SOME-ONE MADE A CALL FOR HIM.
PLUS HIS NAME'S IN THE HOTEL REGISTER IN BLACK AND WHITE.
MASON
WHY WOULD HE MURDER SOMEBODY IN A ROOM UNDER HIS OWN NAME?
HE'S PROBABLY STILL CLOSE BY, HARVEY.
DON'TCHA WANT TO PUT OUT AN APB ON HIM, SIR?
YEAH... YEAH, YOU BET. I'LL CALL IT IN.
LOOKS LIKE WE JUST GOT REAL FREAKIN' LUCKY.

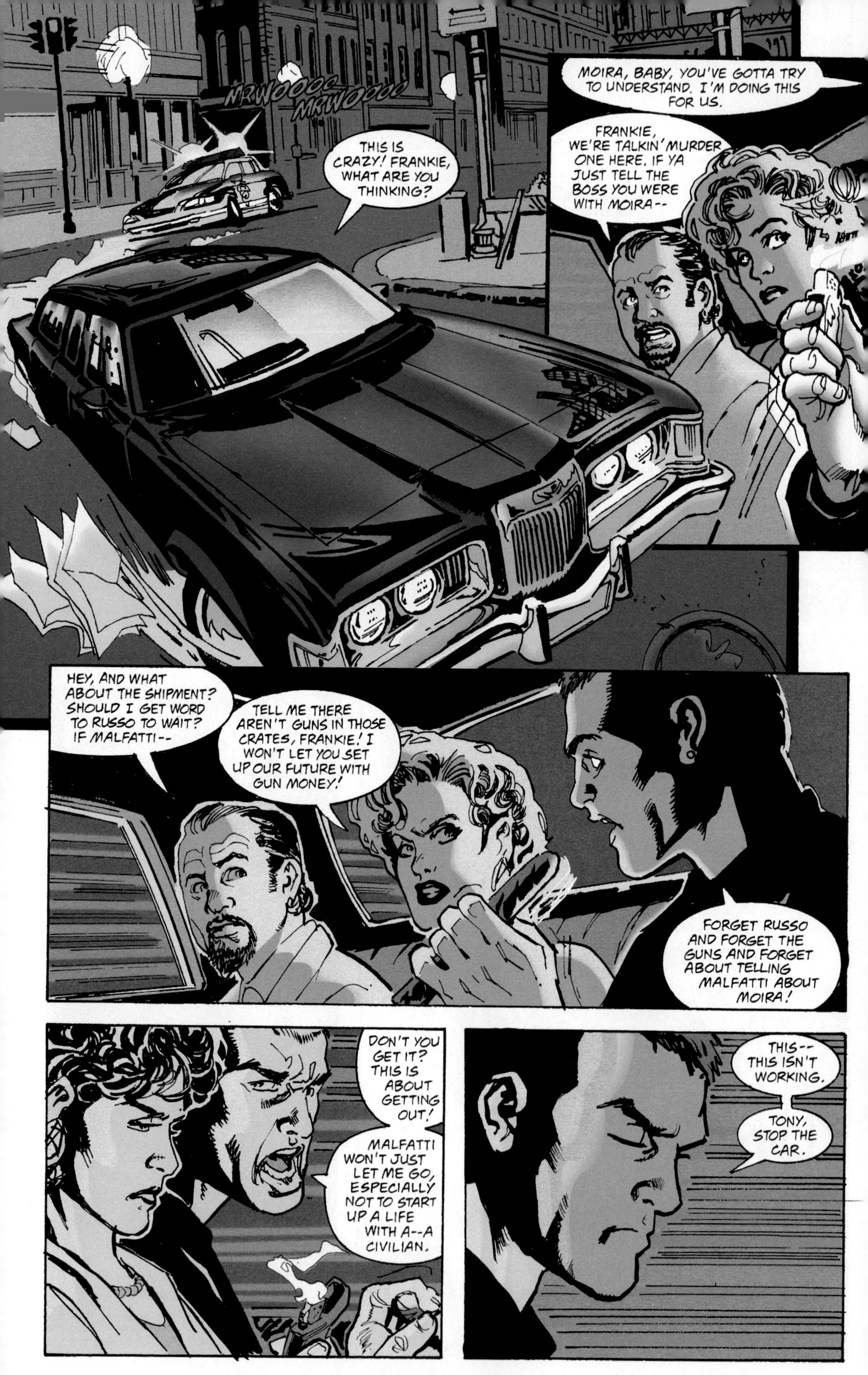
MRWOOOO MRWOOOO
THIS IS CRAZY! FRANKIE, WHAT ARE YOU THINKING?
MOIRA, BABY, YOU'VE GOTTA TRY TO UNDERSTAND. I'M DOING THIS FOR US.
FRANKIE, WE'RE TALKIN' MURDER ONE HERE. IF YA JUST TELL THE BOSS YOU WERE WITH MOIRA--
HEY, AND WHAT ABOUT THE SHIPMENT? SHOULD I GET WORD TO RUSSO TO WAIT? IF MALFATTI--
TELL ME THERE AREN'T GUNS IN THOSE CRATES, FRANKIE! I WON'T LET YOU SET UP OUR FUTURE WITH GUN MONEY!
FORGET RUSSO AND FORGET THE GUNS AND FORGET ABOUT TELLING MALFATTI ABOUT MOIRA!
DON'T YOU GET IT? THIS IS ABOUT GETTING OUT!
MALFATTI WON'T JUST LET ME GO, ESPECIALLY NOT TO START UP A LIFE WITH A--A CIVILIAN.
THIS-- THIS ISN'T WORKING.
TONY, STOP THE CAR.

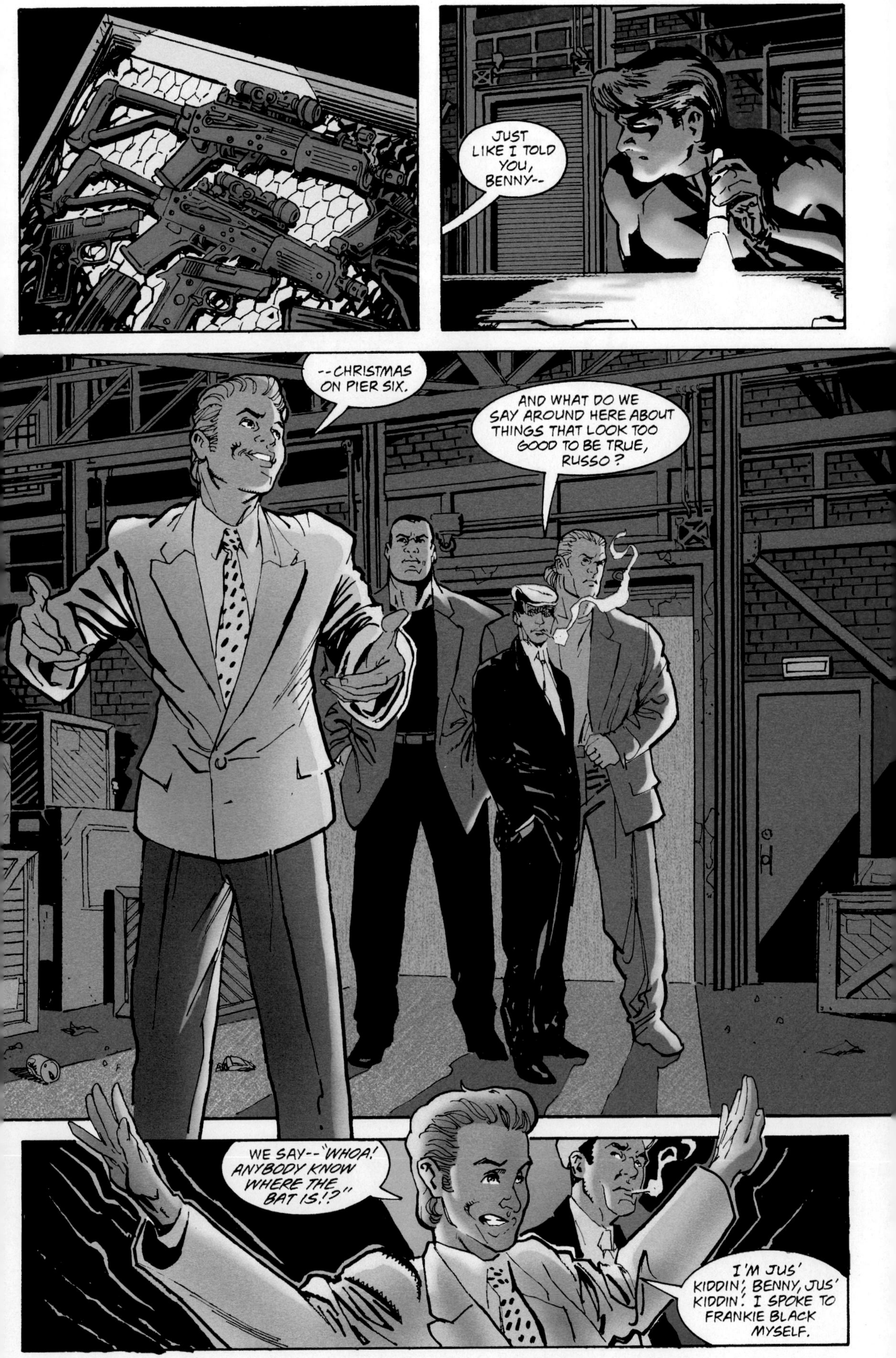
JUST LIKE I TOLD YOU, BENNY--
--CHRISTMAS ON PIER SIX.
AND WHAT DO WE SAY AROUND HERE ABOUT THINGS THAT LOOK TOO GOOD TO BE TRUE, RUSSO?
WE SAY--"WHOA! ANYBODY KNOW WHERE THE BAT IS!?"
I'M JUS' KIDDIN', BENNY, JUS' KIDDIN'. I SPOKE TO FRANKIE BLACK MYSELF.

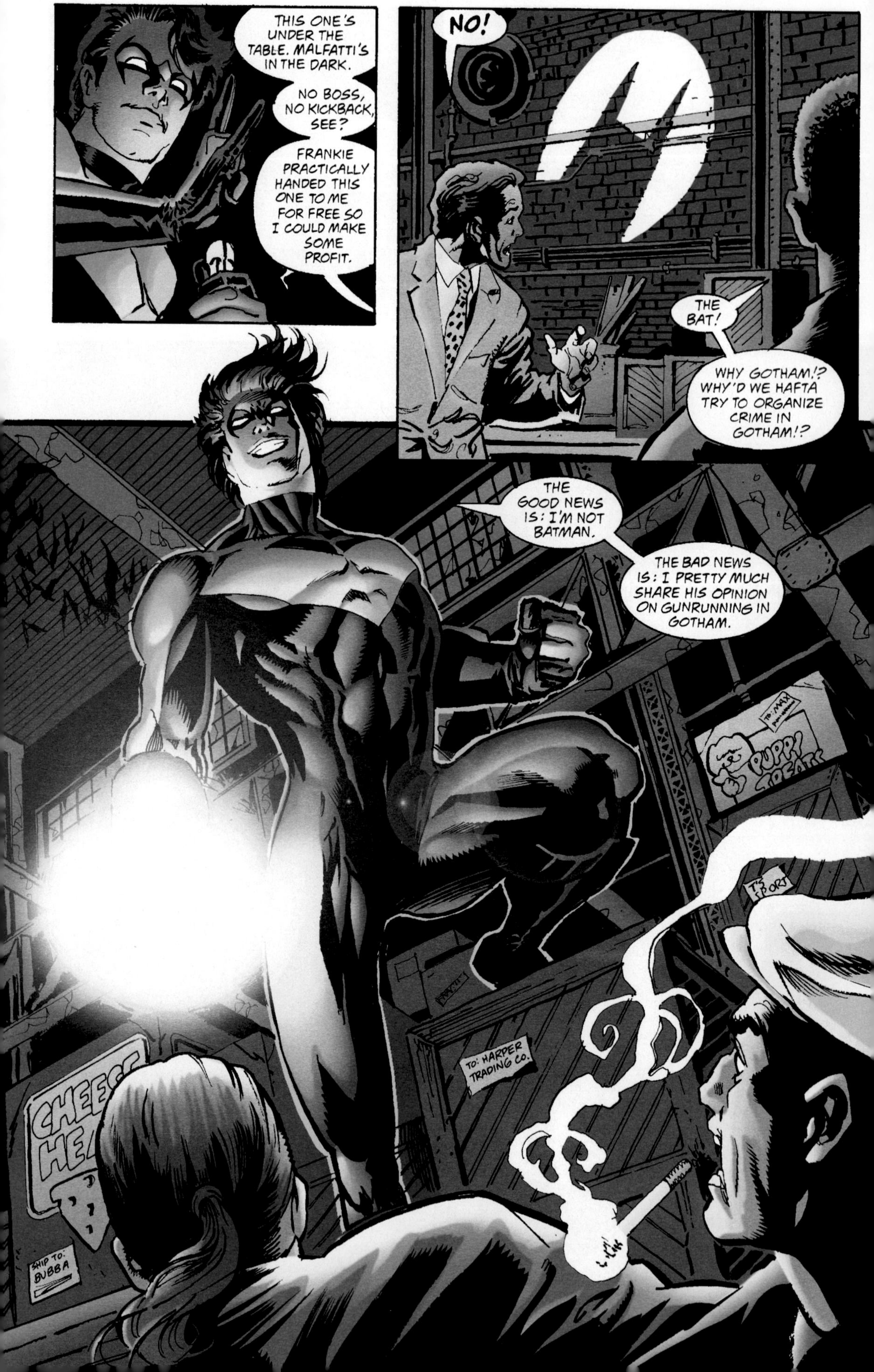

THIS ONE'S UNDER THE TABLE. MALFATTI'S IN THE DARK.
NO BOSS, NO KICKBACK, SEE?
FRANKIE PRACTICALLY HANDED THIS ONE TO ME FOR FREE SO I COULD MAKE SOME PROFIT.
NO!
THE BAT!
WHY GOTHAM!? WHY'D WE HAFTA TRY TO ORGANIZE CRIME IN GOTHAM!?
THE GOOD NEWS IS: I'M NOT BATMAN.
THE BAD NEWS IS: I PRETTY MUCH SHARE HIS OPINION ON GUNRUNNING IN GOTHAM.
TO: MAX
PUPPY
TO: HARPER TRADING CO.
SHIP TO: BUBBA

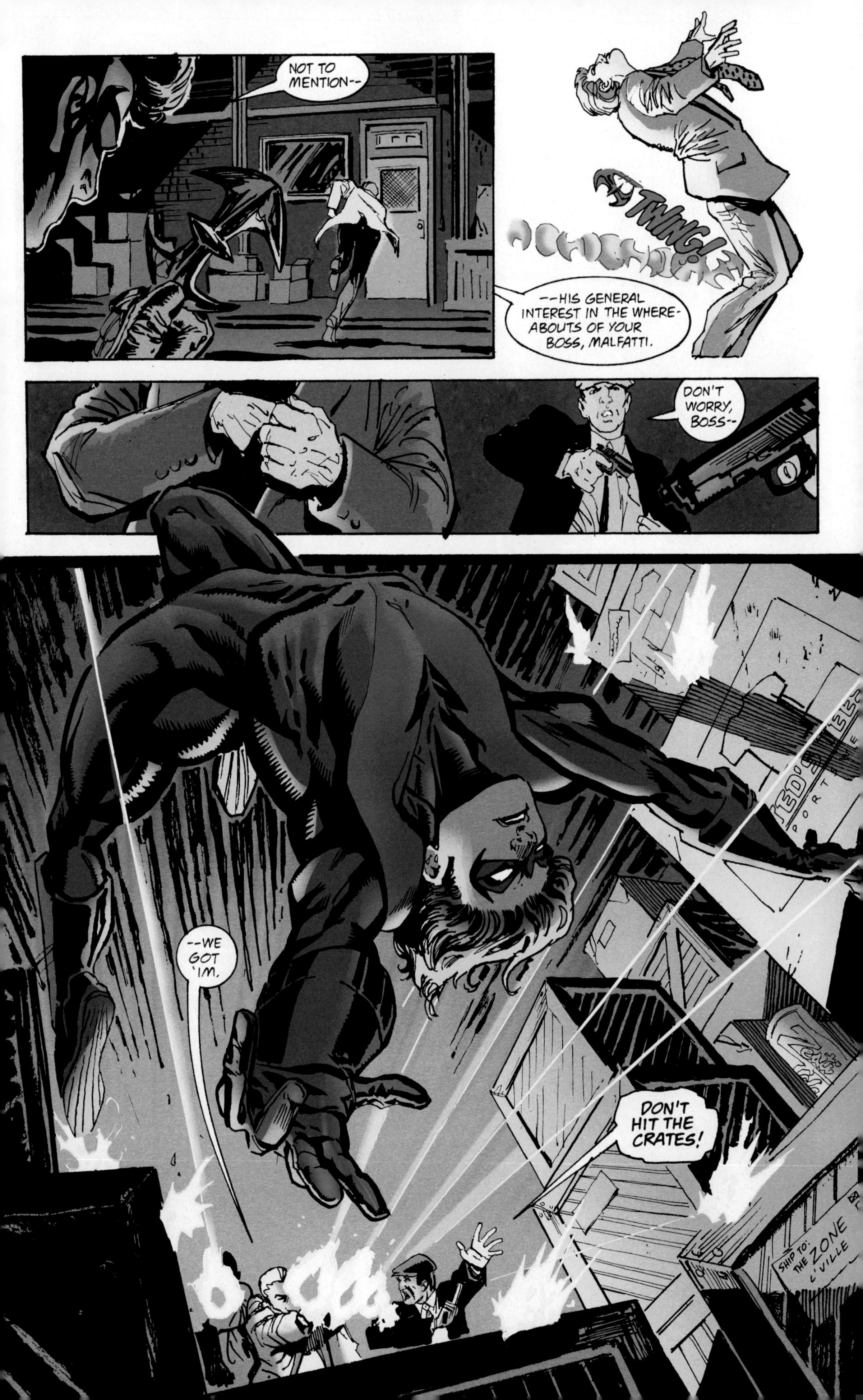
NOT TO MENTION--
TWING!
--HIS GENERAL INTEREST IN THE WHERE-ABOUTS OF YOUR BOSS, MALFATTI.
DON'T WORRY, BOSS--
--WE GOT 'IM.
DON'T HIT THE CRATES!
SHIP TO: THE ZONE L'VILLE

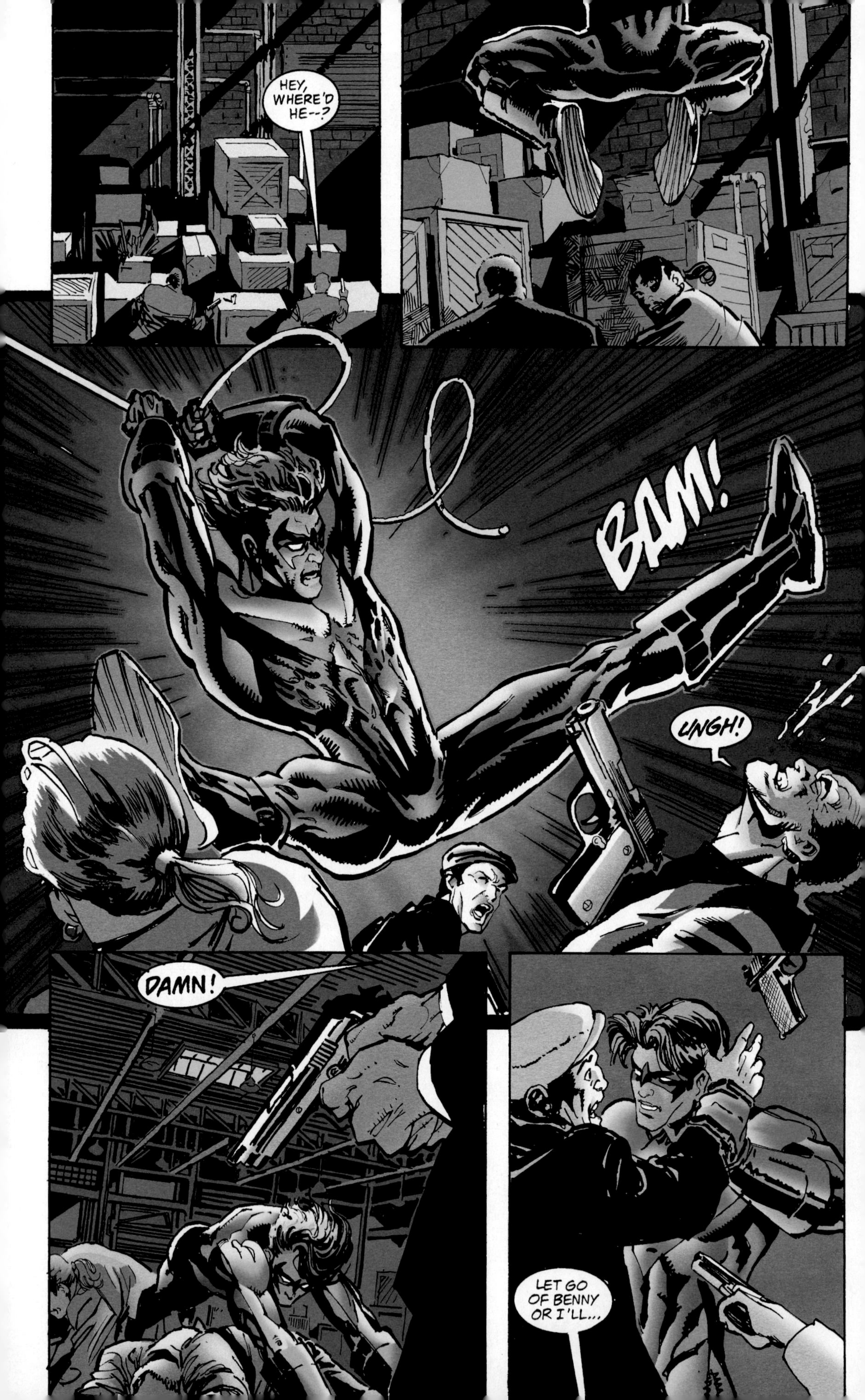
HEY, WHERE'D HE--?
BAM!
UNGH!
DAMN!
LET GO OF BENNY OR I'LL...

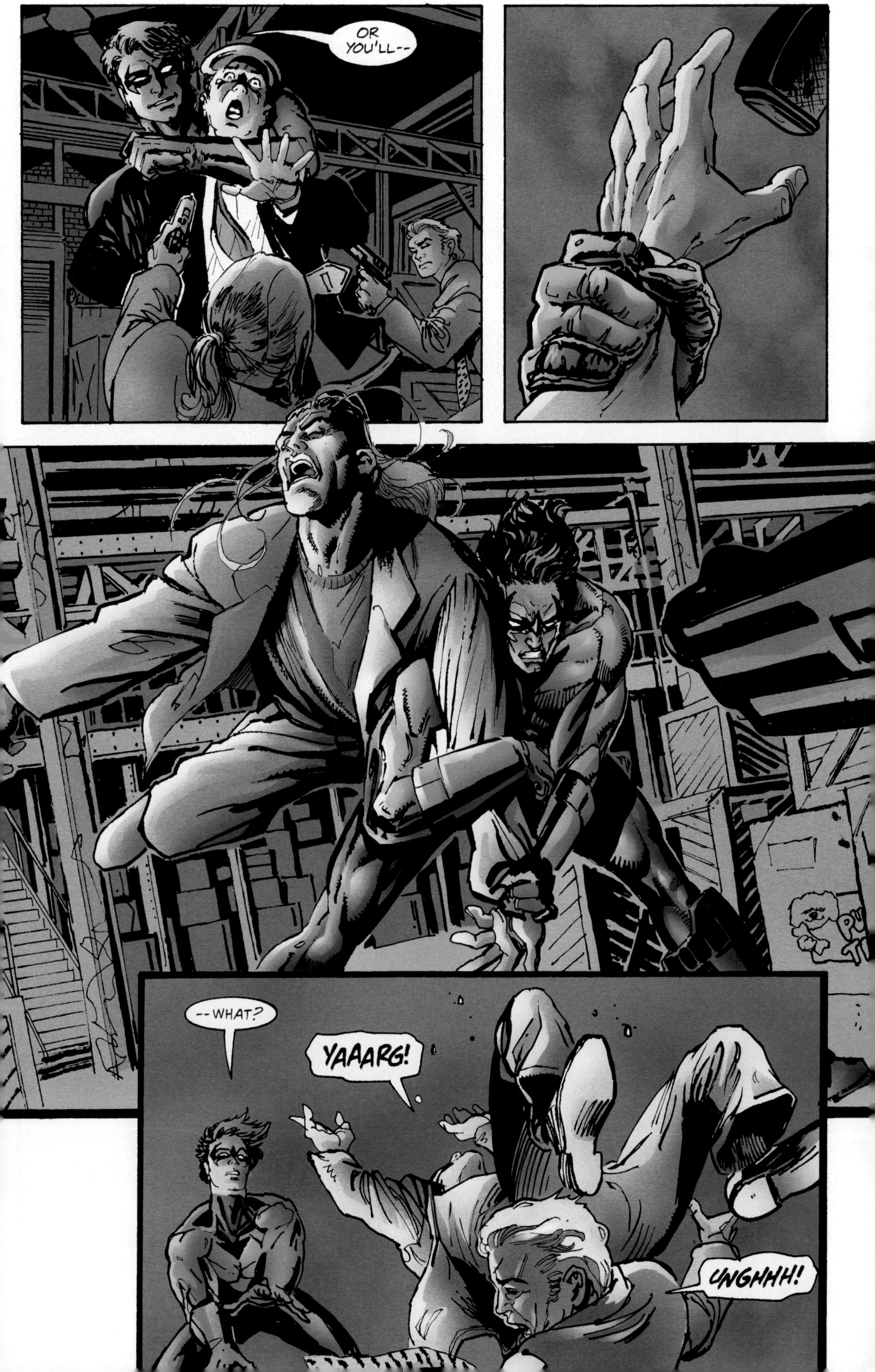
OR YOU'LL--
--WHAT?
YAAARG!
UNGHHH!

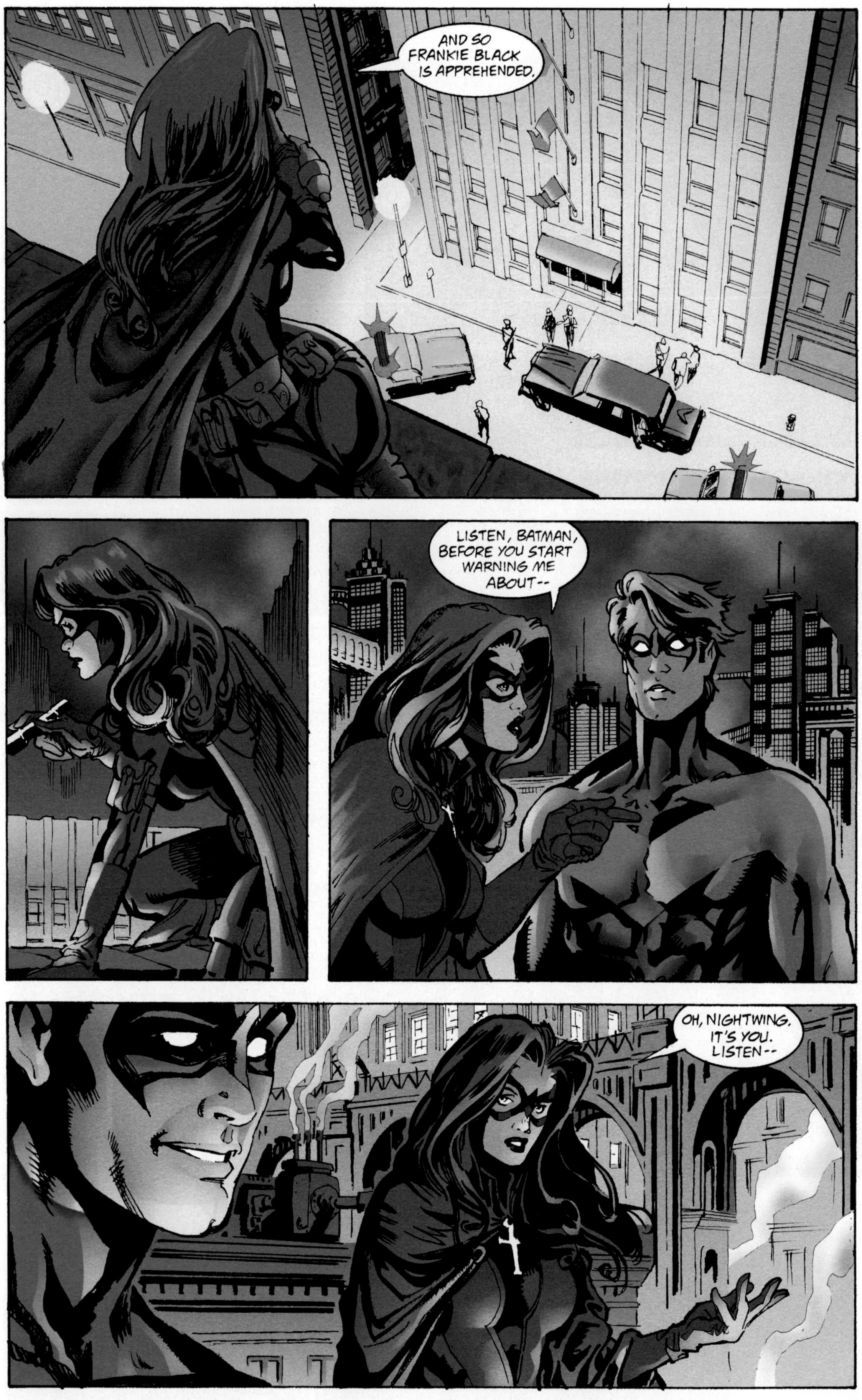
AND SO FRANKIE BLACK IS APPREHENDED.
LISTEN, BATMAN, BEFORE YOU START WARNING ME ABOUT--
OH, NIGHTWING. IT'S YOU. LISTEN--

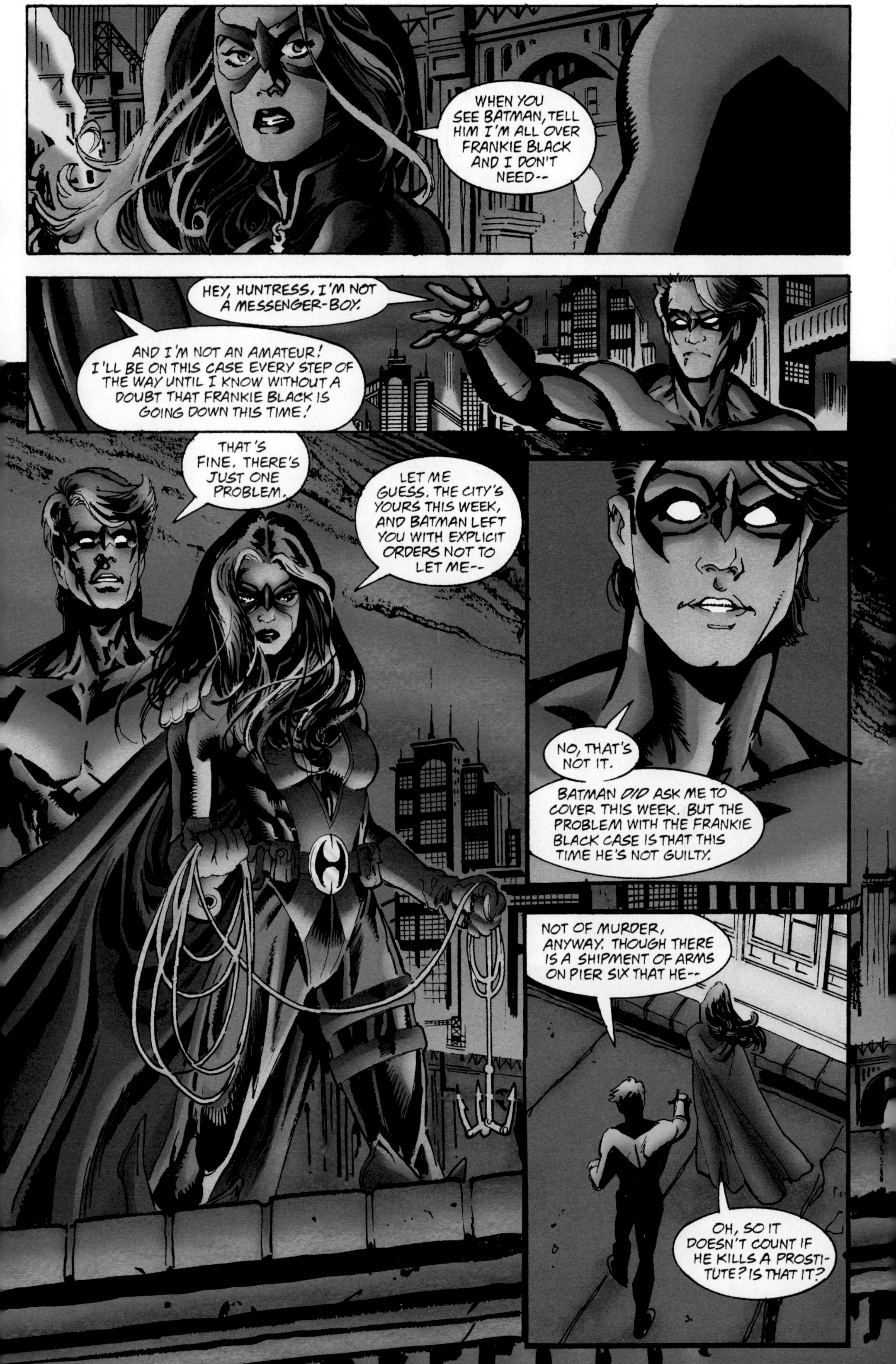
WHEN YOU SEE BATMAN, TELL HIM I'M ALL OVER FRANKIE BLACK AND I DON'T NEED--
HEY, HUNTRESS, I'M NOT A MESSENGER-BOY.
AND I'M NOT AN AMATEUR! I'LL BE ON THIS CASE EVERY STEP OF THE WAY UNTIL I KNOW WITHOUT A DOUBT THAT FRANKIE BLACK IS GOING DOWN THIS TIME!
THAT'S FINE. THERE'S JUST ONE PROBLEM.
LET ME GUESS. THE CITY'S YOURS THIS WEEK, AND BATMAN LEFT YOU WITH EXPLICIT ORDERS NOT TO LET ME--
NO, THAT'S NOT IT.
BATMAN DID ASK ME TO COVER THIS WEEK. BUT THE PROBLEM WITH THE FRANKIE BLACK CASE IS THAT THIS TIME HE'S NOT GUILTY.
NOT OF MURDER, ANYWAY. THOUGH THERE IS A SHIPMENT OF ARMS ON PIER SIX THAT HE--
OH, SO IT DOESN'T COUNT IF HE KILLS A PROSTITUTE? IS THAT IT?

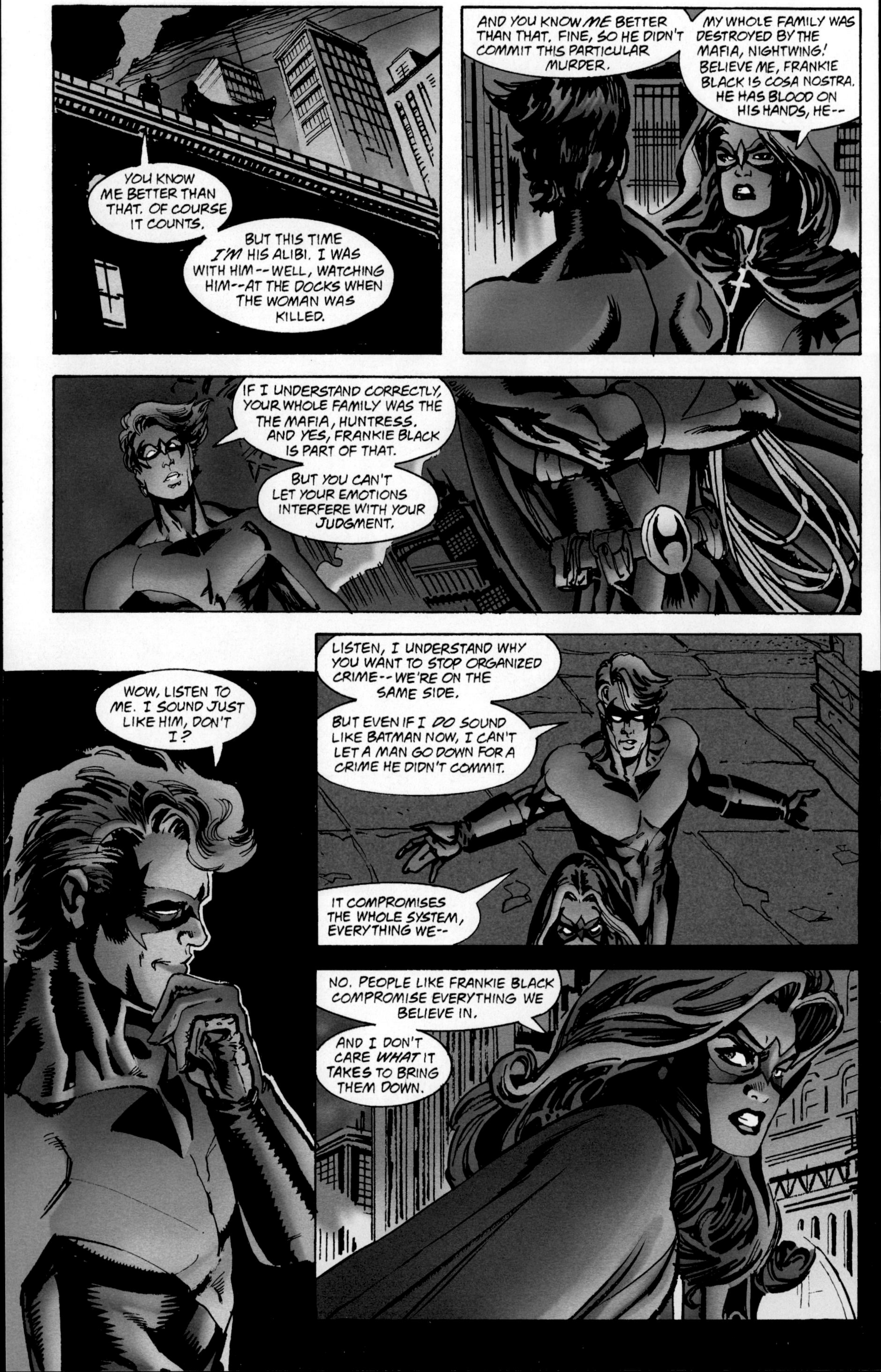
YOU KNOW ME BETTER THAN THAT. OF COURSE IT COUNTS.
BUT THIS TIME I'M HIS ALIBI. I WAS WITH HIM--WELL, WATCHING HIM--AT THE DOCKS WHEN THE WOMAN WAS KILLED.
AND YOU KNOW ME BETTER THAN THAT. FINE, SO HE DIDN'T COMMIT THIS PARTICULAR MURDER.
MY WHOLE FAMILY WAS DESTROYED BY THE MAFIA, NIGHTWING! BELIEVE ME, FRANKIE BLACK IS COSA NOSTRA. HE HAS BLOOD ON HIS HANDS, HE--
IF I UNDERSTAND CORRECTLY, YOUR WHOLE FAMILY WAS THE THE MAFIA, HUNTRESS. AND YES, FRANKIE BLACK IS PART OF THAT.
BUT YOU CAN'T LET YOUR EMOTIONS INTERFERE WITH YOUR JUDGMENT.
LISTEN, I UNDERSTAND WHY YOU WANT TO STOP ORGANIZED CRIME--WE'RE ON THE SAME SIDE.
BUT EVEN IF I DO SOUND LIKE BATMAN NOW, I CAN'T LET A MAN GO DOWN FOR A CRIME HE DIDN'T COMMIT.
IT COMPROMISES THE WHOLE SYSTEM, EVERYTHING WE--
WOW, LISTEN TO ME. I SOUND JUST LIKE HIM, DON'T I?
NO. PEOPLE LIKE FRANKIE BLACK COMPROMISE EVERYTHING WE BELIEVE IN.
AND I DON'T CARE WHAT IT TAKES TO BRING THEM DOWN.

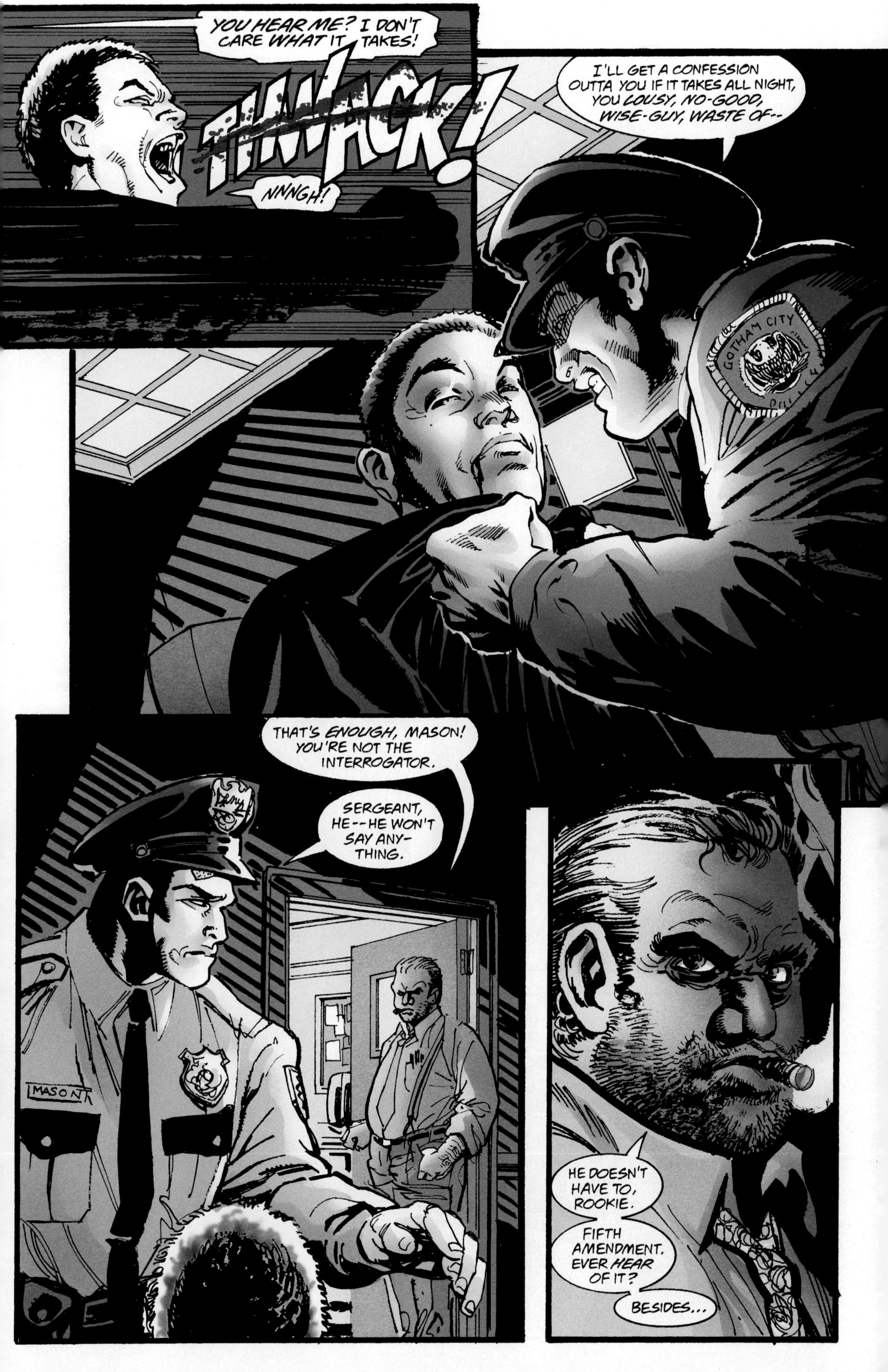

YOU HEAR ME? I DON'T CARE WHAT IT TAKES!
THWACK!
NNNGH!
I'LL GET A CONFESSION OUTTA YOU IF IT TAKES ALL NIGHT, YOU LOUSY, NO-GOOD, WISE-GUY, WASTE OF--
GOTHAM CITY
THAT'S ENOUGH, MASON! YOU'RE NOT THE INTERROGATOR.
SERGEANT, HE--HE WON'T SAY ANY-THING.
MASON
HE DOESN'T HAVE TO, ROOKIE.
FIFTH AMENDMENT. EVER HEAR OF IT?
BESIDES...

...THEY'VE GOT THE HOTEL LEDGER, MALFATTI!

Malfatti's
EST. 1929
RISTORANTE ITALIANO
CLOSED

MM. THE POLICE HAVE THE HOTEL LEDGER.

THE LEDGER HAS FRANKIE BLACK'S SIGNATURE IN IT.

BUT FRANKIE WASN'T AT THE HOTEL.

THE HOTEL WAS AN ALIBI.

YEAH. YEAH, THAT'S IT.

I SEE. AN ALIBI FOR WHAT, PASQUALE?

THE, *UH,* UM, HE...

PASQUALE, HELP ME OUT HERE. BECAUSE I'M STARTING TO THINK IT SOUNDS LIKE HE WAS DOUBLE-CROSSING ME.

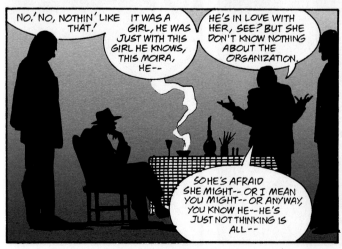

NO,' NO, NOTHIN' LIKE THAT!

IT WAS A GIRL, HE WAS JUST WITH THIS GIRL HE KNOWS, THIS MOIRA, HE--

HE'S IN LOVE WITH HER, SEE? BUT SHE DON'T KNOW NOTHING ABOUT THE ORGANIZATION.

SO HE'S AFRAID SHE MIGHT-- OR I MEAN YOU MIGHT-- OR ANYWAY, YOU KNOW HE--HE'S JUST NOT THINKING IS ALL--

JUST, *UH,* NOT THINKIN' *UH,* TH-THAT'S ALL...

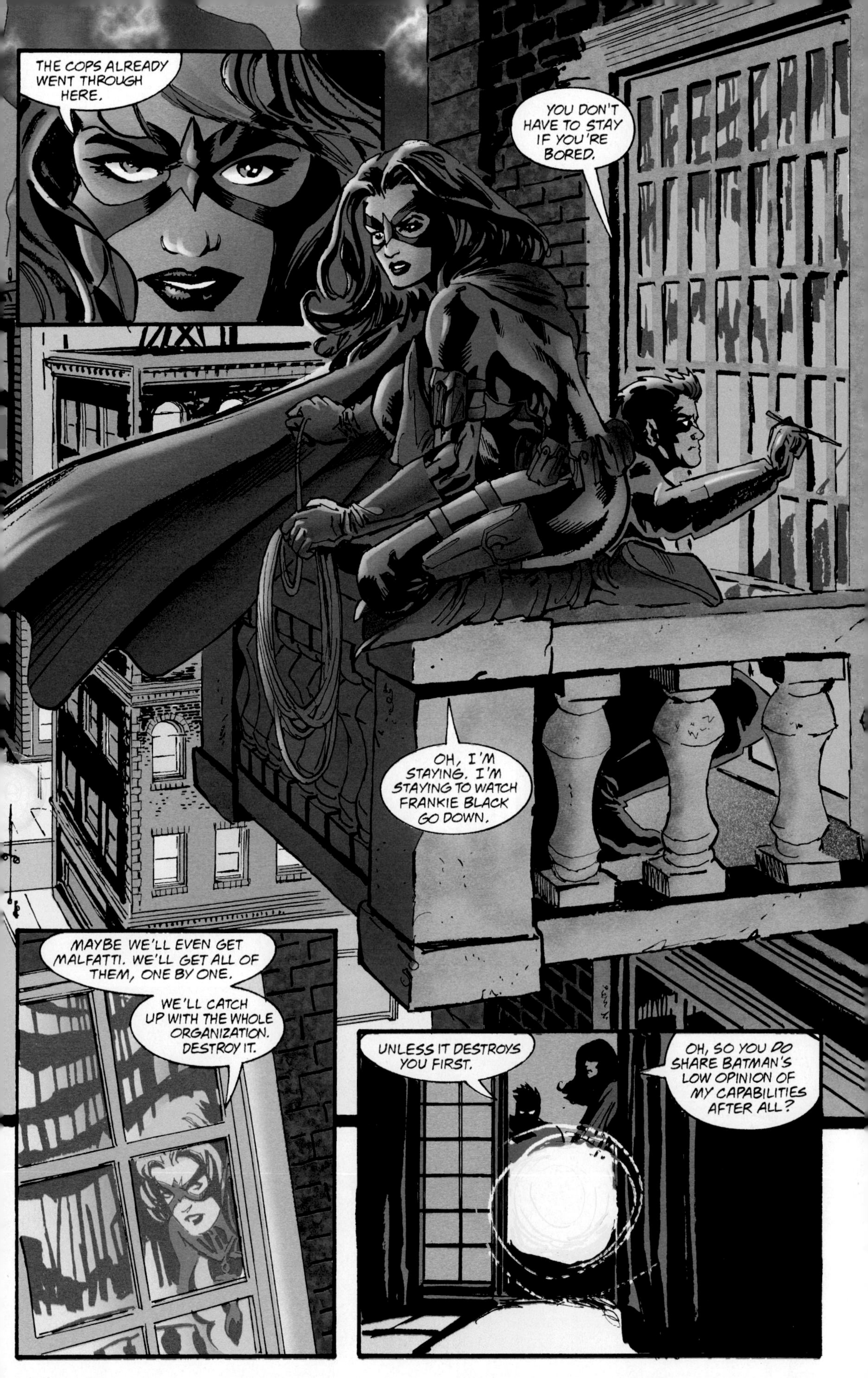
THE COPS ALREADY WENT THROUGH HERE.
YOU DON'T HAVE TO STAY IF YOU'RE BORED.
OH, I'M STAYING. I'M STAYING TO WATCH FRANKIE BLACK GO DOWN.
MAYBE WE'LL EVEN GET MALFATTI. WE'LL GET ALL OF THEM, ONE BY ONE.
WE'LL CATCH UP WITH THE WHOLE ORGANIZATION. DESTROY IT.
UNLESS IT DESTROYS YOU FIRST.
OH, SO YOU DO SHARE BATMAN'S LOW OPINION OF MY CAPABILITIES AFTER ALL?

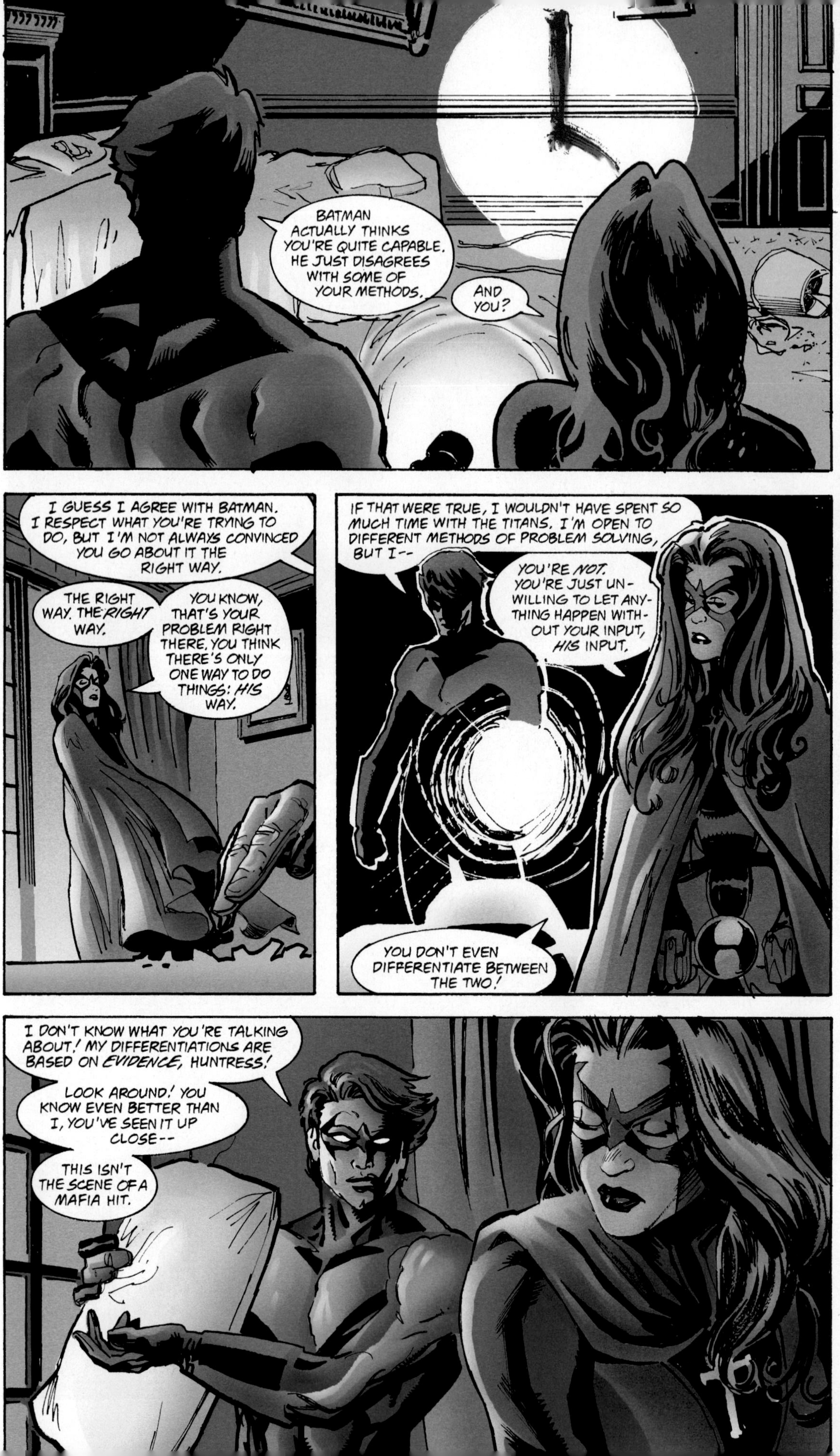
BATMAN ACTUALLY THINKS YOU'RE QUITE CAPABLE. HE JUST DISAGREES WITH SOME OF YOUR METHODS.
AND YOU?
I GUESS I AGREE WITH BATMAN. I RESPECT WHAT YOU'RE TRYING TO DO, BUT I'M NOT ALWAYS CONVINCED YOU GO ABOUT IT THE RIGHT WAY.
THE RIGHT WAY. THE *RIGHT* WAY.
YOU KNOW, THAT'S YOUR PROBLEM RIGHT THERE. YOU THINK THERE'S ONLY ONE WAY TO DO THINGS: *HIS* WAY.
IF THAT WERE TRUE, I WOULDN'T HAVE SPENT SO MUCH TIME WITH THE TITANS. I'M OPEN TO DIFFERENT METHODS OF PROBLEM SOLVING, BUT I--
YOU'RE *NOT.* YOU'RE JUST UNWILLING TO LET ANYTHING HAPPEN WITHOUT YOUR INPUT, *HIS* INPUT.
YOU DON'T EVEN DIFFERENTIATE BETWEEN THE TWO!
I DON'T KNOW WHAT YOU'RE TALKING ABOUT! MY DIFFERENTIATIONS ARE BASED ON *EVIDENCE*, HUNTRESS!
LOOK AROUND! YOU KNOW EVEN BETTER THAN I, YOU'VE SEEN IT UP CLOSE--
THIS ISN'T THE SCENE OF A MAFIA HIT.

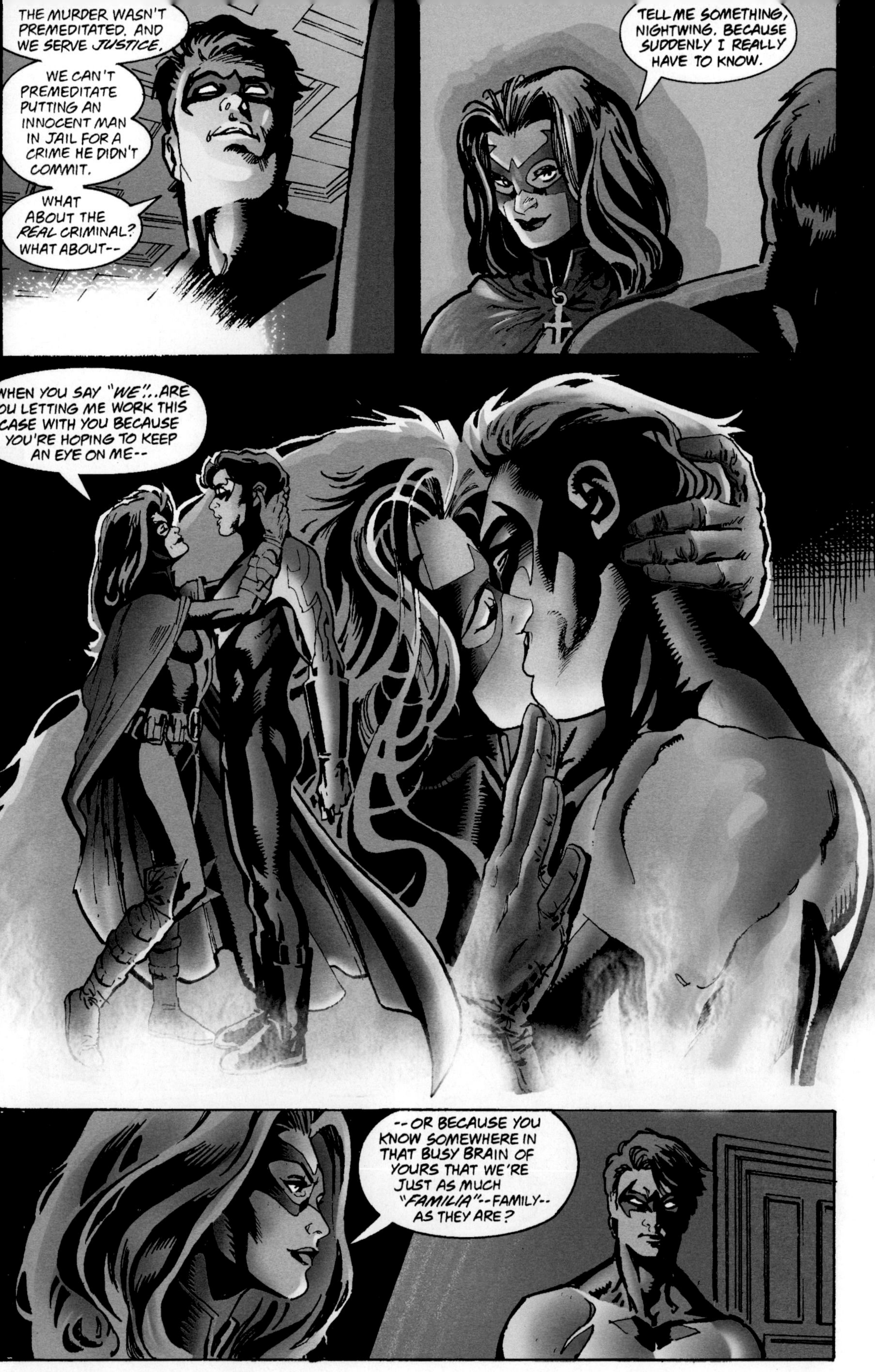
THE MURDER WASN'T PREMEDITATED. AND WE SERVE JUSTICE.
WE CAN'T PREMEDITATE PUTTING AN INNOCENT MAN IN JAIL FOR A CRIME HE DIDN'T COMMIT.
WHAT ABOUT THE REAL CRIMINAL? WHAT ABOUT--
TELL ME SOMETHING, NIGHTWING. BECAUSE SUDDENLY I REALLY HAVE TO KNOW.
WHEN YOU SAY "WE"...ARE YOU LETTING ME WORK THIS CASE WITH YOU BECAUSE YOU'RE HOPING TO KEEP AN EYE ON ME--
--OR BECAUSE YOU KNOW SOMEWHERE IN THAT BUSY BRAIN OF YOURS THAT WE'RE JUST AS MUCH "FAMILIA"--FAMILY--AS THEY ARE?

WHAT D'YA MEAN, "AN ODDLY-SHAPED BATARANG"? HOW MANY YOU EXAMINED UP CLOSE, LADY?

...SO WHEN I CUFFED HIM I SAID, "I SURE HOPE YOUR VOCABULARY IS BIGGER THAN YOUR"--

JUST A JOB HAZARD, YOU KNOW, THE WAY I FIGURE.

I LIKE CATWOMAN FOR IT, BUT OF COURSE THAT'S PRESUMING SHE DIDN'T PULL THE ONE ON MADISON.

HOLD? YEAH, I'LL HOLD--

PARK AND 30TH. COPY.

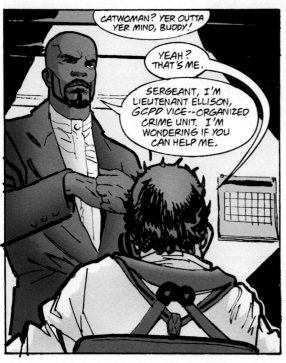

LOOK, IF HE DOESN'T LIKE HIS JOB, HE SHOULD GO GET ANOTHER, YA KNOW?

GUN! BWAH-HA HA!

I'M SENDING A CAR OUT NOW.

I'LL HOLD YOU RESPONSIBLE FOR SCREWIN' UP A MURDER ONE IF YOU DON'T PATCH ME THROUGH THIS SECOND!

SERGEANT BULLOCK?

"LESS RIDGEY THAN USUAL"? OH YEAH, I'M WRITIN' IT DOWN.

CATWOMAN? YER OUTTA YER MIND, BUDDY!

YEAH? THAT'S ME.

SERGEANT, I'M LIEUTENANT ELLISON, GCPD VICE--ORGANIZED CRIME UNIT. I'M WONDERING IF YOU CAN HELP ME.

I'M LOOKING FOR MY PARTNER.

GCPD

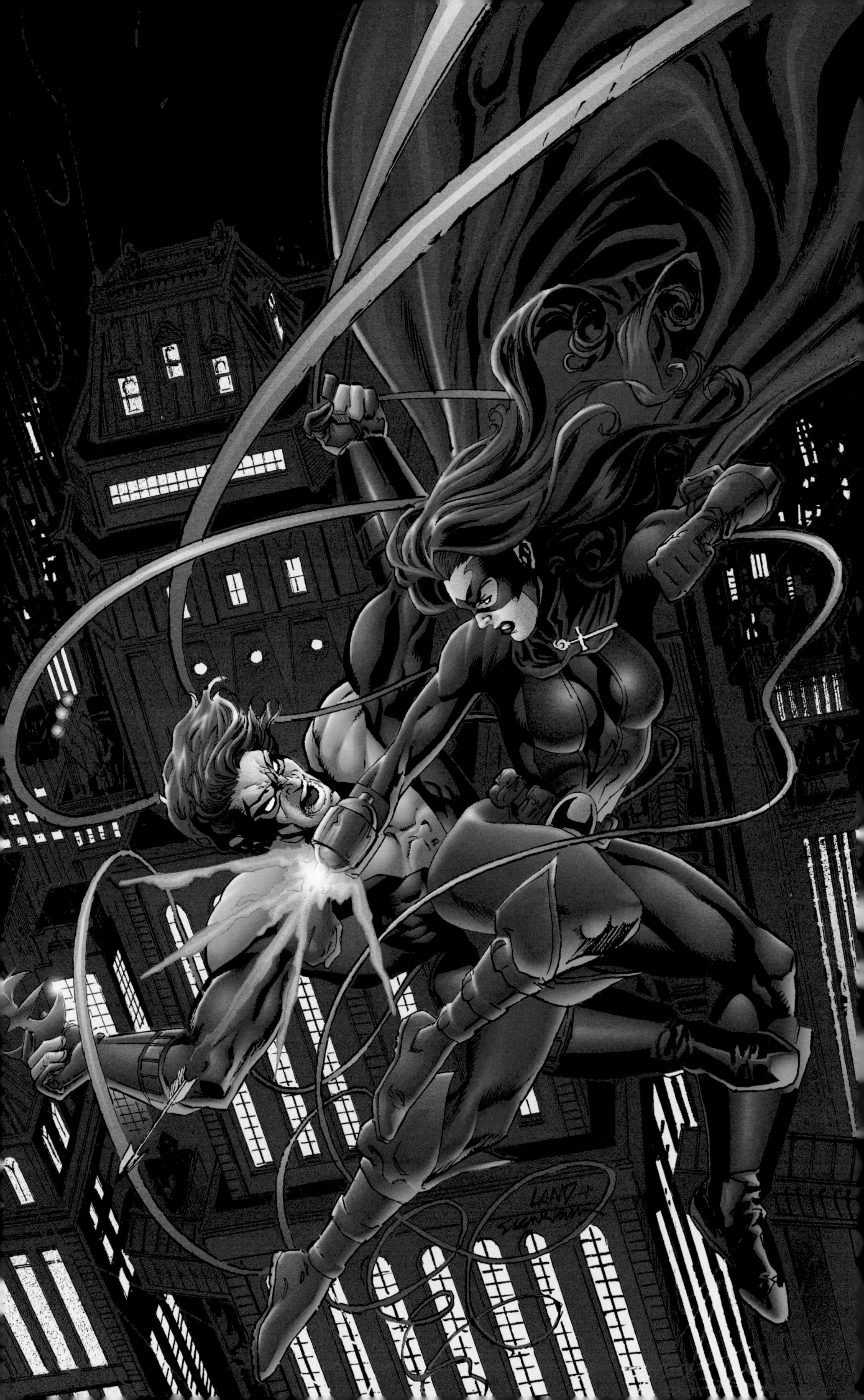

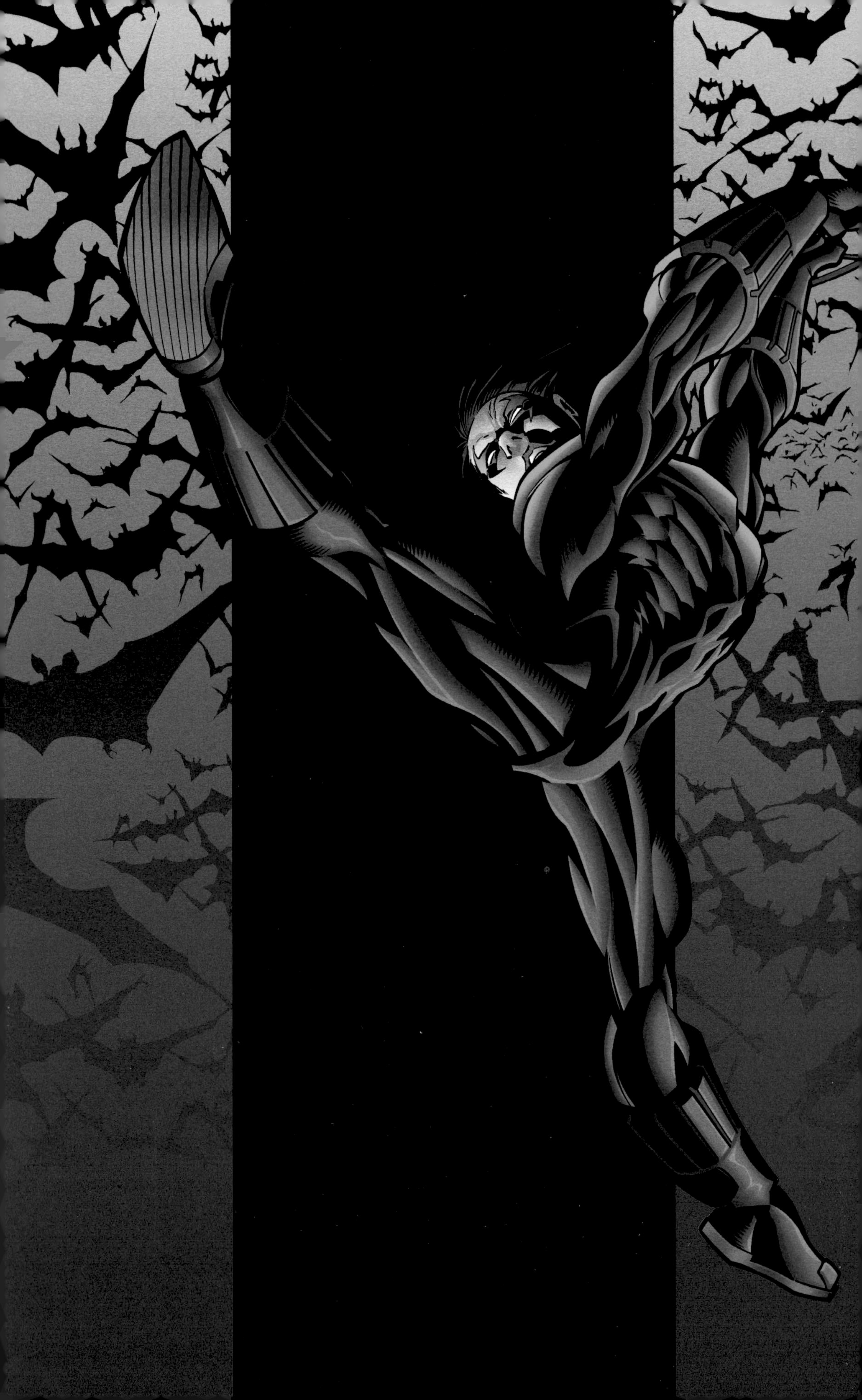

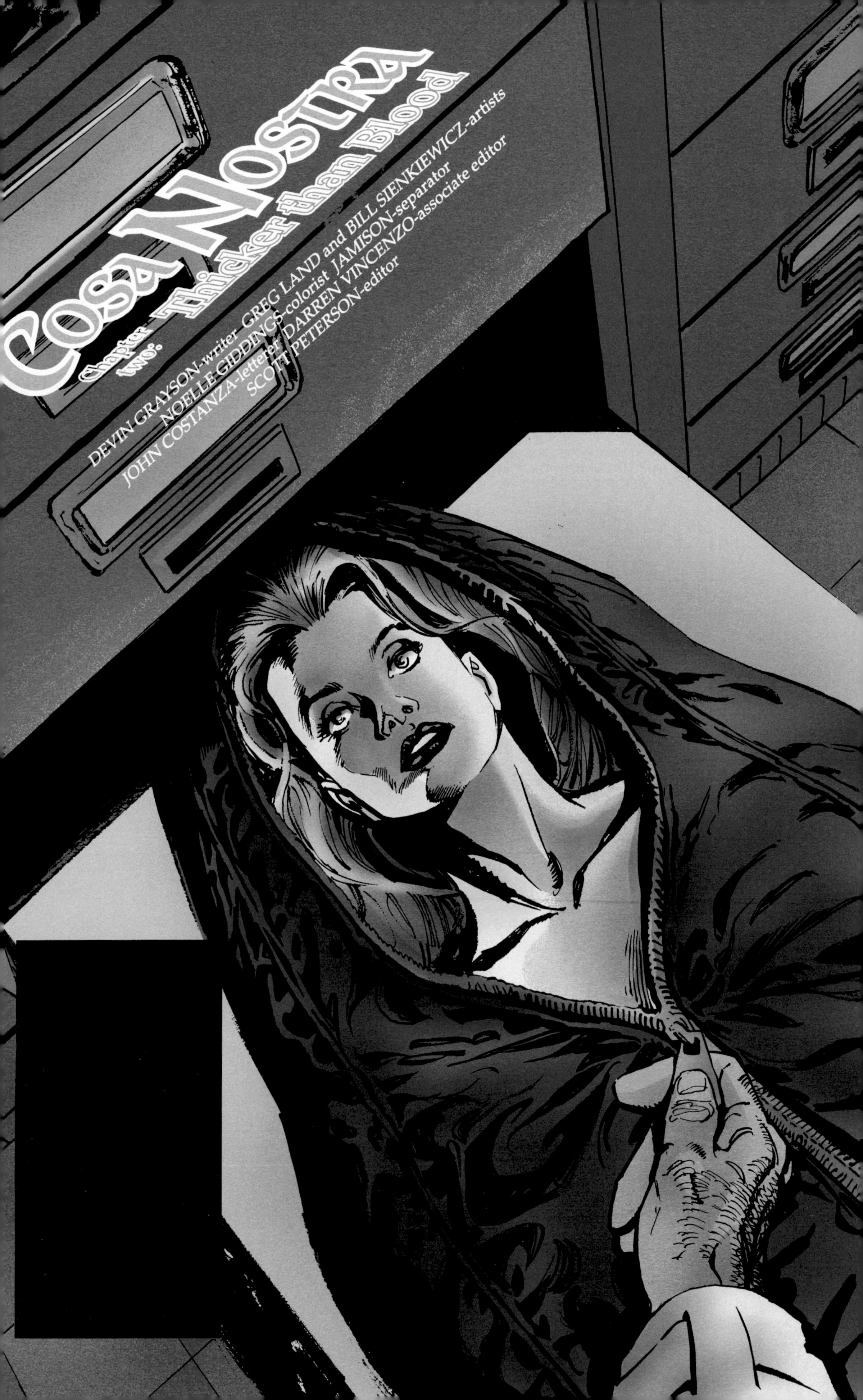
Cosa Nostra
chapter two: Thicker than Blood
DEVIN GRAYSON-writer GREG LAND and BILL SIENKIEWICZ-artists
NOELLE GIDDINGS-colorist JAMISON-separator
JOHN COSTANZA-letterer DARREN VINCENZO-associate editor
SCOTT PETERSON-editor

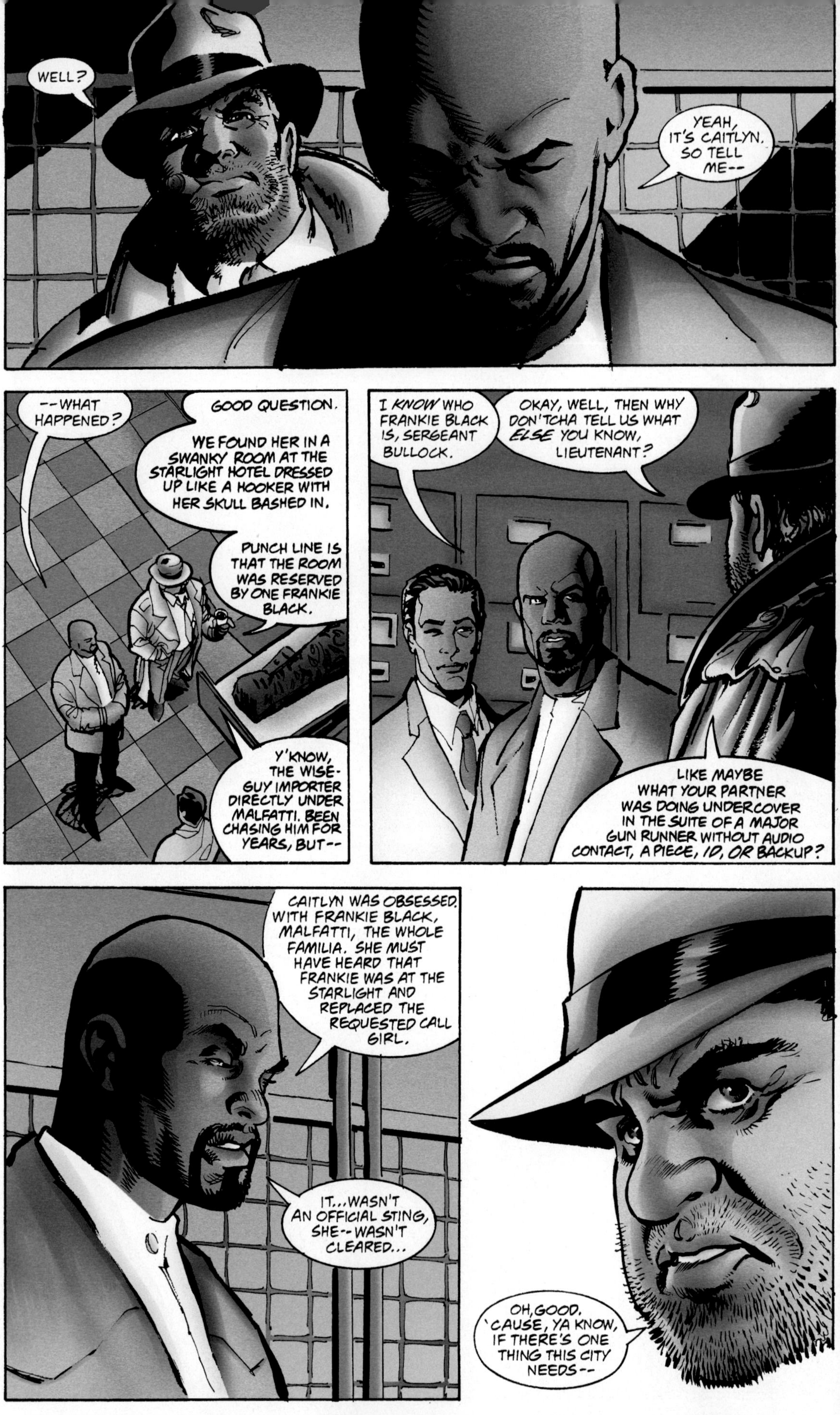
WELL?
YEAH, IT'S CAITLYN. SO TELL ME--
--WHAT HAPPENED?
GOOD QUESTION.
WE FOUND HER IN A SWANKY ROOM AT THE STARLIGHT HOTEL DRESSED UP LIKE A HOOKER WITH HER SKULL BASHED IN.
PUNCH LINE IS THAT THE ROOM WAS RESERVED BY ONE FRANKIE BLACK.
Y'KNOW, THE WISE-GUY IMPORTER DIRECTLY UNDER MALFATTI. BEEN CHASING HIM FOR YEARS, BUT--
I KNOW WHO FRANKIE BLACK IS, SERGEANT BULLOCK.
OKAY, WELL, THEN WHY DON'TCHA TELL US WHAT ELSE YOU KNOW, LIEUTENANT?
LIKE MAYBE WHAT YOUR PARTNER WAS DOING UNDERCOVER IN THE SUITE OF A MAJOR GUN RUNNER WITHOUT AUDIO CONTACT, A PIECE, ID, OR BACKUP?
CAITLYN WAS OBSESSED WITH FRANKIE BLACK, MALFATTI, THE WHOLE FAMILIA. SHE MUST HAVE HEARD THAT FRANKIE WAS AT THE STARLIGHT AND REPLACED THE REQUESTED CALL GIRL.
IT...WASN'T AN OFFICIAL STING, SHE--WASN'T CLEARED...
OH, GOOD. 'CAUSE, YA KNOW, IF THERE'S ONE THING THIS CITY NEEDS--

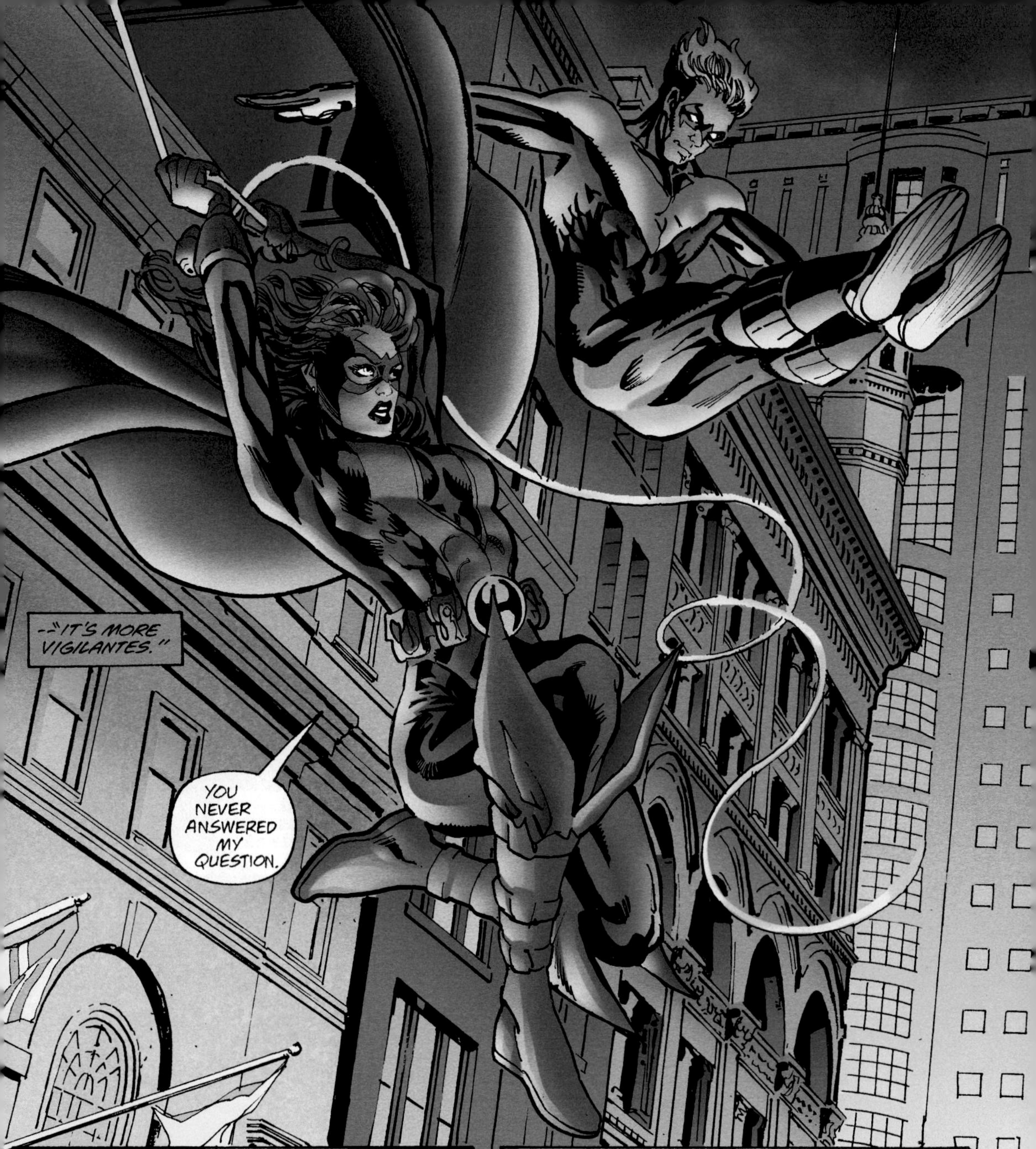

-"IT'S MORE VIGILANTES."
YOU NEVER ANSWERED MY QUESTION.

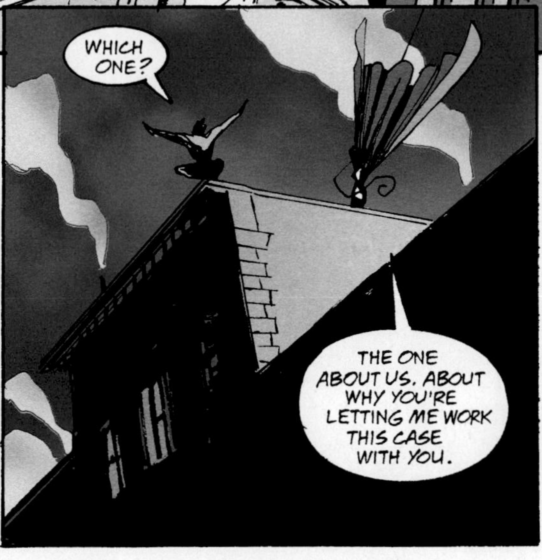

WHICH ONE?
THE ONE ABOUT US. ABOUT WHY YOU'RE LETTING ME WORK THIS CASE WITH YOU.

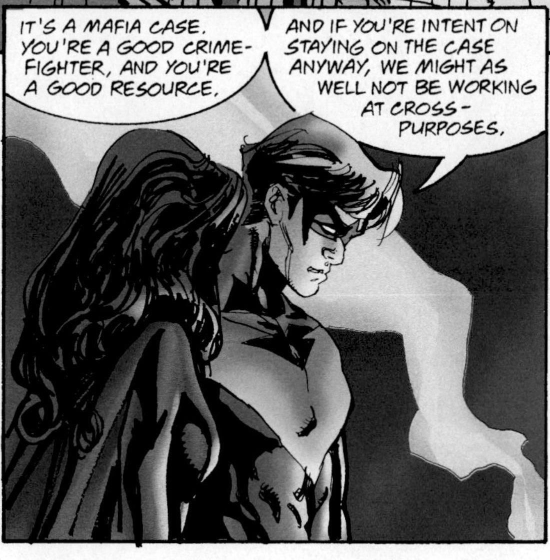

IT'S A MAFIA CASE. YOU'RE A GOOD CRIME-FIGHTER, AND YOU'RE A GOOD RESOURCE.
AND IF YOU'RE INTENT ON STAYING ON THE CASE ANYWAY, WE MIGHT AS WELL NOT BE WORKING AT CROSS-PURPOSES.

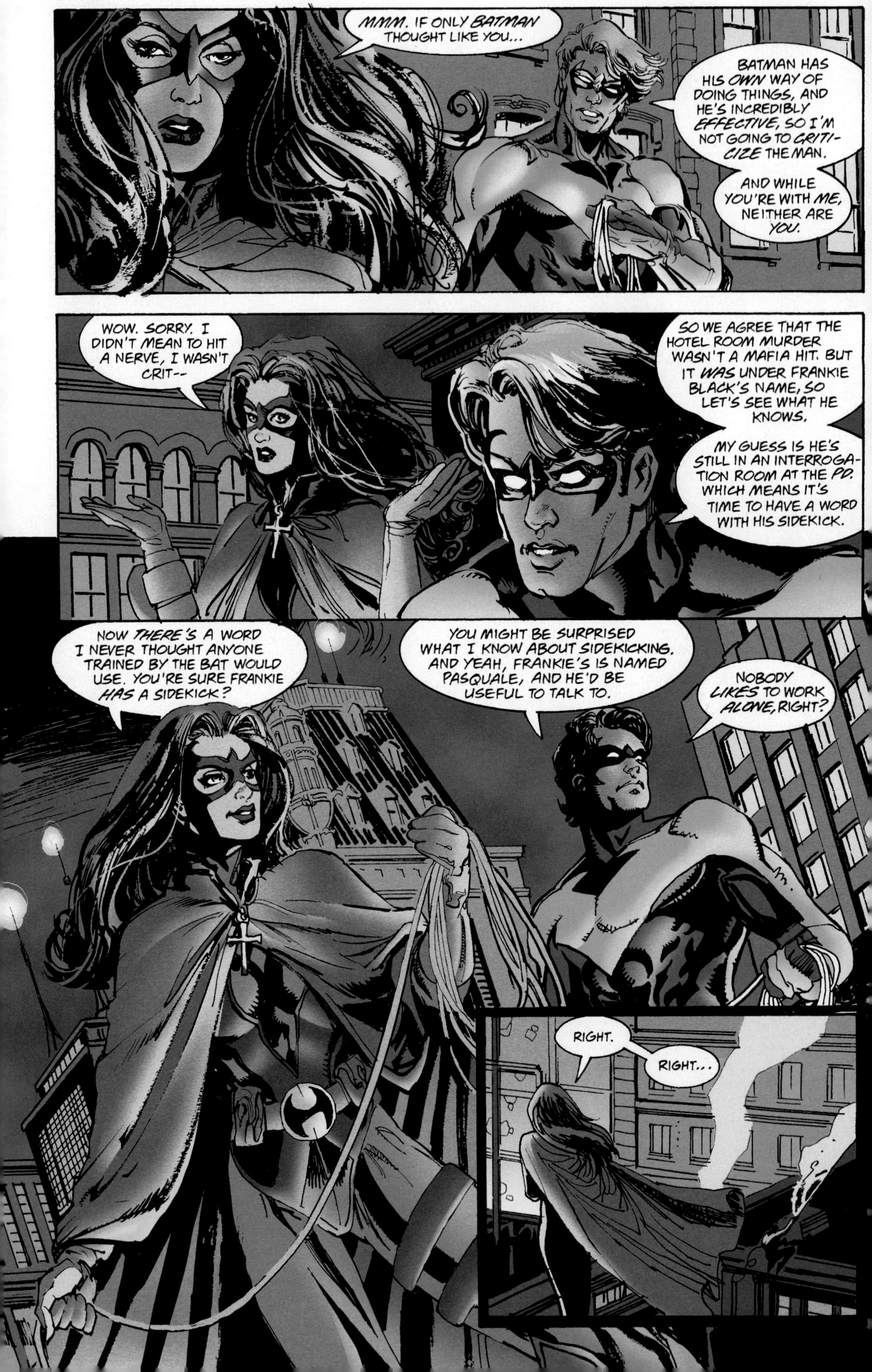
MMM. IF ONLY BATMAN THOUGHT LIKE YOU...
BATMAN HAS HIS OWN WAY OF DOING THINGS, AND HE'S INCREDIBLY EFFECTIVE, SO I'M NOT GOING TO CRITICIZE THE MAN.
AND WHILE YOU'RE WITH ME, NEITHER ARE YOU.
WOW. SORRY. I DIDN'T MEAN TO HIT A NERVE, I WASN'T CRIT--
SO WE AGREE THAT THE HOTEL ROOM MURDER WASN'T A MAFIA HIT. BUT IT WAS UNDER FRANKIE BLACK'S NAME, SO LET'S SEE WHAT HE KNOWS.
MY GUESS IS HE'S STILL IN AN INTERROGATION ROOM AT THE PD. WHICH MEANS IT'S TIME TO HAVE A WORD WITH HIS SIDEKICK.
NOW THERE'S A WORD I NEVER THOUGHT ANYONE TRAINED BY THE BAT WOULD USE. YOU'RE SURE FRANKIE HAS A SIDEKICK?
YOU MIGHT BE SURPRISED WHAT I KNOW ABOUT SIDEKICKING. AND YEAH, FRANKIE'S IS NAMED PASQUALE, AND HE'D BE USEFUL TO TALK TO.
NOBODY LIKES TO WORK ALONE, RIGHT?
RIGHT.
RIGHT...

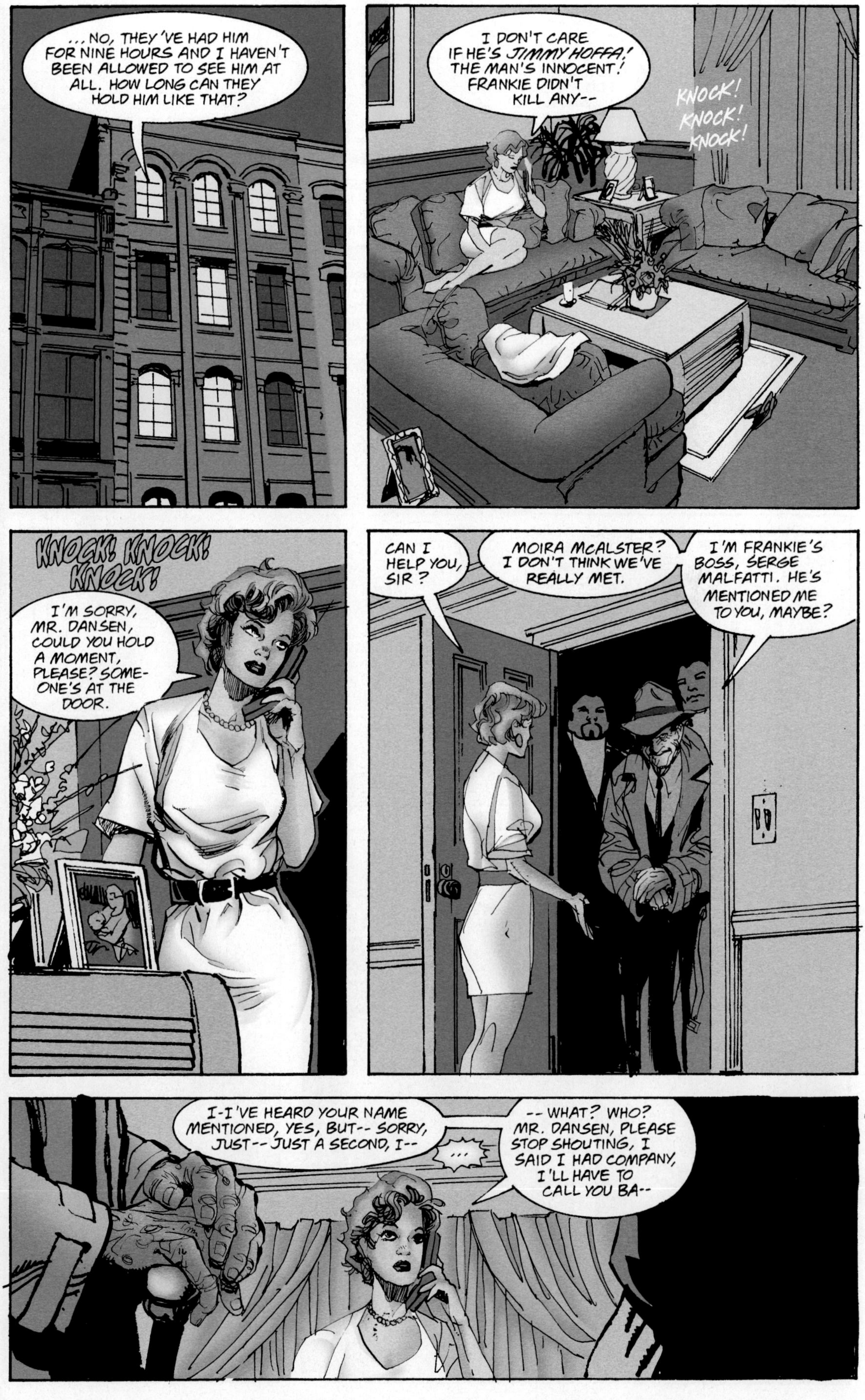
...NO, THEY'VE HAD HIM FOR NINE HOURS AND I HAVEN'T BEEN ALLOWED TO SEE HIM AT ALL. HOW LONG CAN THEY HOLD HIM LIKE THAT?
I DON'T CARE IF HE'S JIMMY HOFFA! THE MAN'S INNOCENT! FRANKIE DIDN'T KILL ANY--
KNOCK! KNOCK! KNOCK!
KNOCK! KNOCK! KNOCK!
I'M SORRY, MR. DANSEN, COULD YOU HOLD A MOMENT, PLEASE? SOME-ONE'S AT THE DOOR.
CAN I HELP YOU, SIR?
MOIRA McALSTER? I DON'T THINK WE'VE REALLY MET.
I'M FRANKIE'S BOSS, SERGE MALFATTI. HE'S MENTIONED ME TO YOU, MAYBE?
I-I'VE HEARD YOUR NAME MENTIONED, YES, BUT-- SORRY, JUST-- JUST A SECOND, I--
...
--WHAT? WHO? MR. DANSEN, PLEASE STOP SHOUTING, I SAID I HAD COMPANY, I'LL HAVE TO CALL YOU BA--

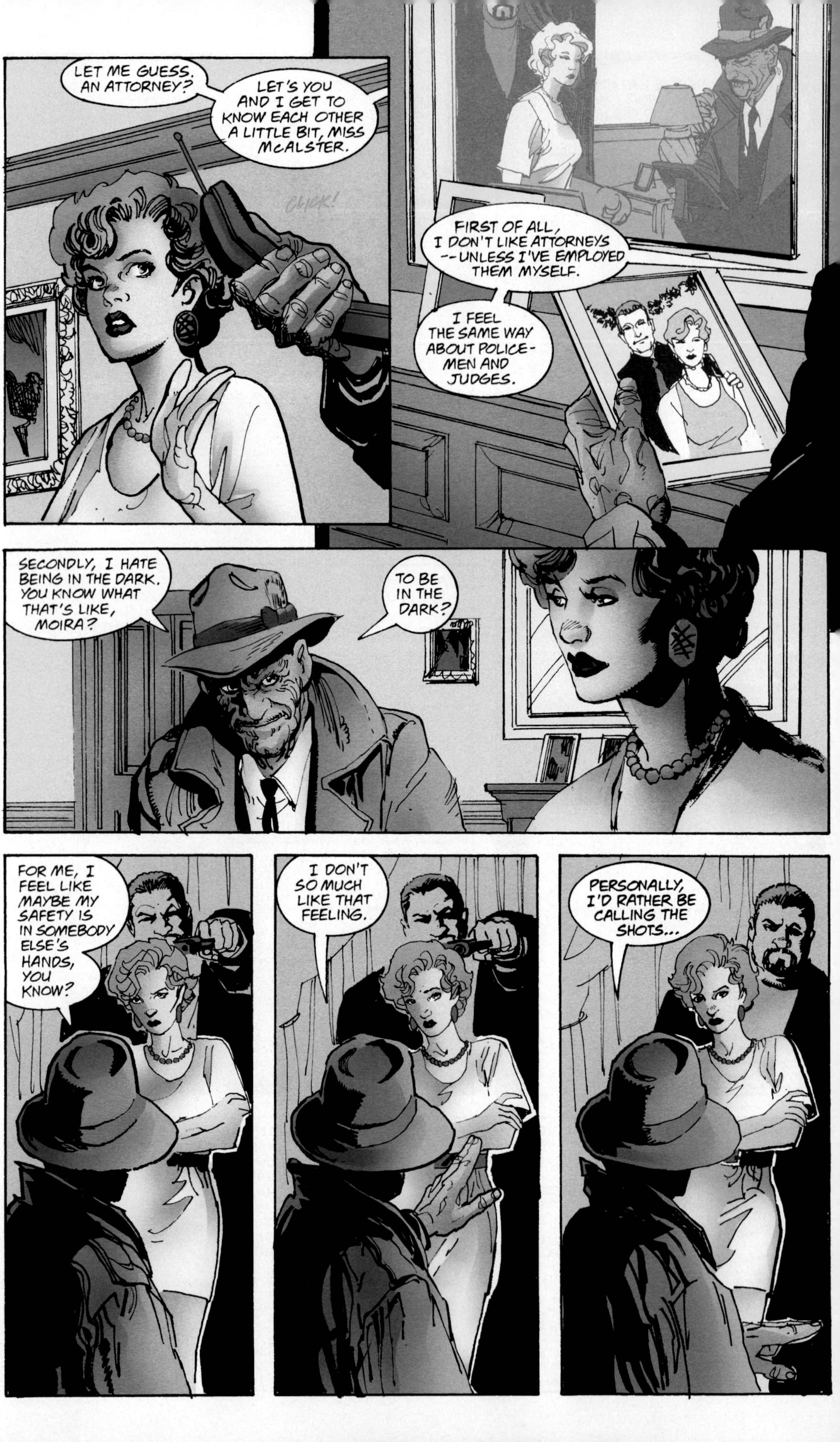
LET ME GUESS. AN ATTORNEY?
LET'S YOU AND I GET TO KNOW EACH OTHER A LITTLE BIT, MISS McALSTER.
CLICK!
FIRST OF ALL, I DON'T LIKE ATTORNEYS --UNLESS I'VE EMPLOYED THEM MYSELF.
I FEEL THE SAME WAY ABOUT POLICEMEN AND JUDGES.
SECONDLY, I HATE BEING IN THE DARK. YOU KNOW WHAT THAT'S LIKE, MOIRA?
TO BE IN THE DARK?
FOR ME, I FEEL LIKE MAYBE MY SAFETY IS IN SOMEBODY ELSE'S HANDS, YOU KNOW?
I DON'T SO MUCH LIKE THAT FEELING.
PERSONALLY, I'D RATHER BE CALLING THE SHOTS...

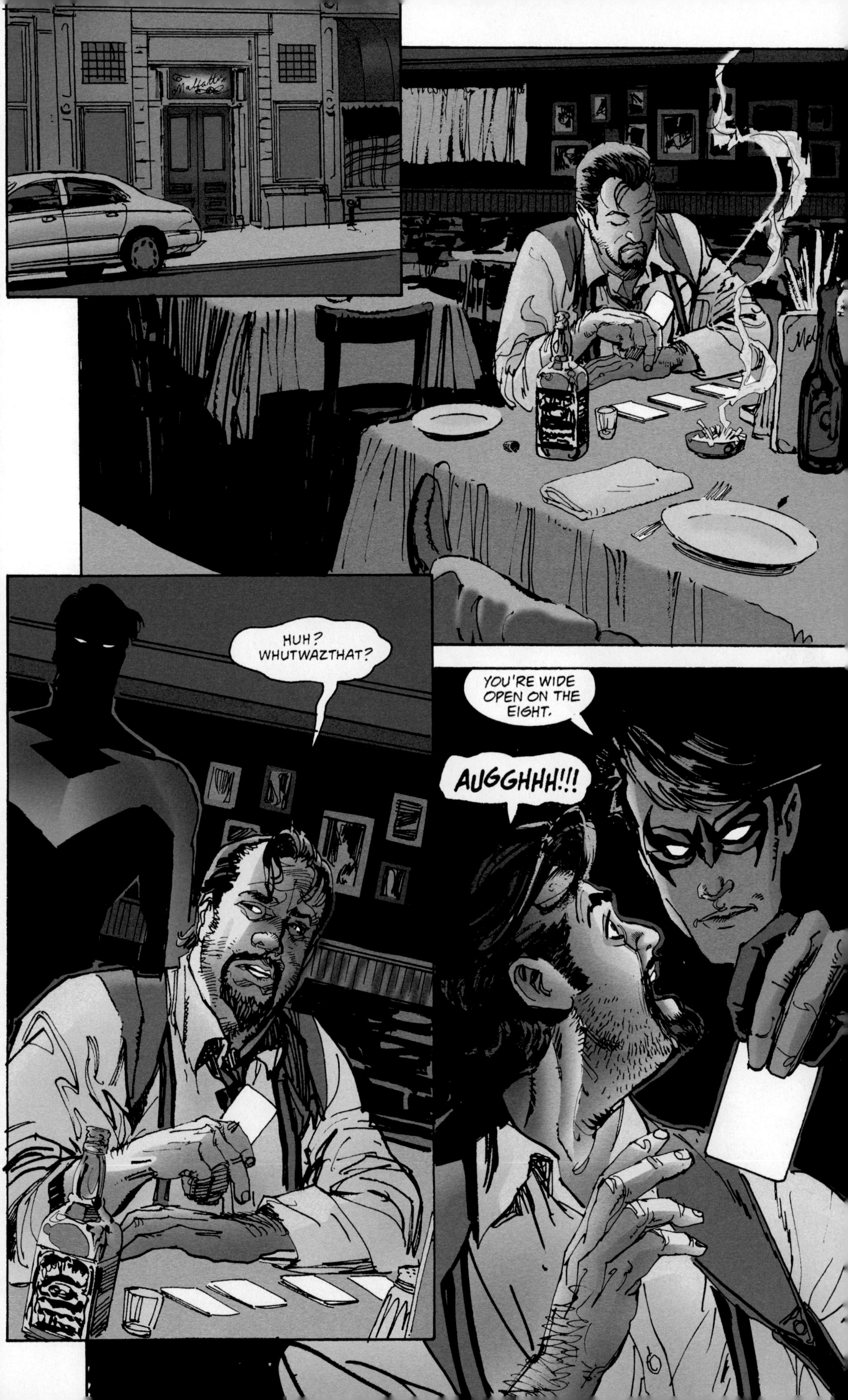

HUH? WHUTWAZTHAT?
YOU'RE WIDE OPEN ON THE EIGHT.
AUGGHHH!!!

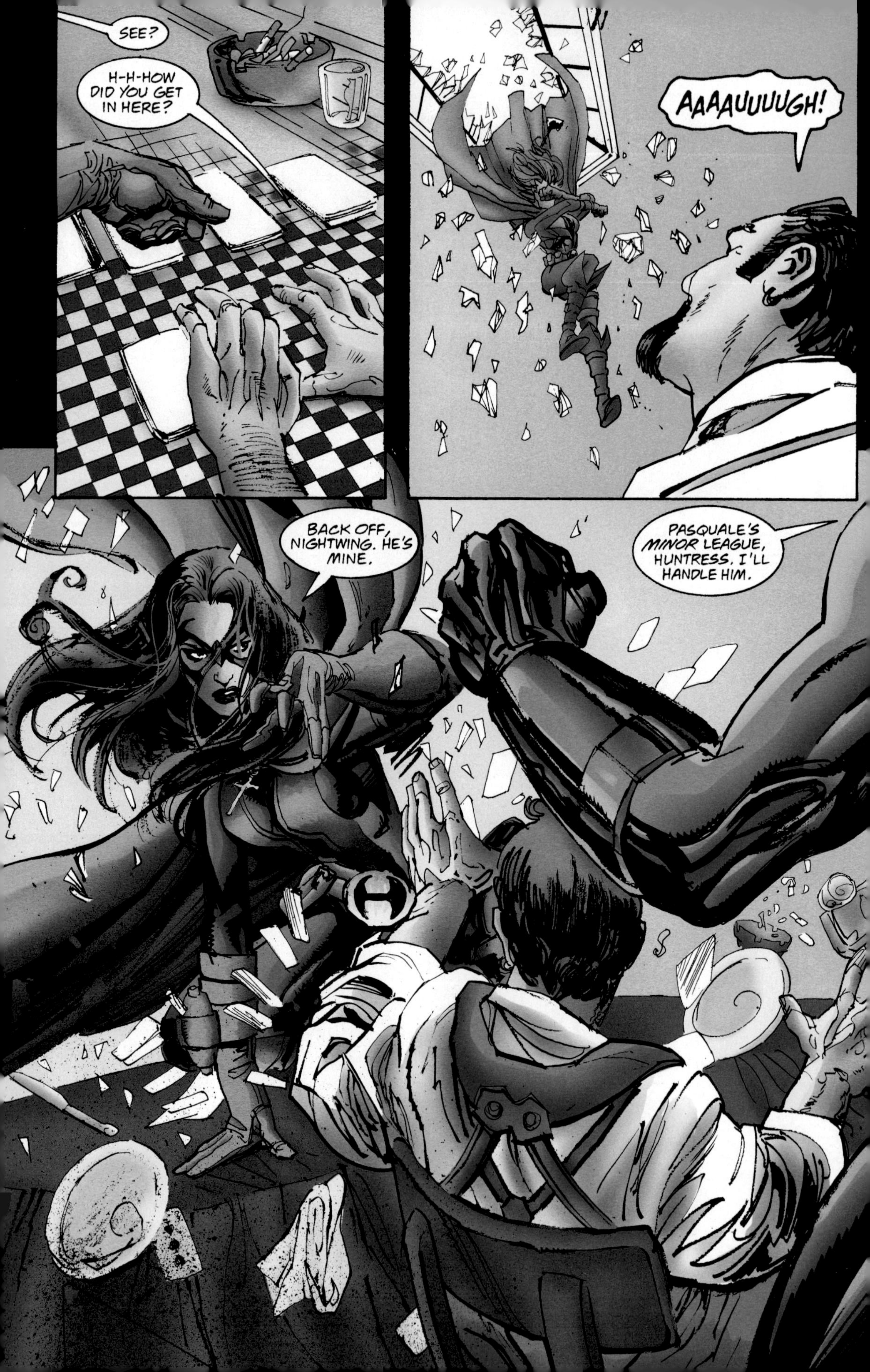
SEE?
H-H-HOW DID YOU GET IN HERE?
AAAAUUUUGH!
BACK OFF, NIGHTWING. HE'S MINE.
PASQUALE'S MINOR LEAGUE, HUNTRESS. I'LL HANDLE HIM.

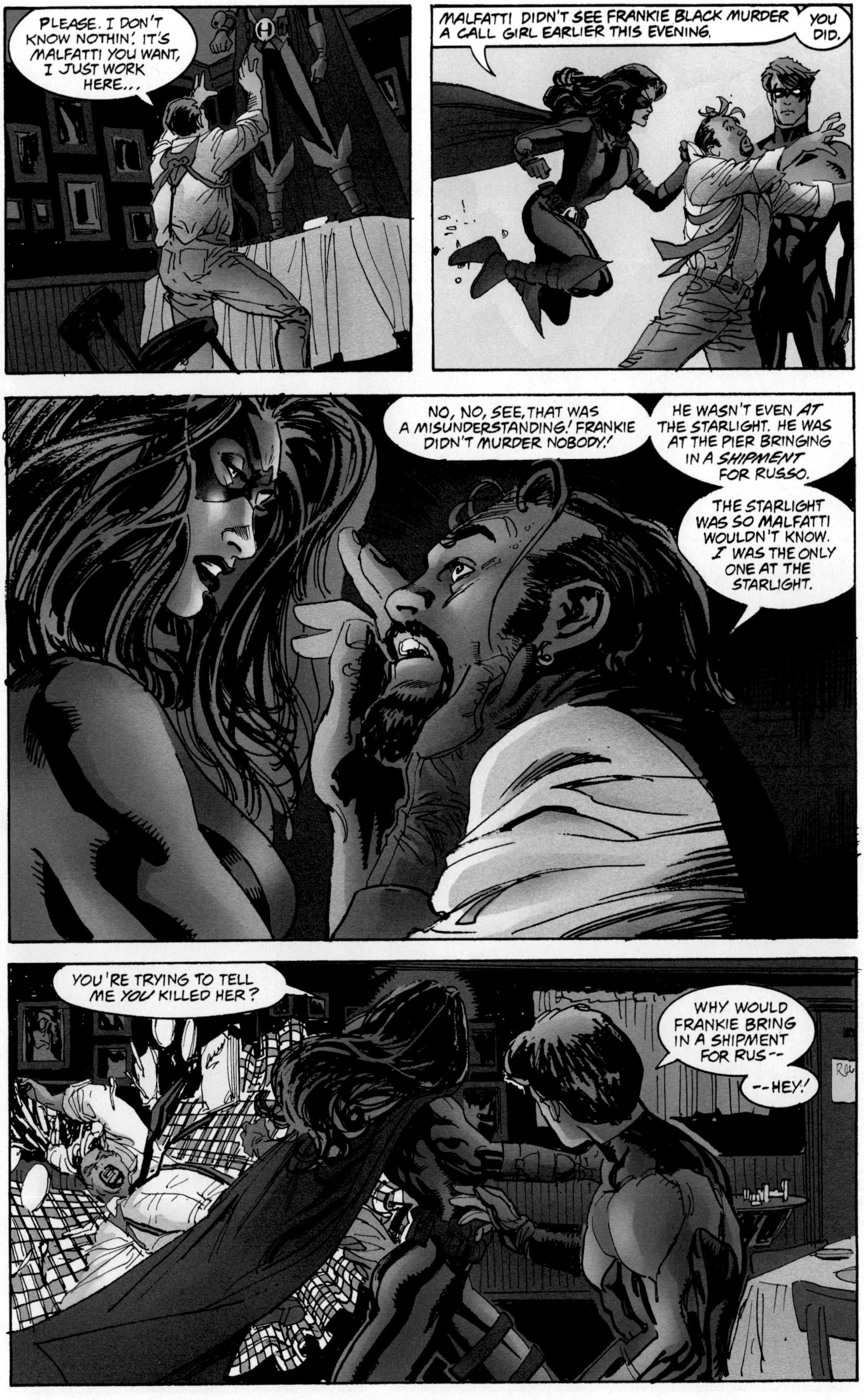
PLEASE. I DON'T KNOW NOTHIN'! IT'S MALFATTI YOU WANT, I JUST WORK HERE...
MALFATTI DIDN'T SEE FRANKIE BLACK MURDER A CALL GIRL EARLIER THIS EVENING.
YOU DID.
NO, NO, SEE, THAT WAS A MISUNDERSTANDING! FRANKIE DIDN'T MURDER NOBODY!
HE WASN'T EVEN AT THE STARLIGHT. HE WAS AT THE PIER BRINGING IN A SHIPMENT FOR RUSSO.
THE STARLIGHT WAS SO MALFATTI WOULDN'T KNOW. I WAS THE ONLY ONE AT THE STARLIGHT.
YOU'RE TRYING TO TELL ME YOU KILLED HER?
WHY WOULD FRANKIE BRING IN A SHIPMENT FOR RUS--
--HEY!

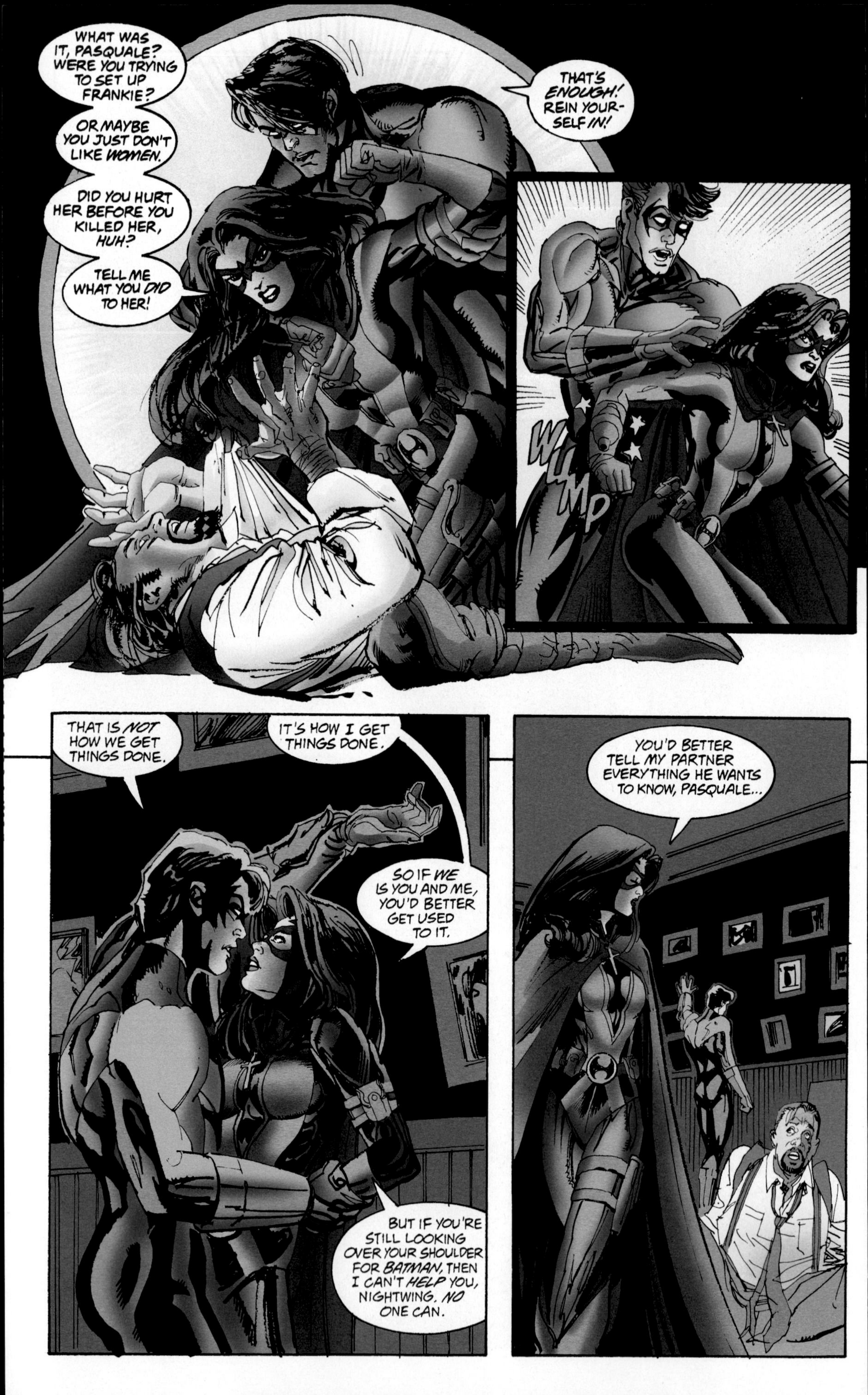

WHAT WAS IT, PASQUALE? WERE YOU TRYING TO SET UP FRANKIE?
OR MAYBE YOU JUST DON'T LIKE WOMEN.
DID YOU HURT HER BEFORE YOU KILLED HER, HUH?
TELL ME WHAT YOU DID TO HER!
THAT'S ENOUGH! REIN YOURSELF IN!
WUMP
THAT IS NOT HOW WE GET THINGS DONE.
IT'S HOW I GET THINGS DONE.
SO IF WE IS YOU AND ME, YOU'D BETTER GET USED TO IT.
BUT IF YOU'RE STILL LOOKING OVER YOUR SHOULDER FOR BATMAN, THEN I CAN'T HELP YOU, NIGHTWING. NO ONE CAN.
YOU'D BETTER TELL MY PARTNER EVERYTHING HE WANTS TO KNOW, PASQUALE...

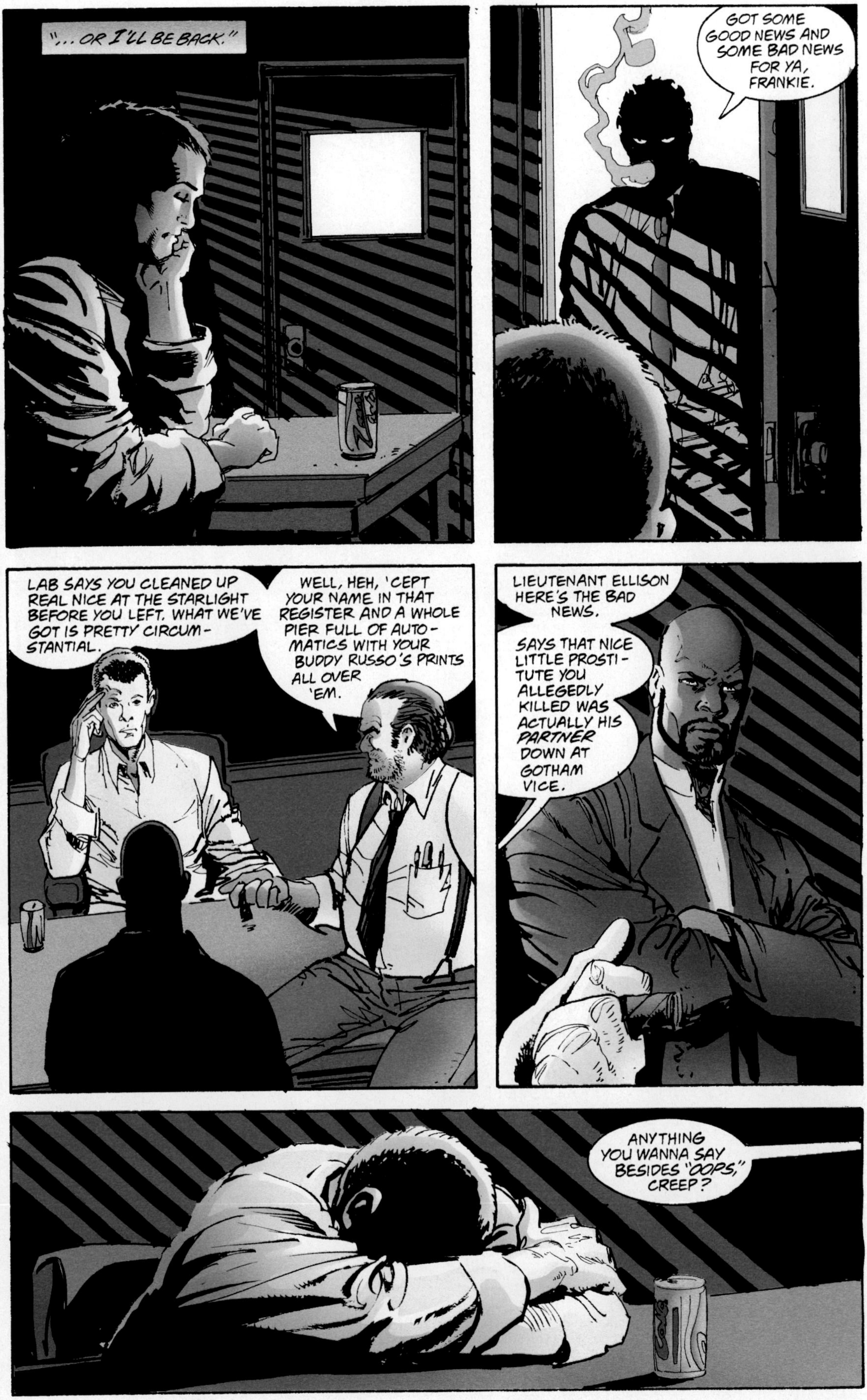
"...OR I'LL BE BACK."
GOT SOME GOOD NEWS AND SOME BAD NEWS FOR YA, FRANKIE.
LAB SAYS YOU CLEANED UP REAL NICE AT THE STARLIGHT BEFORE YOU LEFT. WHAT WE'VE GOT IS PRETTY CIRCUM-STANTIAL.
WELL, HEH, 'CEPT YOUR NAME IN THAT REGISTER AND A WHOLE PIER FULL OF AUTO-MATICS WITH YOUR BUDDY RUSSO'S PRINTS ALL OVER 'EM.
LIEUTENANT ELLISON HERE'S THE BAD NEWS.
SAYS THAT NICE LITTLE PROSTI-TUTE YOU ALLEGEDLY KILLED WAS ACTUALLY HIS PARTNER DOWN AT GOTHAM VICE.
ANYTHING YOU WANNA SAY BESIDES "OOPS," CREEP?

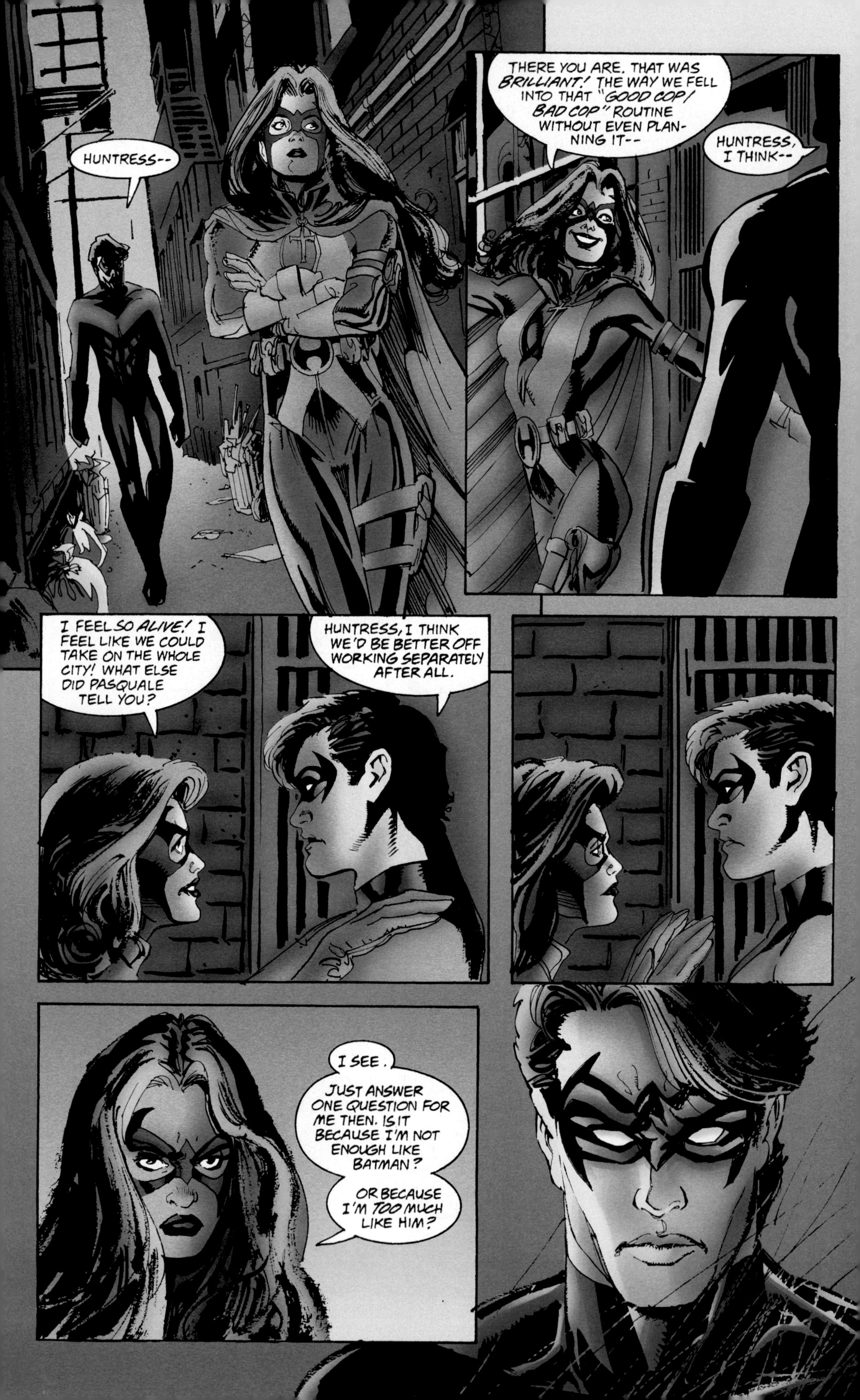

HUNTRESS--
THERE YOU ARE. THAT WAS BRILLIANT! THE WAY WE FELL INTO THAT "GOOD COP/ BAD COP" ROUTINE WITHOUT EVEN PLANNING IT--
HUNTRESS, I THINK--
I FEEL SO ALIVE! I FEEL LIKE WE COULD TAKE ON THE WHOLE CITY! WHAT ELSE DID PASQUALE TELL YOU?
HUNTRESS, I THINK WE'D BE BETTER OFF WORKING SEPARATELY AFTER ALL.
I SEE.
JUST ANSWER ONE QUESTION FOR ME THEN. IS IT BECAUSE I'M NOT ENOUGH LIKE BATMAN?
OR BECAUSE I'M TOO MUCH LIKE HIM?

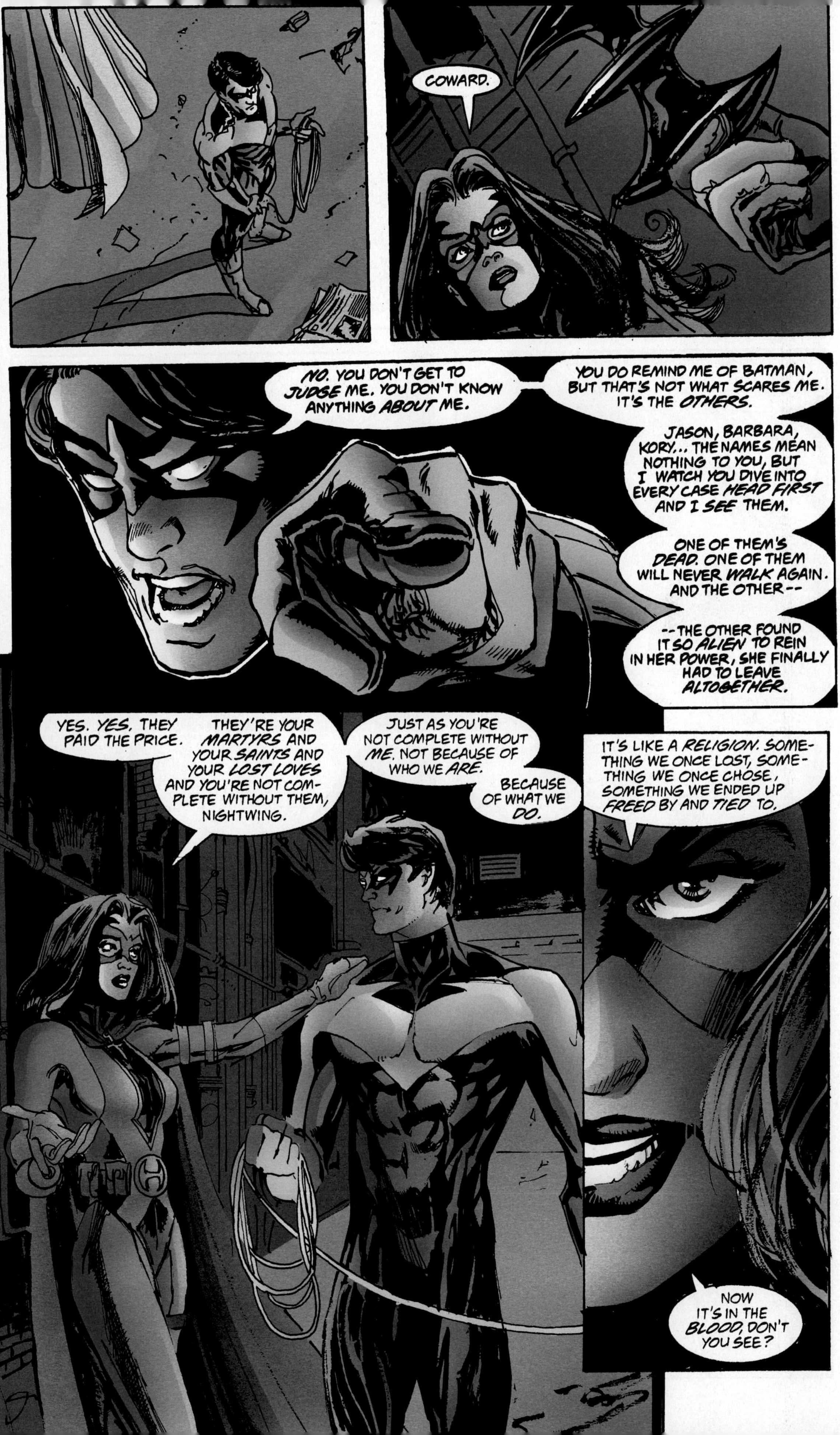
COWARD.
NO. YOU DON'T GET TO JUDGE ME. YOU DON'T KNOW ANYTHING ABOUT ME.
YOU DO REMIND ME OF BATMAN, BUT THAT'S NOT WHAT SCARES ME. IT'S THE OTHERS.
JASON, BARBARA, KORY... THE NAMES MEAN NOTHING TO YOU, BUT I WATCH YOU DIVE INTO EVERY CASE HEAD FIRST AND I SEE THEM.
ONE OF THEM'S DEAD. ONE OF THEM WILL NEVER WALK AGAIN. AND THE OTHER--
--THE OTHER FOUND IT SO ALIEN TO REIN IN HER POWER, SHE FINALLY HAD TO LEAVE ALTOGETHER.
YES. YES. THEY PAID THE PRICE.
THEY'RE YOUR MARTYRS AND YOUR SAINTS AND YOUR LOST LOVES AND YOU'RE NOT COMPLETE WITHOUT THEM, NIGHTWING.
JUST AS YOU'RE NOT COMPLETE WITHOUT ME. NOT BECAUSE OF WHO WE ARE.
BECAUSE OF WHAT WE DO.
IT'S LIKE A RELIGION. SOMETHING WE ONCE LOST, SOMETHING WE ONCE CHOSE, SOMETHING WE ENDED UP FREED BY AND TIED TO.
NOW IT'S IN THE BLOOD, DON'T YOU SEE?

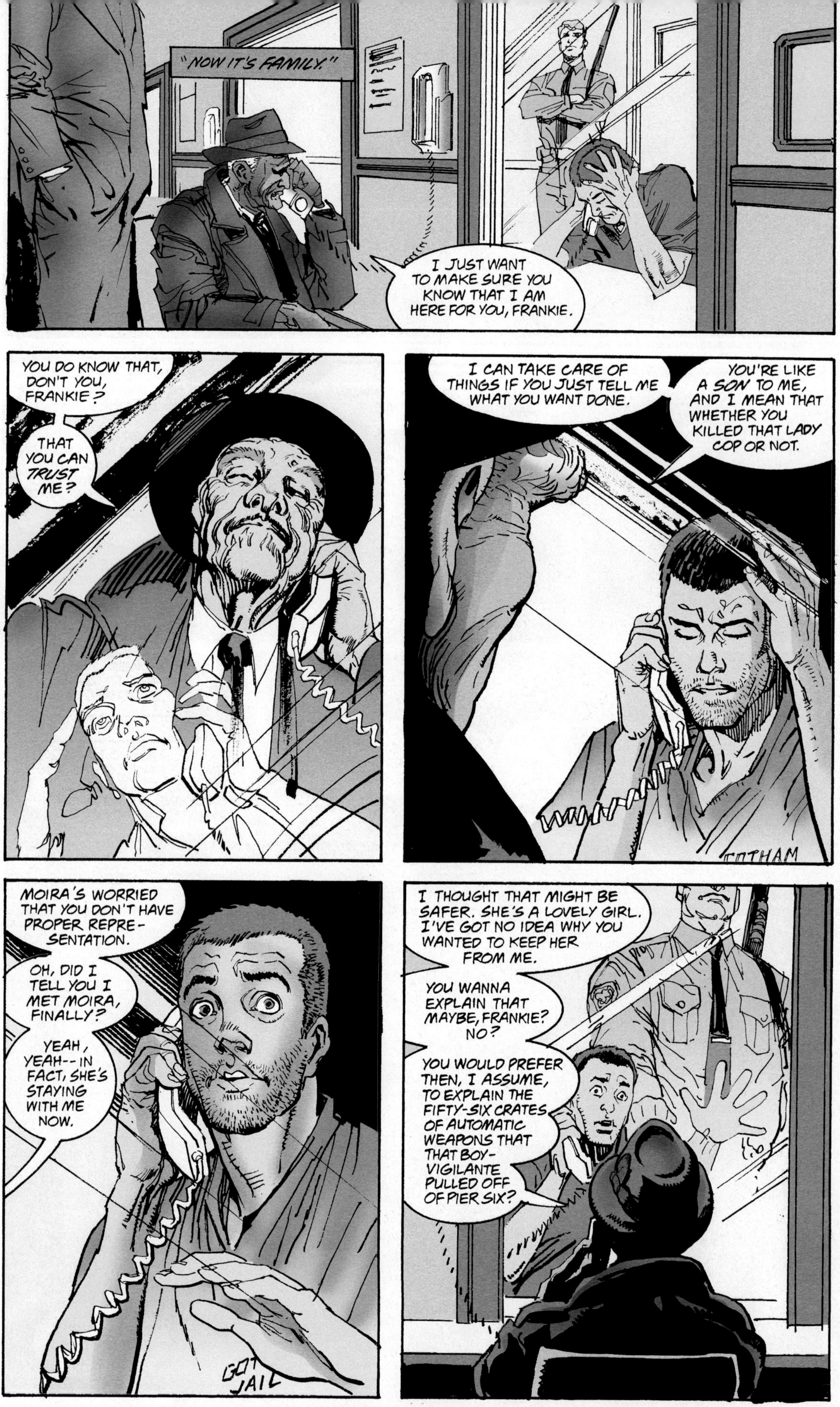
"NOW IT'S FAMILY."
I JUST WANT TO MAKE SURE YOU KNOW THAT I AM HERE FOR YOU, FRANKIE.
YOU DO KNOW THAT, DON'T YOU, FRANKIE?
THAT YOU CAN TRUST ME?
I CAN TAKE CARE OF THINGS IF YOU JUST TELL ME WHAT YOU WANT DONE.
YOU'RE LIKE A SON TO ME, AND I MEAN THAT WHETHER YOU KILLED THAT LADY COP OR NOT.
MOIRA'S WORRIED THAT YOU DON'T HAVE PROPER REPRE-SENTATION.
OH, DID I TELL YOU I MET MOIRA, FINALLY?
YEAH, YEAH--IN FACT, SHE'S STAYING WITH ME NOW.
I THOUGHT THAT MIGHT BE SAFER. SHE'S A LOVELY GIRL. I'VE GOT NO IDEA WHY YOU WANTED TO KEEP HER FROM ME.
YOU WANNA EXPLAIN THAT MAYBE, FRANKIE? NO?
YOU WOULD PREFER THEN, I ASSUME, TO EXPLAIN THE FIFTY-SIX CRATES OF AUTOMATIC WEAPONS THAT THAT BOY-VIGILANTE PULLED OFF OF PIER SIX?

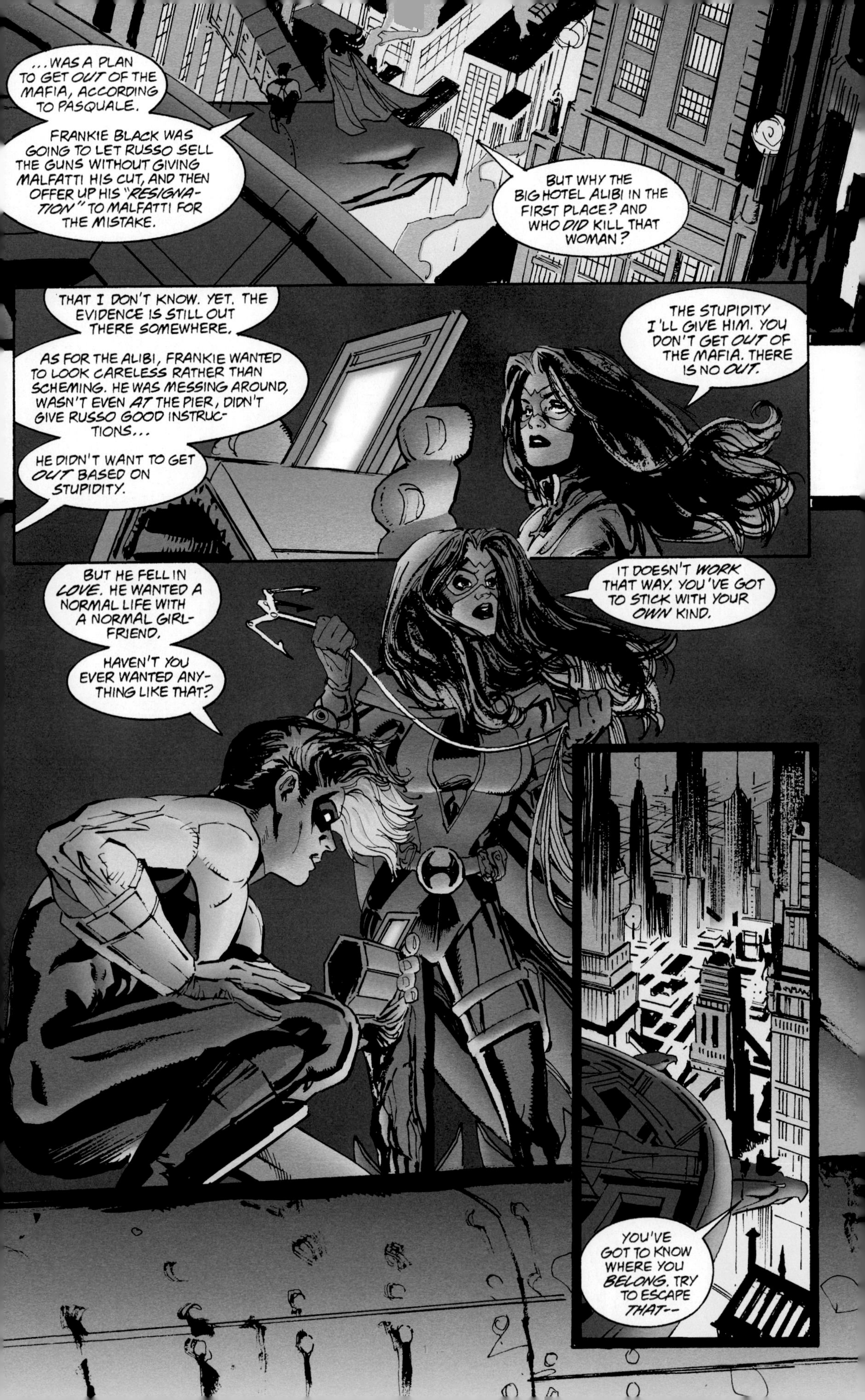
...WAS A PLAN TO GET OUT OF THE MAFIA, ACCORDING TO PASQUALE.
FRANKIE BLACK WAS GOING TO LET RUSSO SELL THE GUNS WITHOUT GIVING MALFATTI HIS CUT, AND THEN OFFER UP HIS "RESIGNATION" TO MALFATTI FOR THE MISTAKE.
BUT WHY THE BIG HOTEL ALIBI IN THE FIRST PLACE? AND WHO DID KILL THAT WOMAN?
THAT I DON'T KNOW. YET. THE EVIDENCE IS STILL OUT THERE SOMEWHERE.
AS FOR THE ALIBI, FRANKIE WANTED TO LOOK CARELESS RATHER THAN SCHEMING. HE WAS MESSING AROUND, WASN'T EVEN AT THE PIER, DIDN'T GIVE RUSSO GOOD INSTRUCTIONS...
HE DIDN'T WANT TO GET OUT BASED ON STUPIDITY.
THE STUPIDITY I'LL GIVE HIM. YOU DON'T GET OUT OF THE MAFIA. THERE IS NO OUT.
BUT HE FELL IN LOVE. HE WANTED A NORMAL LIFE WITH A NORMAL GIRLFRIEND.
HAVEN'T YOU EVER WANTED ANYTHING LIKE THAT?
IT DOESN'T WORK THAT WAY. YOU'VE GOT TO STICK WITH YOUR OWN KIND.
YOU'VE GOT TO KNOW WHERE YOU BELONG. TRY TO ESCAPE THAT--

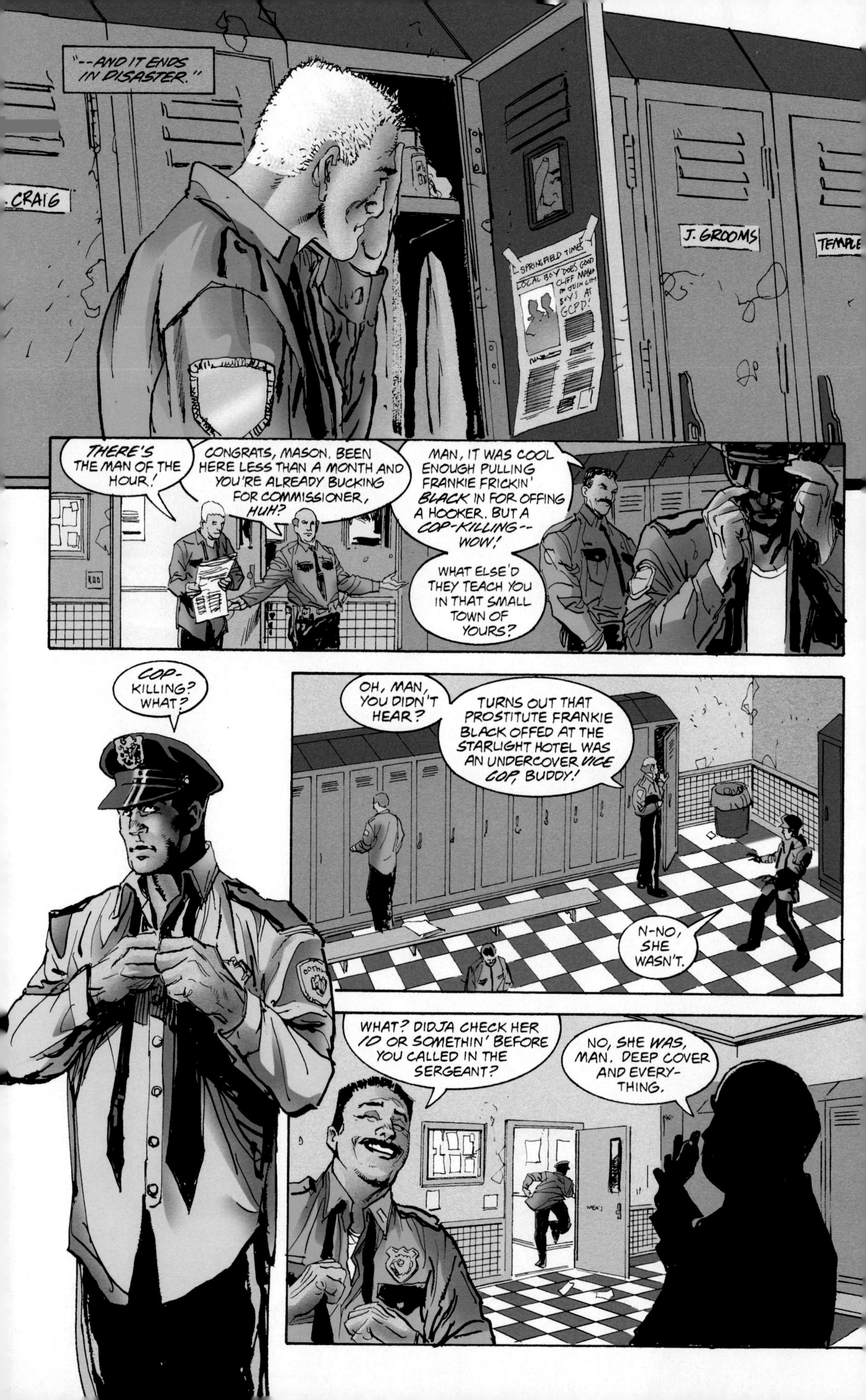
"--AND IT ENDS IN DISASTER."
CRAIG
J. GROOMS
TEMPLE
SPRINGFIELD TIMES
LOCAL BOY DOES GOOD
THERE'S THE MAN OF THE HOUR!
CONGRATS, MASON. BEEN HERE LESS THAN A MONTH AND YOU'RE ALREADY BUCKING FOR COMMISSIONER, HUH?
MAN, IT WAS COOL ENOUGH PULLING FRANKIE FRICKIN' BLACK IN FOR OFFING A HOOKER. BUT A COP-KILLING--WOW!
WHAT ELSE'D THEY TEACH YOU IN THAT SMALL TOWN OF YOURS?
COP-KILLING? WHAT?
OH, MAN, YOU DIDN'T HEAR?
TURNS OUT THAT PROSTITUTE FRANKIE BLACK OFFED AT THE STARLIGHT HOTEL WAS AN UNDERCOVER VICE COP, BUDDY!
N-NO, SHE WASN'T.
WHAT? DIDJA CHECK HER ID OR SOMETHIN' BEFORE YOU CALLED IN THE SERGEANT?
NO, SHE WAS, MAN. DEEP COVER AND EVERY-THING.
MEN'S

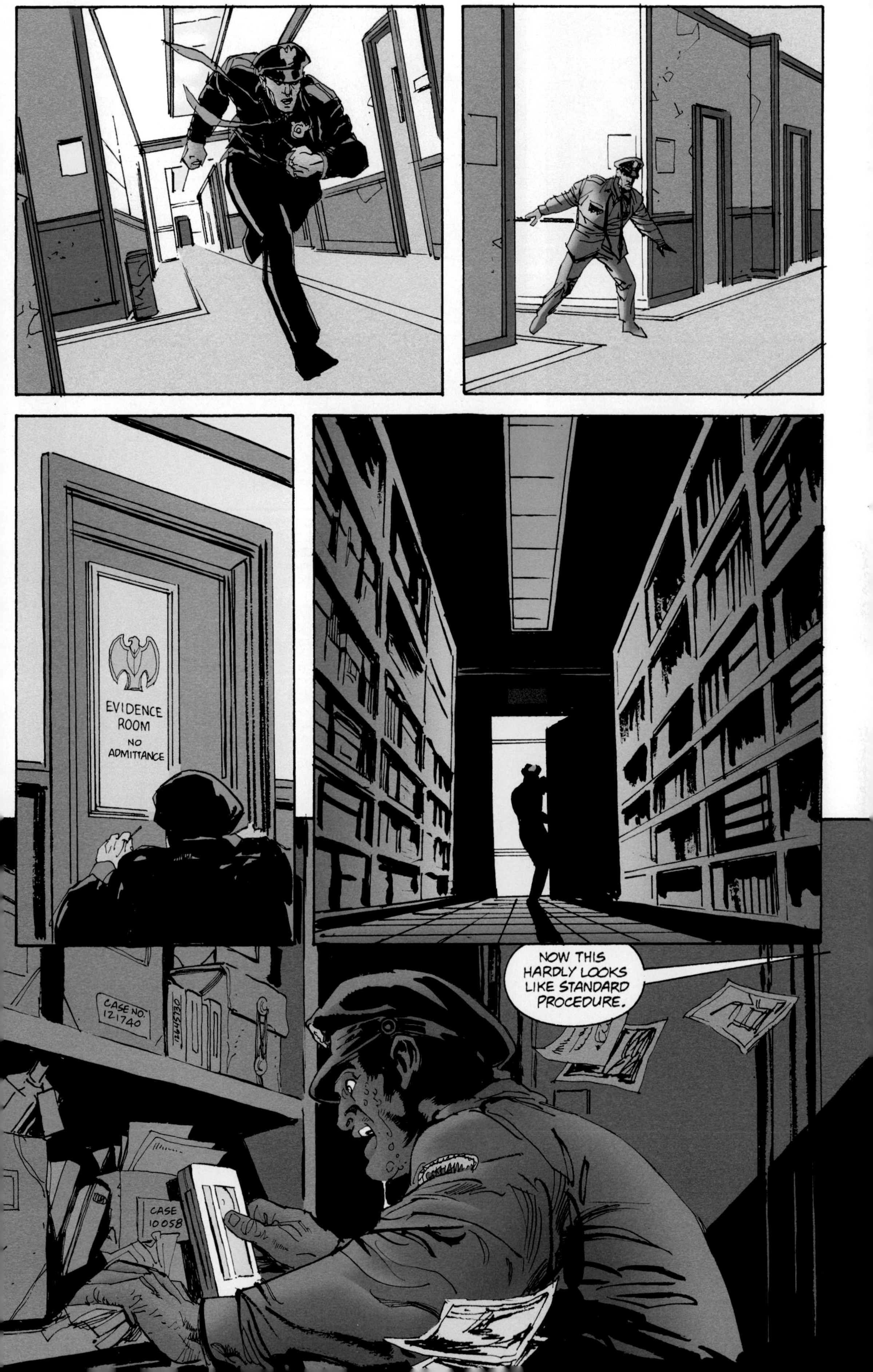
EVIDENCE ROOM
NO ADMITTANCE
NOW THIS HARDLY LOOKS LIKE STANDARD PROCEDURE.
CASE NO. 121740
CASE 10058

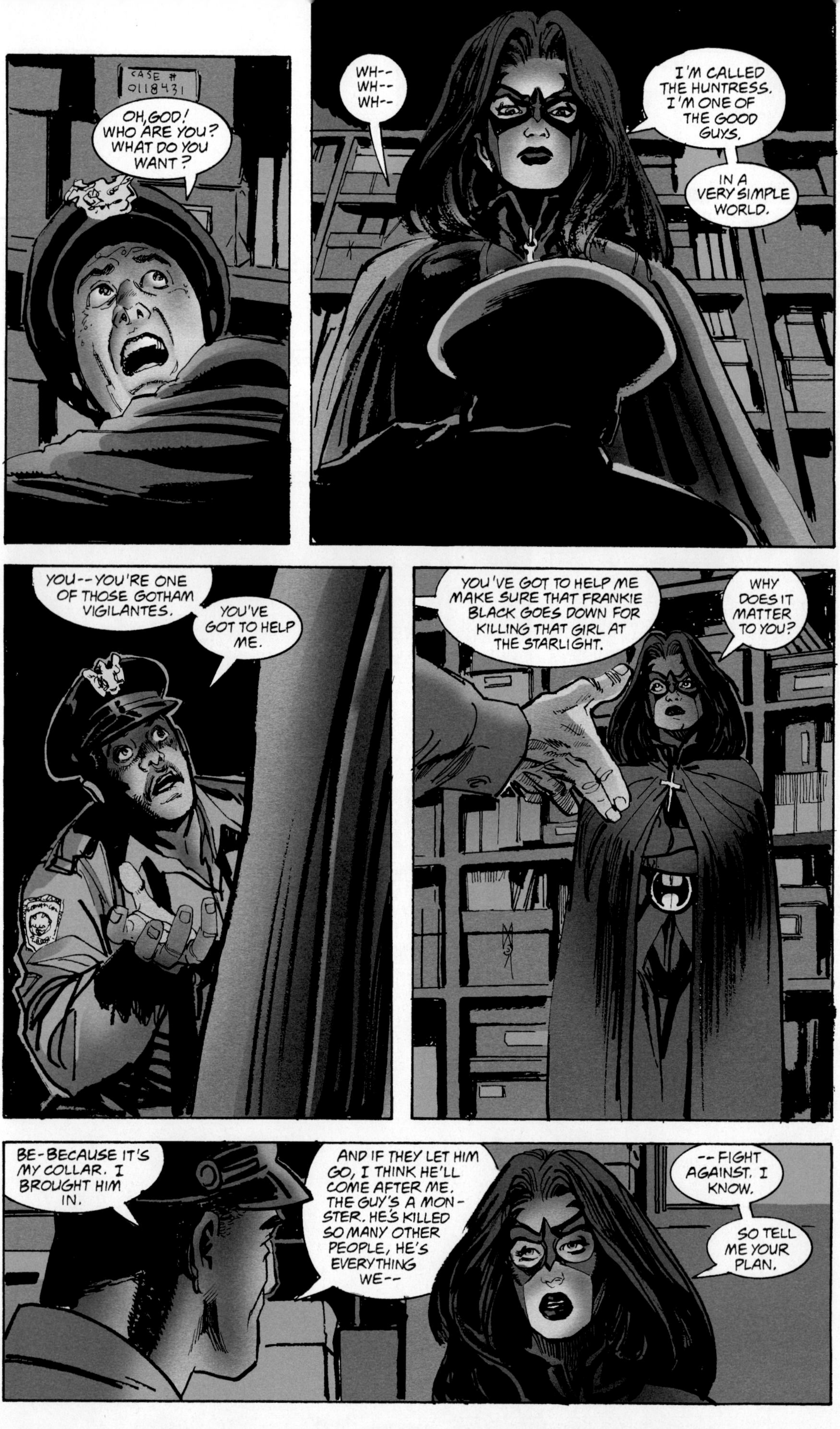
CASE # 0118431
OH, GOD! WHO ARE YOU? WHAT DO YOU WANT?
WH-- WH-- WH--
I'M CALLED THE HUNTRESS. I'M ONE OF THE GOOD GUYS.
IN A VERY SIMPLE WORLD.
YOU--YOU'RE ONE OF THOSE GOTHAM VIGILANTES.
YOU'VE GOT TO HELP ME.
YOU'VE GOT TO HELP ME MAKE SURE THAT FRANKIE BLACK GOES DOWN FOR KILLING THAT GIRL AT THE STARLIGHT.
WHY DOES IT MATTER TO YOU?
BE-BECAUSE IT'S MY COLLAR. I BROUGHT HIM IN.
AND IF THEY LET HIM GO, I THINK HE'LL COME AFTER ME. THE GUY'S A MON-STER. HE'S KILLED SO MANY OTHER PEOPLE, HE'S EVERYTHING WE--
--FIGHT AGAINST. I KNOW.
SO TELL ME YOUR PLAN.

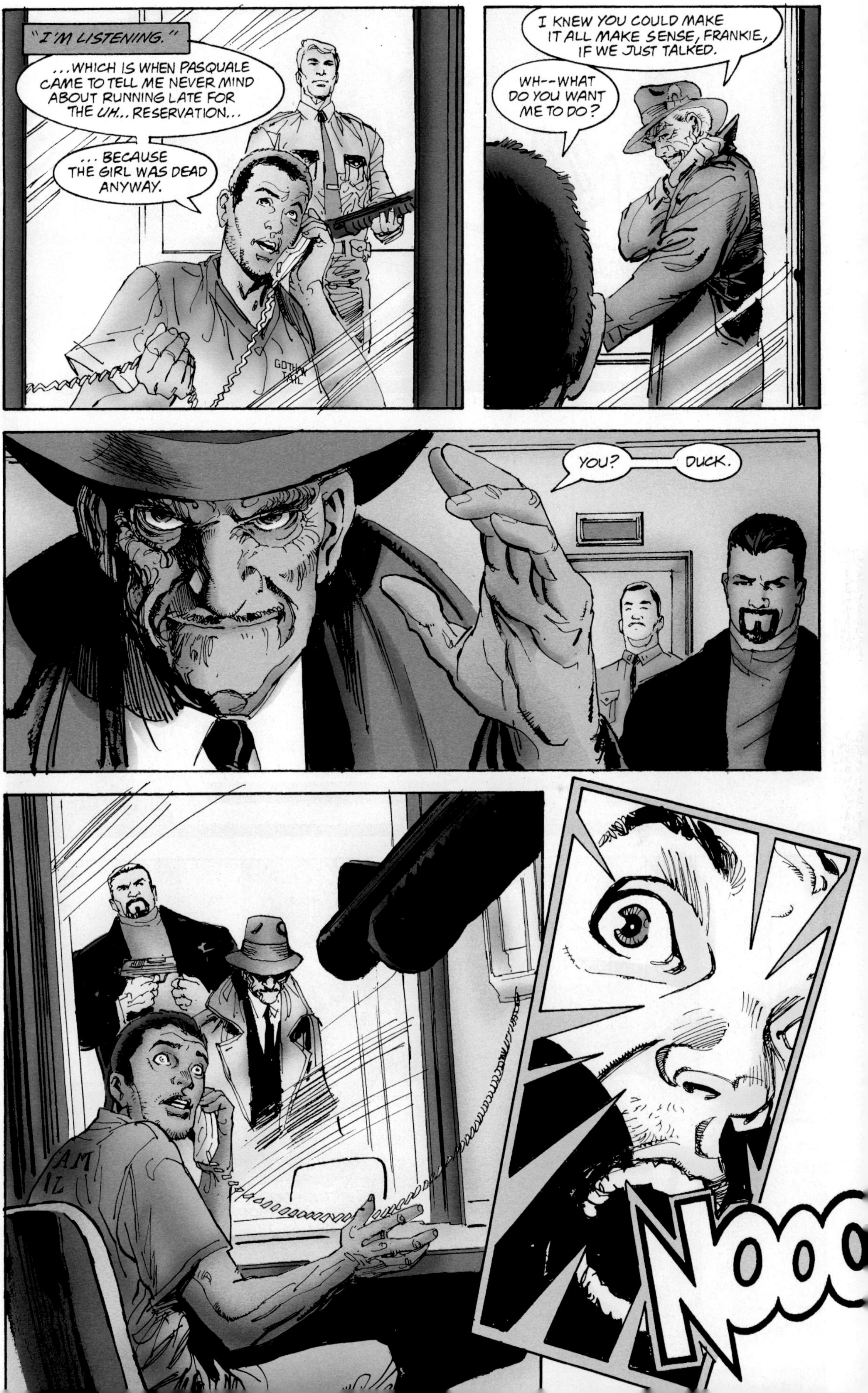
"I'M LISTENING."
...WHICH IS WHEN PASQUALE CAME TO TELL ME NEVER MIND ABOUT RUNNING LATE FOR THE UH... RESERVATION...
...BECAUSE THE GIRL WAS DEAD ANYWAY.
I KNEW YOU COULD MAKE IT ALL MAKE SENSE, FRANKIE, IF WE JUST TALKED.
WH--WHAT DO YOU WANT ME TO DO?
YOU?
DUCK.
NOOO

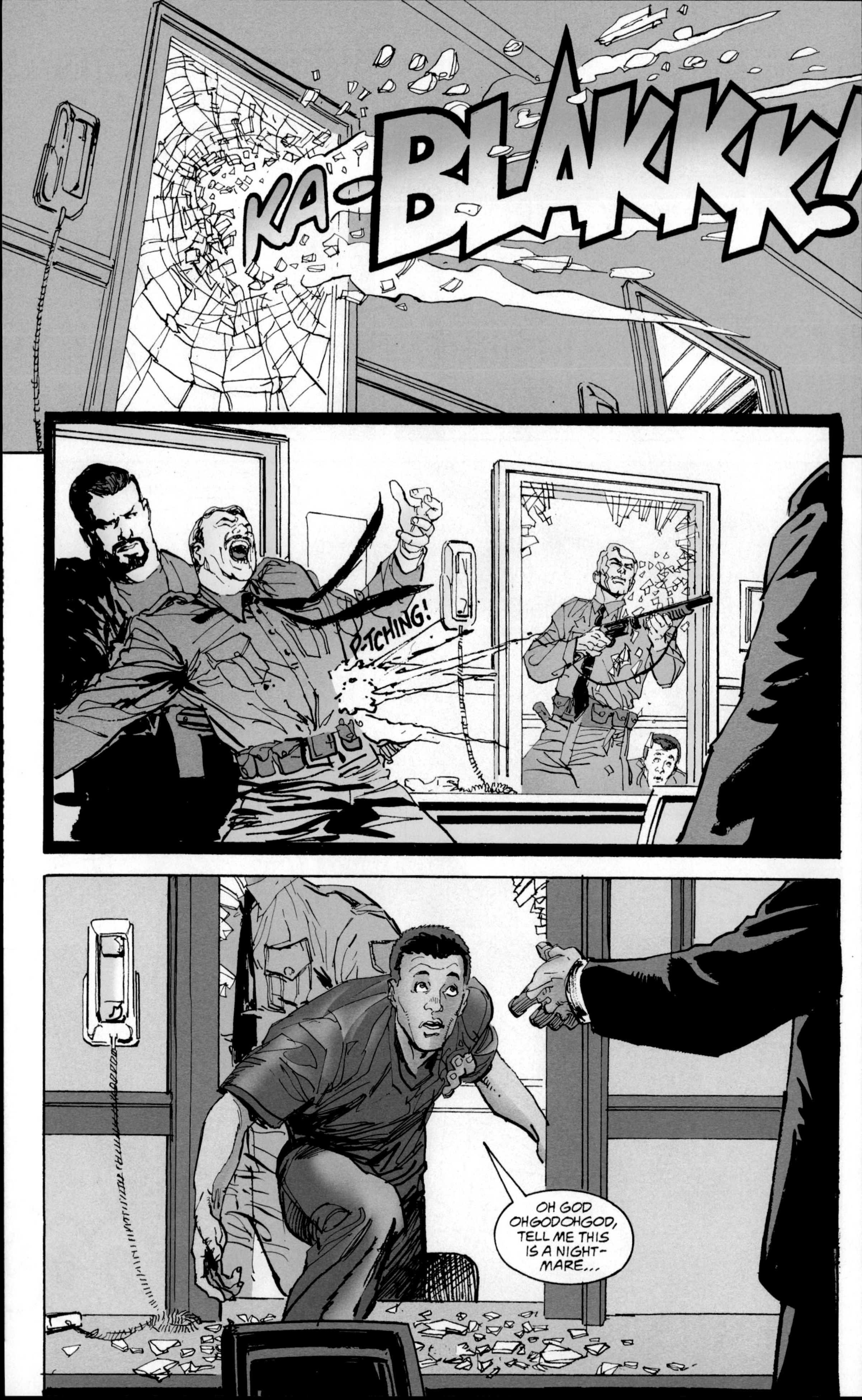
KA-BLAKKK!
P-TCHING!
OH GOD OHGODOHGOD, TELL ME THIS IS A NIGHT-MARE...

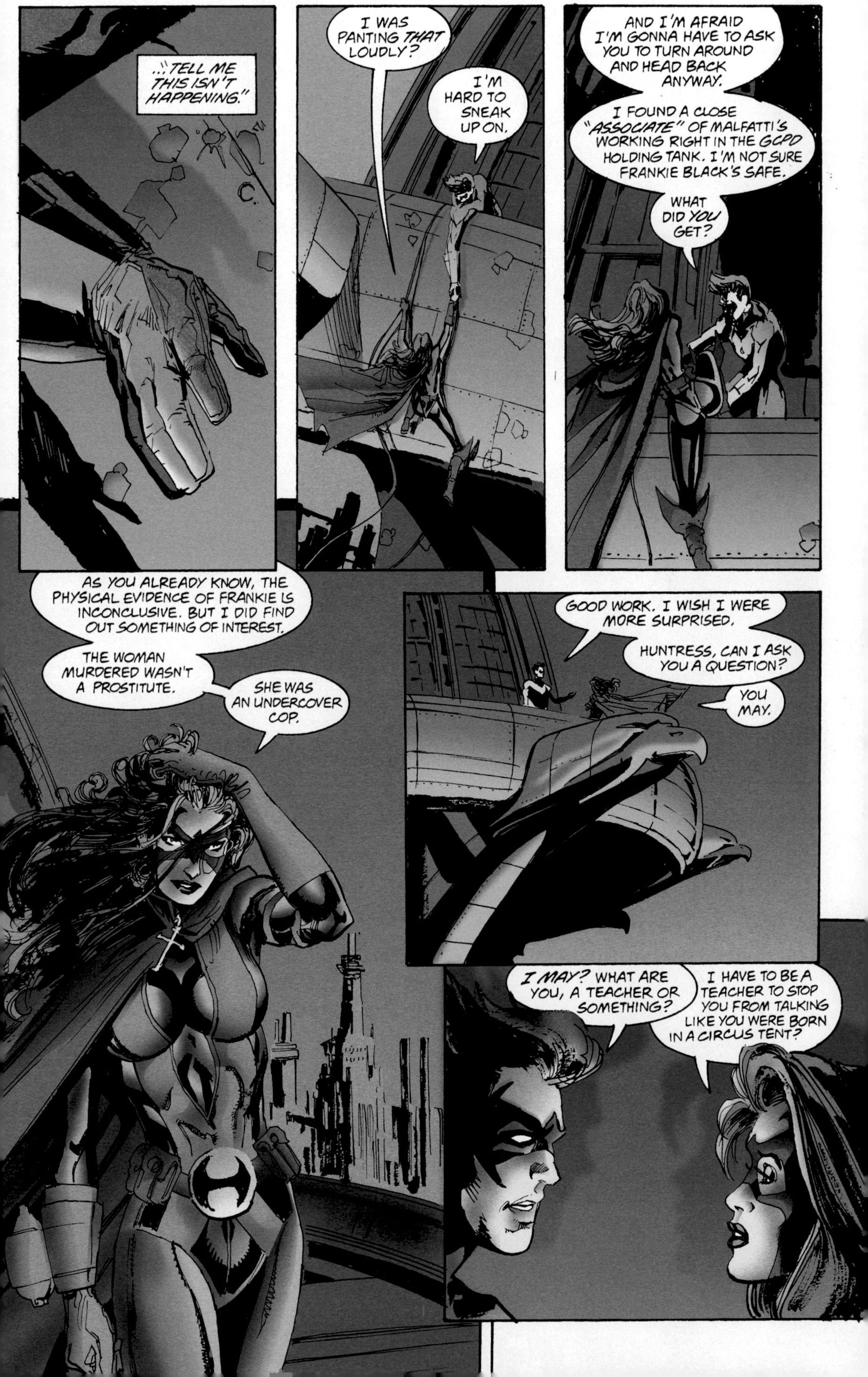

..."TELL ME THIS ISN'T HAPPENING."
I WAS PANTING THAT LOUDLY?
I'M HARD TO SNEAK UP ON.
AND I'M AFRAID I'M GONNA HAVE TO ASK YOU TO TURN AROUND AND HEAD BACK ANYWAY.
I FOUND A CLOSE "ASSOCIATE" OF MALFATTI'S WORKING RIGHT IN THE GCPD HOLDING TANK. I'M NOT SURE FRANKIE BLACK'S SAFE.
WHAT DID YOU GET?
AS YOU ALREADY KNOW, THE PHYSICAL EVIDENCE OF FRANKIE IS INCONCLUSIVE. BUT I DID FIND OUT SOMETHING OF INTEREST.
THE WOMAN MURDERED WASN'T A PROSTITUTE.
SHE WAS AN UNDERCOVER COP.
GOOD WORK. I WISH I WERE MORE SURPRISED.
HUNTRESS, CAN I ASK YOU A QUESTION?
YOU MAY.
I MAY? WHAT ARE YOU, A TEACHER OR SOMETHING?
I HAVE TO BE A TEACHER TO STOP YOU FROM TALKING LIKE YOU WERE BORN IN A CIRCUS TENT?

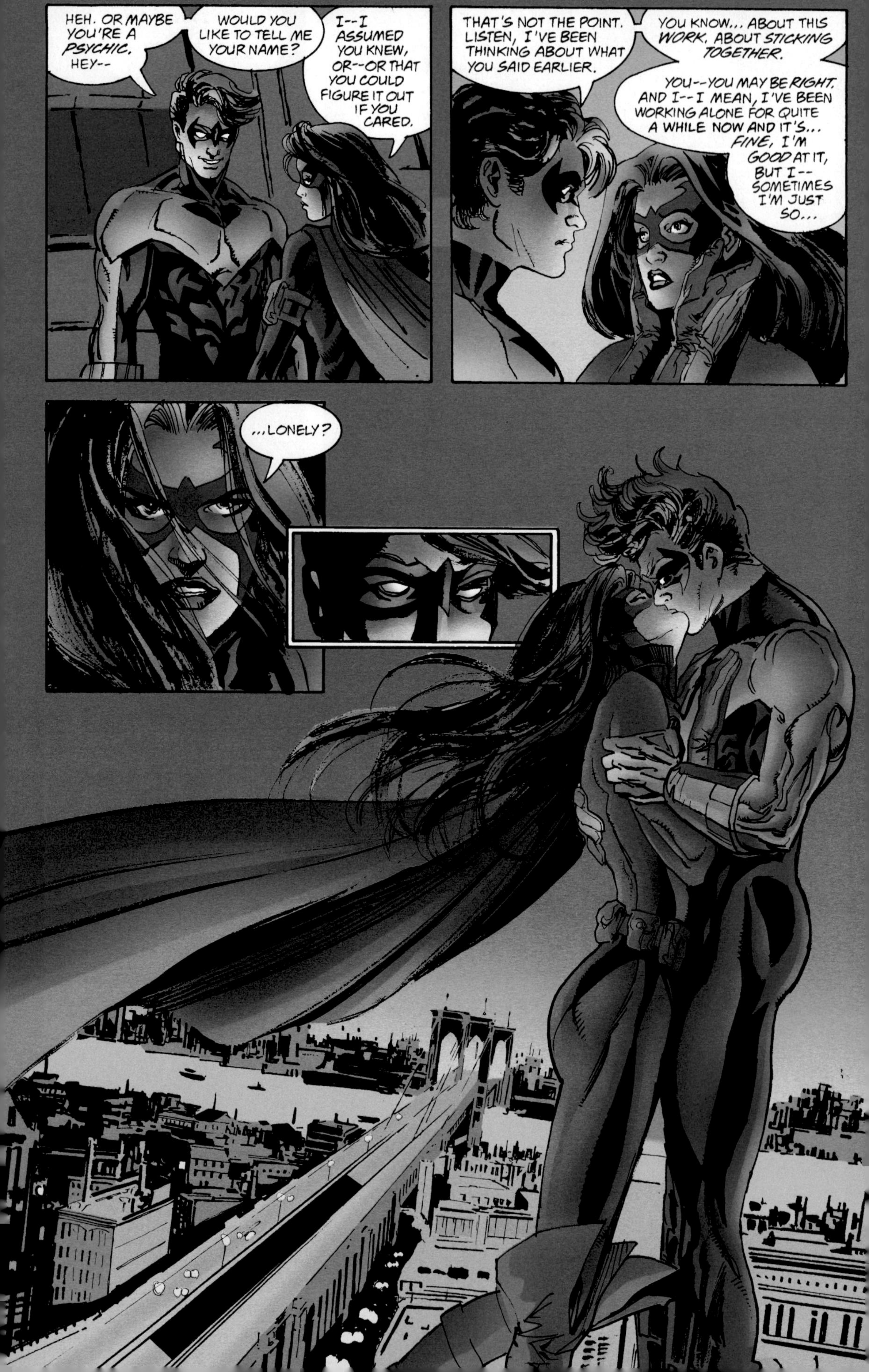
HEH. OR MAYBE YOU'RE A PSYCHIC. HEY--
WOULD YOU LIKE TO TELL ME YOUR NAME?
I--I ASSUMED YOU KNEW, OR--OR THAT YOU COULD FIGURE IT OUT IF YOU CARED.
THAT'S NOT THE POINT. LISTEN, I'VE BEEN THINKING ABOUT WHAT YOU SAID EARLIER.
YOU KNOW... ABOUT THIS WORK. ABOUT STICKING TOGETHER.
YOU--YOU MAY BE RIGHT. AND I--I MEAN, I'VE BEEN WORKING ALONE FOR QUITE A WHILE NOW AND IT'S... FINE, I'M GOOD AT IT, BUT I--SOMETIMES I'M JUST SO...
...LONELY?

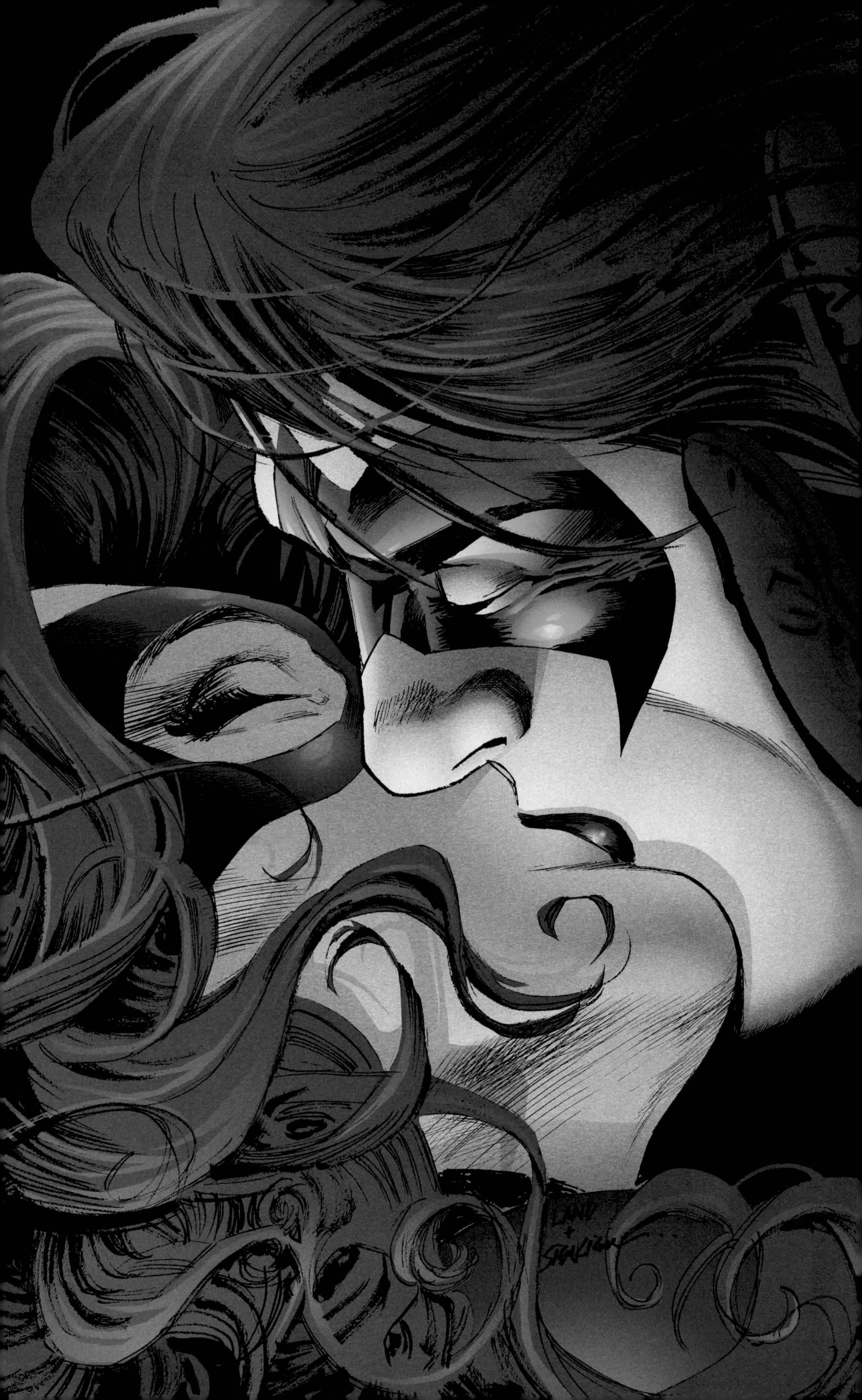

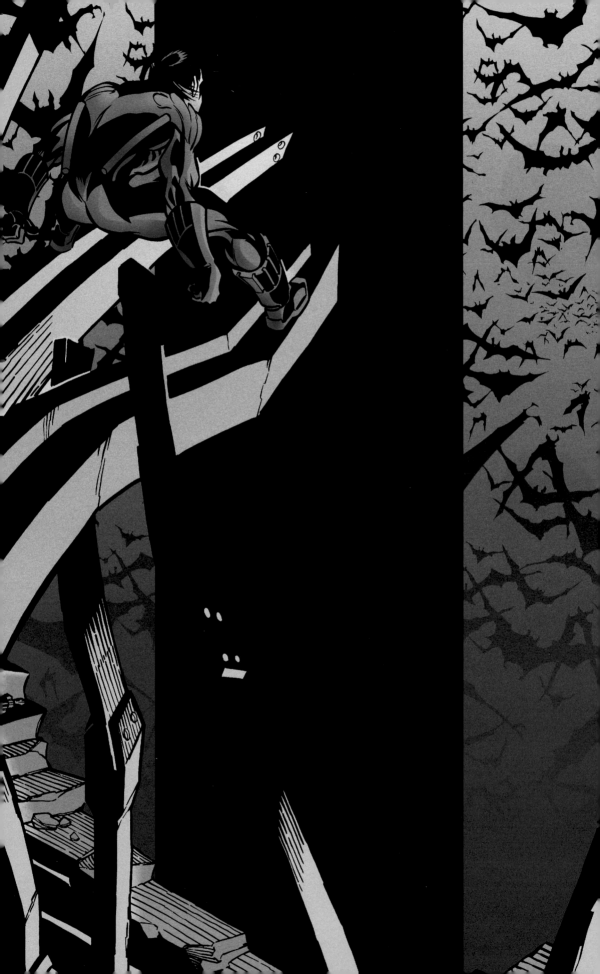

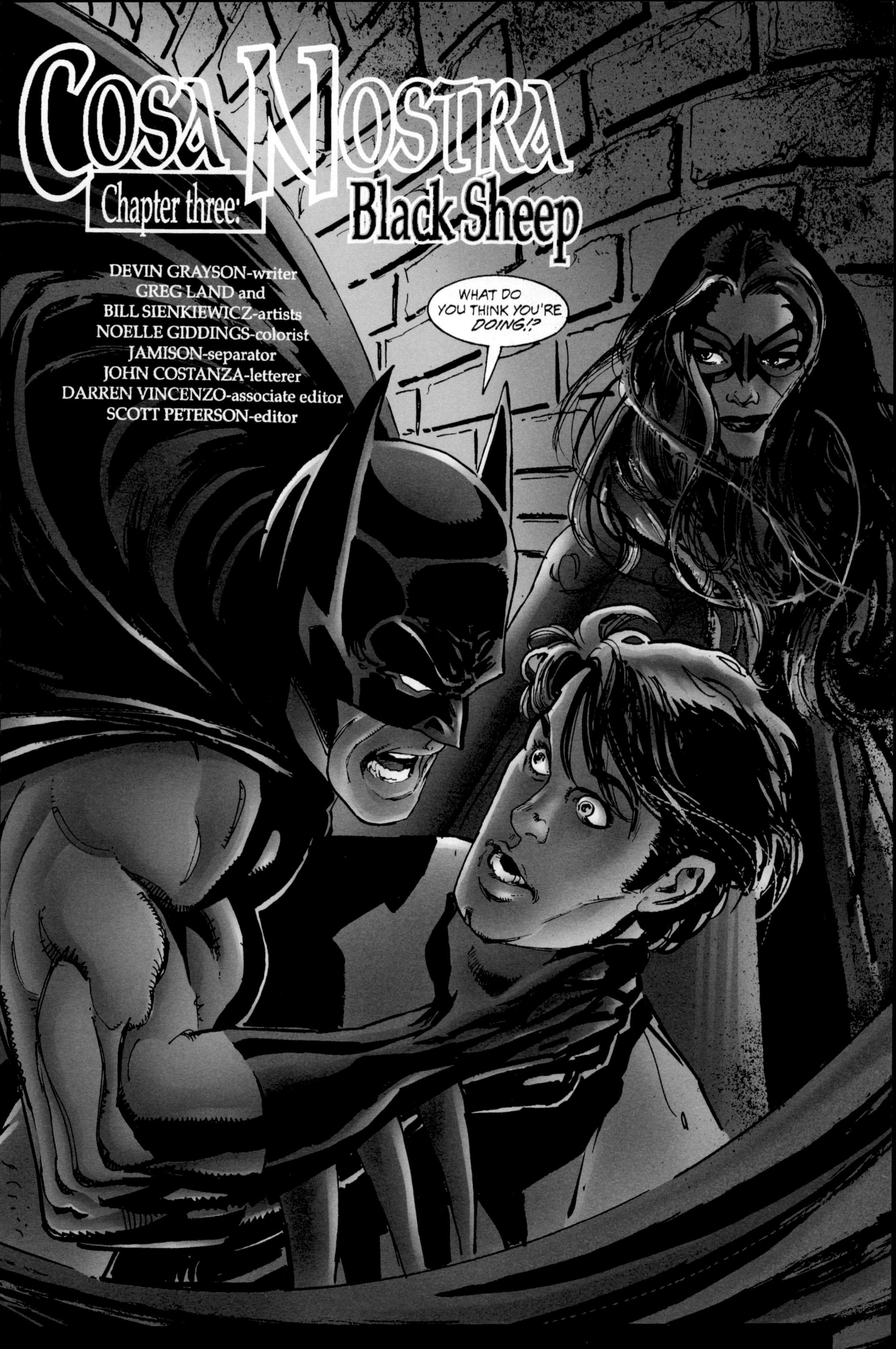
Cosa Nostra
Chapter three: Black Sheep
DEVIN GRAYSON-writer
GREG LAND and
BILL SIENKIEWICZ-artists
NOELLE GIDDINGS-colorist
JAMISON-separator
JOHN COSTANZA-letterer
DARREN VINCENZO-associate editor
SCOTT PETERSON-editor
WHAT DO YOU THINK YOU'RE DOING!?

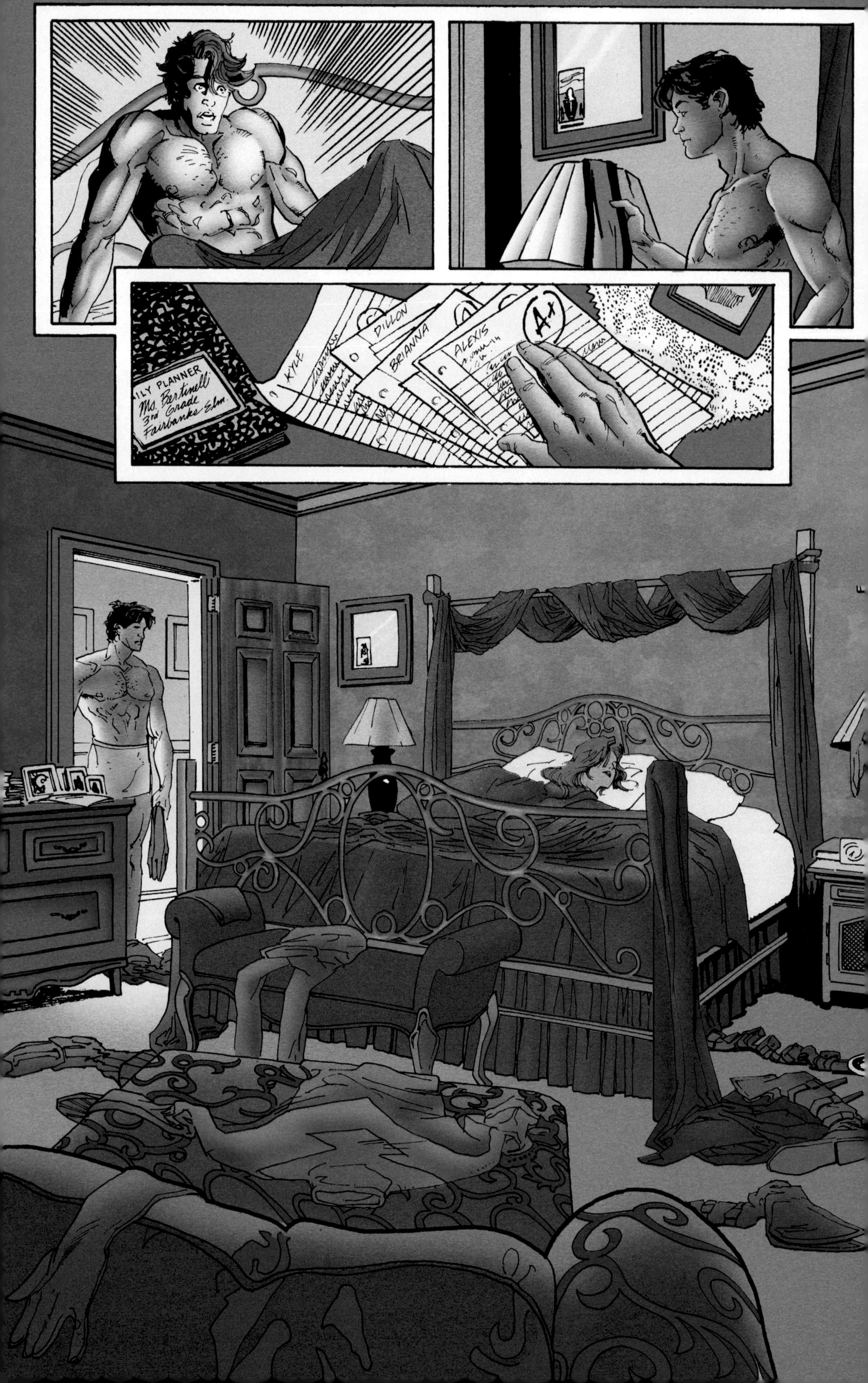
ILY PLANNER
Ms. Bertinelli
3rd Grade
Fairbanks Elm.
KYLE
DILLON
BRIANNA
ALEXIS
A+

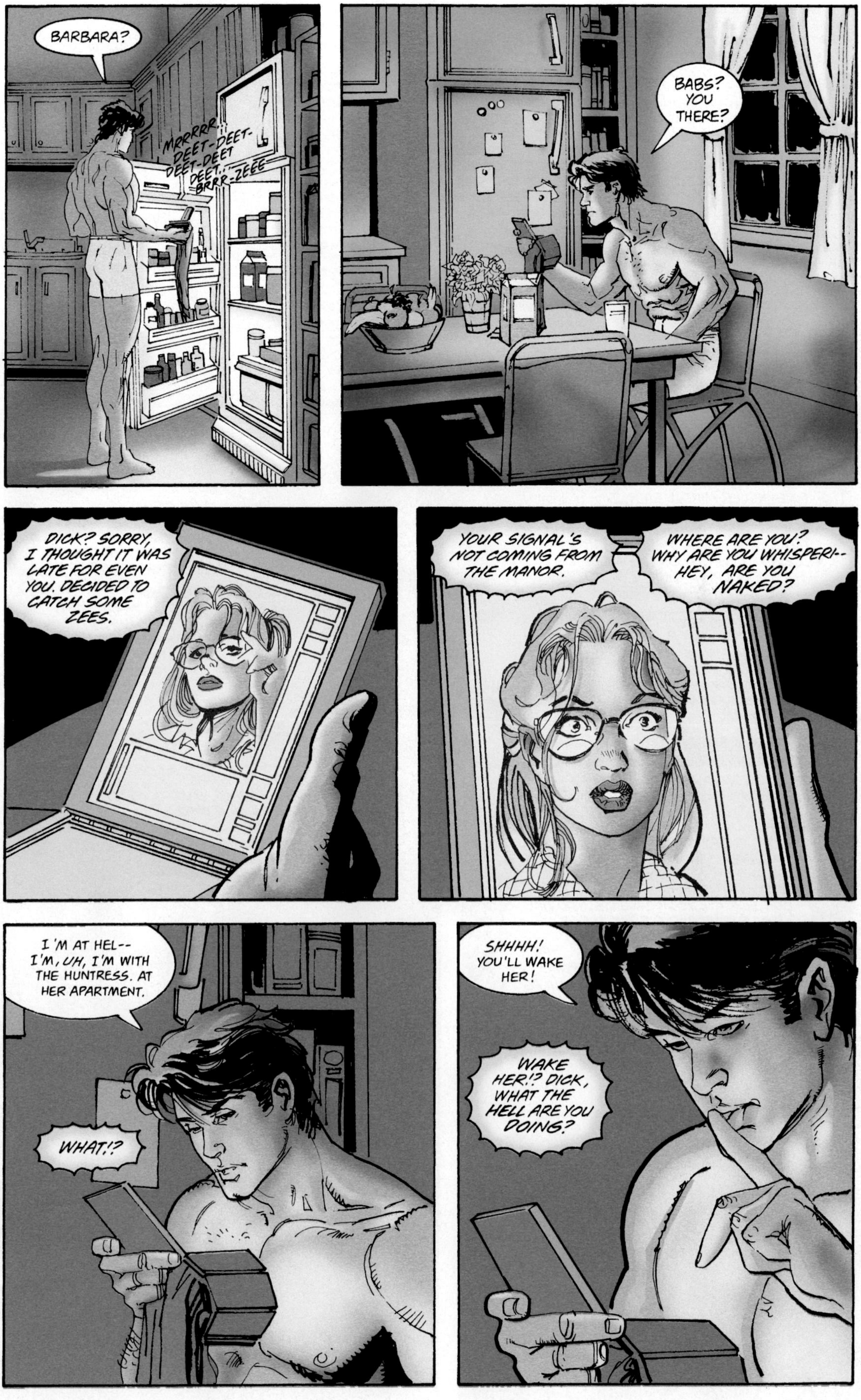
BARBARA?
MRRRRR... DEET-DEET-DEET-DEET DEET... BRRR-ZEEE
BABS? YOU THERE?
DICK? SORRY, I THOUGHT IT WAS LATE FOR EVEN YOU. DECIDED TO CATCH SOME ZEES.
YOUR SIGNAL'S NOT COMING FROM THE MANOR.
WHERE ARE YOU? WHY ARE YOU WHISPERI-- HEY, ARE YOU NAKED?
I'M AT HEL-- I'M, UH, I'M WITH THE HUNTRESS. AT HER APARTMENT.
WHAT!?
SHHHH! YOU'LL WAKE HER!
WAKE HER!? DICK, WHAT THE HELL ARE YOU DOING?

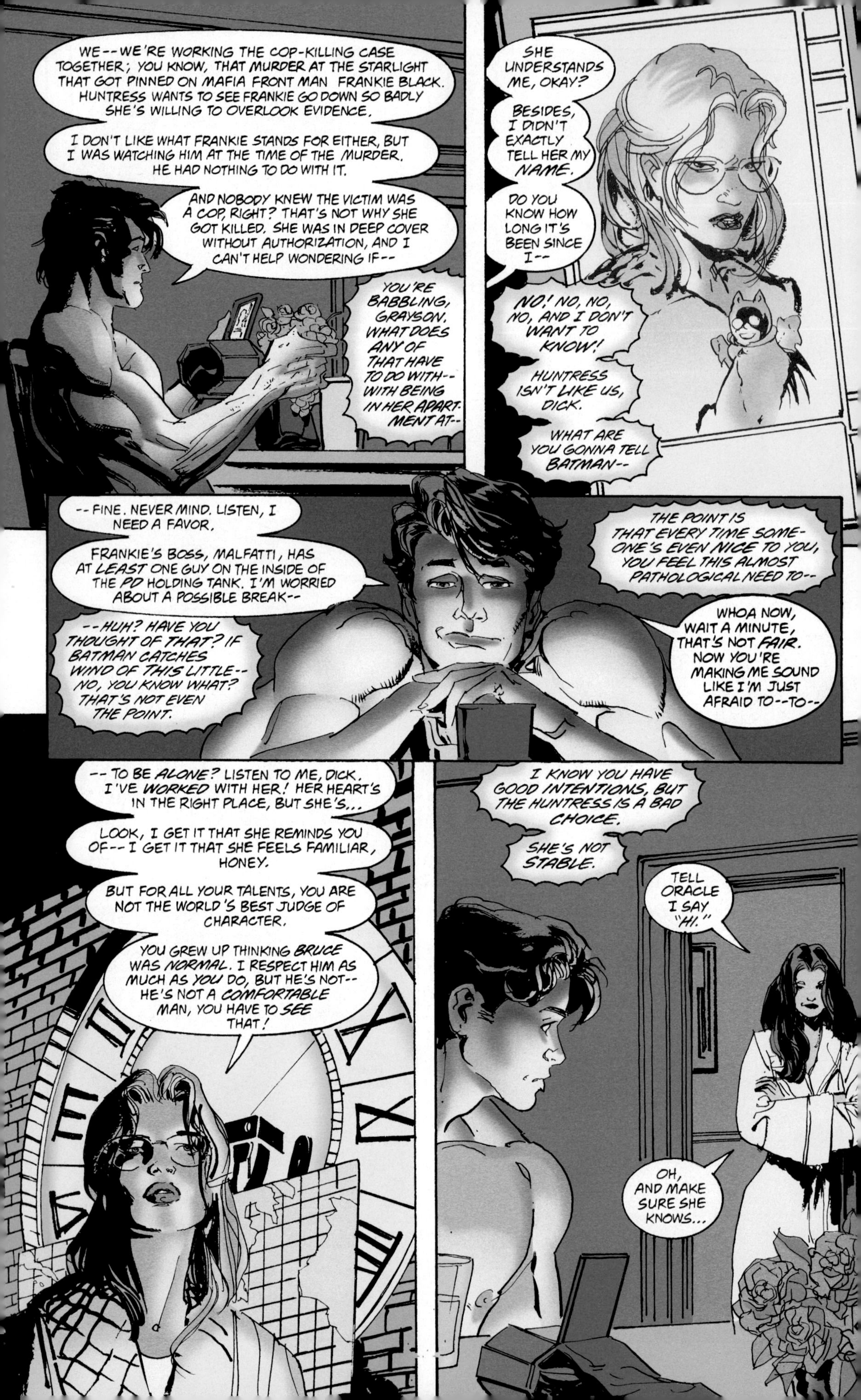

WE--WE'RE WORKING THE COP-KILLING CASE TOGETHER; YOU KNOW, THAT MURDER AT THE STARLIGHT THAT GOT PINNED ON MAFIA FRONT MAN FRANKIE BLACK. HUNTRESS WANTS TO SEE FRANKIE GO DOWN SO BADLY SHE'S WILLING TO OVERLOOK EVIDENCE.
I DON'T LIKE WHAT FRANKIE STANDS FOR EITHER, BUT I WAS WATCHING HIM AT THE TIME OF THE MURDER. HE HAD NOTHING TO DO WITH IT.
AND NOBODY KNEW THE VICTIM WAS A COP, RIGHT? THAT'S NOT WHY SHE GOT KILLED. SHE WAS IN DEEP COVER WITHOUT AUTHORIZATION, AND I CAN'T HELP WONDERING IF--
YOU'RE BABBLING, GRAYSON. WHAT DOES ANY OF THAT HAVE TO DO WITH--WITH BEING IN HER APARTMENT AT--
SHE UNDERSTANDS ME, OKAY?
BESIDES, I DIDN'T EXACTLY TELL HER MY NAME.
DO YOU KNOW HOW LONG IT'S BEEN SINCE I--
NO! NO, NO, NO, AND I DON'T WANT TO KNOW!
HUNTRESS ISN'T LIKE US, DICK.
WHAT ARE YOU GONNA TELL BATMAN--
--FINE. NEVER MIND. LISTEN, I NEED A FAVOR.
FRANKIE'S BOSS, MALFATTI, HAS AT LEAST ONE GUY ON THE INSIDE OF THE PD HOLDING TANK. I'M WORRIED ABOUT A POSSIBLE BREAK--
--HUH? HAVE YOU THOUGHT OF THAT? IF BATMAN CATCHES WIND OF THIS LITTLE-- NO, YOU KNOW WHAT? THAT'S NOT EVEN THE POINT.
THE POINT IS THAT EVERY TIME SOME-ONE'S EVEN NICE TO YOU, YOU FEEL THIS ALMOST PATHOLOGICAL NEED TO--
WHOA NOW, WAIT A MINUTE, THAT'S NOT FAIR. NOW YOU'RE MAKING ME SOUND LIKE I'M JUST AFRAID TO--TO--
--TO BE ALONE? LISTEN TO ME, DICK. I'VE WORKED WITH HER! HER HEART'S IN THE RIGHT PLACE, BUT SHE'S...
LOOK, I GET IT THAT SHE REMINDS YOU OF-- I GET IT THAT SHE FEELS FAMILIAR, HONEY.
BUT FOR ALL YOUR TALENTS, YOU ARE NOT THE WORLD'S BEST JUDGE OF CHARACTER.
YOU GREW UP THINKING BRUCE WAS NORMAL. I RESPECT HIM AS MUCH AS YOU DO, BUT HE'S NOT-- HE'S NOT A COMFORTABLE MAN, YOU HAVE TO SEE THAT!
I KNOW YOU HAVE GOOD INTENTIONS, BUT THE HUNTRESS IS A BAD CHOICE.
SHE'S NOT STABLE.
TELL ORACLE I SAY "HI."
OH, AND MAKE SURE SHE KNOWS...

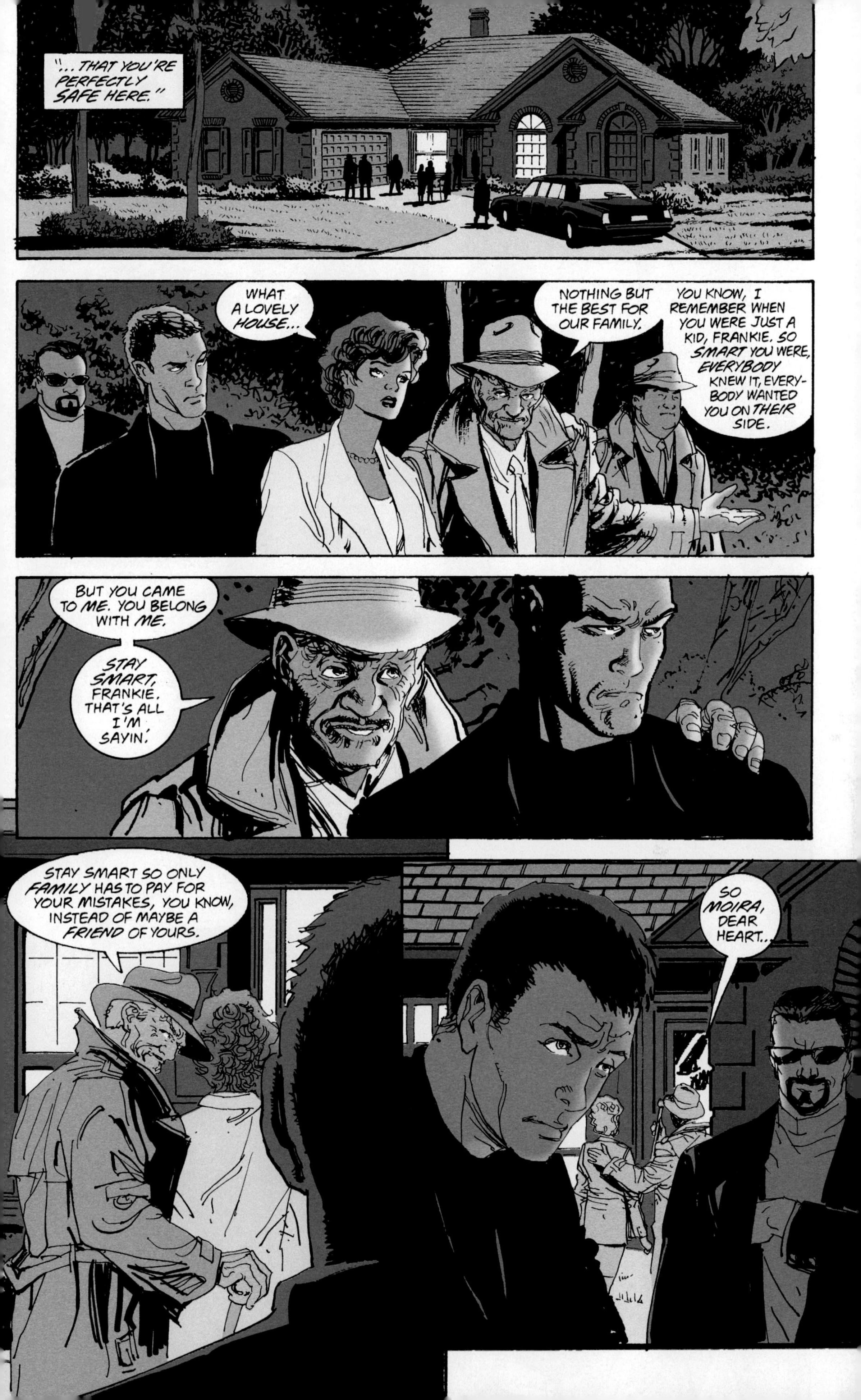
"...THAT YOU'RE PERFECTLY SAFE HERE."
WHAT A LOVELY HOUSE...
NOTHING BUT THE BEST FOR OUR FAMILY.
YOU KNOW, I REMEMBER WHEN YOU WERE JUST A KID, FRANKIE. SO SMART YOU WERE, EVERYBODY KNEW IT, EVERYBODY WANTED YOU ON THEIR SIDE.
BUT YOU CAME TO ME. YOU BELONG WITH ME.
STAY SMART, FRANKIE. THAT'S ALL I'M SAYIN'.
STAY SMART SO ONLY FAMILY HAS TO PAY FOR YOUR MISTAKES, YOU KNOW, INSTEAD OF MAYBE A FRIEND OF YOURS.
SO MOIRA, DEAR HEART...

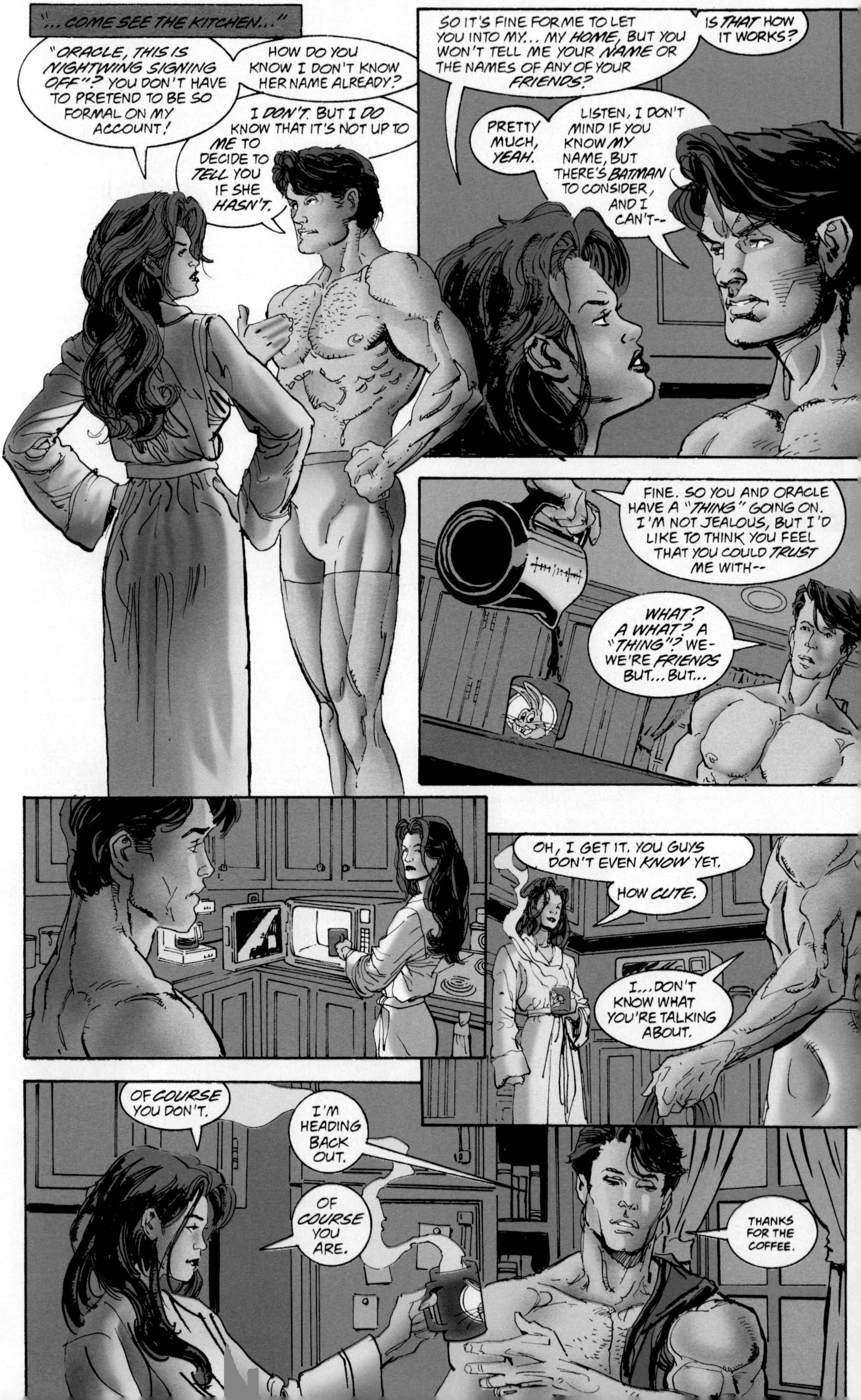
"...COME SEE THE KITCHEN..."
"ORACLE, THIS IS NIGHTWING SIGNING OFF"? YOU DON'T HAVE TO PRETEND TO BE SO FORMAL ON MY ACCOUNT!
HOW DO YOU KNOW I DON'T KNOW HER NAME ALREADY?
I DON'T. BUT I DO KNOW THAT IT'S NOT UP TO ME TO DECIDE TO TELL YOU IF SHE HASN'T.
SO IT'S FINE FOR ME TO LET YOU INTO MY... MY HOME, BUT YOU WON'T TELL ME YOUR NAME OR THE NAMES OF ANY OF YOUR FRIENDS?
IS THAT HOW IT WORKS?
PRETTY MUCH, YEAH.
LISTEN, I DON'T MIND IF YOU KNOW MY NAME, BUT THERE'S BATMAN TO CONSIDER, AND I CAN'T--
FINE. SO YOU AND ORACLE HAVE A "THING" GOING ON. I'M NOT JEALOUS, BUT I'D LIKE TO THINK YOU FEEL THAT YOU COULD TRUST ME WITH--
WHAT? A WHAT? A "THING"? WE-WE'RE FRIENDS BUT... BUT...
OH, I GET IT. YOU GUYS DON'T EVEN KNOW YET.
HOW CUTE.
I... DON'T KNOW WHAT YOU'RE TALKING ABOUT.
OF COURSE YOU DON'T.
I'M HEADING BACK OUT.
OF COURSE YOU ARE.
THANKS FOR THE COFFEE.

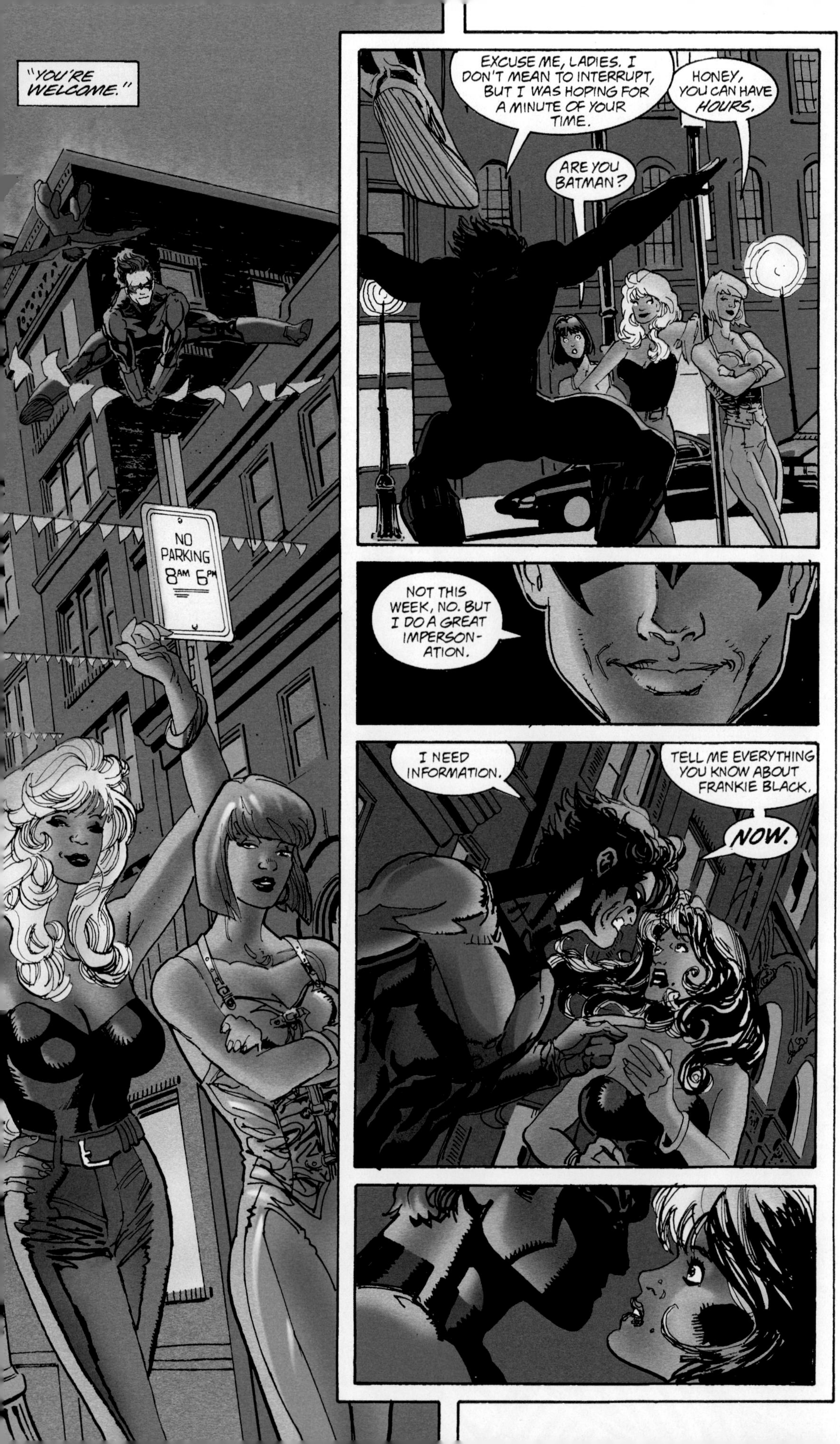
"YOU'RE WELCOME."
NO PARKING 8AM 6PM
EXCUSE ME, LADIES. I DON'T MEAN TO INTERRUPT, BUT I WAS HOPING FOR A MINUTE OF YOUR TIME.
HONEY, YOU CAN HAVE HOURS.
ARE YOU BATMAN?
NOT THIS WEEK, NO. BUT I DO A GREAT IMPERSON-ATION.
I NEED INFORMATION.
TELL ME EVERYTHING YOU KNOW ABOUT FRANKIE BLACK.
NOW.

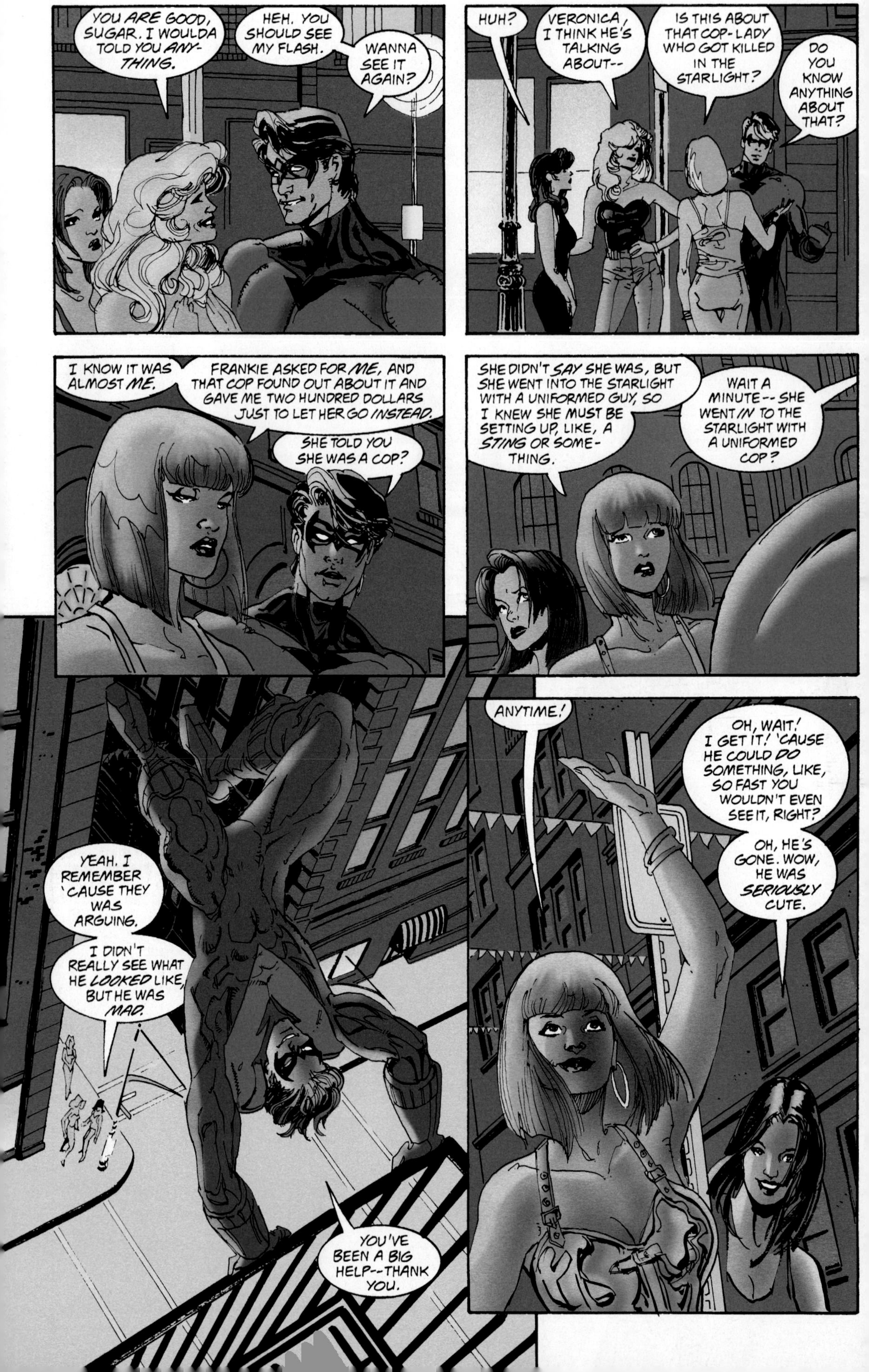
YOU ARE GOOD, SUGAR. I WOULDA TOLD YOU ANYTHING.
HEH. YOU SHOULD SEE MY FLASH.
WANNA SEE IT AGAIN?
HUH?
VERONICA, I THINK HE'S TALKING ABOUT--
IS THIS ABOUT THAT COP-LADY WHO GOT KILLED IN THE STARLIGHT?
DO YOU KNOW ANYTHING ABOUT THAT?
I KNOW IT WAS ALMOST ME.
FRANKIE ASKED FOR ME, AND THAT COP FOUND OUT ABOUT IT AND GAVE ME TWO HUNDRED DOLLARS JUST TO LET HER GO INSTEAD.
SHE TOLD YOU SHE WAS A COP?
SHE DIDN'T SAY SHE WAS, BUT SHE WENT INTO THE STARLIGHT WITH A UNIFORMED GUY, SO I KNEW SHE MUST BE SETTING UP, LIKE, A STING OR SOMETHING.
WAIT A MINUTE-- SHE WENT IN TO THE STARLIGHT WITH A UNIFORMED COP?
YEAH. I REMEMBER 'CAUSE THEY WAS ARGUING.
I DIDN'T REALLY SEE WHAT HE LOOKED LIKE, BUT HE WAS MAD.
YOU'VE BEEN A BIG HELP--THANK YOU.
ANYTIME!
OH, WAIT! I GET IT! 'CAUSE HE COULD DO SOMETHING, LIKE, SO FAST YOU WOULDN'T EVEN SEE IT, RIGHT?
OH, HE'S GONE. WOW, HE WAS SERIOUSLY CUTE.

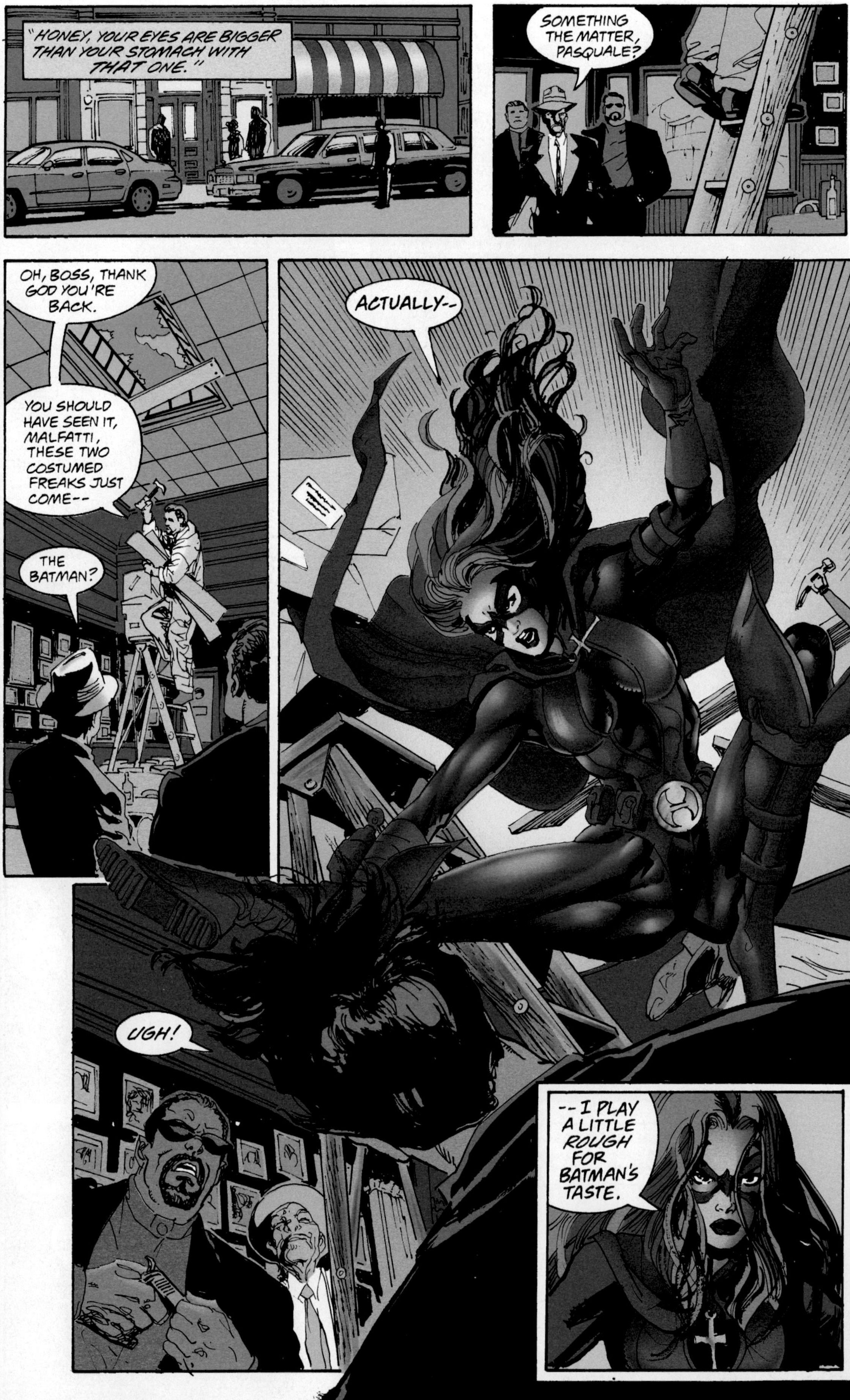
"HONEY, YOUR EYES ARE BIGGER THAN YOUR STOMACH WITH THAT ONE."
SOMETHING THE MATTER, PASQUALE?
OH, BOSS, THANK GOD YOU'RE BACK.
YOU SHOULD HAVE SEEN IT, MALFATTI, THESE TWO COSTUMED FREAKS JUST COME--
THE BATMAN?
ACTUALLY--
UGH!
--I PLAY A LITTLE ROUGH FOR BATMAN'S TASTE.

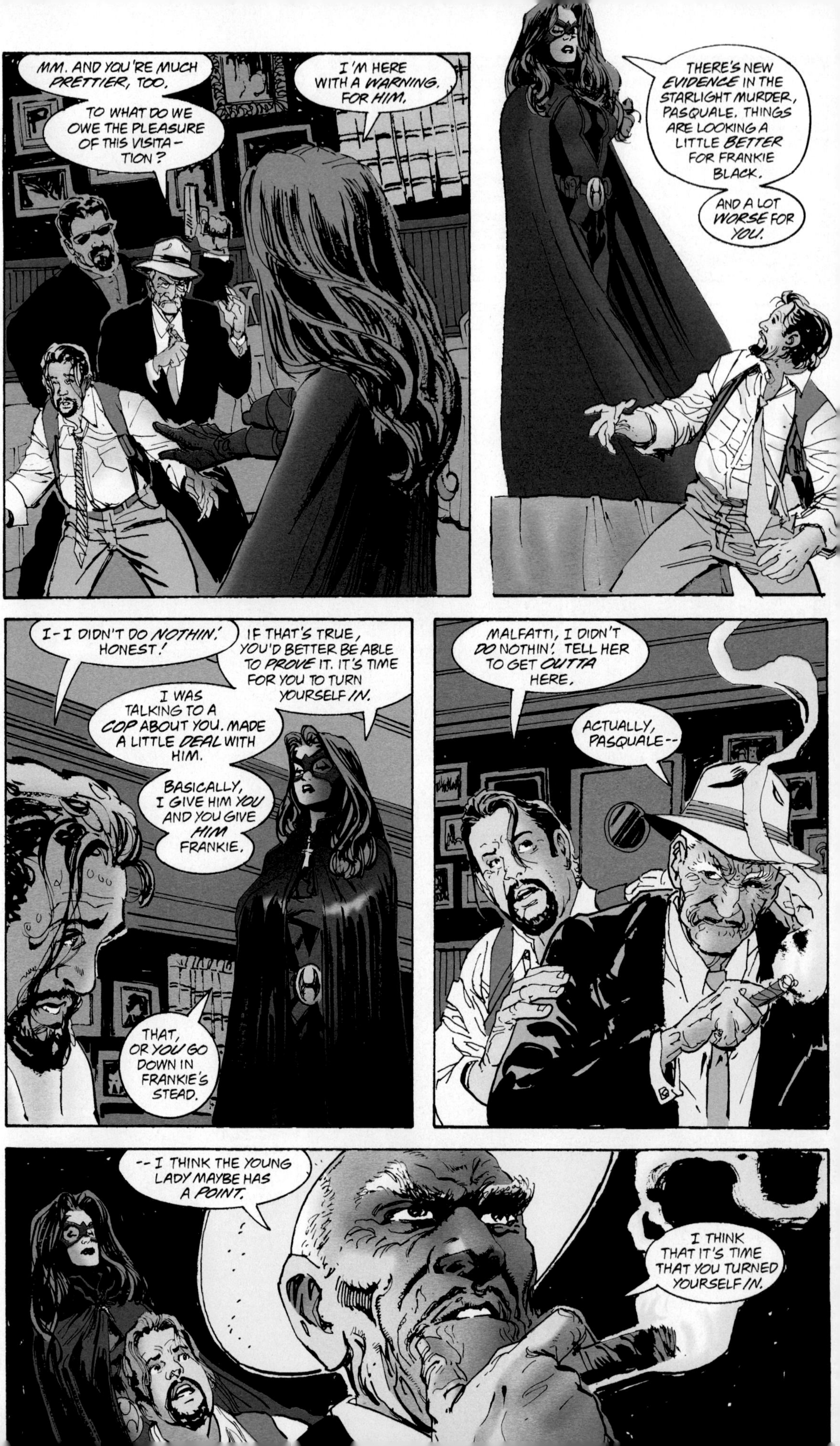
MM. AND YOU'RE MUCH PRETTIER, TOO.
TO WHAT DO WE OWE THE PLEASURE OF THIS VISITA-TION?
I'M HERE WITH A WARNING. FOR HIM.
THERE'S NEW EVIDENCE IN THE STARLIGHT MURDER, PASQUALE. THINGS ARE LOOKING A LITTLE BETTER FOR FRANKIE BLACK.
AND A LOT WORSE FOR YOU.
I-I DIDN'T DO NOTHIN'. HONEST!
IF THAT'S TRUE, YOU'D BETTER BE ABLE TO PROVE IT. IT'S TIME FOR YOU TO TURN YOURSELF IN.
I WAS TALKING TO A COP ABOUT YOU. MADE A LITTLE DEAL WITH HIM.
BASICALLY, I GIVE HIM YOU AND YOU GIVE HIM FRANKIE.
THAT, OR YOU GO DOWN IN FRANKIE'S STEAD.
MALFATTI, I DIDN'T DO NOTHIN'. TELL HER TO GET OUTTA HERE.
ACTUALLY, PASQUALE--
--I THINK THE YOUNG LADY MAYBE HAS A POINT.
I THINK THAT IT'S TIME THAT YOU TURNED YOURSELF IN.

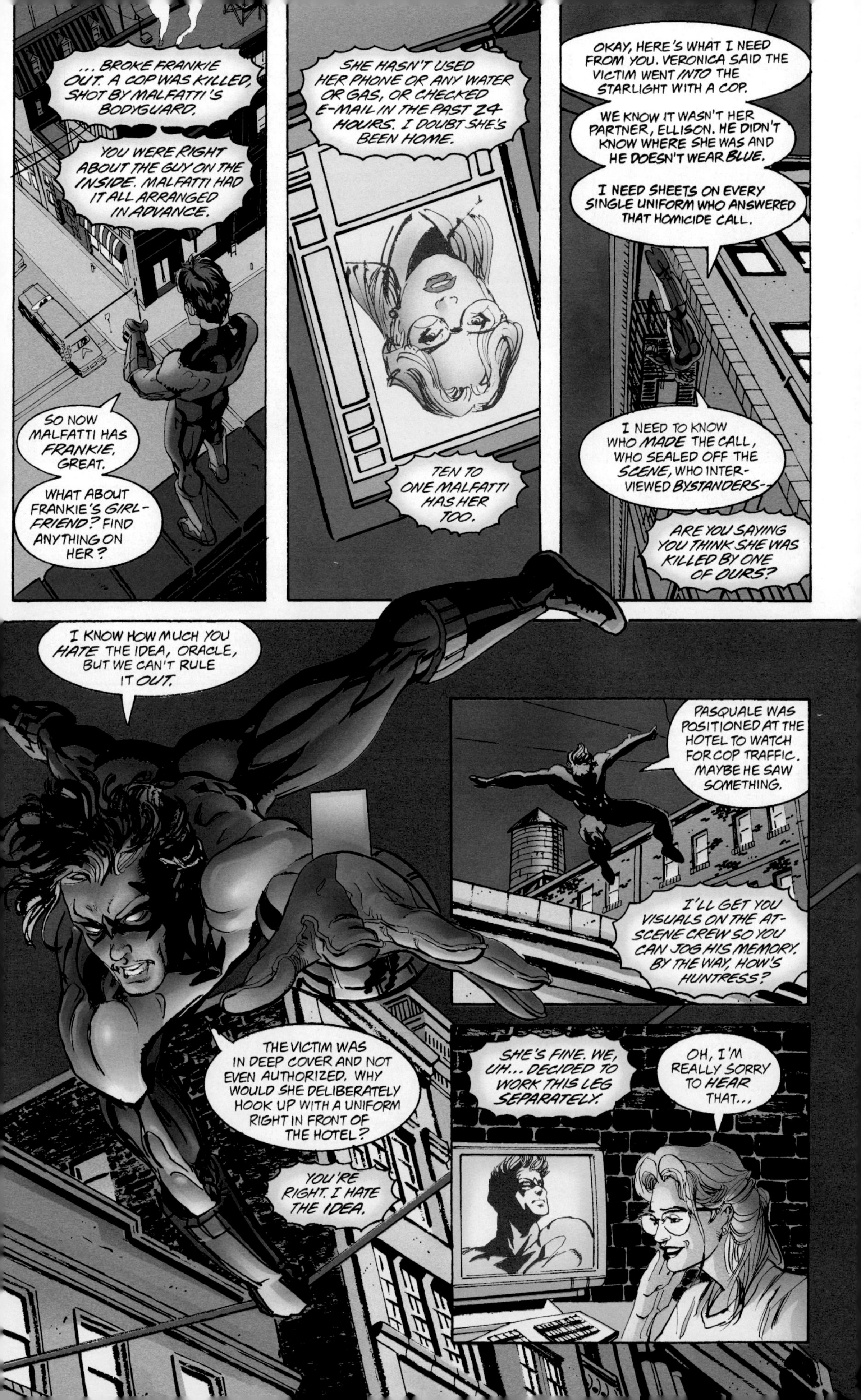
...BROKE FRANKIE OUT. A COP WAS KILLED, SHOT BY MALFATTI'S BODYGUARD.
YOU WERE RIGHT ABOUT THE GUY ON THE INSIDE. MALFATTI HAD IT ALL ARRANGED IN ADVANCE.
SO NOW MALFATTI HAS FRANKIE, GREAT.
WHAT ABOUT FRANKIE'S GIRL-FRIEND? FIND ANYTHING ON HER?
SHE HASN'T USED HER PHONE OR ANY WATER OR GAS, OR CHECKED E-MAIL IN THE PAST 24 HOURS. I DOUBT SHE'S BEEN HOME.
TEN TO ONE MALFATTI HAS HER TOO.
OKAY, HERE'S WHAT I NEED FROM YOU. VERONICA SAID THE VICTIM WENT INTO THE STARLIGHT WITH A COP.
WE KNOW IT WASN'T HER PARTNER, ELLISON. HE DIDN'T KNOW WHERE SHE WAS AND HE DOESN'T WEAR BLUE.
I NEED SHEETS ON EVERY SINGLE UNIFORM WHO ANSWERED THAT HOMICIDE CALL.
I NEED TO KNOW WHO MADE THE CALL, WHO SEALED OFF THE SCENE, WHO INTER-VIEWED BYSTANDERS--
ARE YOU SAYING YOU THINK SHE WAS KILLED BY ONE OF OURS?
I KNOW HOW MUCH YOU HATE THE IDEA, ORACLE, BUT WE CAN'T RULE IT OUT.
THE VICTIM WAS IN DEEP COVER AND NOT EVEN AUTHORIZED. WHY WOULD SHE DELIBERATELY HOOK UP WITH A UNIFORM RIGHT IN FRONT OF THE HOTEL?
YOU'RE RIGHT. I HATE THE IDEA.
PASQUALE WAS POSITIONED AT THE HOTEL TO WATCH FOR COP TRAFFIC. MAYBE HE SAW SOMETHING.
I'LL GET YOU VISUALS ON THE AT-SCENE CREW SO YOU CAN JOG HIS MEMORY. BY THE WAY, HOW'S HUNTRESS?
SHE'S FINE. WE, UH... DECIDED TO WORK THIS LEG SEPARATELY.
OH, I'M REALLY SORRY TO HEAR THAT...

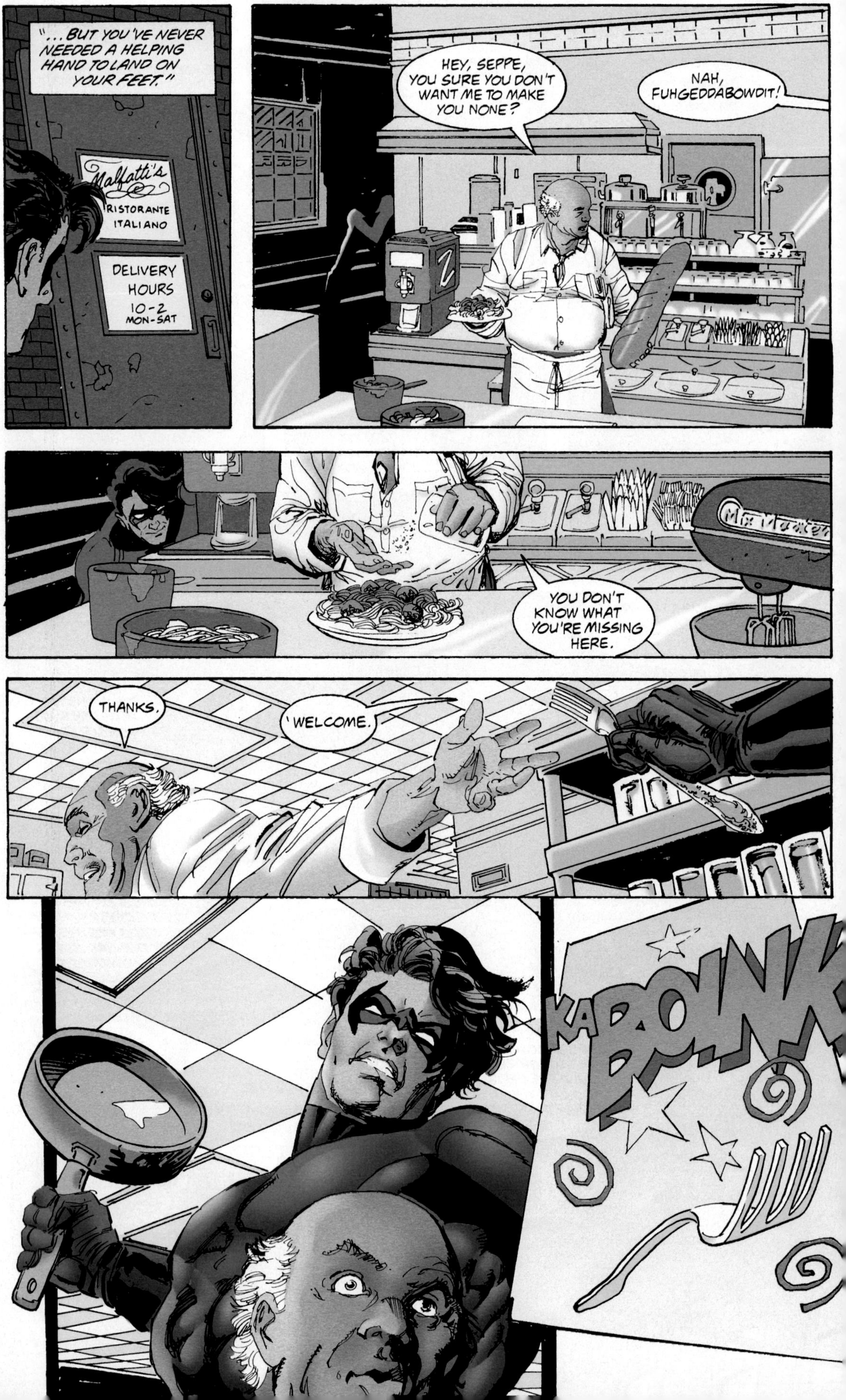
"...BUT YOU'VE NEVER NEEDED A HELPING HAND TO LAND ON YOUR FEET."
Malfatti's RISTORANTE ITALIANO
DELIVERY HOURS 10-2 MON-SAT
HEY, SEPPE, YOU SURE YOU DON'T WANT ME TO MAKE YOU NONE?
NAH, FUHGEDDABOWDIT!
YOU DON'T KNOW WHAT YOU'RE MISSING HERE.
THANKS.
'WELCOME.
KA-BOINK

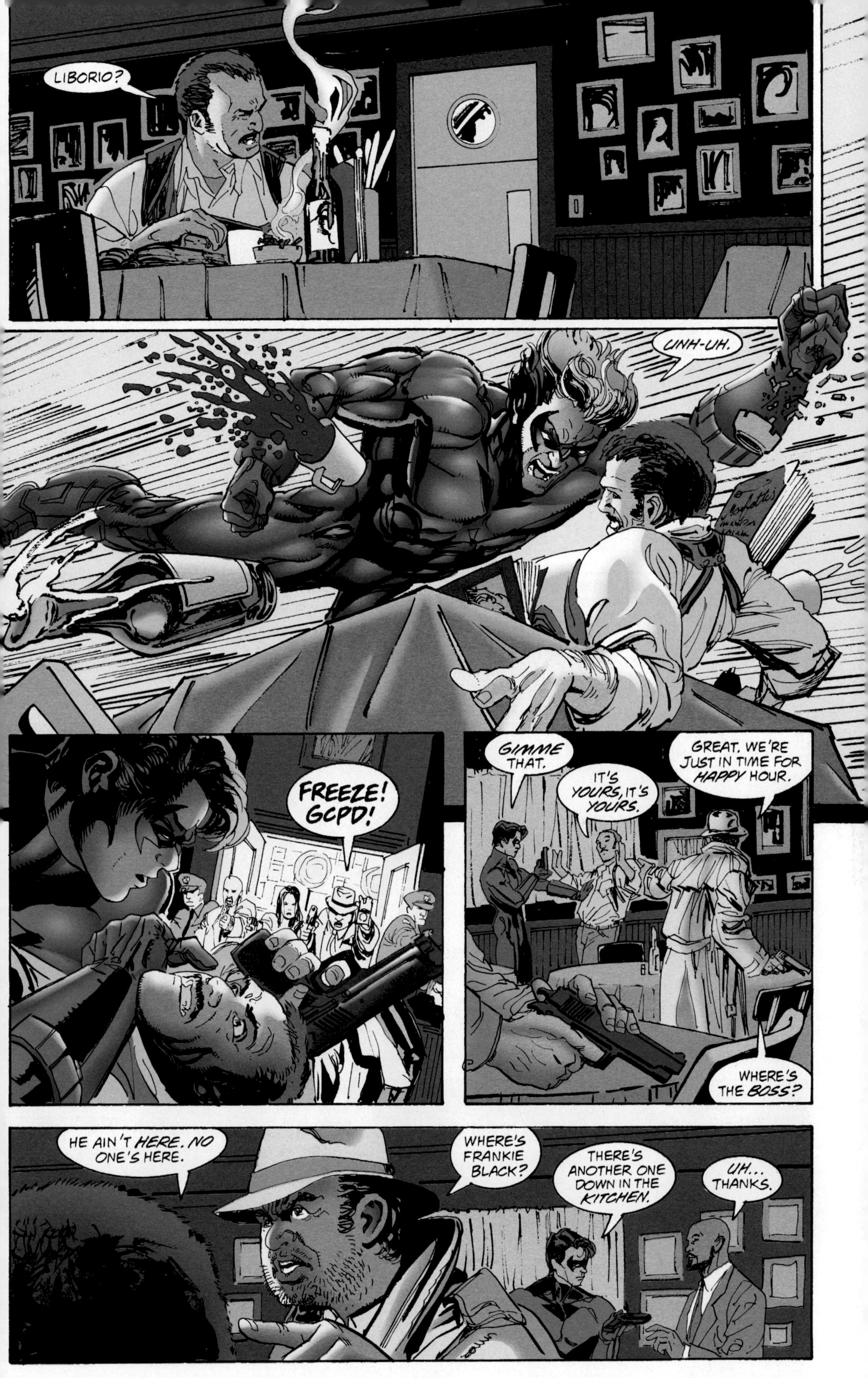
LIBORIO?
UNH-UH.
FREEZE! GCPD!
GIMME THAT.
IT'S YOURS, IT'S YOURS.
GREAT. WE'RE JUST IN TIME FOR HAPPY HOUR.
WHERE'S THE BOSS?
HE AIN'T HERE. NO ONE'S HERE.
WHERE'S FRANKIE BLACK?
THERE'S ANOTHER ONE DOWN IN THE KITCHEN.
UH... THANKS.

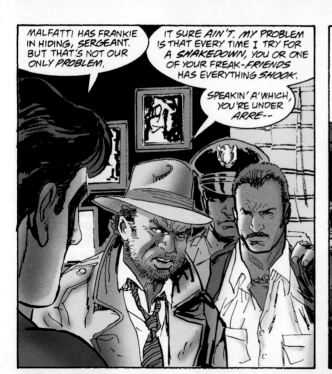

MALFATTI HAS FRANKIE IN HIDING, SERGEANT. BUT THAT'S NOT OUR ONLY *PROBLEM*.

IT SURE *AIN'T*. MY PROBLEM IS THAT EVERY TIME I TRY FOR A *SHAKEDOWN*, YOU OR ONE OF YOUR FREAK-FRIENDS HAS EVERYTHING *SHOOK*.

SPEAKIN' A' WHICH, YOU'RE UNDER *ARRE*--

--YEAH, YEAH, YEAH. SPARE ME THE *MIRANDA*, HARVEY, I'M *GOING*. PASQUALE ISN'T HERE *ANYWAY*.

BUT TELL THE COMMISSIONER THAT THE REPLACED PROSTITUTE SAW CAITLYN BECKER GO INTO THE STARLIGHT WITH A UNIFORMED *COP*. ONE OF OURS.

PASQUALE TURNED HIMSELF *IN* FOR THE MURDER OF LIEUTENANT CAITLYN BECKER AN *HOUR* AGO, HOT SHOT.

WHAT? BUT-- BUT *PASQUALE* DIDN'T DO IT!

HE *COULDN'T* HAVE! LOOK AT THE STRANGULATION ANGLE ON THE FORENSICS REPORT! HE'S TOO *SHORT*!

HARVEY?

YEAH?

THIS PLACE LOOKS CLEAN, PARTNER.

WE'RE NOT FINDING--

D'OH! HE'S GONE! I CAN'T BELIEVE I FELL FOR THAT! WHAT'RE YOU-- WORKING *WITH* THE VIGILANTE NOW, MONTOYA?

THE KID'S FAST. BUT HE *IS* TRYING TO *HELP*, ISN'T HE?

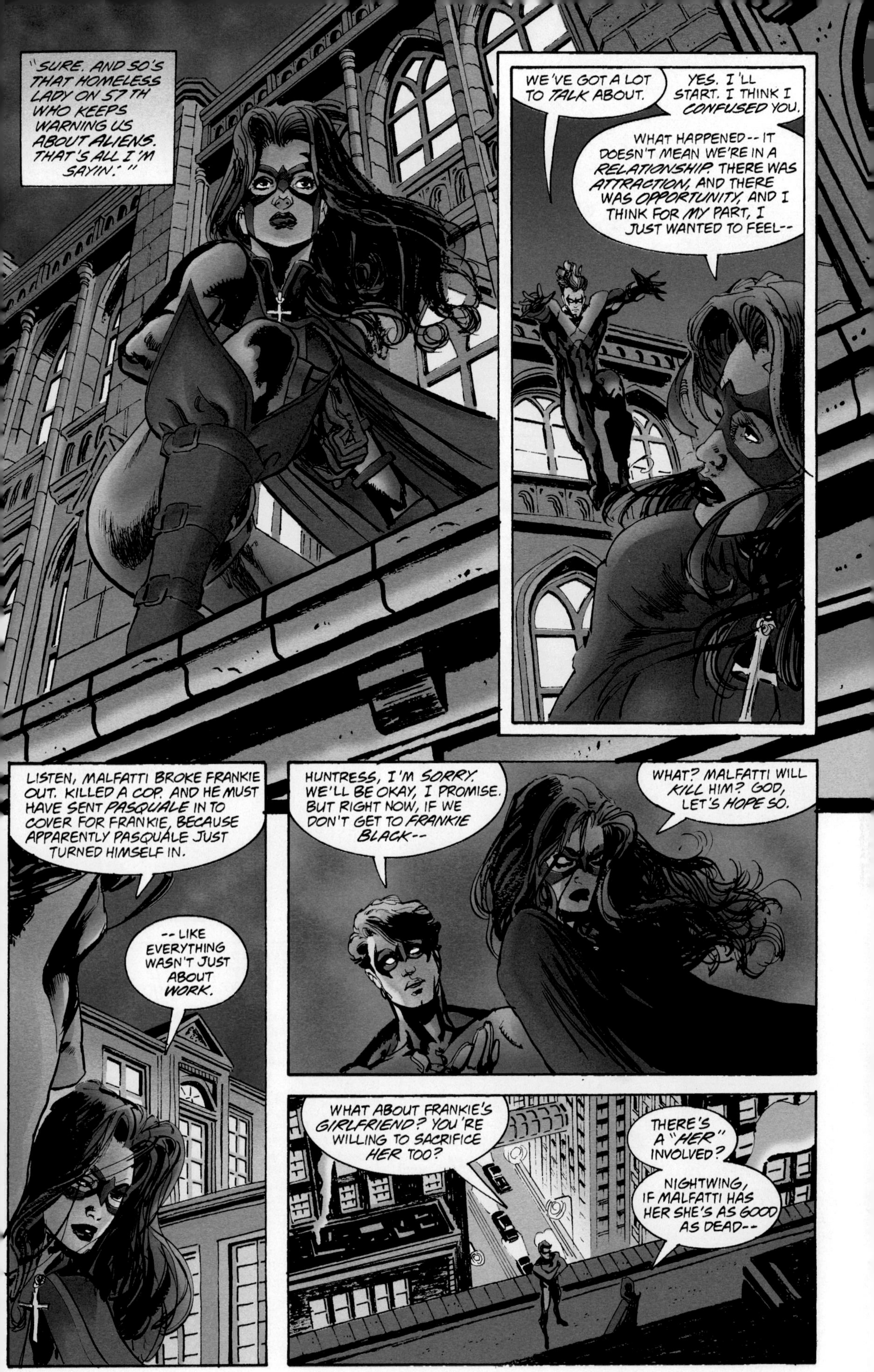
"SURE. AND SO'S THAT HOMELESS LADY ON 57TH WHO KEEPS WARNING US ABOUT ALIENS. THAT'S ALL I'M SAYIN.'"
WE'VE GOT A LOT TO TALK ABOUT.
YES. I'LL START. I THINK I CONFUSED YOU.
WHAT HAPPENED-- IT DOESN'T MEAN WE'RE IN A RELATIONSHIP. THERE WAS ATTRACTION, AND THERE WAS OPPORTUNITY, AND I THINK FOR MY PART, I JUST WANTED TO FEEL--
LISTEN, MALFATTI BROKE FRANKIE OUT. KILLED A COP. AND HE MUST HAVE SENT PASQUALE IN TO COVER FOR FRANKIE, BECAUSE APPARENTLY PASQUALE JUST TURNED HIMSELF IN.
--LIKE EVERYTHING WASN'T JUST ABOUT WORK.
HUNTRESS, I'M SORRY. WE'LL BE OKAY, I PROMISE. BUT RIGHT NOW, IF WE DON'T GET TO FRANKIE BLACK--
WHAT? MALFATTI WILL KILL HIM? GOD, LET'S HOPE SO.
WHAT ABOUT FRANKIE'S GIRLFRIEND? YOU'RE WILLING TO SACRIFICE HER TOO?
THERE'S A "HER" INVOLVED?
NIGHTWING, IF MALFATTI HAS HER SHE'S AS GOOD AS DEAD--

"-- IT'S INEVITABLE."

-- WANNA TELL US WHY, SCUMBAG?

I DIDN'T LIKE THE WAY SHE WAS LOOKIN' AT ME. I DON'T KNOW. IT WAS AN ACCIDENT.

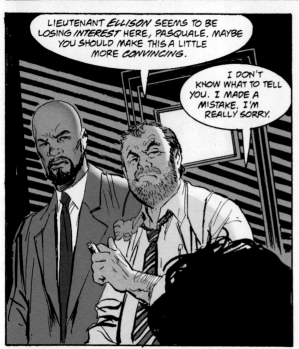

LIEUTENANT ELLISON SEEMS TO BE LOSING INTEREST HERE, PASQUALE. MAYBE YOU SHOULD MAKE THIS A LITTLE MORE CONVINCING.

I DON'T KNOW WHAT TO TELL YOU. I MADE A MISTAKE. I'M REALLY SORRY.

THIS WHOLE THING IS NUTS.

I CAN'T STOP THINKING ABOUT WHAT THAT VIGILANTE SAID: "ONE OF OURS..."

INTERR RO

BUT BULLOCK'S RIGHT. I DIDN'T TRAIN FOR VICE TO TAKE POINTERS FROM A GUY IN TIGHTS.

INTE RO LOC RO

THE KID'S WRONG. HE HAS TO BE WRONG.

HE WORKS OUTSIDE THE LAW AND HE CAN'T POSSIBLY UNDERSTAND WHAT HAPPENS INSIDE.

OCKER OOM

STILL, I HAVE THIS *GUT FEELING* THAT HE KNOWS WHAT HE'S *TALKING* ABOUT. CAITLYN KNEW THE *MOB* LIKE THE BACK OF HER HAND-- SHE WOULD HAVE BEEN ON GUARD, PREPARED.

IT WOULD HAVE TAKEN SOMETHING *UNEXPECTED...*

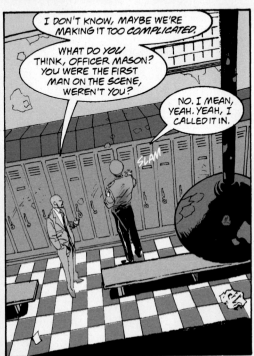

I DON'T KNOW, MAYBE WE'RE MAKING IT TOO *COMPLICATED.*

WHAT DO *YOU* THINK, OFFICER MASON? YOU WERE THE FIRST MAN ON THE SCENE, WEREN'T YOU?

NO. I MEAN, YEAH. YEAH, I CALLED IT IN.

SLAM

BACK AT *VICE,* WE USED TO HAVE THESE *SESSIONS* IN THE LOCKER ROOM. WE'D JUST START THROWING OUT THE MOST *RIDICULOUS* HYPOTHESES ABOUT EACH OTHER'S CASES.

MOSTLY TO BLOW OFF STEAM, YOU KNOW, BUT SOMETIMES SOMETHING WOULD *CLICK.*

WHAT'S *YOUR* THEORY ON MY PARTNER'S *MURDER,* OFFICER?

CLICK

WELL, I-- I THINK FRANKIE BLACK DID IT, YOU KNOW? AND THEY'VE GOT THIS, *UM,* PASQUALE GUY TRYING TO *COVER.*

BUT HE'LL *SLIP,* YOU KNOW, WHEN *NEW EVIDENCE* COMES UP--

NEW EVIDENCE? LIKE WHAT?

Mason

WELL, *UH,* LIKE THAT *PILLOWCASE* FOR INSTANCE, YOU KNOW?

PILLOWCASE? OH, YEAH, YOU'RE RIGHT-- ONE WAS *MISSING* FROM THE BED.

THAT'S QUITE A MEMORY YOU'VE GOT, PATROLMAN. YOU MUST BE TAKING THIS CASE VERY *SERIOUSLY.*

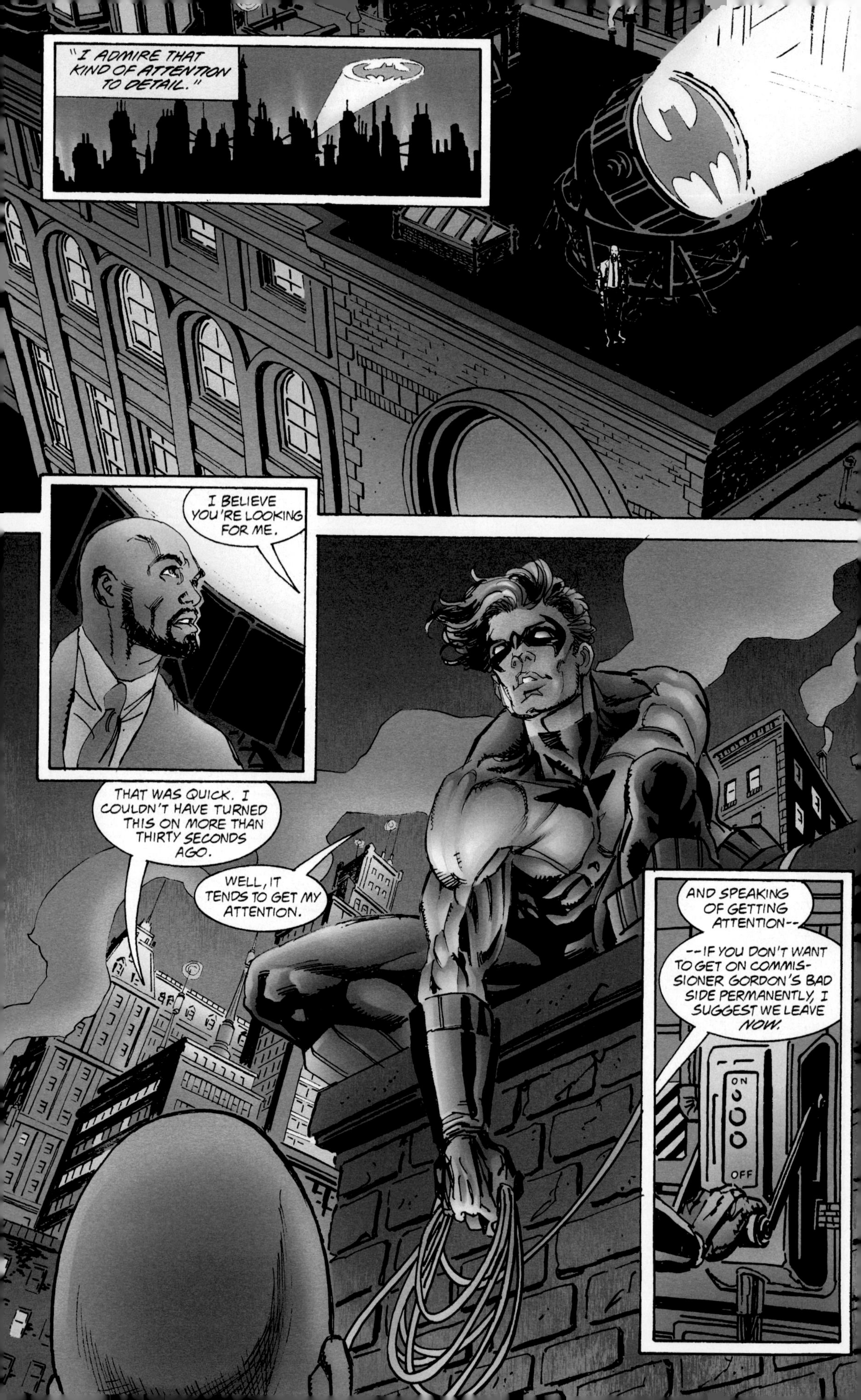
"I ADMIRE THAT KIND OF ATTENTION TO DETAIL."
I BELIEVE YOU'RE LOOKING FOR ME.
THAT WAS QUICK. I COULDN'T HAVE TURNED THIS ON MORE THAN THIRTY SECONDS AGO.
WELL, IT TENDS TO GET MY ATTENTION.
AND SPEAKING OF GETTING ATTENTION--
--IF YOU DON'T WANT TO GET ON COMMISSIONER GORDON'S BAD SIDE PERMANENTLY, I SUGGEST WE LEAVE NOW.
ON
OFF

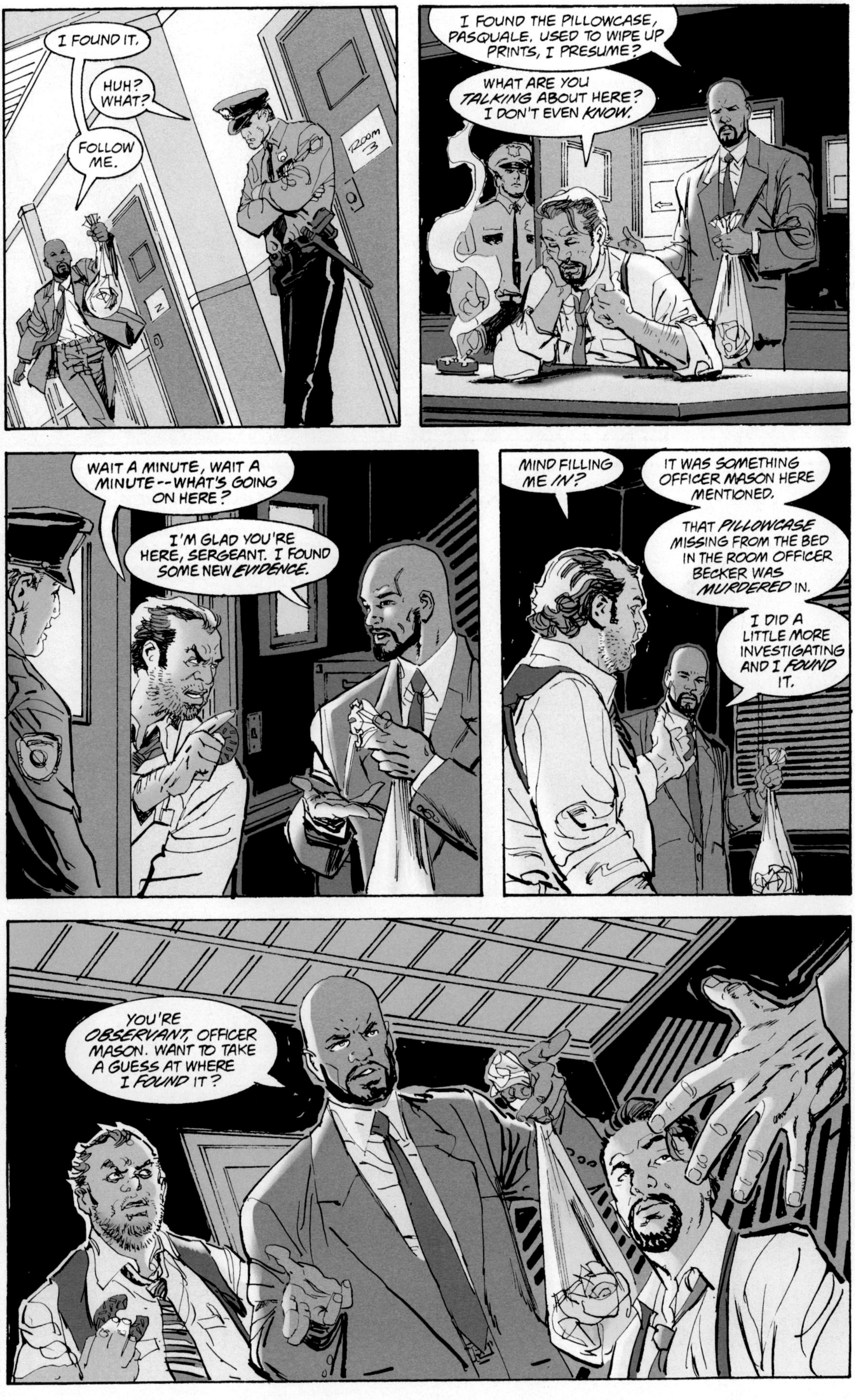
I FOUND IT.
HUH? WHAT?
FOLLOW ME.
ROOM 3
2
I FOUND THE PILLOWCASE, PASQUALE. USED TO WIPE UP PRINTS, I PRESUME?
WHAT ARE YOU TALKING ABOUT HERE? I DON'T EVEN KNOW.
WAIT A MINUTE, WAIT A MINUTE--WHAT'S GOING ON HERE?
I'M GLAD YOU'RE HERE, SERGEANT. I FOUND SOME NEW EVIDENCE.
MIND FILLING ME IN?
IT WAS SOMETHING OFFICER MASON HERE MENTIONED.
THAT PILLOWCASE MISSING FROM THE BED IN THE ROOM OFFICER BECKER WAS MURDERED IN.
I DID A LITTLE MORE INVESTIGATING AND I FOUND IT.
YOU'RE OBSERVANT, OFFICER MASON. WANT TO TAKE A GUESS AT WHERE I FOUND IT?

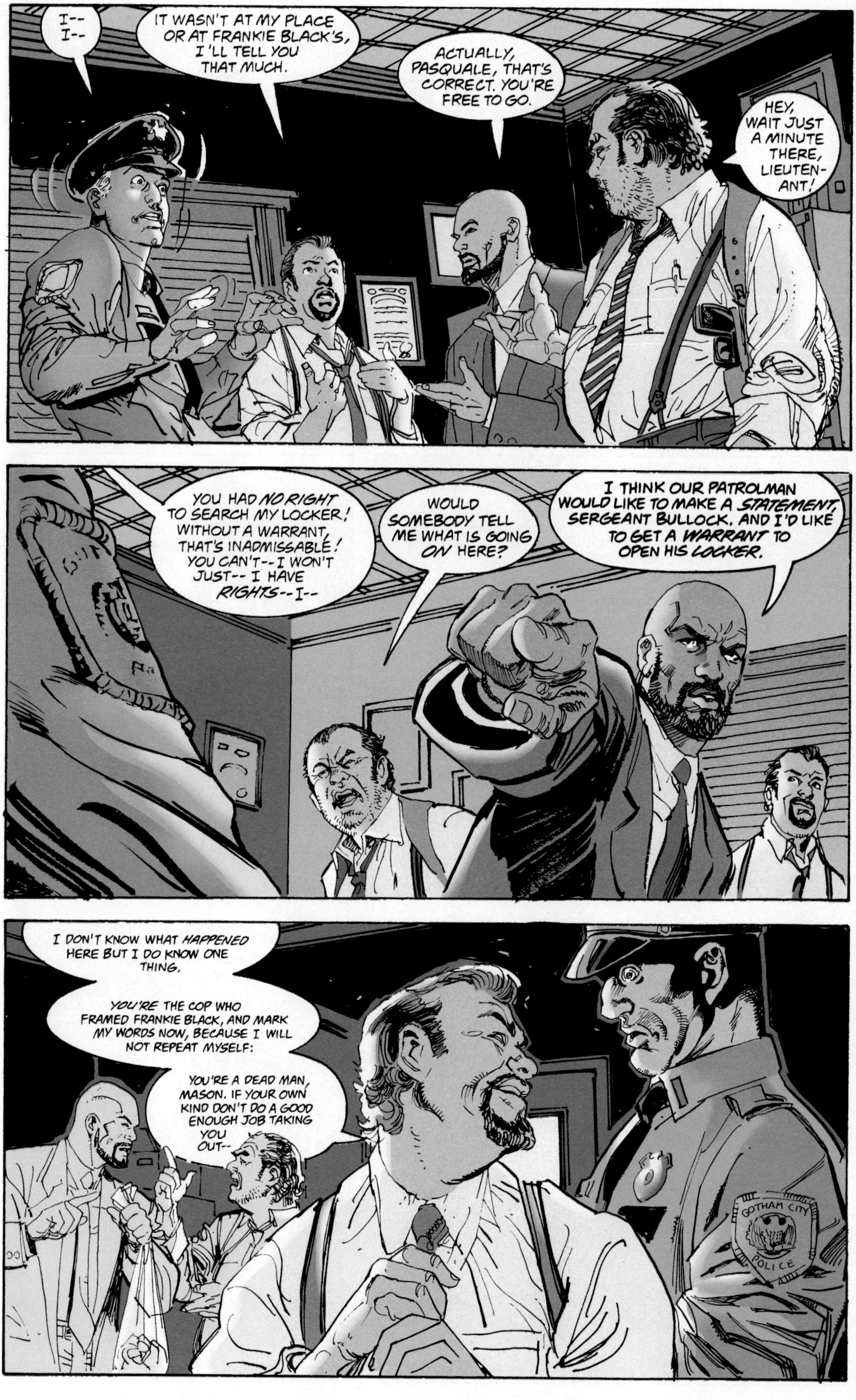
I-- I--
IT WASN'T AT MY PLACE OR AT FRANKIE BLACK'S, I'LL TELL YOU THAT MUCH.
ACTUALLY, PASQUALE, THAT'S CORRECT. YOU'RE FREE TO GO.
HEY, WAIT JUST A MINUTE THERE, LIEUTENANT!
YOU HAD NO RIGHT TO SEARCH MY LOCKER! WITHOUT A WARRANT, THAT'S INADMISSABLE! YOU CAN'T--I WON'T JUST-- I HAVE RIGHTS--I--
WOULD SOMEBODY TELL ME WHAT IS GOING ON HERE?
I THINK OUR PATROLMAN WOULD LIKE TO MAKE A STATEMENT, SERGEANT BULLOCK. AND I'D LIKE TO GET A WARRANT TO OPEN HIS LOCKER.
I DON'T KNOW WHAT HAPPENED HERE BUT I DO KNOW ONE THING.
YOU'RE THE COP WHO FRAMED FRANKIE BLACK, AND MARK MY WORDS NOW, BECAUSE I WILL NOT REPEAT MYSELF:
YOU'RE A DEAD MAN, MASON. IF YOUR OWN KIND DON'T DO A GOOD ENOUGH JOB TAKING YOU OUT--
GOTHAM CITY POLICE

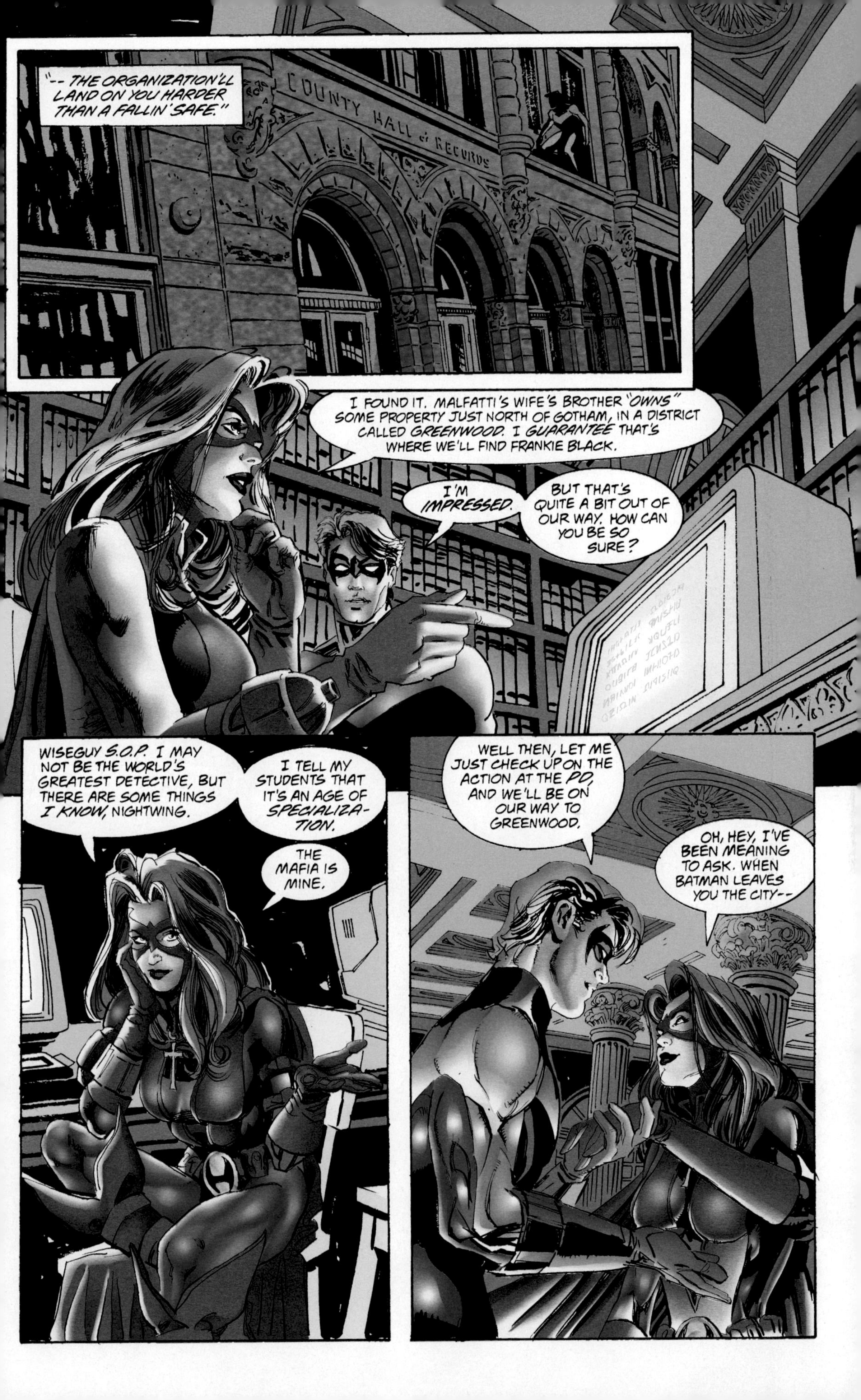
"-- THE ORGANIZATION'LL LAND ON YOU HARDER THAN A FALLIN' SAFE."
COUNTY HALL of RECORDS
I FOUND IT. MALFATTI'S WIFE'S BROTHER "OWNS" SOME PROPERTY JUST NORTH OF GOTHAM, IN A DISTRICT CALLED GREENWOOD. I GUARANTEE THAT'S WHERE WE'LL FIND FRANKIE BLACK.
I'M IMPRESSED.
BUT THAT'S QUITE A BIT OUT OF OUR WAY. HOW CAN YOU BE SO SURE?
WISEGUY S.O.P. I MAY NOT BE THE WORLD'S GREATEST DETECTIVE, BUT THERE ARE SOME THINGS I KNOW, NIGHTWING.
I TELL MY STUDENTS THAT IT'S AN AGE OF SPECIALIZA-TION.
THE MAFIA IS MINE.
WELL THEN, LET ME JUST CHECK UP ON THE ACTION AT THE PD, AND WE'LL BE ON OUR WAY TO GREENWOOD.
OH, HEY, I'VE BEEN MEANING TO ASK. WHEN BATMAN LEAVES YOU THE CITY--

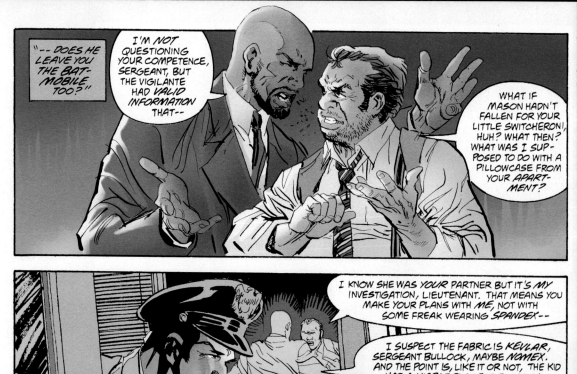

"-- DOES HE LEAVE YOU THE BAT-MOBILE TOO?"

I'M *NOT* QUESTIONING YOUR COMPETENCE, SERGEANT, BUT THE VIGILANTE HAD *VALID* INFORMATION THAT--

WHAT IF MASON HADN'T *FALLEN* FOR YOUR LITTLE SWITCHERONI, HUH? WHAT THEN? WHAT WAS I SUP-POSED TO DO WITH A PILLOWCASE FROM YOUR *APART-MENT*?

I KNOW SHE WAS *YOUR* PARTNER BUT IT'S *MY* INVESTIGATION, LIEUTENANT. THAT MEANS YOU MAKE YOUR PLANS WITH *ME*, NOT WITH SOME FREAK WEARING *SPANDEX*--

I SUSPECT THE FABRIC IS *KEVLAR*, SERGEANT BULLOCK, MAYBE *NOMEX*. AND THE POINT IS, LIKE IT OR NOT, THE KID HAD A *VIABLE* PLAN FOR FLUSHING OUT *MASON*.

I FOLLOWED HIS *ADVICE* AND IT *WORKED*--

CAN I TALK YOU INTO GOING ALL THE WAY OUT TO *GREENWOOD*, BUDDY?

WELL, DON'T JUST SIT THERE--

--FOLLOW THAT CAR!

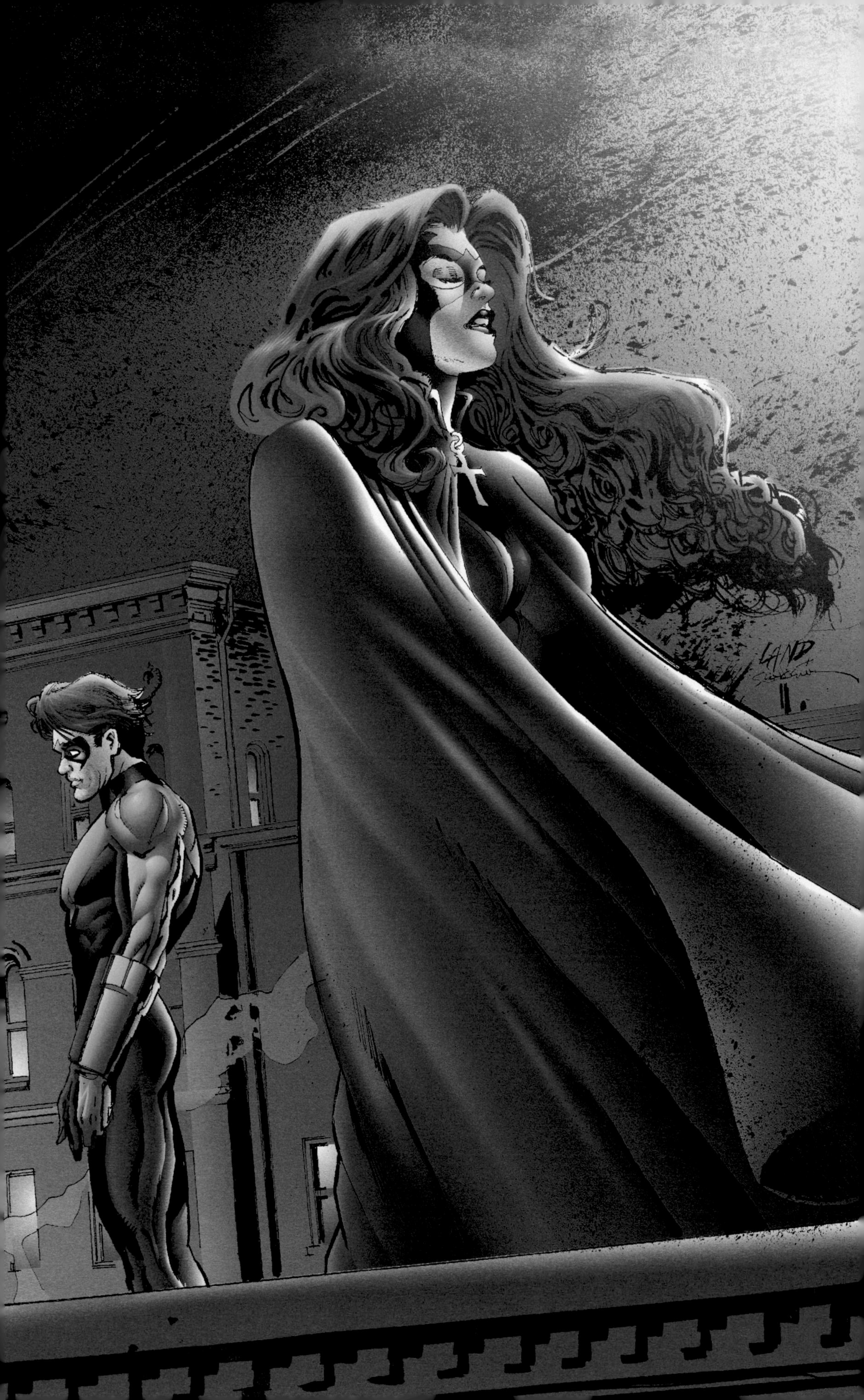

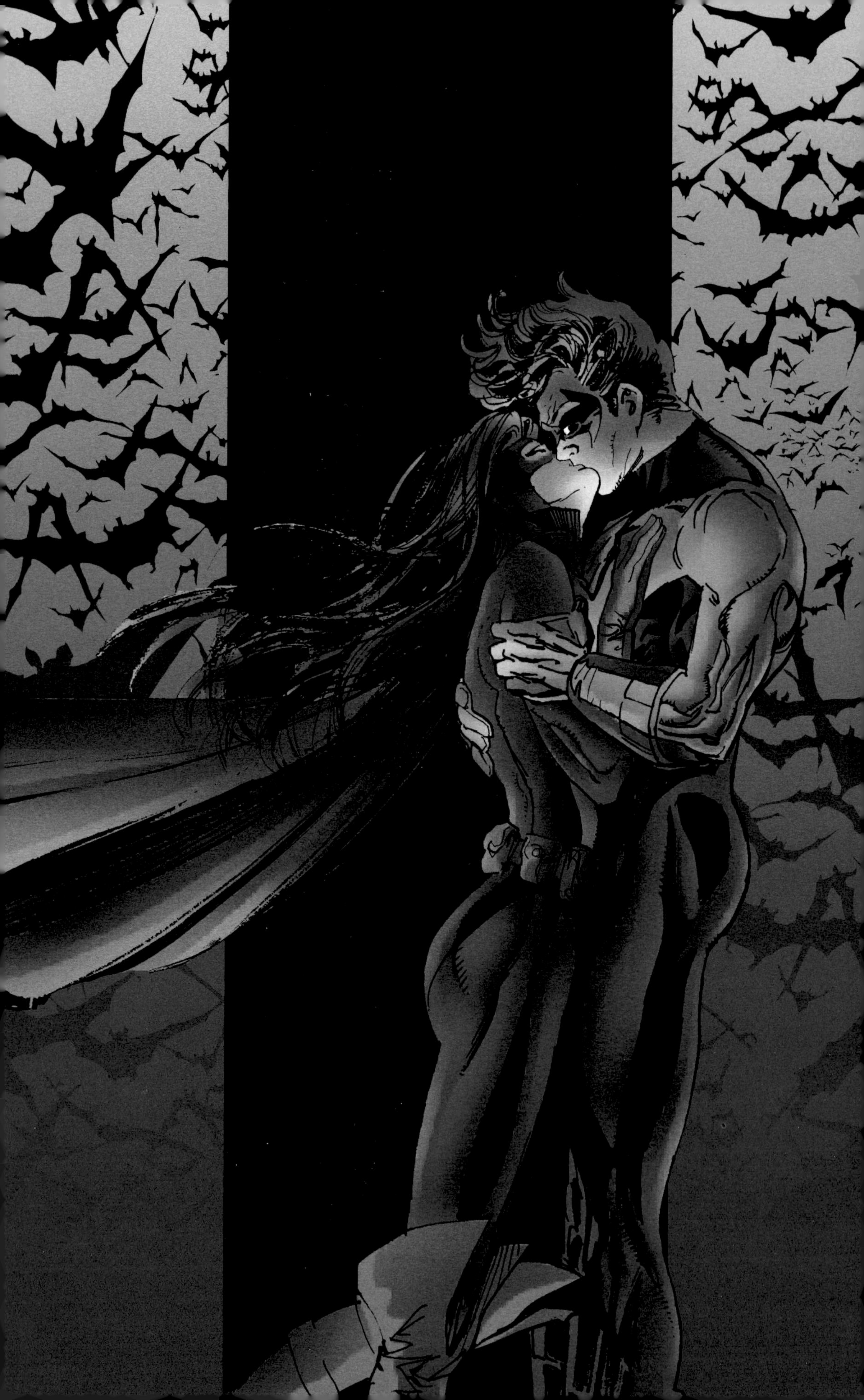

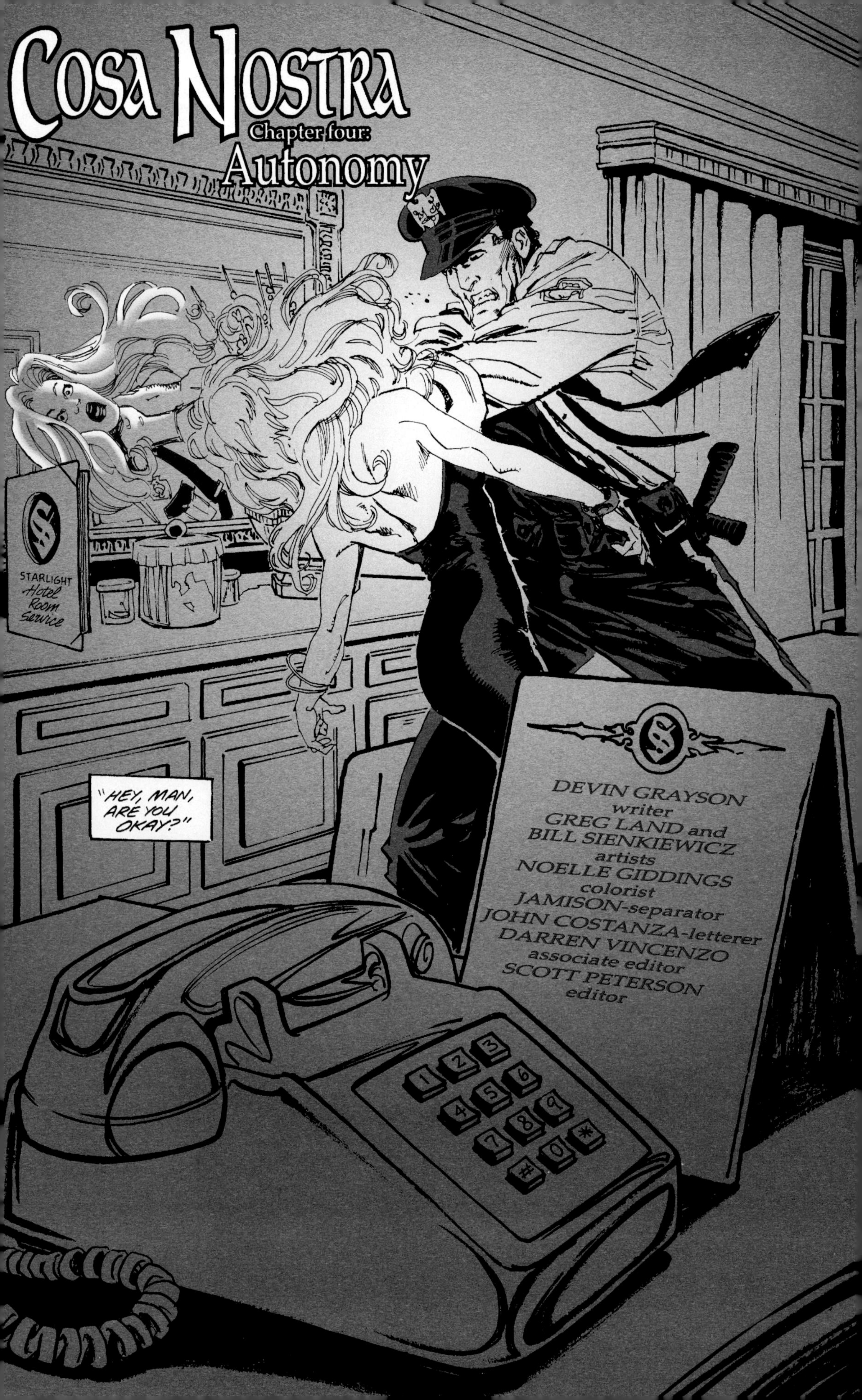
COSA NOSTRA
Chapter four:
Autonomy
STARLIGHT Hotel Room Service
"HEY, MAN, ARE YOU OKAY?"
DEVIN GRAYSON writer
GREG LAND and BILL SIENKIEWICZ artists
NOELLE GIDDINGS colorist
JAMISON-separator
JOHN COSTANZA-letterer
DARREN VINCENZO associate editor
SCOTT PETERSON editor

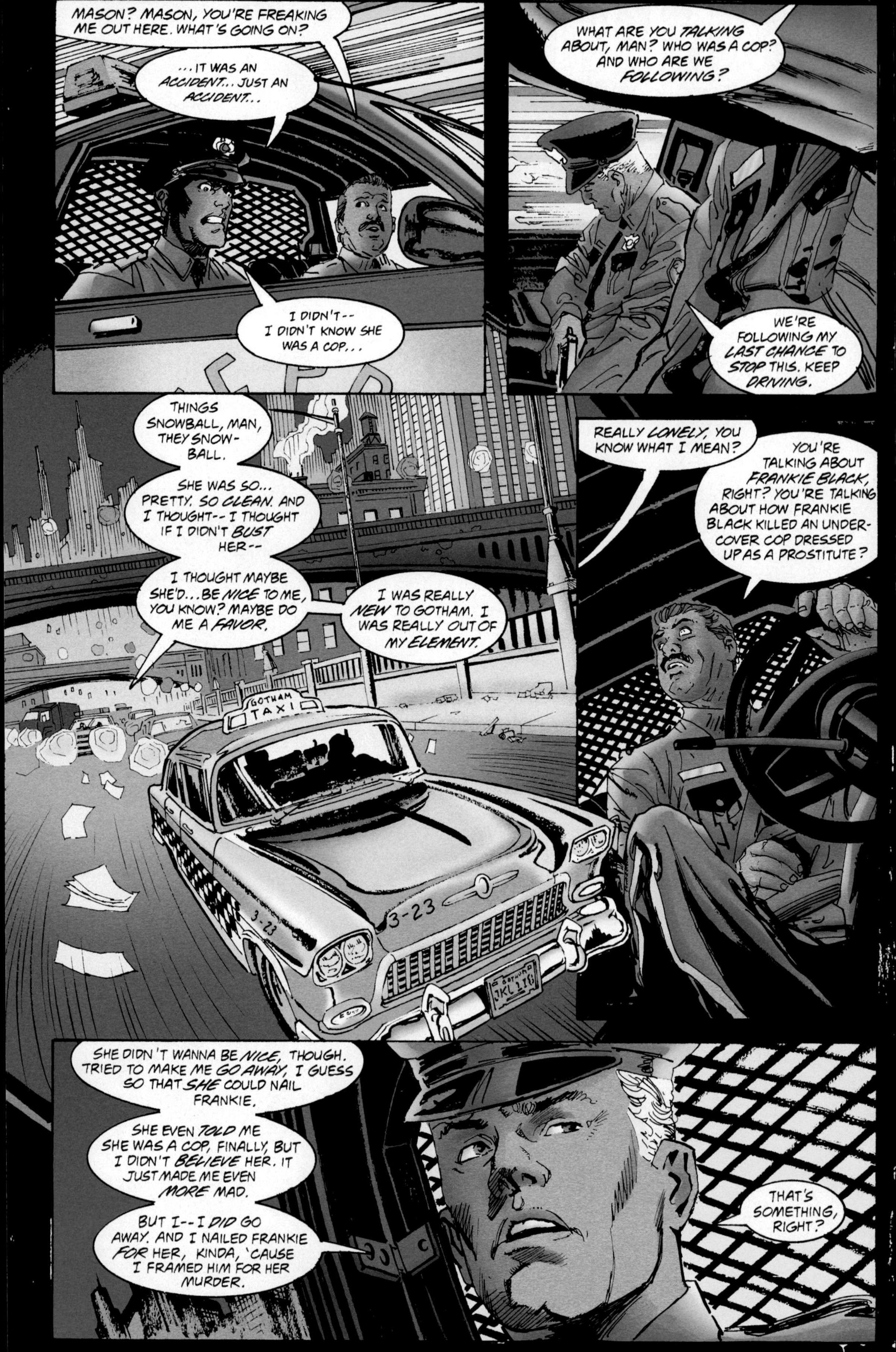
MASON? MASON, YOU'RE FREAKING ME OUT HERE. WHAT'S GOING ON?
...IT WAS AN ACCIDENT... JUST AN ACCIDENT...
I DIDN'T-- I DIDN'T KNOW SHE WAS A COP...
WHAT ARE YOU TALKING ABOUT, MAN? WHO WAS A COP? AND WHO ARE WE FOLLOWING?
WE'RE FOLLOWING MY LAST CHANCE TO STOP THIS. KEEP DRIVING.
THINGS SNOWBALL, MAN, THEY SNOW-BALL.
SHE WAS SO... PRETTY. SO CLEAN. AND I THOUGHT-- I THOUGHT IF I DIDN'T BUST HER--
I THOUGHT MAYBE SHE'D... BE NICE TO ME, YOU KNOW? MAYBE DO ME A FAVOR.
I WAS REALLY NEW TO GOTHAM. I WAS REALLY OUT OF MY ELEMENT.
GOTHAM TAXI
3-23
REALLY LONELY, YOU KNOW WHAT I MEAN?
YOU'RE TALKING ABOUT FRANKIE BLACK, RIGHT? YOU'RE TALKING ABOUT HOW FRANKIE BLACK KILLED AN UNDER-COVER COP DRESSED UP AS A PROSTITUTE?
SHE DIDN'T WANNA BE NICE, THOUGH. TRIED TO MAKE ME GO AWAY, I GUESS SO THAT SHE COULD NAIL FRANKIE.
SHE EVEN TOLD ME SHE WAS A COP, FINALLY, BUT I DIDN'T BELIEVE HER. IT JUST MADE ME EVEN MORE MAD.
BUT I-- I DID GO AWAY. AND I NAILED FRANKIE FOR HER, KINDA, 'CAUSE I FRAMED HIM FOR HER MURDER.
THAT'S SOMETHING, RIGHT?

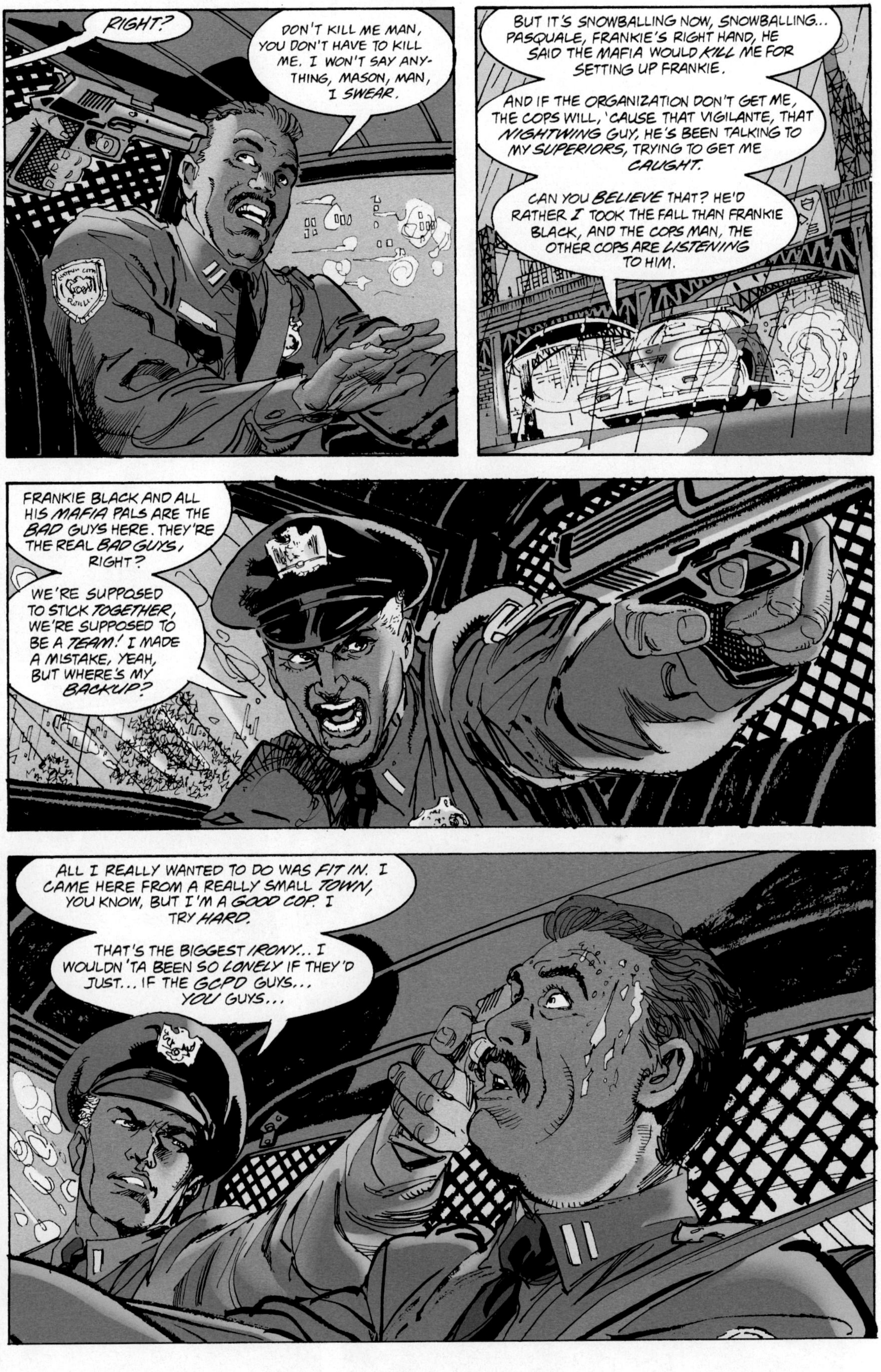
RIGHT?
DON'T KILL ME MAN, YOU DON'T HAVE TO KILL ME. I WON'T SAY ANYTHING, MASON, MAN, I SWEAR.
BUT IT'S SNOWBALLING NOW, SNOWBALLING... PASQUALE, FRANKIE'S RIGHT HAND, HE SAID THE MAFIA WOULD KILL ME FOR SETTING UP FRANKIE.
AND IF THE ORGANIZATION DON'T GET ME, THE COPS WILL, 'CAUSE THAT VIGILANTE, THAT NIGHTWING GUY, HE'S BEEN TALKING TO MY SUPERIORS, TRYING TO GET ME CAUGHT.
CAN YOU BELIEVE THAT? HE'D RATHER I TOOK THE FALL THAN FRANKIE BLACK, AND THE COPS MAN, THE OTHER COPS ARE LISTENING TO HIM.
FRANKIE BLACK AND ALL HIS MAFIA PALS ARE THE BAD GUYS HERE. THEY'RE THE REAL BAD GUYS, RIGHT?
WE'RE SUPPOSED TO STICK TOGETHER, WE'RE SUPPOSED TO BE A TEAM! I MADE A MISTAKE, YEAH, BUT WHERE'S MY BACKUP?
ALL I REALLY WANTED TO DO WAS FIT IN. I CAME HERE FROM A REALLY SMALL TOWN, YOU KNOW, BUT I'M A GOOD COP. I TRY HARD.
THAT'S THE BIGGEST IRONY... I WOULDN'TA BEEN SO LONELY IF THEY'D JUST... IF THE GCPD GUYS... YOU GUYS...

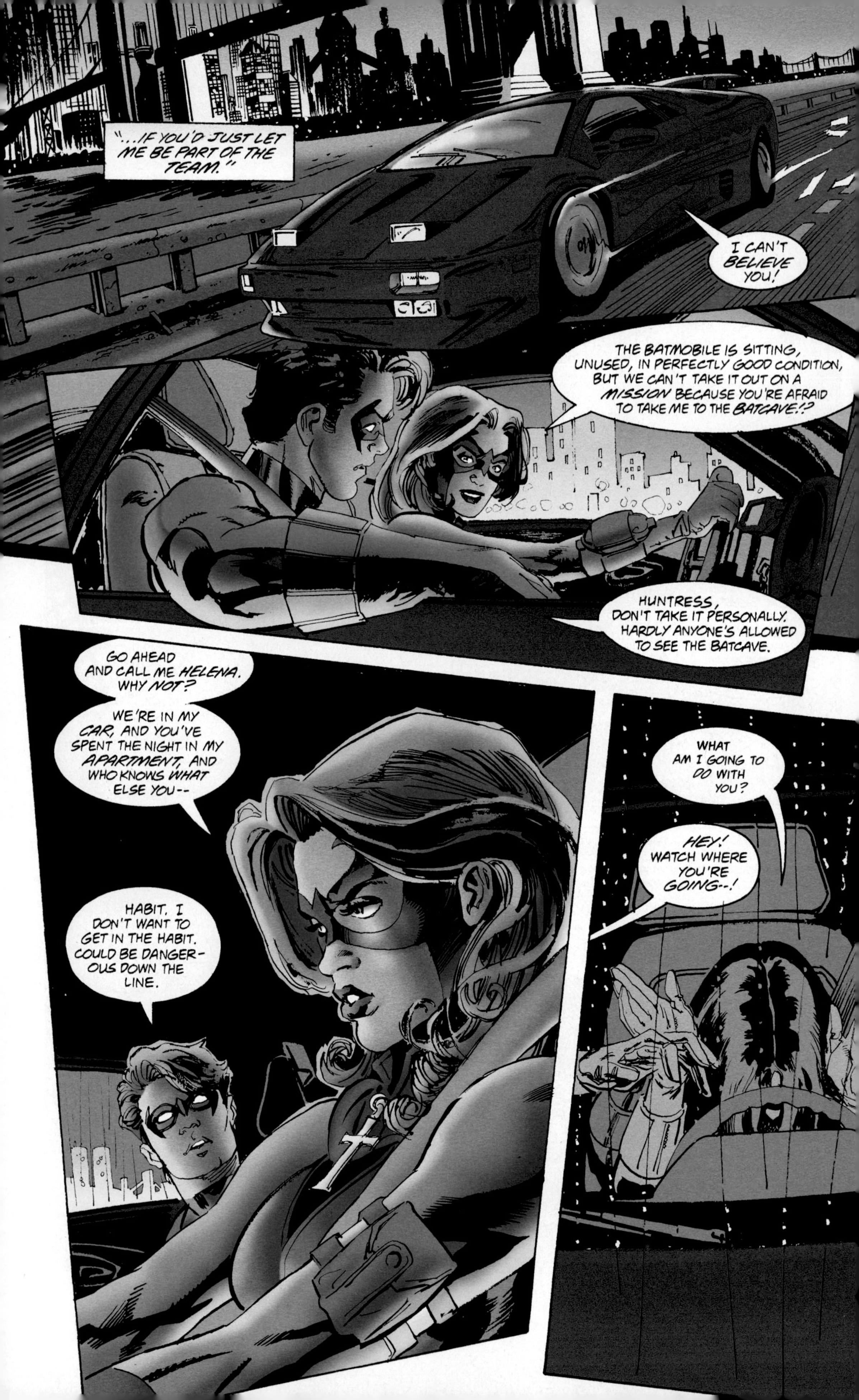
"...IF YOU'D JUST LET ME BE PART OF THE TEAM."
I CAN'T BELIEVE YOU!
THE BATMOBILE IS SITTING, UNUSED, IN PERFECTLY GOOD CONDITION, BUT WE CAN'T TAKE IT OUT ON A MISSION BECAUSE YOU'RE AFRAID TO TAKE ME TO THE BATCAVE!?
HUNTRESS, DON'T TAKE IT PERSONALLY. HARDLY ANYONE'S ALLOWED TO SEE THE BATCAVE.
GO AHEAD AND CALL ME HELENA. WHY NOT?
WE'RE IN MY CAR, AND YOU'VE SPENT THE NIGHT IN MY APARTMENT, AND WHO KNOWS WHAT ELSE YOU--
HABIT. I DON'T WANT TO GET IN THE HABIT. COULD BE DANGER-OUS DOWN THE LINE.
WHAT AM I GOING TO DO WITH YOU?
HEY! WATCH WHERE YOU'RE GOING--!

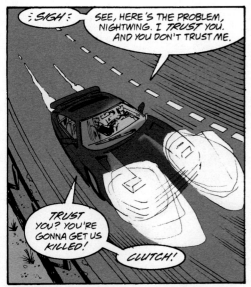

:SIGH: SEE, HERE'S THE PROBLEM, NIGHTWING. I *TRUST* YOU. AND YOU DON'T TRUST ME.

TRUST YOU? YOU'RE GONNA GET US *KILLED!*

CLUTCH!

NO. WE'RE NOT EVEN IN *DANGER* NOW. I COULD CRAWL OUT ONTO THE *HOOD* AND YOU'D *STILL* KEEP CONTROL OF THE CAR.

YOU WON'T LET US GET *HURT,* AND YOU WON'T TELL ANYONE MY SECRET IDEN-*TITY...*

...AND IF I TOLD YOU I DON'T WANT TO BE *ALONE* TONIGHT, YOU'D COME *HOME* WITH ME, WHEREAS IF I TOLD YOU I NEVER WANTED TO *SEE* YOU AGAIN, YOU'D LEAVE ME *ALONE.*

UH...SO YOU'RE SAYING YOU...?

YOU'RE A *GOOD* MAN, AND A *GREAT* FRIEND. I UNDERSTAND WHY BATMAN AND THE TITANS *TRUST* YOU.

YOU'RE LOYAL TO A *FAULT,* WHICH IS EXACTLY WHY YOU'LL NEVER GIVE ME THE ONE THING I REALLY *WANT.*

YOU'LL NEVER LET ME *IN.*

I GREW UP *PART* OF *SOMETHING,* NIGHTWING.

IT WAS THE *MAFIA,* SO MAYBE IT WASN'T A *GREAT* THING, BUT IT WAS... A *FAMILY* OF SORTS. PEOPLE WERE *THERE* FOR EACH OTHER, YOU COULD *COUNT* ON IT.

NOT UNLIKE WHAT YOU AND BATMAN AND ROBIN AND ORACLE HAVE *NOW.*

YOU... HAVE OBVIOUSLY BEEN VERY *LONELY* IN YOUR TIME, OH HEIR APPAR-ENT--

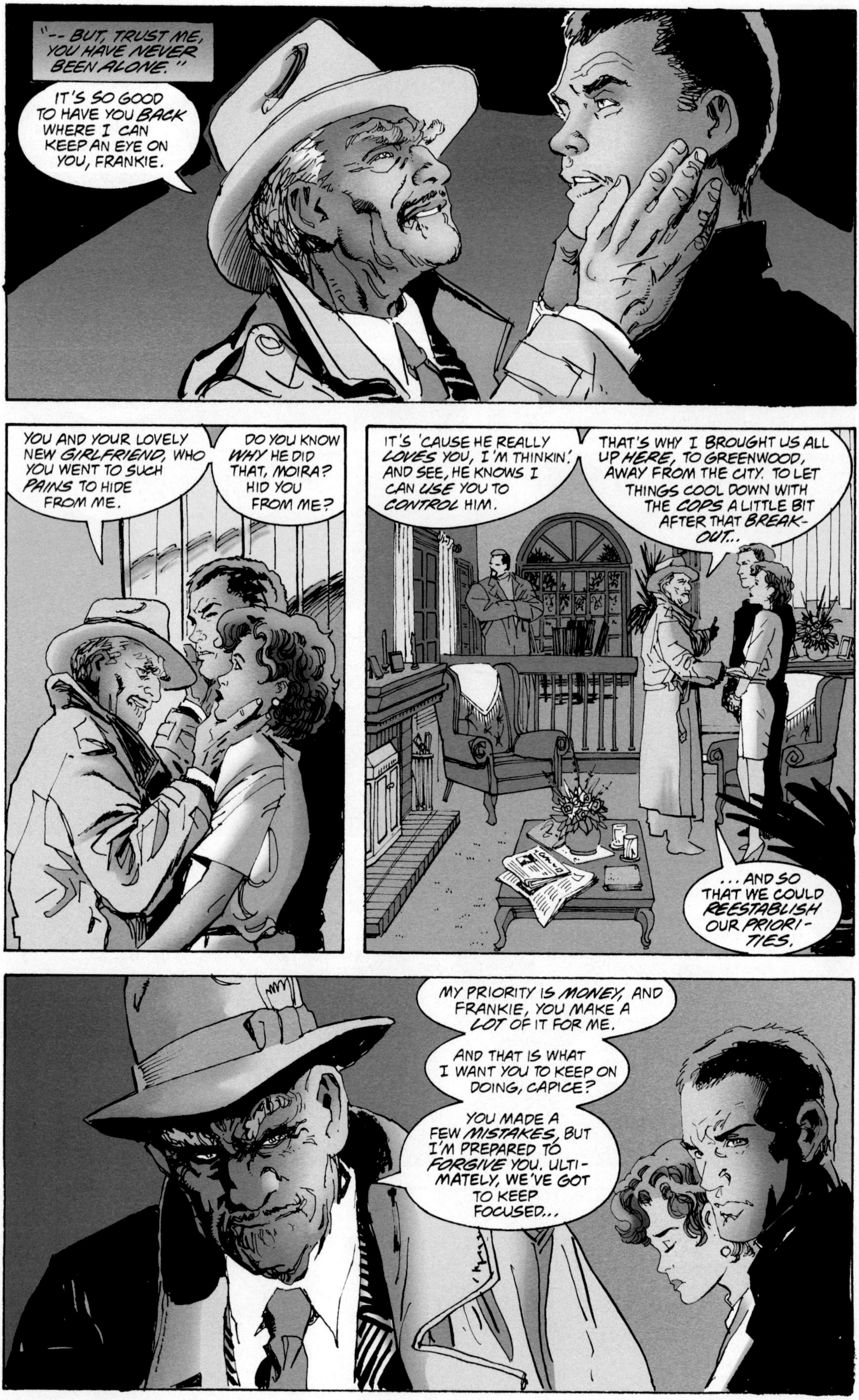
"-- BUT, TRUST ME, YOU HAVE NEVER BEEN ALONE."
IT'S SO GOOD TO HAVE YOU BACK WHERE I CAN KEEP AN EYE ON YOU, FRANKIE.
YOU AND YOUR LOVELY NEW GIRLFRIEND, WHO YOU WENT TO SUCH PAINS TO HIDE FROM ME.
DO YOU KNOW WHY HE DID THAT, MOIRA? HID YOU FROM ME?
IT'S 'CAUSE HE REALLY LOVES YOU, I'M THINKIN'. AND SEE, HE KNOWS I CAN USE YOU TO CONTROL HIM.
THAT'S WHY I BROUGHT US ALL UP HERE, TO GREENWOOD, AWAY FROM THE CITY. TO LET THINGS COOL DOWN WITH THE COPS A LITTLE BIT AFTER THAT BREAK-OUT...
...AND SO THAT WE COULD REESTABLISH OUR PRIORI-TIES.
MY PRIORITY IS MONEY, AND FRANKIE, YOU MAKE A LOT OF IT FOR ME.
AND THAT IS WHAT I WANT YOU TO KEEP ON DOING, CAPICE?
YOU MADE A FEW MISTAKES, BUT I'M PREPARED TO FORGIVE YOU. ULTI-MATELY, WE'VE GOT TO KEEP FOCUSED...

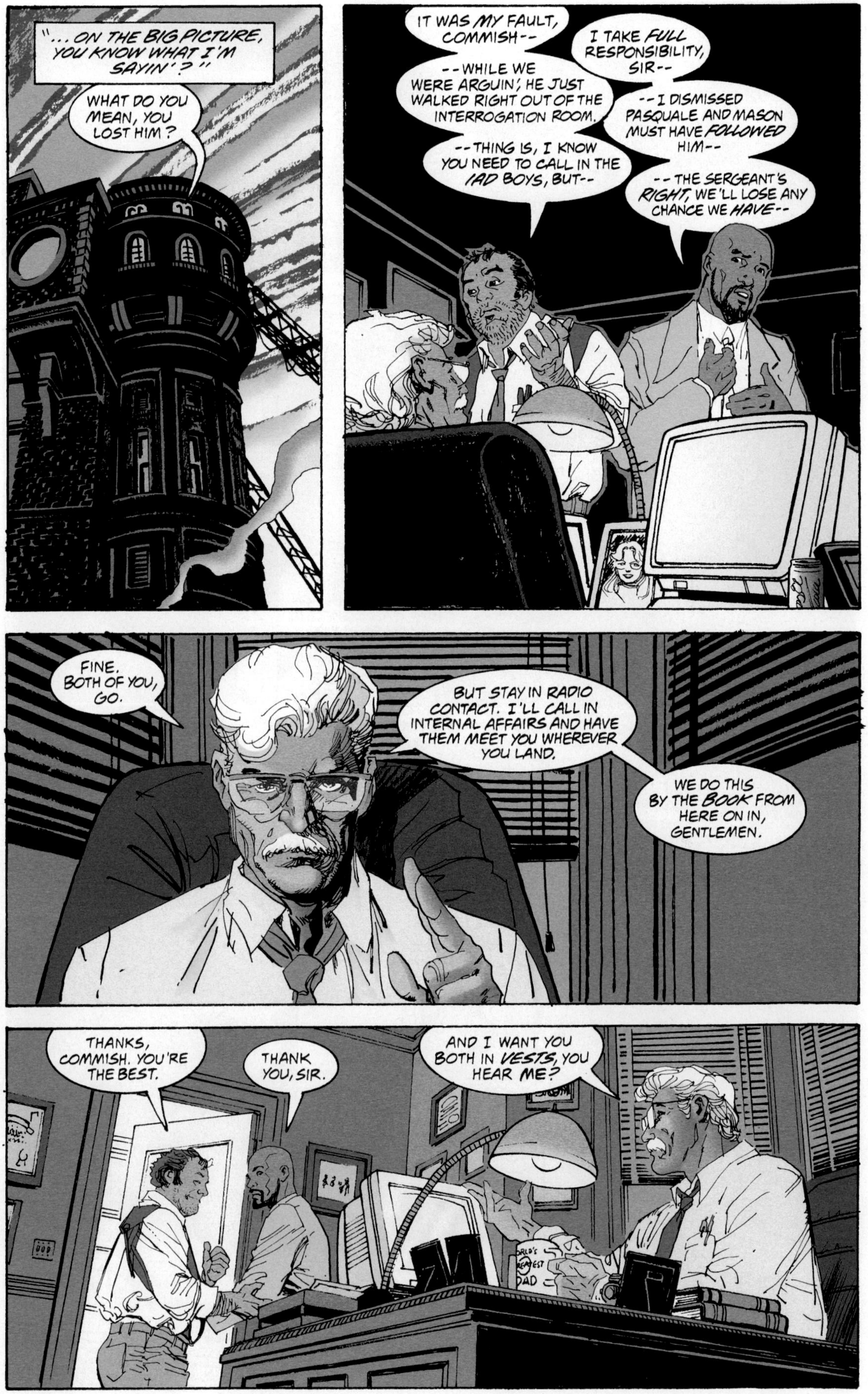
"... ON THE BIG PICTURE, YOU KNOW WHAT I'M SAYIN'?"
WHAT DO YOU MEAN, YOU LOST HIM?
IT WAS MY FAULT, COMMISH--
--WHILE WE WERE ARGUIN', HE JUST WALKED RIGHT OUT OF THE INTERROGATION ROOM.
--THING IS, I KNOW YOU NEED TO CALL IN THE IAD BOYS, BUT--
I TAKE FULL RESPONSIBILITY, SIR--
--I DISMISSED PASQUALE AND MASON MUST HAVE FOLLOWED HIM--
--THE SERGEANT'S RIGHT, WE'LL LOSE ANY CHANCE WE HAVE--
FINE. BOTH OF YOU, GO.
BUT STAY IN RADIO CONTACT. I'LL CALL IN INTERNAL AFFAIRS AND HAVE THEM MEET YOU WHEREVER YOU LAND.
WE DO THIS BY THE BOOK FROM HERE ON IN, GENTLEMEN.
THANKS, COMMISH. YOU'RE THE BEST.
THANK YOU, SIR.
AND I WANT YOU BOTH IN VESTS, YOU HEAR ME?

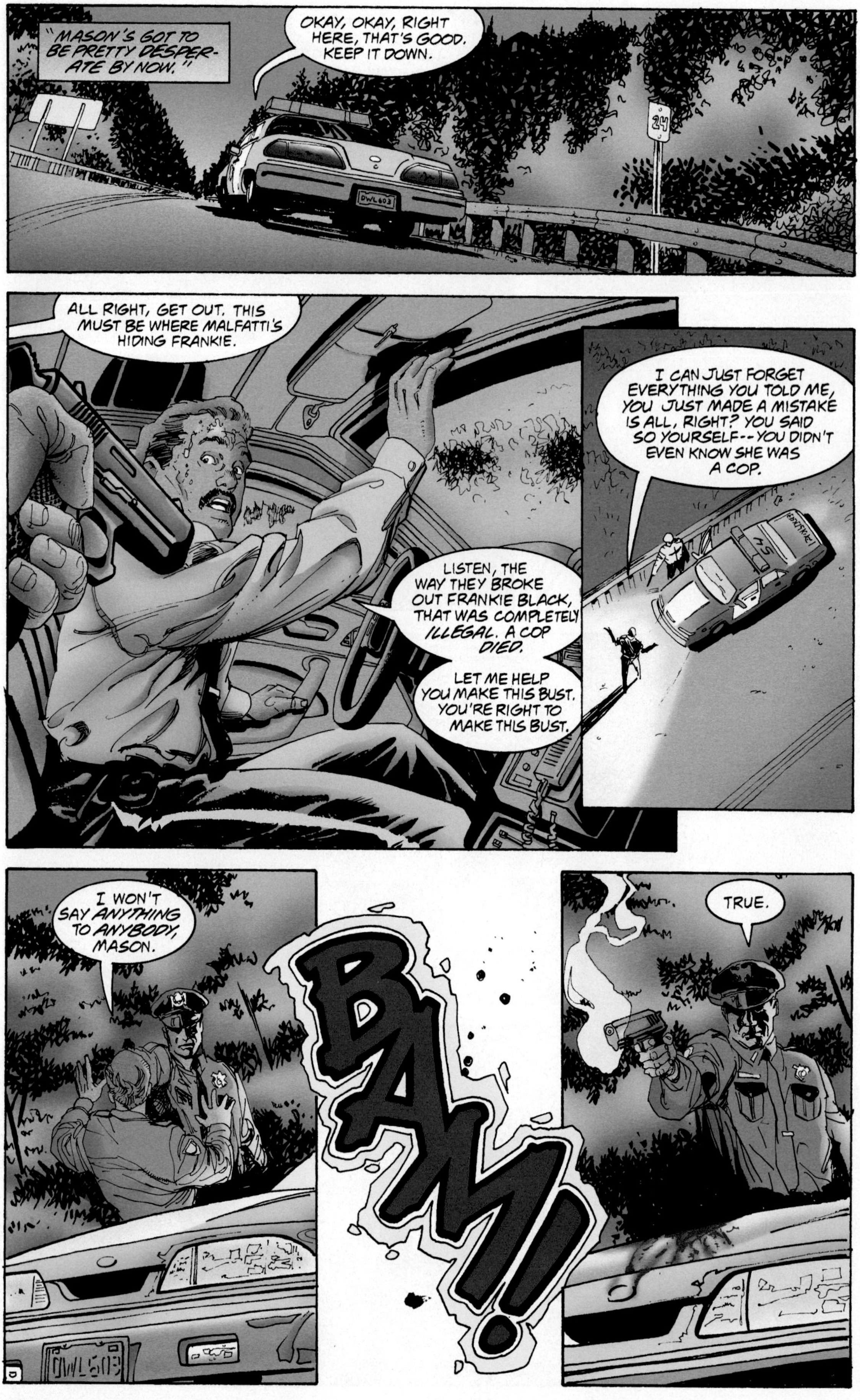
"MASON'S GOT TO BE PRETTY DESPERATE BY NOW."
OKAY, OKAY, RIGHT HERE, THAT'S GOOD. KEEP IT DOWN.
24
DWL603
ALL RIGHT, GET OUT. THIS MUST BE WHERE MALFATTI'S HIDING FRANKIE.
LISTEN, THE WAY THEY BROKE OUT FRANKIE BLACK, THAT WAS COMPLETELY ILLEGAL. A COP DIED.
LET ME HELP YOU MAKE THIS BUST. YOU'RE RIGHT TO MAKE THIS BUST.
I CAN JUST FORGET EVERYTHING YOU TOLD ME, YOU JUST MADE A MISTAKE IS ALL, RIGHT? YOU SAID SO YOURSELF--YOU DIDN'T EVEN KNOW SHE WAS A COP.
I WON'T SAY ANYTHING TO ANYBODY, MASON.
DWL603
BAM!
TRUE.

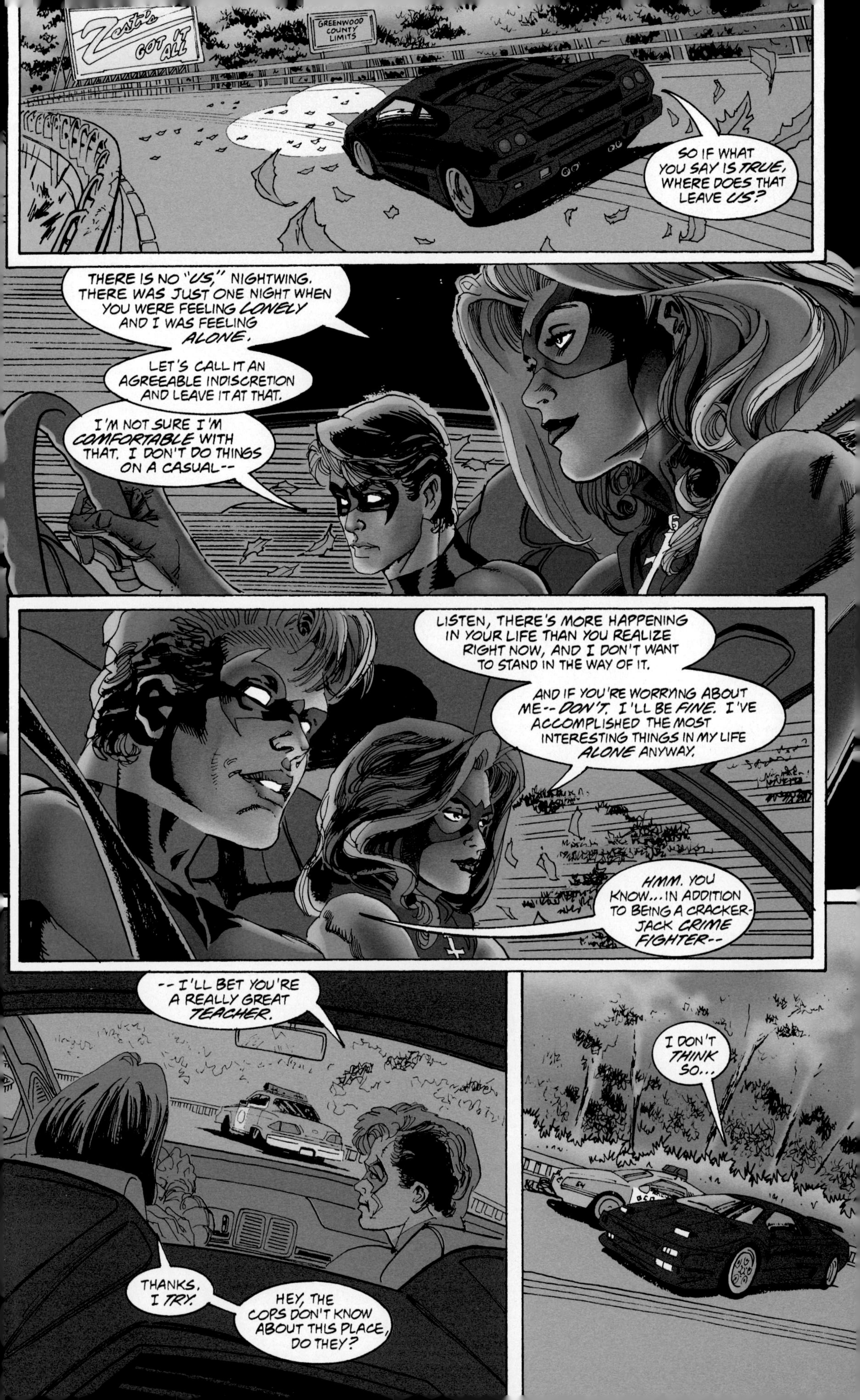
Zest's GOT IT ALL
GREENWOOD COUNTY LIMITS
SO IF WHAT YOU SAY IS TRUE, WHERE DOES THAT LEAVE US?
THERE IS NO "US," NIGHTWING. THERE WAS JUST ONE NIGHT WHEN YOU WERE FEELING LONELY AND I WAS FEELING ALONE.
LET'S CALL IT AN AGREEABLE INDISCRETION AND LEAVE IT AT THAT.
I'M NOT SURE I'M COMFORTABLE WITH THAT. I DON'T DO THINGS ON A CASUAL--
LISTEN, THERE'S MORE HAPPENING IN YOUR LIFE THAN YOU REALIZE RIGHT NOW, AND I DON'T WANT TO STAND IN THE WAY OF IT.
AND IF YOU'RE WORRYING ABOUT ME--DON'T. I'LL BE FINE. I'VE ACCOMPLISHED THE MOST INTERESTING THINGS IN MY LIFE ALONE ANYWAY.
HMM. YOU KNOW... IN ADDITION TO BEING A CRACKER-JACK CRIME FIGHTER--
--I'LL BET YOU'RE A REALLY GREAT TEACHER.
THANKS. I TRY.
HEY, THE COPS DON'T KNOW ABOUT THIS PLACE, DO THEY?
I DON'T THINK SO...

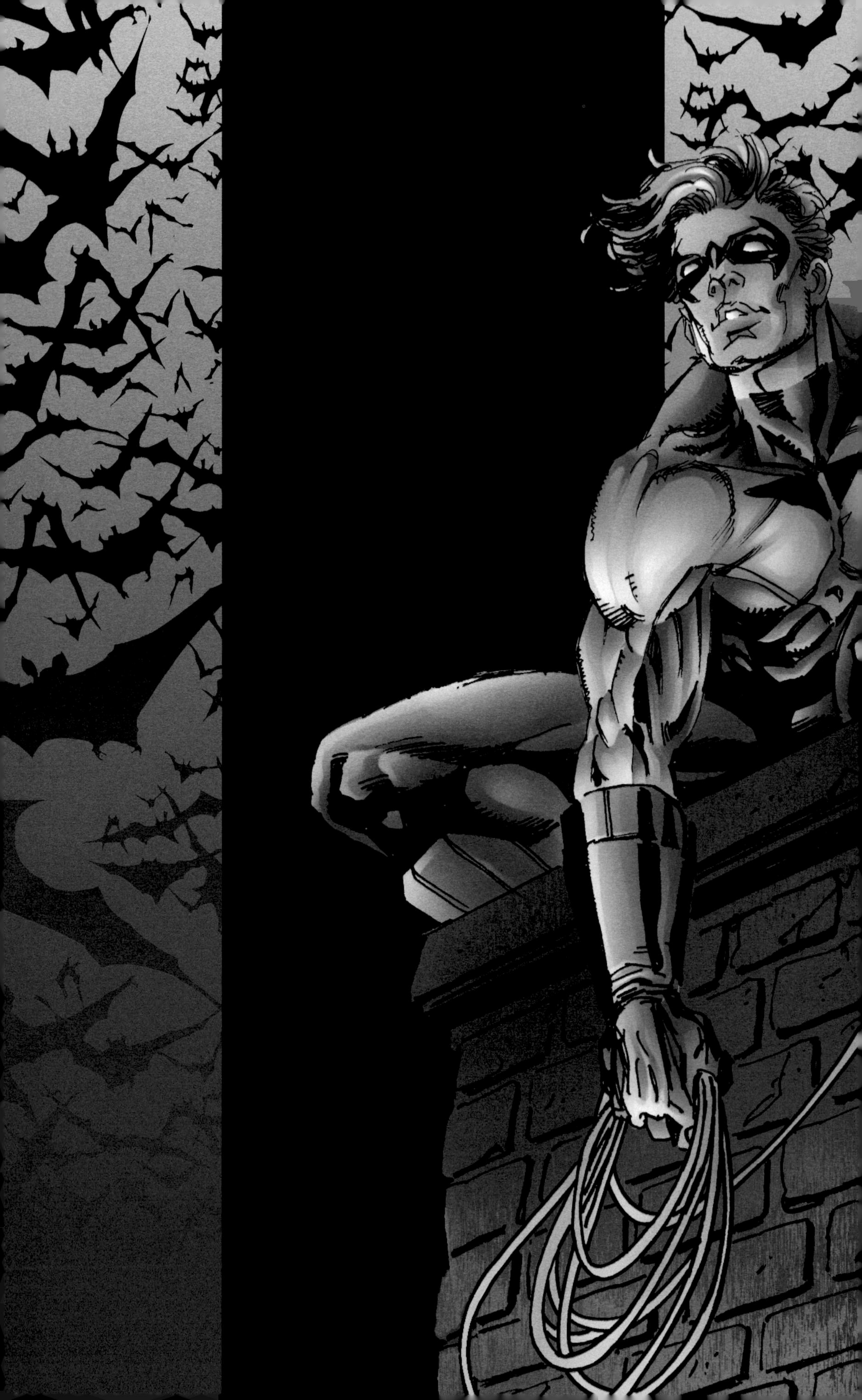

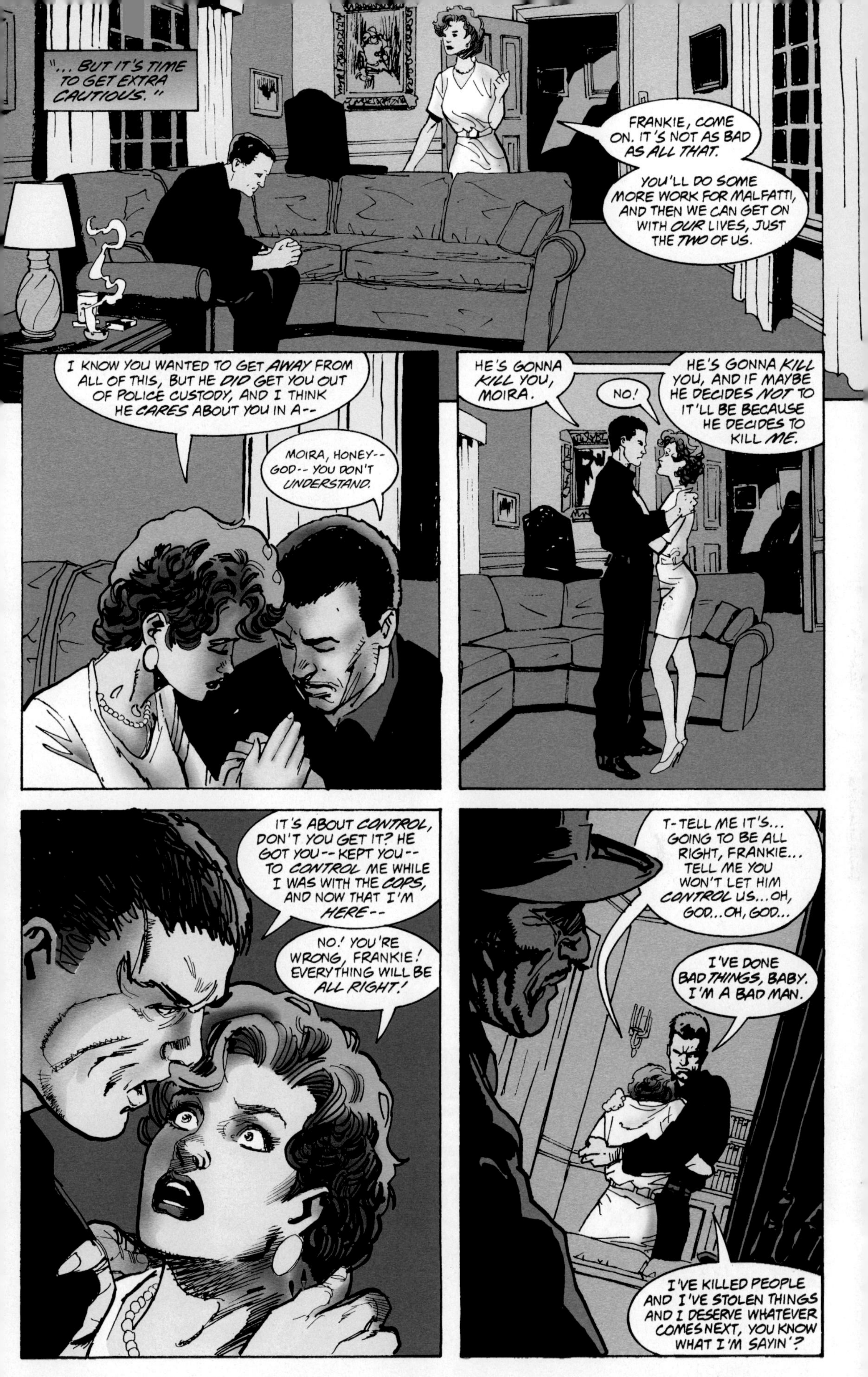
"...BUT IT'S TIME TO GET EXTRA CAUTIOUS."
FRANKIE, COME ON. IT'S NOT AS BAD AS ALL THAT.
YOU'LL DO SOME MORE WORK FOR MALFATTI, AND THEN WE CAN GET ON WITH OUR LIVES, JUST THE TWO OF US.
I KNOW YOU WANTED TO GET AWAY FROM ALL OF THIS, BUT HE DID GET YOU OUT OF POLICE CUSTODY, AND I THINK HE CARES ABOUT YOU IN A--
MOIRA, HONEY-- GOD-- YOU DON'T UNDERSTAND.
HE'S GONNA KILL YOU, MOIRA.
NO!
HE'S GONNA KILL YOU, AND IF MAYBE HE DECIDES NOT TO IT'LL BE BECAUSE HE DECIDES TO KILL ME.
IT'S ABOUT CONTROL, DON'T YOU GET IT? HE GOT YOU--KEPT YOU-- TO CONTROL ME WHILE I WAS WITH THE COPS, AND NOW THAT I'M HERE--
NO! YOU'RE WRONG, FRANKIE! EVERYTHING WILL BE ALL RIGHT!
T-TELL ME IT'S... GOING TO BE ALL RIGHT, FRANKIE... TELL ME YOU WON'T LET HIM CONTROL US...OH, GOD...OH, GOD...
I'VE DONE BAD THINGS, BABY. I'M A BAD MAN.
I'VE KILLED PEOPLE AND I'VE STOLEN THINGS AND I DESERVE WHATEVER COMES NEXT, YOU KNOW WHAT I'M SAYIN'?

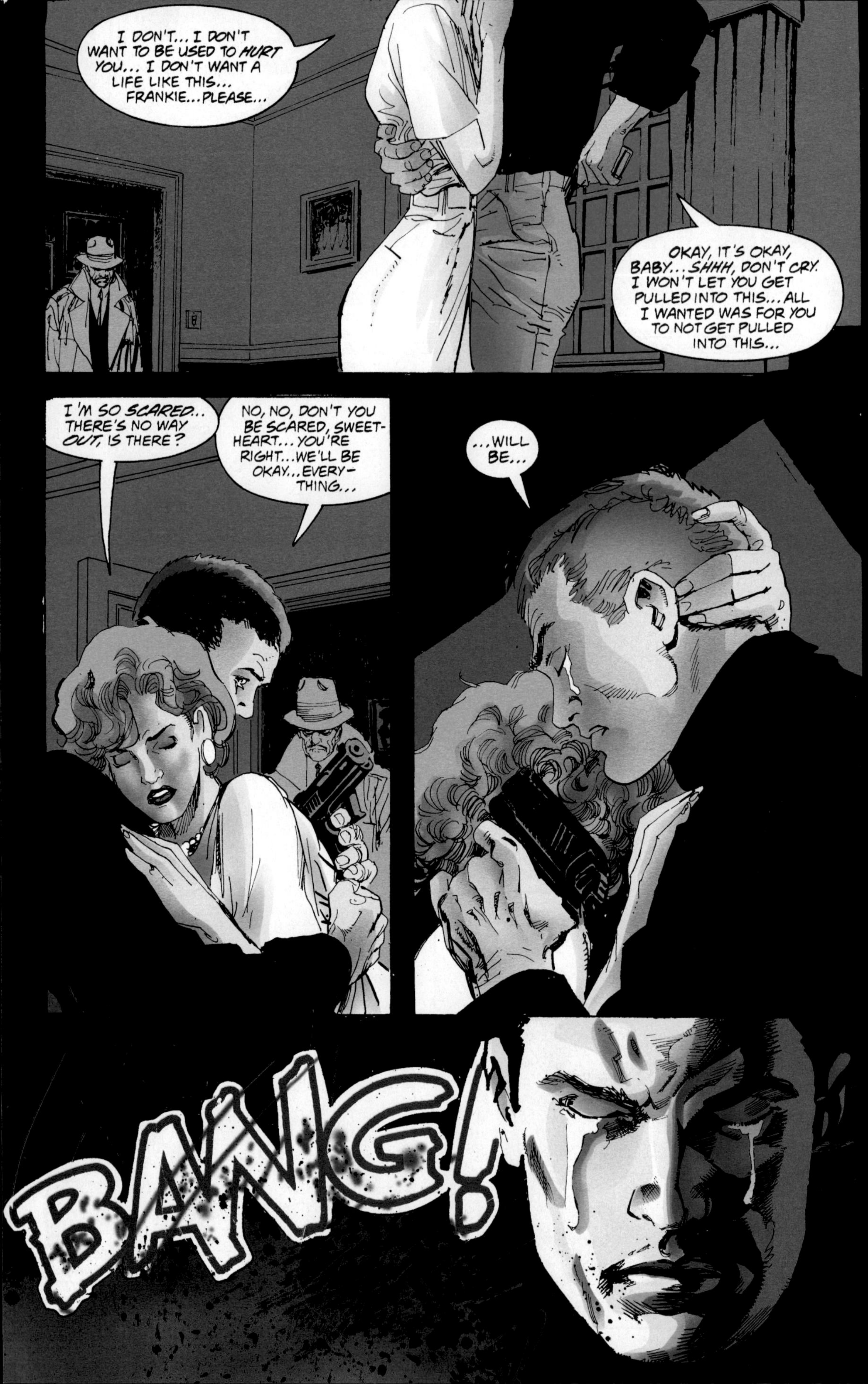
I DON'T... I DON'T WANT TO BE USED TO HURT YOU... I DON'T WANT A LIFE LIKE THIS... FRANKIE...PLEASE...
OKAY, IT'S OKAY, BABY... SHHH, DON'T CRY. I WON'T LET YOU GET PULLED INTO THIS...ALL I WANTED WAS FOR YOU TO NOT GET PULLED INTO THIS...
I'M SO SCARED... THERE'S NO WAY OUT, IS THERE?
NO, NO, DON'T YOU BE SCARED, SWEET-HEART... YOU'RE RIGHT...WE'LL BE OKAY...EVERY-THING...
...WILL BE...
BANG!

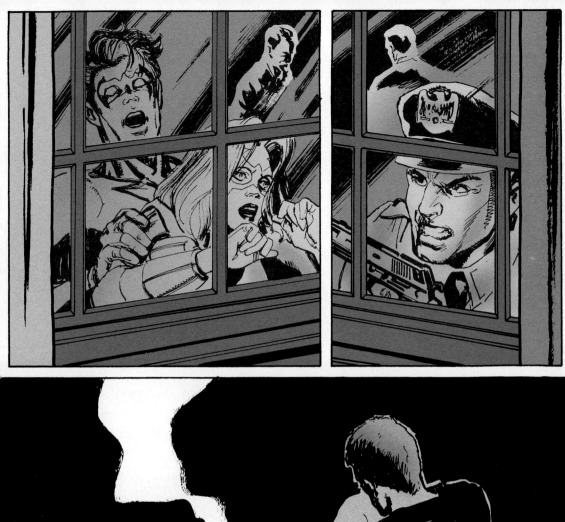

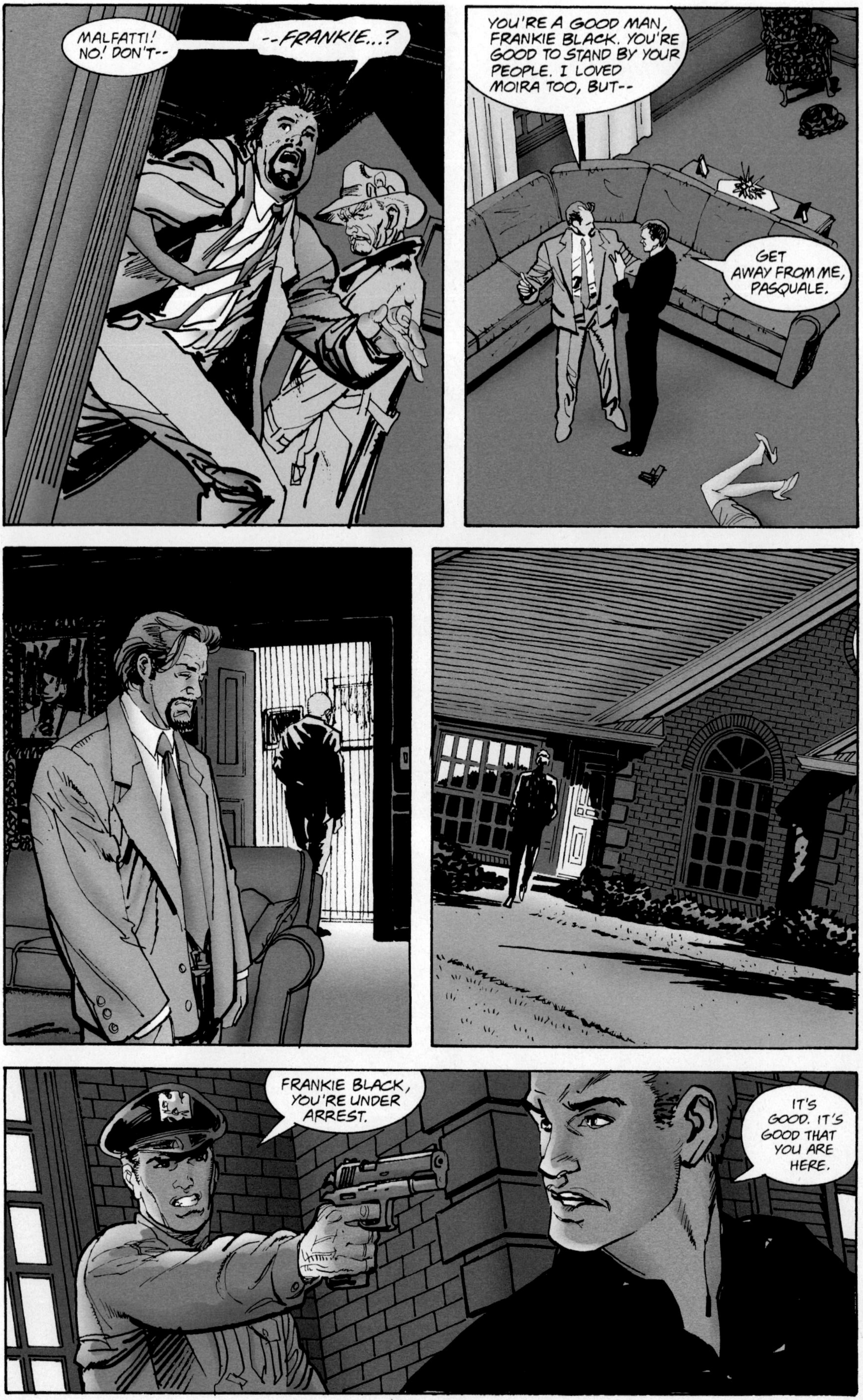
MALFATTI! NO! DON'T--
--FRANKIE...?
YOU'RE A GOOD MAN, FRANKIE BLACK. YOU'RE GOOD TO STAND BY YOUR PEOPLE. I LOVED MOIRA TOO, BUT--
GET AWAY FROM ME, PASQUALE.
FRANKIE BLACK, YOU'RE UNDER ARREST.
IT'S GOOD. IT'S GOOD THAT YOU ARE HERE.

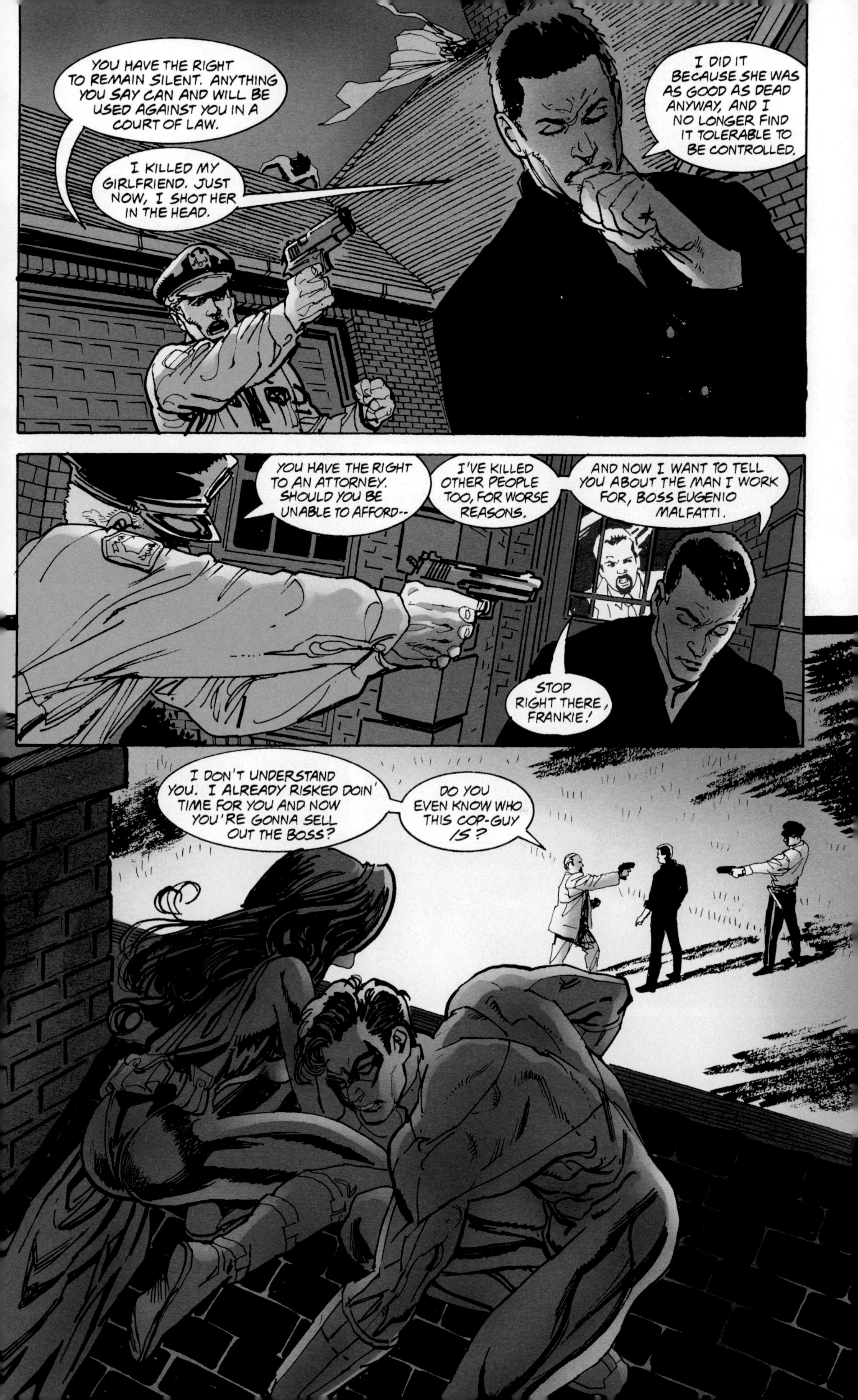
YOU HAVE THE RIGHT TO REMAIN SILENT. ANYTHING YOU SAY CAN AND WILL BE USED AGAINST YOU IN A COURT OF LAW.
I KILLED MY GIRLFRIEND. JUST NOW, I SHOT HER IN THE HEAD.
I DID IT BECAUSE SHE WAS AS GOOD AS DEAD ANYWAY, AND I NO LONGER FIND IT TOLERABLE TO BE CONTROLLED.
YOU HAVE THE RIGHT TO AN ATTORNEY. SHOULD YOU BE UNABLE TO AFFORD--
I'VE KILLED OTHER PEOPLE TOO, FOR WORSE REASONS.
AND NOW I WANT TO TELL YOU ABOUT THE MAN I WORK FOR, BOSS EUGENIO MALFATTI.
STOP RIGHT THERE, FRANKIE!
I DON'T UNDERSTAND YOU. I ALREADY RISKED DOIN' TIME FOR YOU AND NOW YOU'RE GONNA SELL OUT THE BOSS?
DO YOU EVEN KNOW WHO THIS COP-GUY IS?

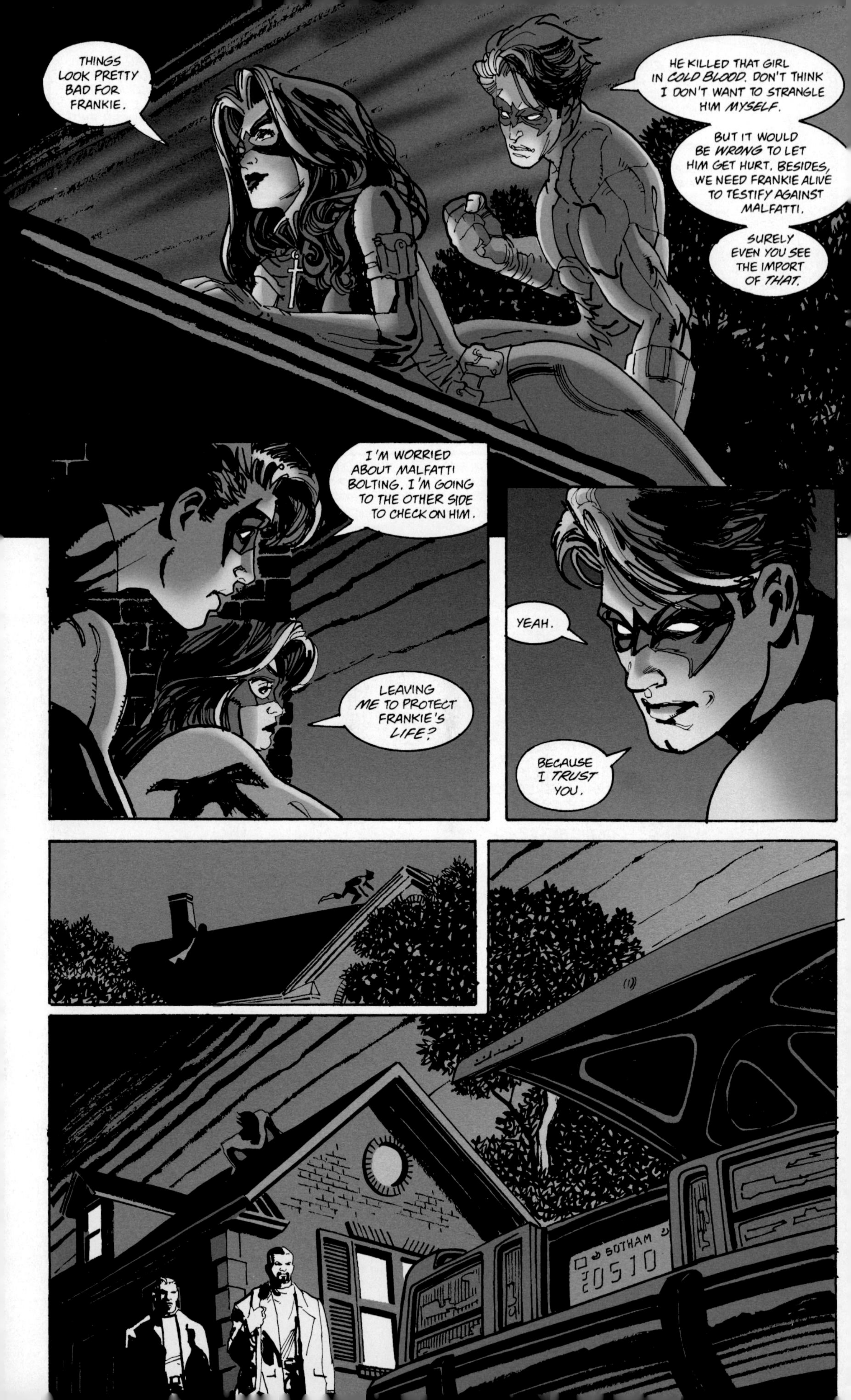

THINGS LOOK PRETTY BAD FOR FRANKIE.
HE KILLED THAT GIRL IN COLD BLOOD. DON'T THINK I DON'T WANT TO STRANGLE HIM MYSELF.
BUT IT WOULD BE WRONG TO LET HIM GET HURT. BESIDES, WE NEED FRANKIE ALIVE TO TESTIFY AGAINST MALFATTI.
SURELY EVEN YOU SEE THE IMPORT OF THAT.
I'M WORRIED ABOUT MALFATTI BOLTING. I'M GOING TO THE OTHER SIDE TO CHECK ON HIM.
LEAVING ME TO PROTECT FRANKIE'S LIFE?
YEAH.
BECAUSE I TRUST YOU.
GOTHAM
0510

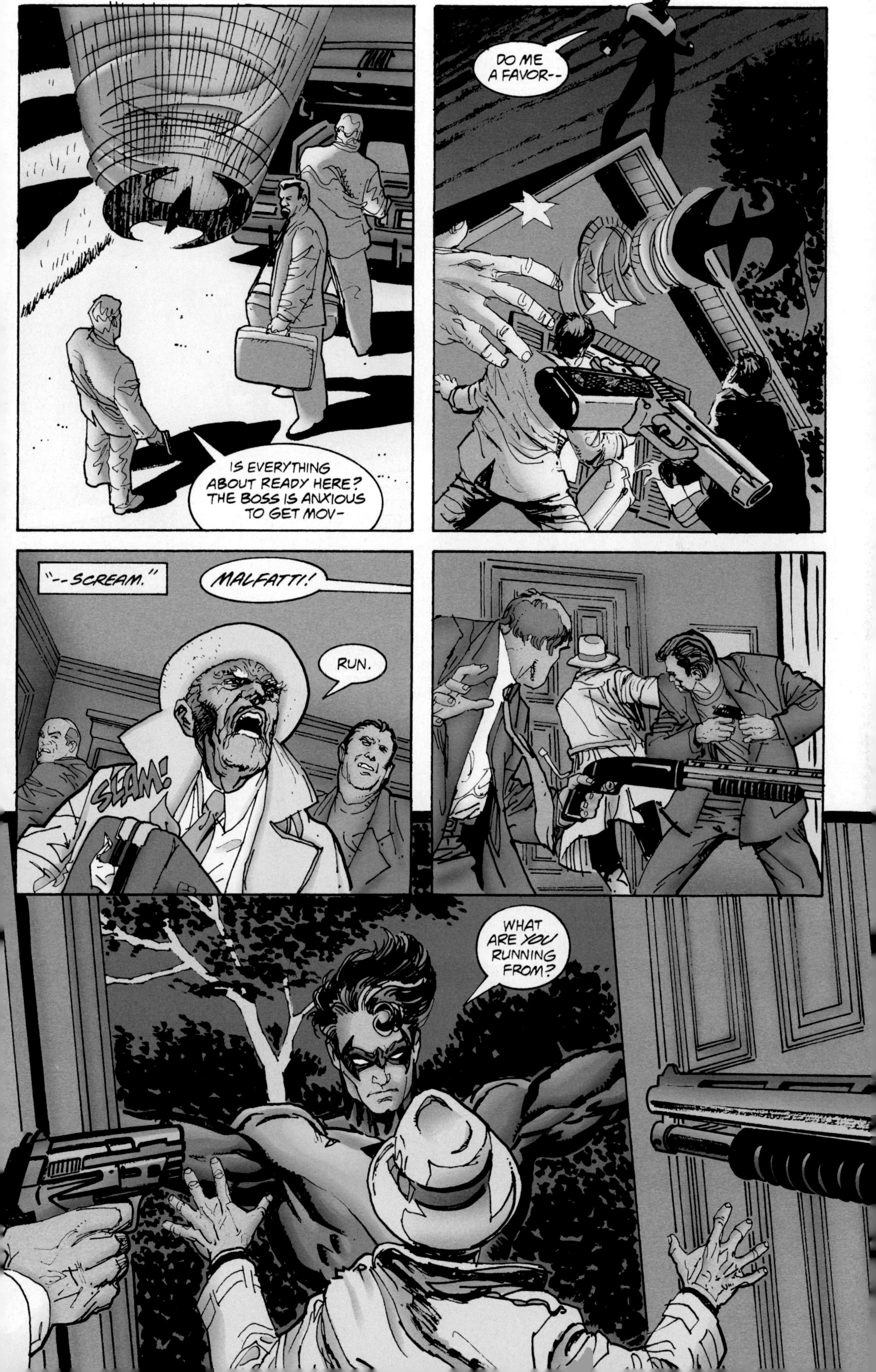
IS EVERYTHING ABOUT READY HERE? THE BOSS IS ANXIOUS TO GET MOV-
DO ME A FAVOR--
"--SCREAM."
MALFATTI!
RUN.
WHAT ARE YOU RUNNING FROM?
SLAM!

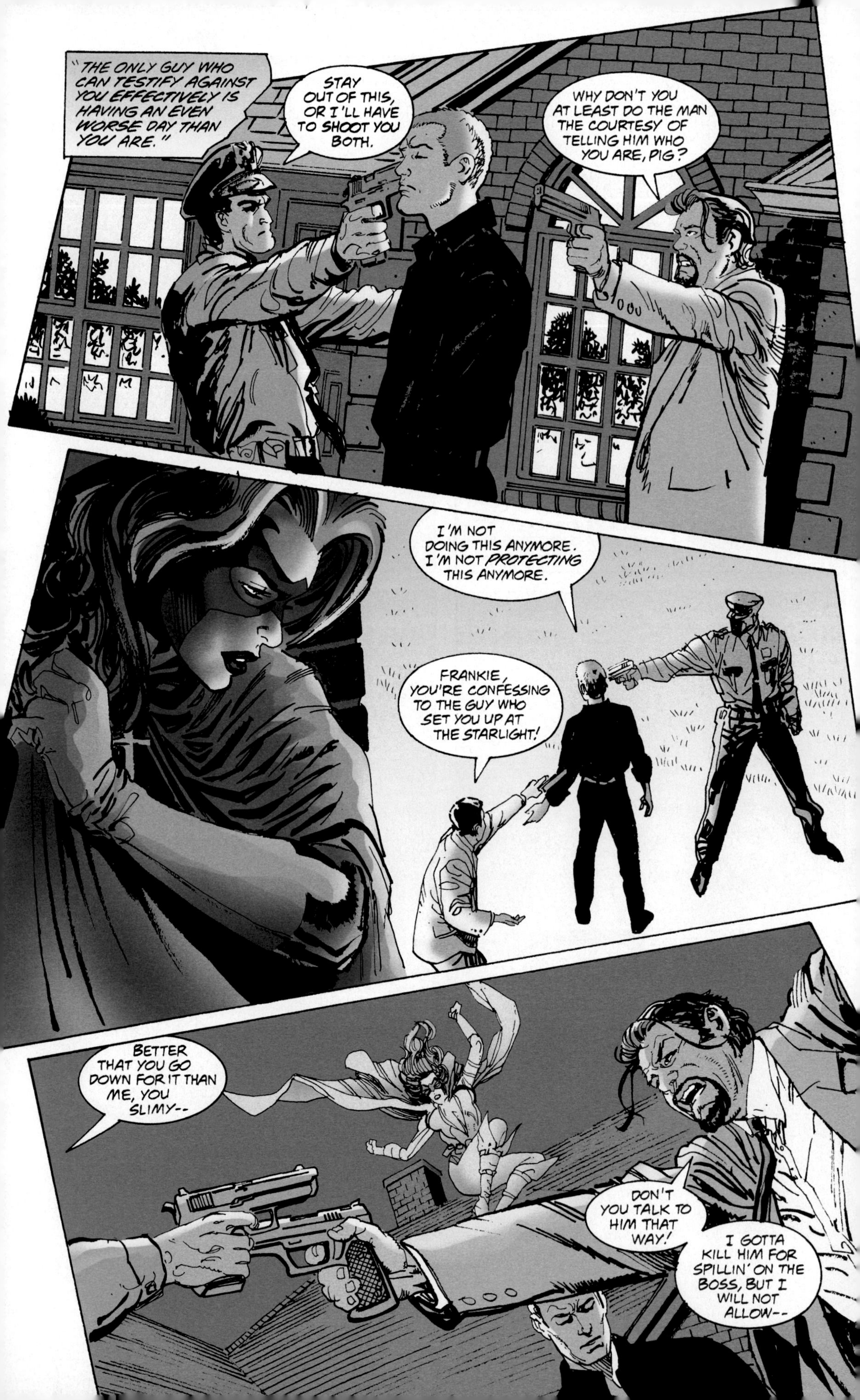
"THE ONLY GUY WHO CAN TESTIFY AGAINST YOU EFFECTIVELY IS HAVING AN EVEN WORSE DAY THAN YOU ARE."
STAY OUT OF THIS, OR I'LL HAVE TO SHOOT YOU BOTH.
WHY DON'T YOU AT LEAST DO THE MAN THE COURTESY OF TELLING HIM WHO YOU ARE, PIG?
I'M NOT DOING THIS ANYMORE. I'M NOT PROTECTING THIS ANYMORE.
FRANKIE, YOU'RE CONFESSING TO THE GUY WHO SET YOU UP AT THE STARLIGHT!
BETTER THAT YOU GO DOWN FOR IT THAN ME, YOU SLIMY--
DON'T YOU TALK TO HIM THAT WAY!
I GOTTA KILL HIM FOR SPILLIN' ON THE BOSS, BUT I WILL NOT ALLOW--

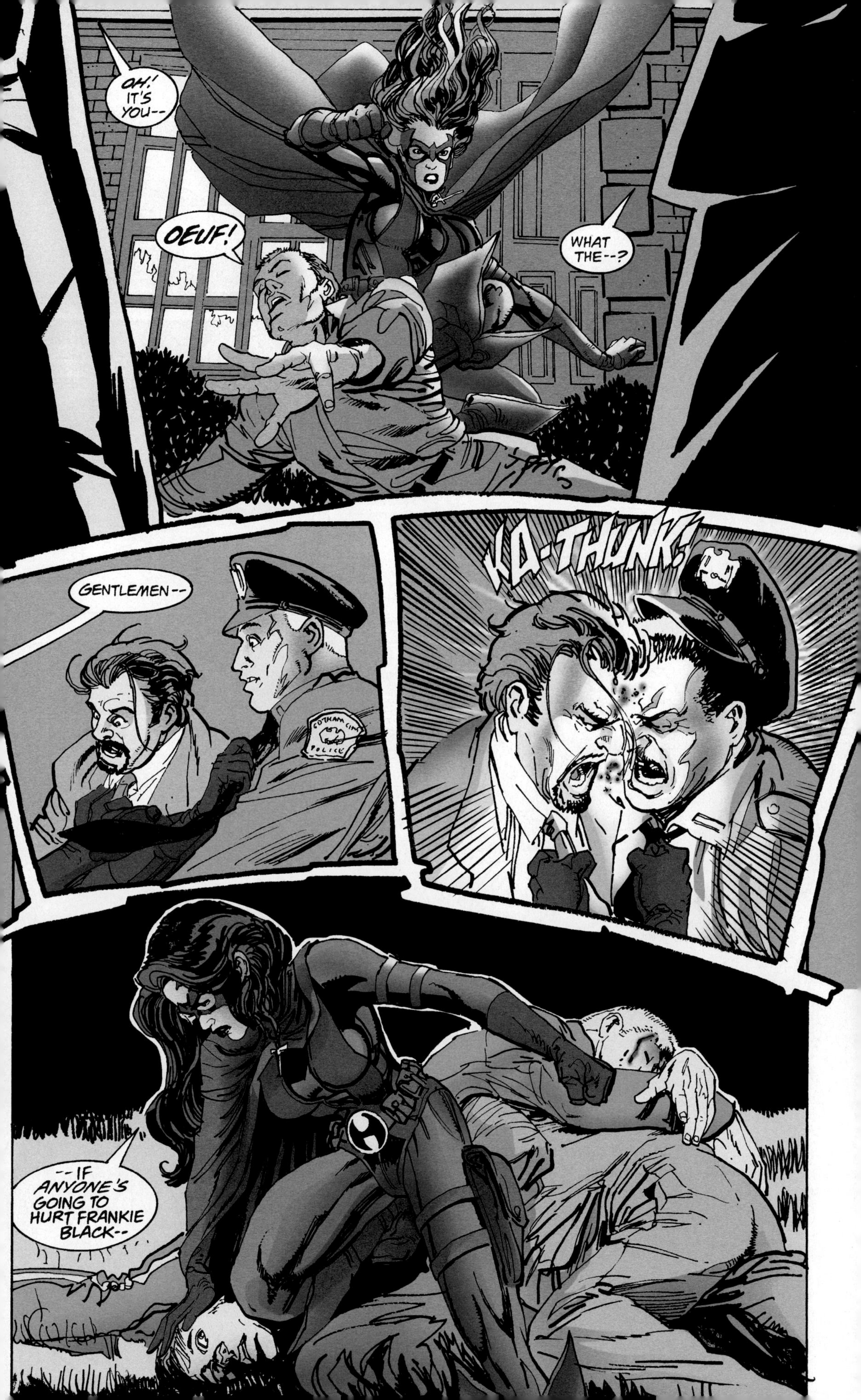
OH! IT'S YOU--
OEUF!
WHAT THE--?
GENTLEMEN--
K-A-THUNK!
--IF ANYONE'S GOING TO HURT FRANKIE BLACK--

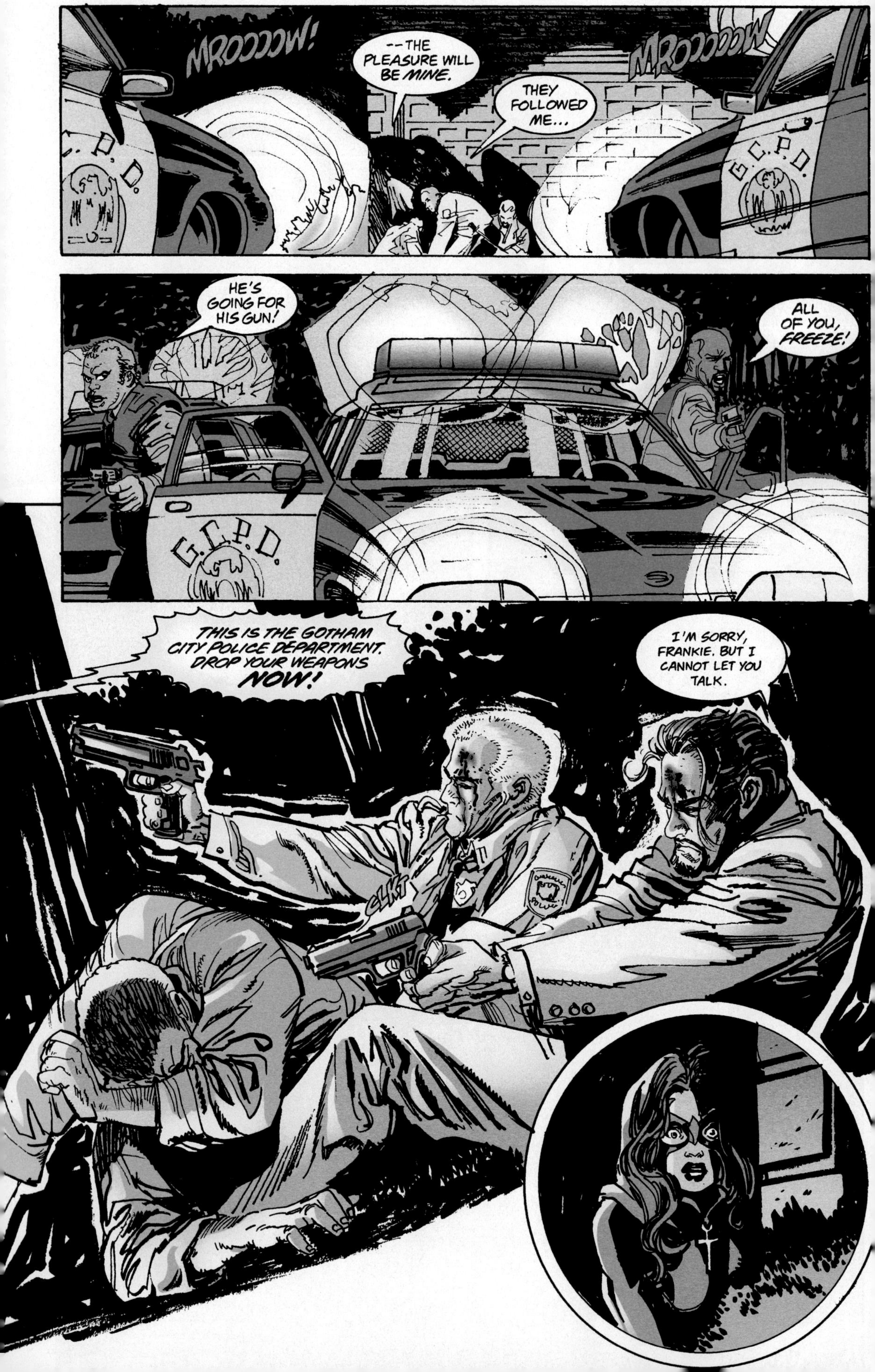
MROOOOOW!
--THE PLEASURE WILL BE MINE.
THEY FOLLOWED ME...
MROOOOOOW
HE'S GOING FOR HIS GUN!
ALL OF YOU, FREEZE!
THIS IS THE GOTHAM CITY POLICE DEPARTMENT. DROP YOUR WEAPONS NOW!
I'M SORRY, FRANKIE. BUT I CANNOT LET YOU TALK.
CLIK

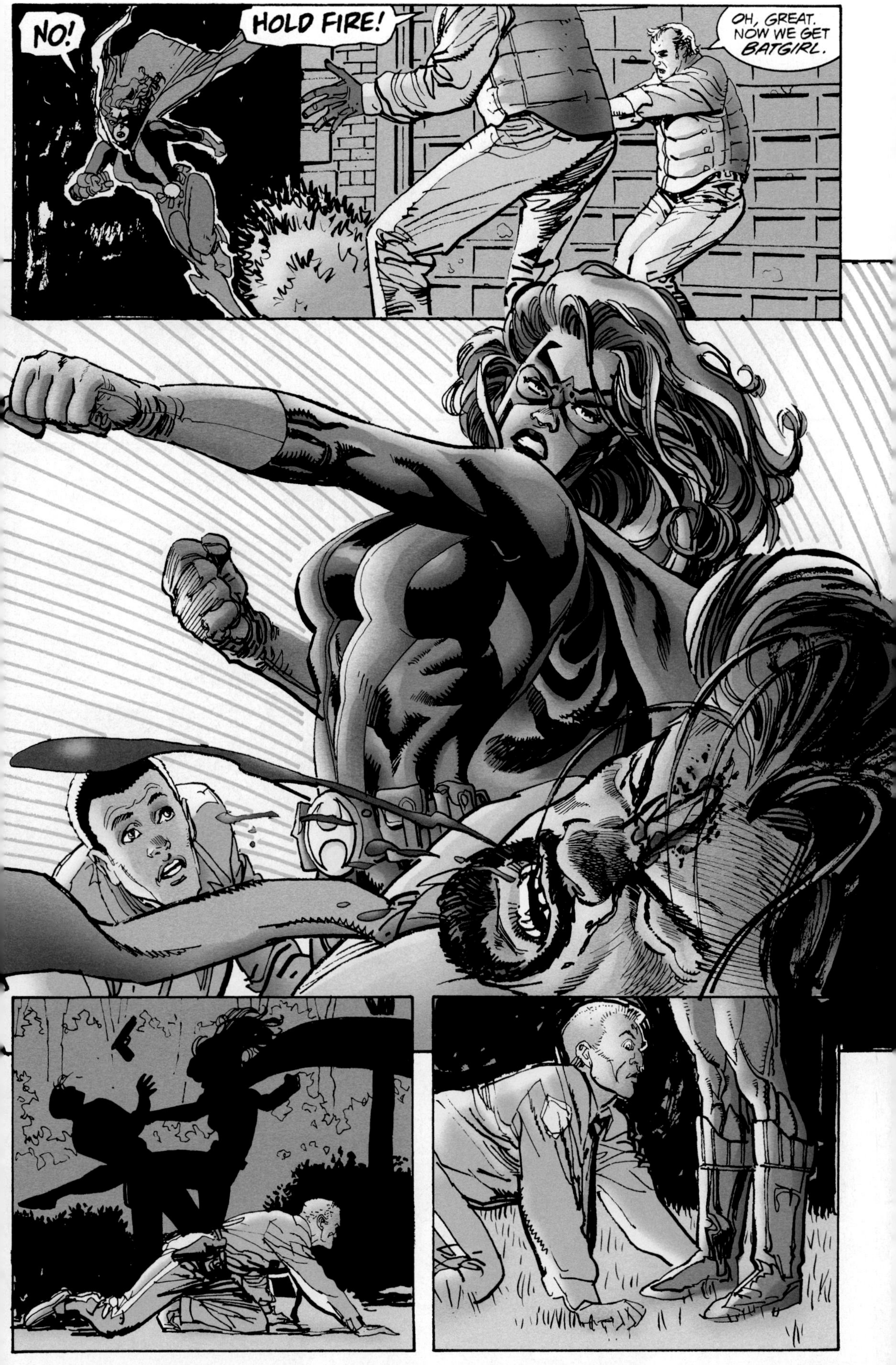
NO!
HOLD FIRE!
OH, GREAT. NOW WE GET BATGIRL.

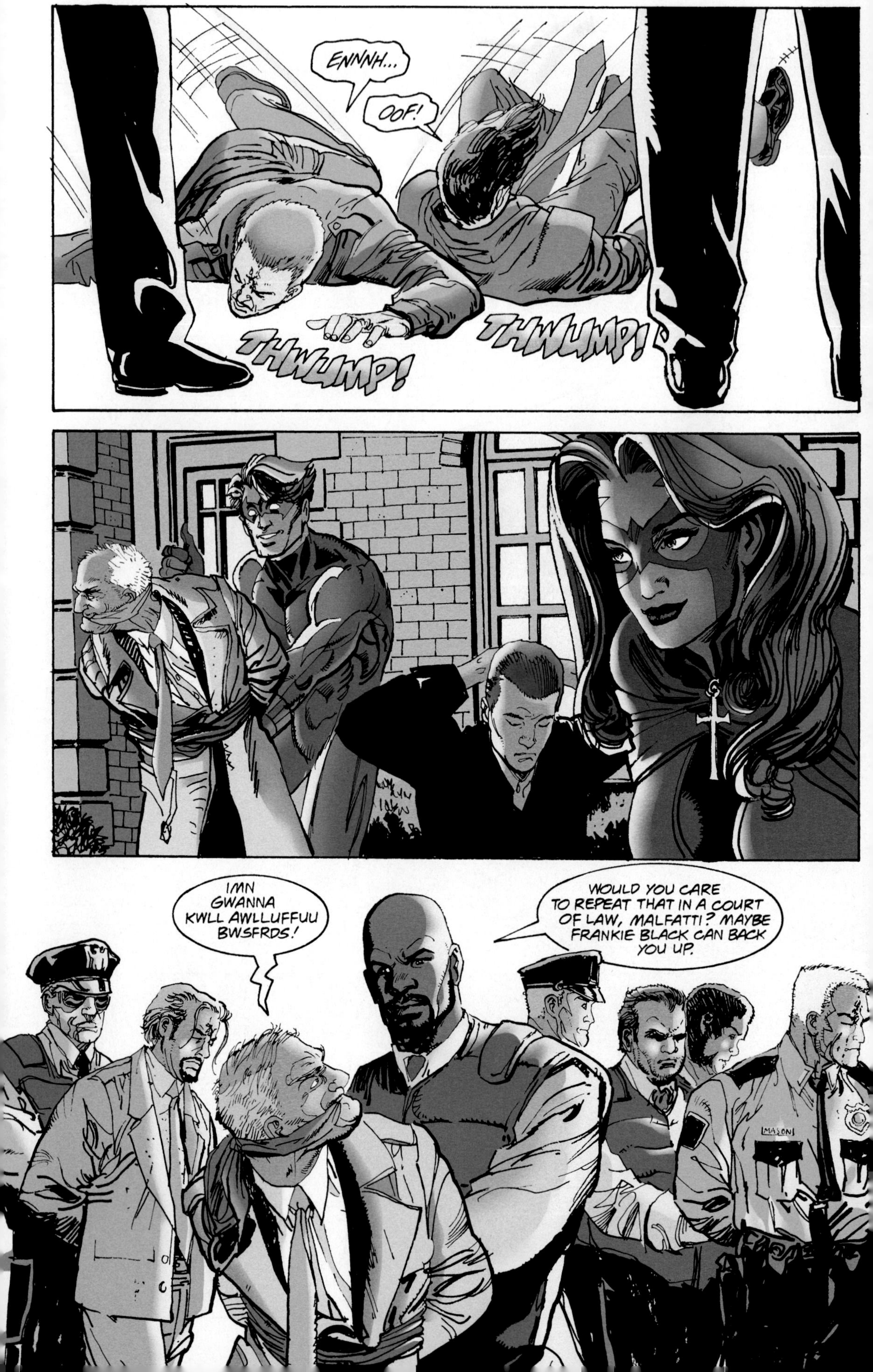
ENNNH...
OOF!
THWUMP!
THWUMP!
IMN GWANNA KWLL AWLLUFFUU BWSFRDS!
WOULD YOU CARE TO REPEAT THAT IN A COURT OF LAW, MALFATTI? MAYBE FRANKIE BLACK CAN BACK YOU UP.
MASON

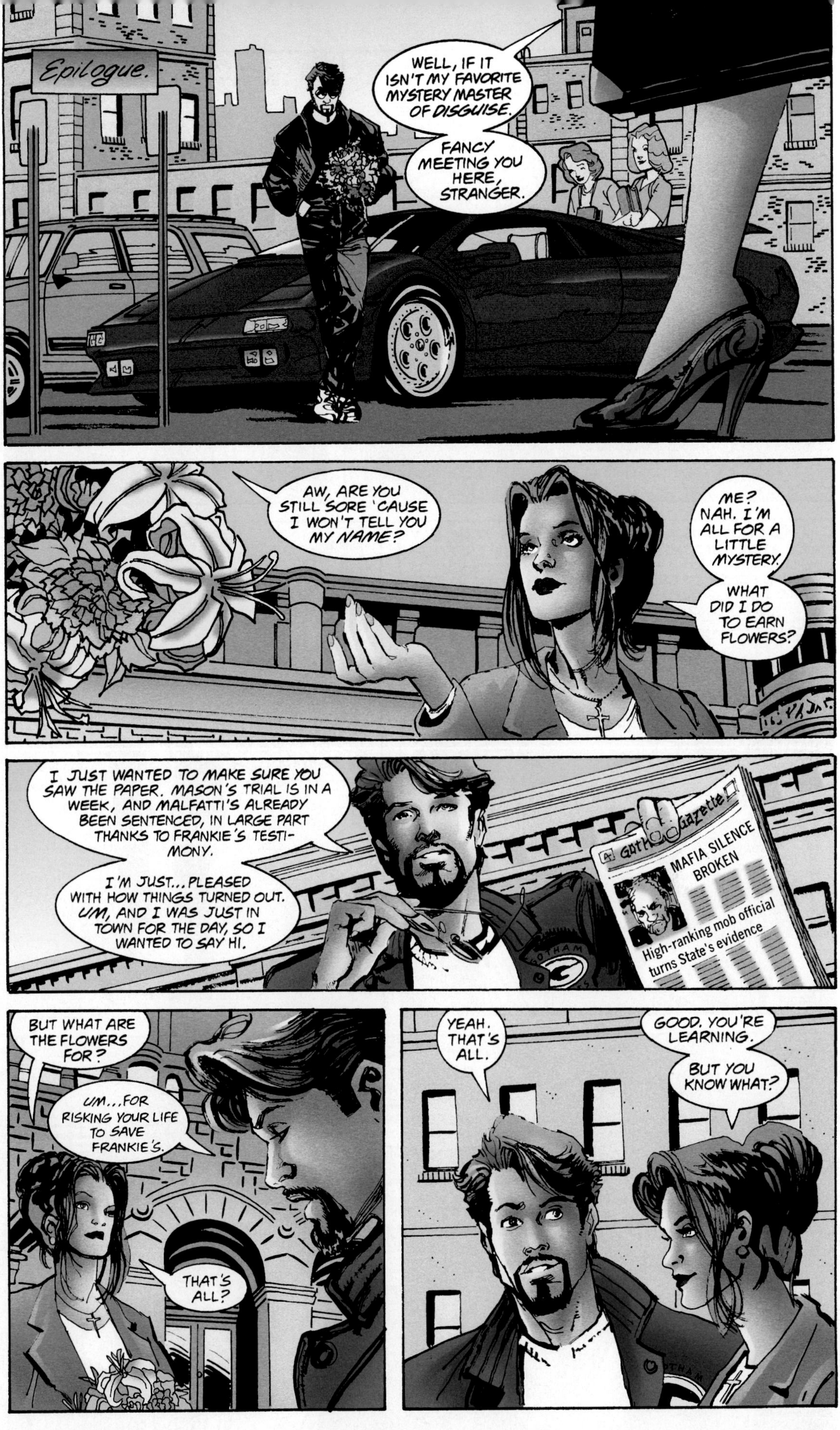

Epilogue.
WELL, IF IT ISN'T MY FAVORITE MYSTERY MASTER OF DISGUISE.
FANCY MEETING YOU HERE, STRANGER.
AW, ARE YOU STILL SORE 'CAUSE I WON'T TELL YOU MY NAME?
ME? NAH. I'M ALL FOR A LITTLE MYSTERY.
WHAT DID I DO TO EARN FLOWERS?
I JUST WANTED TO MAKE SURE YOU SAW THE PAPER. MASON'S TRIAL IS IN A WEEK, AND MALFATTI'S ALREADY BEEN SENTENCED, IN LARGE PART THANKS TO FRANKIE'S TESTI-MONY.
I'M JUST... PLEASED WITH HOW THINGS TURNED OUT. UM, AND I WAS JUST IN TOWN FOR THE DAY, SO I WANTED TO SAY HI.
MAFIA SILENCE BROKEN
High-ranking mob official turns State's evidence
BUT WHAT ARE THE FLOWERS FOR?
UM... FOR RISKING YOUR LIFE TO SAVE FRANKIE'S.
THAT'S ALL?
YEAH. THAT'S ALL.
GOOD. YOU'RE LEARNING.
BUT YOU KNOW WHAT?

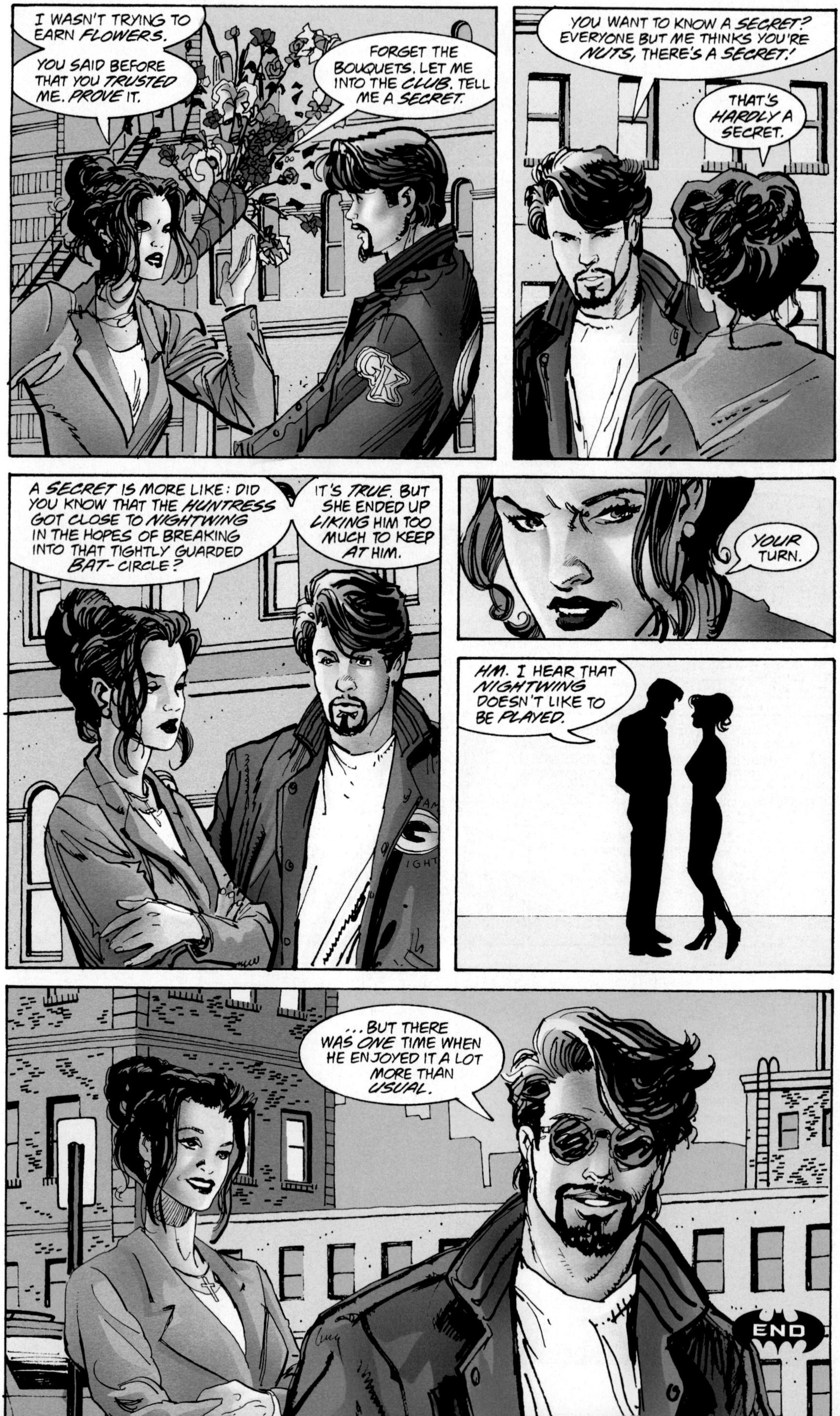

I WASN'T TRYING TO EARN FLOWERS.
YOU SAID BEFORE THAT YOU TRUSTED ME. PROVE IT.
FORGET THE BOUQUETS. LET ME INTO THE CLUB. TELL ME A SECRET.
YOU WANT TO KNOW A SECRET? EVERYONE BUT ME THINKS YOU'RE NUTS, THERE'S A SECRET!
THAT'S HARDLY A SECRET.
A SECRET IS MORE LIKE: DID YOU KNOW THAT THE HUNTRESS GOT CLOSE TO NIGHTWING IN THE HOPES OF BREAKING INTO THAT TIGHTLY GUARDED BAT-CIRCLE?
IT'S TRUE. BUT SHE ENDED UP LIKING HIM TOO MUCH TO KEEP AT HIM.
YOUR TURN.
HM. I HEAR THAT NIGHTWING DOESN'T LIKE TO BE PLAYED.
...BUT THERE WAS ONE TIME WHEN HE ENJOYED IT A LOT MORE THAN USUAL.
END

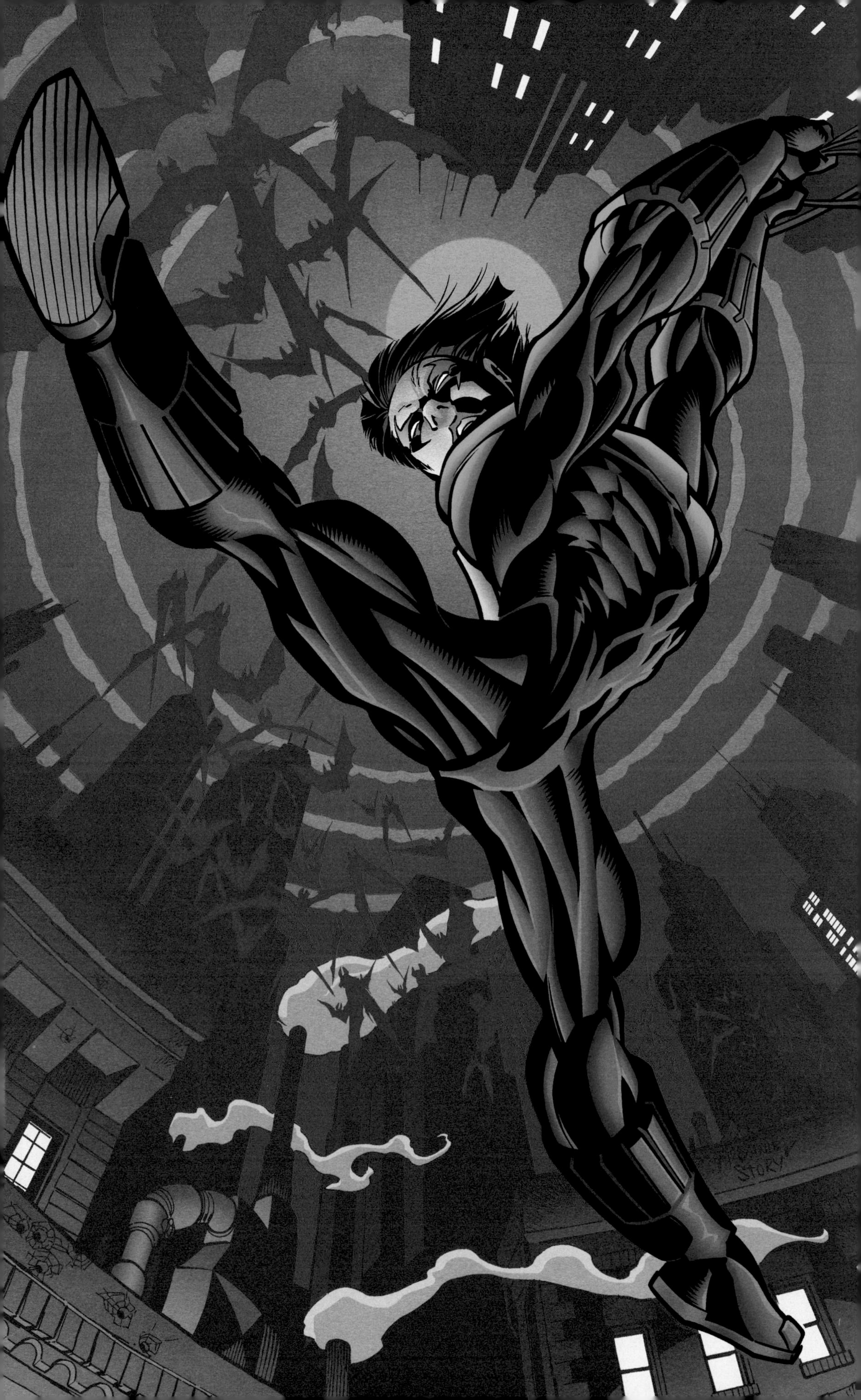

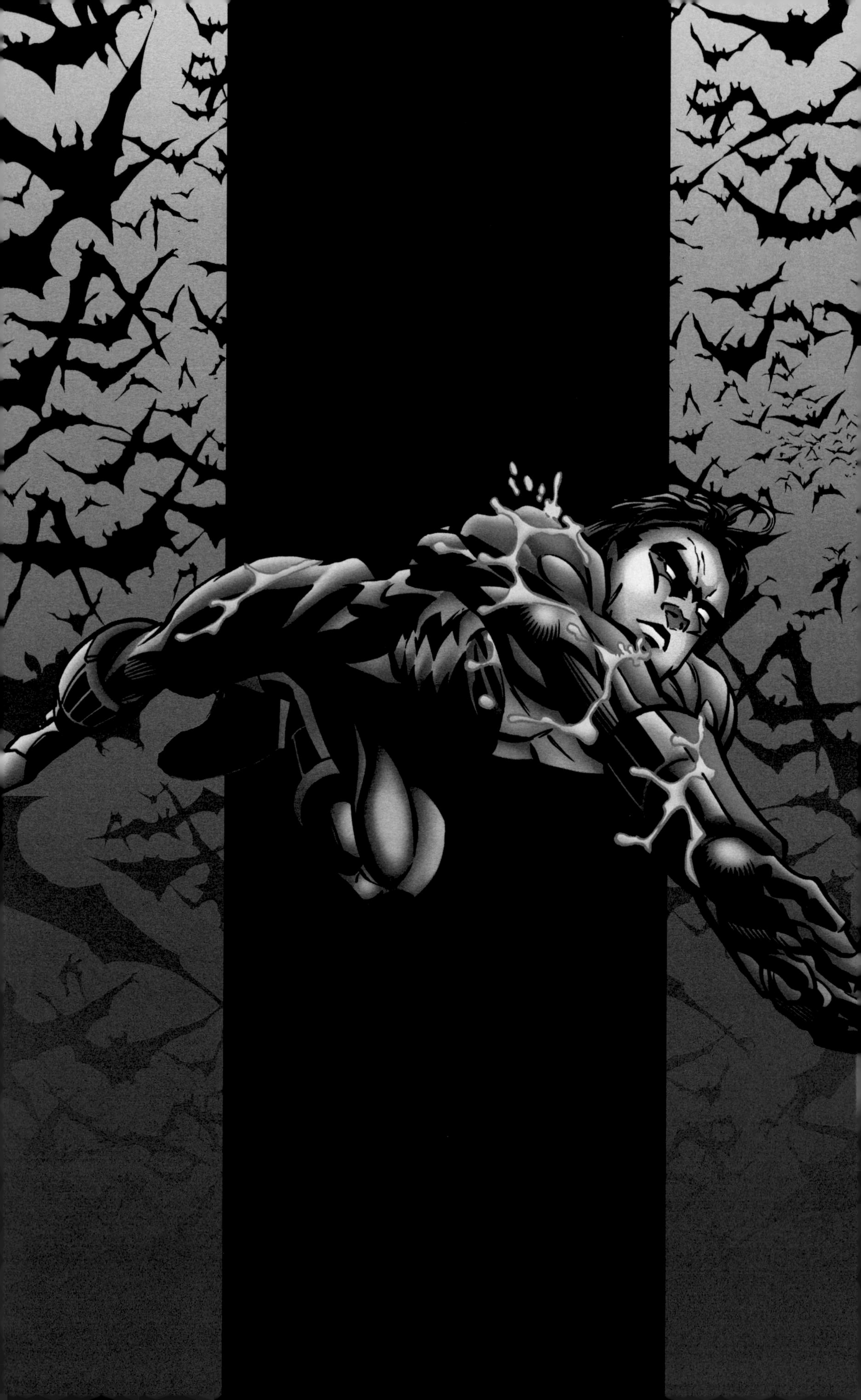

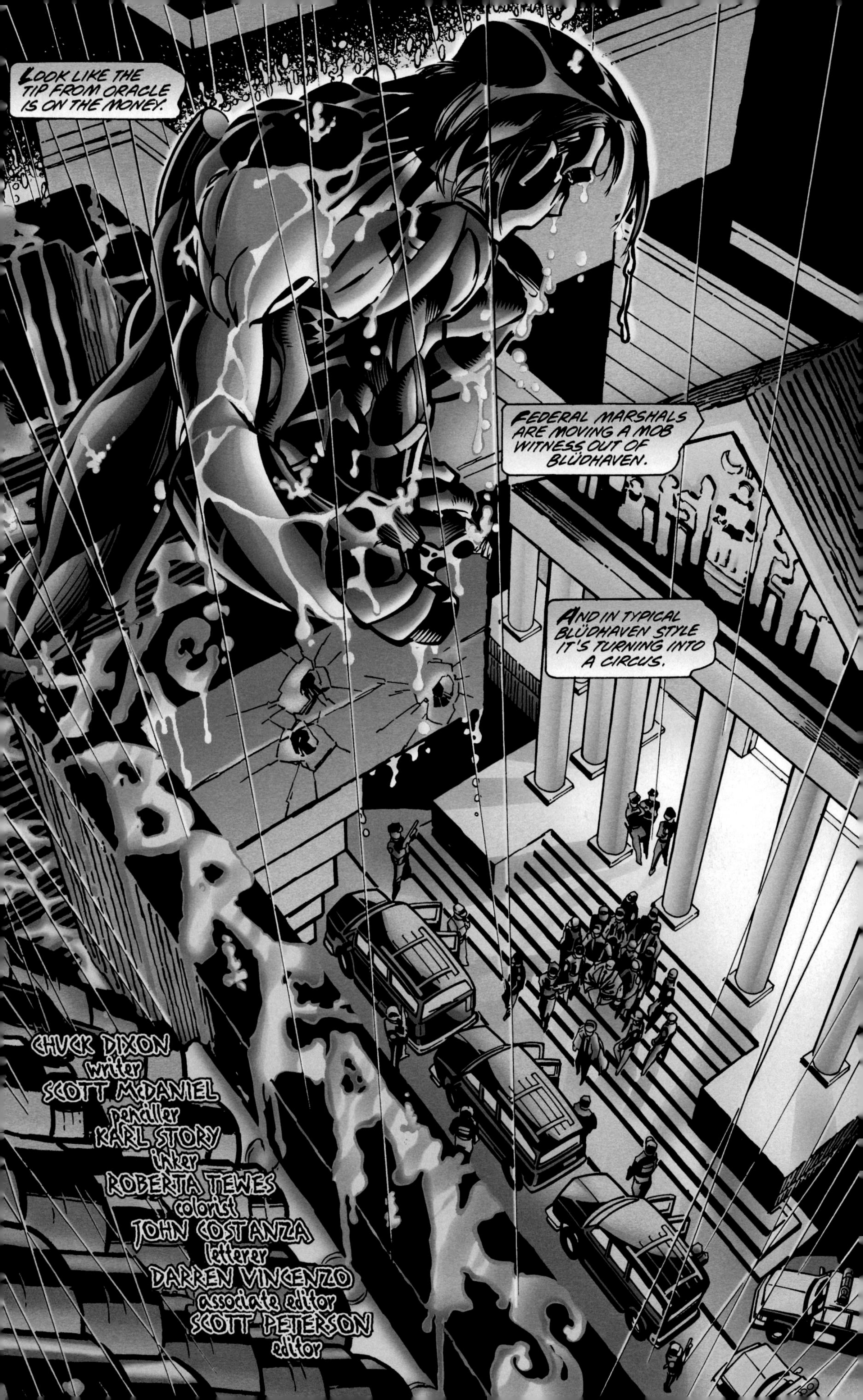
LOOK LIKE THE TIP FROM ORACLE IS ON THE MONEY.
FEDERAL MARSHALS ARE MOVING A MOB WITNESS OUT OF BLÜDHAVEN.
AND IN TYPICAL BLÜDHAVEN STYLE IT'S TURNING INTO A CIRCUS.
CHUCK DIXON writer
SCOTT McDANIEL penciller
KARL STORY inker
ROBERTA TEWES colorist
JOHN COSTANZA letterer
DARREN VINCENZO associate editor
SCOTT PETERSON editor

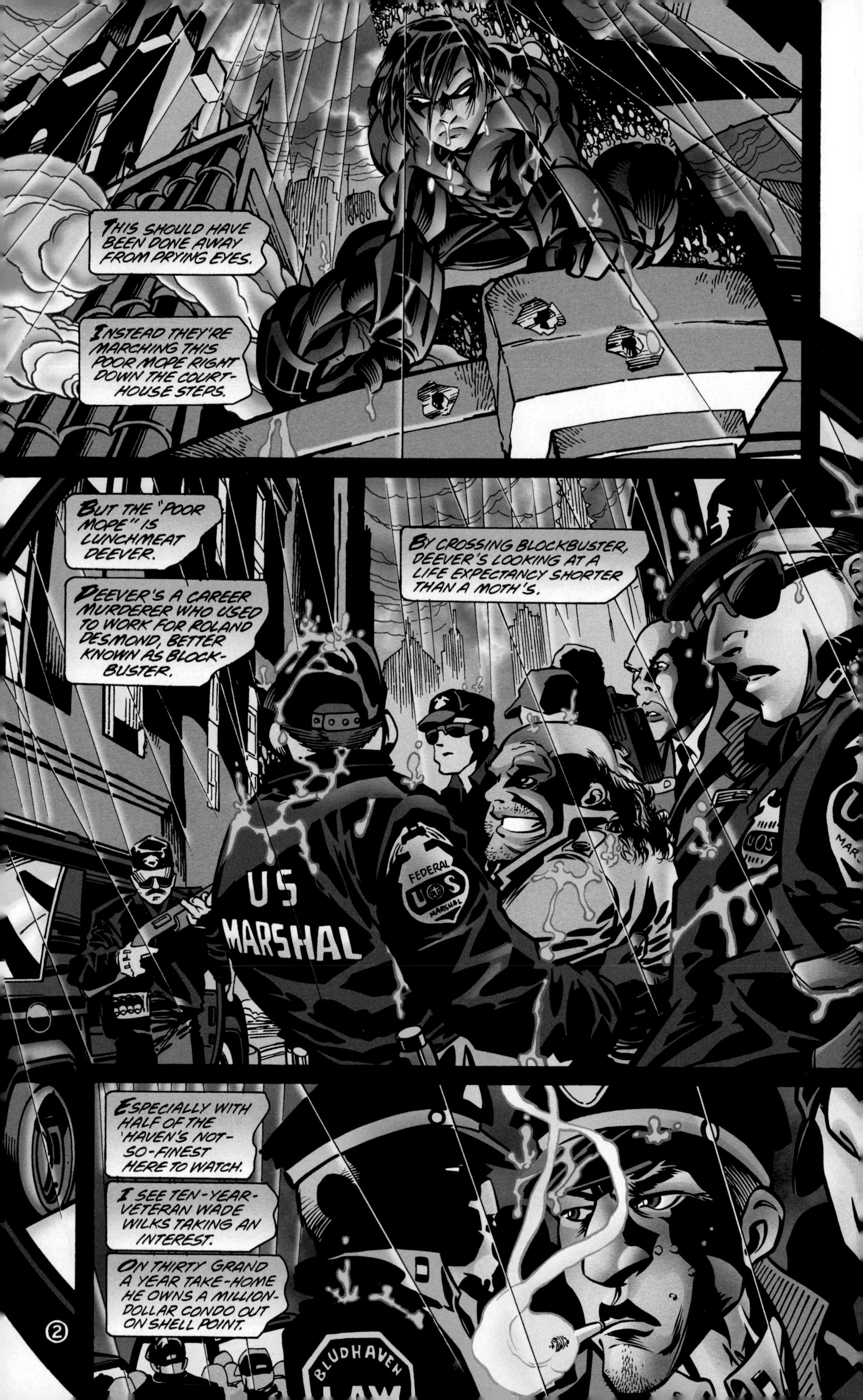
THIS SHOULD HAVE BEEN DONE AWAY FROM PRYING EYES.
INSTEAD THEY'RE MARCHING THIS POOR MOPE RIGHT DOWN THE COURT-HOUSE STEPS.
BUT THE "POOR MOPE" IS LUNCHMEAT DEEVER.
DEEVER'S A CAREER MURDERER WHO USED TO WORK FOR ROLAND DESMOND, BETTER KNOWN AS BLOCK-BUSTER.
BY CROSSING BLOCKBUSTER, DEEVER'S LOOKING AT A LIFE EXPECTANCY SHORTER THAN A MOTH'S.
US MARSHAL
FEDERAL
MARSHAL
ESPECIALLY WITH HALF OF THE 'HAVEN'S NOT-SO-FINEST HERE TO WATCH.
I SEE TEN-YEAR-VETERAN WADE WILKS TAKING AN INTEREST.
ON THIRTY GRAND A YEAR TAKE-HOME HE OWNS A MILLION-DOLLAR CONDO OUT ON SHELL POINT.
BLUDHAVEN
LAW

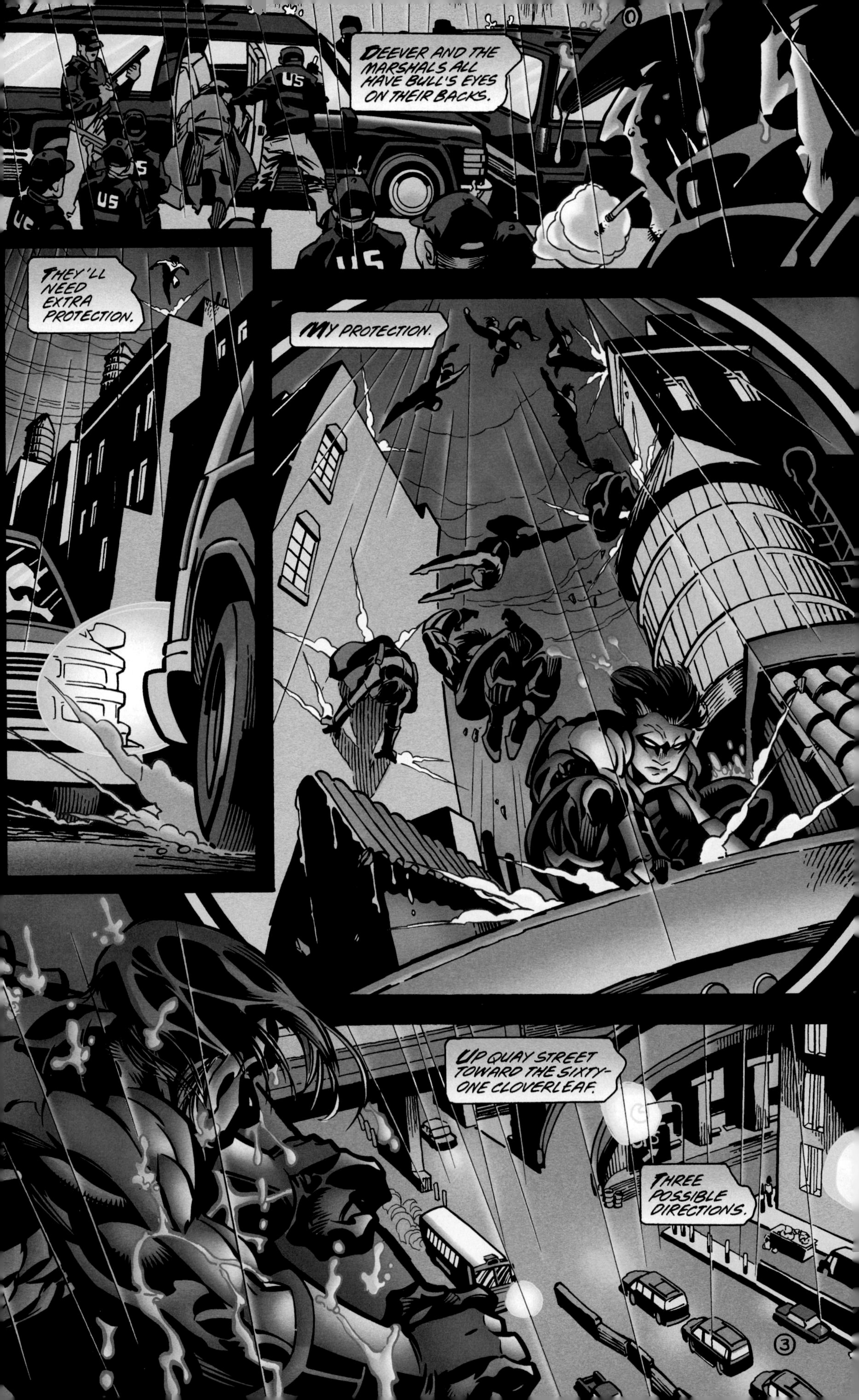
DEEVER AND THE MARSHALS ALL HAVE BULL'S EYES ON THEIR BACKS.
THEY'LL NEED EXTRA PROTECTION.
MY PROTECTION.
UP QUAY STREET TOWARD THE SIXTY-ONE CLOVERLEAF.
THREE POSSIBLE DIRECTIONS.
3

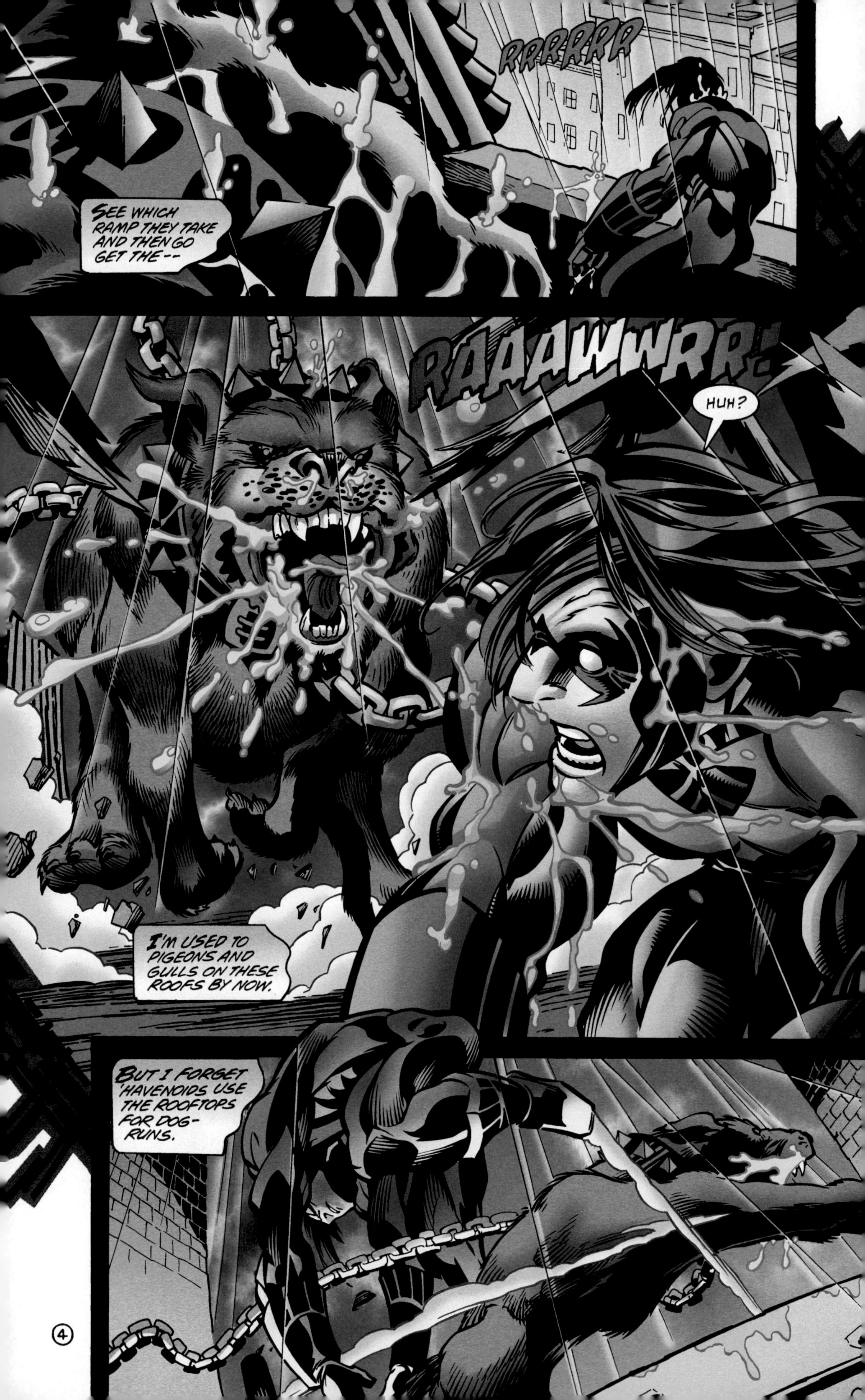

RRRRRR
SEE WHICH RAMP THEY TAKE AND THEN GO GET THE--
RAAAWWRR!
HUH?
I'M USED TO PIGEONS AND GULLS ON THESE ROOFS BY NOW.
BUT I FORGET 'HAVENOIDS USE THE ROOFTOPS FOR DOG-RUNS.

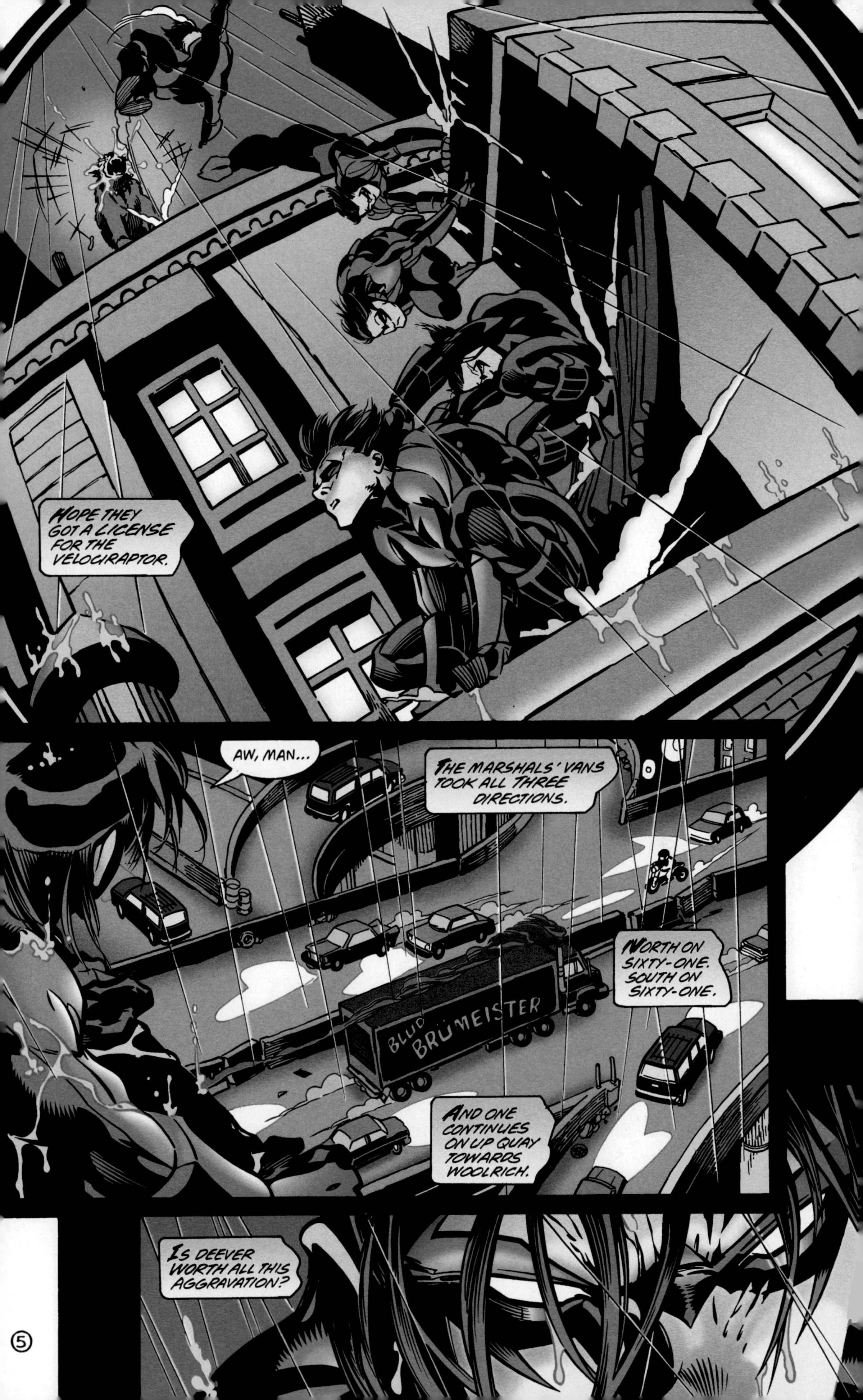
HOPE THEY GOT A LICENSE FOR THE VELOCIRAPTOR.
AW, MAN...
THE MARSHALS' VANS TOOK ALL THREE DIRECTIONS.
NORTH ON SIXTY-ONE. SOUTH ON SIXTY-ONE.
BLUD BRÜMEISTER
AND ONE CONTINUES ON UP QUAY TOWARDS WOOLRICH.
IS DEEVER WORTH ALL THIS AGGRAVATION?
5

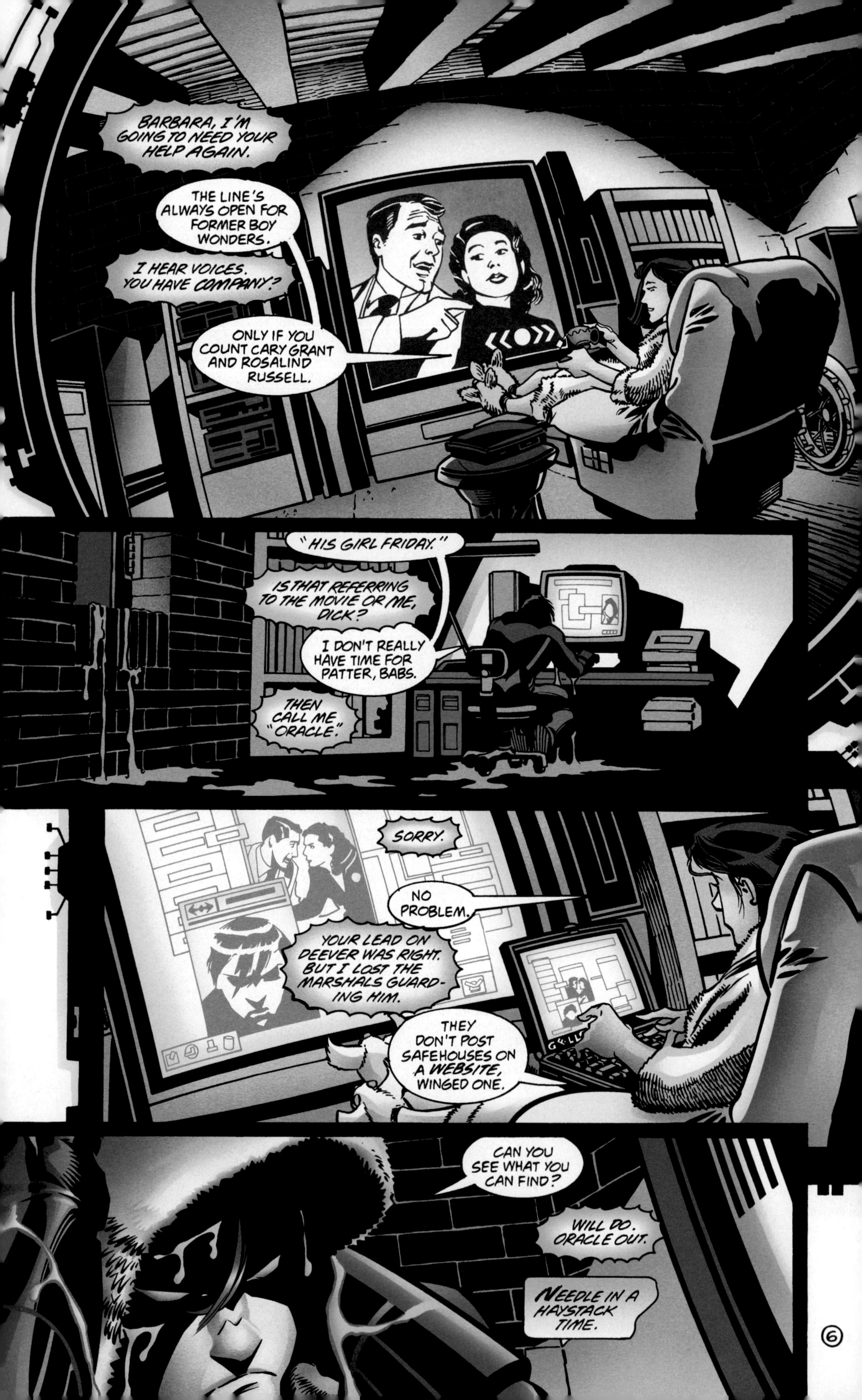
BARBARA, I'M GOING TO NEED YOUR HELP AGAIN.
THE LINE'S ALWAYS OPEN FOR FORMER BOY WONDERS.
I HEAR VOICES. YOU HAVE COMPANY?
ONLY IF YOU COUNT CARY GRANT AND ROSALIND RUSSELL.
"HIS GIRL FRIDAY."
IS THAT REFERRING TO THE MOVIE OR ME, DICK?
I DON'T REALLY HAVE TIME FOR PATTER, BABS.
THEN CALL ME "ORACLE."
SORRY.
NO PROBLEM.
YOUR LEAD ON DEEVER WAS RIGHT. BUT I LOST THE MARSHALS GUARDING HIM.
THEY DON'T POST SAFEHOUSES ON A WEBSITE, WINGED ONE.
CAN YOU SEE WHAT YOU CAN FIND?
WILL DO. ORACLE OUT.
NEEDLE IN A HAYSTACK TIME.

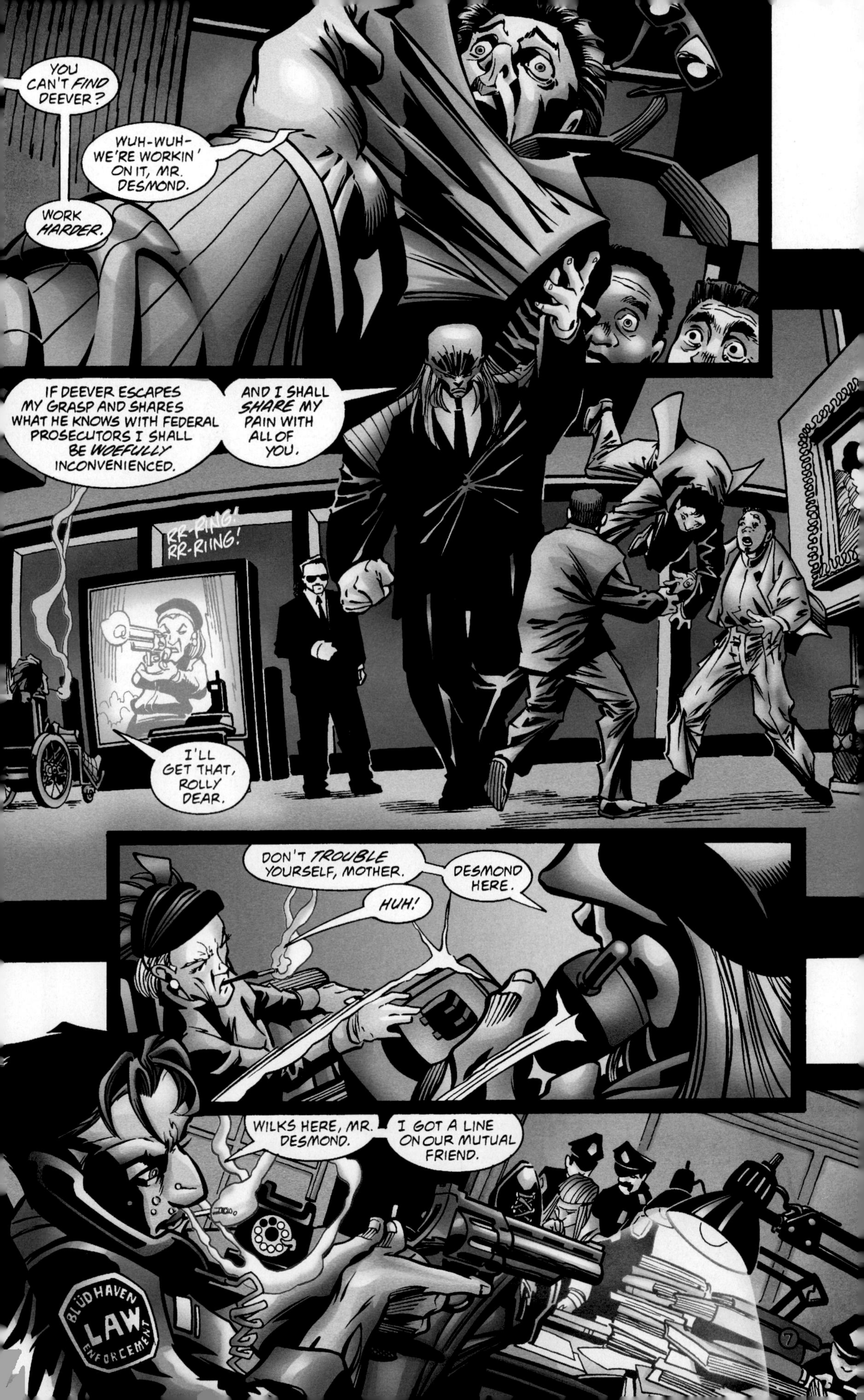
YOU CAN'T *FIND* DEEVER?
WUH-WUH- WE'RE WORKIN' ON IT, MR. DESMOND.
WORK *HARDER*.
IF DEEVER ESCAPES MY GRASP AND SHARES WHAT HE KNOWS WITH FEDERAL PROSECUTORS I SHALL BE *WOEFULLY* INCONVENIENCED.
AND I SHALL *SHARE* MY PAIN WITH ALL OF YOU.
RR-RING! RR-RIING!
I'LL GET THAT, ROLLY DEAR.
DON'T *TROUBLE* YOURSELF, MOTHER.
HUH!
DESMOND HERE.
WILKS HERE, MR. DESMOND.
I GOT A LINE ON OUR MUTUAL FRIEND.
BLÜDHAVEN LAW ENFORCEMENT
7

WORK IT, FELLA!

HEY! HOW LONG HAVE YOU BEEN ON LINE, BABS?

LONG ENOUGH, HANDSOME. WOOF!

OTHER THAN GIVING ME TIME TO GET OUT A DRY OUTFIT--

-- WHAT ELSE HAVE YOU DONE?

SOMETIMES I THINK THE FEDS SHOULD CALL IT THE EYEWITLESS PROGRAM.

LISTEN TO THIS EXAMPLE OF YOUR TAX DOLLARS AT WORK.

SOMEBODY RENTED OUT THREE DIFFERENT HOTEL ROOMS AROUND BLÜDHAVEN USING THE SAME NAME.

AND THE SAME GOVERNMENT CHARGE CARD.

BUT WHICH HOTEL'S THE RIGHT ONE?

WHO WOULD ORDER OUT FOR A LARGE PEPPERONI AND SAUSAGE PIZZA WITH EXTRA CHOLESTEROL?

LUNCHMEAT.

NOK! NOK!

UH... I GOTTA GO.

ORACLE OUT, SPEEDO-BOY.

YOU WERE WATCHING.

HEE!

8

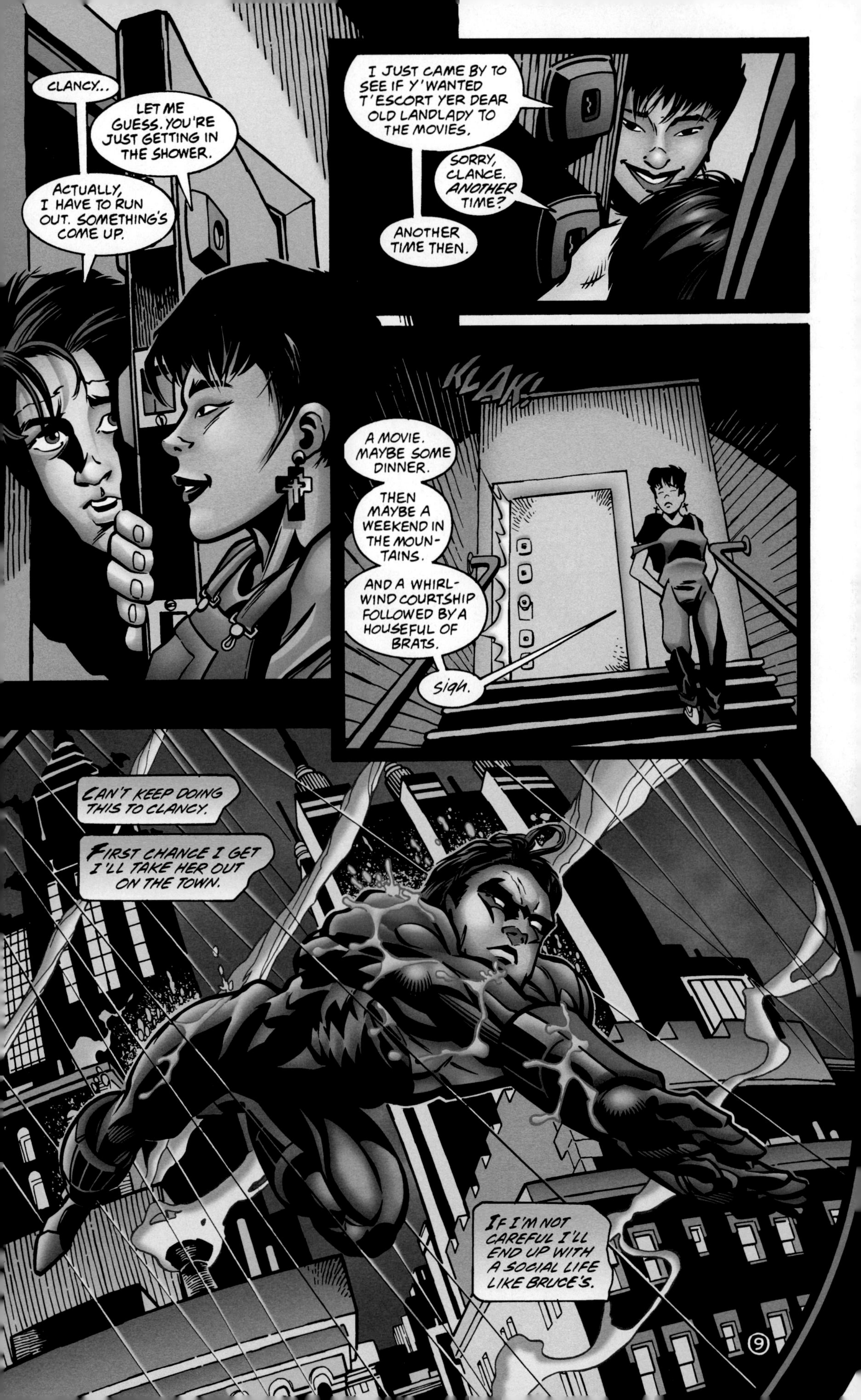

CLANCY...
LET ME GUESS. YOU'RE JUST GETTING IN THE SHOWER.
ACTUALLY, I HAVE TO RUN OUT. SOMETHING'S COME UP.
I JUST CAME BY TO SEE IF Y'WANTED T'ESCORT YER DEAR OLD LANDLADY TO THE MOVIES.
SORRY, CLANCE. ANOTHER TIME?
ANOTHER TIME THEN.
KLAK!
A MOVIE. MAYBE SOME DINNER.
THEN MAYBE A WEEKEND IN THE MOUNTAINS.
AND A WHIRLWIND COURTSHIP FOLLOWED BY A HOUSEFUL OF BRATS.
sigh.
CAN'T KEEP DOING THIS TO CLANCY.
FIRST CHANCE I GET I'LL TAKE HER OUT ON THE TOWN.
IF I'M NOT CAREFUL I'LL END UP WITH A SOCIAL LIFE LIKE BRUCE'S.
9

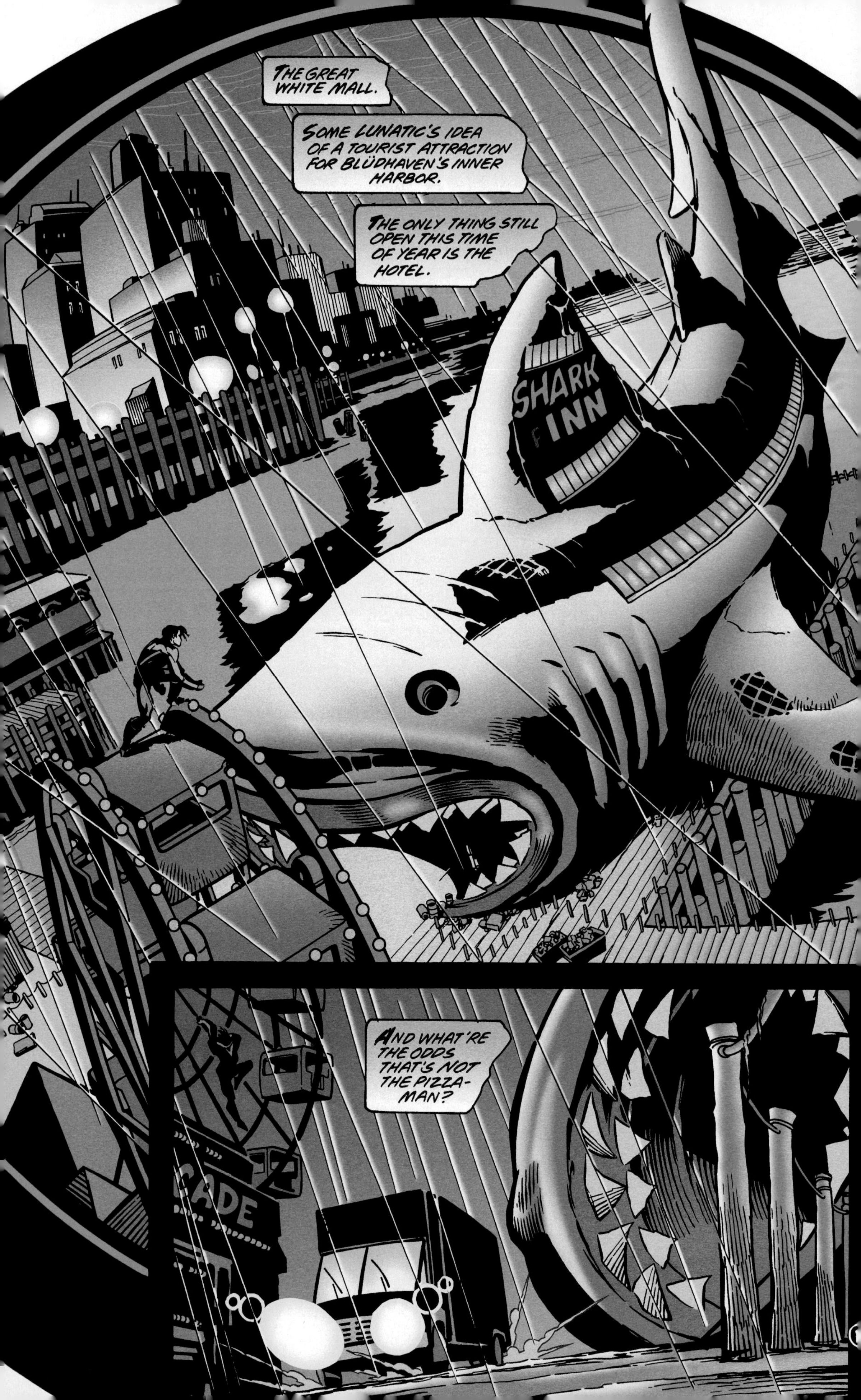
THE GREAT WHITE MALL.
SOME LUNATIC'S IDEA OF A TOURIST ATTRACTION FOR BLÜDHAVEN'S INNER HARBOR.
THE ONLY THING STILL OPEN THIS TIME OF YEAR IS THE HOTEL.
SHARK FINN
AND WHAT'RE THE ODDS THAT'S NOT THE PIZZA-MAN?
CADE

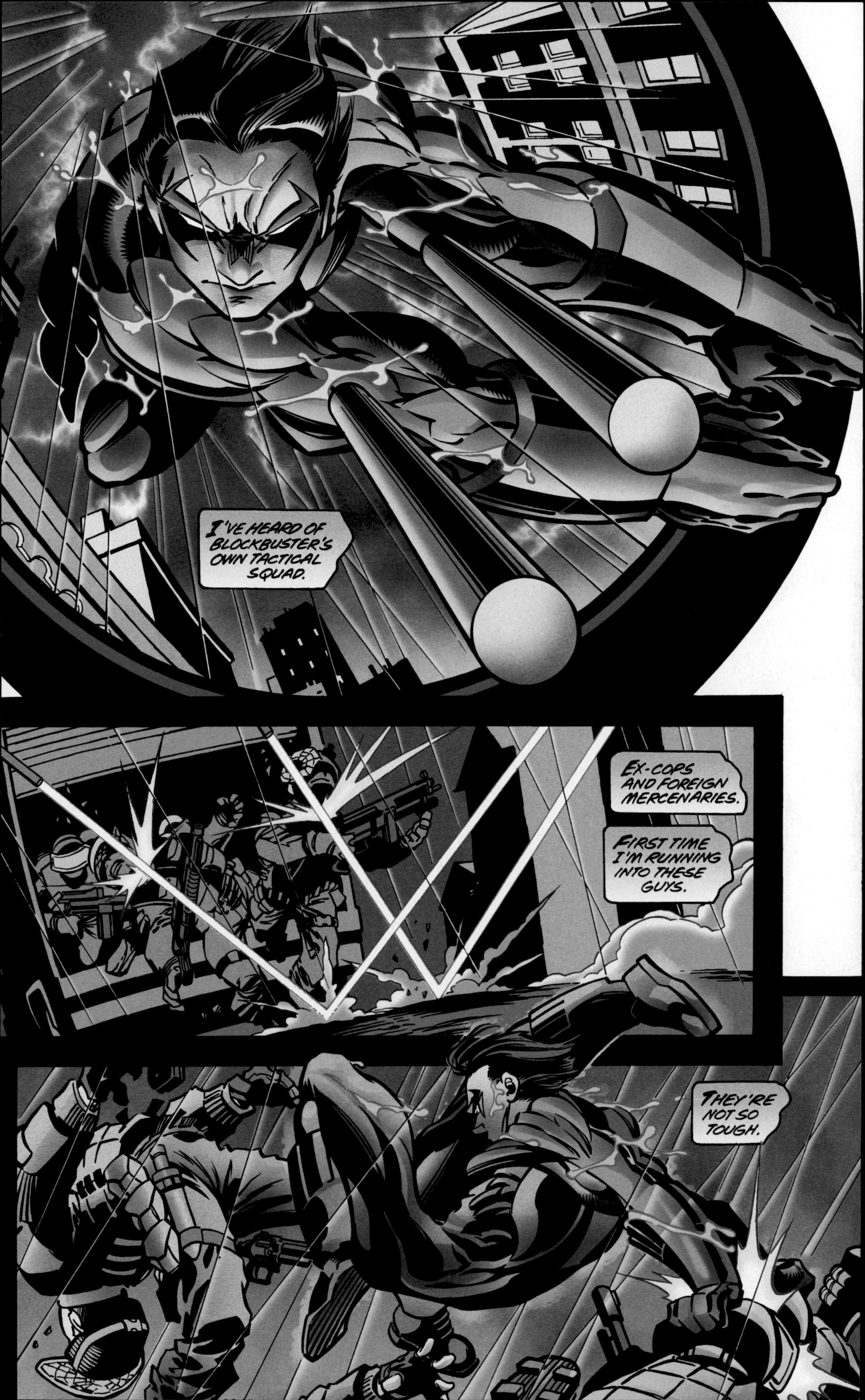
I'VE HEARD OF BLOCKBUSTER'S OWN TACTICAL SQUAD.
EX-COPS AND FOREIGN MERCENARIES.
FIRST TIME I'M RUNNING INTO THESE GUYS.
THEY'RE NOT SO TOUGH.

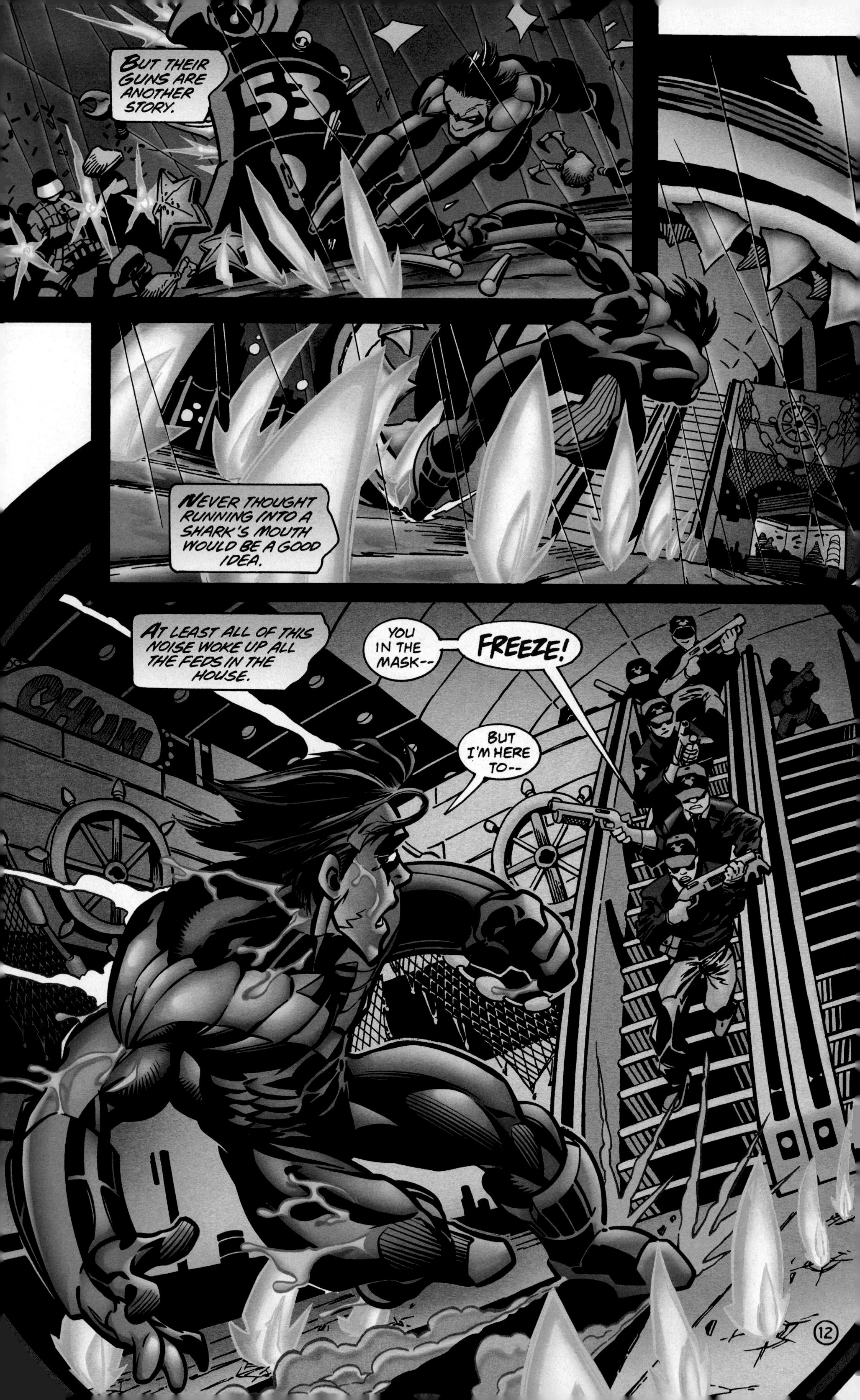

BUT THEIR GUNS ARE ANOTHER STORY.
NEVER THOUGHT RUNNING INTO A SHARK'S MOUTH WOULD BE A GOOD IDEA.
AT LEAST ALL OF THIS NOISE WOKE UP ALL THE FEDS IN THE HOUSE.
YOU IN THE MASK--
FREEZE!
BUT I'M HERE TO--
CHUM

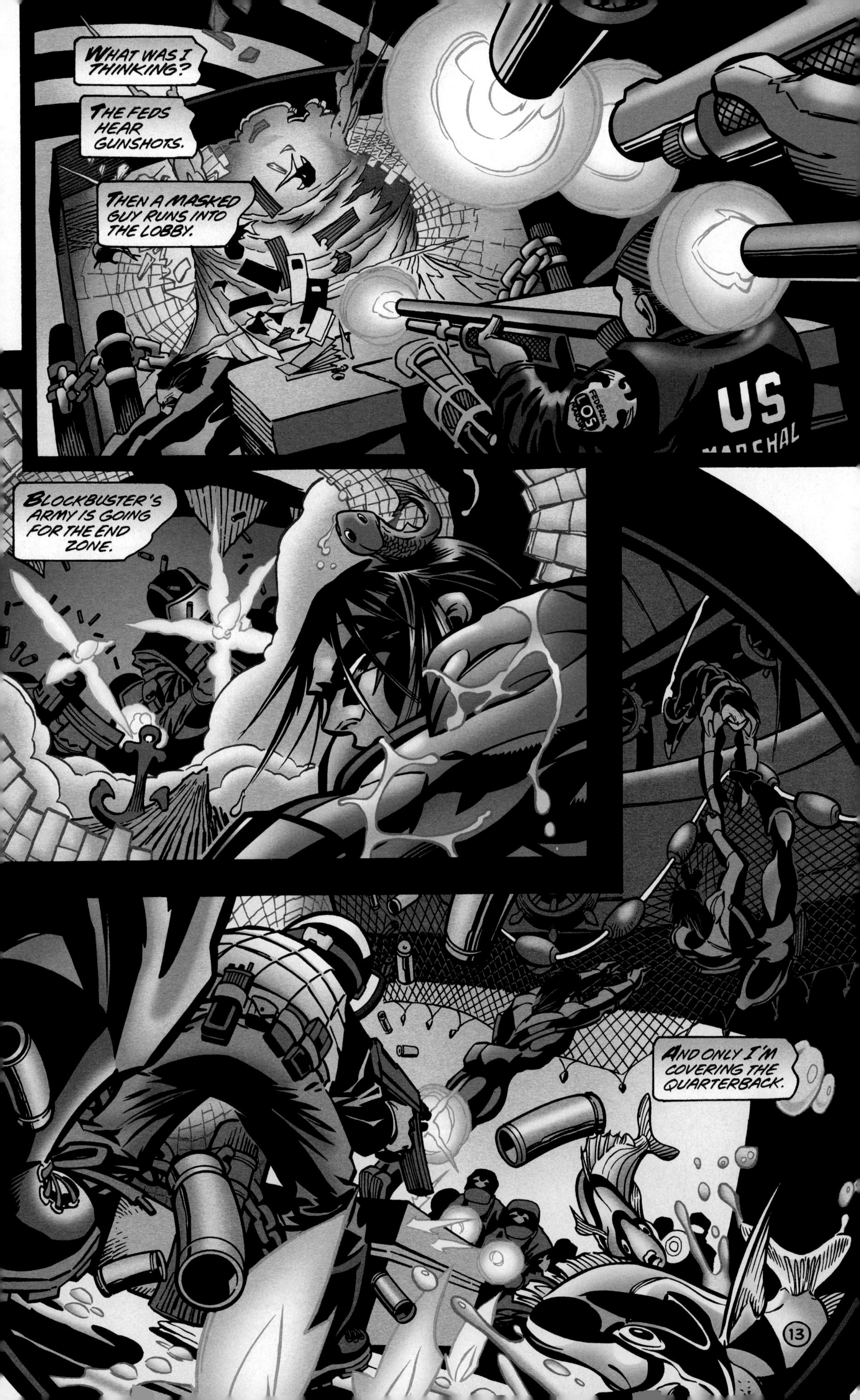

WHAT WAS I THINKING?
THE FEDS HEAR GUNSHOTS.
THEN A MASKED GUY RUNS INTO THE LOBBY.
FEDERAL
US MARSHAL
BLOCKBUSTER'S ARMY IS GOING FOR THE END ZONE.
AND ONLY I'M COVERING THE QUARTERBACK.

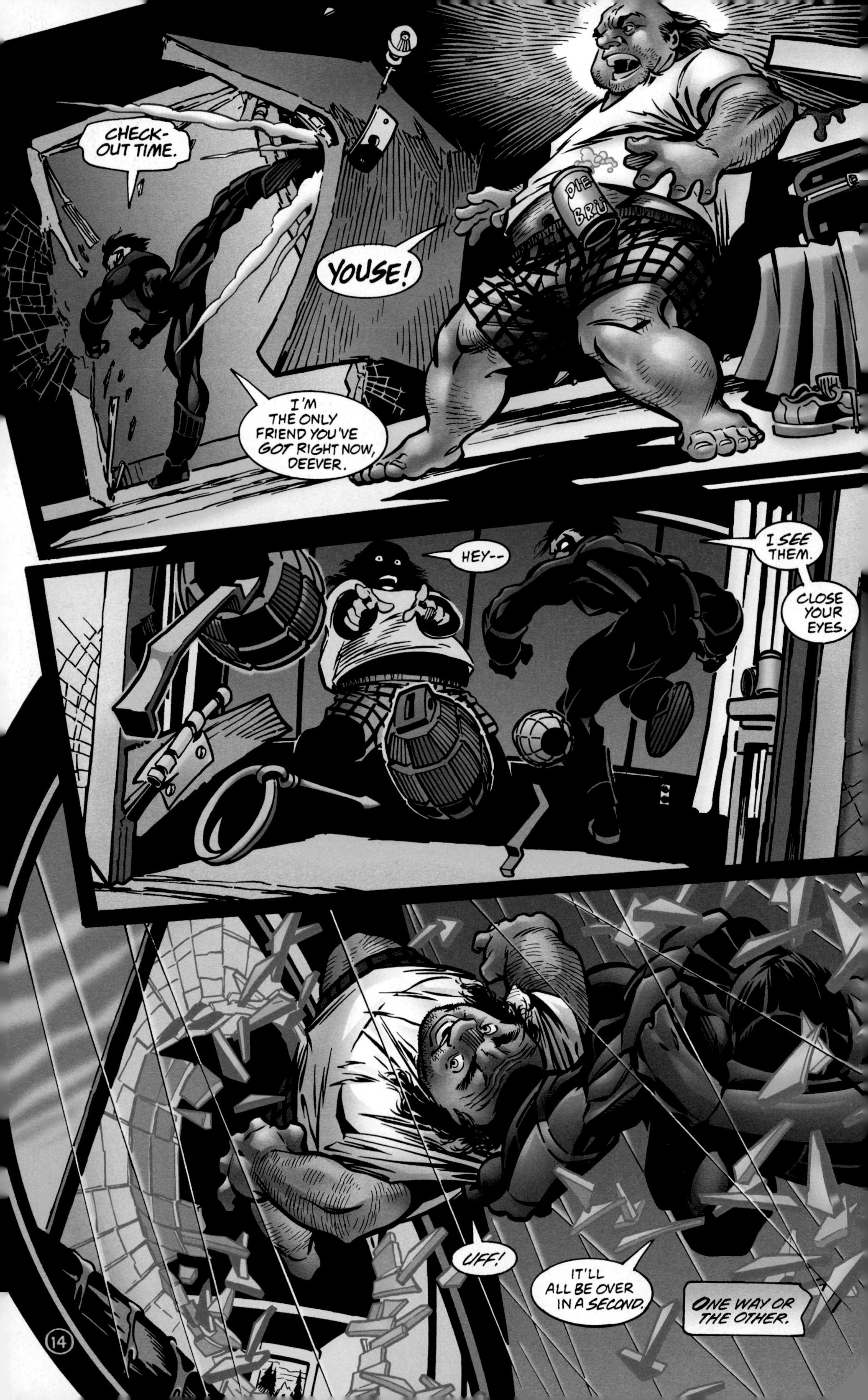
CHECK-OUT TIME.
YOUSE!
I'M THE ONLY FRIEND YOU'VE GOT RIGHT NOW, DEEVER.
HEY--
I SEE THEM.
CLOSE YOUR EYES.
UFF!
IT'LL ALL BE OVER IN A SECOND.
ONE WAY OR THE OTHER.

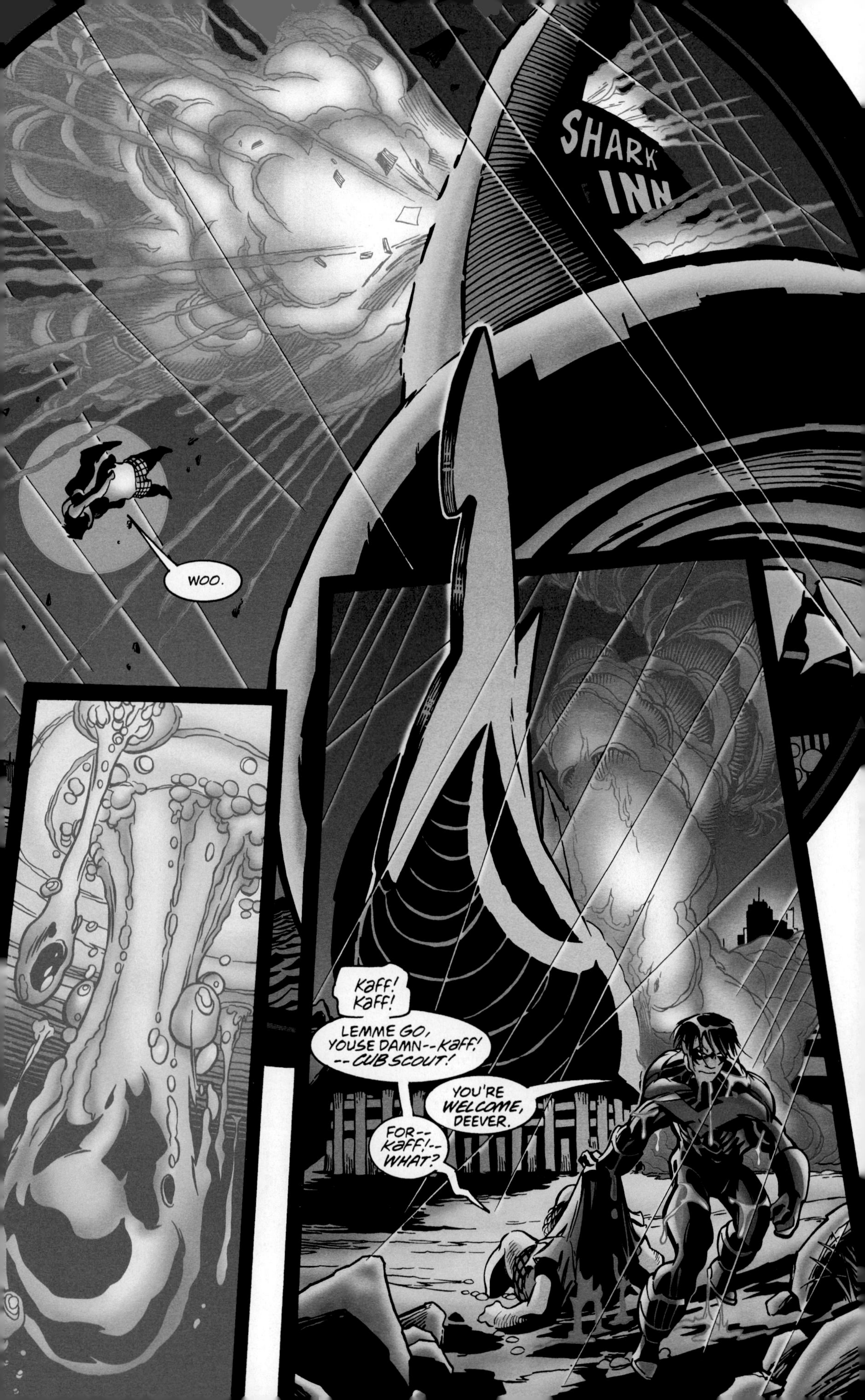
SHARK INN
WOO.
KAFF! KAFF!
LEMME GO, YOUSE DAMN--KAFF! --CUB SCOUT!
YOU'RE WELCOME, DEEVER.
FOR--KAFF!--WHAT?

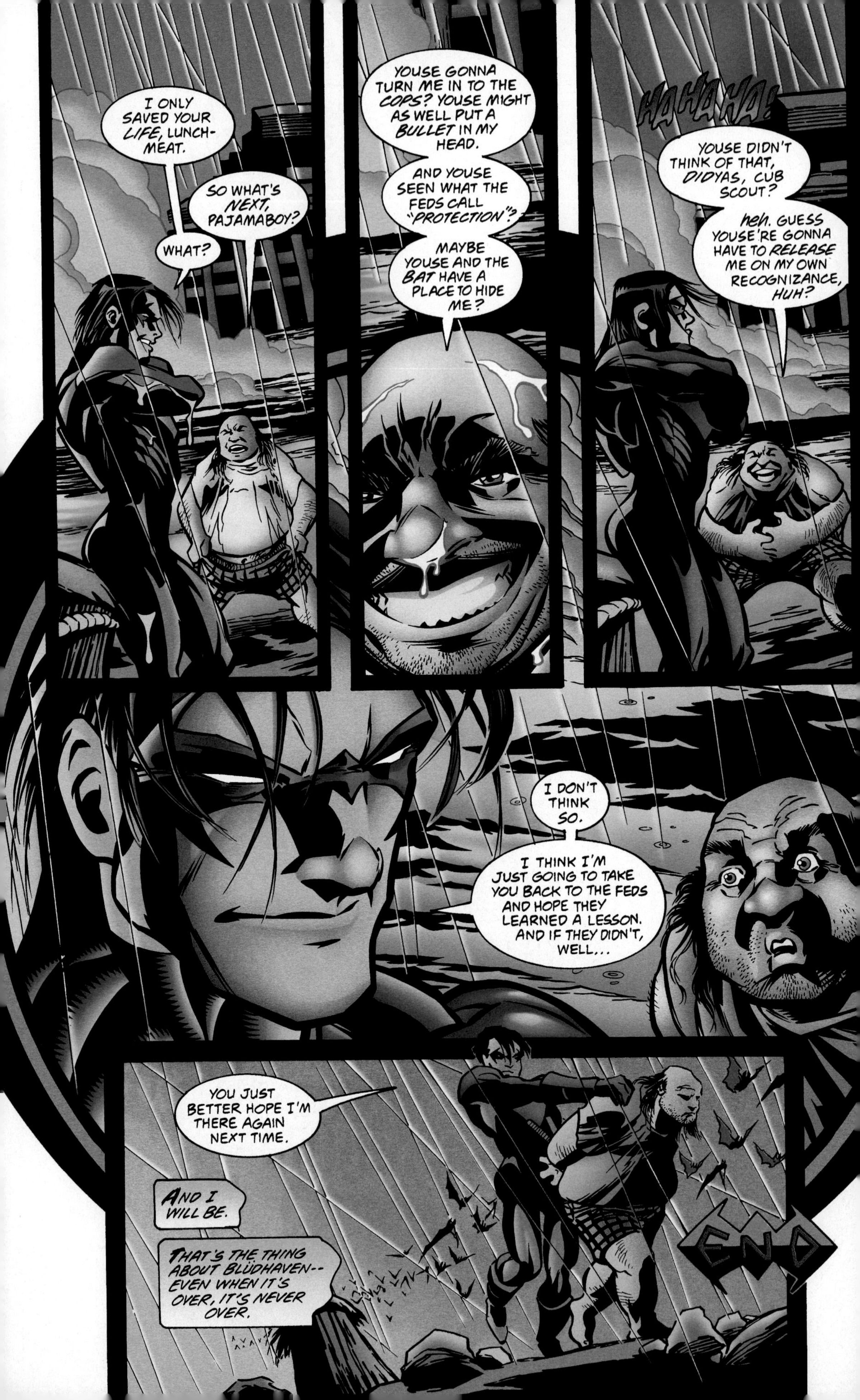
I ONLY SAVED YOUR LIFE, LUNCH-MEAT.
WHAT?
SO WHAT'S NEXT, PAJAMABOY?
YOUSE GONNA TURN ME IN TO THE COPS? YOUSE MIGHT AS WELL PUT A BULLET IN MY HEAD.
AND YOUSE SEEN WHAT THE FEDS CALL "PROTECTION"?
MAYBE YOUSE AND THE BAT HAVE A PLACE TO HIDE ME?
HAHAHA!
YOUSE DIDN'T THINK OF THAT, DIDYAS, CUB SCOUT?
heh. GUESS YOUSE'RE GONNA HAVE TO RELEASE ME ON MY OWN RECOGNIZANCE, HUH?
I DON'T THINK SO.
I THINK I'M JUST GOING TO TAKE YOU BACK TO THE FEDS AND HOPE THEY LEARNED A LESSON. AND IF THEY DIDN'T, WELL...
YOU JUST BETTER HOPE I'M THERE AGAIN NEXT TIME.
AND I WILL BE.
THAT'S THE THING ABOUT BLÜDHAVEN-- EVEN WHEN IT'S OVER, IT'S NEVER OVER.
END

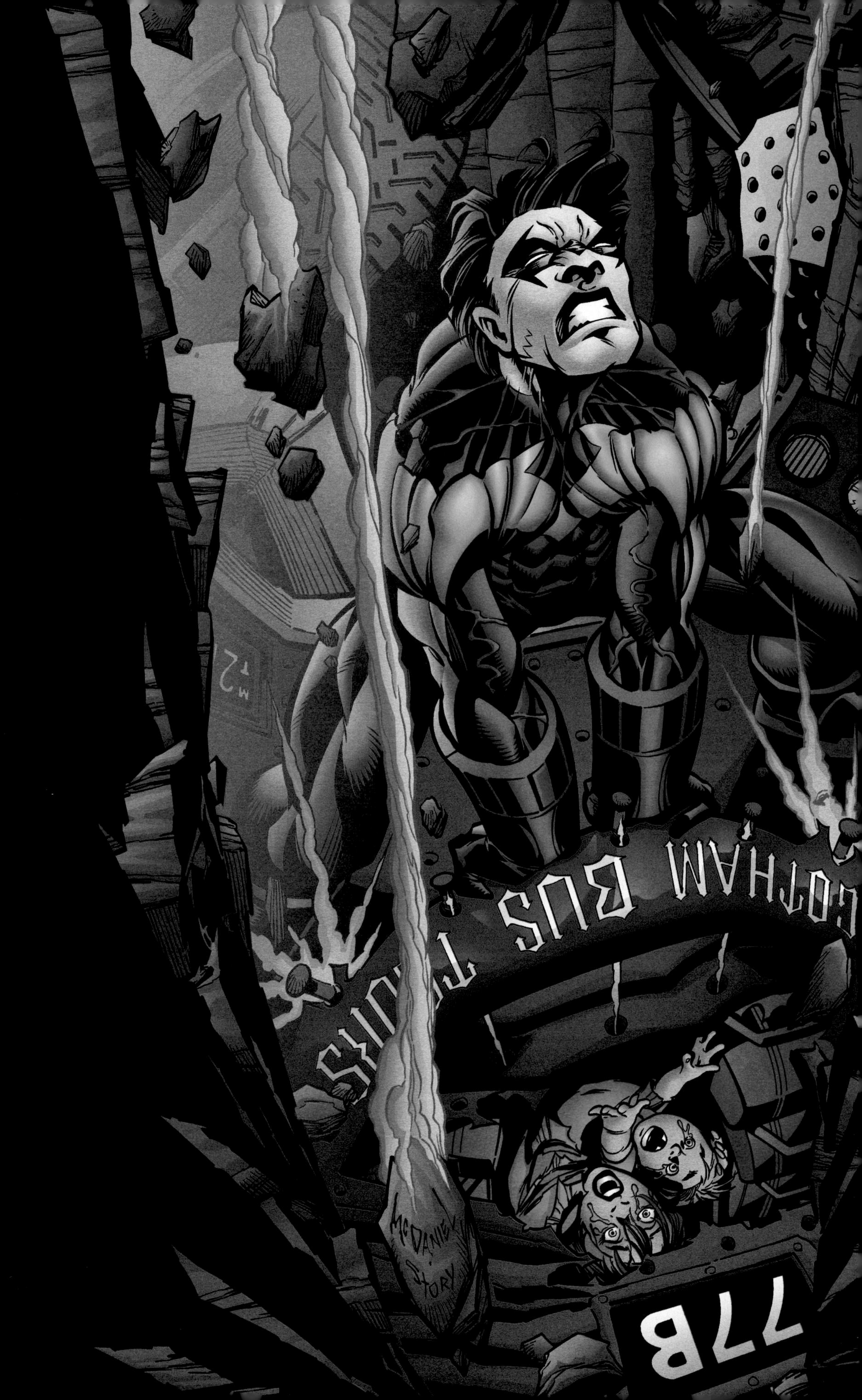
GOTHAM BUS TOURS
77B

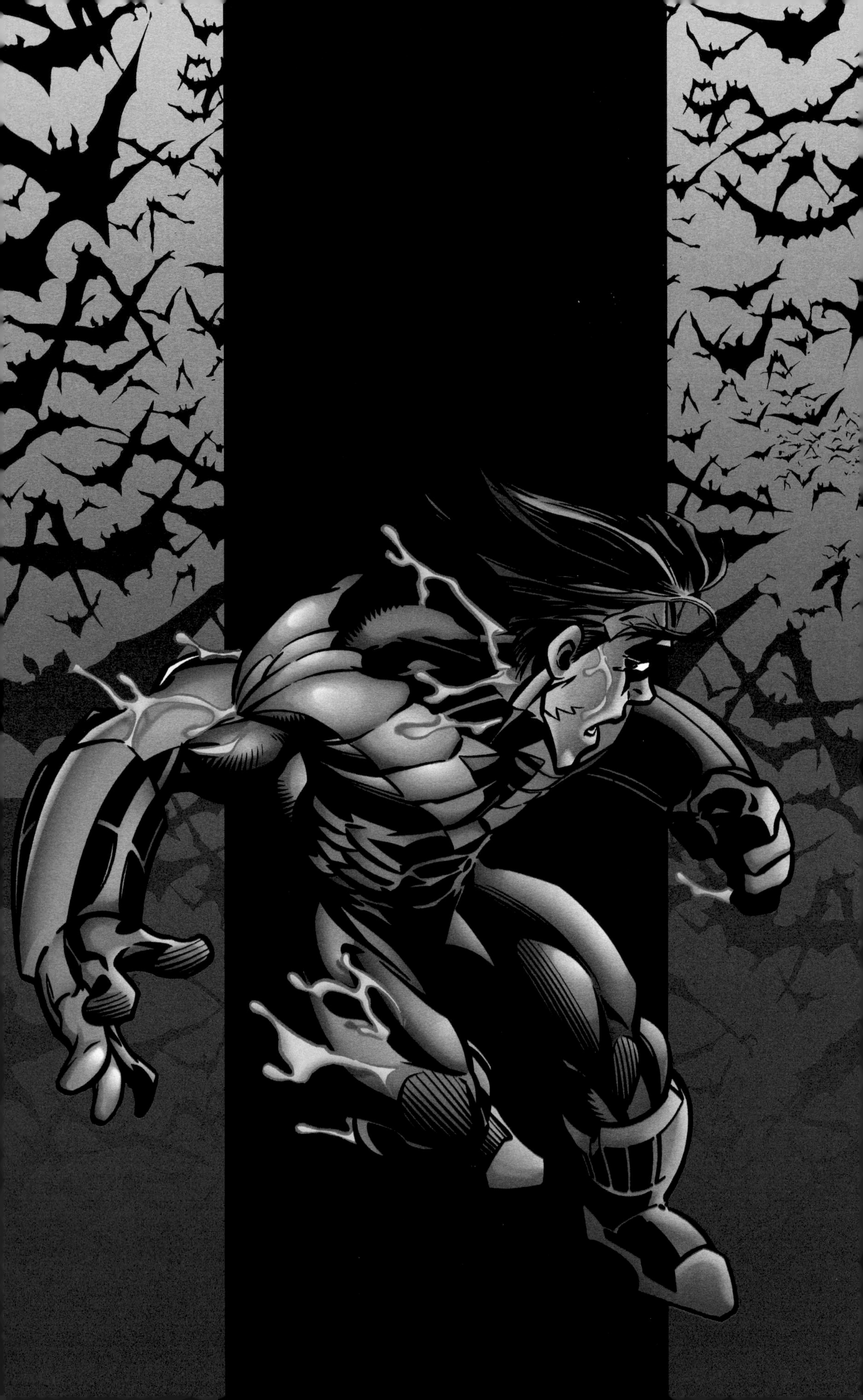

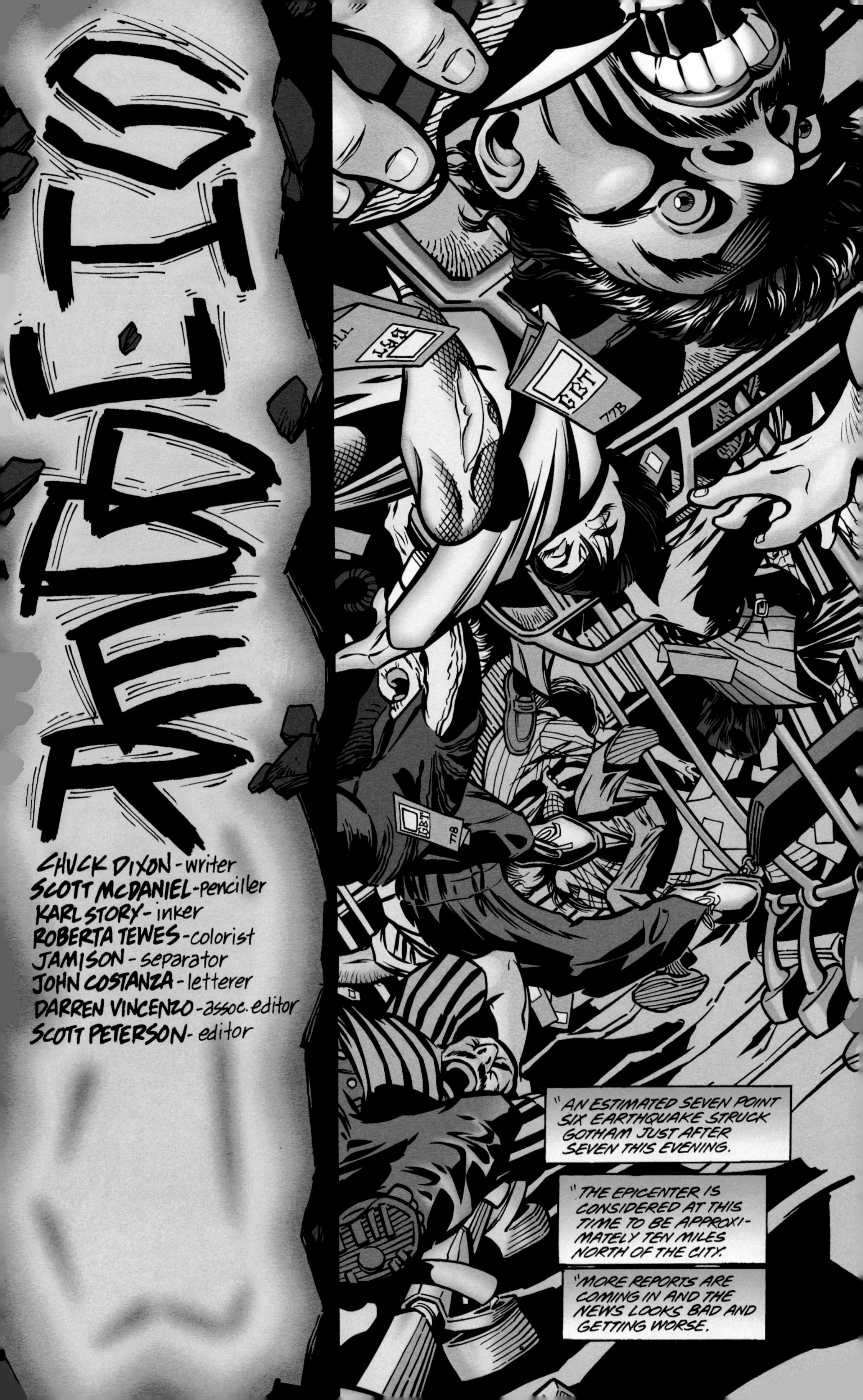
CHUCK DIXON - writer
SCOTT McDANIEL - penciller
KARL STORY - inker
ROBERTA TEWES - colorist
JAMISON - separator
JOHN COSTANZA - letterer
DARREN VINCENZO - assoc. editor
SCOTT PETERSON - editor
"AN ESTIMATED SEVEN POINT SIX EARTHQUAKE STRUCK GOTHAM JUST AFTER SEVEN THIS EVENING.
"THE EPICENTER IS CONSIDERED AT THIS TIME TO BE APPROXIMATELY TEN MILES NORTH OF THE CITY.
"MORE REPORTS ARE COMING IN AND THE NEWS LOOKS BAD AND GETTING WORSE.

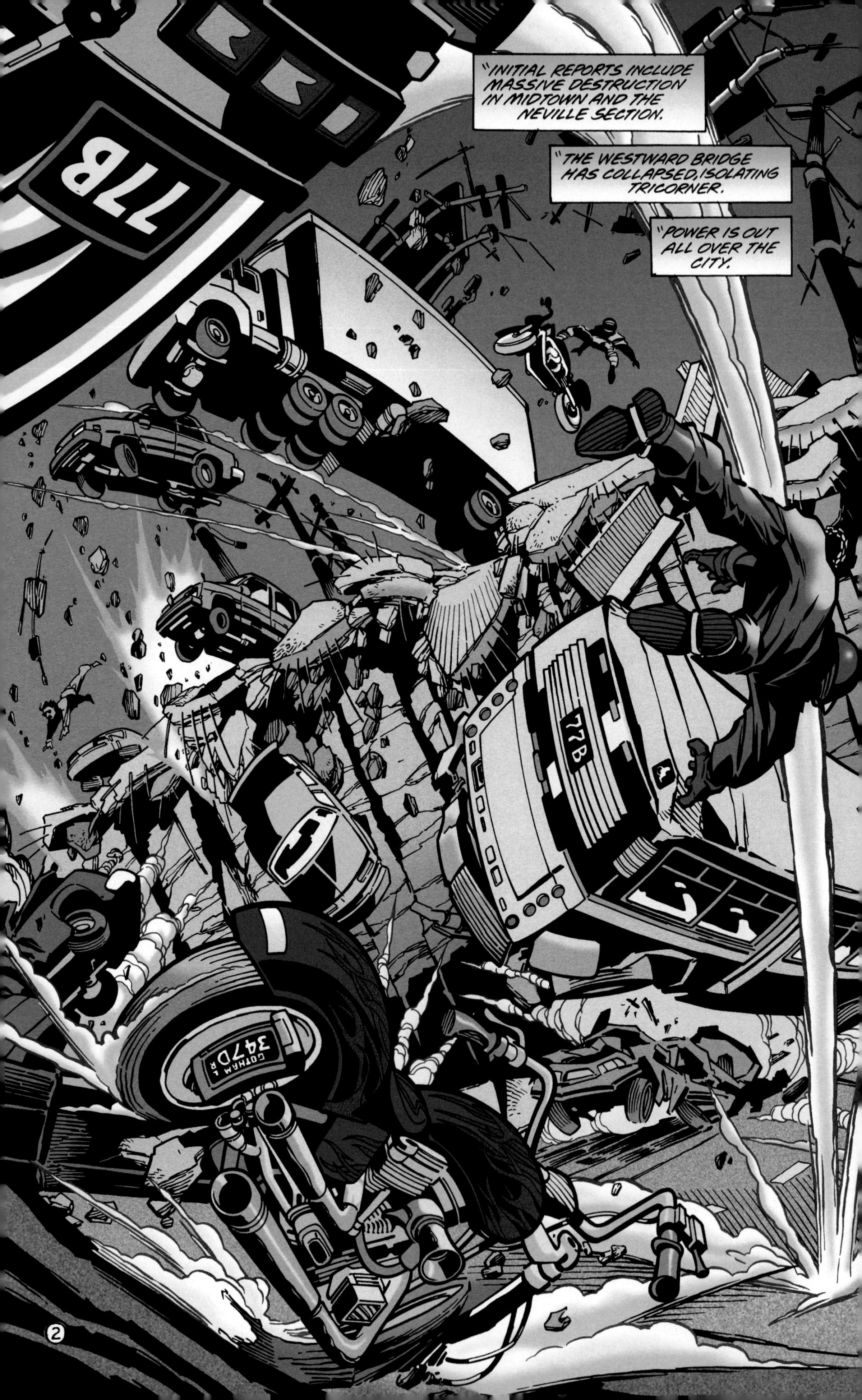
"INITIAL REPORTS INCLUDE MASSIVE DESTRUCTION IN MIDTOWN AND THE NEVILLE SECTION.
"THE WESTWARD BRIDGE HAS COLLAPSED, ISOLATING TRICORNER.
"POWER IS OUT ALL OVER THE CITY.
77B
77B
GOTHAM
347D

2

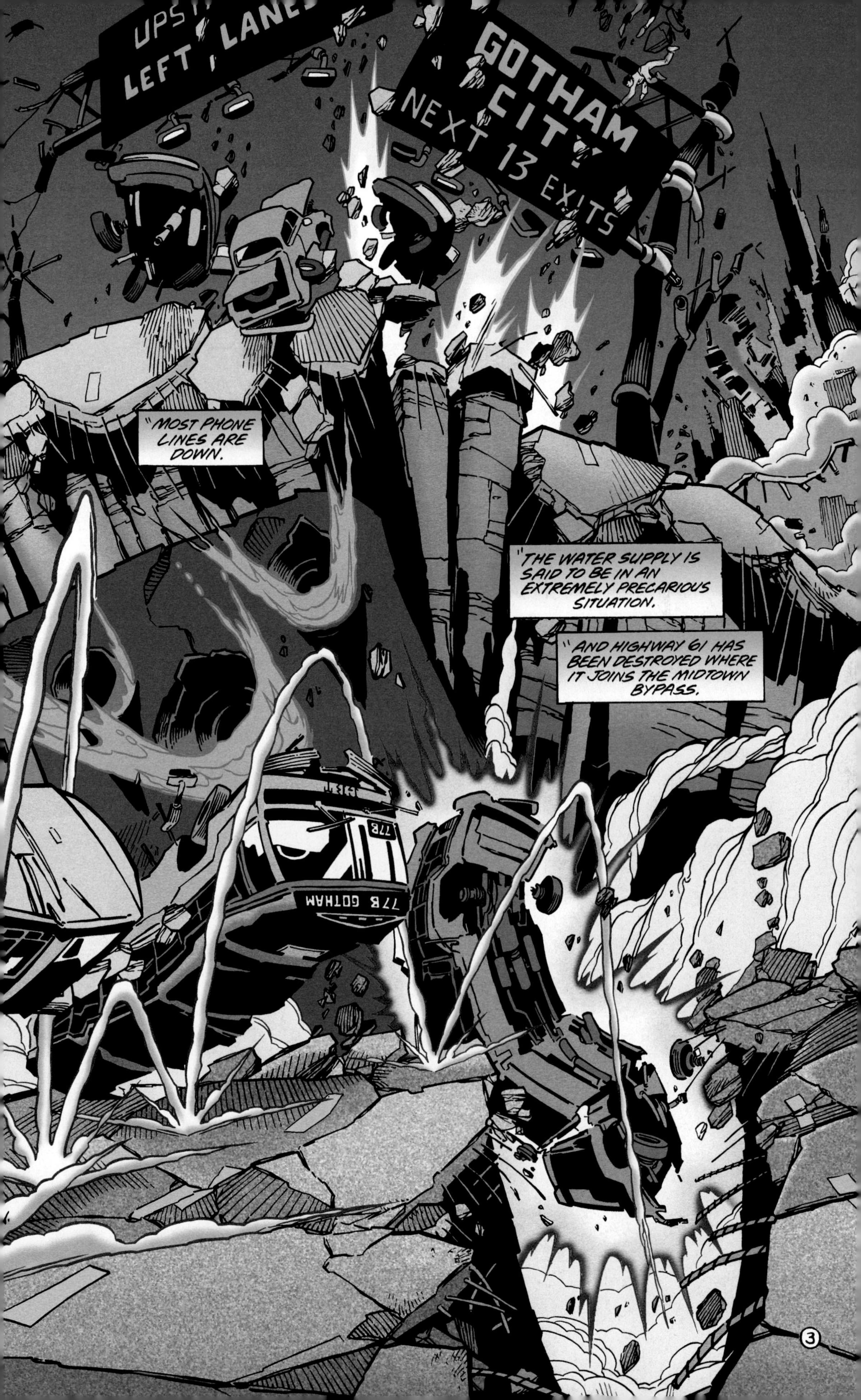
UPST
LEFT LANE
GOTHAM CITY
NEXT 13 EXITS
"MOST PHONE LINES ARE DOWN.
"THE WATER SUPPLY IS SAID TO BE IN AN EXTREMELY PRECARIOUS SITUATION.
"AND HIGHWAY 61 HAS BEEN DESTROYED WHERE IT JOINS THE MIDTOWN BYPASS.
77B GOTHAM
77B

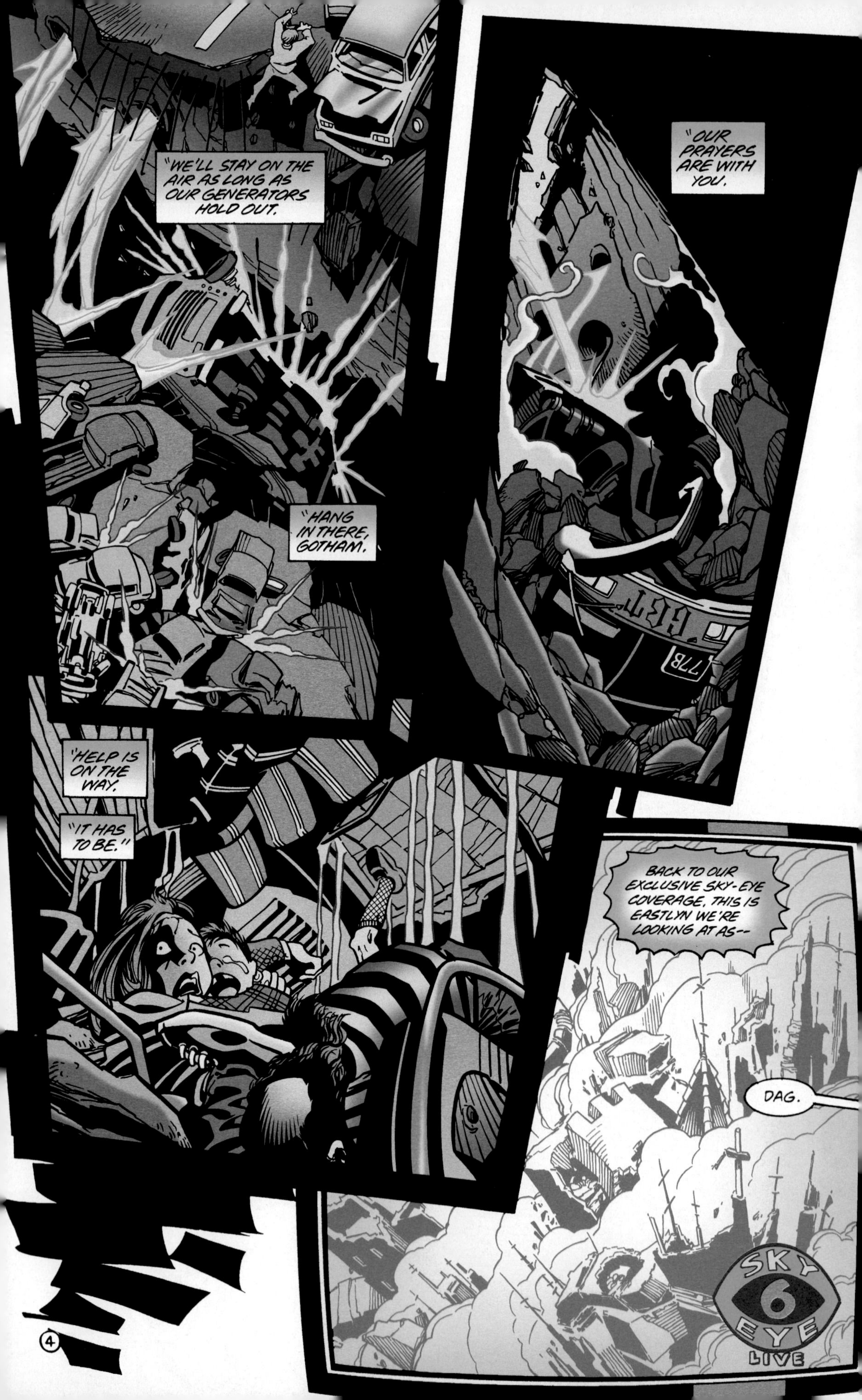
"WE'LL STAY ON THE AIR AS LONG AS OUR GENERATORS HOLD OUT.
"OUR PRAYERS ARE WITH YOU.
"HANG IN THERE, GOTHAM.
"HELP IS ON THE WAY.
"IT HAS TO BE."
BACK TO OUR EXCLUSIVE SKY-EYE COVERAGE. THIS IS EASTLYN WE'RE LOOKING AT AS--
DAG.
SKY 6 EYE
LIVE

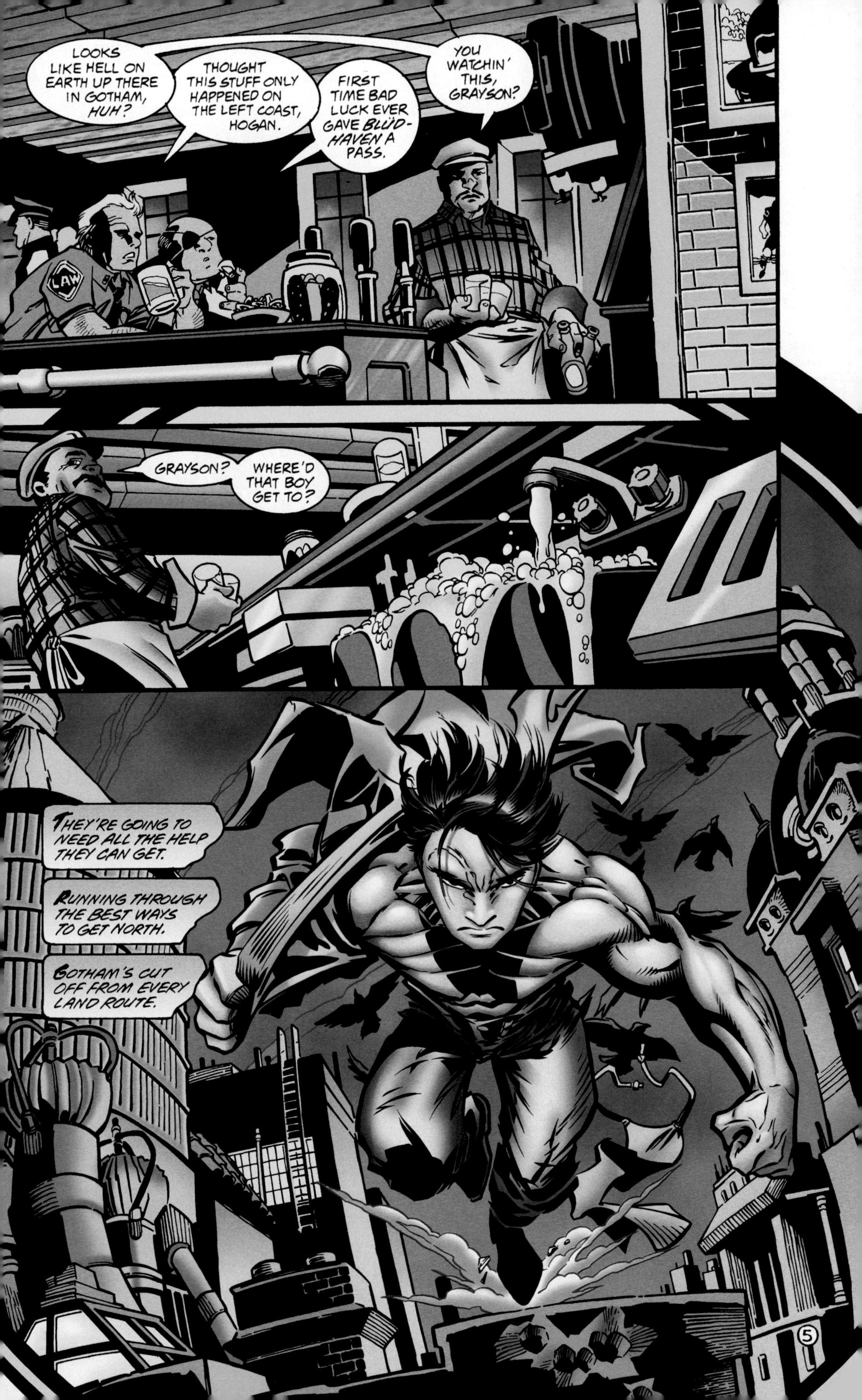
LOOKS LIKE HELL ON EARTH UP THERE IN GOTHAM, HUH?
THOUGHT THIS STUFF ONLY HAPPENED ON THE LEFT COAST, HOGAN.
FIRST TIME BAD LUCK EVER GAVE BLÜDHAVEN A PASS.
YOU WATCHIN' THIS, GRAYSON?
LAW
GRAYSON?
WHERE'D THAT BOY GET TO?
THEY'RE GOING TO NEED ALL THE HELP THEY CAN GET.
RUNNING THROUGH THE BEST WAYS TO GET NORTH.
GOTHAM'S CUT OFF FROM EVERY LAND ROUTE.
5

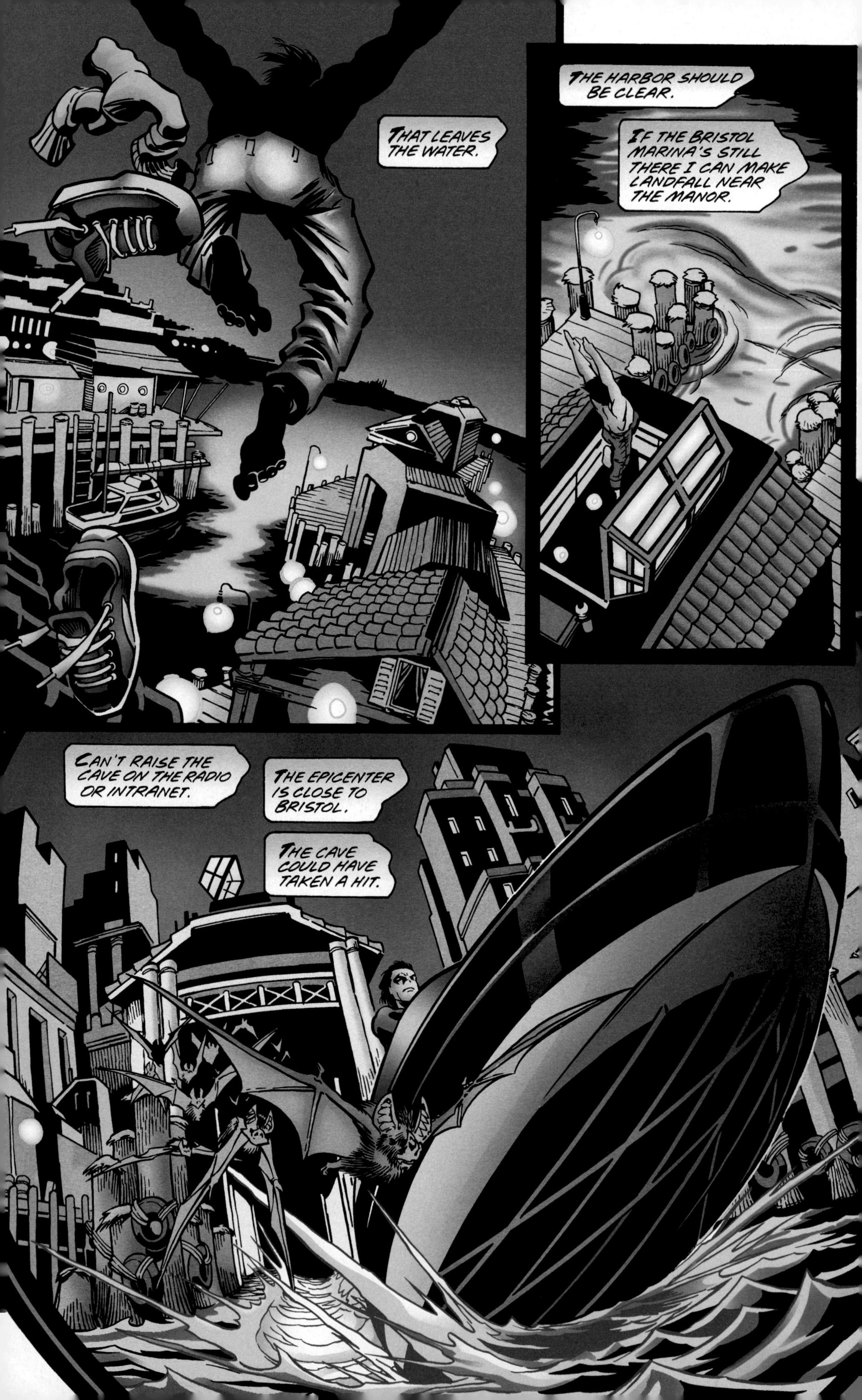
THAT LEAVES THE WATER.
THE HARBOR SHOULD BE CLEAR.
IF THE BRISTOL MARINA'S STILL THERE I CAN MAKE LANDFALL NEAR THE MANOR.
CAN'T RAISE THE CAVE ON THE RADIO OR INTRANET.
THE EPICENTER IS CLOSE TO BRISTOL.
THE CAVE COULD HAVE TAKEN A HIT.

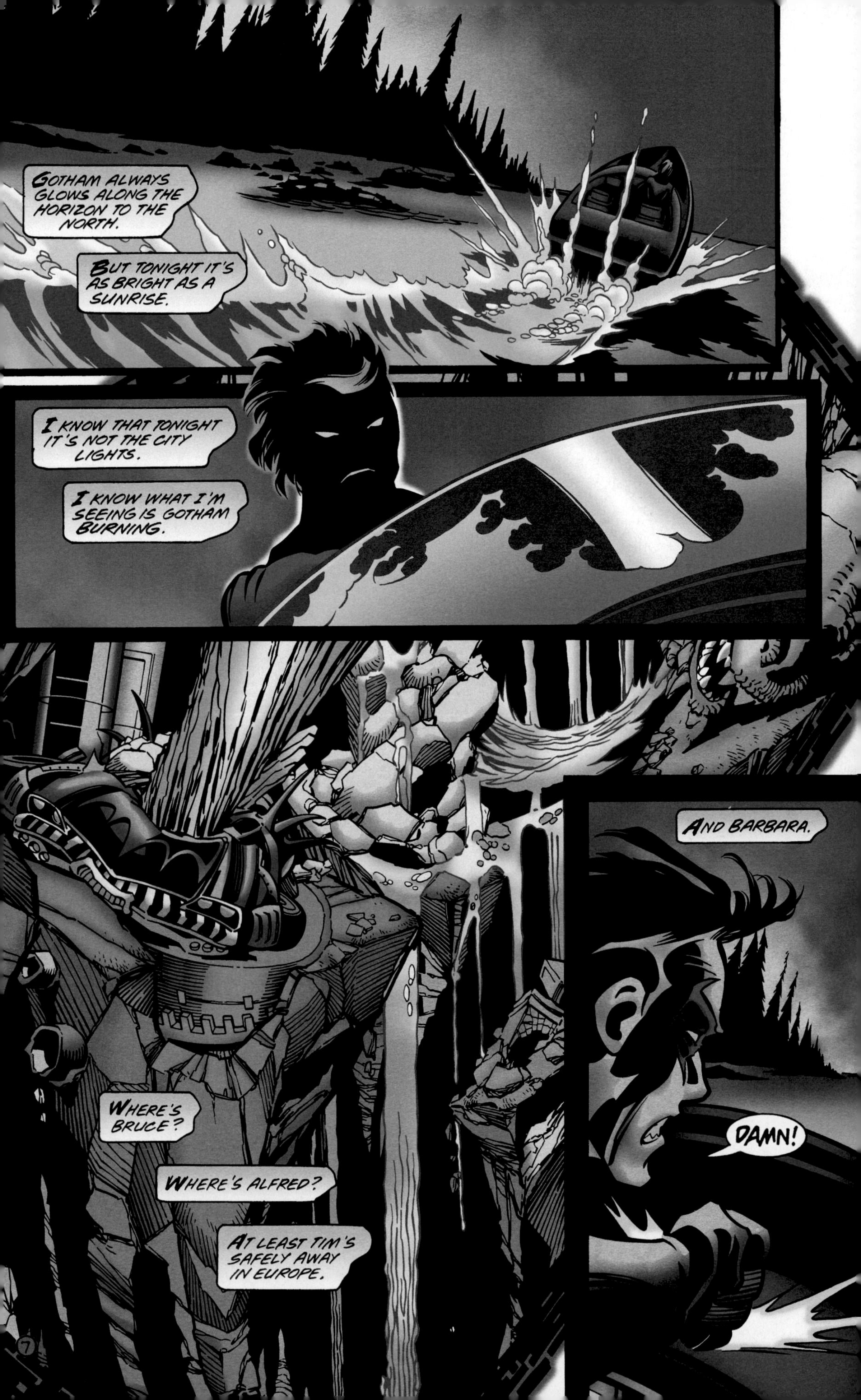
GOTHAM ALWAYS GLOWS ALONG THE HORIZON TO THE NORTH.
BUT TONIGHT IT'S AS BRIGHT AS A SUNRISE.
I KNOW THAT TONIGHT IT'S NOT THE CITY LIGHTS.
I KNOW WHAT I'M SEEING IS GOTHAM BURNING.
WHERE'S BRUCE?
WHERE'S ALFRED?
AT LEAST TIM'S SAFELY AWAY IN EUROPE.
AND BARBARA.
DAMN!

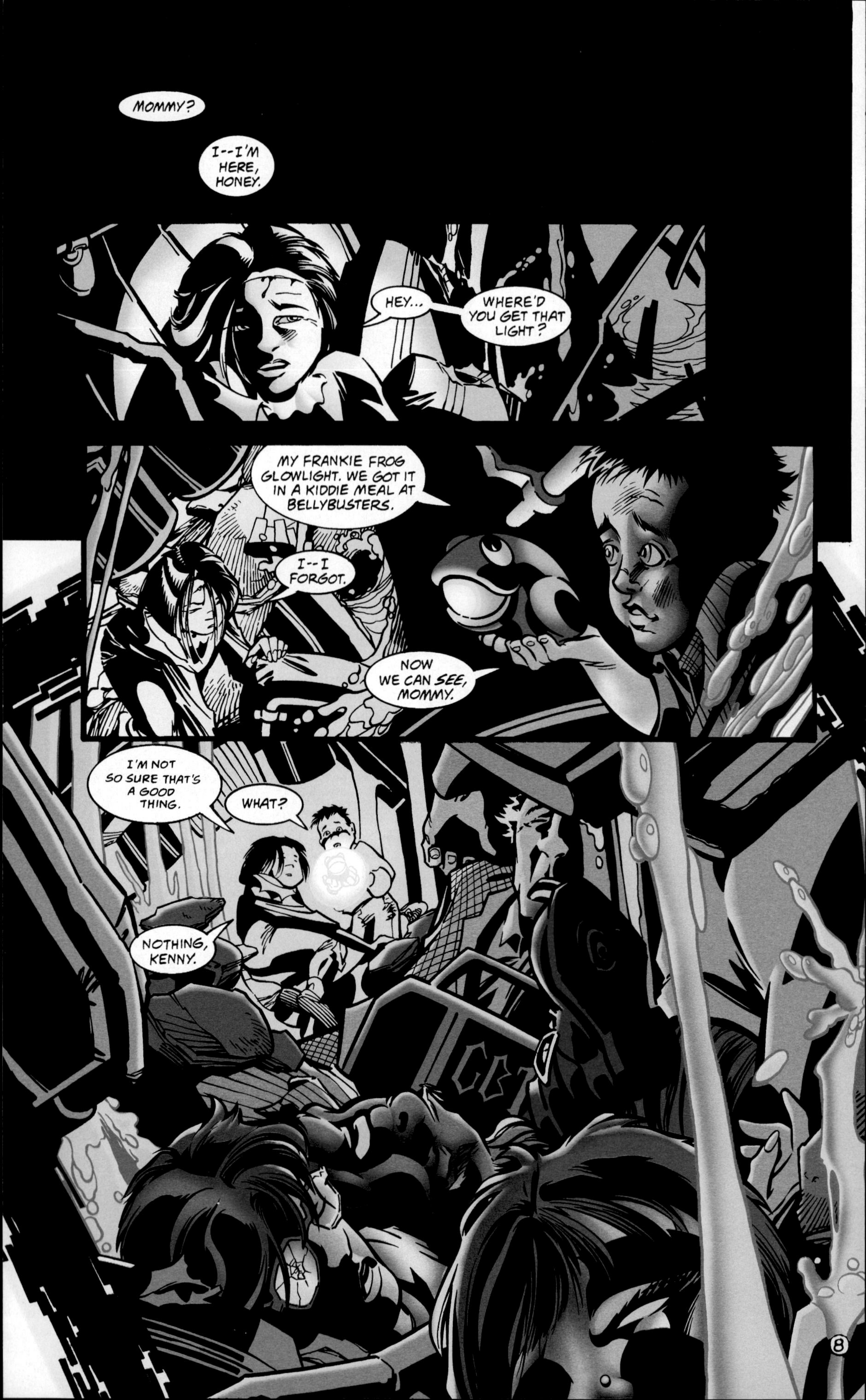
MOMMY?
I--I'M HERE, HONEY.
HEY...
WHERE'D YOU GET THAT LIGHT?
MY FRANKIE FROG GLOWLIGHT. WE GOT IT IN A KIDDIE MEAL AT BELLYBUSTERS.
I--I FORGOT.
NOW WE CAN SEE, MOMMY.
I'M NOT SO SURE THAT'S A GOOD THING.
WHAT?
NOTHING, KENNY.

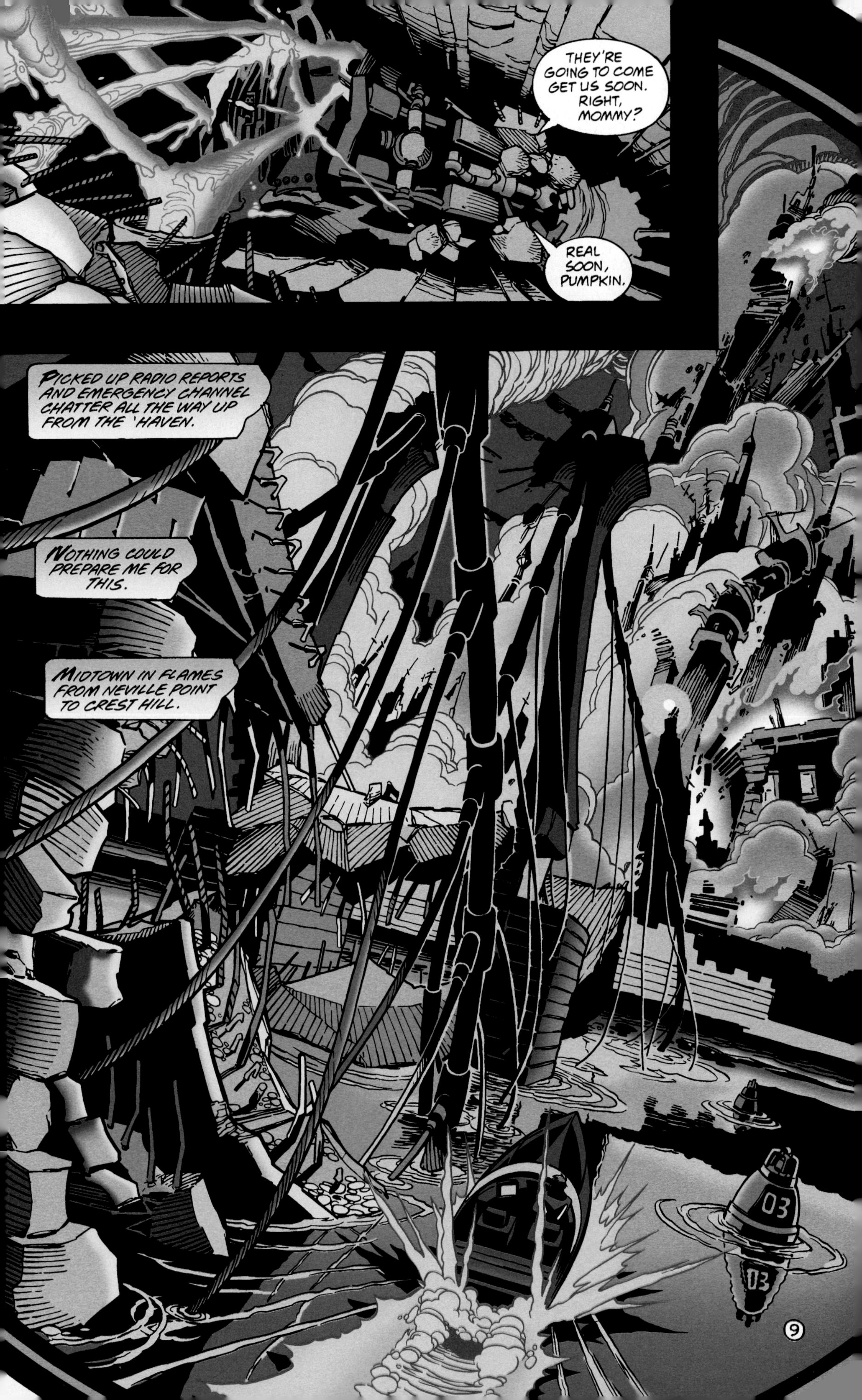
THEY'RE GOING TO COME GET US SOON. RIGHT, MOMMY?
REAL SOON, PUMPKIN.
PICKED UP RADIO REPORTS AND EMERGENCY CHANNEL CHATTER ALL THE WAY UP FROM THE 'HAVEN.
NOTHING COULD PREPARE ME FOR THIS.
MIDTOWN IN FLAMES FROM NEVILLE POINT TO CREST HILL.
03
03

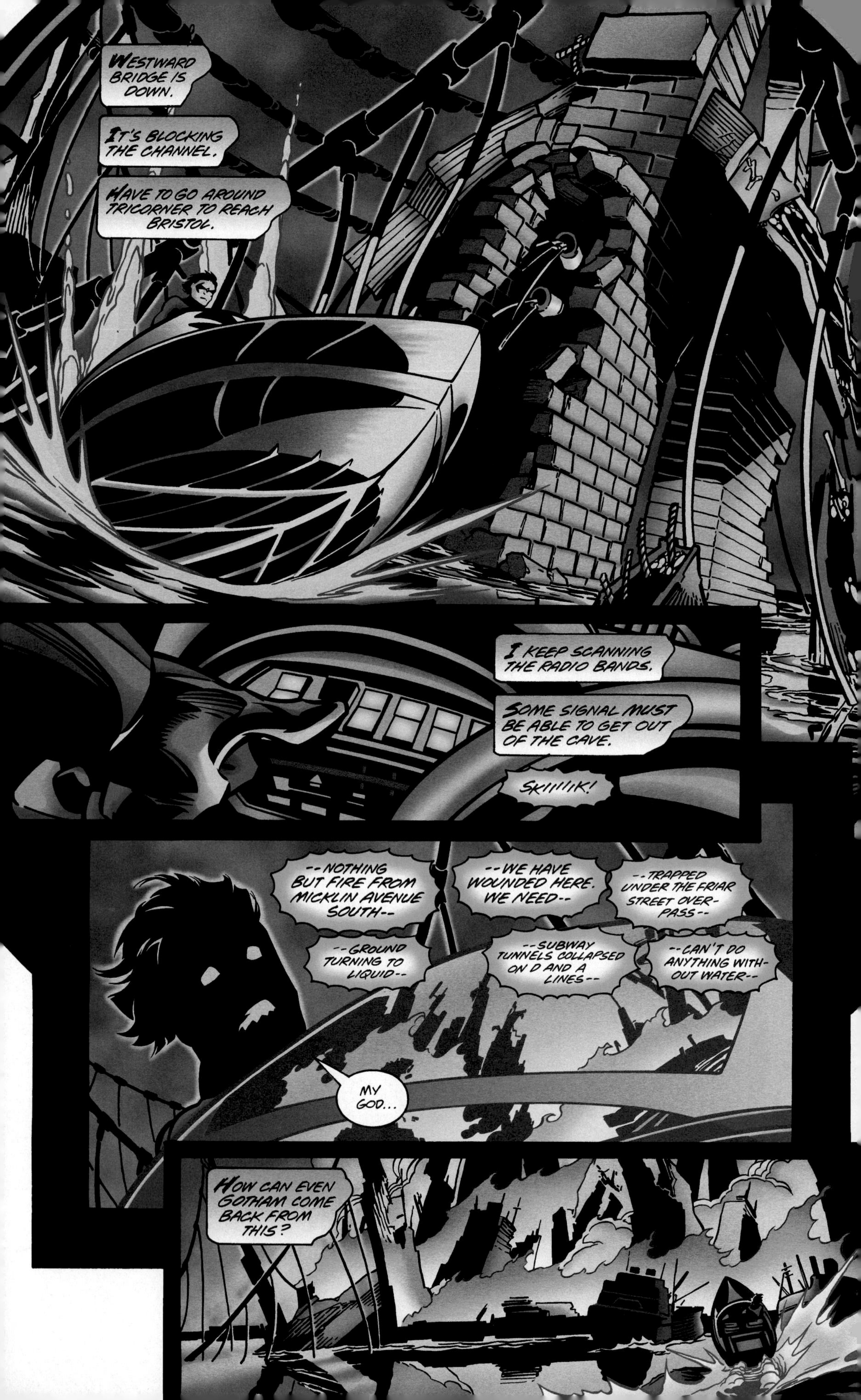
WESTWARD BRIDGE IS DOWN.
IT'S BLOCKING THE CHANNEL.
HAVE TO GO AROUND TRICORNER TO REACH BRISTOL.
I KEEP SCANNING THE RADIO BANDS.
SOME SIGNAL MUST BE ABLE TO GET OUT OF THE CAVE.
SKIIIIIK!
--NOTHING BUT FIRE FROM MICKLIN AVENUE SOUTH--
--WE HAVE WOUNDED HERE. WE NEED--
--TRAPPED UNDER THE FRIAR STREET OVER-PASS--
--GROUND TURNING TO LIQUID--
--SUBWAY TUNNELS COLLAPSED ON D AND A LINES--
--CAN'T DO ANYTHING WITH-OUT WATER--
MY GOD...
HOW CAN EVEN GOTHAM COME BACK FROM THIS?

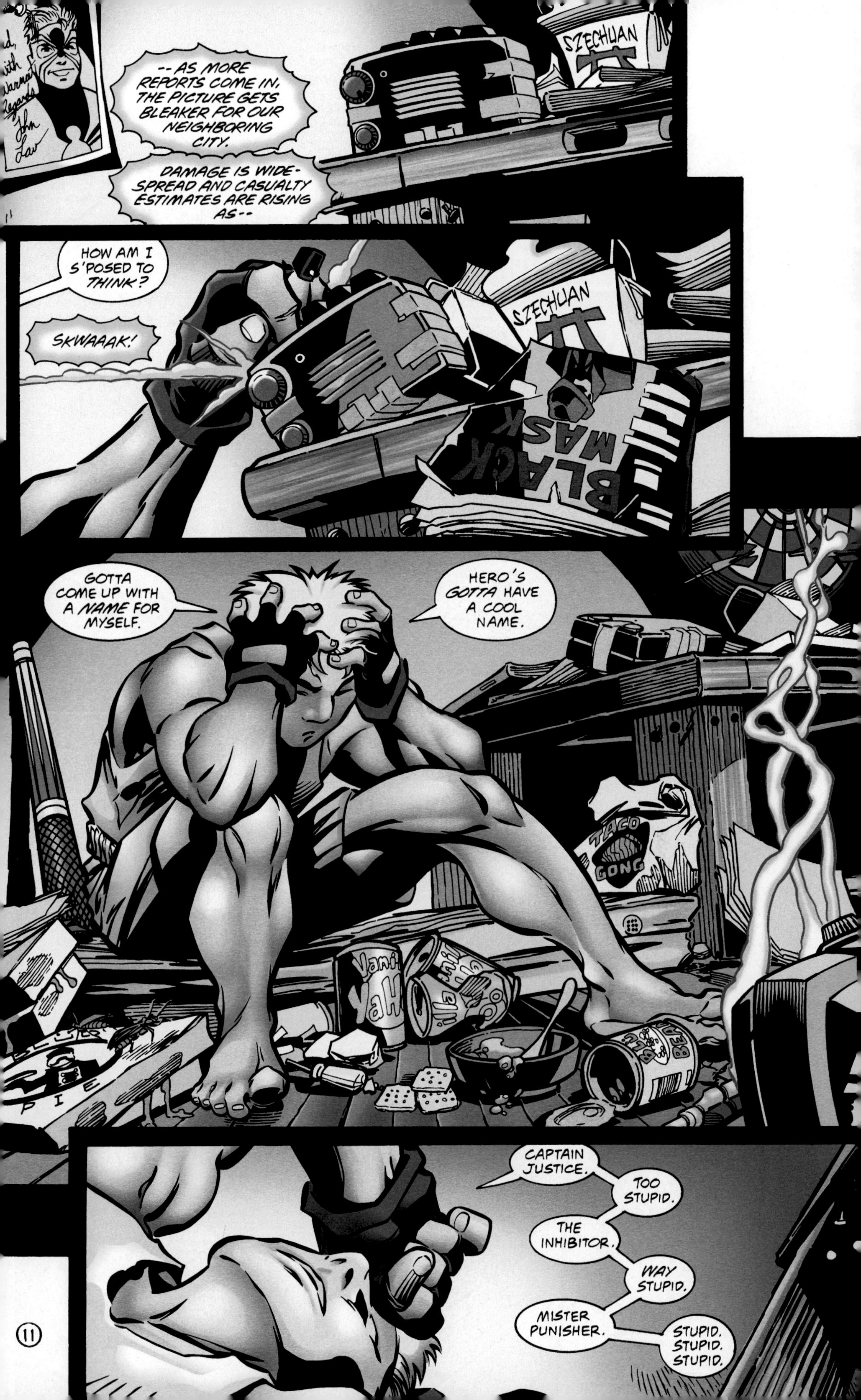

With Warmest Regards John Law
-- AS MORE REPORTS COME IN, THE PICTURE GETS BLEAKER FOR OUR NEIGHBORING CITY.
DAMAGE IS WIDE-SPREAD AND CASUALTY ESTIMATES ARE RISING AS--
SZECHUAN
HOW AM I S'POSED TO THINK?
SKWAAAK!
SZECHUAN
BLACK MASK
GOTTA COME UP WITH A NAME FOR MYSELF.
HERO'S GOTTA HAVE A COOL NAME.
TACO GONG
CAPTAIN JUSTICE.
TOO STUPID.
THE INHIBITOR.
WAY STUPID.
MISTER PUNISHER.
STUPID. STUPID. STUPID.

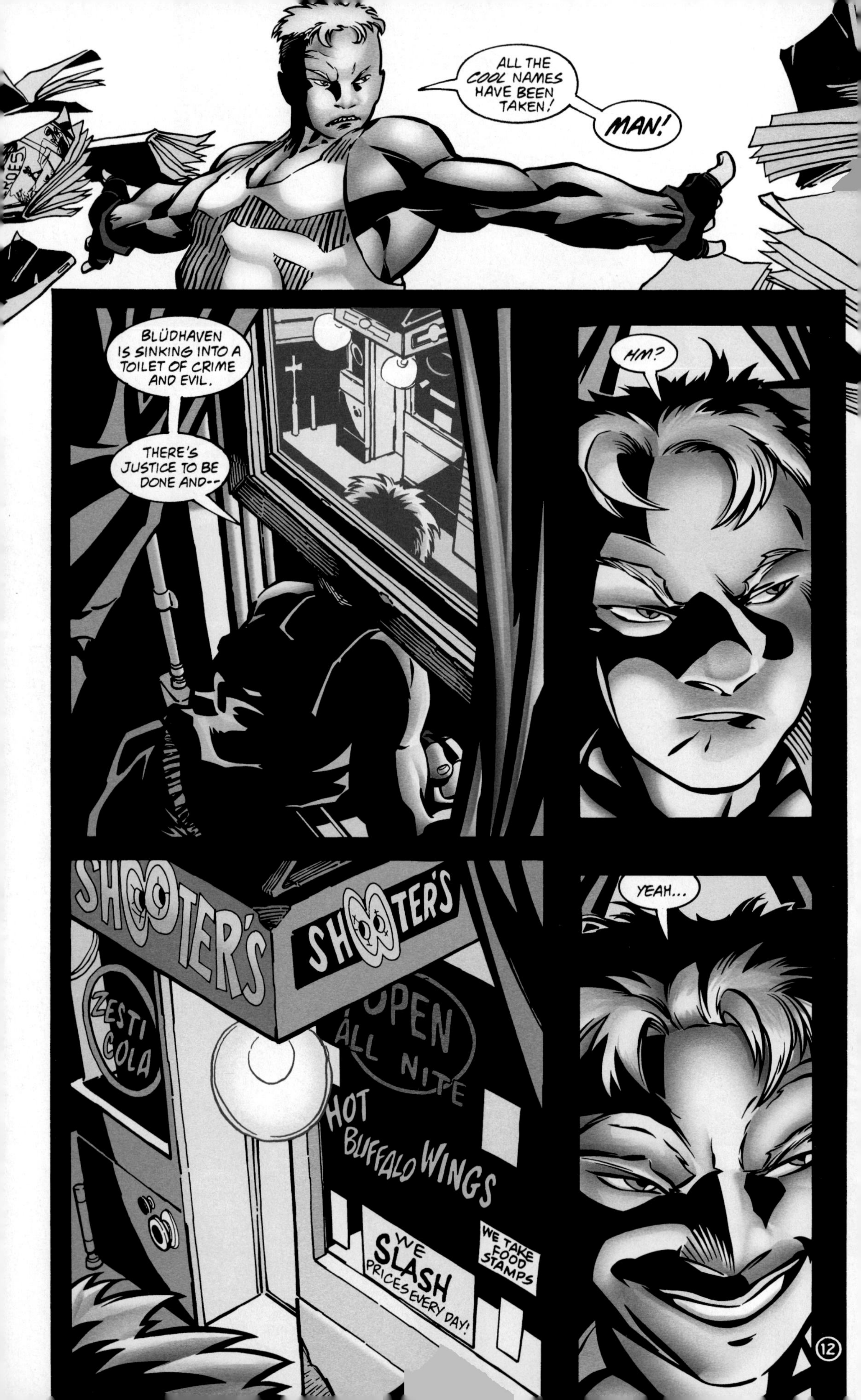
ALL THE COOL NAMES HAVE BEEN TAKEN!
MAN!
BLÜDHAVEN IS SINKING INTO A TOILET OF CRIME AND EVIL.
THERE'S JUSTICE TO BE DONE AND--
HM?
SHOOTER'S
SHOOTER'S
ZESTI COLA
OPEN ALL NITE
HOT BUFFALO WINGS
WE SLASH PRICES EVERY DAY!
WE TAKE FOOD STAMPS
YEAH...

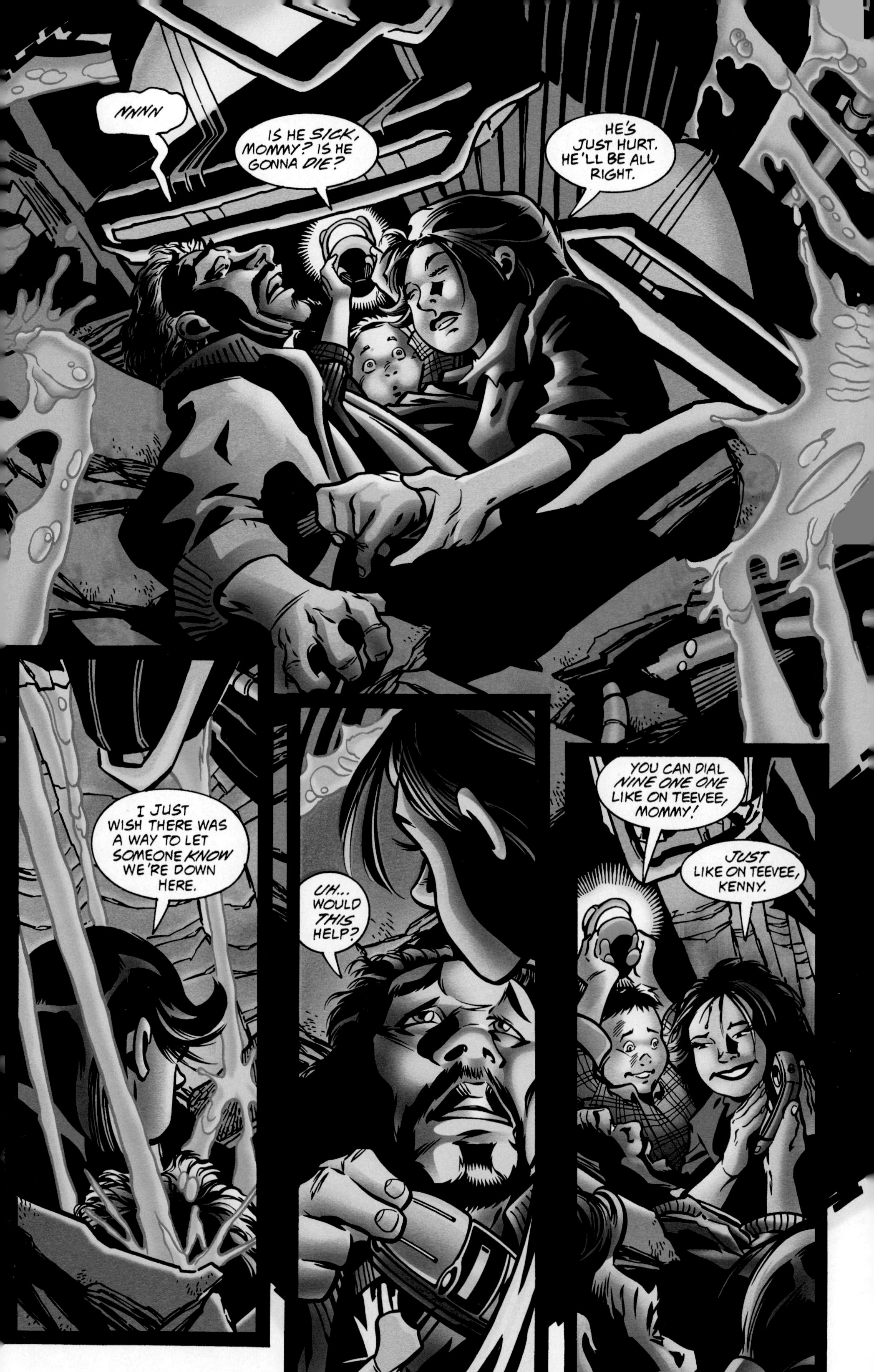
NNNN
IS HE SICK, MOMMY? IS HE GONNA DIE?
HE'S JUST HURT. HE'LL BE ALL RIGHT.
I JUST WISH THERE WAS A WAY TO LET SOMEONE KNOW WE'RE DOWN HERE.
UH... WOULD THIS HELP?
YOU CAN DIAL NINE ONE ONE LIKE ON TEEVEE, MOMMY!
JUST LIKE ON TEEVEE, KENNY.

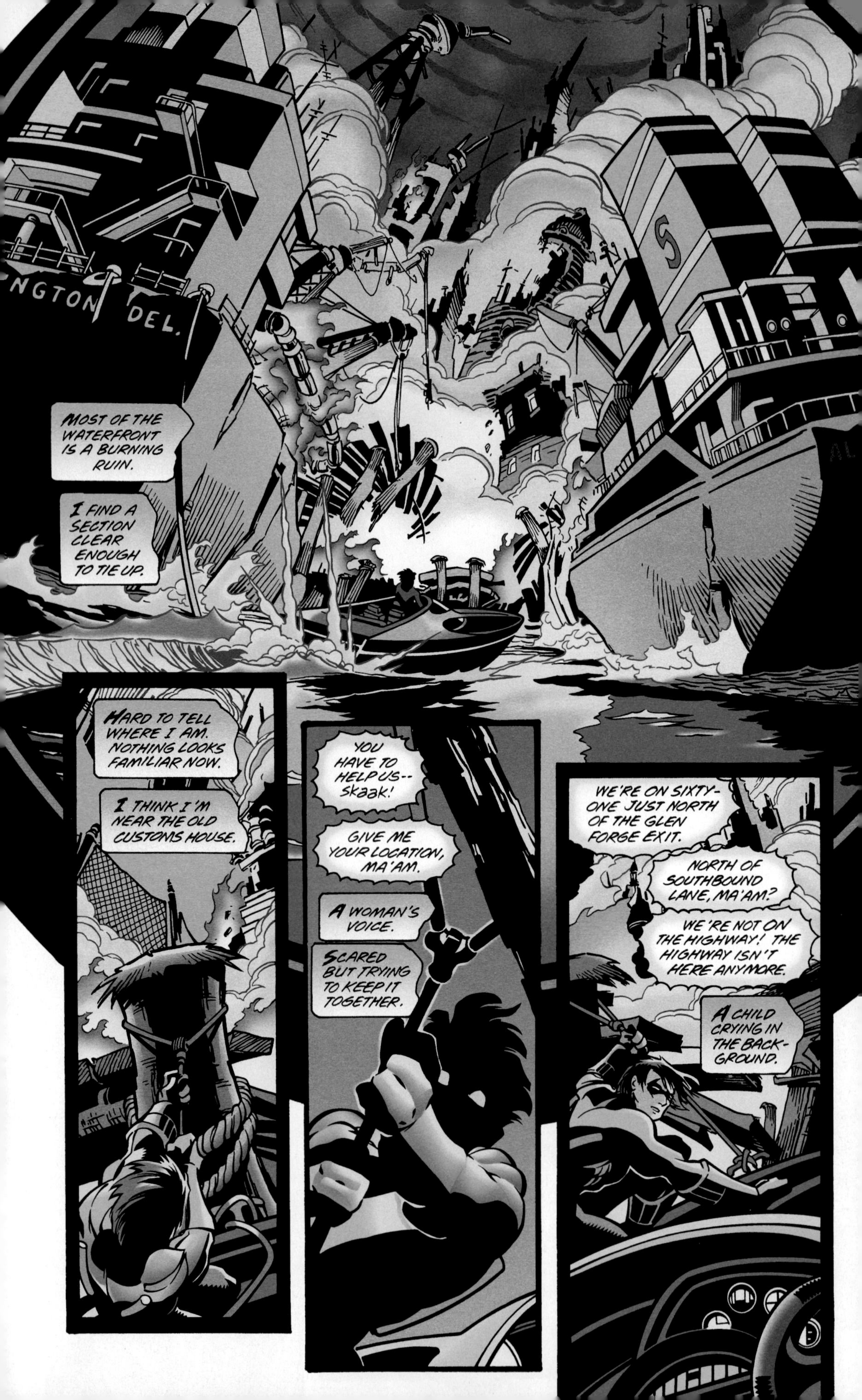
NGTON DEL.
MOST OF THE WATERFRONT IS A BURNING RUIN.
I FIND A SECTION CLEAR ENOUGH TO TIE UP.
HARD TO TELL WHERE I AM. NOTHING LOOKS FAMILIAR NOW.
I THINK I'M NEAR THE OLD CUSTOMS HOUSE.
YOU HAVE TO HELP US-- skaak!
GIVE ME YOUR LOCATION, MA'AM.
A WOMAN'S VOICE.
SCARED BUT TRYING TO KEEP IT TOGETHER.
WE'RE ON SIXTY-ONE JUST NORTH OF THE GLEN FORGE EXIT.
NORTH OF SOUTHBOUND LANE, MA'AM?
WE'RE NOT ON THE HIGHWAY! THE HIGHWAY ISN'T HERE ANYMORE.
A CHILD CRYING IN THE BACK-GROUND.

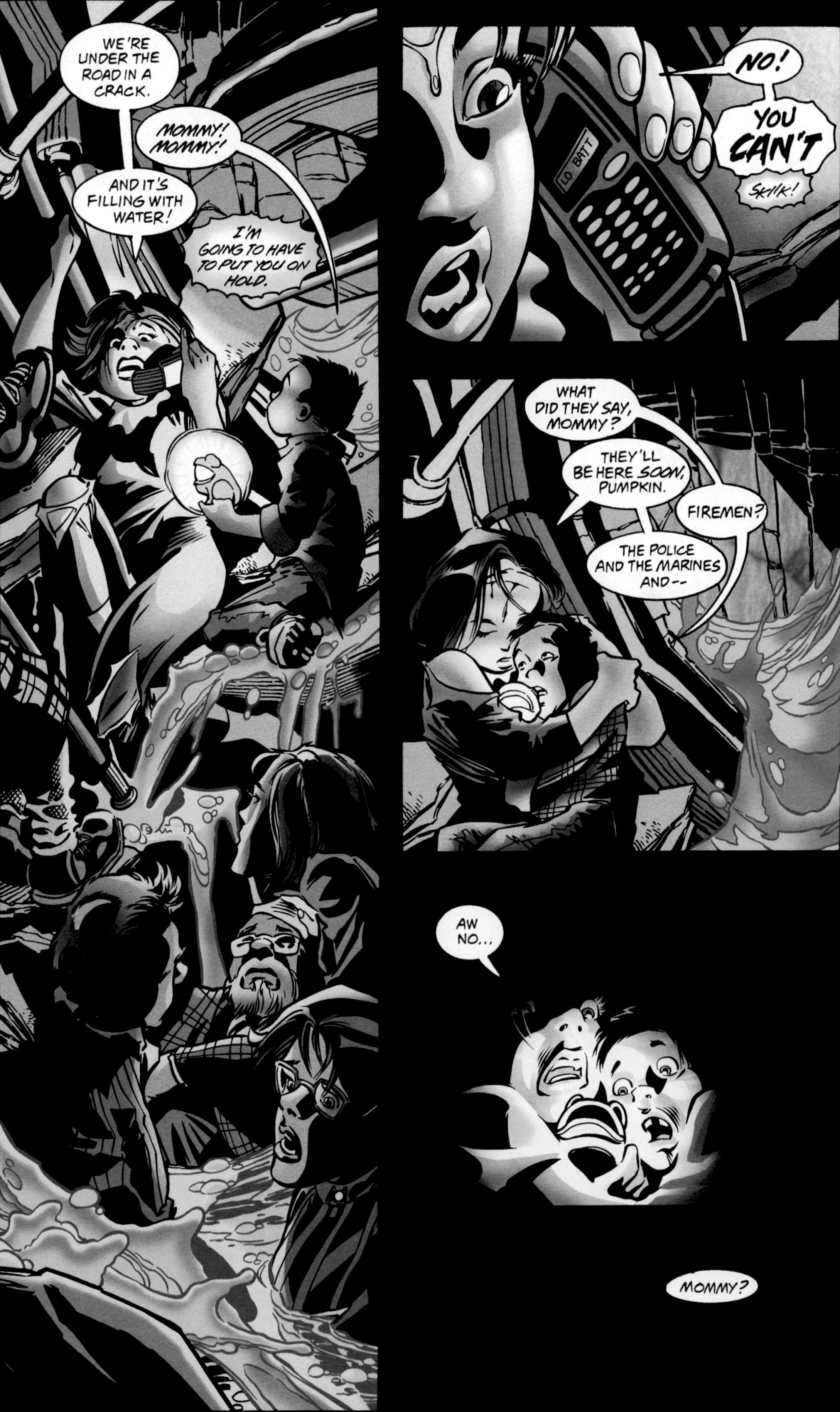
WE'RE UNDER THE ROAD IN A CRACK.
MOMMY! MOMMY!
AND IT'S FILLING WITH WATER!
I'M GOING TO HAVE TO PUT YOU ON HOLD.
LO BATT
NO!
YOU CAN'T
SKLIK!
WHAT DID THEY SAY, MOMMY?
THEY'LL BE HERE SOON, PUMPKIN.
FIREMEN?
THE POLICE AND THE MARINES AND--
AW NO...
MOMMY?

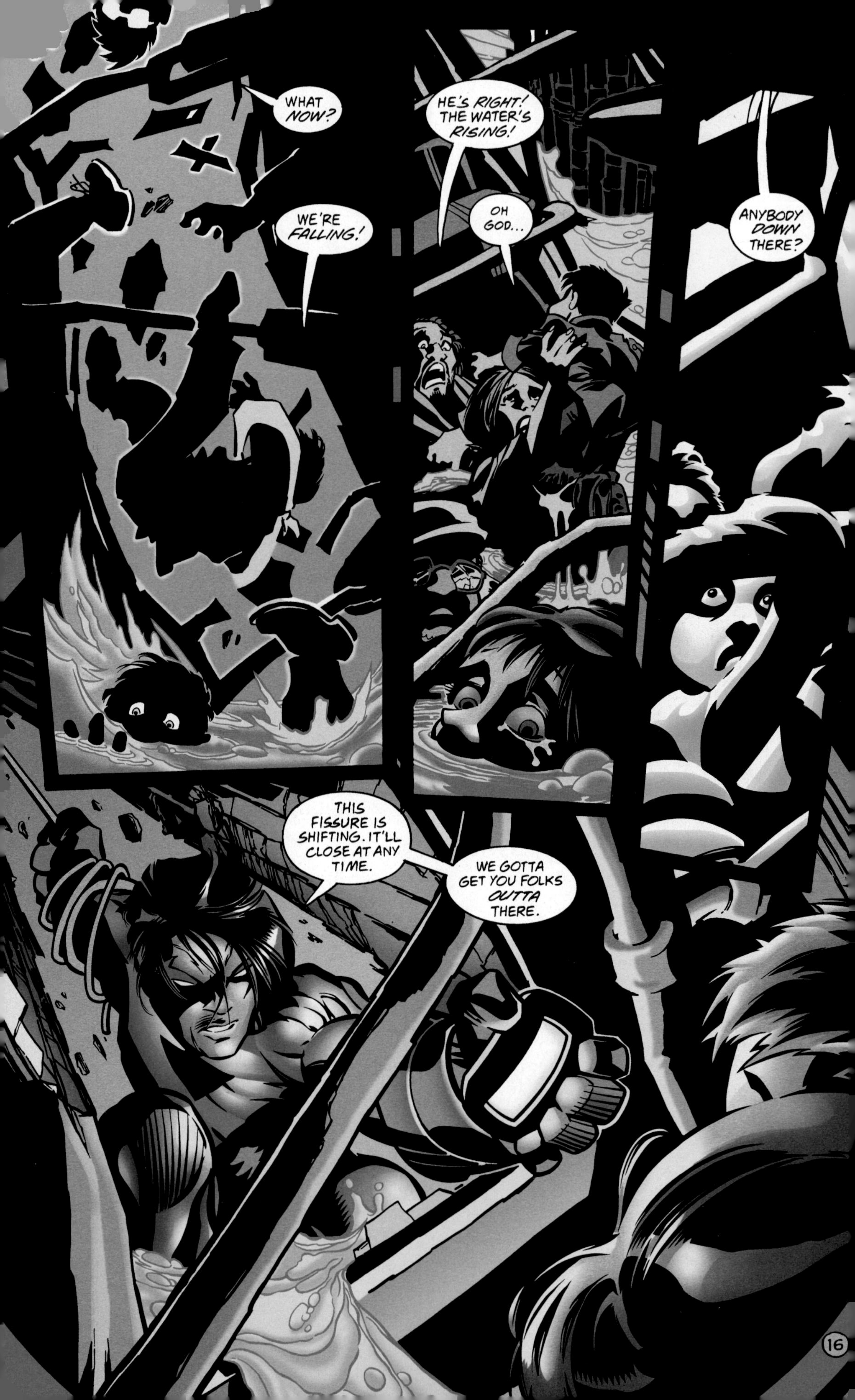
WHAT NOW?
WE'RE FALLING!
HE'S RIGHT! THE WATER'S RISING!
OH GOD...
ANYBODY DOWN THERE?
THIS FISSURE IS SHIFTING. IT'LL CLOSE AT ANY TIME.
WE GOTTA GET YOU FOLKS OUTTA THERE.

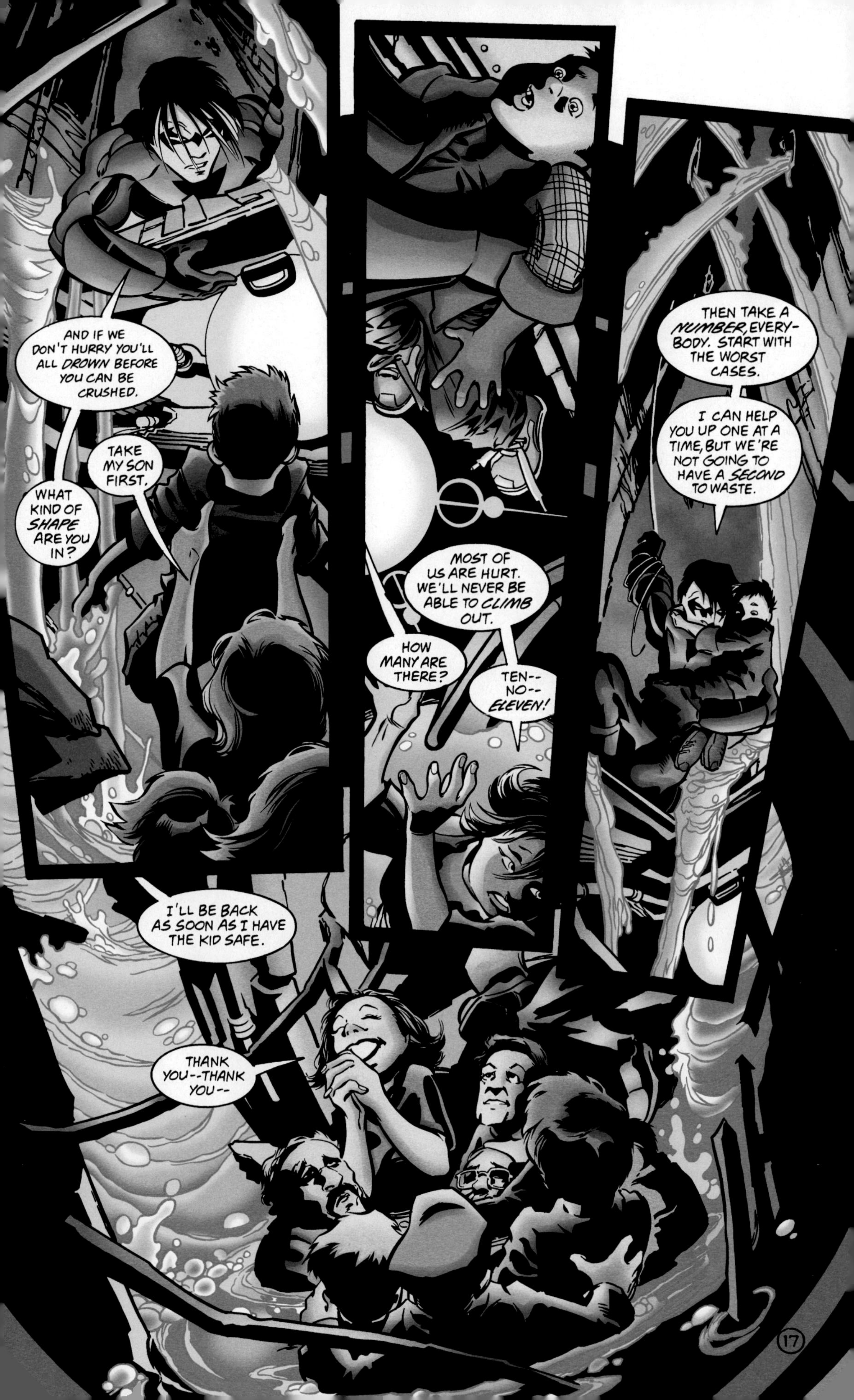
AND IF WE DON'T HURRY YOU'LL ALL DROWN BEFORE YOU CAN BE CRUSHED.
TAKE MY SON FIRST.
WHAT KIND OF SHAPE ARE YOU IN?
MOST OF US ARE HURT. WE'LL NEVER BE ABLE TO CLIMB OUT.
HOW MANY ARE THERE?
TEN-- NO-- ELEVEN!
THEN TAKE A NUMBER, EVERY-BODY. START WITH THE WORST CASES.
I CAN HELP YOU UP ONE AT A TIME, BUT WE'RE NOT GOING TO HAVE A SECOND TO WASTE.
I'LL BE BACK AS SOON AS I HAVE THE KID SAFE.
THANK YOU--THANK YOU--

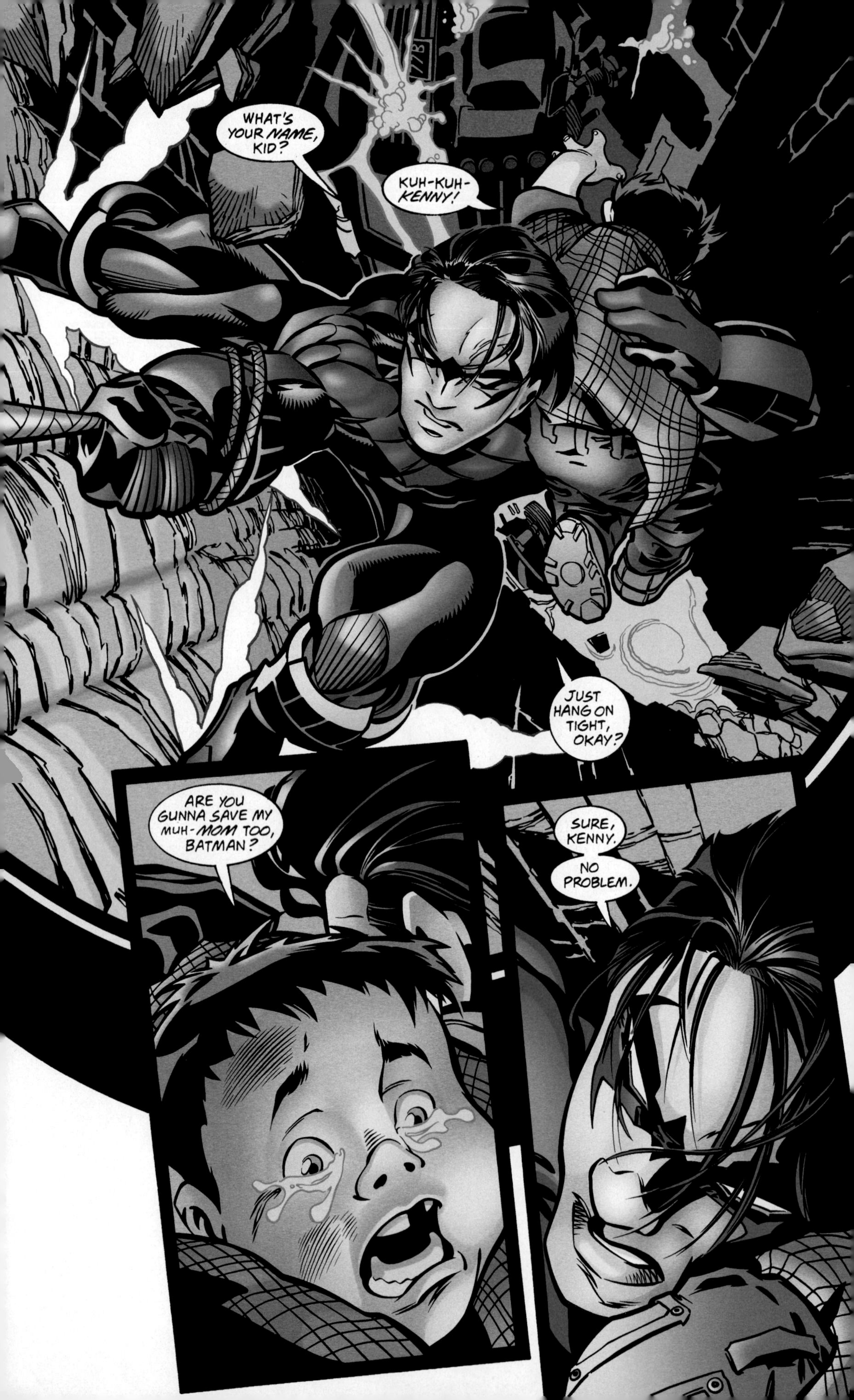
WHAT'S YOUR NAME, KID?
KUH-KUH-KENNY!
JUST HANG ON TIGHT, OKAY?
ARE YOU GUNNA SAVE MY MUH-MOM TOO, BATMAN?
SURE, KENNY.
NO PROBLEM.

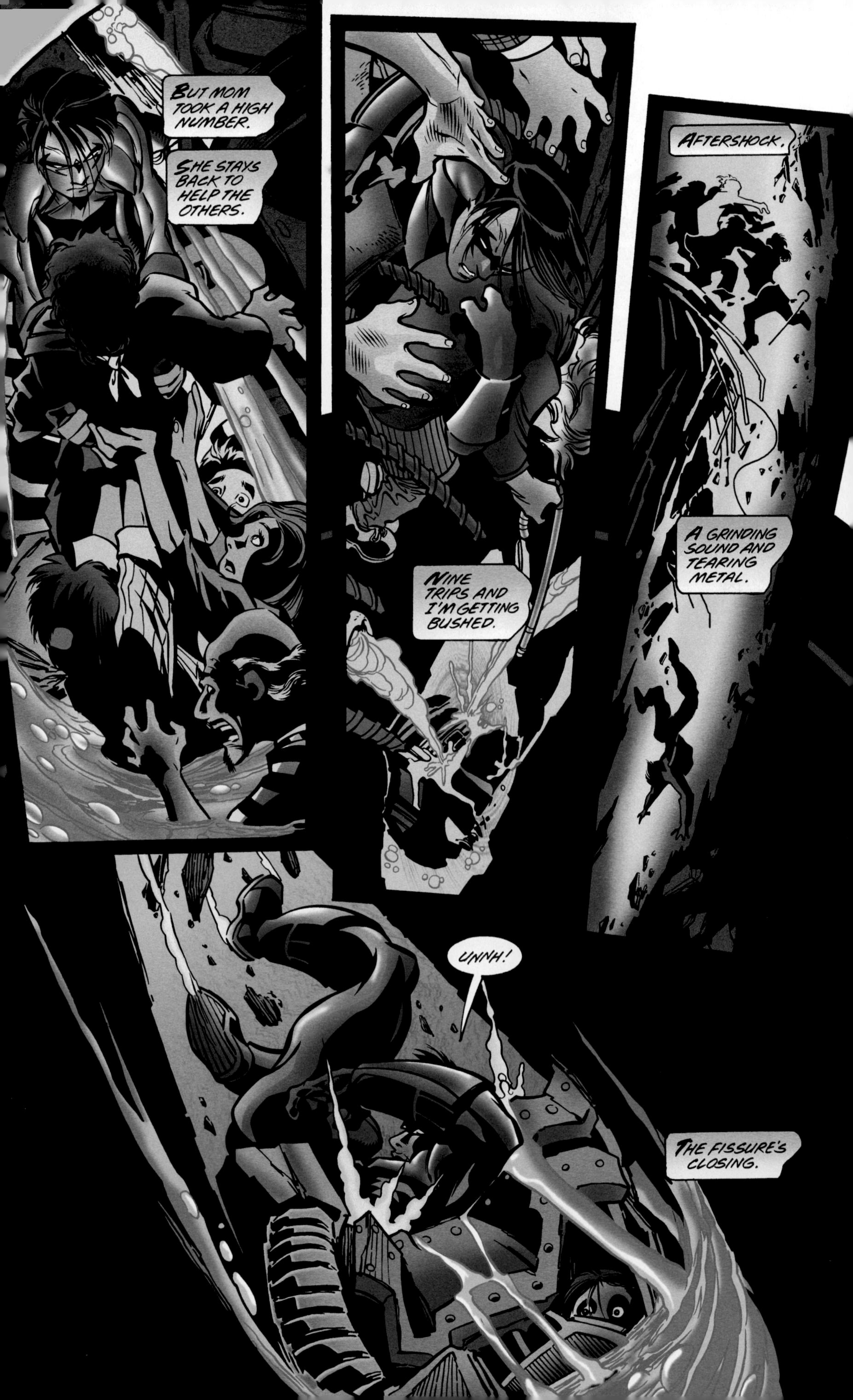
BUT MOM TOOK A HIGH NUMBER.
SHE STAYS BACK TO HELP THE OTHERS.
NINE TRIPS AND I'M GETTING BUSHED.
AFTERSHOCK.
A GRINDING SOUND AND TEARING METAL.
UNNH!
THE FISSURE'S CLOSING.

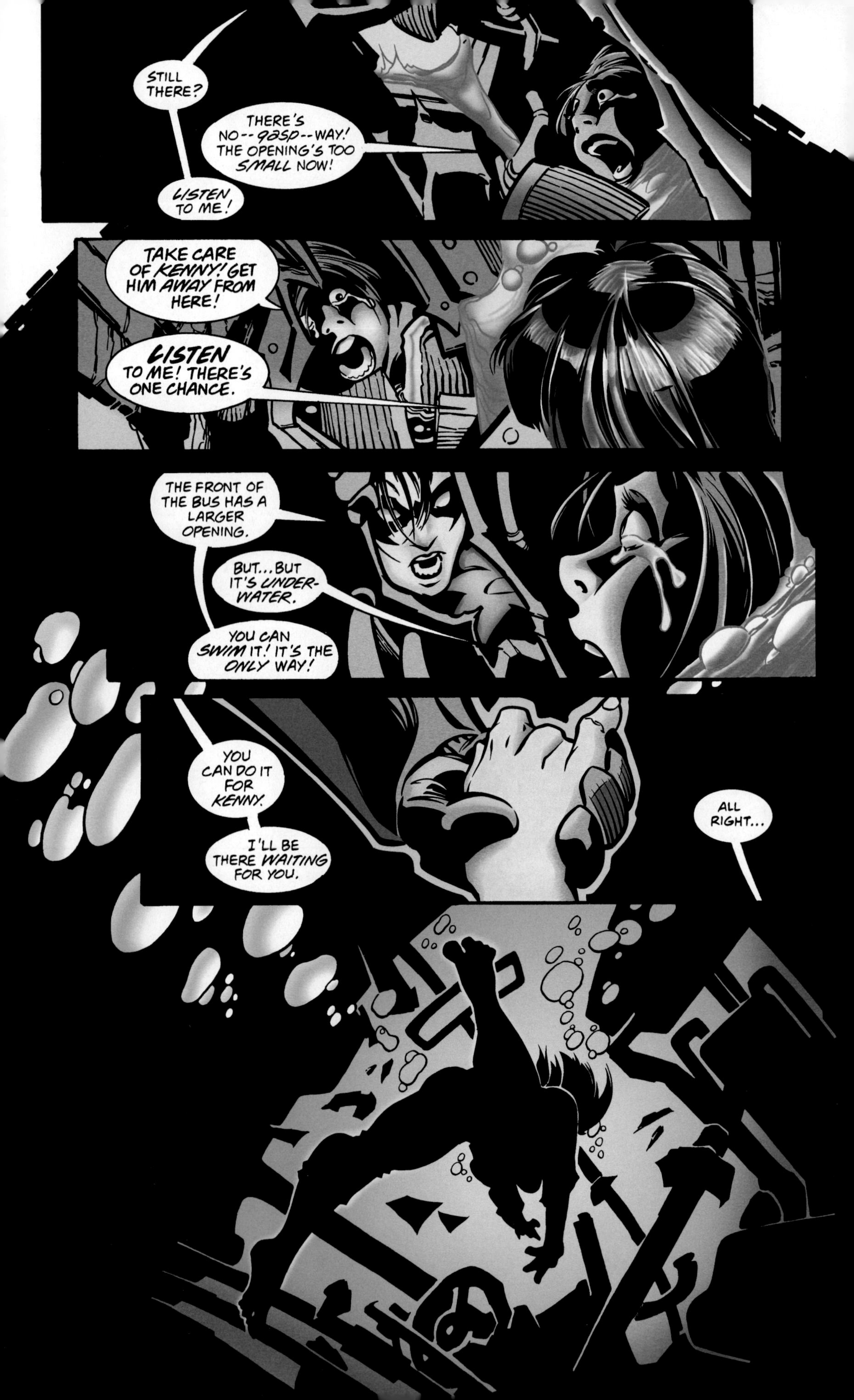
STILL THERE?
THERE'S NO--gasp--WAY! THE OPENING'S TOO SMALL NOW!
LISTEN TO ME!
TAKE CARE OF KENNY! GET HIM AWAY FROM HERE!
LISTEN TO ME! THERE'S ONE CHANCE.
THE FRONT OF THE BUS HAS A LARGER OPENING.
BUT...BUT IT'S UNDER-WATER.
YOU CAN SWIM IT! IT'S THE ONLY WAY!
YOU CAN DO IT FOR KENNY.
I'LL BE THERE WAITING FOR YOU.
ALL RIGHT...

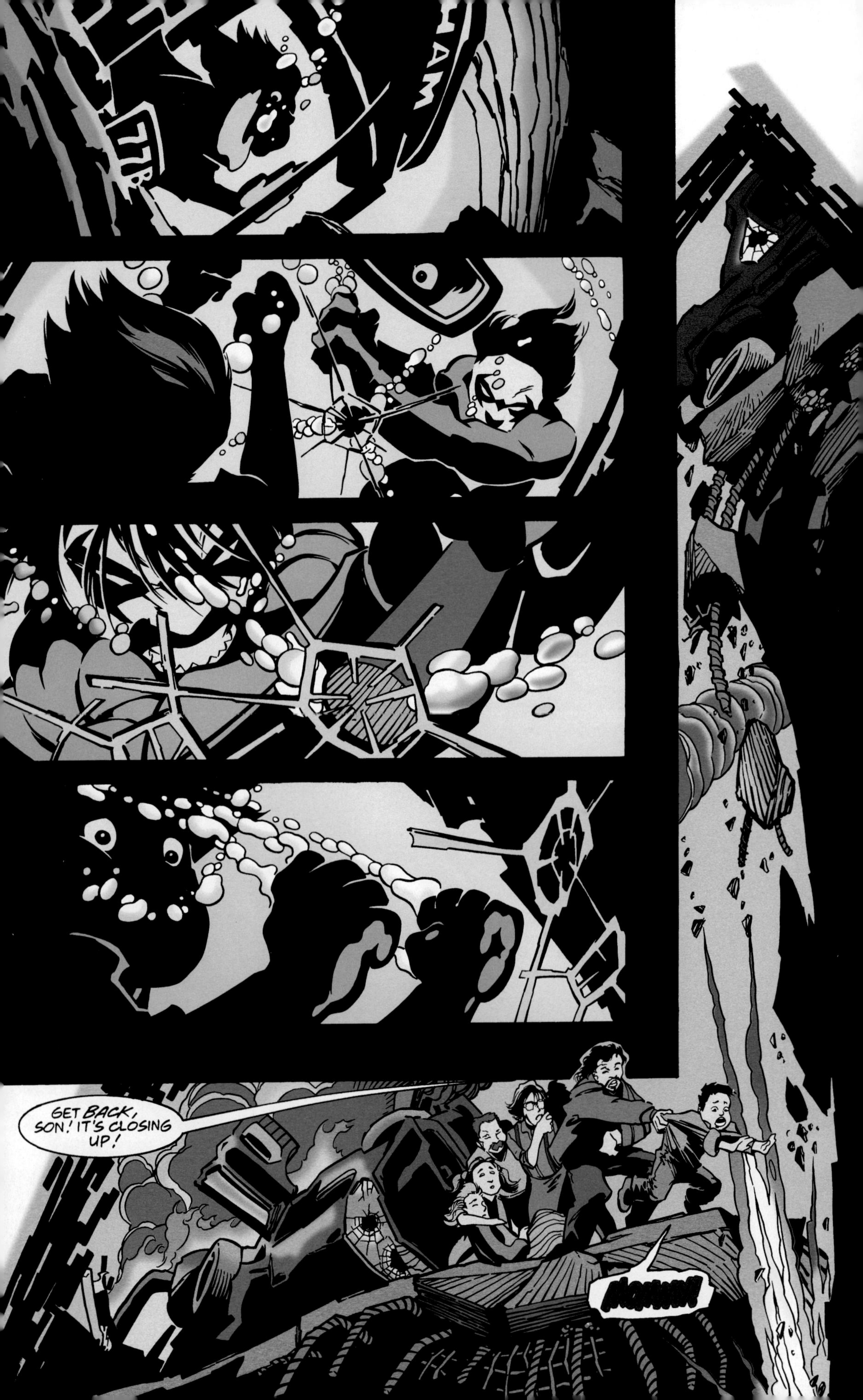
GET BACK, SON! IT'S CLOSING UP!
PLOMMM!

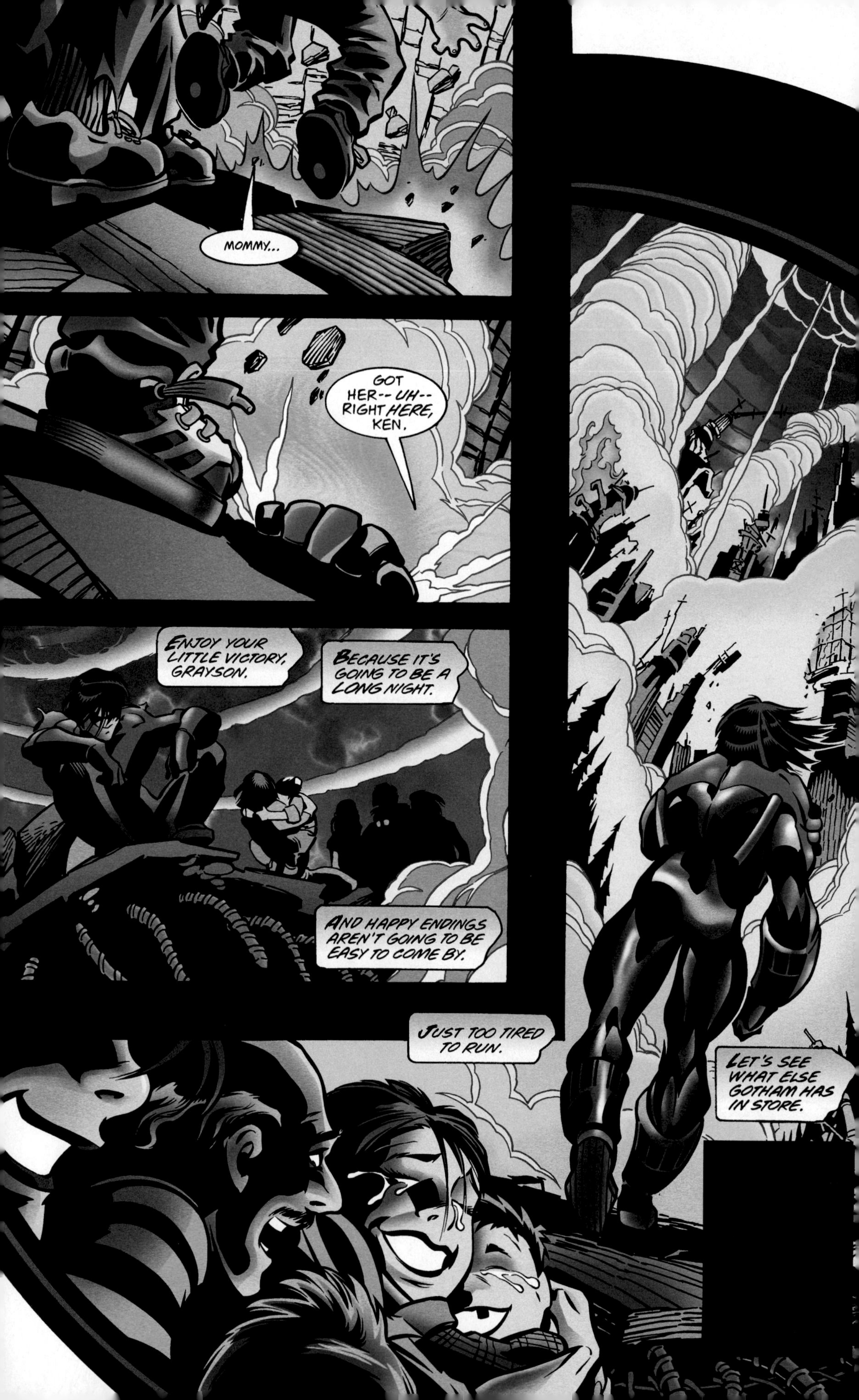
MOMMY...
GOT HER-- UH-- RIGHT HERE, KEN.
ENJOY YOUR LITTLE VICTORY, GRAYSON.
BECAUSE IT'S GOING TO BE A LONG NIGHT.
AND HAPPY ENDINGS AREN'T GOING TO BE EASY TO COME BY.
JUST TOO TIRED TO RUN.
LET'S SEE WHAT ELSE GOTHAM HAS IN STORE.

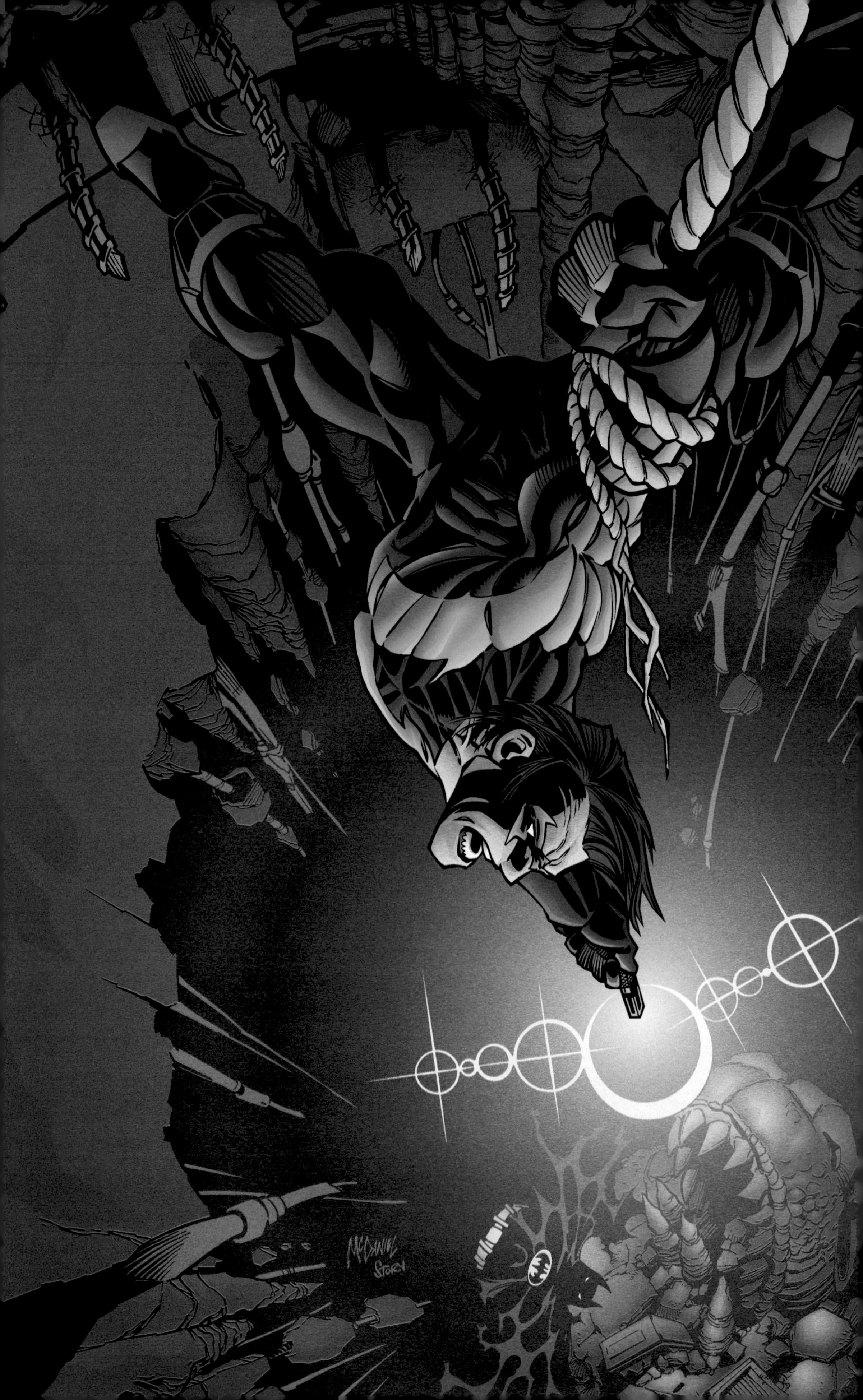
McDANIEL
STORY

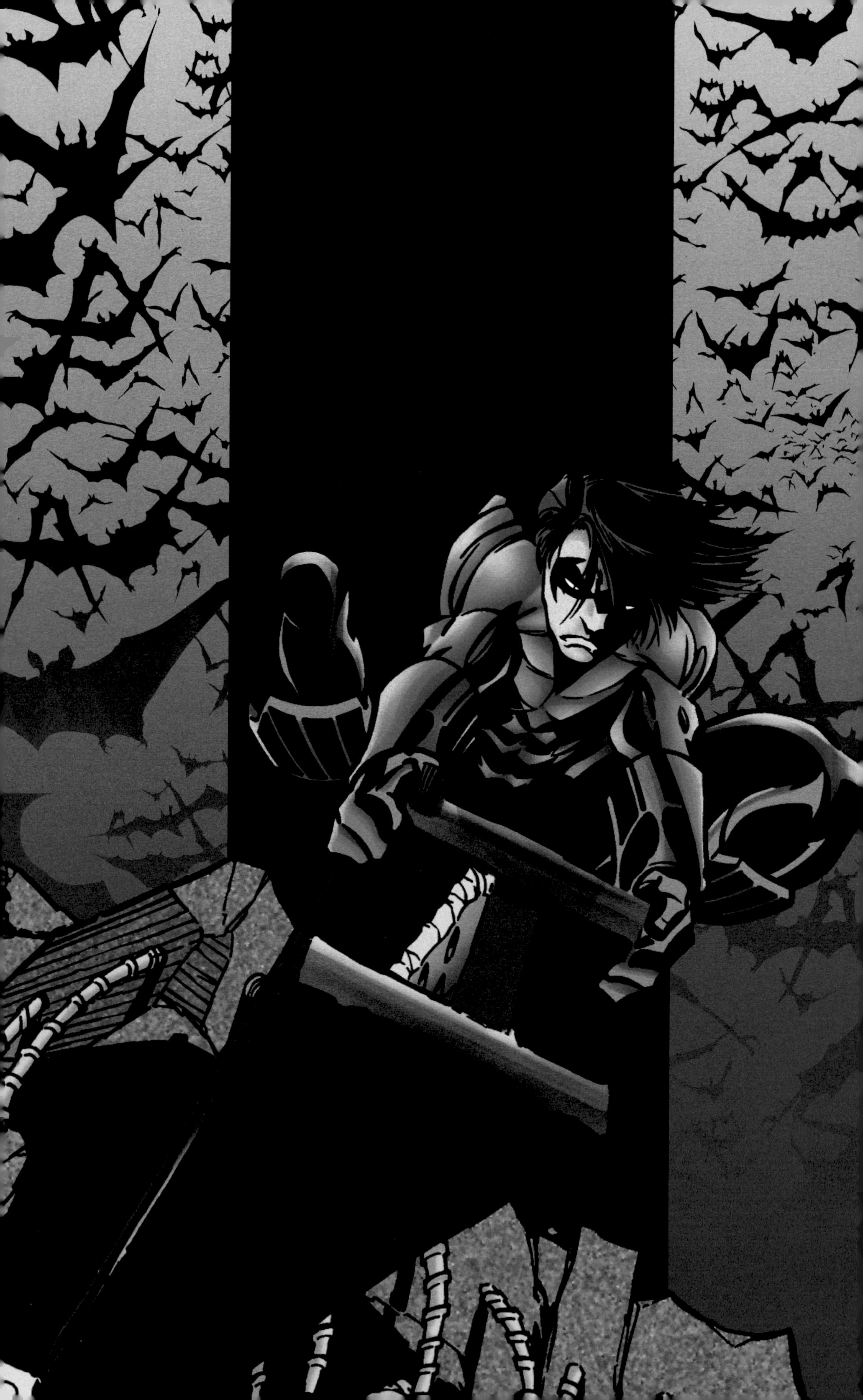

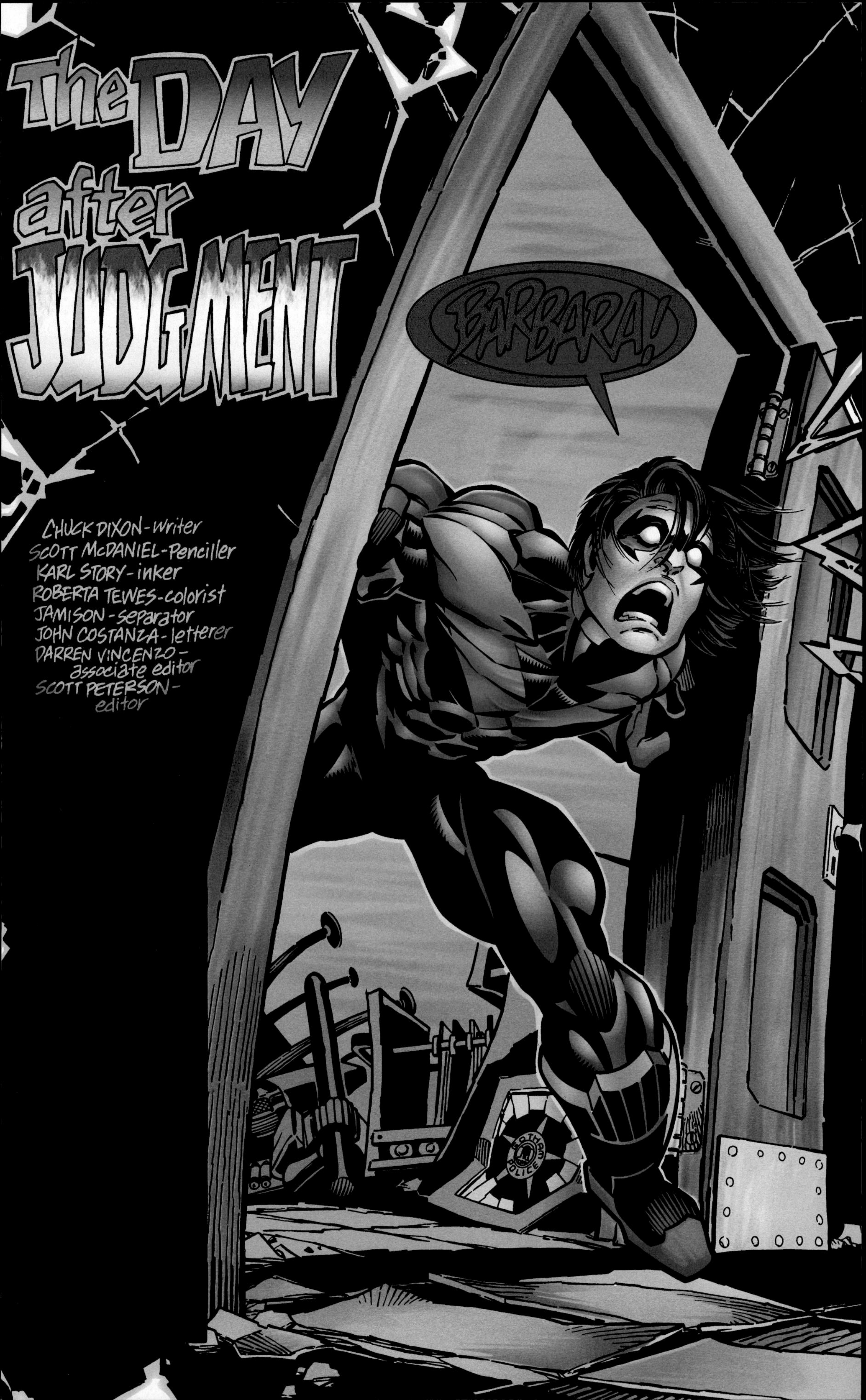
The DAY after JUDGMENT
BARBARA!
CHUCK DIXON-writer
SCOTT McDANIEL-Penciller
KARL STORY-inker
ROBERTA TEWES-colorist
JAMISON-separator
JOHN COSTANZA-letterer
DARREN VINCENZO-associate editor
SCOTT PETERSON-editor
GOTHAM POLICE

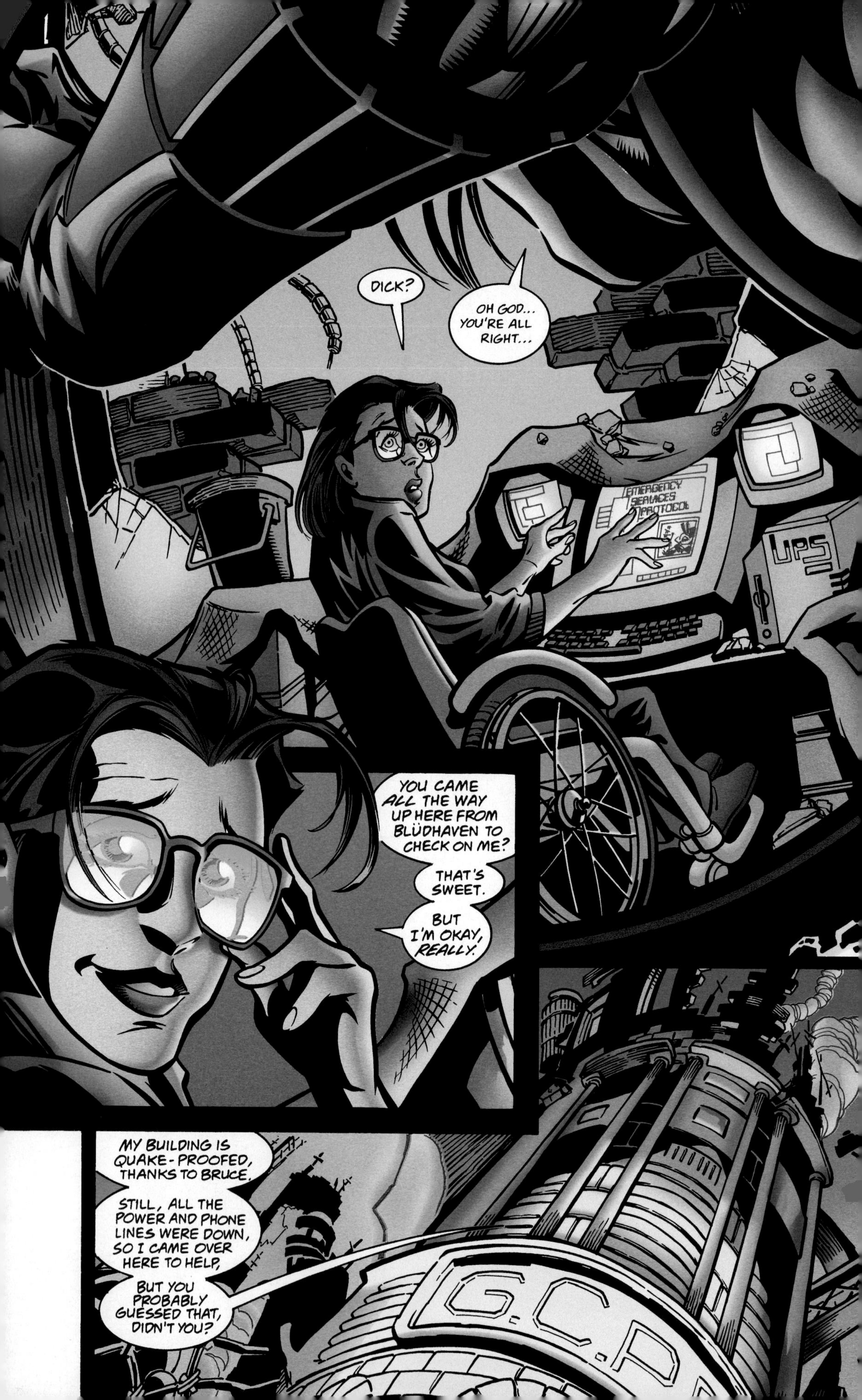
DICK?
OH GOD... YOU'RE ALL RIGHT...
EMERGENCY SERVICES PROTOCOL
UPS
YOU CAME ALL THE WAY UP HERE FROM BLÜDHAVEN TO CHECK ON ME?
THAT'S SWEET.
BUT I'M OKAY, REALLY.
MY BUILDING IS QUAKE-PROOFED, THANKS TO BRUCE.
STILL, ALL THE POWER AND PHONE LINES WERE DOWN, SO I CAME OVER HERE TO HELP,
BUT YOU PROBABLY GUESSED THAT, DIDN'T YOU?
G.C.P.D.

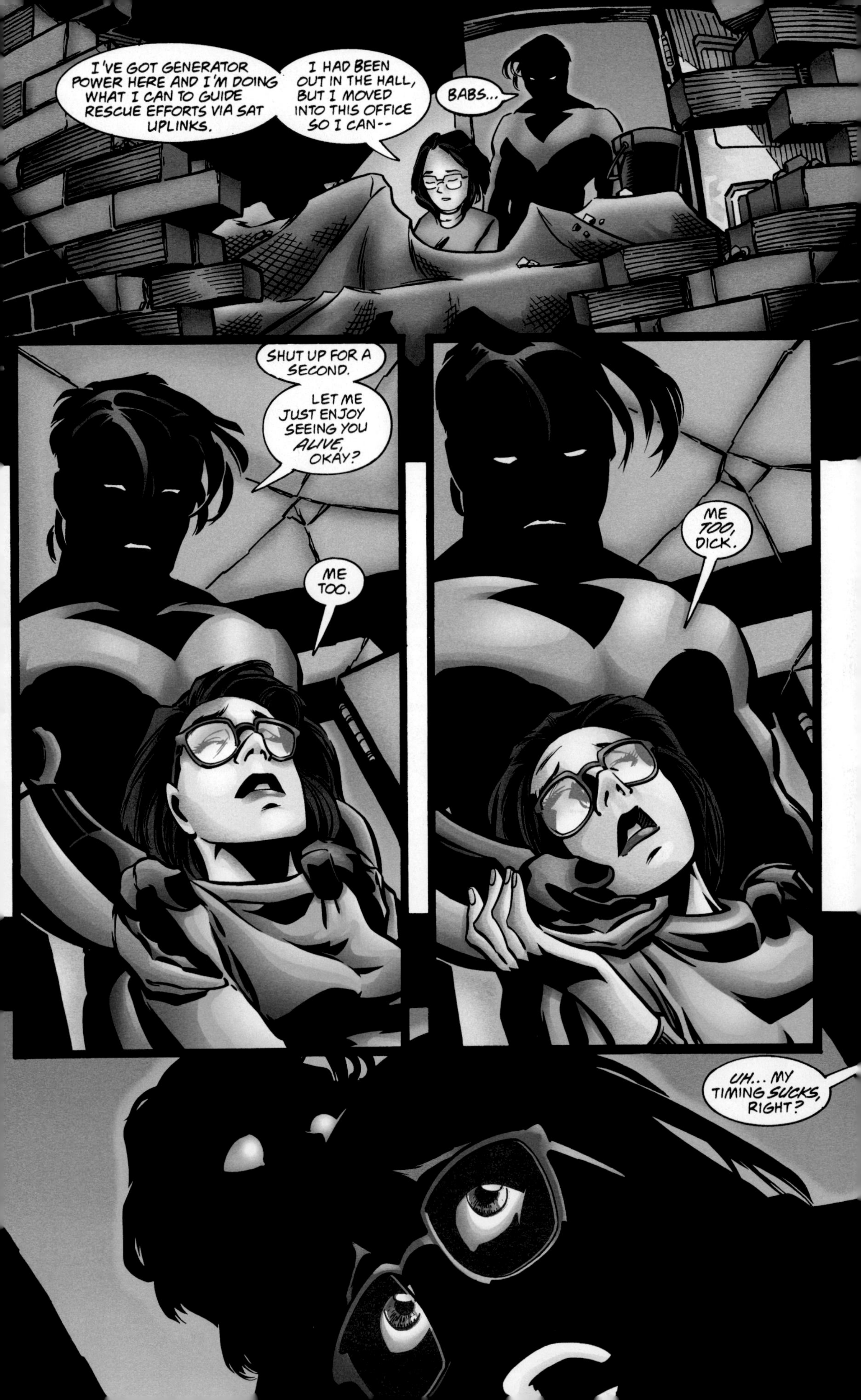
I'VE GOT GENERATOR POWER HERE AND I'M DOING WHAT I CAN TO GUIDE RESCUE EFFORTS VIA SAT UPLINKS.
I HAD BEEN OUT IN THE HALL, BUT I MOVED INTO THIS OFFICE SO I CAN--
BABS...
SHUT UP FOR A SECOND.
LET ME JUST ENJOY SEEING YOU *ALIVE*, OKAY?
ME TOO.
ME *TOO*, DICK.
UH... MY TIMING *SUCKS*, RIGHT?

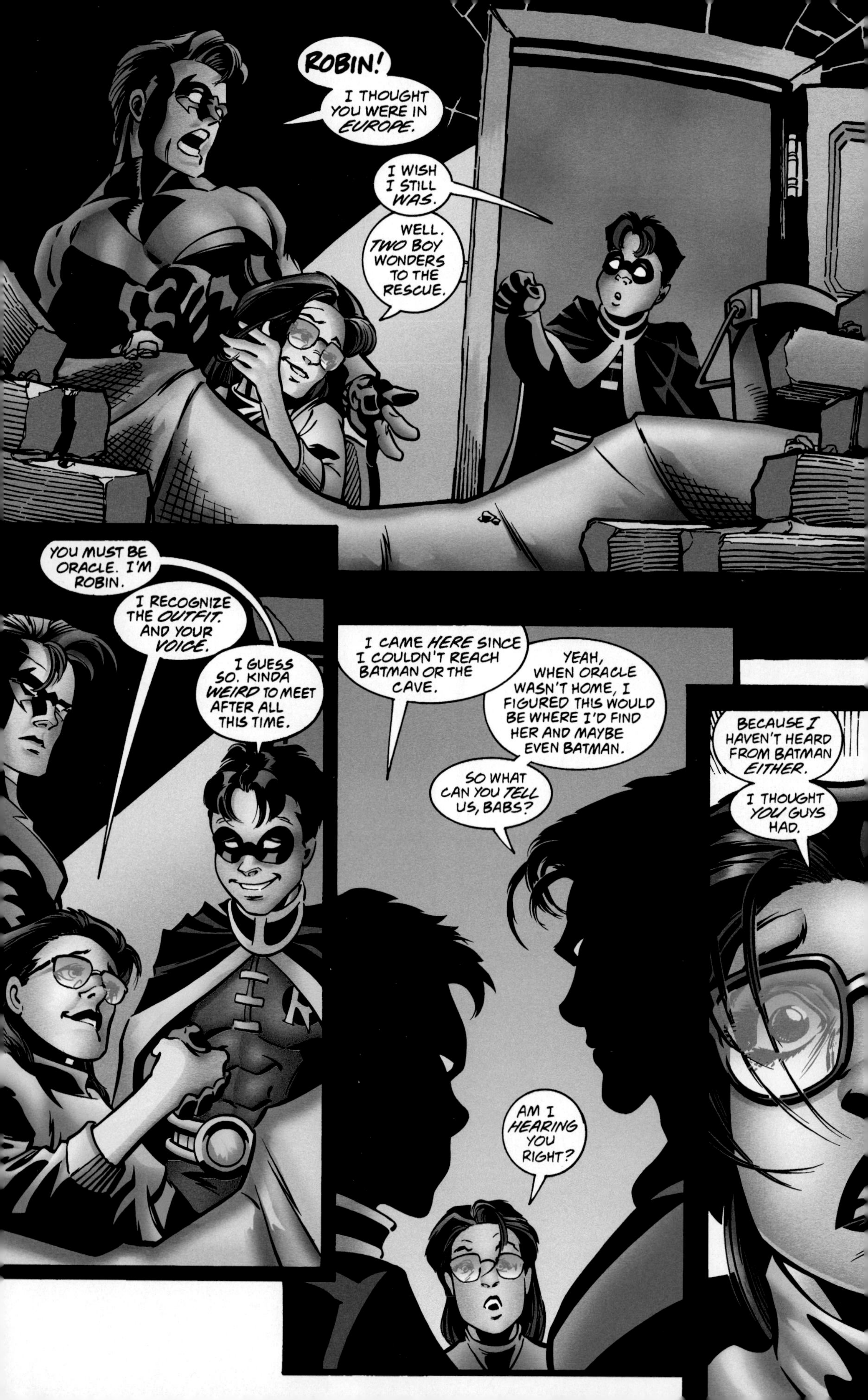
ROBIN!
I THOUGHT YOU WERE IN EUROPE.
I WISH I STILL WAS.
WELL. TWO BOY WONDERS TO THE RESCUE.
YOU MUST BE ORACLE. I'M ROBIN.
I RECOGNIZE THE OUTFIT. AND YOUR VOICE.
I GUESS SO. KINDA WEIRD TO MEET AFTER ALL THIS TIME.
I CAME HERE SINCE I COULDN'T REACH BATMAN OR THE CAVE.
YEAH, WHEN ORACLE WASN'T HOME, I FIGURED THIS WOULD BE WHERE I'D FIND HER AND MAYBE EVEN BATMAN.
SO WHAT CAN YOU TELL US, BABS?
AM I HEARING YOU RIGHT?
BECAUSE I HAVEN'T HEARD FROM BATMAN EITHER.
I THOUGHT YOU GUYS HAD.

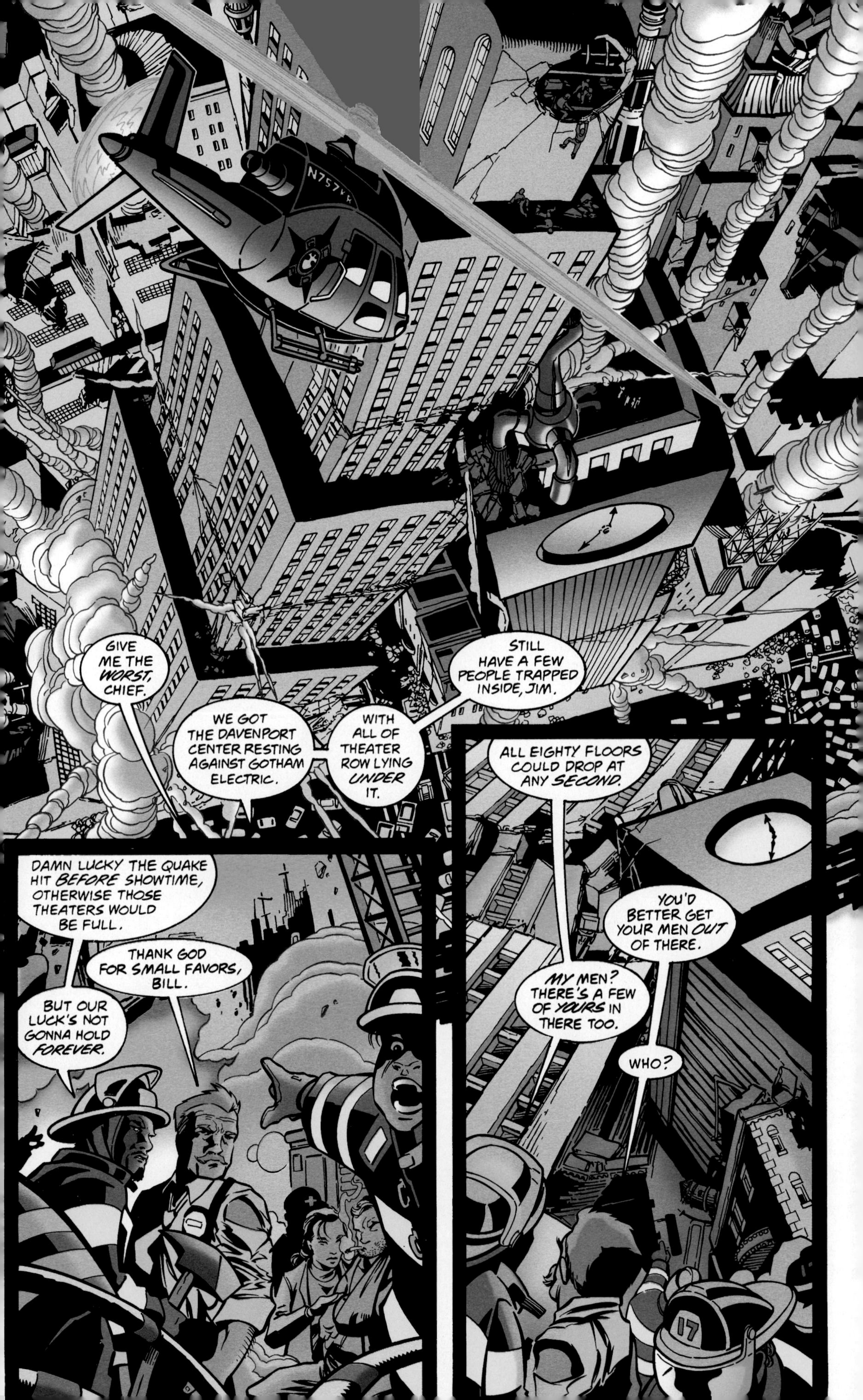
GIVE ME THE WORST, CHIEF.
WE GOT THE DAVENPORT CENTER RESTING AGAINST GOTHAM ELECTRIC.
WITH ALL OF THEATER ROW LYING UNDER IT.
STILL HAVE A FEW PEOPLE TRAPPED INSIDE, JIM.
DAMN LUCKY THE QUAKE HIT BEFORE SHOWTIME, OTHERWISE THOSE THEATERS WOULD BE FULL.
THANK GOD FOR SMALL FAVORS, BILL.
BUT OUR LUCK'S NOT GONNA HOLD FOREVER.
ALL EIGHTY FLOORS COULD DROP AT ANY SECOND.
YOU'D BETTER GET YOUR MEN OUT OF THERE.
MY MEN? THERE'S A FEW OF YOURS IN THERE TOO.
WHO?

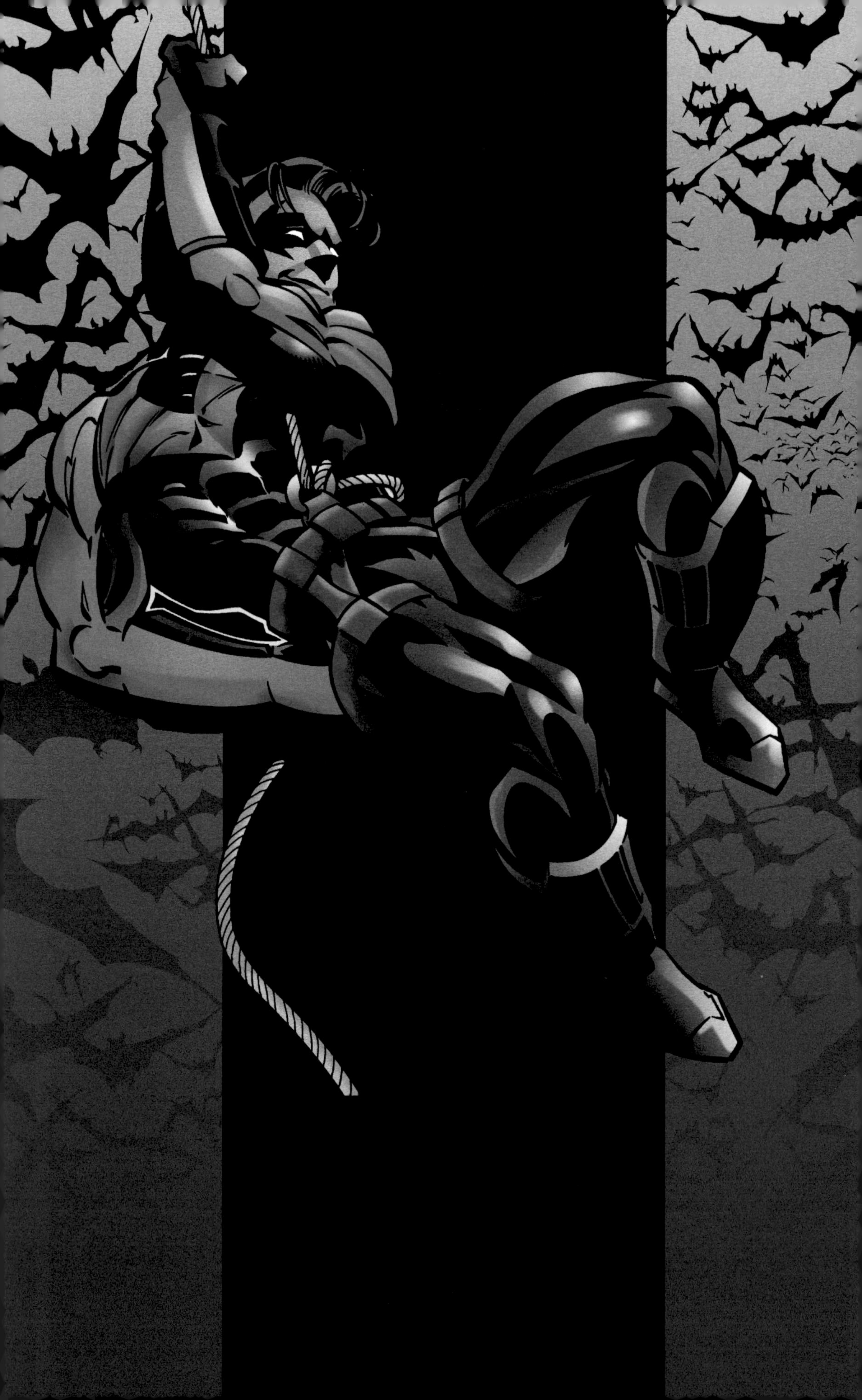

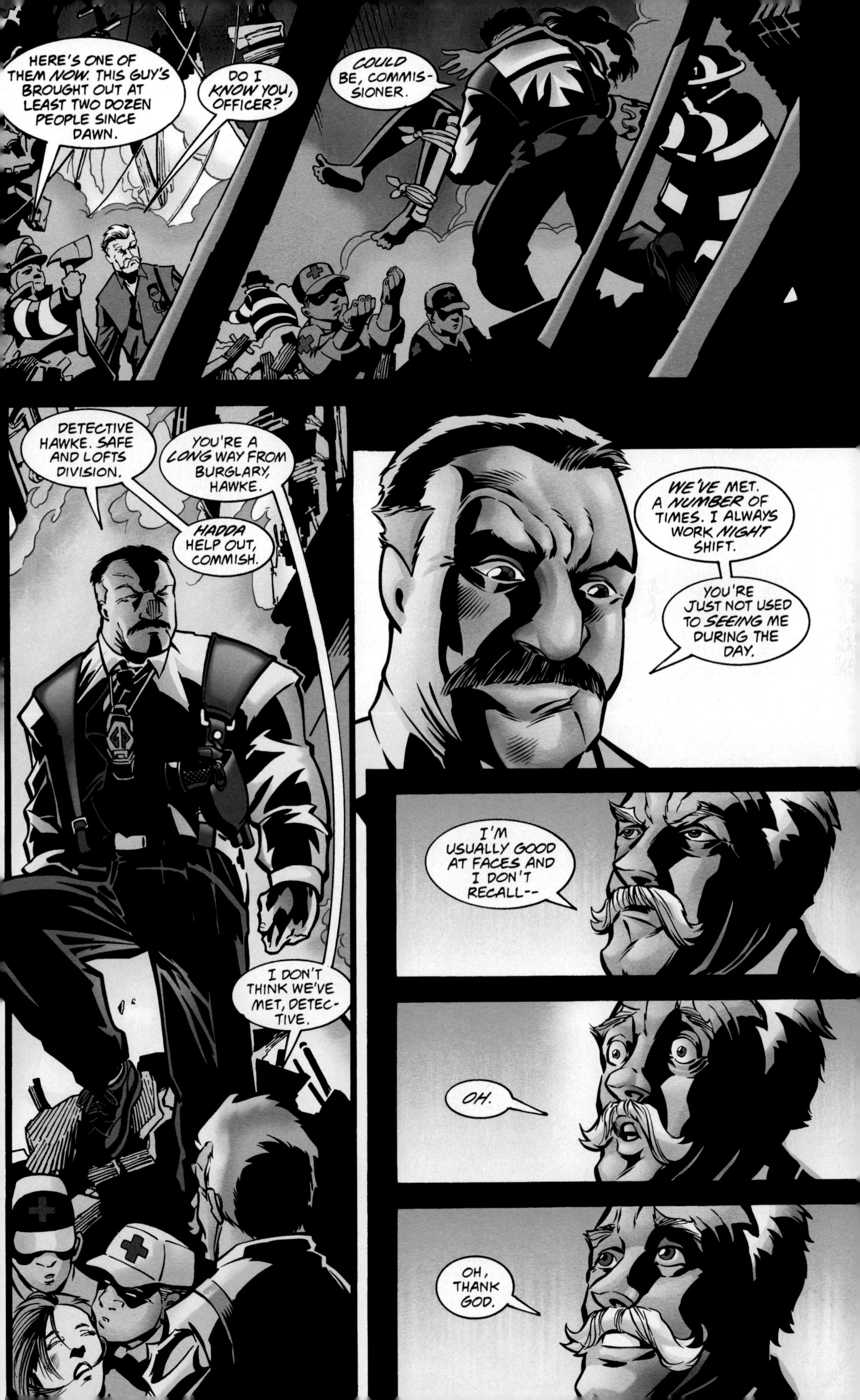
HERE'S ONE OF THEM NOW. THIS GUY'S BROUGHT OUT AT LEAST TWO DOZEN PEOPLE SINCE DAWN.
DO I KNOW YOU, OFFICER?
COULD BE, COMMIS-SIONER.
DETECTIVE HAWKE. SAFE AND LOFTS DIVISION.
YOU'RE A LONG WAY FROM BURGLARY, HAWKE.
HADDA HELP OUT, COMMISH.
I DON'T THINK WE'VE MET, DETEC-TIVE.
WE'VE MET. A NUMBER OF TIMES. I ALWAYS WORK NIGHT SHIFT.
YOU'RE JUST NOT USED TO SEEING ME DURING THE DAY.
I'M USUALLY GOOD AT FACES AND I DON'T RECALL--
OH.
OH, THANK GOD.

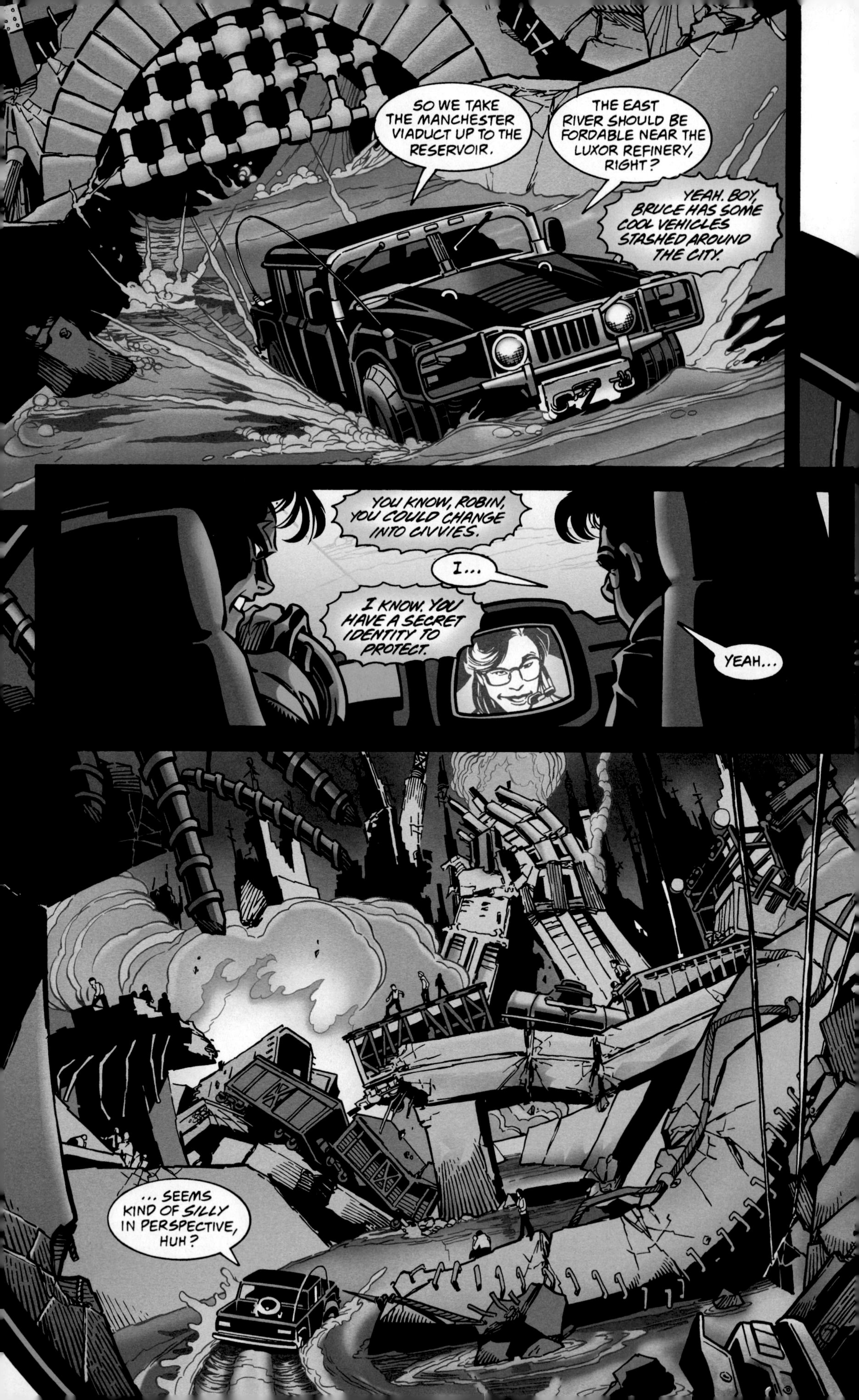
SO WE TAKE THE MANCHESTER VIADUCT UP TO THE RESERVOIR.
THE EAST RIVER SHOULD BE FORDABLE NEAR THE LUXOR REFINERY, RIGHT?
YEAH. BOY, BRUCE HAS SOME COOL VEHICLES STASHED AROUND THE CITY.
YOU KNOW, ROBIN, YOU COULD CHANGE INTO CIVVIES.
I...
I KNOW. YOU HAVE A SECRET IDENTITY TO PROTECT.
YEAH...
... SEEMS KIND OF SILLY IN PERSPECTIVE, HUH?

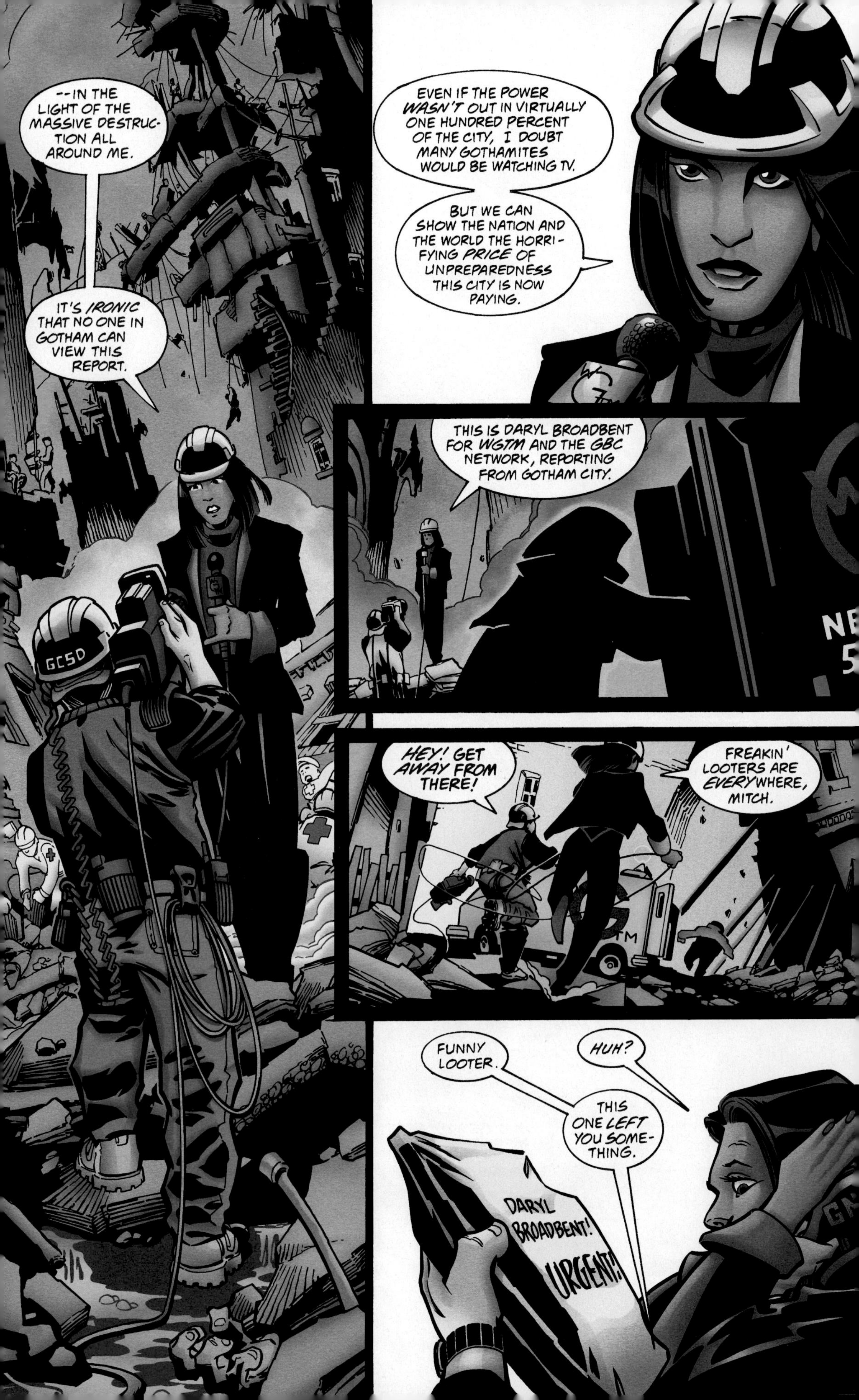
--IN THE LIGHT OF THE MASSIVE DESTRUCTION ALL AROUND ME.
IT'S IRONIC THAT NO ONE IN GOTHAM CAN VIEW THIS REPORT.
EVEN IF THE POWER WASN'T OUT IN VIRTUALLY ONE HUNDRED PERCENT OF THE CITY, I DOUBT MANY GOTHAMITES WOULD BE WATCHING TV.
BUT WE CAN SHOW THE NATION AND THE WORLD THE HORRIFYING PRICE OF UNPREPAREDNESS THIS CITY IS NOW PAYING.
GCSD
THIS IS DARYL BROADBENT FOR WGTM AND THE GBC NETWORK, REPORTING FROM GOTHAM CITY.
HEY! GET AWAY FROM THERE!
FREAKIN' LOOTERS ARE EVERYWHERE, MITCH.
FUNNY LOOTER.
HUH?
THIS ONE LEFT YOU SOMETHING.
DARYL BROADBENT! URGENT!

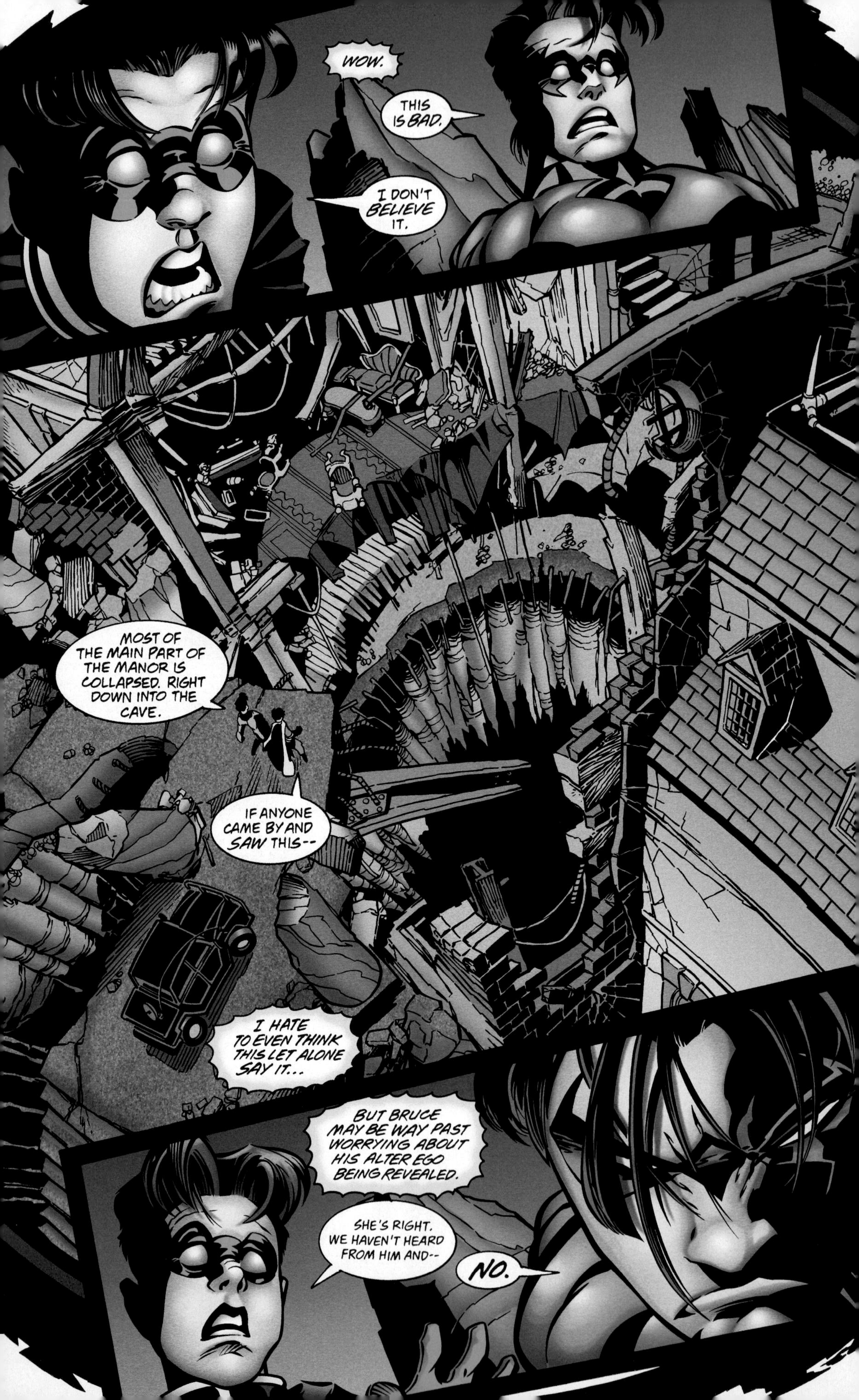
WOW.
THIS IS BAD.
I DON'T BELIEVE IT.
MOST OF THE MAIN PART OF THE MANOR IS COLLAPSED. RIGHT DOWN INTO THE CAVE.
IF ANYONE CAME BY AND SAW THIS--
I HATE TO EVEN THINK THIS LET ALONE SAY IT...
BUT BRUCE MAY BE WAY PAST WORRYING ABOUT HIS ALTER EGO BEING REVEALED.
SHE'S RIGHT. WE HAVEN'T HEARD FROM HIM AND--
NO.

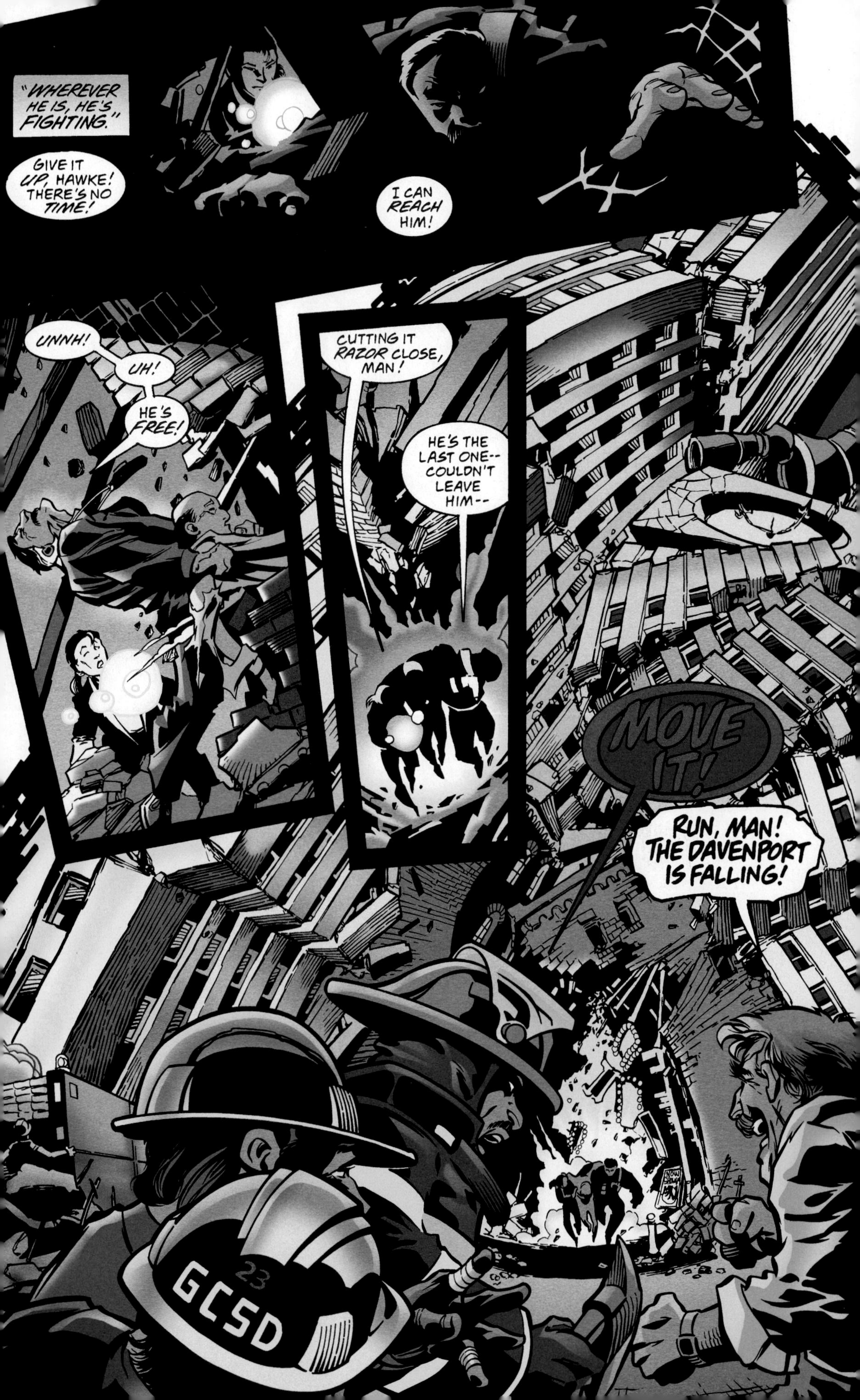
"WHEREVER HE IS, HE'S FIGHTING."
GIVE IT UP, HAWKE! THERE'S NO TIME!
I CAN REACH HIM!
UNNH!
UH!
HE'S FREE!
CUTTING IT RAZOR CLOSE, MAN!
HE'S THE LAST ONE-- COULDN'T LEAVE HIM--
MOVE IT!
RUN, MAN! THE DAVENPORT IS FALLING!
GCSD
23

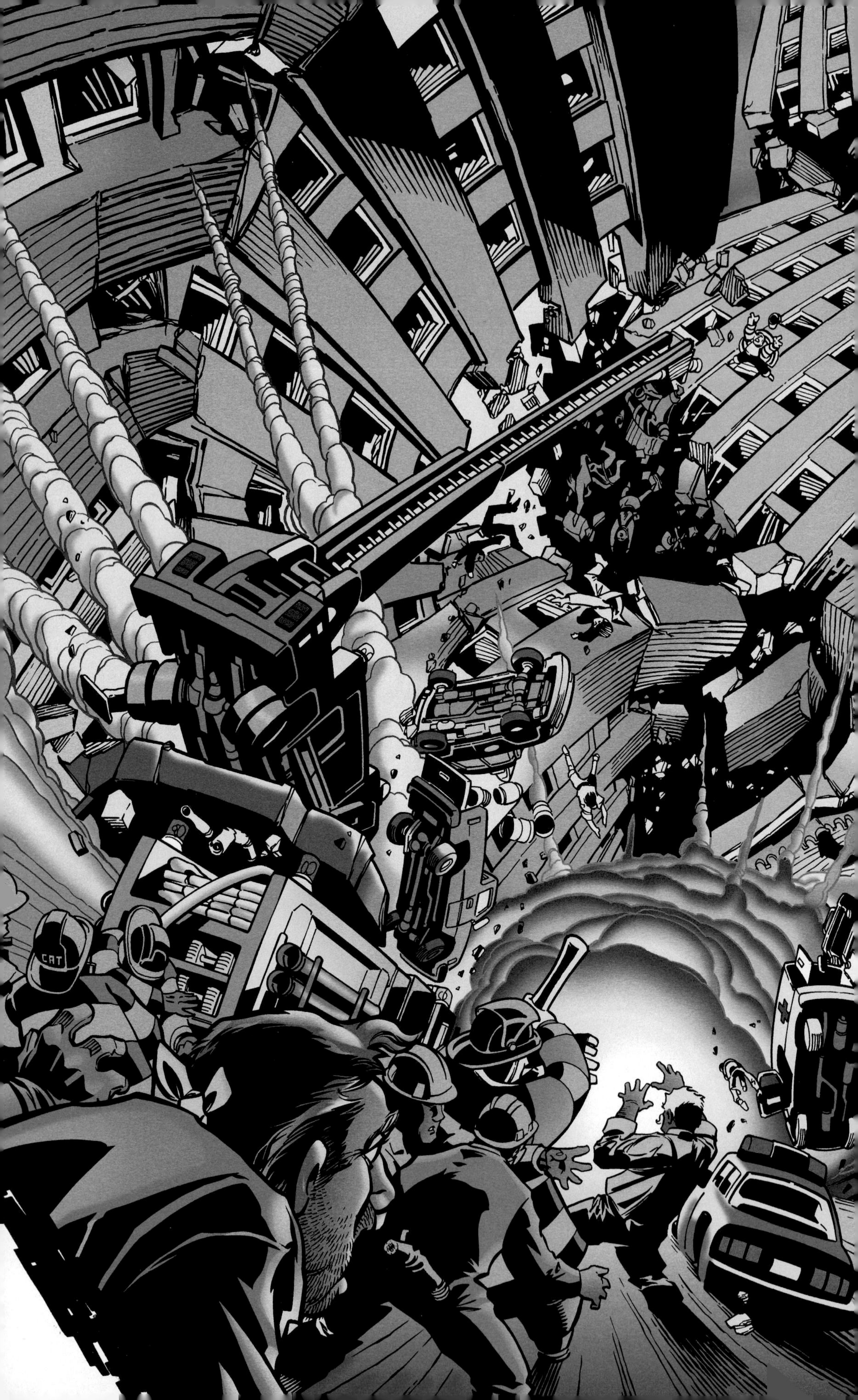
CAT

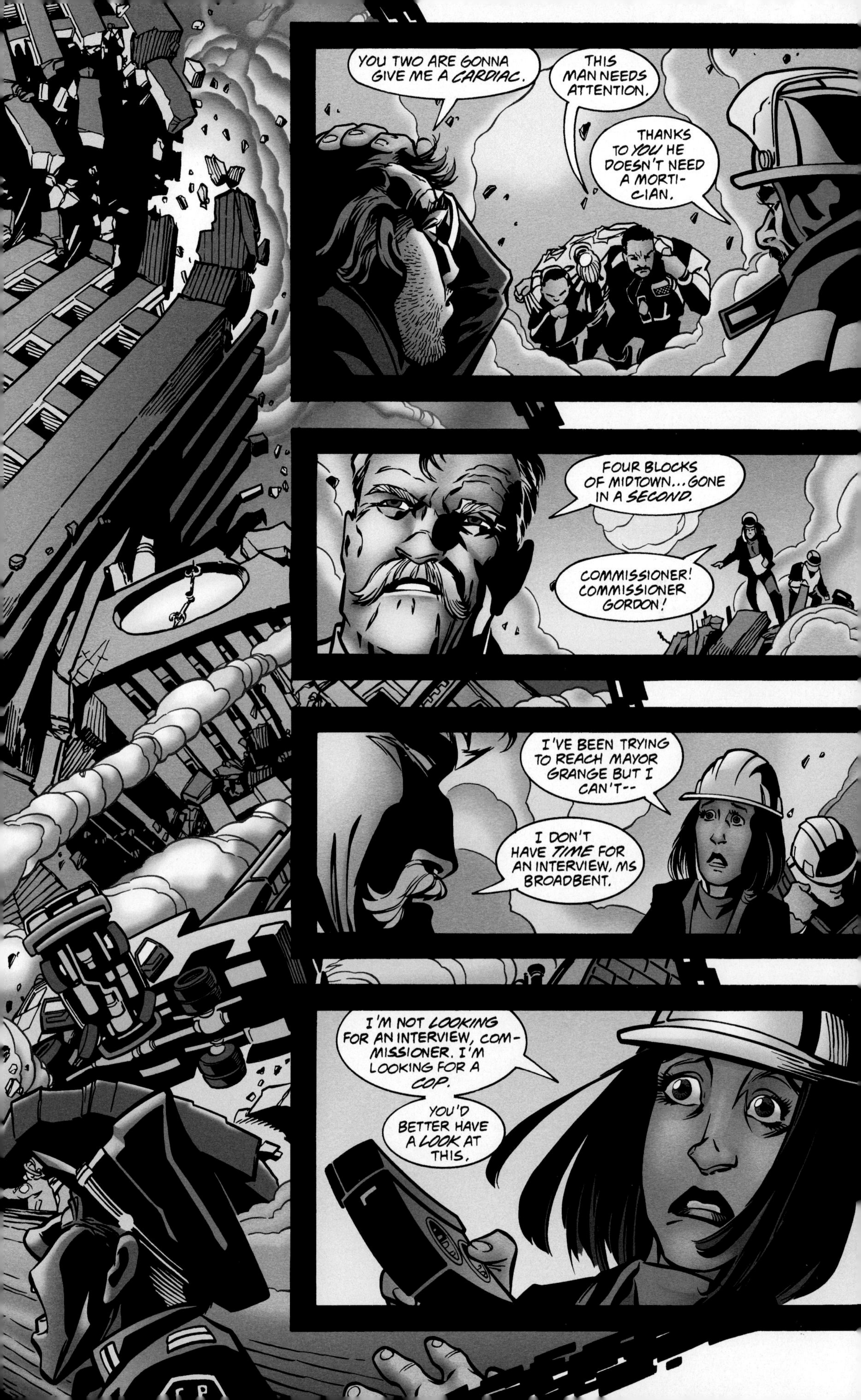
YOU TWO ARE GONNA GIVE ME A CARDIAC.
THIS MAN NEEDS ATTENTION.
THANKS TO YOU HE DOESN'T NEED A MORTI-CIAN.
FOUR BLOCKS OF MIDTOWN... GONE IN A SECOND.
COMMISSIONER! COMMISSIONER GORDON!
I'VE BEEN TRYING TO REACH MAYOR GRANGE BUT I CAN'T--
I DON'T HAVE TIME FOR AN INTERVIEW, MS BROADBENT.
I'M NOT LOOKING FOR AN INTERVIEW, COM-MISSIONER. I'M LOOKING FOR A COP.
YOU'D BETTER HAVE A LOOK AT THIS.

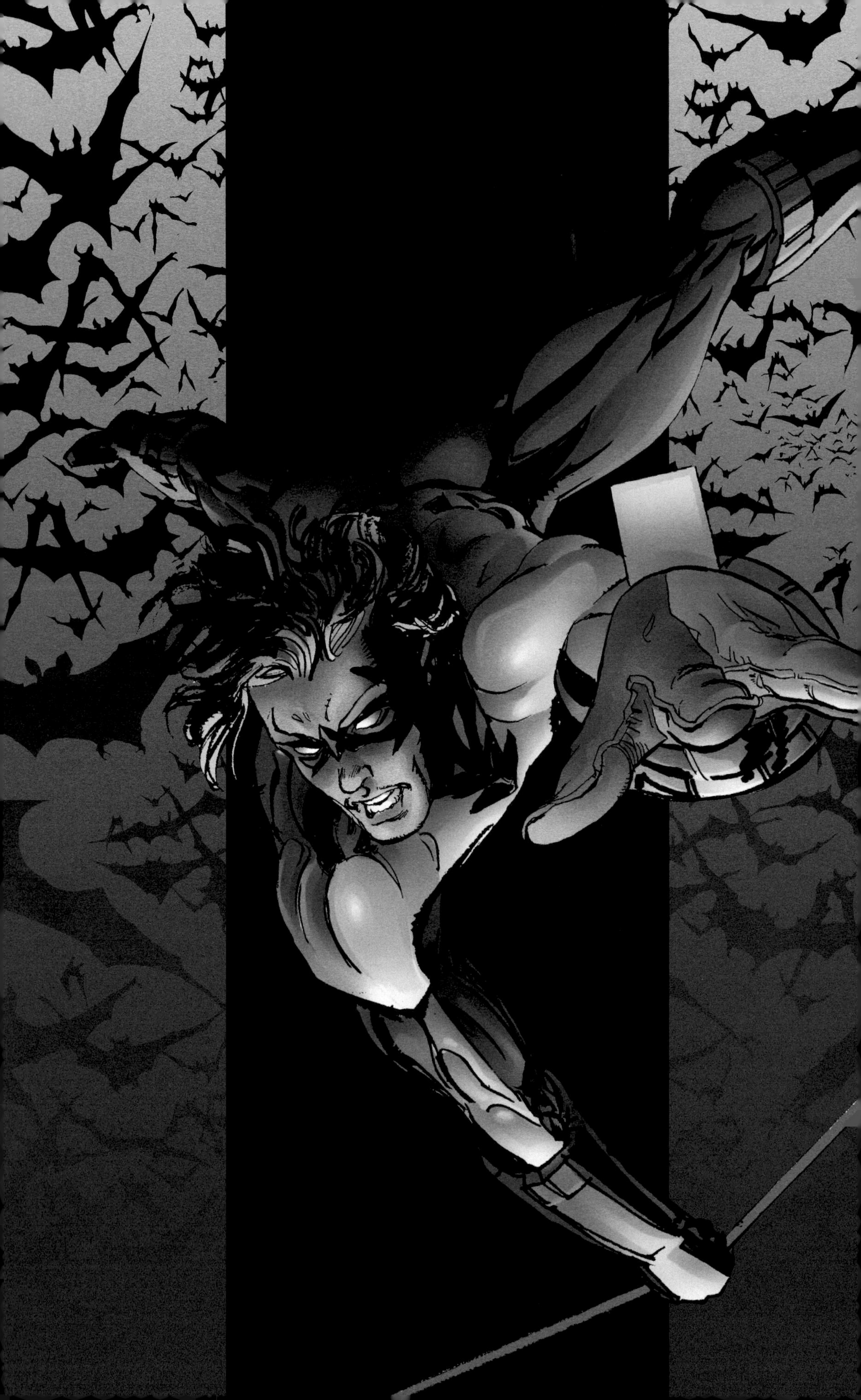

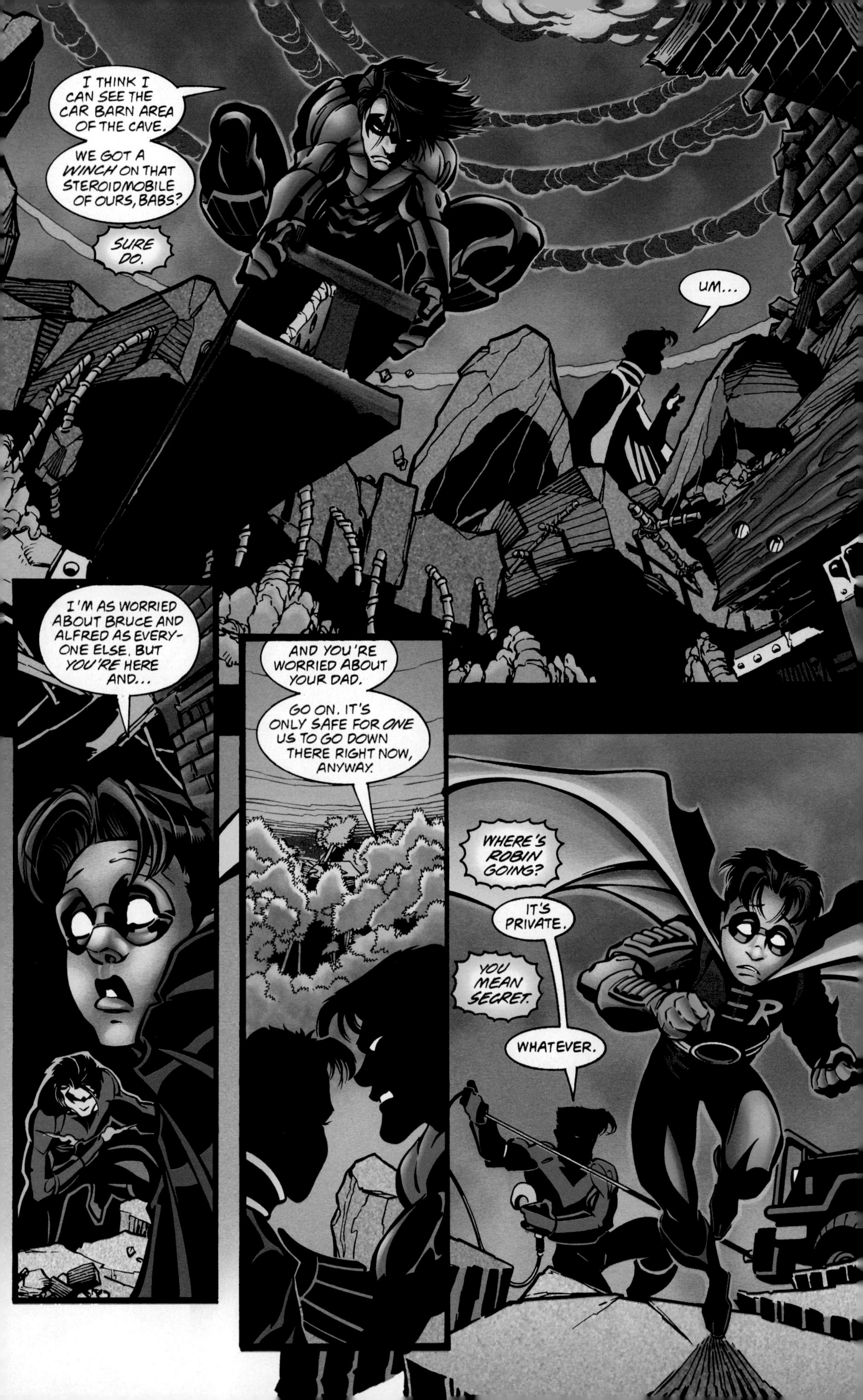

I THINK I CAN SEE THE CAR BARN AREA OF THE CAVE.
WE GOT A *WINCH* ON THAT STEROIDMOBILE OF OURS, BABS?
SURE DO.
UM...
I'M AS WORRIED ABOUT BRUCE AND ALFRED AS EVERY-ONE ELSE. BUT *YOU'RE* HERE AND...
AND YOU'RE WORRIED ABOUT YOUR DAD.
GO ON. IT'S ONLY SAFE FOR *ONE* US TO GO DOWN THERE RIGHT NOW, ANYWAY.
WHERE'S ROBIN GOING?
IT'S PRIVATE.
YOU MEAN SECRET.
WHATEVER.

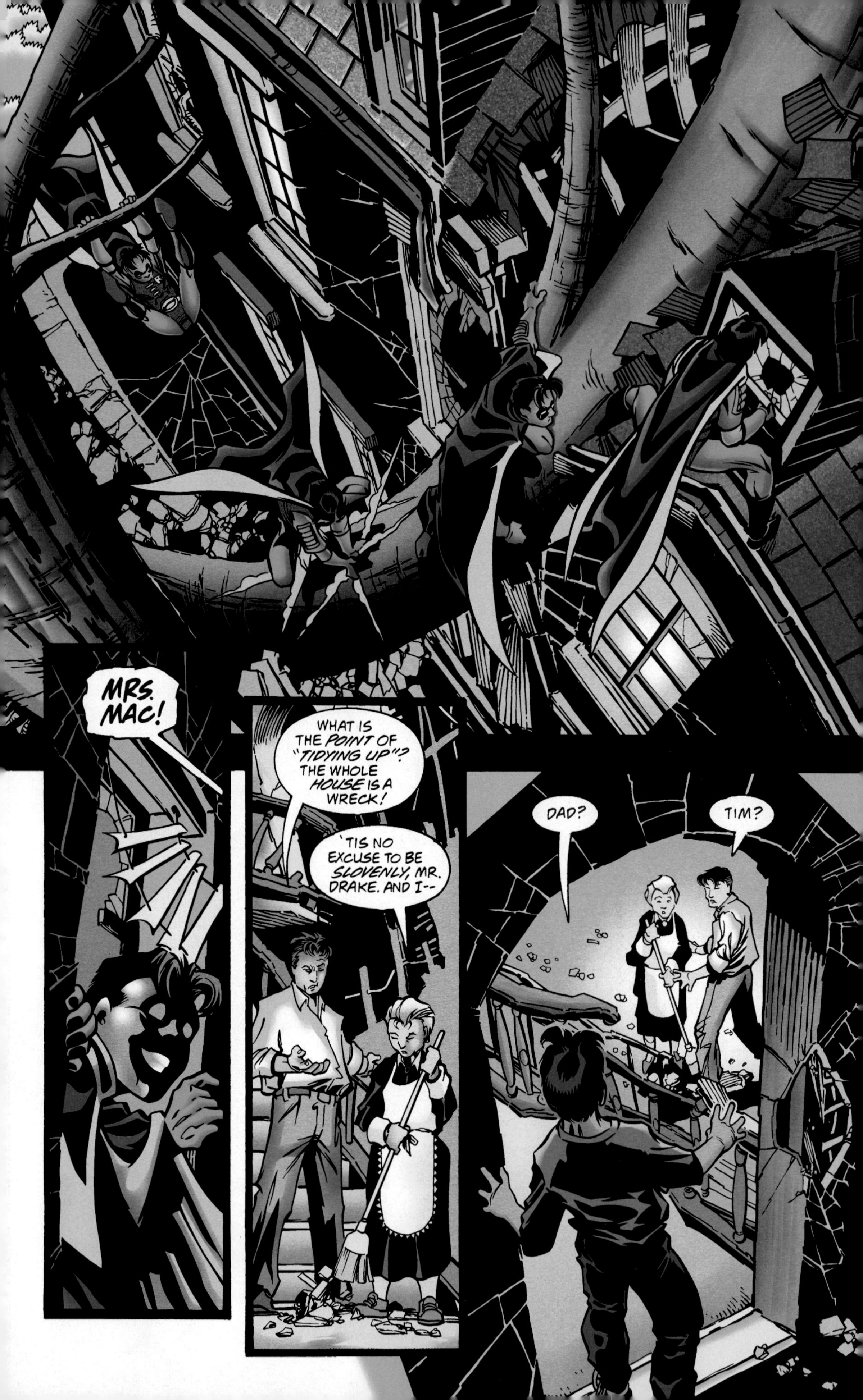
MRS. MAC!
WHAT IS THE POINT OF "TIDYING UP"? THE WHOLE HOUSE IS A WRECK!
'TIS NO EXCUSE TO BE SLOVENLY, MR. DRAKE. AND I--
DAD?
TIM?

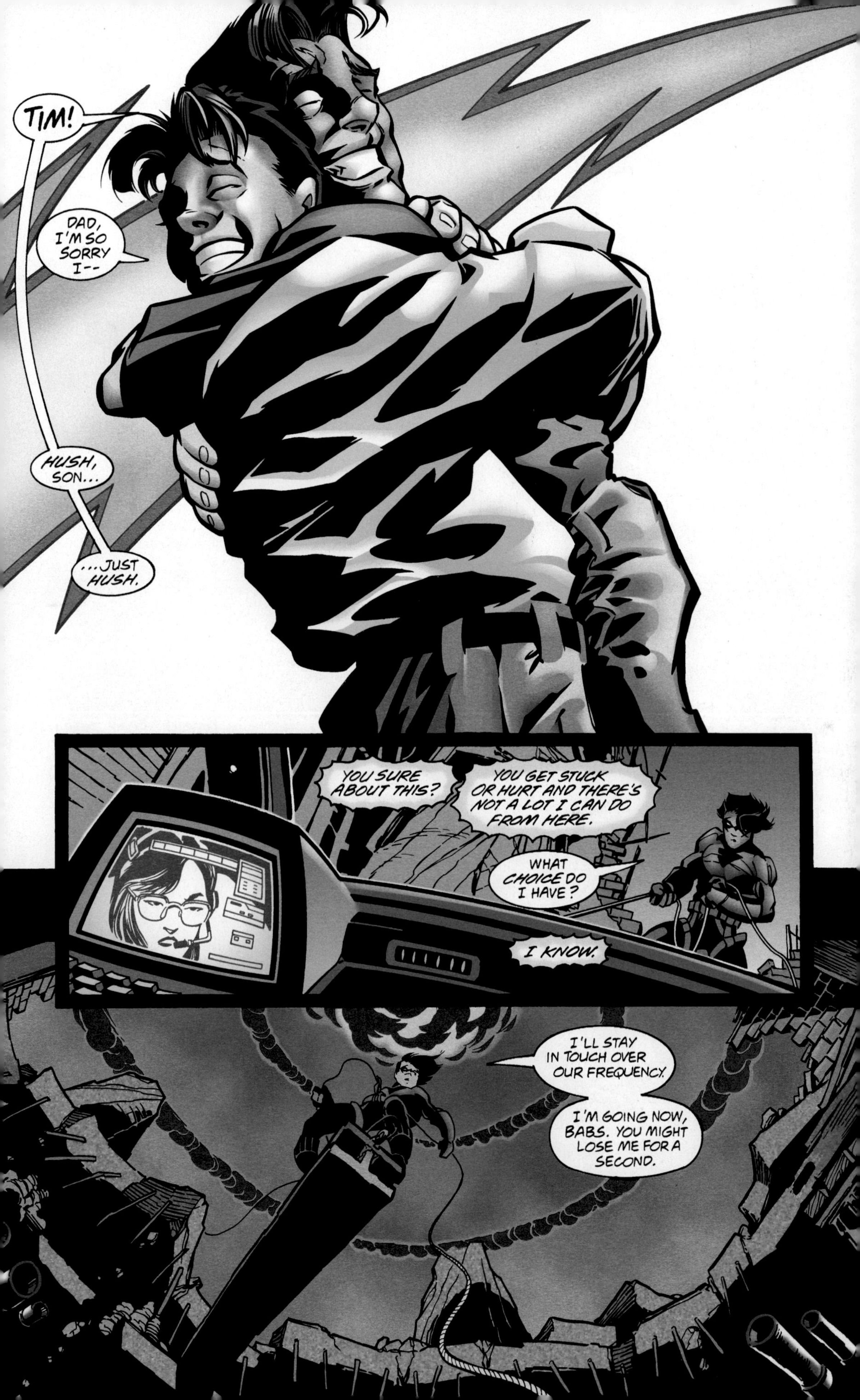
TIM!
DAD, I'M SO SORRY I--
HUSH, SON...
...JUST HUSH.
YOU SURE ABOUT THIS?
YOU GET STUCK OR HURT AND THERE'S NOT A LOT I CAN DO FROM HERE.
WHAT CHOICE DO I HAVE?
I KNOW.
I'LL STAY IN TOUCH OVER OUR FREQUENCY.
I'M GOING NOW, BABS. YOU MIGHT LOSE ME FOR A SECOND.

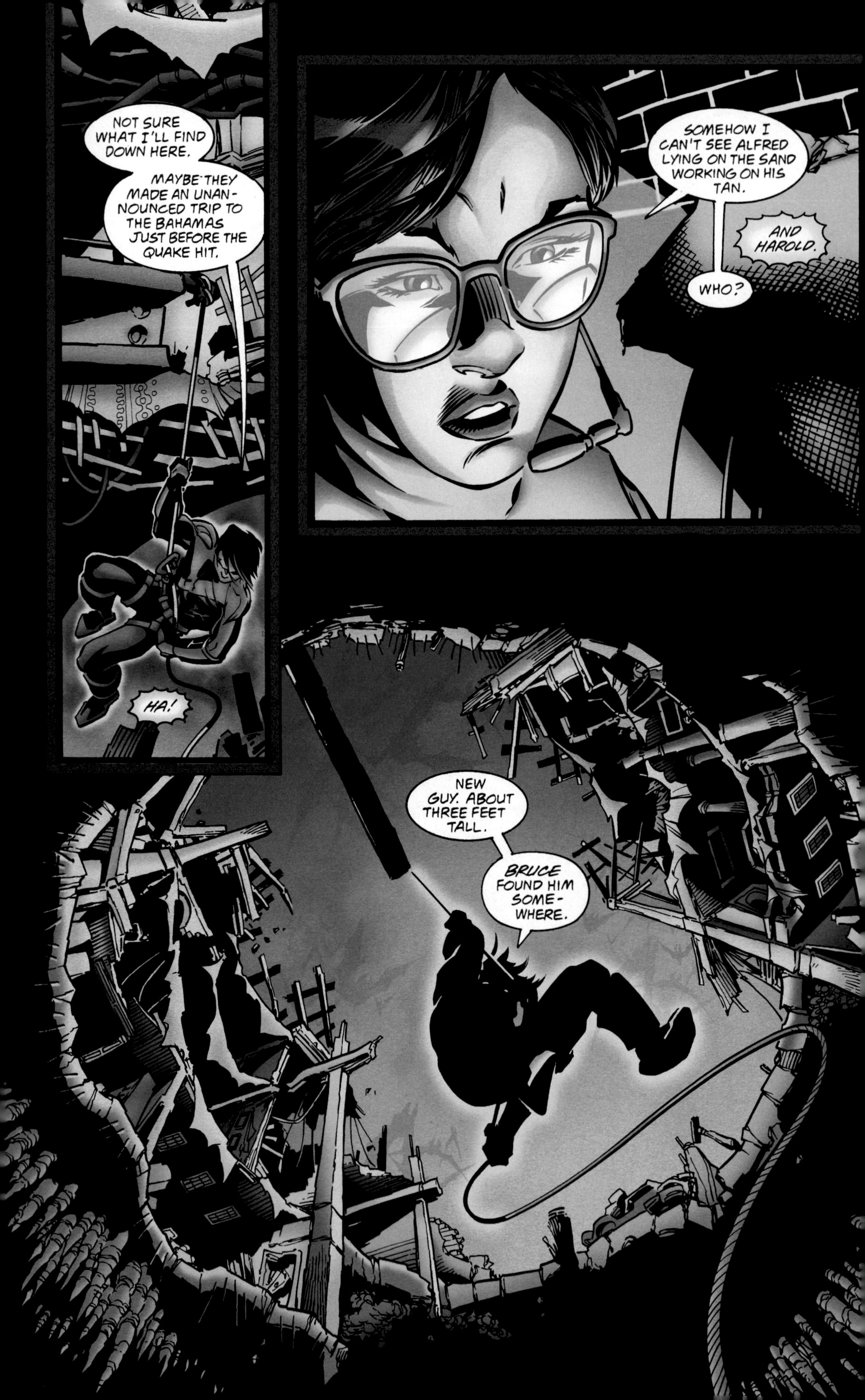
NOT SURE WHAT I'LL FIND DOWN HERE.
MAYBE THEY MADE AN UNANNOUNCED TRIP TO THE BAHAMAS JUST BEFORE THE QUAKE HIT.
SOMEHOW I CAN'T SEE ALFRED LYING ON THE SAND WORKING ON HIS TAN.
AND HAROLD.
WHO?
HA!
NEW GUY. ABOUT THREE FEET TALL.
BRUCE FOUND HIM SOMEWHERE.

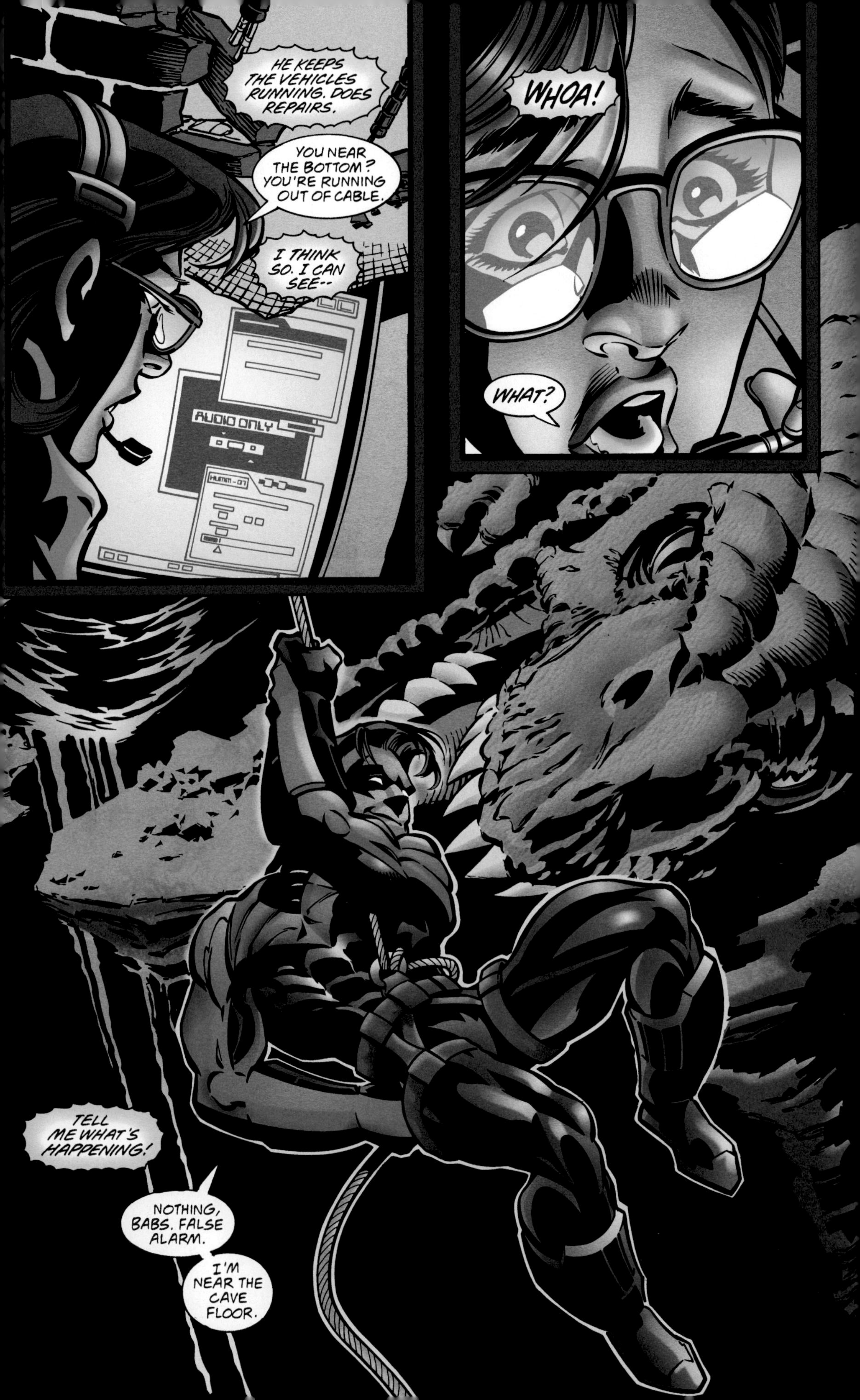
HE KEEPS THE VEHICLES RUNNING. DOES REPAIRS.
YOU NEAR THE BOTTOM? YOU'RE RUNNING OUT OF CABLE.
I THINK SO. I CAN SEE--
AUDIO ONLY
WHOA!
WHAT?
TELL ME WHAT'S HAPPENING!
NOTHING, BABS. FALSE ALARM.
I'M NEAR THE CAVE FLOOR.

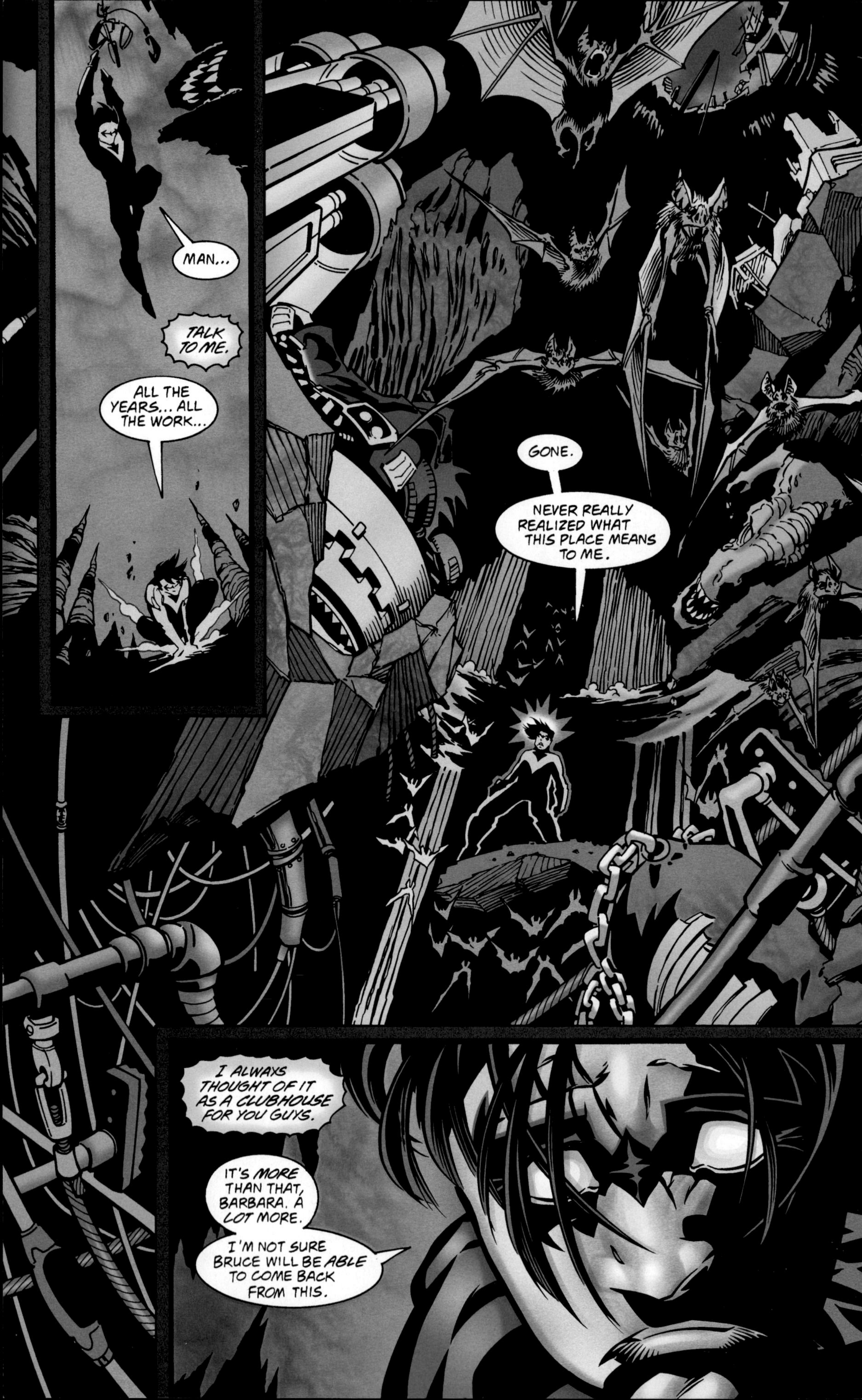
MAN...
TALK TO ME.
ALL THE YEARS... ALL THE WORK...
GONE.
NEVER REALLY REALIZED WHAT THIS PLACE MEANS TO ME.
I ALWAYS THOUGHT OF IT AS A CLUBHOUSE FOR YOU GUYS.
IT'S MORE THAN THAT, BARBARA. A LOT MORE.
I'M NOT SURE BRUCE WILL BE ABLE TO COME BACK FROM THIS.

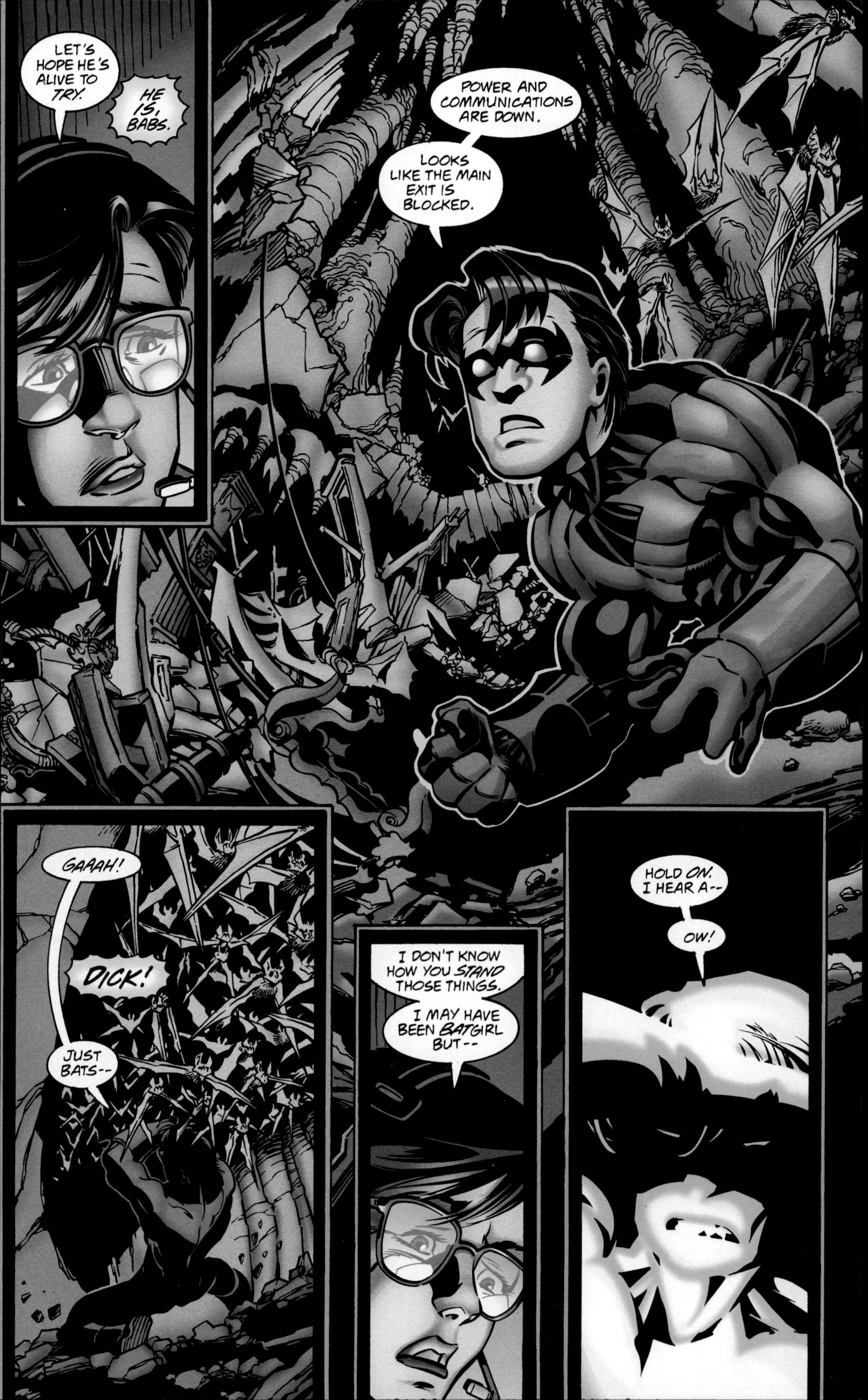
LET'S HOPE HE'S ALIVE TO TRY.
HE IS, BABS.
POWER AND COMMUNICATIONS ARE DOWN.
LOOKS LIKE THE MAIN EXIT IS BLOCKED.
GAAAH!
DICK!
JUST BATS--
I DON'T KNOW HOW YOU STAND THOSE THINGS.
I MAY HAVE BEEN BATGIRL BUT--
HOLD ON. I HEAR A--
OW!

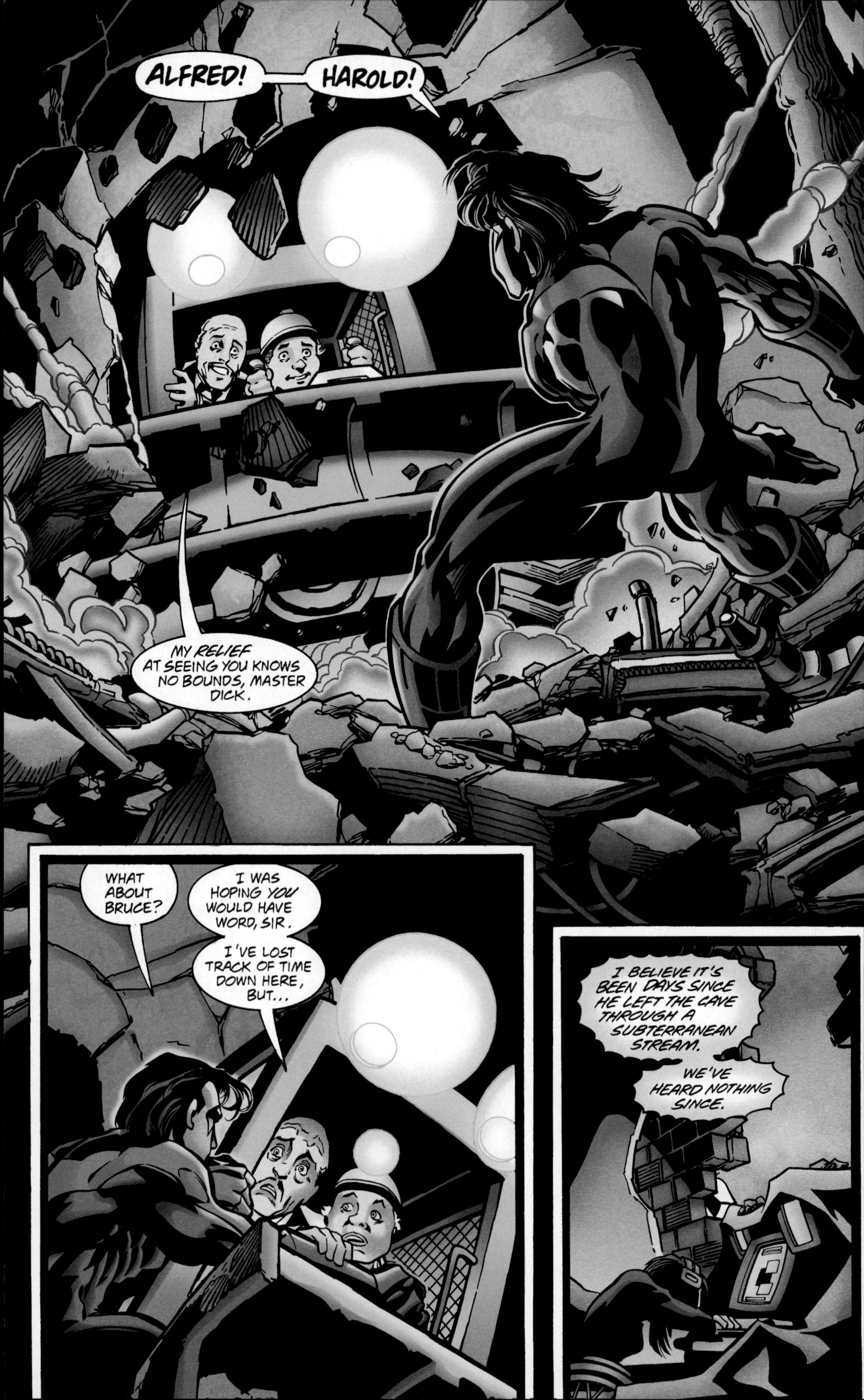
ALFRED!
HAROLD!
MY RELIEF AT SEEING YOU KNOWS NO BOUNDS, MASTER DICK.
WHAT ABOUT BRUCE?
I WAS HOPING YOU WOULD HAVE WORD, SIR.
I'VE LOST TRACK OF TIME DOWN HERE, BUT...
I BELIEVE IT'S BEEN DAYS SINCE HE LEFT THE CAVE THROUGH A SUBTERRANEAN STREAM.
WE'VE HEARD NOTHING SINCE.

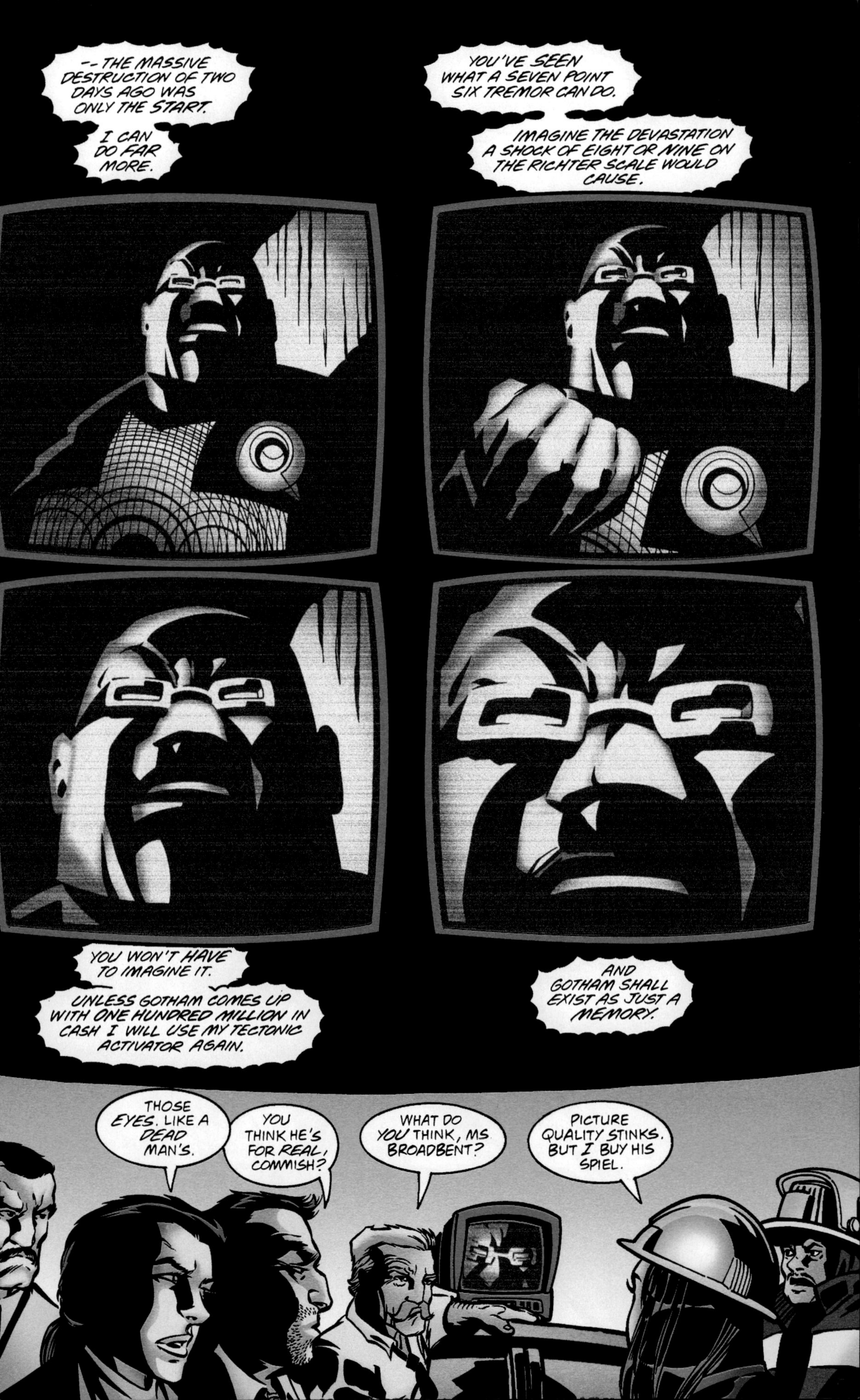
--THE MASSIVE DESTRUCTION OF TWO DAYS AGO WAS ONLY THE START.
I CAN DO FAR MORE.
YOU'VE SEEN WHAT A SEVEN POINT SIX TREMOR CAN DO.
IMAGINE THE DEVASTATION A SHOCK OF EIGHT OR NINE ON THE RICHTER SCALE WOULD CAUSE.
YOU WON'T HAVE TO IMAGINE IT.
UNLESS GOTHAM COMES UP WITH ONE HUNDRED MILLION IN CASH I WILL USE MY TECTONIC ACTIVATOR AGAIN.
AND GOTHAM SHALL EXIST AS JUST A MEMORY.
THOSE EYES. LIKE A DEAD MAN'S.
YOU THINK HE'S FOR REAL, COMMISH?
WHAT DO YOU THINK, MS. BROADBENT?
PICTURE QUALITY STINKS. BUT I BUY HIS SPIEL.

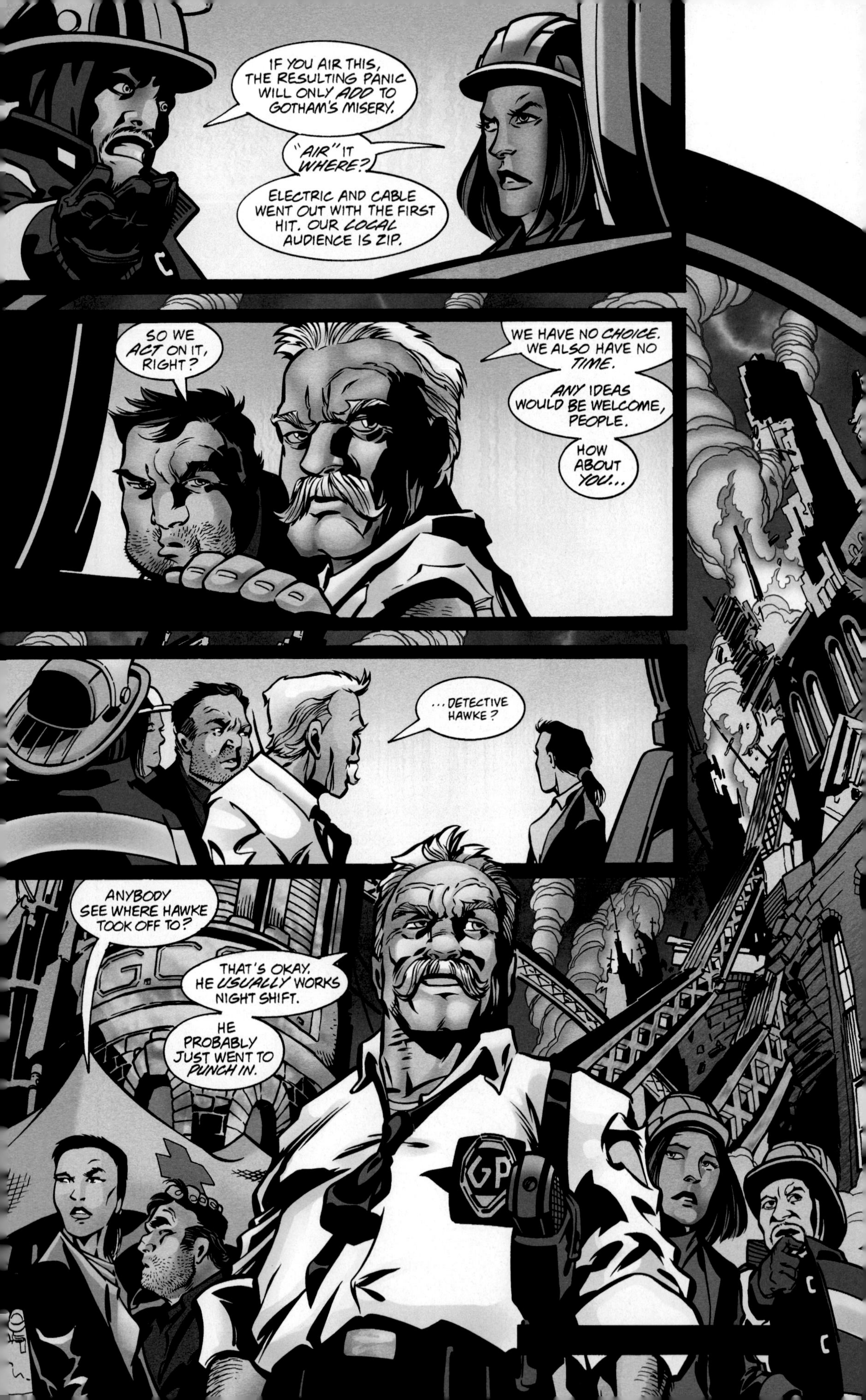
IF YOU AIR THIS, THE RESULTING PANIC WILL ONLY *ADD* TO GOTHAM'S MISERY.
"*AIR*" IT *WHERE?*
ELECTRIC AND CABLE WENT OUT WITH THE FIRST HIT. OUR *LOCAL* AUDIENCE IS ZIP.
SO WE *ACT* ON IT, RIGHT?
WE HAVE NO *CHOICE.* WE ALSO HAVE NO *TIME.*
ANY IDEAS WOULD BE WELCOME, PEOPLE.
HOW ABOUT *YOU*...
...DETECTIVE HAWKE?
ANYBODY SEE WHERE HAWKE TOOK OFF TO?
THAT'S OKAY. HE *USUALLY* WORKS NIGHT SHIFT.
HE PROBABLY JUST WENT TO *PUNCH IN.*

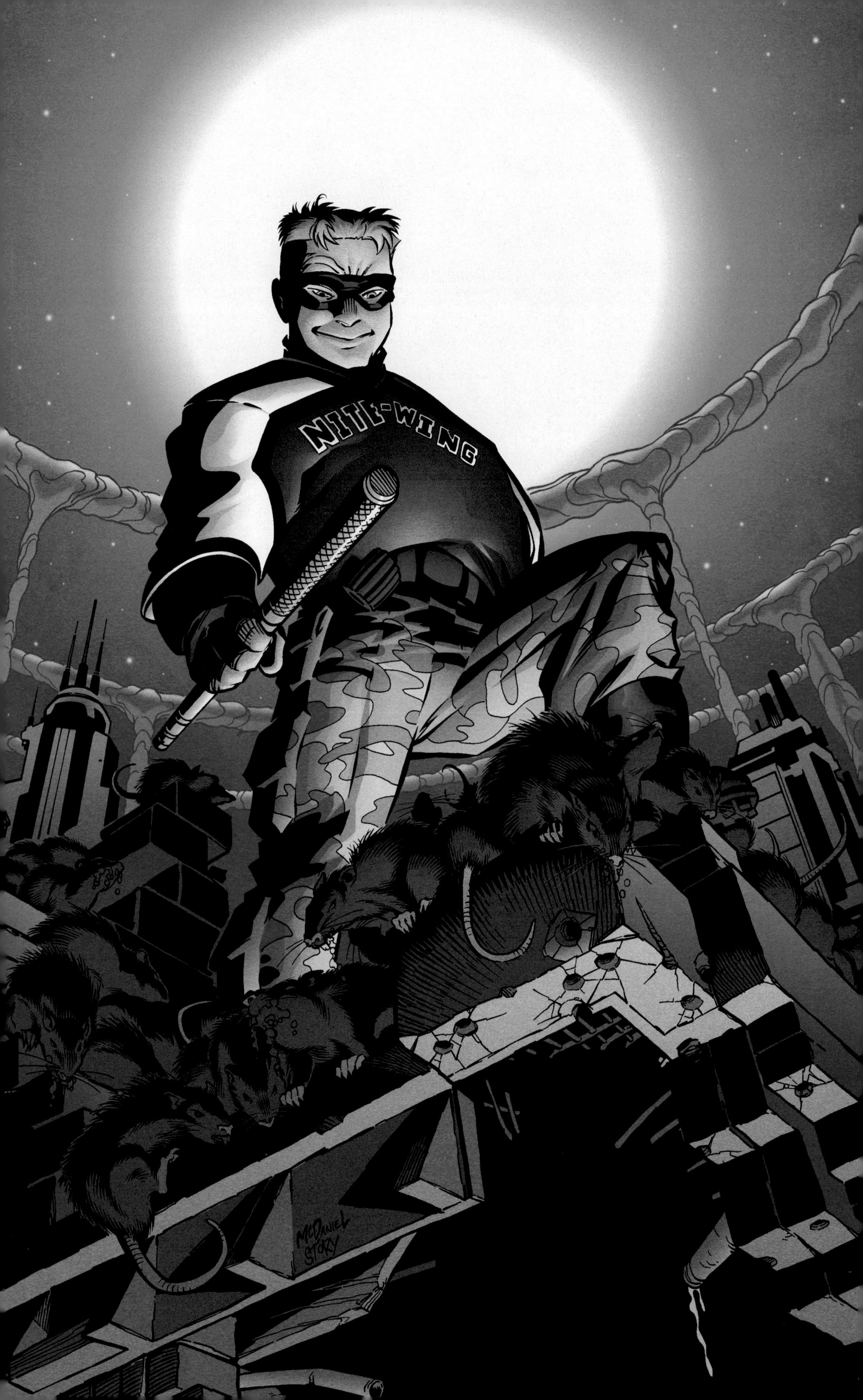
NITE-WING
McDANIEL
STORY

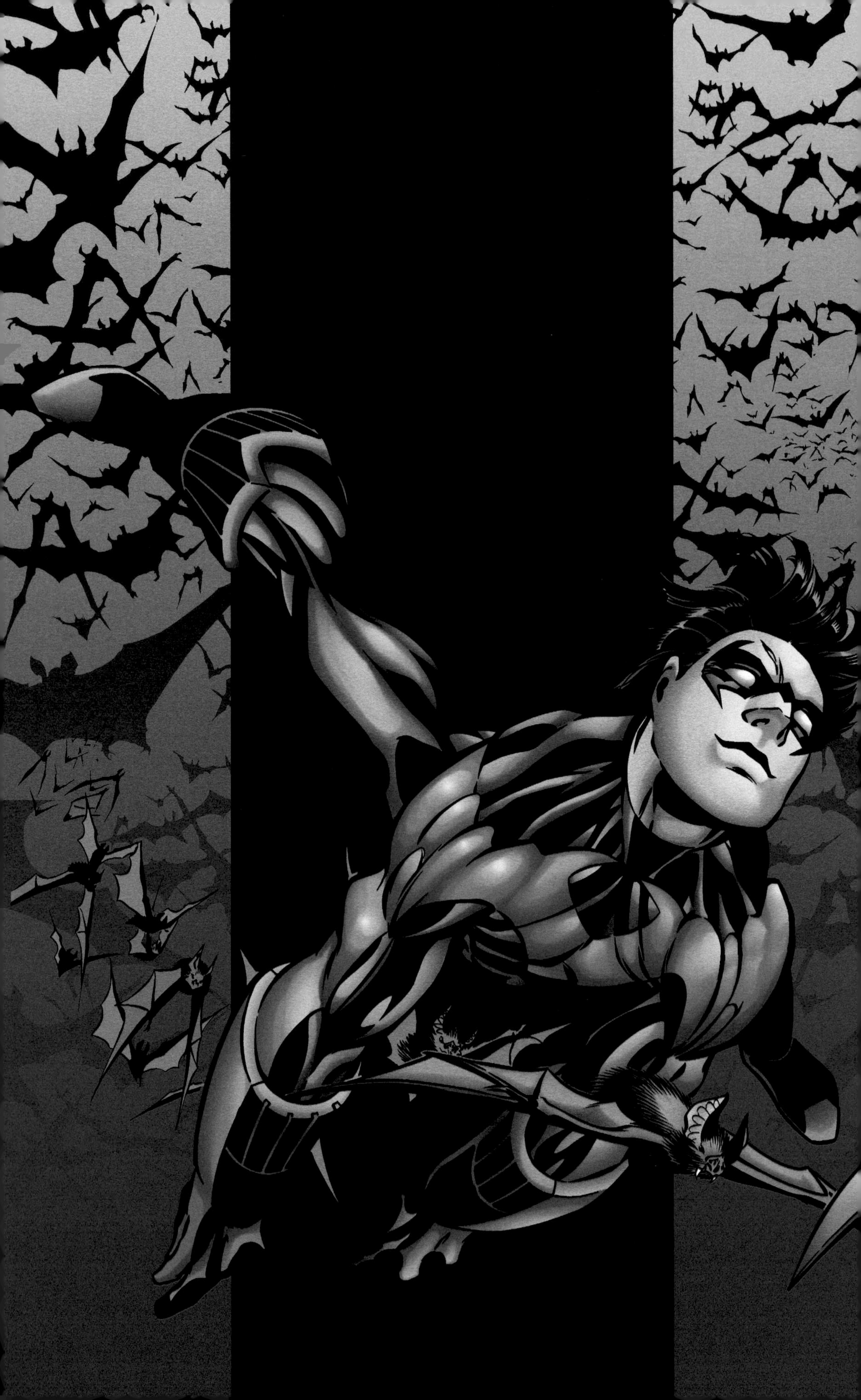

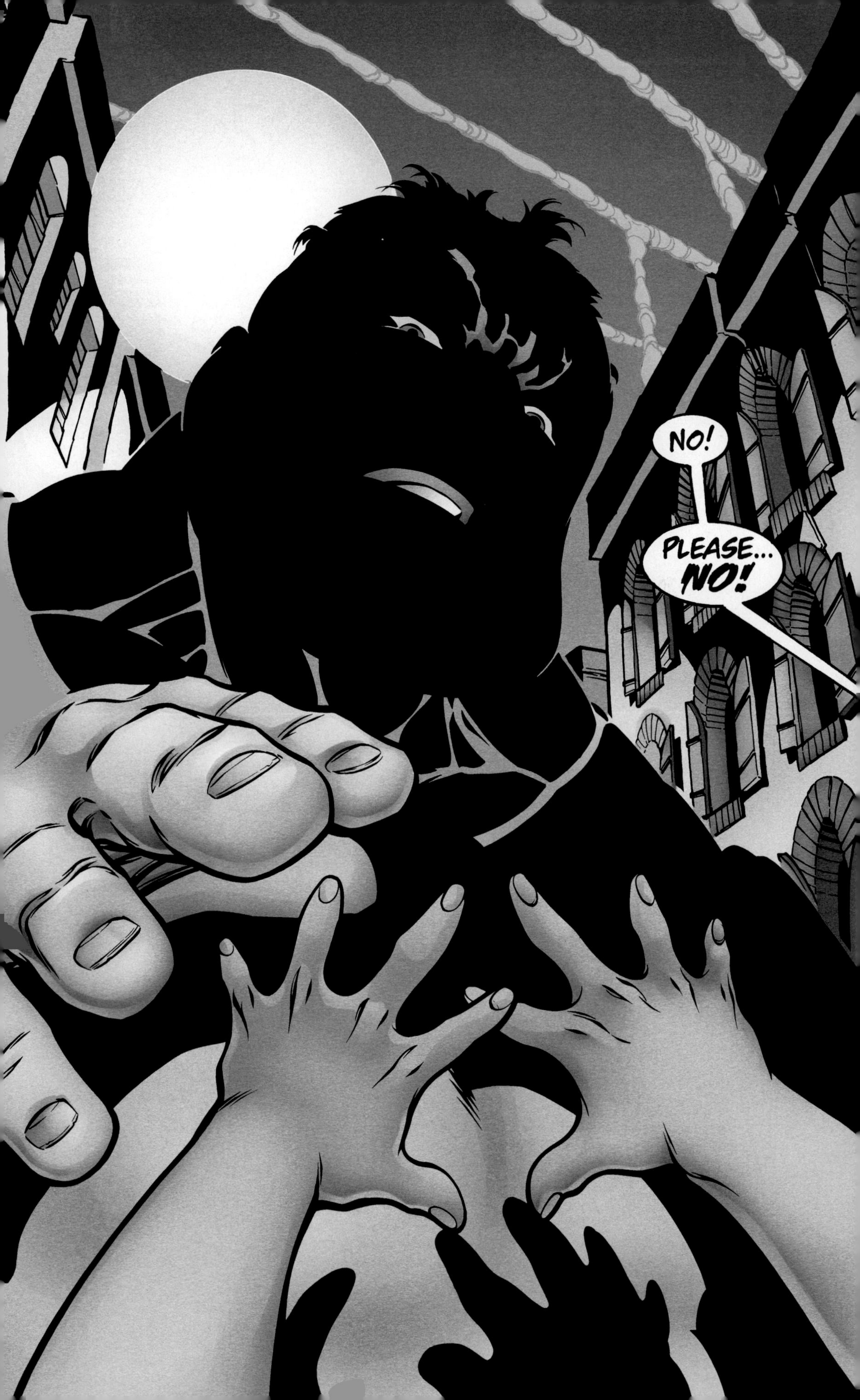
NO!
PLEASE... NO!

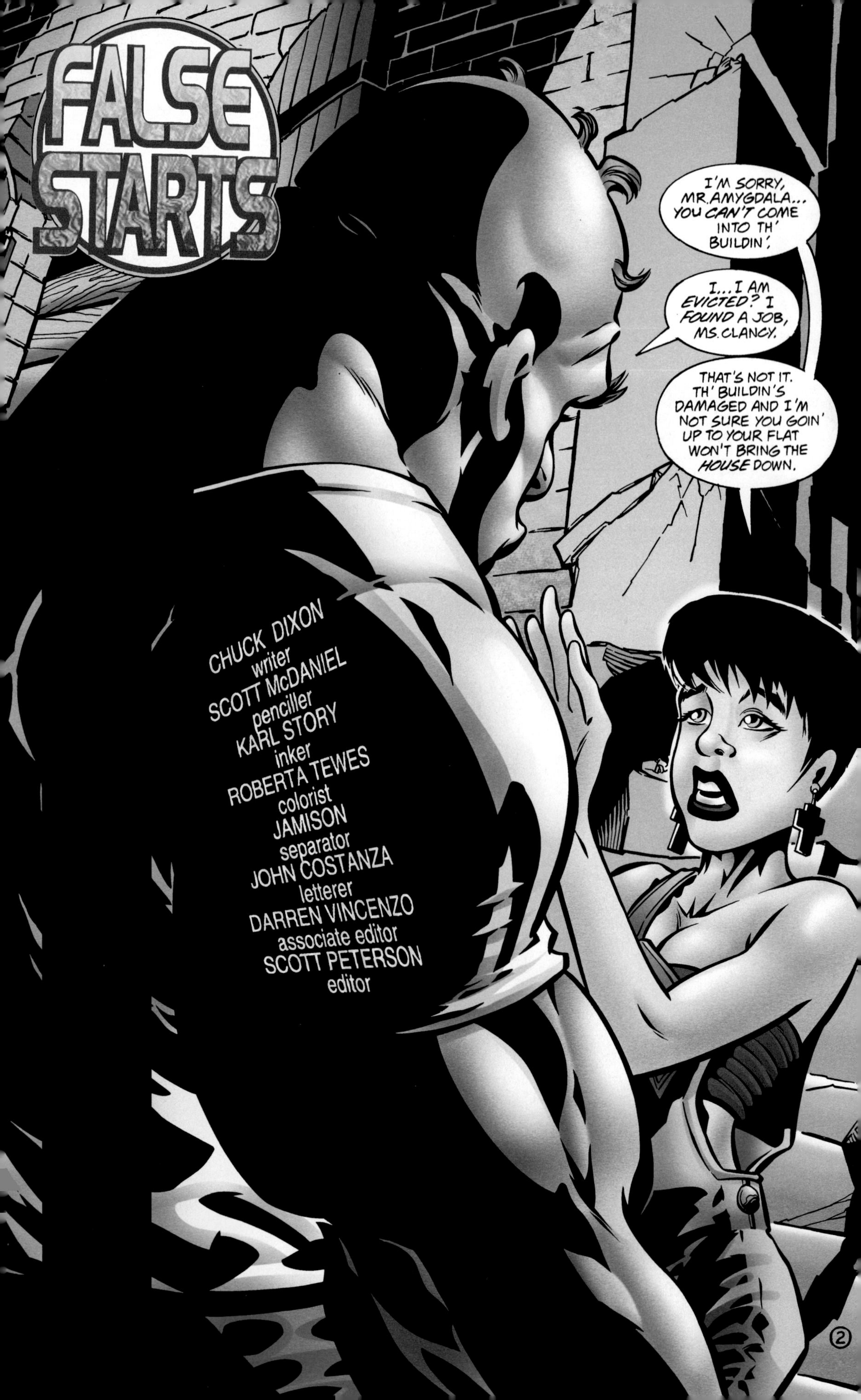
FALSE STARTS
I'M SORRY, MR. AMYGDALA... YOU CAN'T COME INTO TH' BUILDIN'.
I...I AM EVICTED? I FOUND A JOB, MS. CLANCY.
THAT'S NOT IT. TH' BUILDIN'S DAMAGED AND I'M NOT SURE YOU GOIN' UP TO YOUR FLAT WON'T BRING THE HOUSE DOWN.
CHUCK DIXON writer
SCOTT McDANIEL penciller
KARL STORY inker
ROBERTA TEWES colorist
JAMISON separator
JOHN COSTANZA letterer
DARREN VINCENZO associate editor
SCOTT PETERSON editor
2

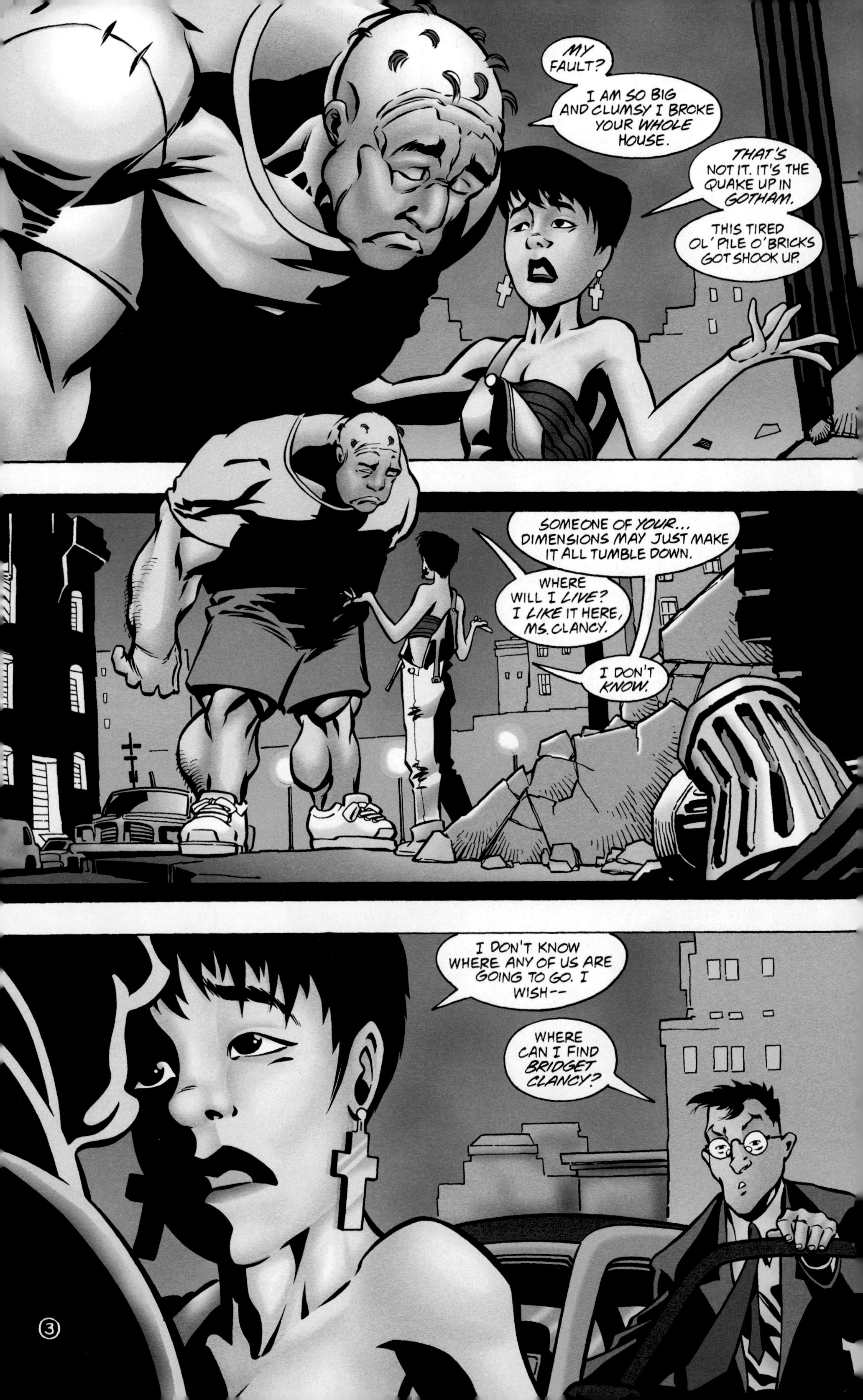
MY FAULT?
I AM SO BIG AND CLUMSY I BROKE YOUR WHOLE HOUSE.
THAT'S NOT IT. IT'S THE QUAKE UP IN GOTHAM.
THIS TIRED OL' PILE O'BRICKS GOT SHOOK UP.
SOMEONE OF YOUR... DIMENSIONS MAY JUST MAKE IT ALL TUMBLE DOWN.
WHERE WILL I LIVE? I LIKE IT HERE, MS. CLANCY.
I DON'T KNOW.
I DON'T KNOW WHERE ANY OF US ARE GOING TO GO. I WISH--
WHERE CAN I FIND BRIDGET CLANCY?
3

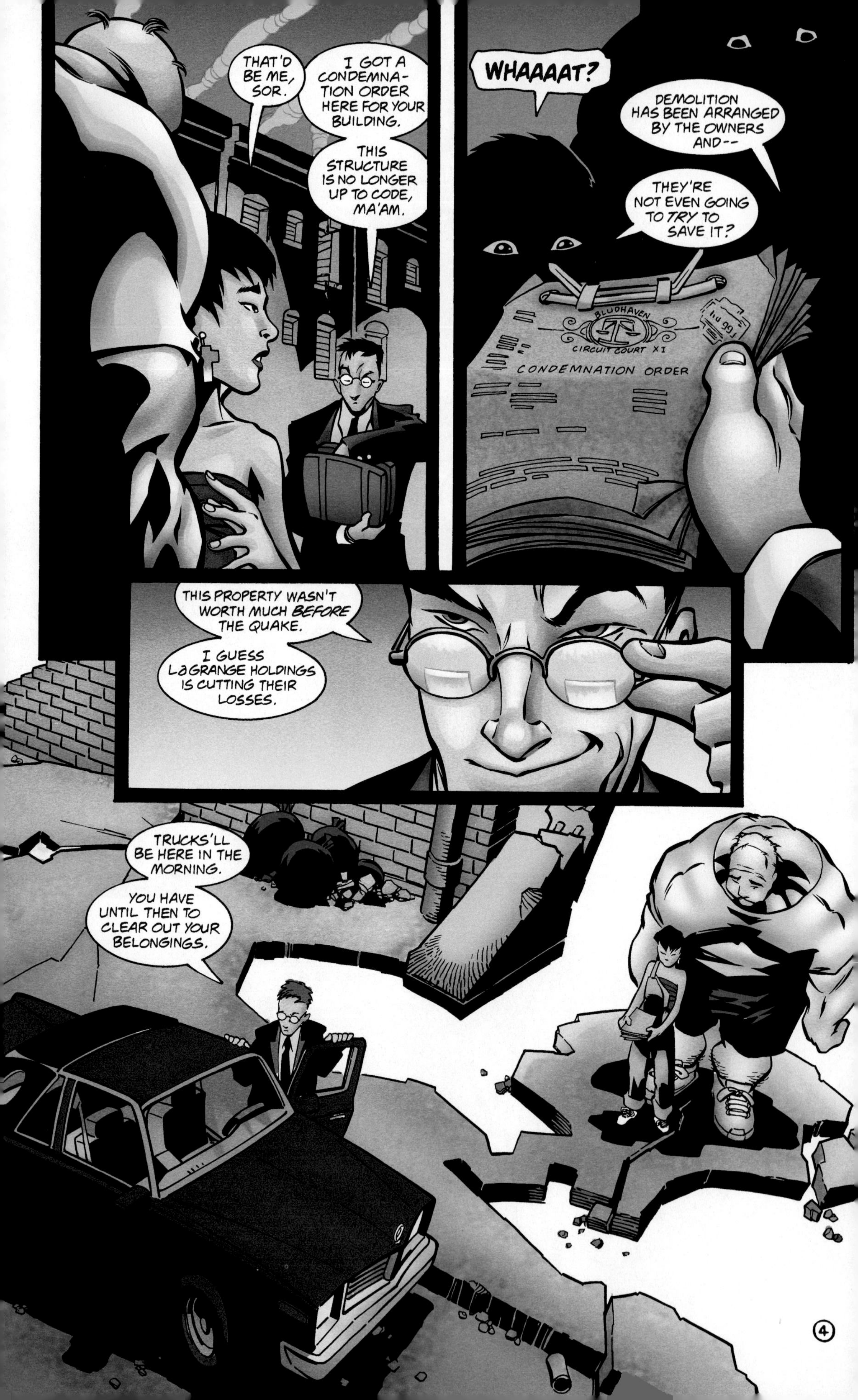
THAT'D BE ME, SOR.
I GOT A CONDEMNATION ORDER HERE FOR YOUR BUILDING.
THIS STRUCTURE IS NO LONGER UP TO CODE, MA'AM.
WHAAAAT?
DEMOLITION HAS BEEN ARRANGED BY THE OWNERS AND--
THEY'RE NOT EVEN GOING TO TRY TO SAVE IT?
BLUDHAVEN
CIRCUIT COURT XI
CONDEMNATION ORDER
THIS PROPERTY WASN'T WORTH MUCH BEFORE THE QUAKE.
I GUESS LaGRANGE HOLDINGS IS CUTTING THEIR LOSSES.
TRUCKS'LL BE HERE IN THE MORNING.
YOU HAVE UNTIL THEN TO CLEAR OUT YOUR BELONGINGS.

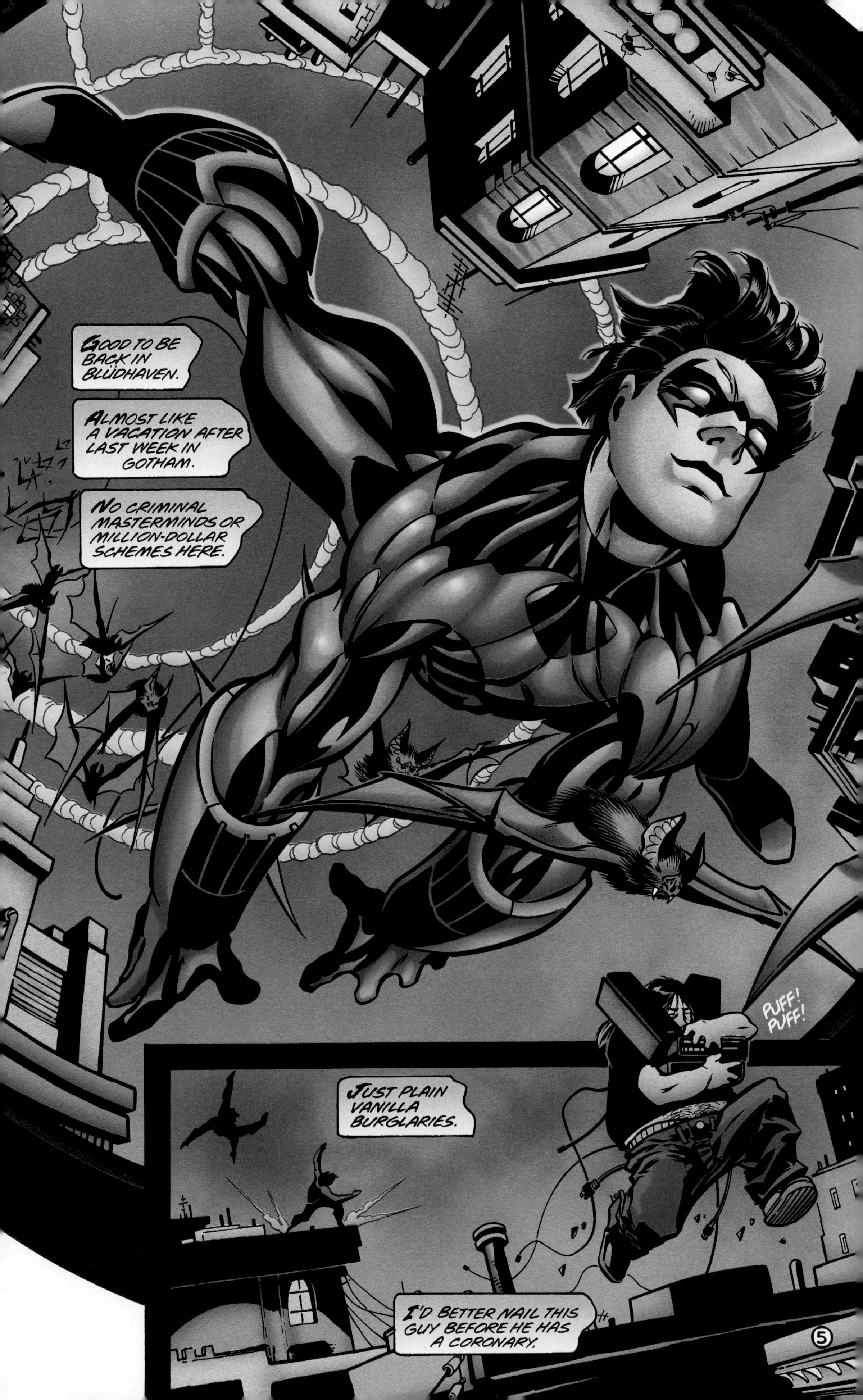
GOOD TO BE BACK IN BLÜDHAVEN.
ALMOST LIKE A VACATION AFTER LAST WEEK IN GOTHAM.
NO CRIMINAL MASTERMINDS OR MILLION-DOLLAR SCHEMES HERE.
PUFF! PUFF!
JUST PLAIN VANILLA BURGLARIES.
I'D BETTER NAIL THIS GUY BEFORE HE HAS A CORONARY.
5

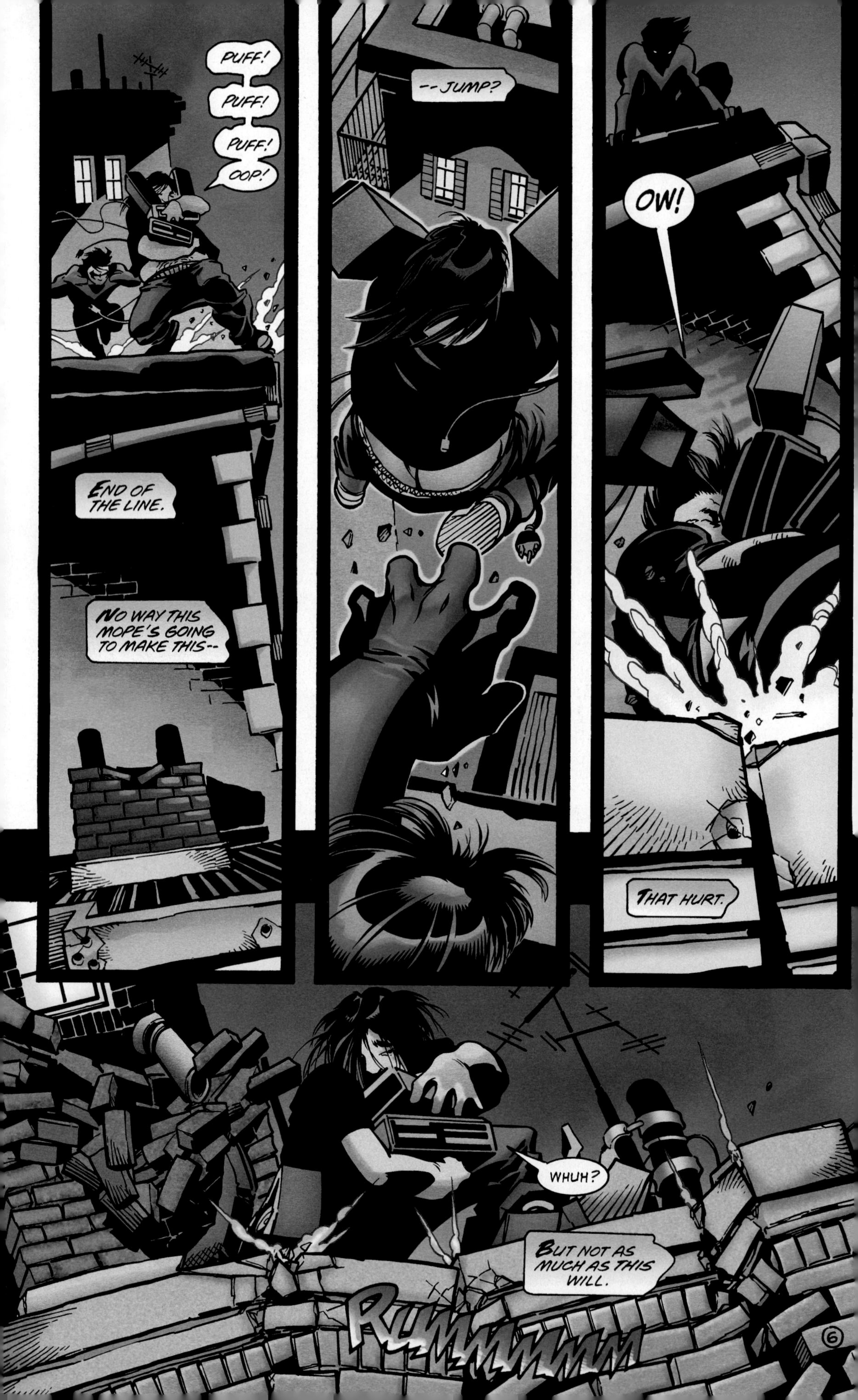
PUFF!
PUFF!
PUFF!
OOP!
END OF THE LINE.
NO WAY THIS MOPE'S GOING TO MAKE THIS--
--JUMP?
OW!
THAT HURT.
WHUH?
BUT NOT AS MUCH AS THIS WILL.
RUMMMMMM
6

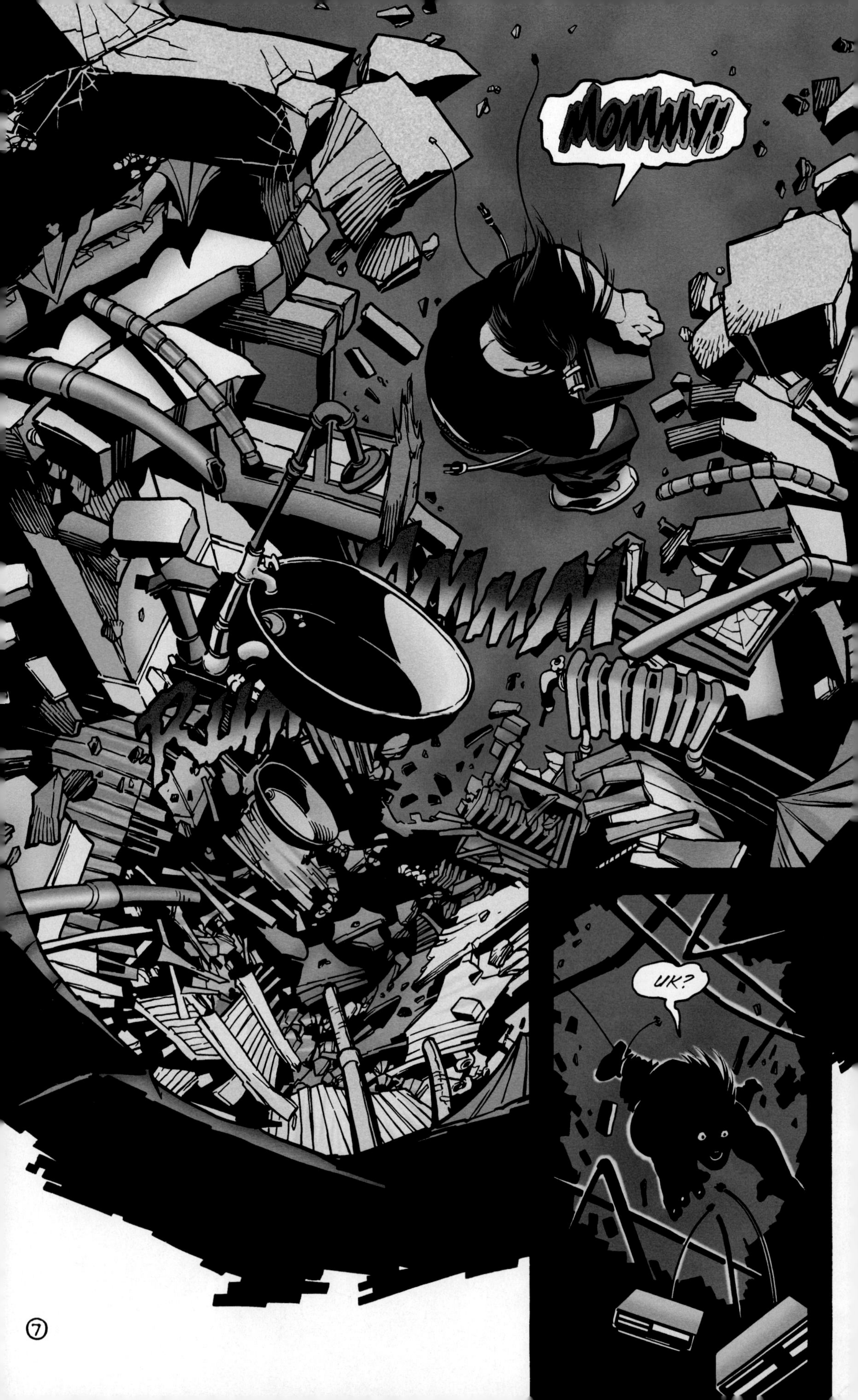
MOMMY!
MMMMM
UK?

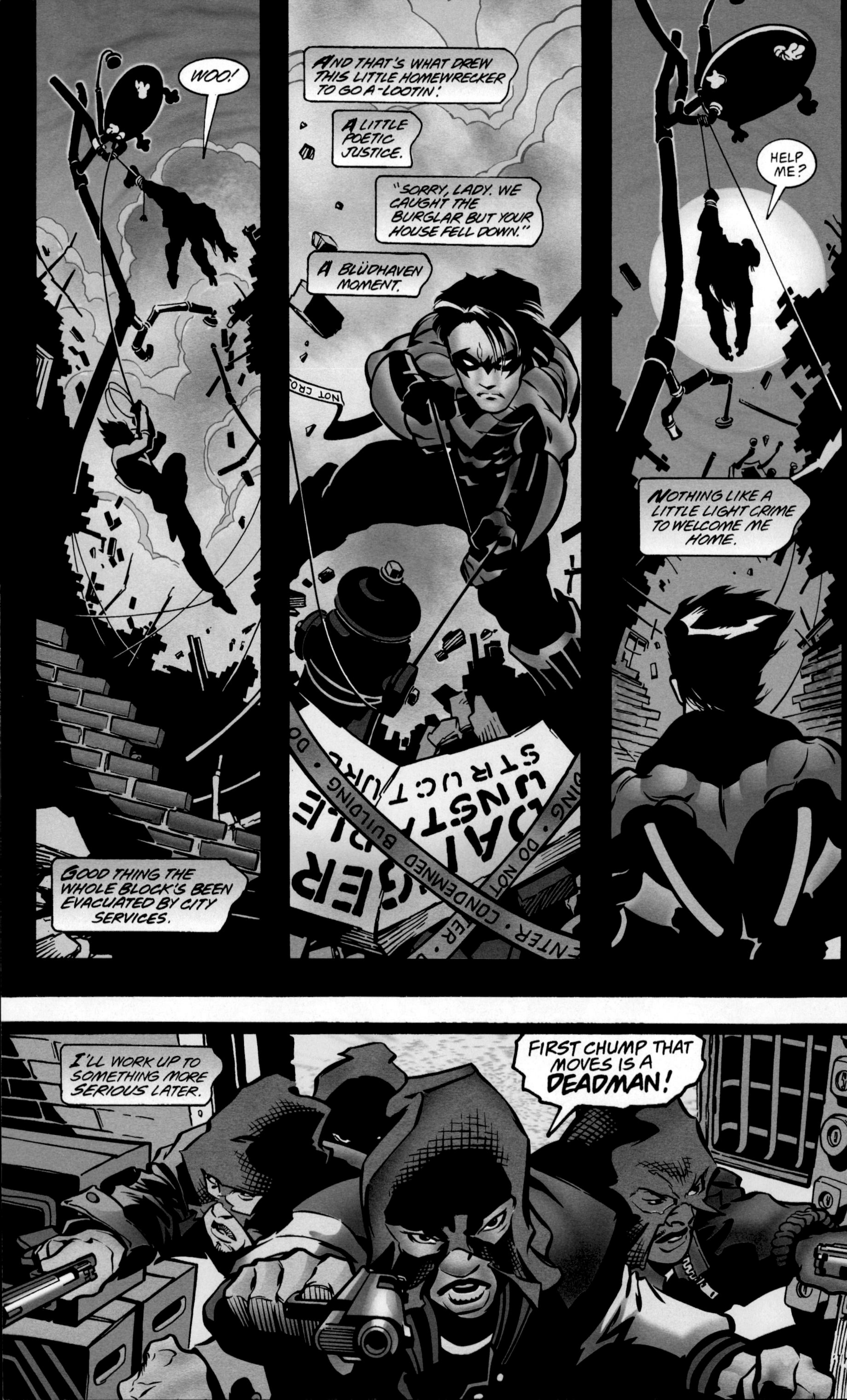
WOO!
GOOD THING THE WHOLE BLOCK'S BEEN EVACUATED BY CITY SERVICES.
AND THAT'S WHAT DREW THIS LITTLE HOMEWRECKER TO GO A-LOOTIN'.
A LITTLE POETIC JUSTICE.
"SORRY, LADY. WE CAUGHT THE BURGLAR BUT YOUR HOUSE FELL DOWN."
A BLÜDHAVEN MOMENT.
HELP ME?
NOTHING LIKE A LITTLE LIGHT CRIME TO WELCOME ME HOME.
I'LL WORK UP TO SOMETHING MORE SERIOUS LATER.
FIRST CHUMP THAT MOVES IS A DEADMAN!

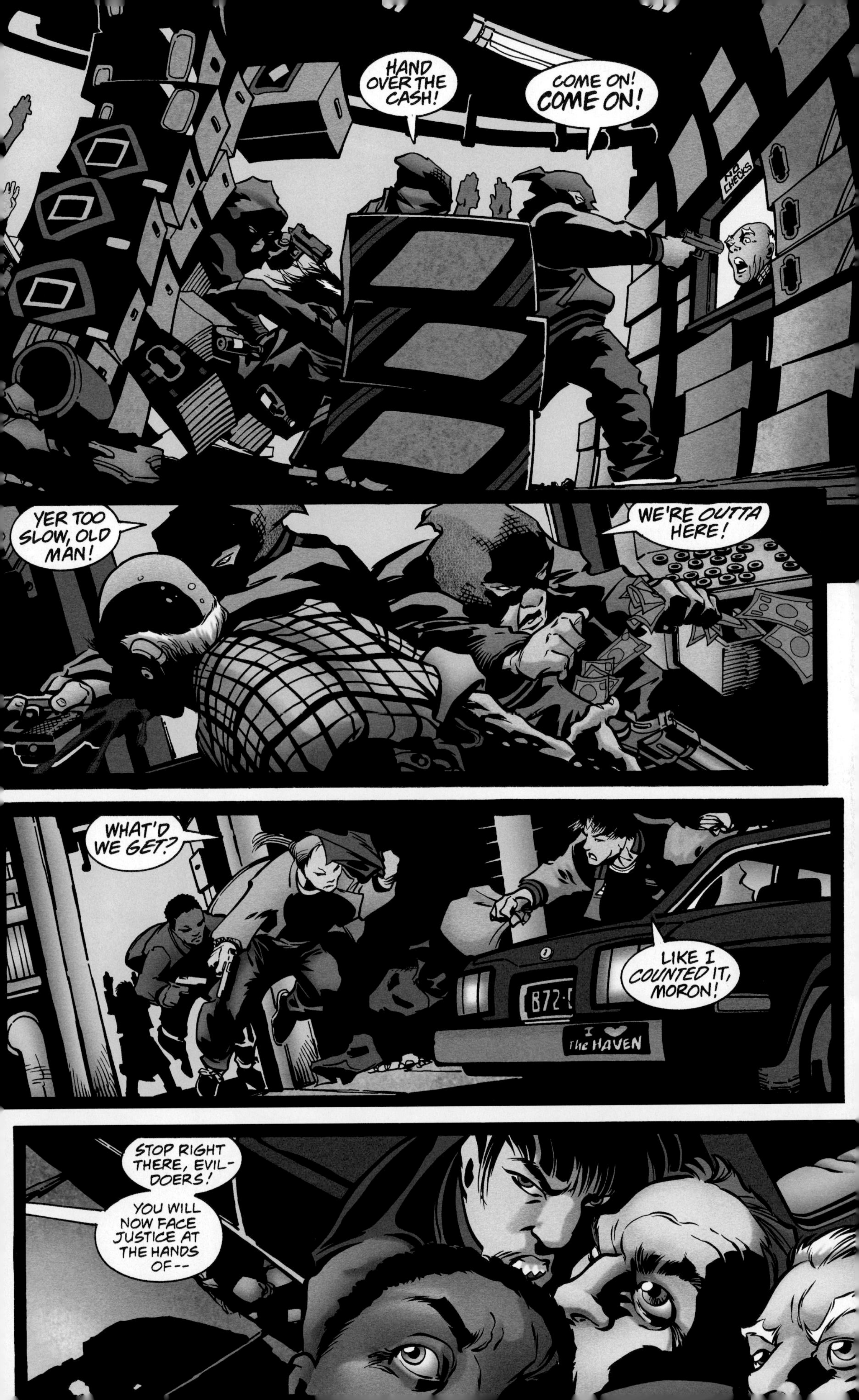
HAND OVER THE CASH!
COME ON! COME ON!
NO CHECKS
YER TOO SLOW, OLD MAN!
WE'RE OUTTA HERE!
WHAT'D WE GET?
LIKE I COUNTED IT, MORON!
B72-
I ♥ The HAVEN
STOP RIGHT THERE, EVIL-DOERS!
YOU WILL NOW FACE JUSTICE AT THE HANDS OF--

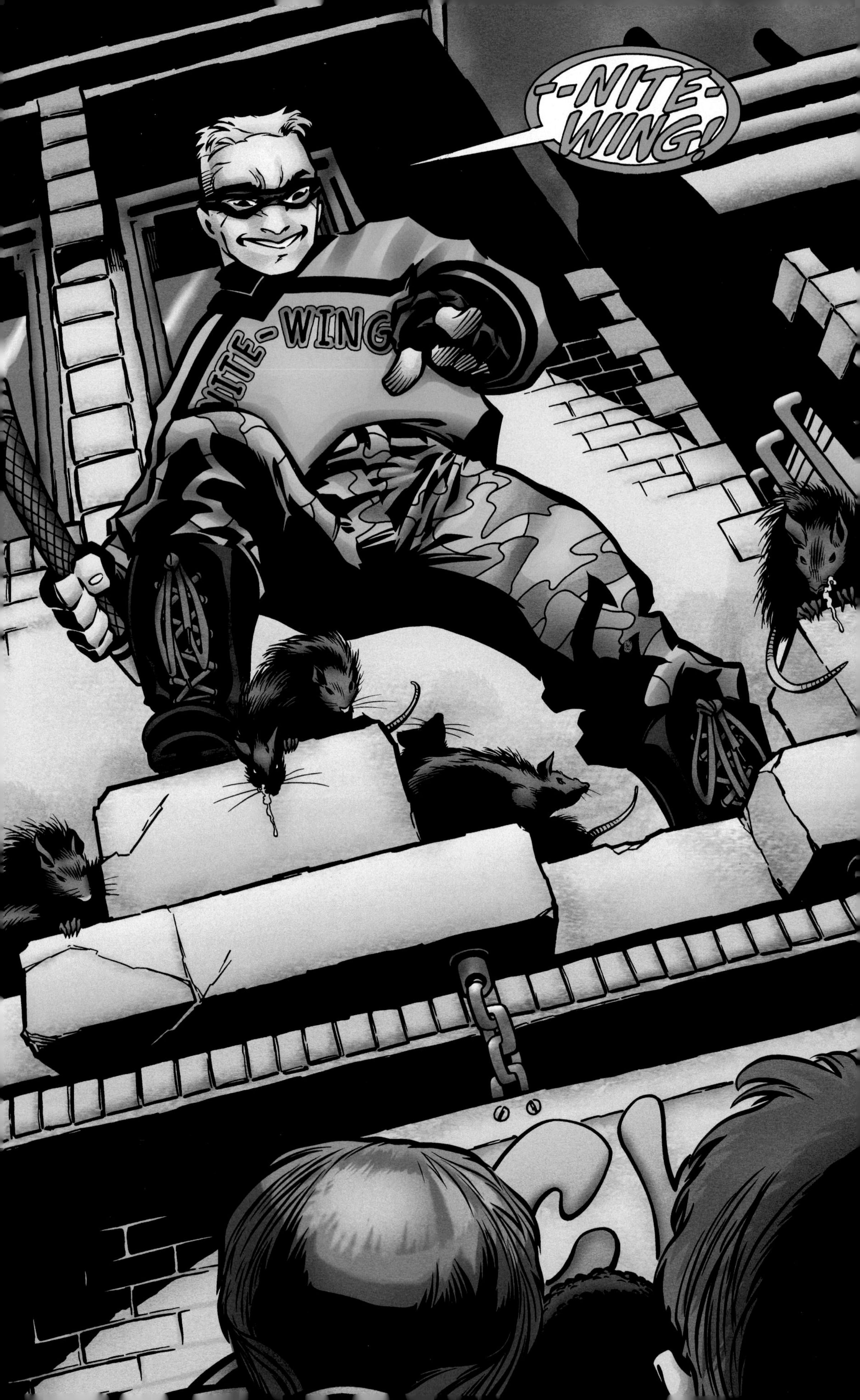
-NITE-WING!
NITE-WING

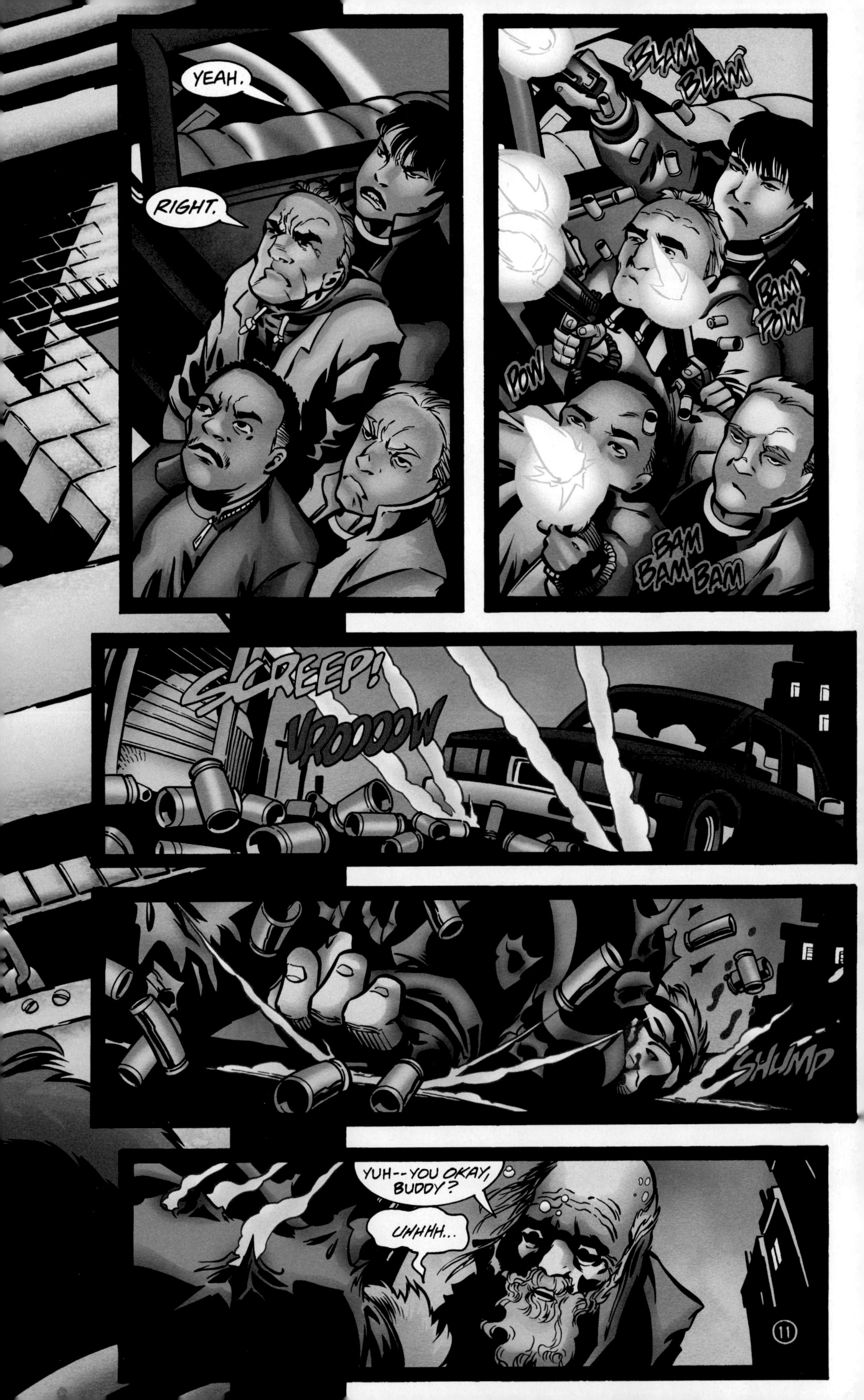
YEAH.
RIGHT.
BLAM
BLAM
BAM
POW
POW
BAM
BAM
BAM
SCREEP!
VROOOOW
SHUMP
YUH--YOU OKAY, BUDDY?
UHHHH...
11

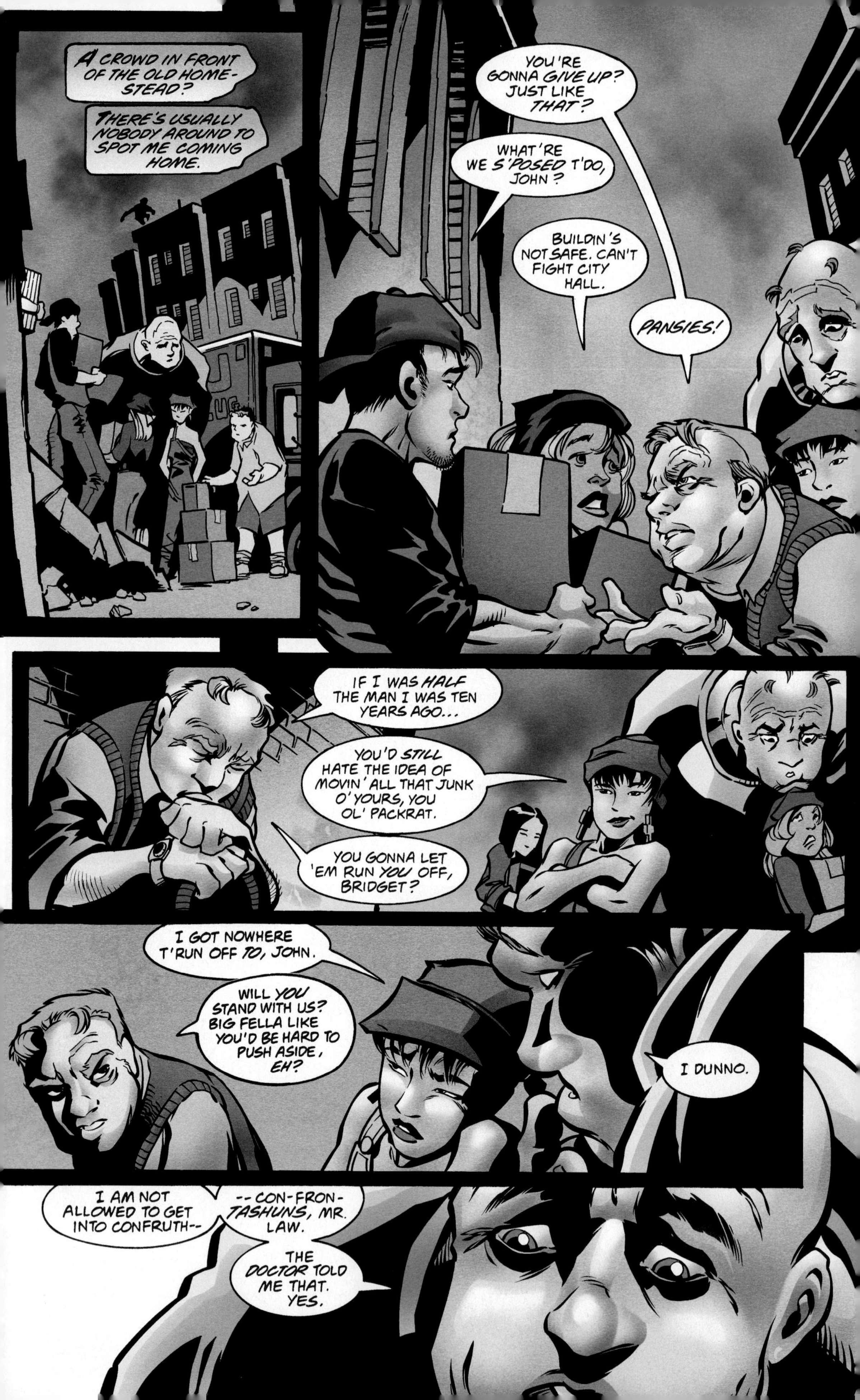
A CROWD IN FRONT OF THE OLD HOME-STEAD?
THERE'S USUALLY NOBODY AROUND TO SPOT ME COMING HOME.
YOU'RE GONNA GIVE UP? JUST LIKE THAT?
WHAT'RE WE S'POSED T'DO, JOHN?
BUILDIN'S NOT SAFE. CAN'T FIGHT CITY HALL.
PANSIES!
IF I WAS HALF THE MAN I WAS TEN YEARS AGO...
YOU'D STILL HATE THE IDEA OF MOVIN' ALL THAT JUNK O' YOURS, YOU OL' PACKRAT.
YOU GONNA LET 'EM RUN YOU OFF, BRIDGET?
I GOT NOWHERE T'RUN OFF TO, JOHN.
WILL YOU STAND WITH US? BIG FELLA LIKE YOU'D BE HARD TO PUSH ASIDE, EH?
I DUNNO.
I AM NOT ALLOWED TO GET INTO CONFRUTH--
--CON-FRON-TASHUNS, MR. LAW.
THE DOCTOR TOLD ME THAT. YES.

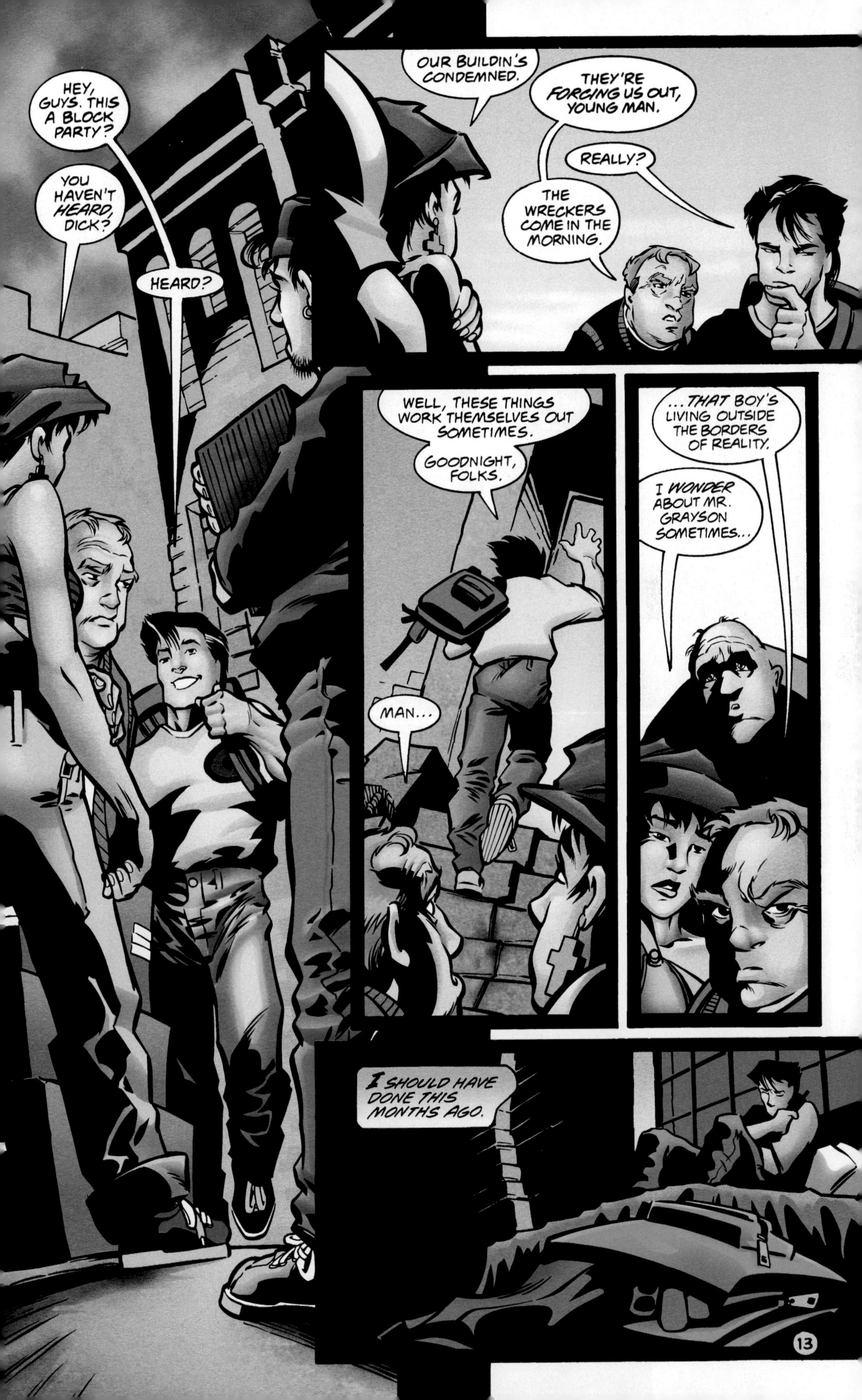
HEY, GUYS. THIS A BLOCK PARTY?
YOU HAVEN'T HEARD, DICK?
HEARD?
OUR BUILDIN'S CONDEMNED.
THEY'RE FORCING US OUT, YOUNG MAN.
REALLY?
THE WRECKERS COME IN THE MORNING.
WELL, THESE THINGS WORK THEMSELVES OUT SOMETIMES.
GOODNIGHT, FOLKS.
MAN...
...THAT BOY'S LIVING OUTSIDE THE BORDERS OF REALITY.
I WONDER ABOUT MR. GRAYSON SOMETIMES...
I SHOULD HAVE DONE THIS MONTHS AGO.

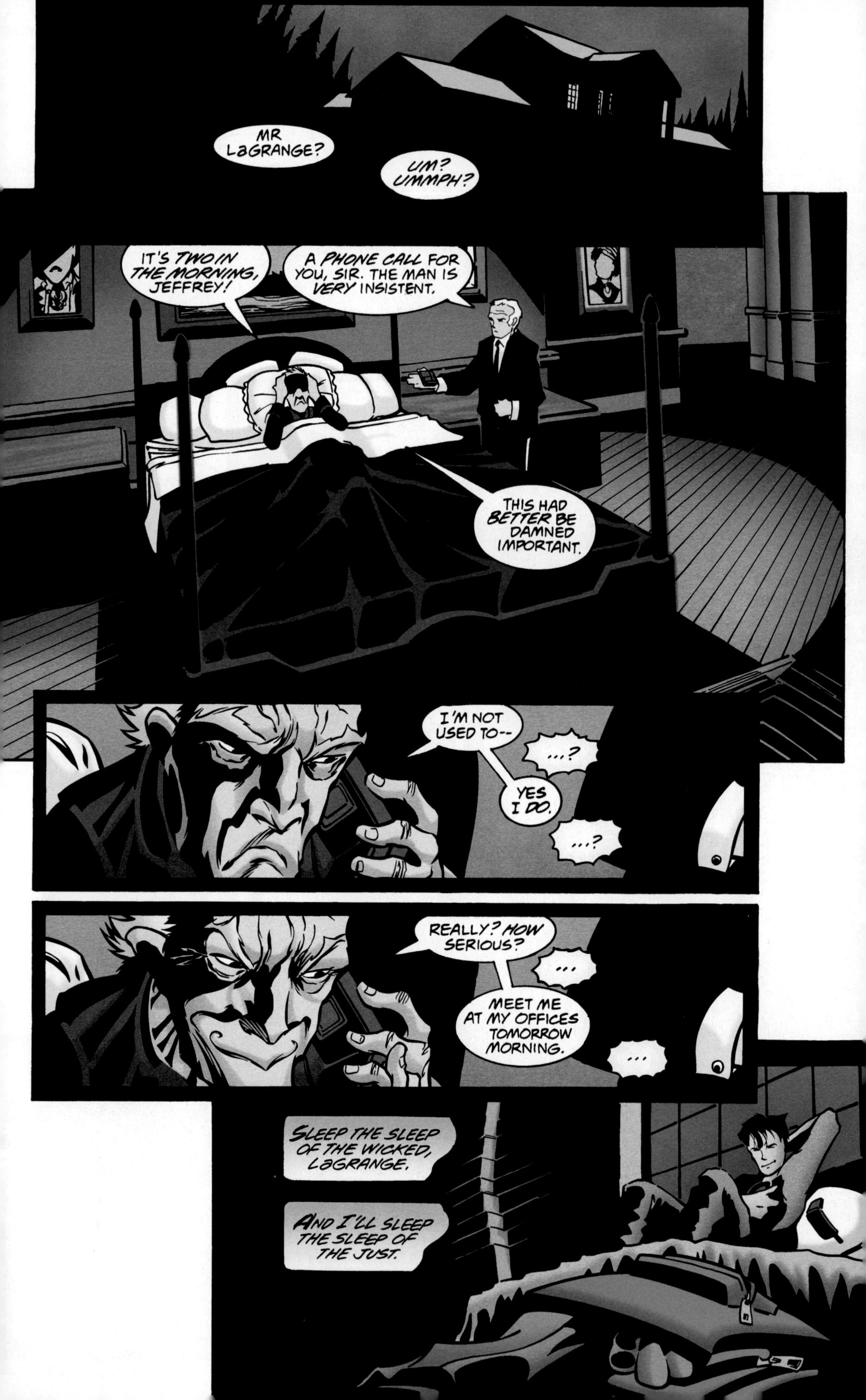
MR LaGRANGE?
UM? UMMPH?
IT'S TWO IN THE MORNING, JEFFREY!
A PHONE CALL FOR YOU, SIR. THE MAN IS VERY INSISTENT.
THIS HAD BETTER BE DAMNED IMPORTANT.
I'M NOT USED TO--
...?
YES I DO.
...?
REALLY? HOW SERIOUS?
...
MEET ME AT MY OFFICES TOMORROW MORNING.
...
SLEEP THE SLEEP OF THE WICKED, LaGRANGE.
AND I'LL SLEEP THE SLEEP OF THE JUST.

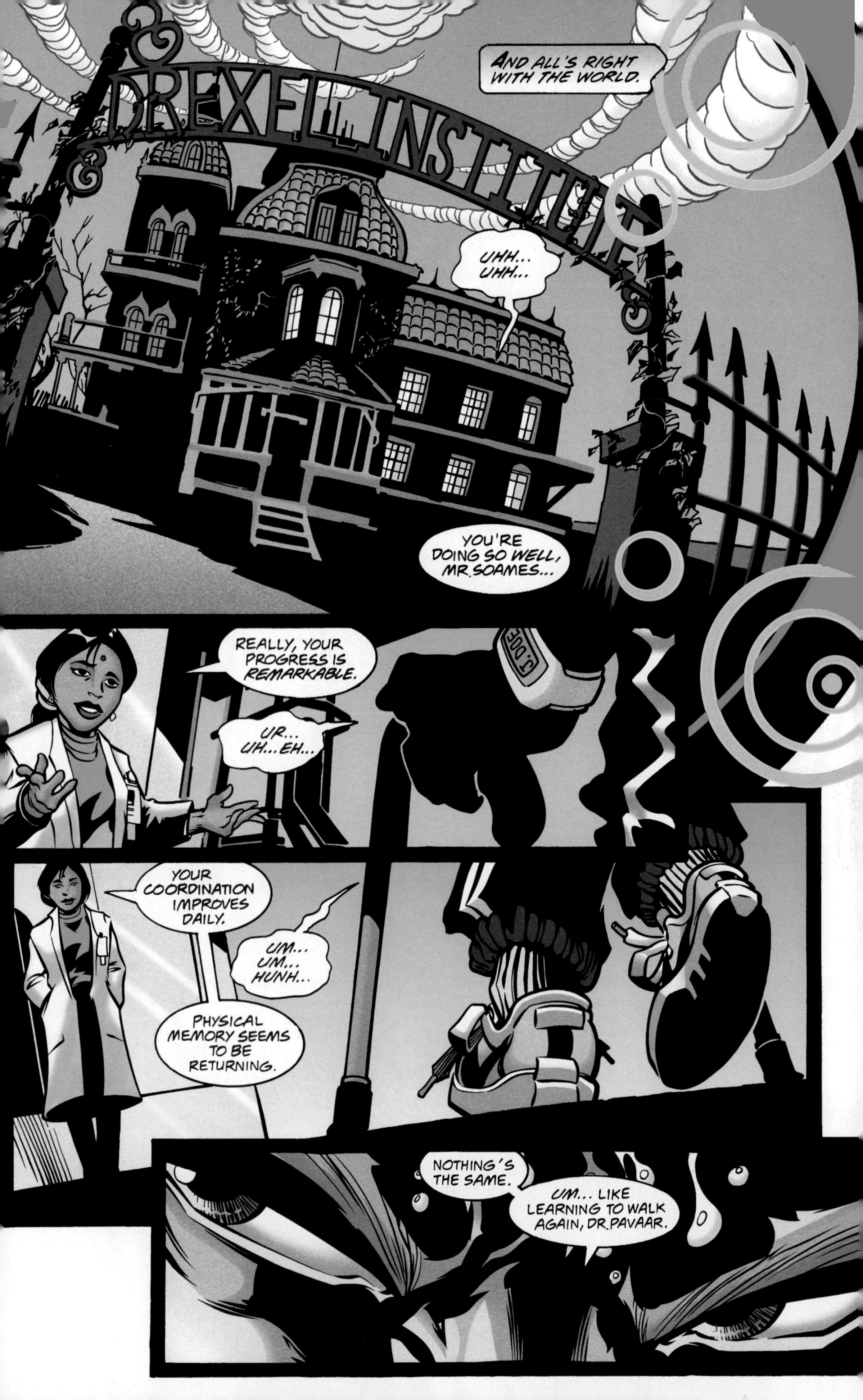
DREXEL INSTITUTE
AND ALL'S RIGHT WITH THE WORLD.
UHH... UHH...
YOU'RE DOING SO WELL, MR. SOAMES...
REALLY, YOUR PROGRESS IS REMARKABLE.
UR... UH...EH...
YOUR COORDINATION IMPROVES DAILY.
UM... UM... HUNH...
PHYSICAL MEMORY SEEMS TO BE RETURNING.
NOTHING'S THE SAME.
UM... LIKE LEARNING TO WALK AGAIN, DR. PAVAAR.

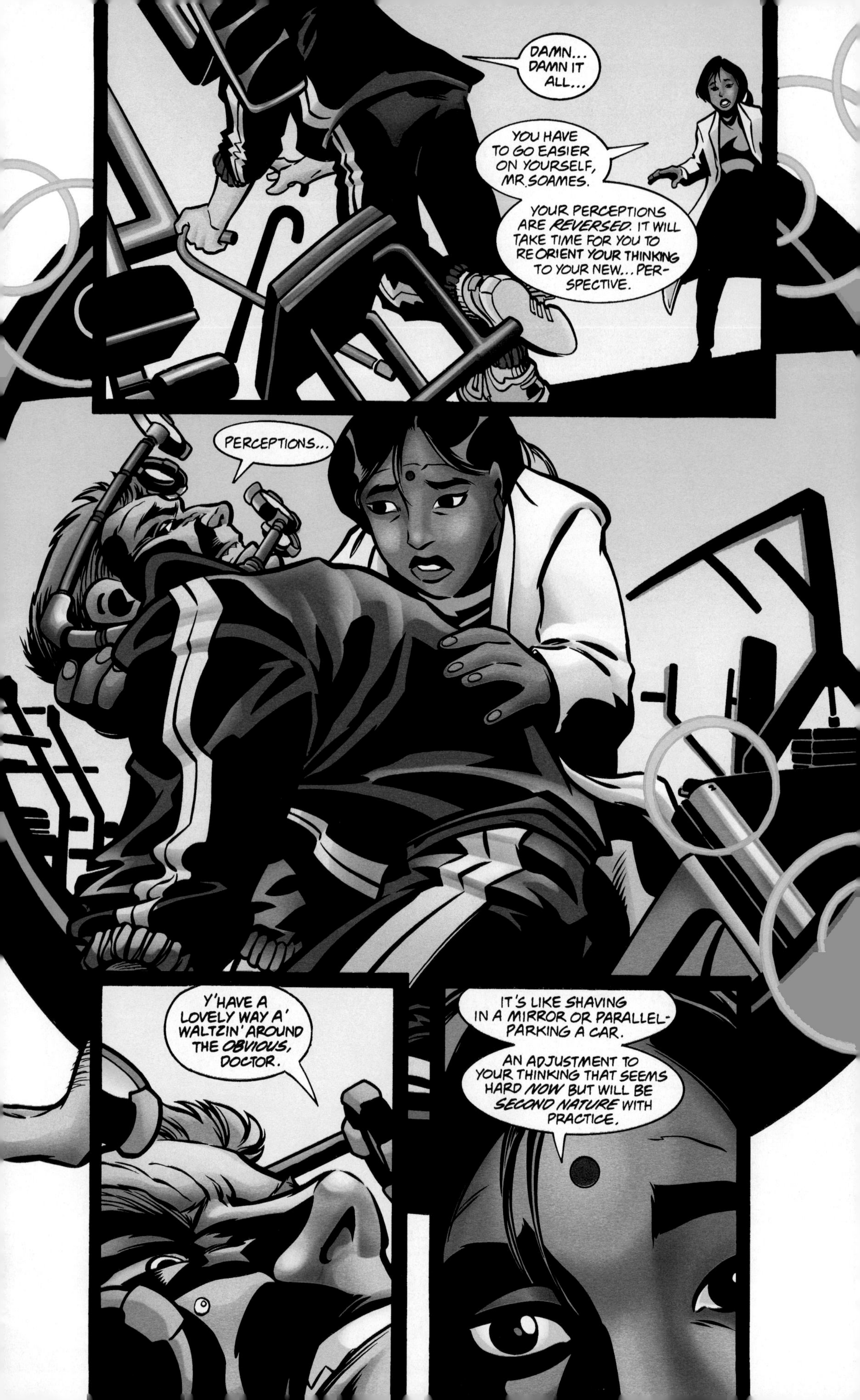
DAMN... DAMN IT ALL...
YOU HAVE TO GO EASIER ON YOURSELF, MR. SOAMES.
YOUR PERCEPTIONS ARE REVERSED. IT WILL TAKE TIME FOR YOU TO REORIENT YOUR THINKING TO YOUR NEW... PERSPECTIVE.
PERCEPTIONS...
Y'HAVE A LOVELY WAY A' WALTZIN' AROUND THE OBVIOUS, DOCTOR.
IT'S LIKE SHAVING IN A MIRROR OR PARALLEL-PARKING A CAR.
AN ADJUSTMENT TO YOUR THINKING THAT SEEMS HARD NOW BUT WILL BE SECOND NATURE WITH PRACTICE.

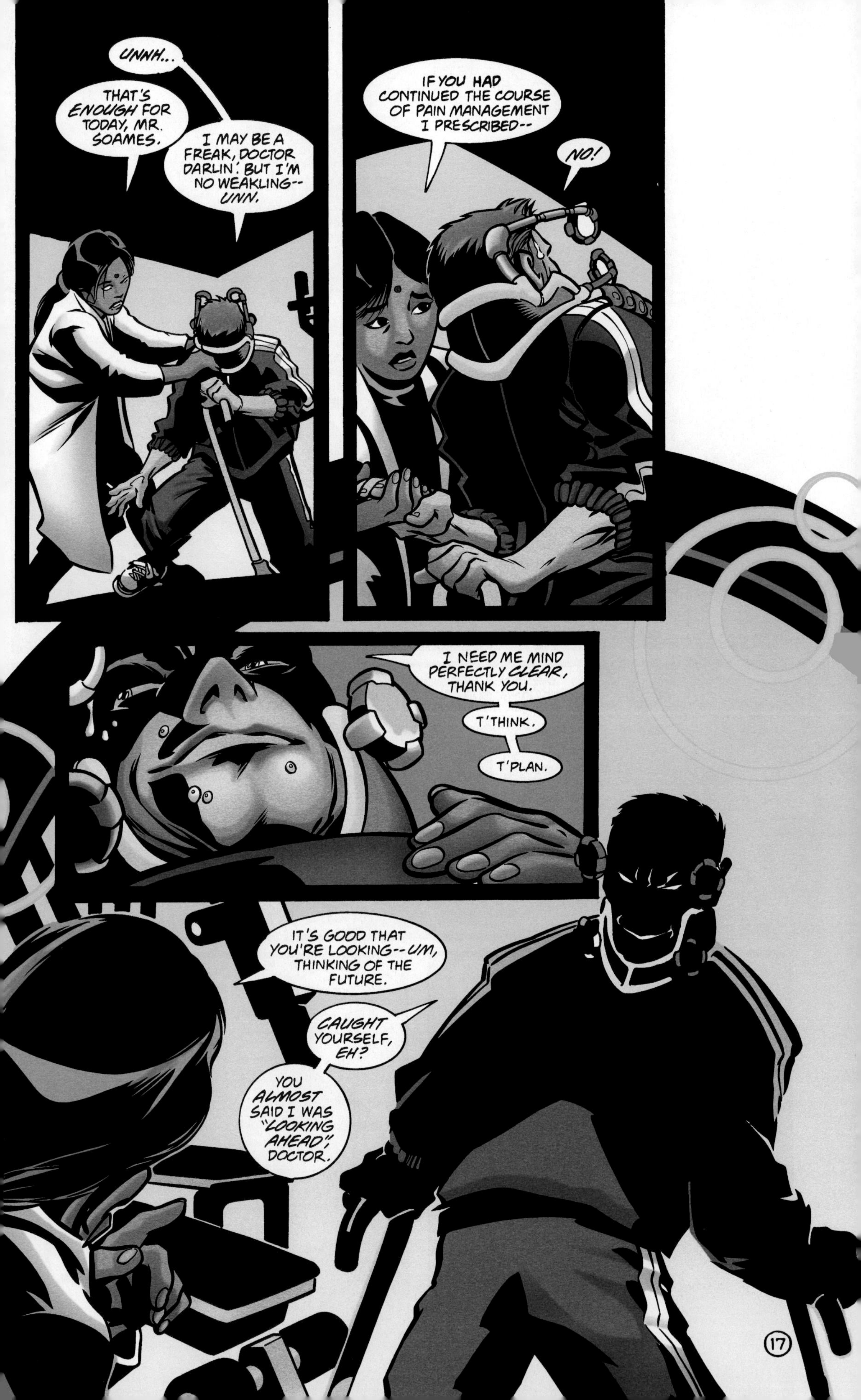
UNNH...
THAT'S ENOUGH FOR TODAY, MR. SOAMES.
I MAY BE A FREAK, DOCTOR DARLIN'. BUT I'M NO WEAKLING-- UNN.
IF YOU HAD CONTINUED THE COURSE OF PAIN MANAGEMENT I PRESCRIBED--
NO!
I NEED ME MIND PERFECTLY CLEAR, THANK YOU.
T'THINK.
T'PLAN.
IT'S GOOD THAT YOU'RE LOOKING--UM, THINKING OF THE FUTURE.
CAUGHT YOURSELF, EH?
YOU ALMOST SAID I WAS "LOOKING AHEAD", DOCTOR.
17

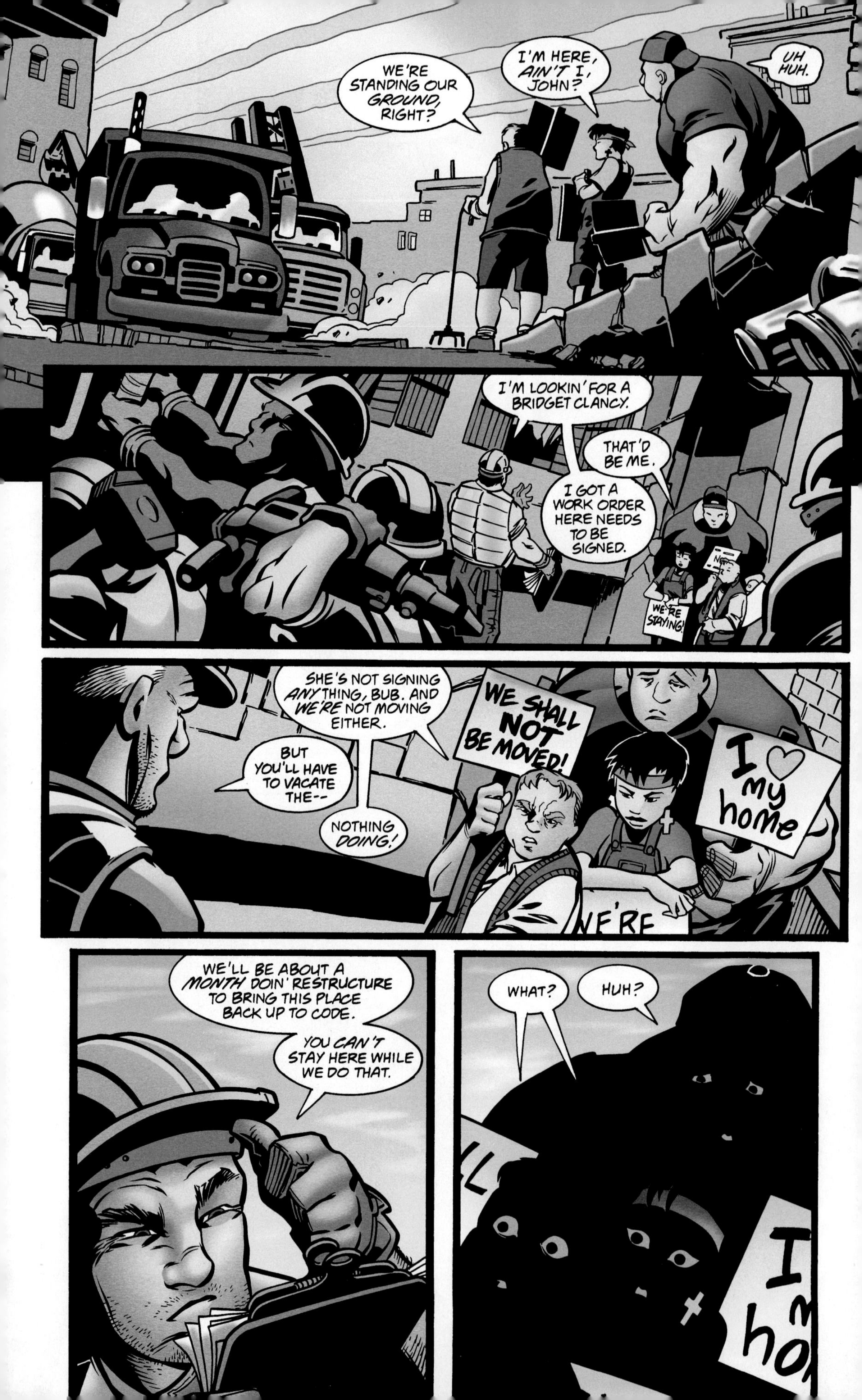

WE'RE STANDING OUR GROUND, RIGHT?
I'M HERE, AIN'T I, JOHN?
UH HUH.
I'M LOOKIN' FOR A BRIDGET CLANCY.
THAT'D BE ME.
I GOT A WORK ORDER HERE NEEDS TO BE SIGNED.
WE'RE STAYING!
SHE'S NOT SIGNING ANYTHING, BUB. AND WE'RE NOT MOVING EITHER.
WE SHALL NOT BE MOVED!
I ♥ my home
BUT YOU'LL HAVE TO VACATE THE--
NOTHING DOING!
WE'LL BE ABOUT A MONTH DOIN' RESTRUCTURE TO BRING THIS PLACE BACK UP TO CODE.
YOU CAN'T STAY HERE WHILE WE DO THAT.
WHAT?
HUH?

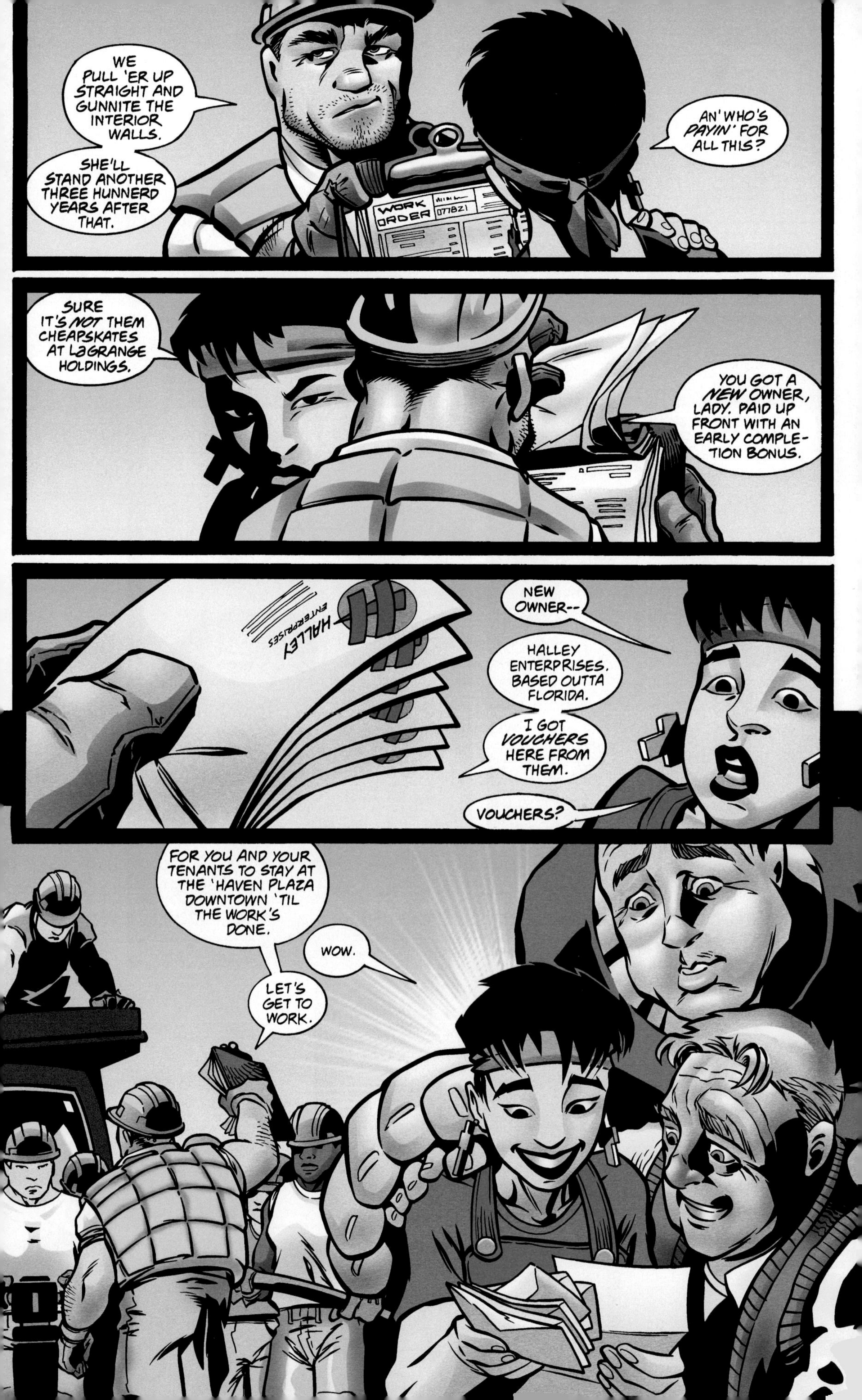
WE PULL 'ER UP STRAIGHT AND GUNNITE THE INTERIOR WALLS.
SHE'LL STAND ANOTHER THREE HUNNERD YEARS AFTER THAT.
WORK ORDER 077B21
AN' WHO'S PAYIN' FOR ALL THIS?
SURE IT'S NOT THEM CHEAPSKATES AT LaGRANGE HOLDINGS.
YOU GOT A NEW OWNER, LADY. PAID UP FRONT WITH AN EARLY COMPLETION BONUS.
HALLEY ENTERPRISES
NEW OWNER--
HALLEY ENTERPRISES. BASED OUTTA FLORIDA.
I GOT VOUCHERS HERE FROM THEM.
VOUCHERS?
FOR YOU AND YOUR TENANTS TO STAY AT THE 'HAVEN PLAZA DOWNTOWN 'TIL THE WORK'S DONE.
WOW.
LET'S GET TO WORK.

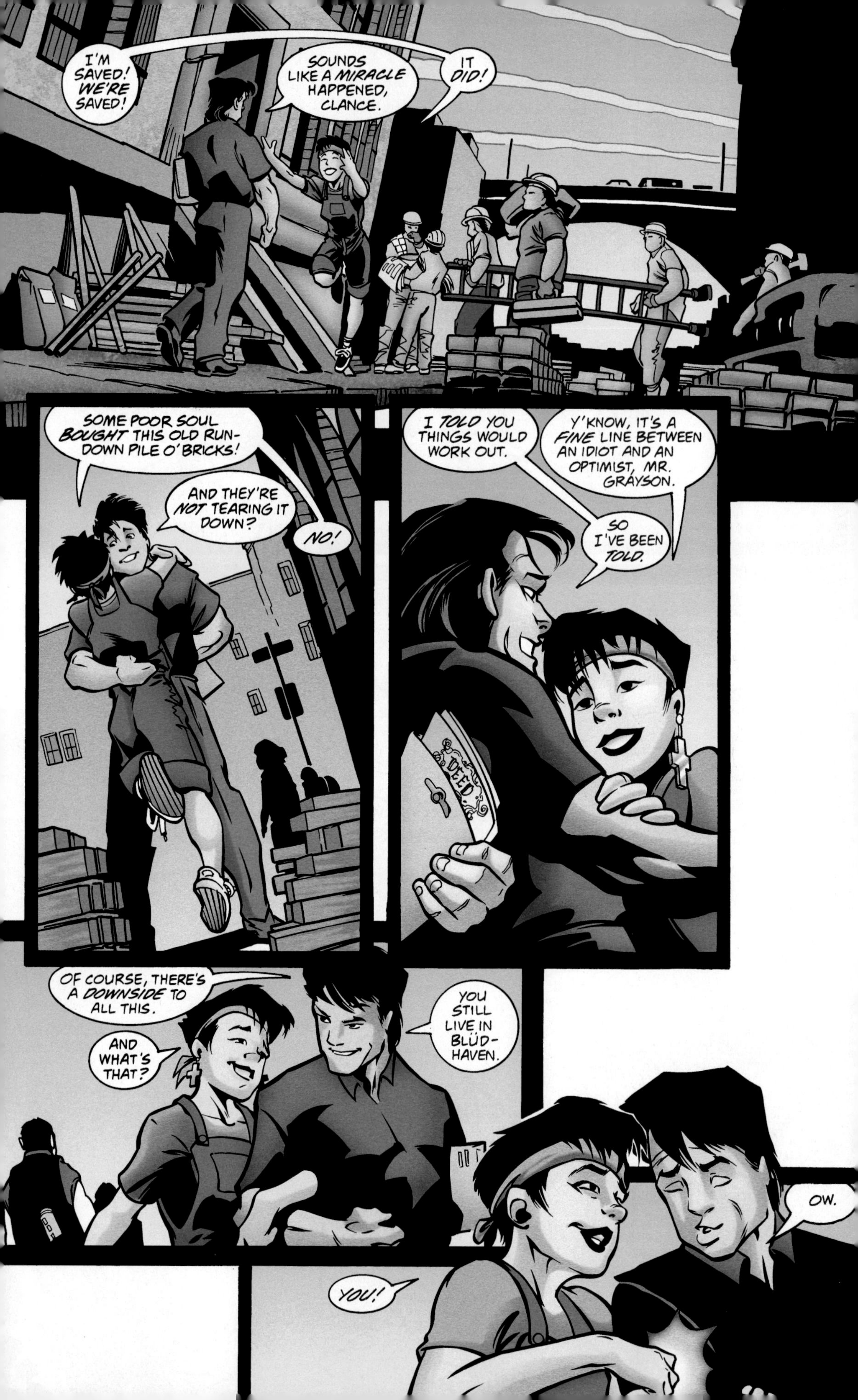
I'M SAVED! WE'RE SAVED!
SOUNDS LIKE A MIRACLE HAPPENED, CLANCE.
IT DID!
SOME POOR SOUL BOUGHT THIS OLD RUN-DOWN PILE O' BRICKS!
AND THEY'RE NOT TEARING IT DOWN?
NO!
I TOLD YOU THINGS WOULD WORK OUT.
Y'KNOW, IT'S A FINE LINE BETWEEN AN IDIOT AND AN OPTIMIST, MR. GRAYSON.
SO I'VE BEEN TOLD.
DEED
OF COURSE, THERE'S A DOWNSIDE TO ALL THIS.
AND WHAT'S THAT?
YOU STILL LIVE IN BLÜD-HAVEN.
OW.
YOU!

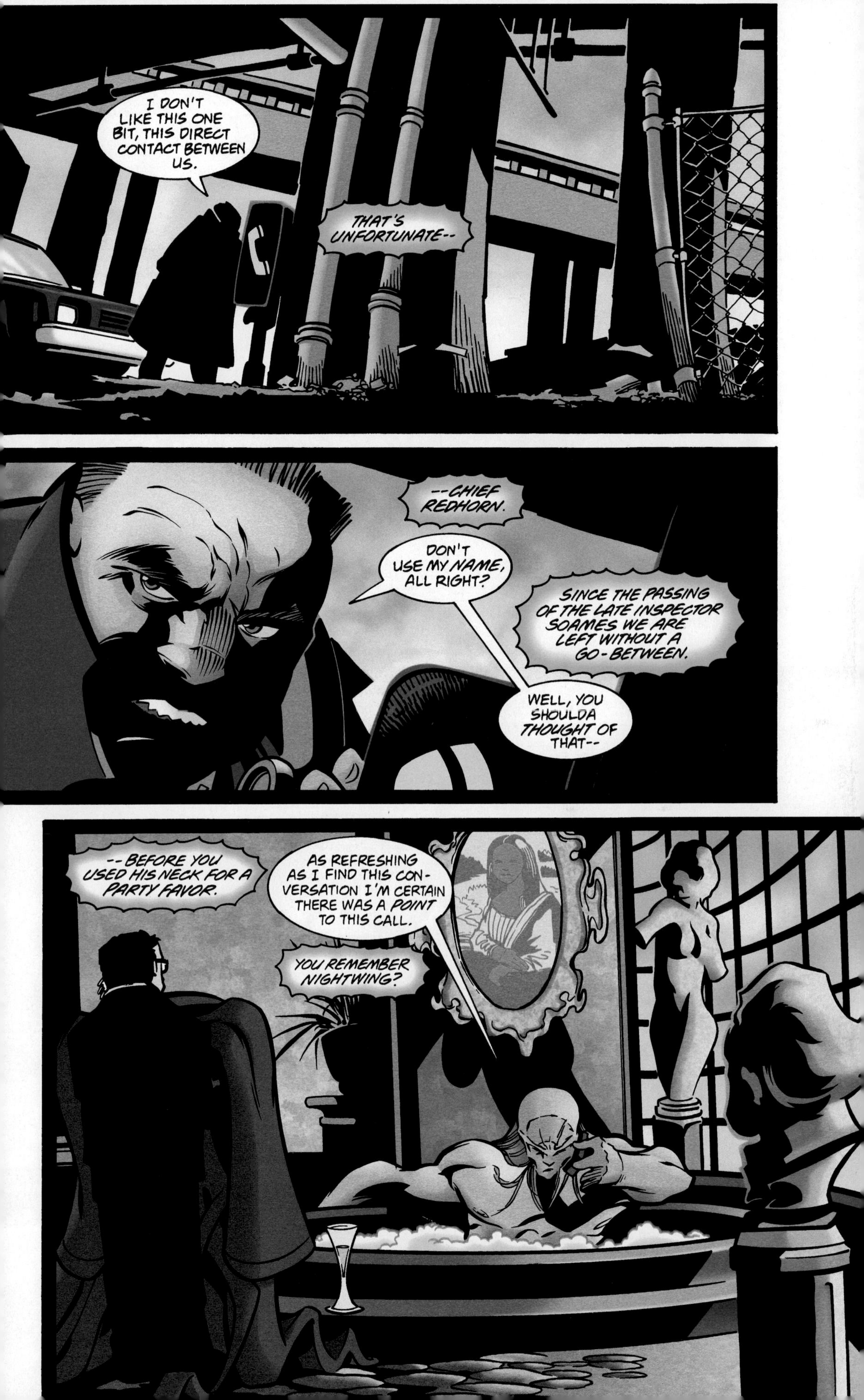

I DON'T LIKE THIS ONE BIT, THIS DIRECT CONTACT BETWEEN US.
THAT'S UNFORTUNATE--
--CHIEF REDHORN.
DON'T USE MY NAME, ALL RIGHT?
SINCE THE PASSING OF THE LATE INSPECTOR SOAMES WE ARE LEFT WITHOUT A GO-BETWEEN.
WELL, YOU SHOULDA THOUGHT OF THAT--
--BEFORE YOU USED HIS NECK FOR A PARTY FAVOR.
AS REFRESHING AS I FIND THIS CON-VERSATION I'M CERTAIN THERE WAS A POINT TO THIS CALL.
YOU REMEMBER NIGHTWING?

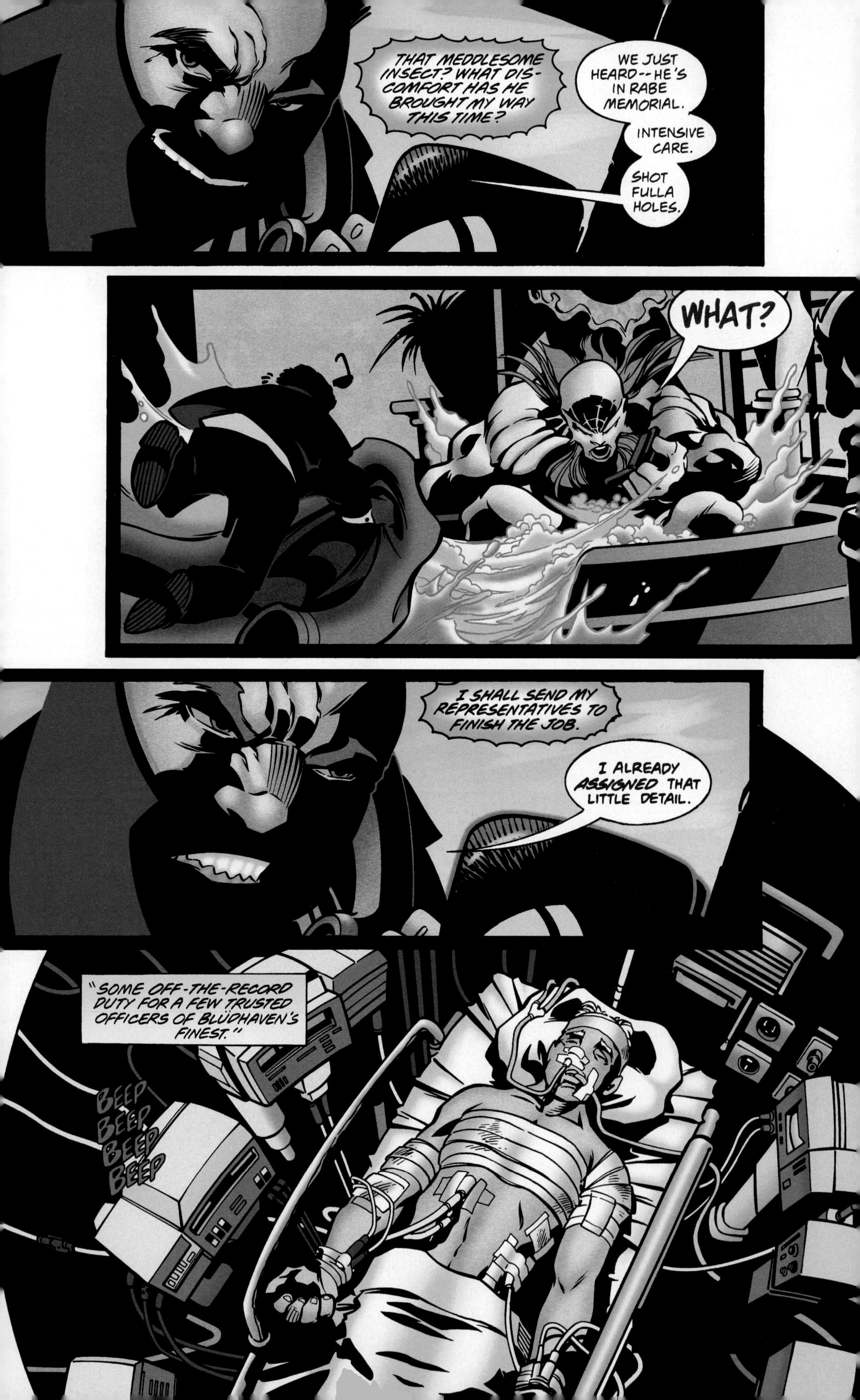
THAT MEDDLESOME INSECT? WHAT DIS-COMFORT HAS HE BROUGHT MY WAY THIS TIME?
WE JUST HEARD--HE'S IN RABE MEMORIAL.
INTENSIVE CARE.
SHOT FULLA HOLES.
WHAT?
I SHALL SEND MY REPRESENTATIVES TO FINISH THE JOB.
I ALREADY ASSIGNED THAT LITTLE DETAIL.
"SOME OFF-THE-RECORD DUTY FOR A FEW TRUSTED OFFICERS OF BLÜDHAVEN'S FINEST."
BEEP
BEEP
BEEP
BEEP

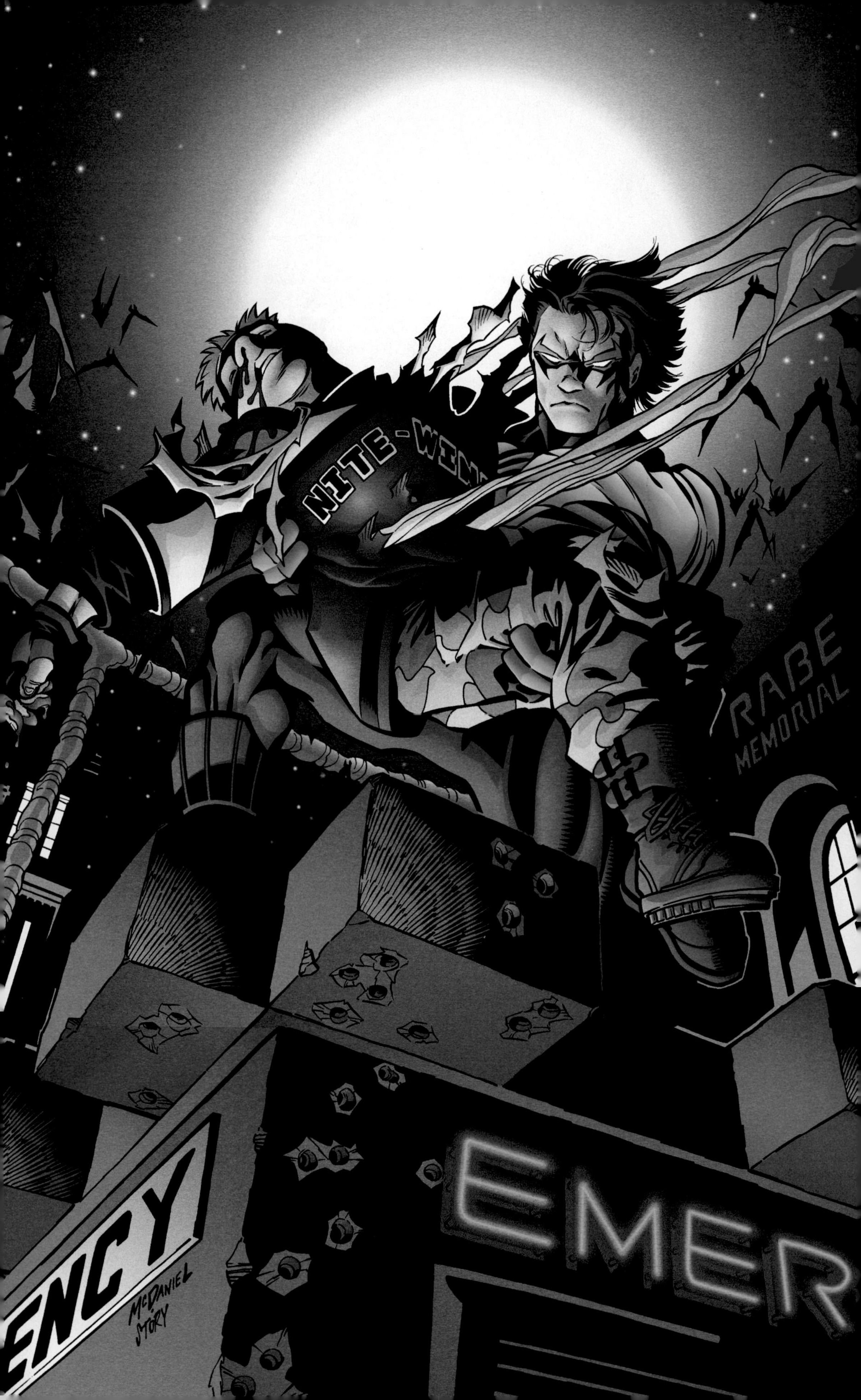
NITE-WIN
RABE
MEMORIAL
ENCY
EMER
McDANIEL
STORY

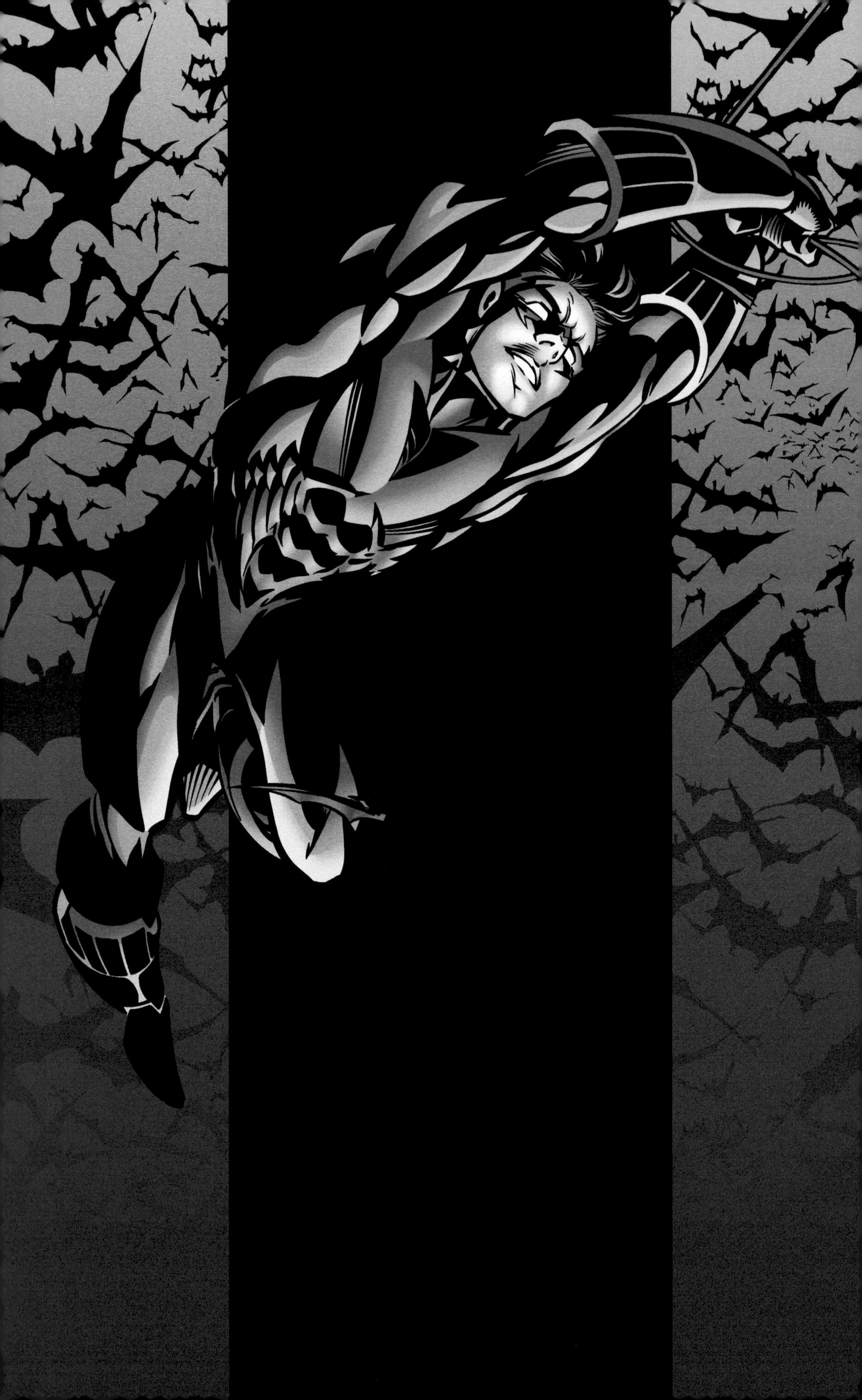

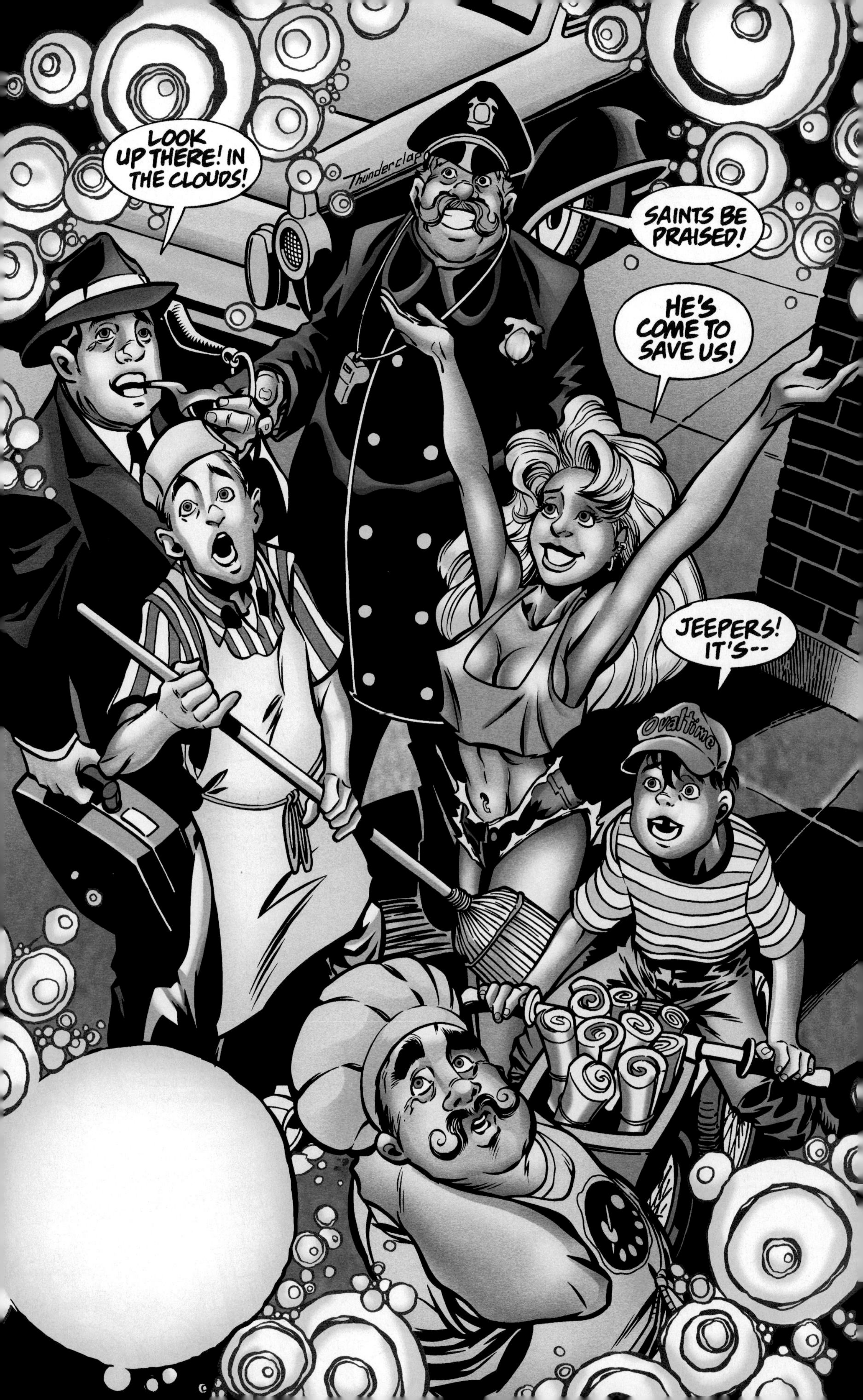
LOOK UP THERE! IN THE CLOUDS!
SAINTS BE PRAISED!
HE'S COME TO SAVE US!
JEEPERS! IT'S--
Thunderclap
Ovaltime

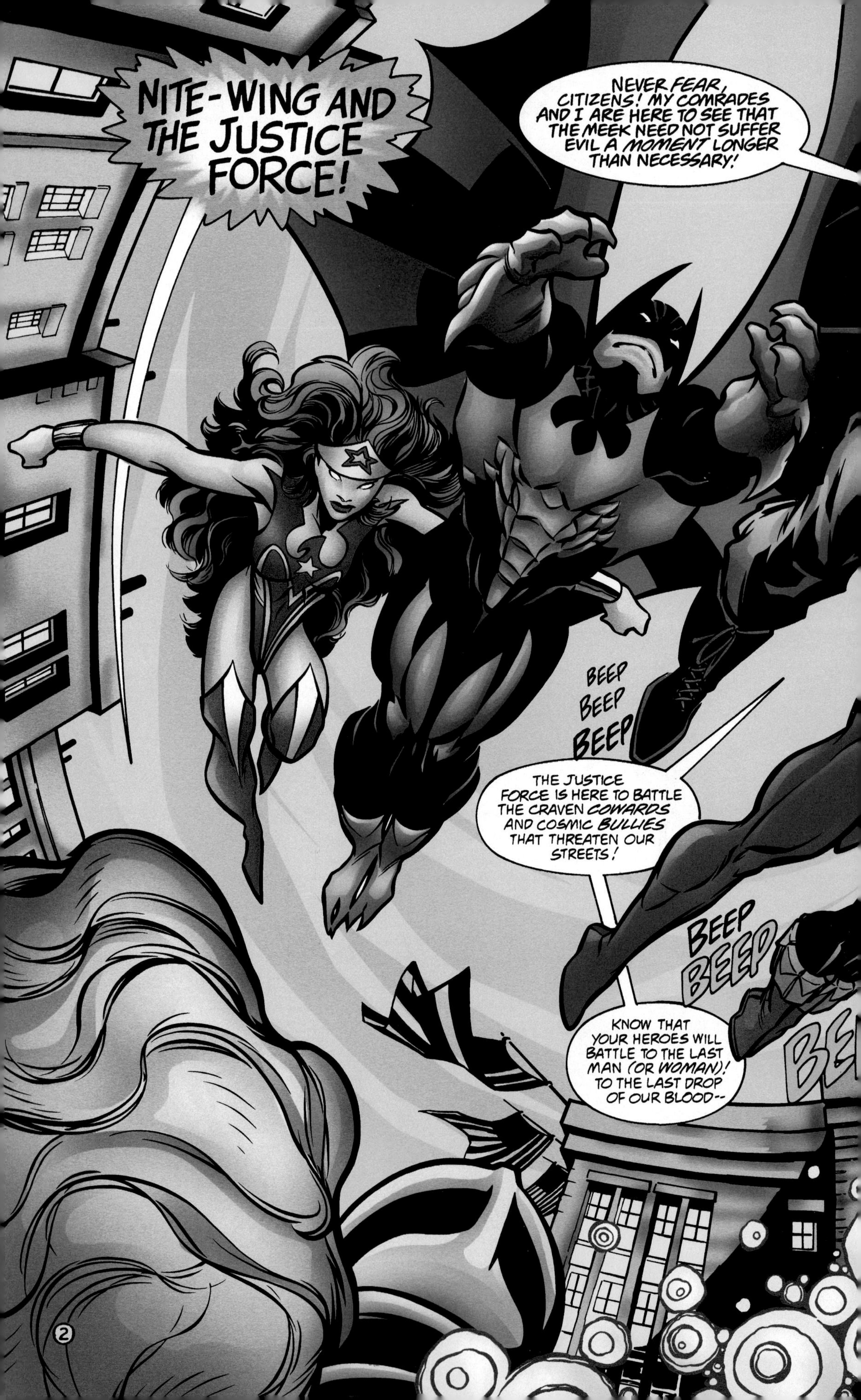
NITE-WING AND THE JUSTICE FORCE!
NEVER FEAR, CITIZENS! MY COMRADES AND I ARE HERE TO SEE THAT THE MEEK NEED NOT SUFFER EVIL A MOMENT LONGER THAN NECESSARY!
BEEP BEEP BEEP
THE JUSTICE FORCE IS HERE TO BATTLE THE CRAVEN COWARDS AND COSMIC BULLIES THAT THREATEN OUR STREETS!
BEEP BEEP
KNOW THAT YOUR HEROES WILL BATTLE TO THE LAST MAN (OR WOMAN)! TO THE LAST DROP OF OUR BLOOD--

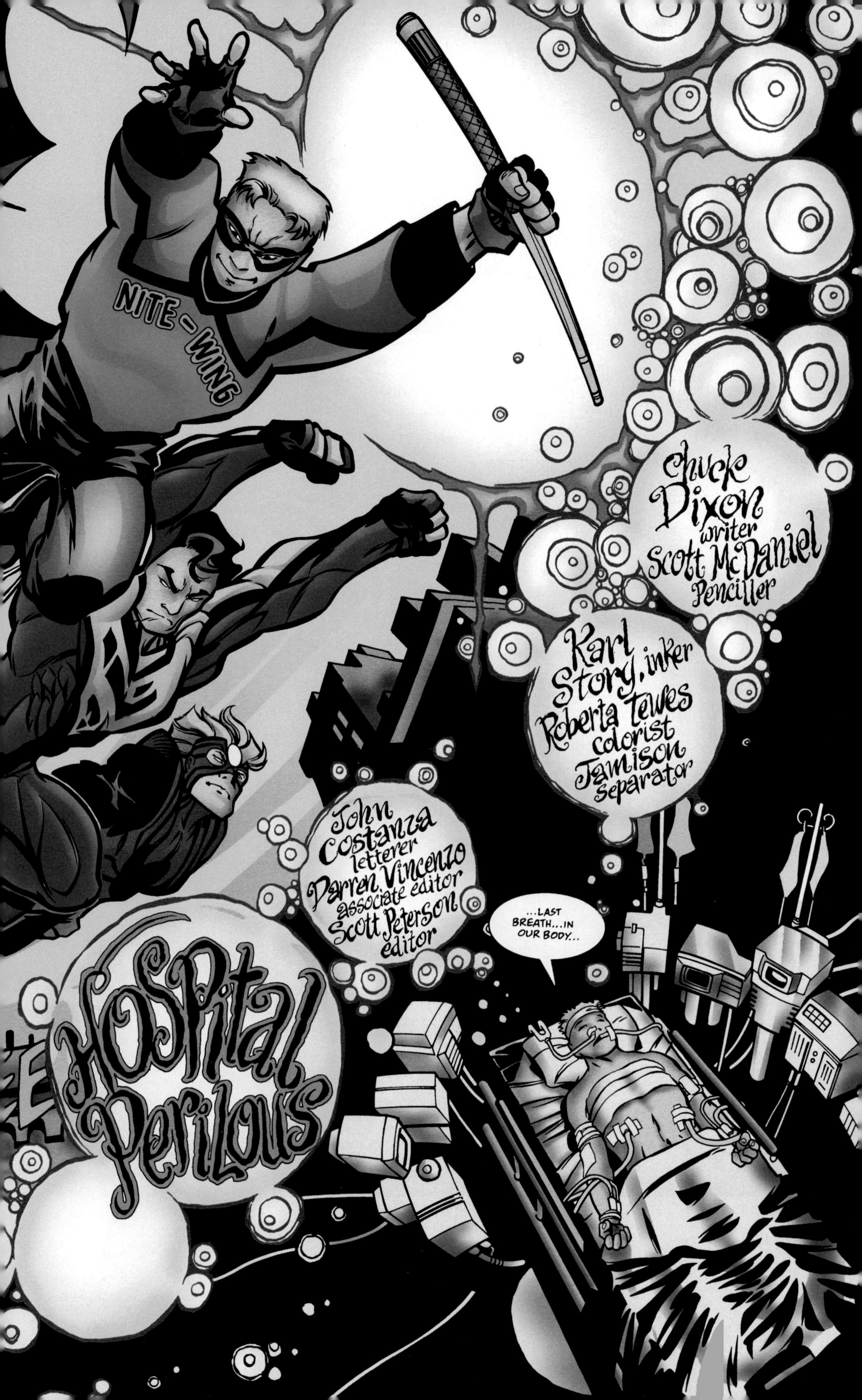
NITE-WING
Chuck Dixon writer
Scott McDaniel Penciller
Karl Story, inker
Roberta Tewes colorist
Jamison separator
John Costanza letterer
Darren Vincenzo associate editor
Scott Peterson editor
...LAST BREATH...IN OUR BODY...
Hospital Perilous

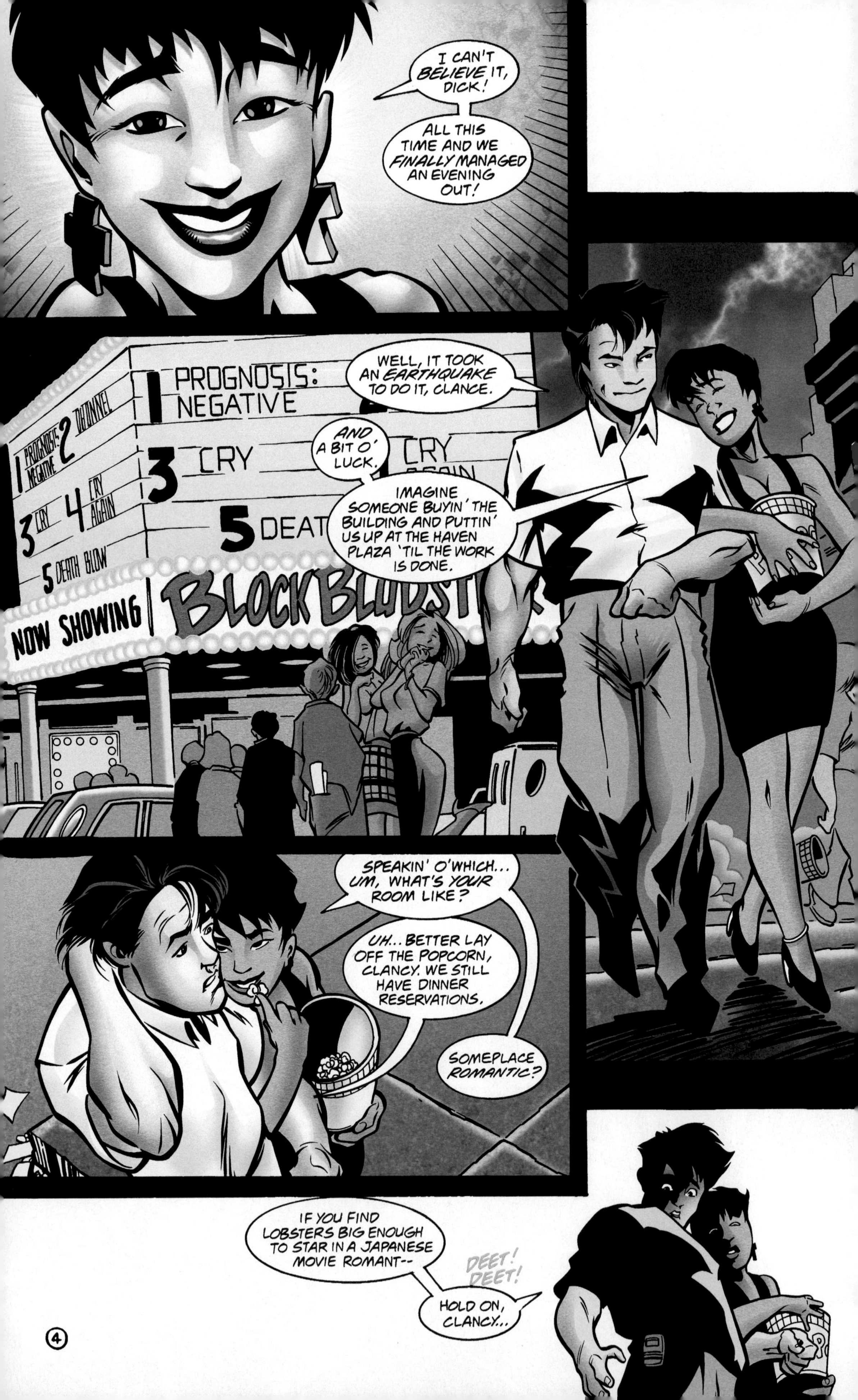
I CAN'T BELIEVE IT, DICK!
ALL THIS TIME AND WE FINALLY MANAGED AN EVENING OUT!
1 PROGNOSIS: NEGATIVE
3 CRY
5 DEAT
1 PROGNOSIS NEGATIVE 2
3 CRY 4 CRY AGAIN
5 DEATH BLOW
NOW SHOWING
BLOCKBLUDSTE
WELL, IT TOOK AN EARTHQUAKE TO DO IT, CLANCE.
AND A BIT O' LUCK.
IMAGINE SOMEONE BUYIN' THE BUILDING AND PUTTIN' US UP AT THE HAVEN PLAZA 'TIL THE WORK IS DONE.
SPEAKIN' O'WHICH... UM, WHAT'S YOUR ROOM LIKE?
UH... BETTER LAY OFF THE POPCORN, CLANCY. WE STILL HAVE DINNER RESERVATIONS.
SOMEPLACE ROMANTIC?
IF YOU FIND LOBSTERS BIG ENOUGH TO STAR IN A JAPANESE MOVIE ROMANT--
DEET! DEET!
HOLD ON, CLANCY...

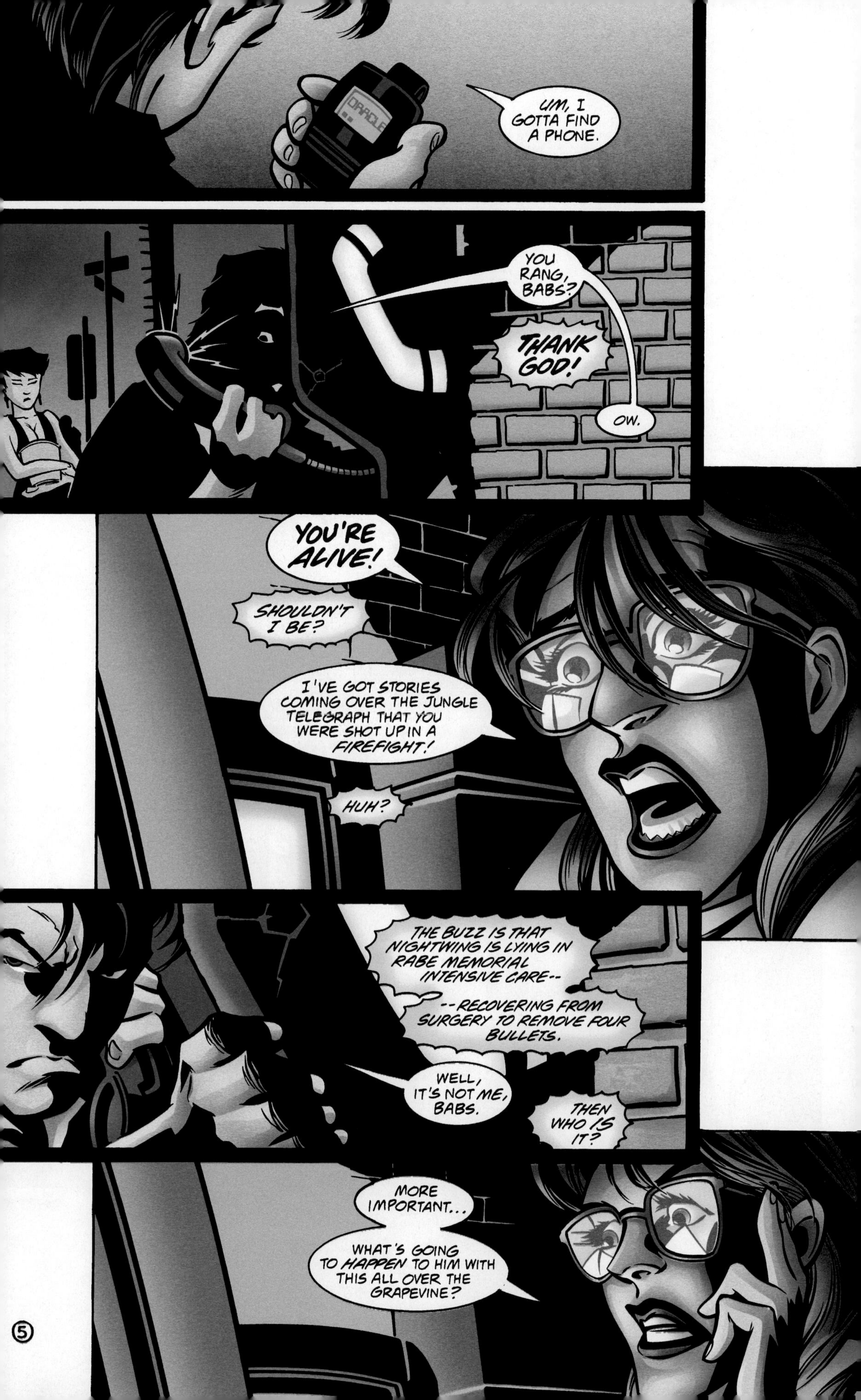
ORACLE
UM, I GOTTA FIND A PHONE.
YOU RANG, BABS?
THANK GOD!
OW.
YOU'RE ALIVE!
SHOULDN'T I BE?
I'VE GOT STORIES COMING OVER THE JUNGLE TELEGRAPH THAT YOU WERE SHOT UP IN A FIREFIGHT!
HUH?
THE BUZZ IS THAT NIGHTWING IS LYING IN RABE MEMORIAL INTENSIVE CARE--
--RECOVERING FROM SURGERY TO REMOVE FOUR BULLETS.
WELL, IT'S NOT ME, BABS.
THEN WHO IS IT?
MORE IMPORTANT...
WHAT'S GOING TO HAPPEN TO HIM WITH THIS ALL OVER THE GRAPEVINE?

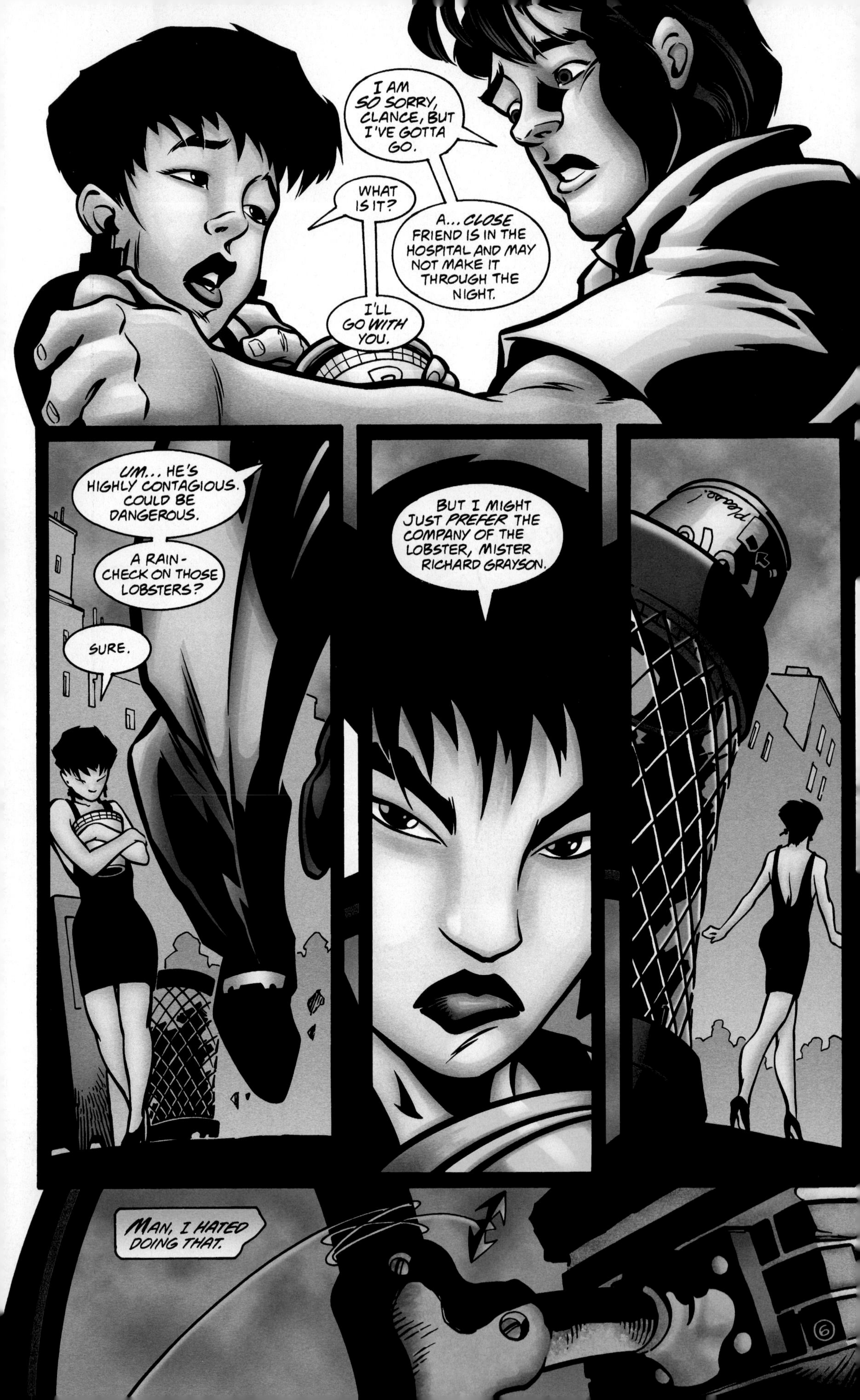
I AM SO SORRY, CLANCE, BUT I'VE GOTTA GO.
WHAT IS IT?
A... CLOSE FRIEND IS IN THE HOSPITAL AND MAY NOT MAKE IT THROUGH THE NIGHT.
I'LL GO WITH YOU.
UM... HE'S HIGHLY CONTAGIOUS. COULD BE DANGEROUS.
A RAIN-CHECK ON THOSE LOBSTERS?
SURE.
BUT I MIGHT JUST PREFER THE COMPANY OF THE LOBSTER, MISTER RICHARD GRAYSON.
MAN, I HATED DOING THAT.
6

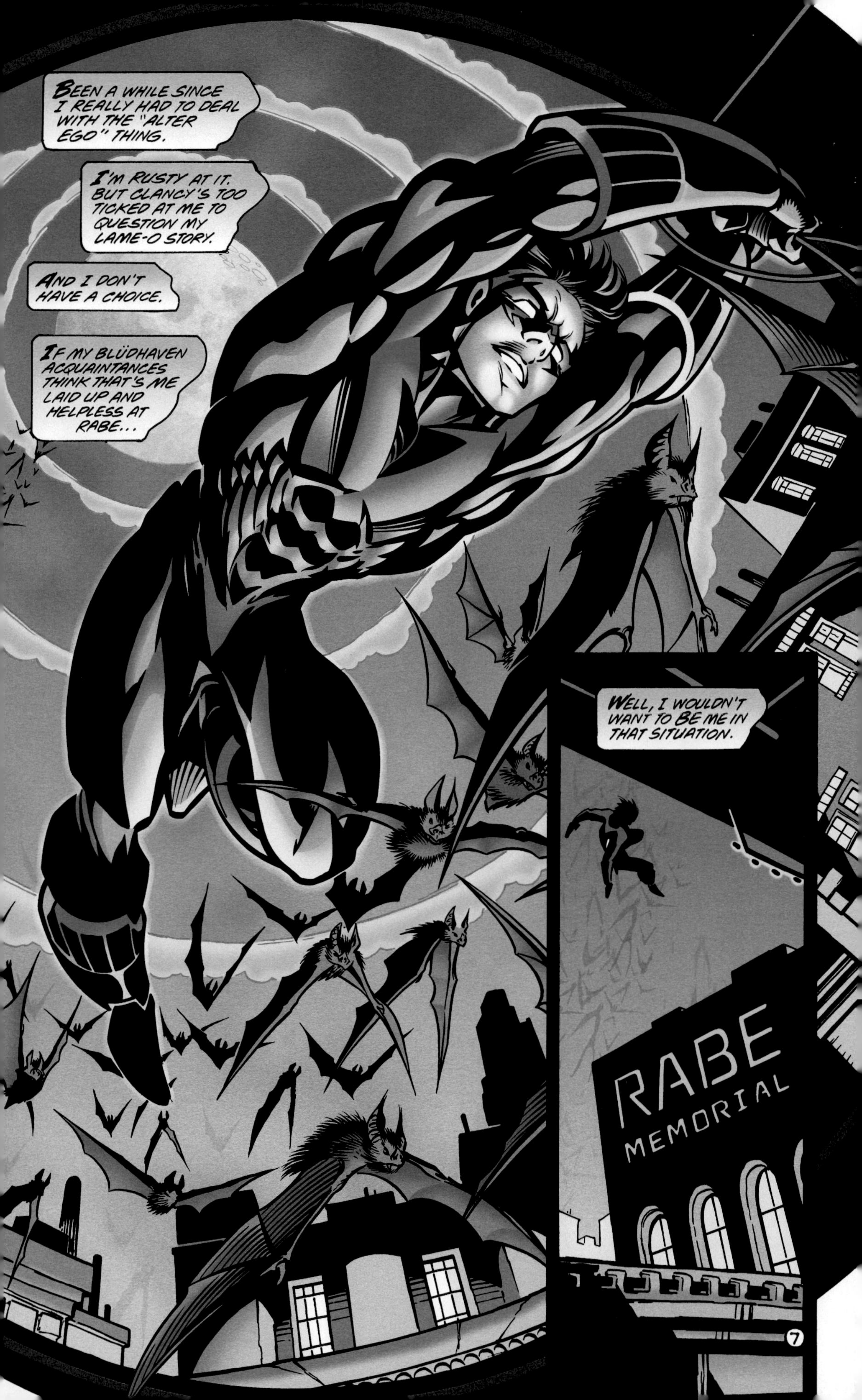
BEEN A WHILE SINCE I REALLY HAD TO DEAL WITH THE "ALTER EGO" THING.
I'M RUSTY AT IT. BUT CLANCY'S TOO TICKED AT ME TO QUESTION MY LAME-O STORY.
AND I DON'T HAVE A CHOICE.
IF MY BLÜDHAVEN ACQUAINTANCES THINK THAT'S ME LAID UP AND HELPLESS AT RABE...
WELL, I WOULDN'T WANT TO BE ME IN THAT SITUATION.
RABE MEMORIAL

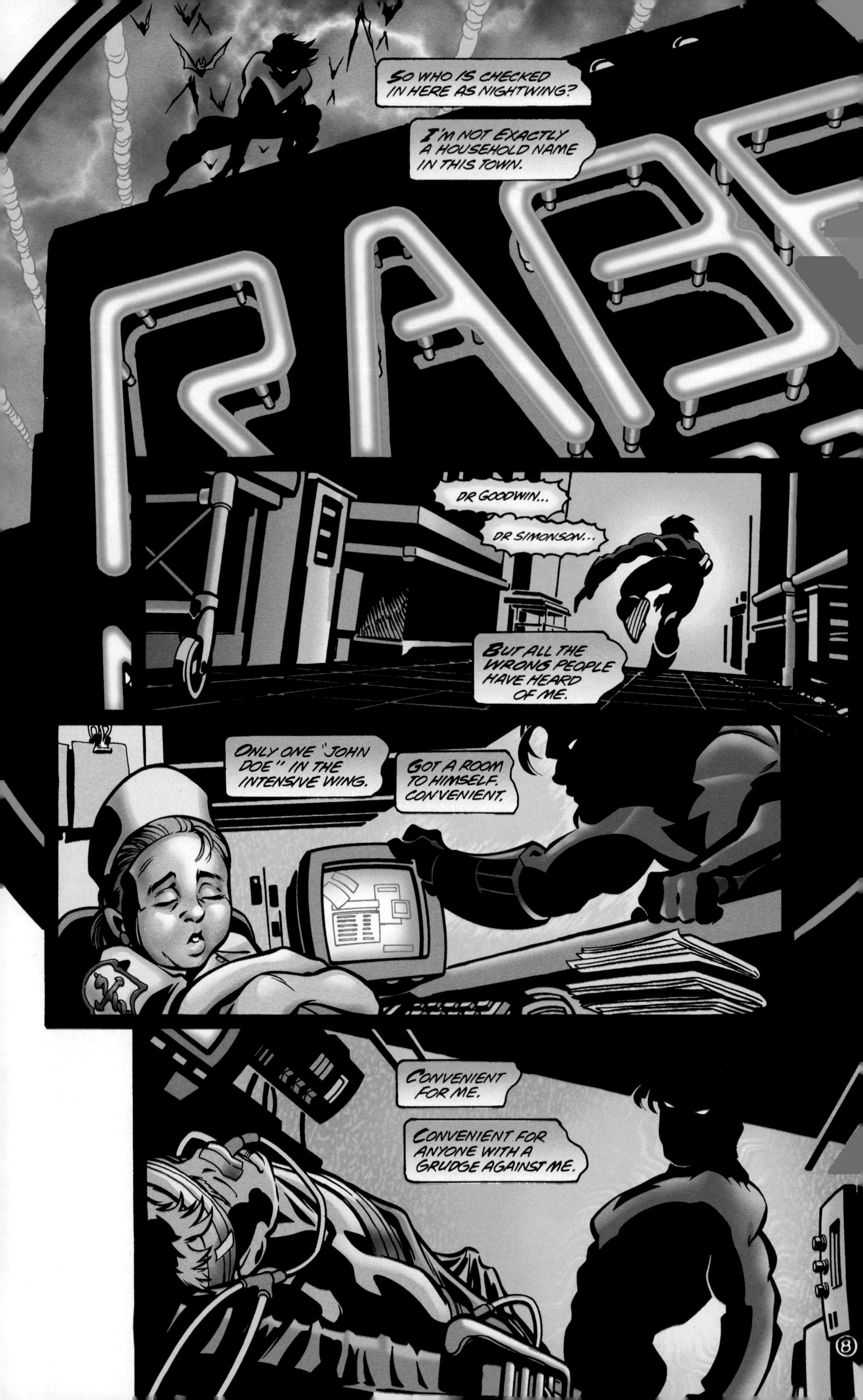

SO WHO IS CHECKED IN HERE AS NIGHTWING?
I'M NOT EXACTLY A HOUSEHOLD NAME IN THIS TOWN.
DR GOODWIN...
DR SIMONSON...
BUT ALL THE WRONG PEOPLE HAVE HEARD OF ME.
ONLY ONE "JOHN DOE" IN THE INTENSIVE WING.
GOT A ROOM TO HIMSELF. CONVENIENT.
CONVENIENT FOR ME.
CONVENIENT FOR ANYONE WITH A GRUDGE AGAINST ME.

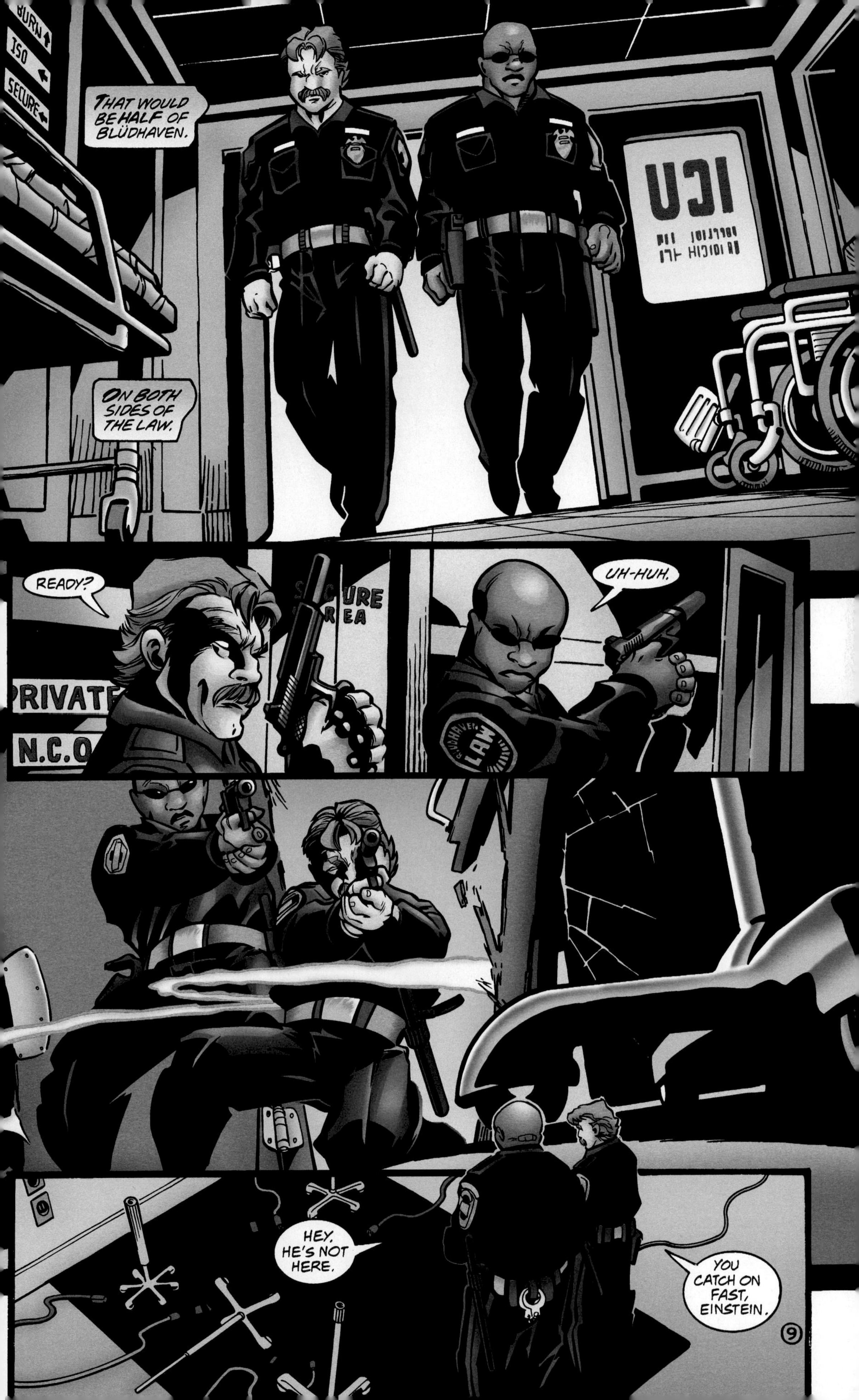
BURN
ISO
SECURE
THAT WOULD BE HALF OF BLÜDHAVEN.
UCI
ON BOTH SIDES OF THE LAW.
READY?
SECURE AREA
PRIVATE
N.C.O
UH-HUH.
LAW
HEY. HE'S NOT HERE.
YOU CATCH ON FAST, EINSTEIN.
9

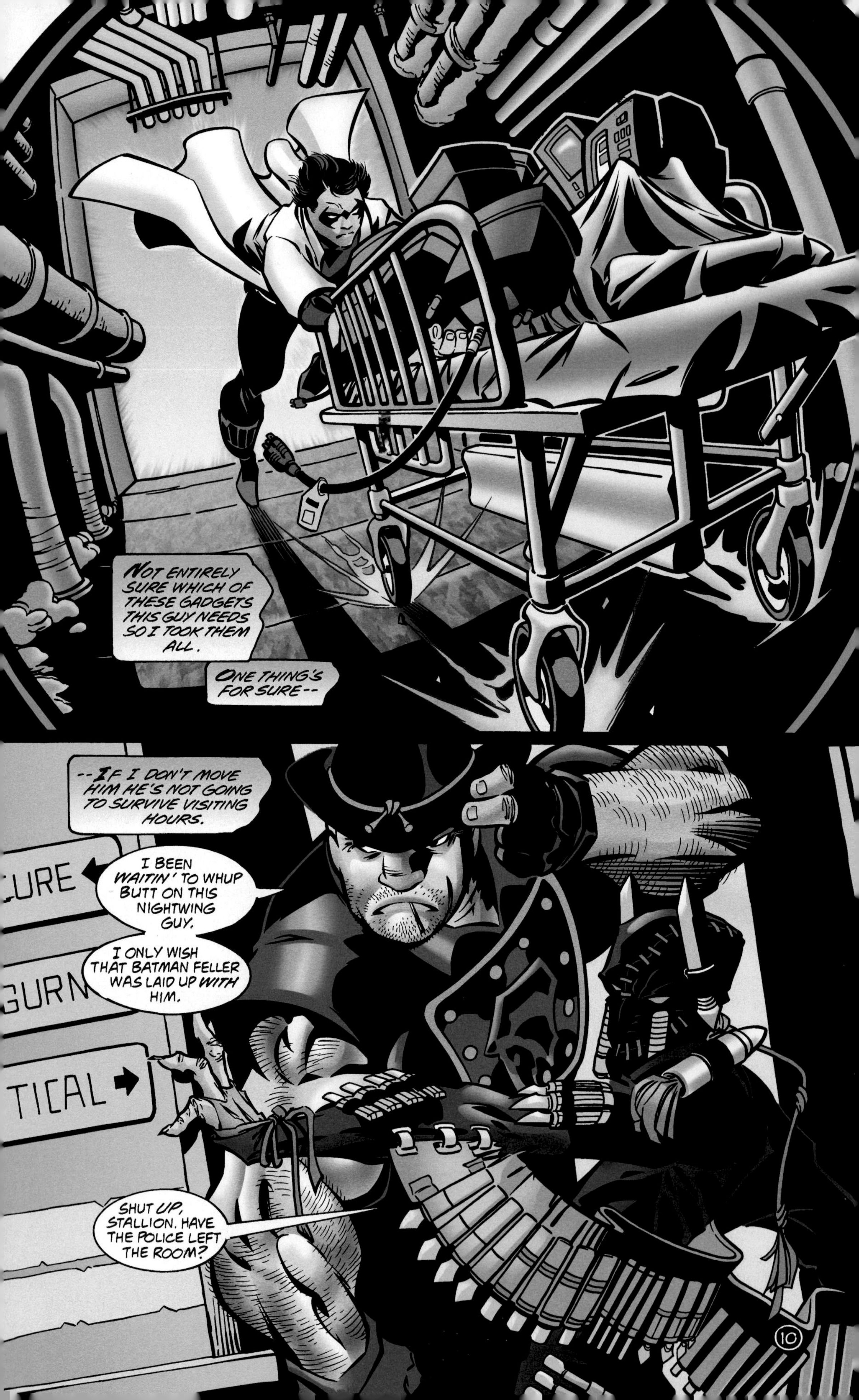
NOT ENTIRELY SURE WHICH OF THESE GADGETS THIS GUY NEEDS SO I TOOK THEM ALL.
ONE THING'S FOR SURE--
--IF I DON'T MOVE HIM HE'S NOT GOING TO SURVIVE VISITING HOURS.
CURE
GURN
TICAL
I BEEN WAITIN' TO WHUP BUTT ON THIS NIGHTWING GUY.
I ONLY WISH THAT BATMAN FELLER WAS LAID UP WITH HIM.
SHUT UP, STALLION. HAVE THE POLICE LEFT THE ROOM?
10

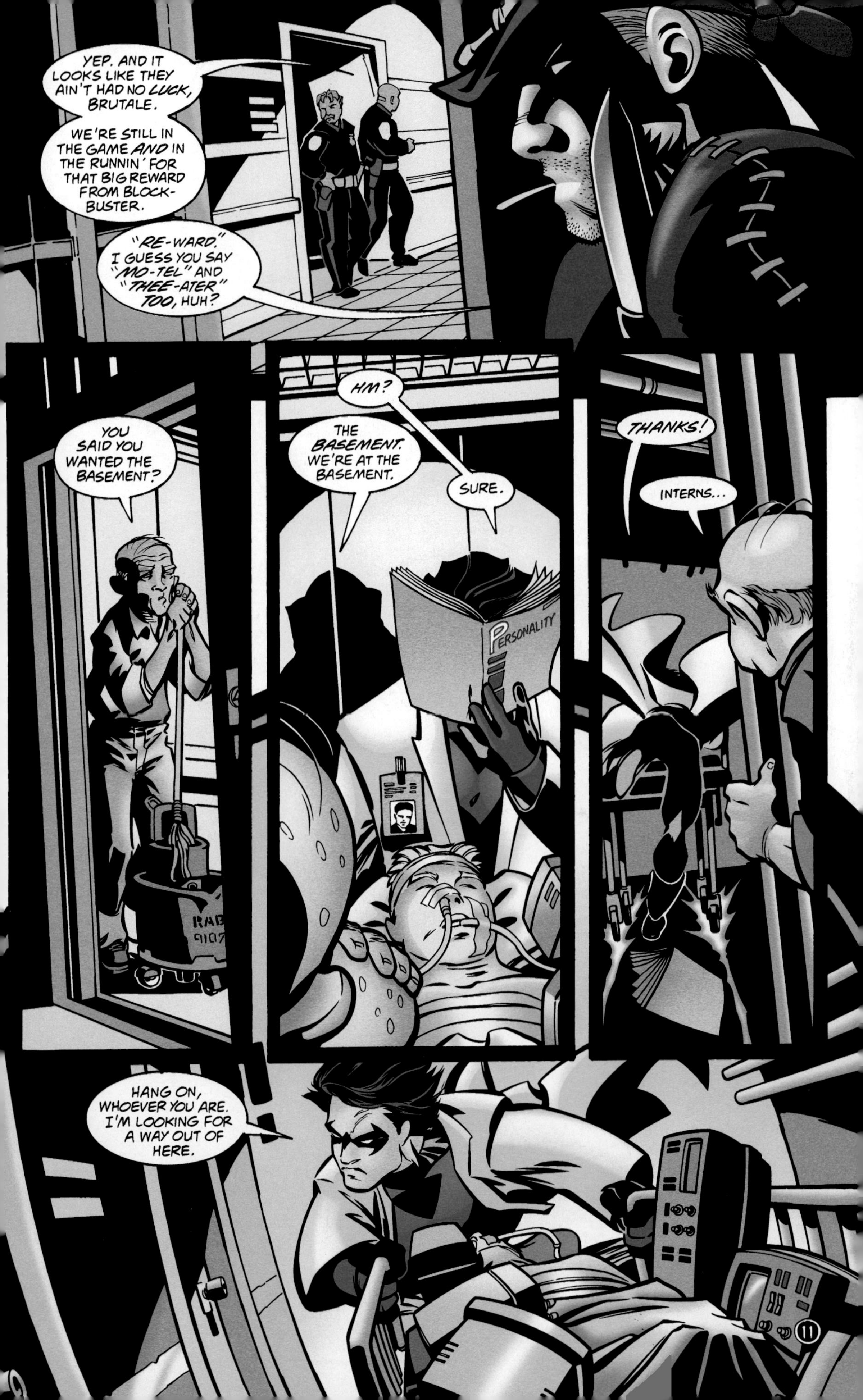
YEP. AND IT LOOKS LIKE THEY AIN'T HAD NO *LUCK*, BRUTALE.
WE'RE STILL IN THE GAME *AND* IN THE RUNNIN' FOR THAT BIG REWARD FROM BLOCK-BUSTER.
"RE-WARD." I GUESS YOU SAY "MO-TEL" AND "THEE-ATER" TOO, HUH?
YOU SAID YOU WANTED THE BASEMENT?
HM?
THE *BASEMENT*. WE'RE AT THE BASEMENT.
SURE.
PERSONALITY
THANKS!
INTERNS...
HANG ON, WHOEVER YOU ARE. I'M LOOKING FOR A WAY OUT OF HERE.
11

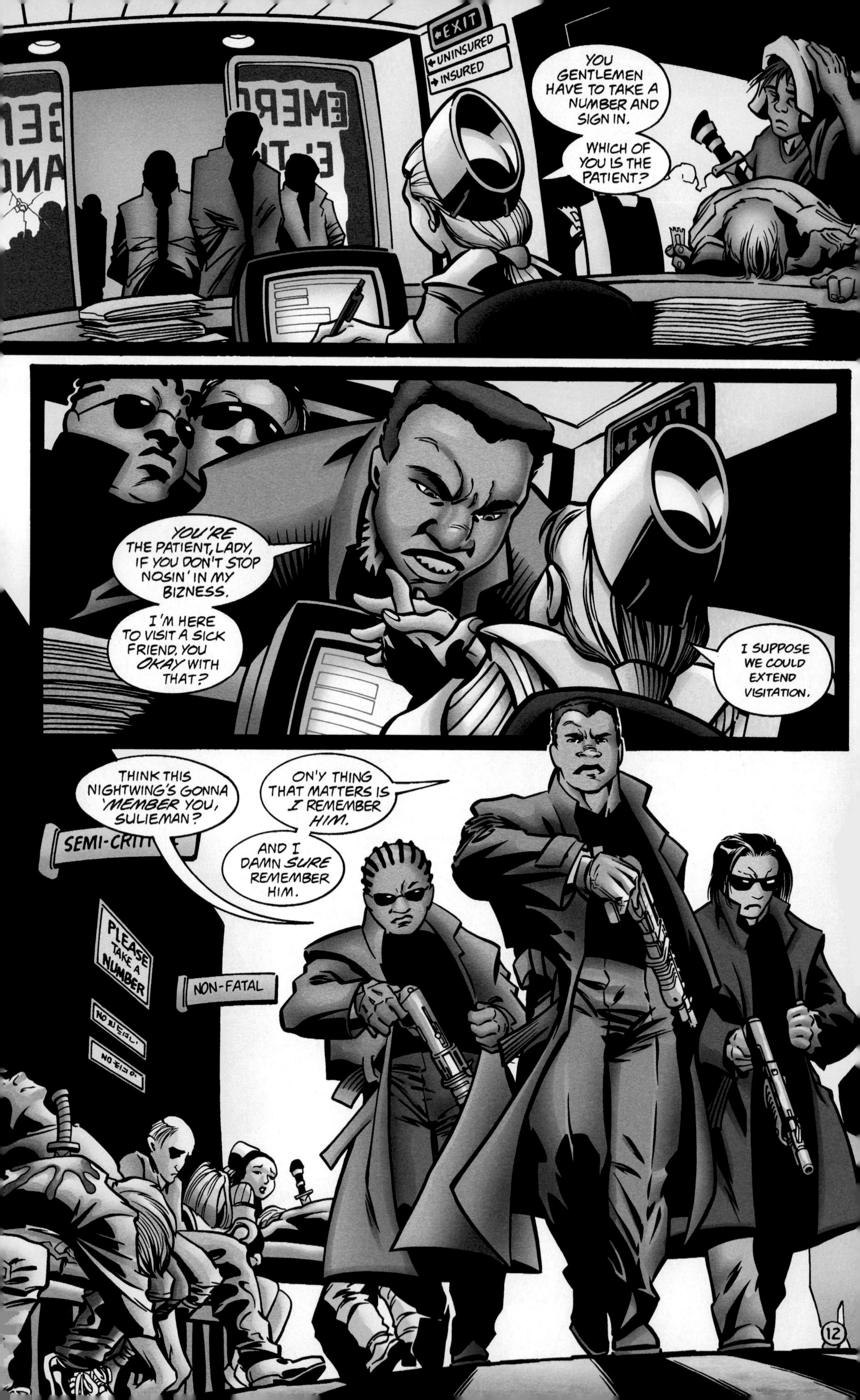
EXIT
UNINSURED
INSURED
YOU GENTLEMEN HAVE TO TAKE A NUMBER AND SIGN IN.
WHICH OF YOU IS THE PATIENT?
YOU'RE THE PATIENT, LADY, IF YOU DON'T STOP NOSIN' IN MY BIZNESS.
I'M HERE TO VISIT A SICK FRIEND. YOU OKAY WITH THAT?
I SUPPOSE WE COULD EXTEND VISITATION.
THINK THIS NIGHTWING'S GONNA 'MEMBER YOU, SULIEMAN?
ON'Y THING THAT MATTERS IS I REMEMBER HIM.
AND I DAMN SURE REMEMBER HIM.
PLEASE TAKE A NUMBER
NON-FATAL
12

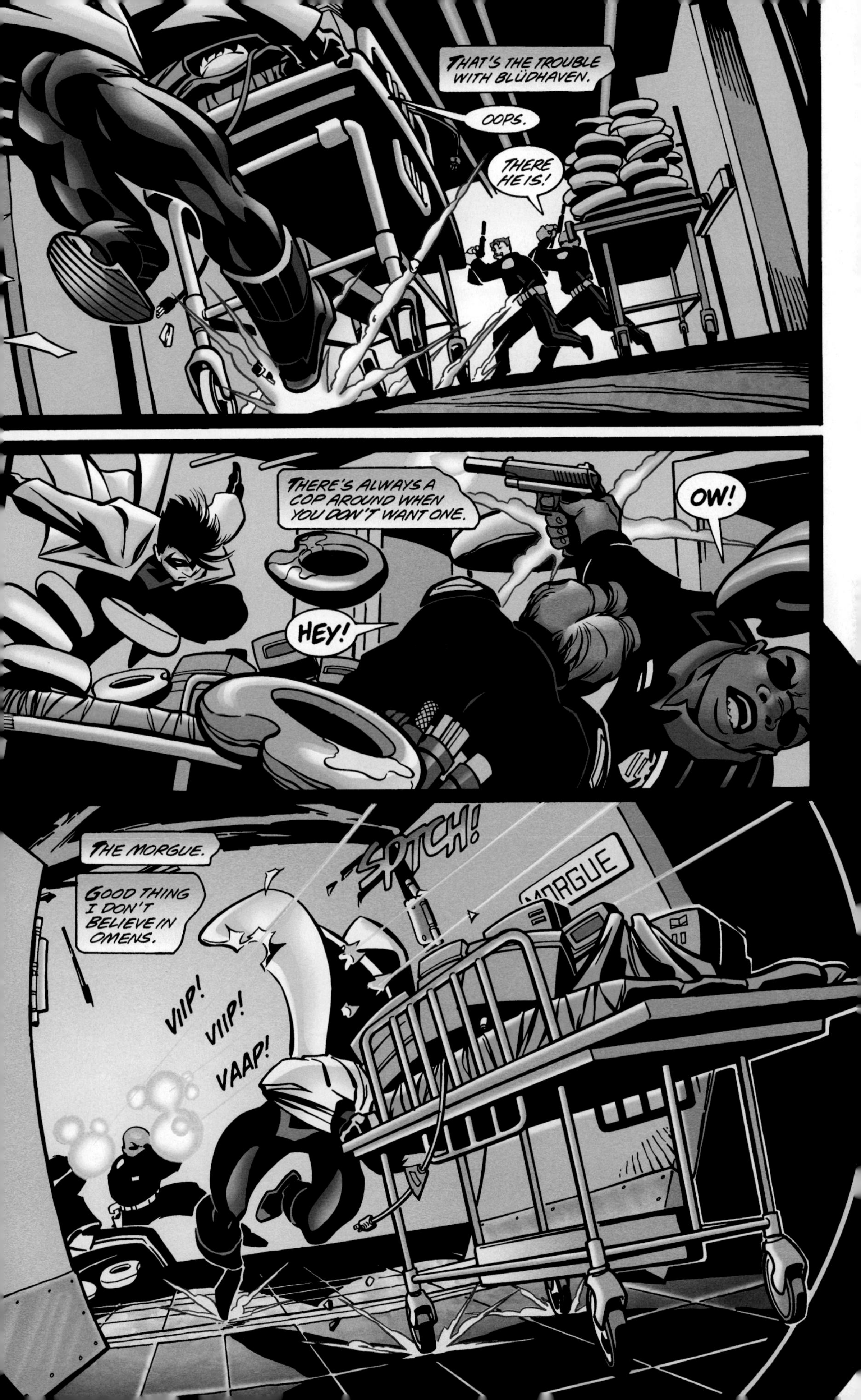
THAT'S THE TROUBLE WITH BLÜDHAVEN.
OOPS.
THERE HE IS!
THERE'S ALWAYS A COP AROUND WHEN YOU DON'T WANT ONE.
OW!
HEY!
THE MORGUE.
GOOD THING I DON'T BELIEVE IN OMENS.
SPTCH!
MORGUE
VIIP!
VIIP!
VAAP!

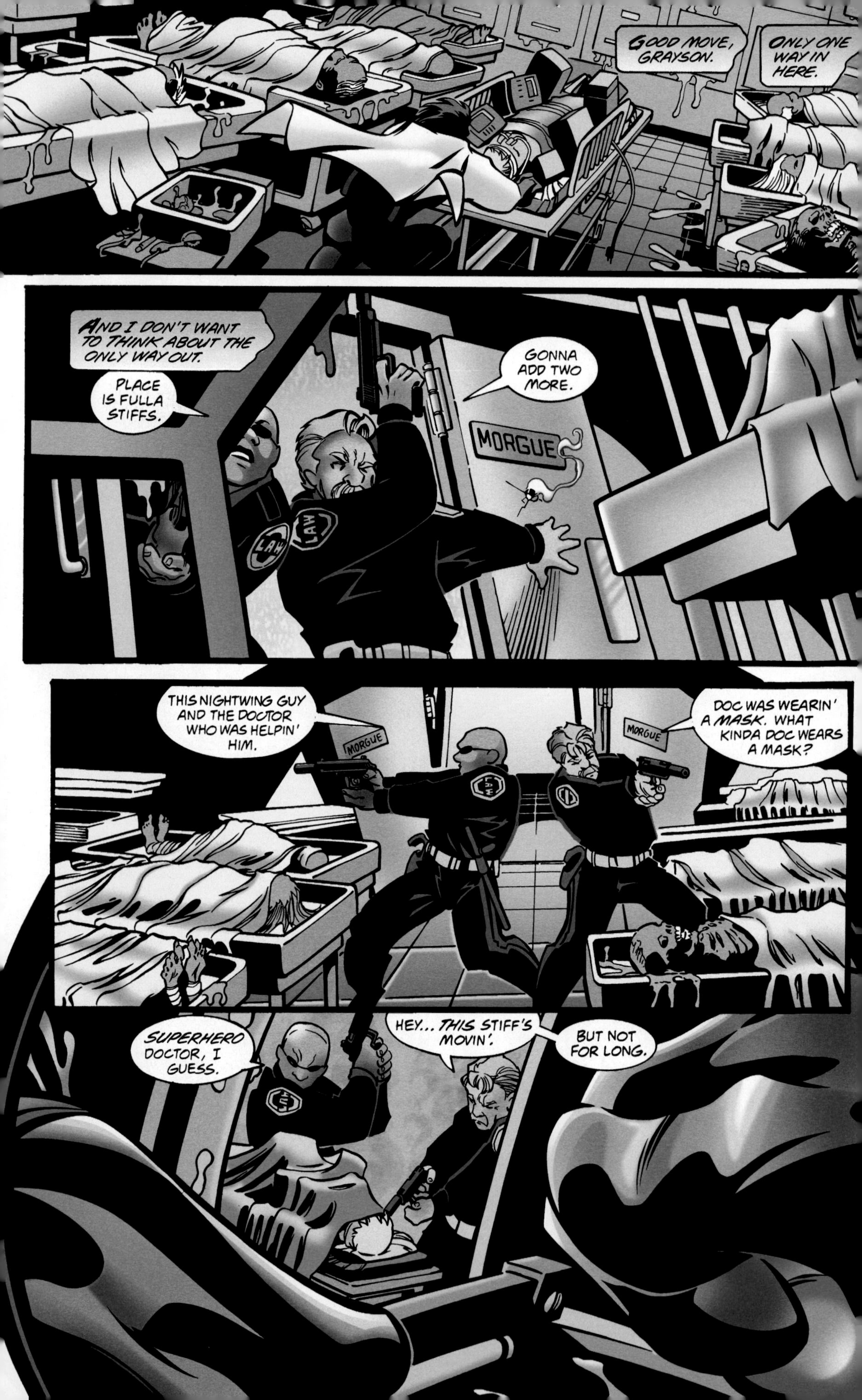
GOOD MOVE, GRAYSON.
ONLY ONE WAY IN HERE.
AND I DON'T WANT TO THINK ABOUT THE ONLY WAY OUT.
PLACE IS FULLA STIFFS.
GONNA ADD TWO MORE.
MORGUE
THIS NIGHTWING GUY AND THE DOCTOR WHO WAS HELPIN' HIM.
MORGUE
MORGUE
DOC WAS WEARIN' A MASK. WHAT KINDA DOC WEARS A MASK?
SUPERHERO DOCTOR, I GUESS.
HEY... THIS STIFF'S MOVIN'.
BUT NOT FOR LONG.

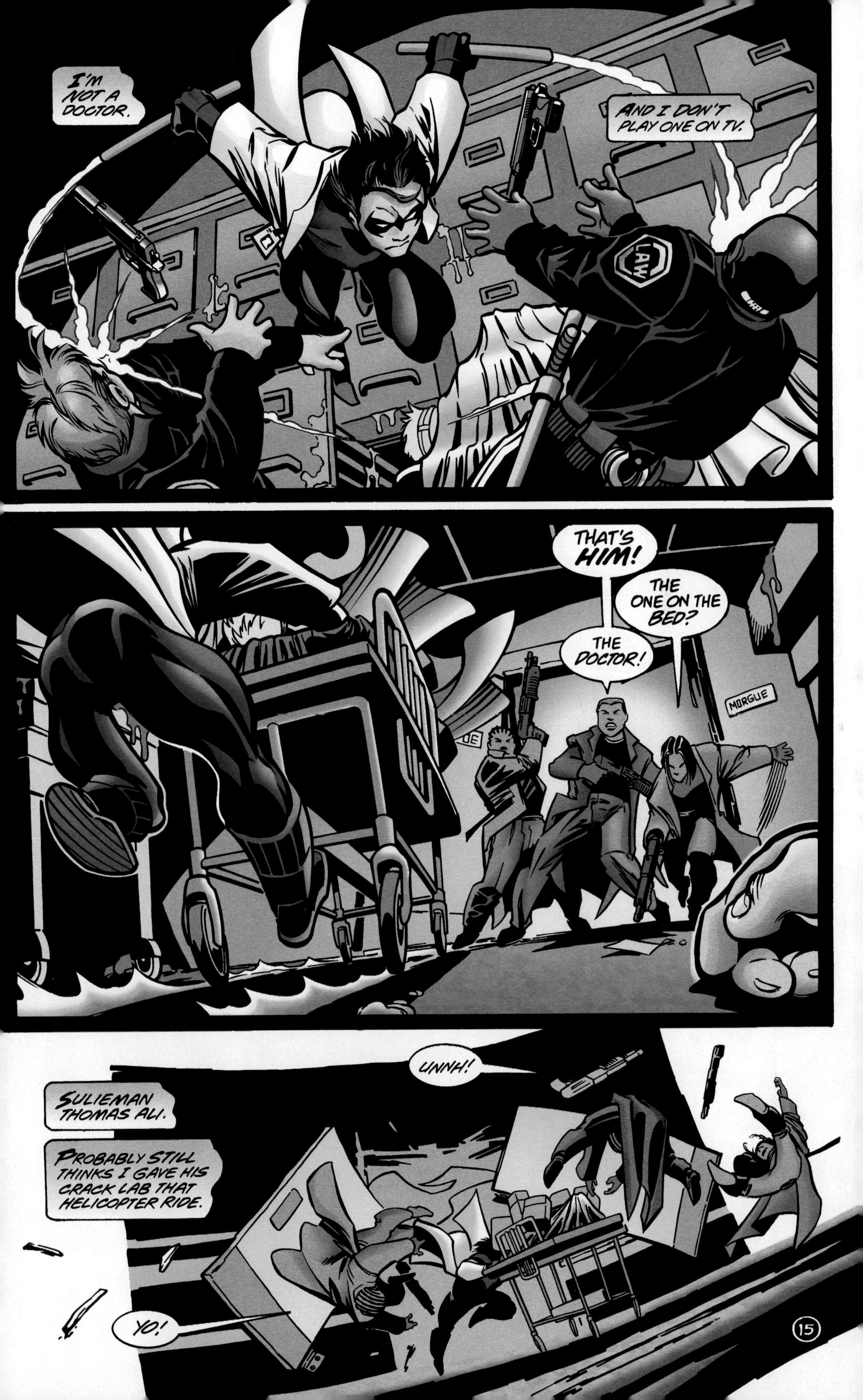
I'M NOT A DOCTOR.
AND I DON'T PLAY ONE ON TV.
LAW
THAT'S HIM!
THE ONE ON THE BED?
THE DOCTOR!
MORGUE
UNNH!
SULIEMAN THOMAS ALI.
PROBABLY STILL THINKS I GAVE HIS CRACK LAB THAT HELICOPTER RIDE.
YO!

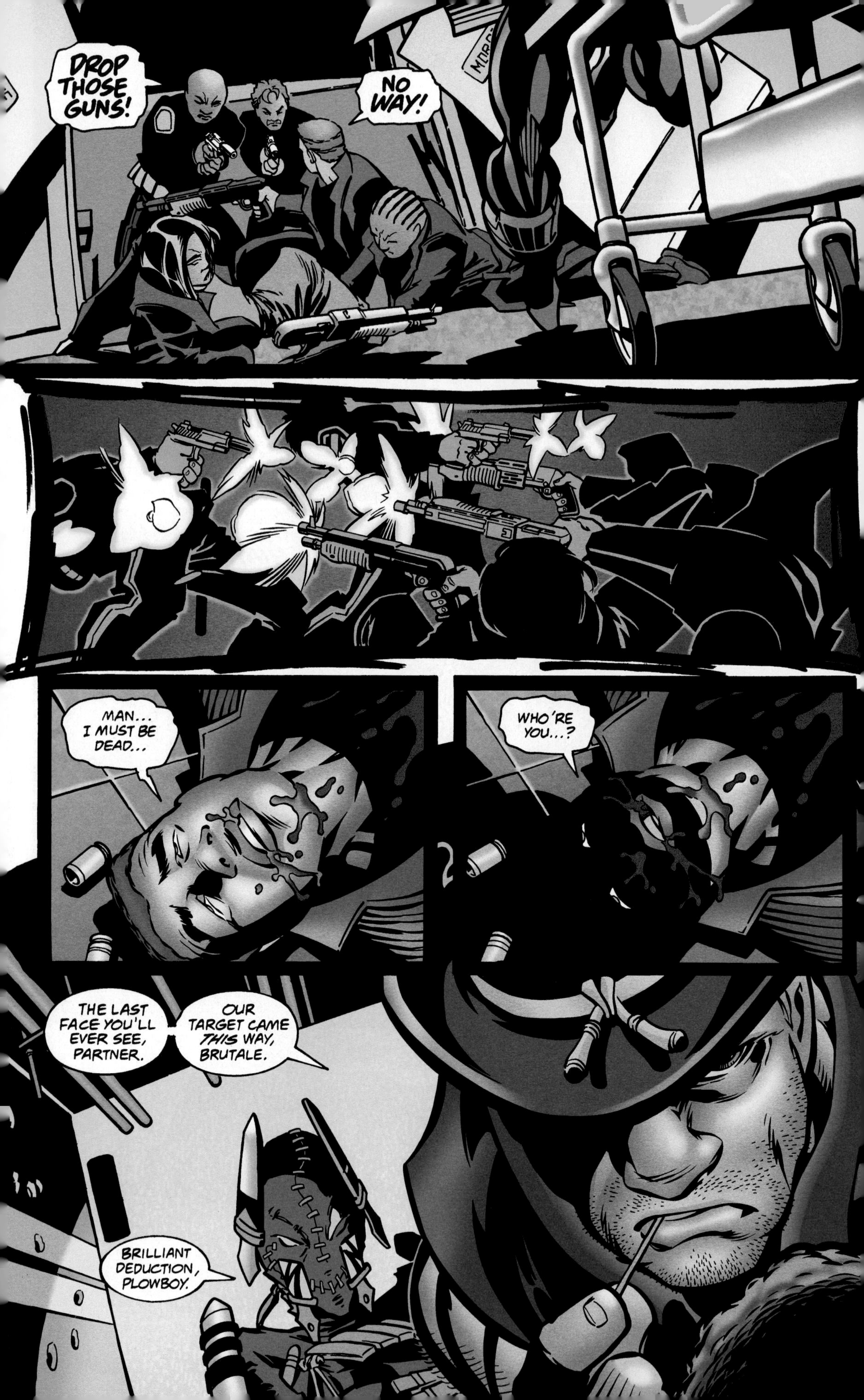
DROP THOSE GUNS!
NO WAY!
MAN... I MUST BE DEAD...
WHO'RE YOU...?
THE LAST FACE YOU'LL EVER SEE, PARTNER.
OUR TARGET CAME THIS WAY, BRUTALE.
BRILLIANT DEDUCTION, PLOWBOY.

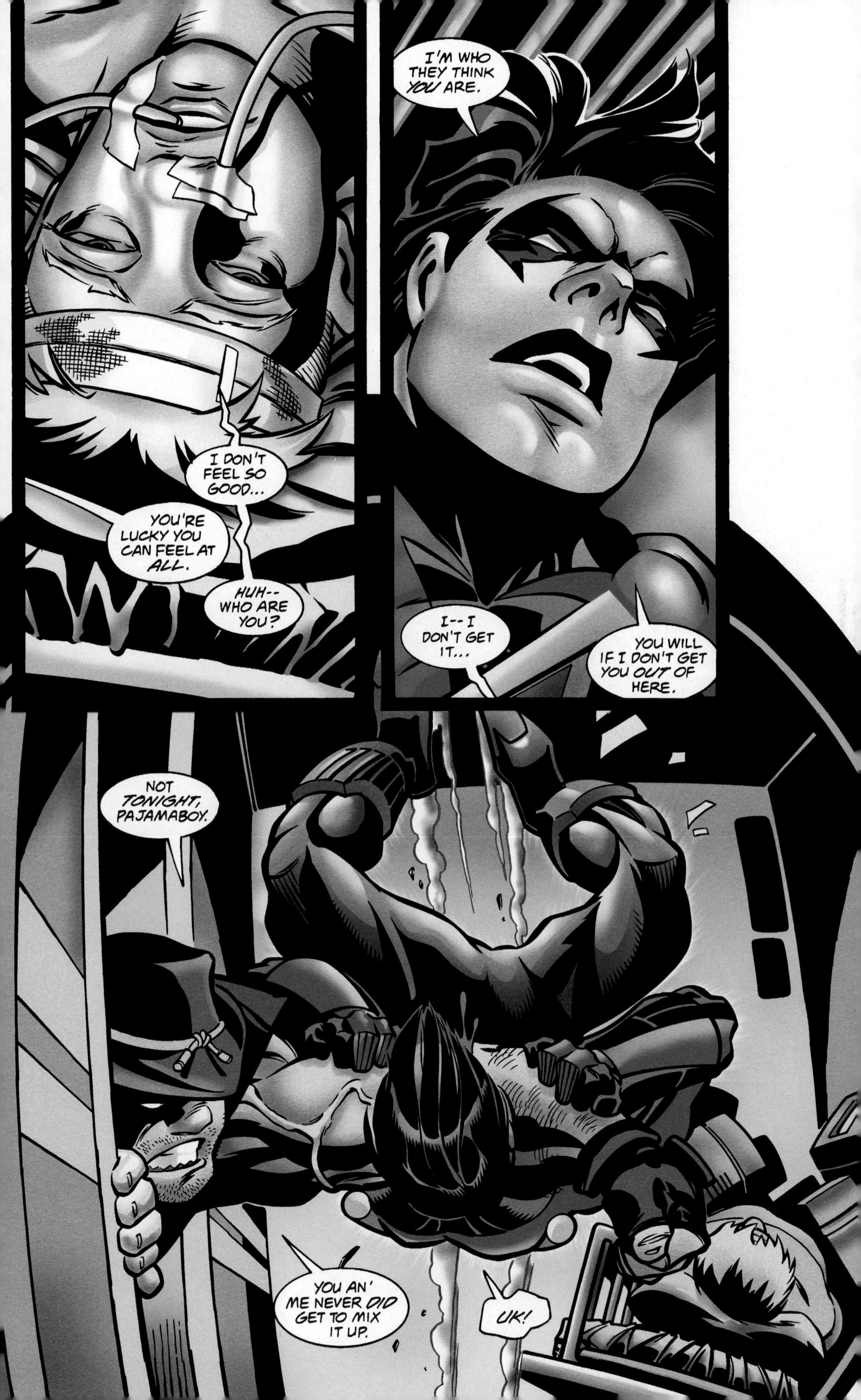
I DON'T FEEL SO GOOD...
YOU'RE LUCKY YOU CAN FEEL AT ALL.
HUH-- WHO ARE YOU?
I'M WHO THEY THINK YOU ARE.
I-- I DON'T GET IT...
YOU WILL IF I DON'T GET YOU OUT OF HERE.
NOT TONIGHT, PAJAMABOY.
YOU AN' ME NEVER DID GET TO MIX IT UP.
UK!

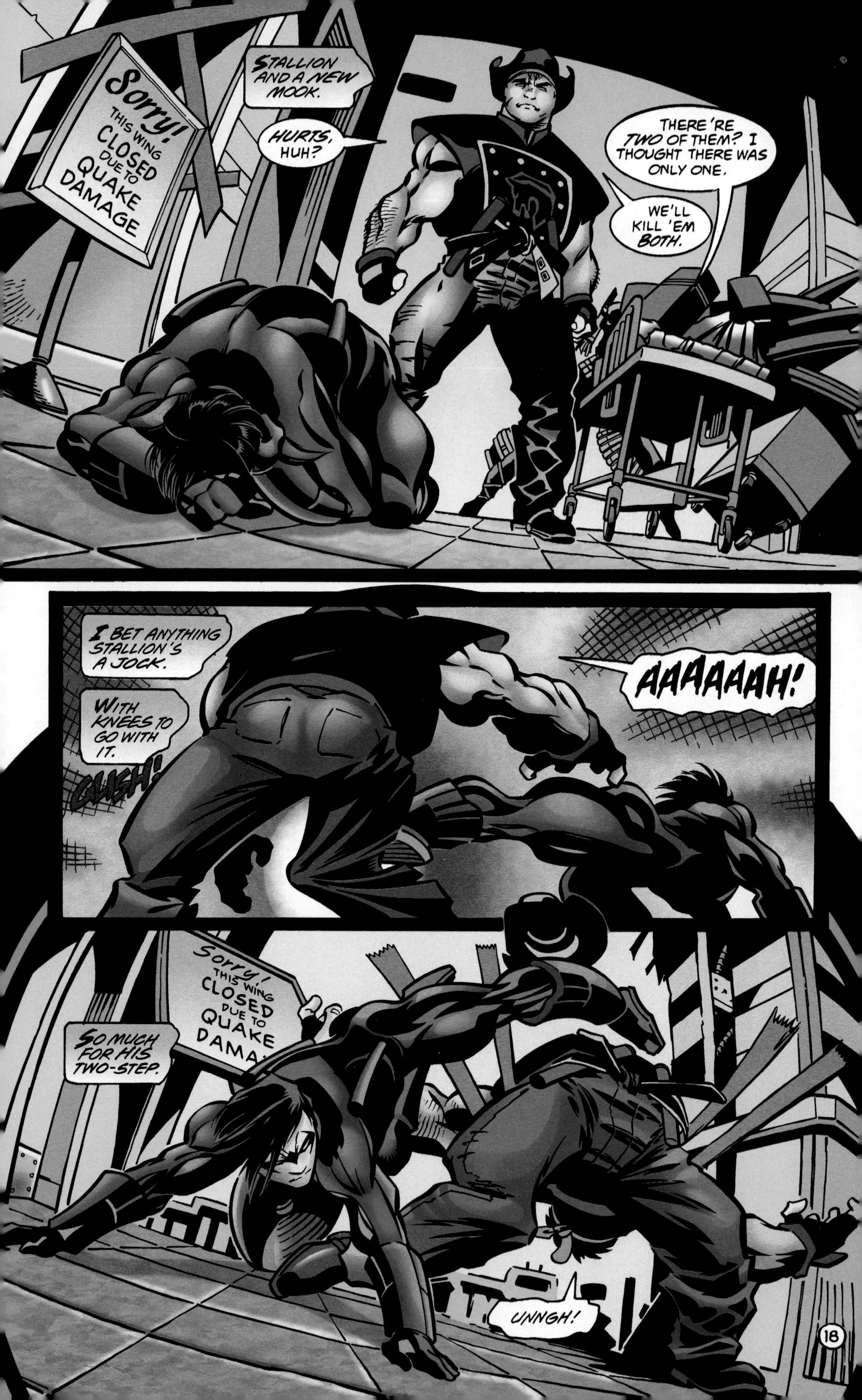
Sorry! This wing CLOSED due to QUAKE DAMAGE
STALLION AND A NEW MOOK.
HURTS, HUH?
THERE'RE TWO OF THEM? I THOUGHT THERE WAS ONLY ONE.
WE'LL KILL 'EM BOTH.
I BET ANYTHING STALLION'S A JOCK.
WITH KNEES TO GO WITH IT.
CLISH!
AAAAAAH!
Sorry! This wing CLOSED due to QUAKE DAMA
SO MUCH FOR HIS TWO-STEP.
UNNGH!
18

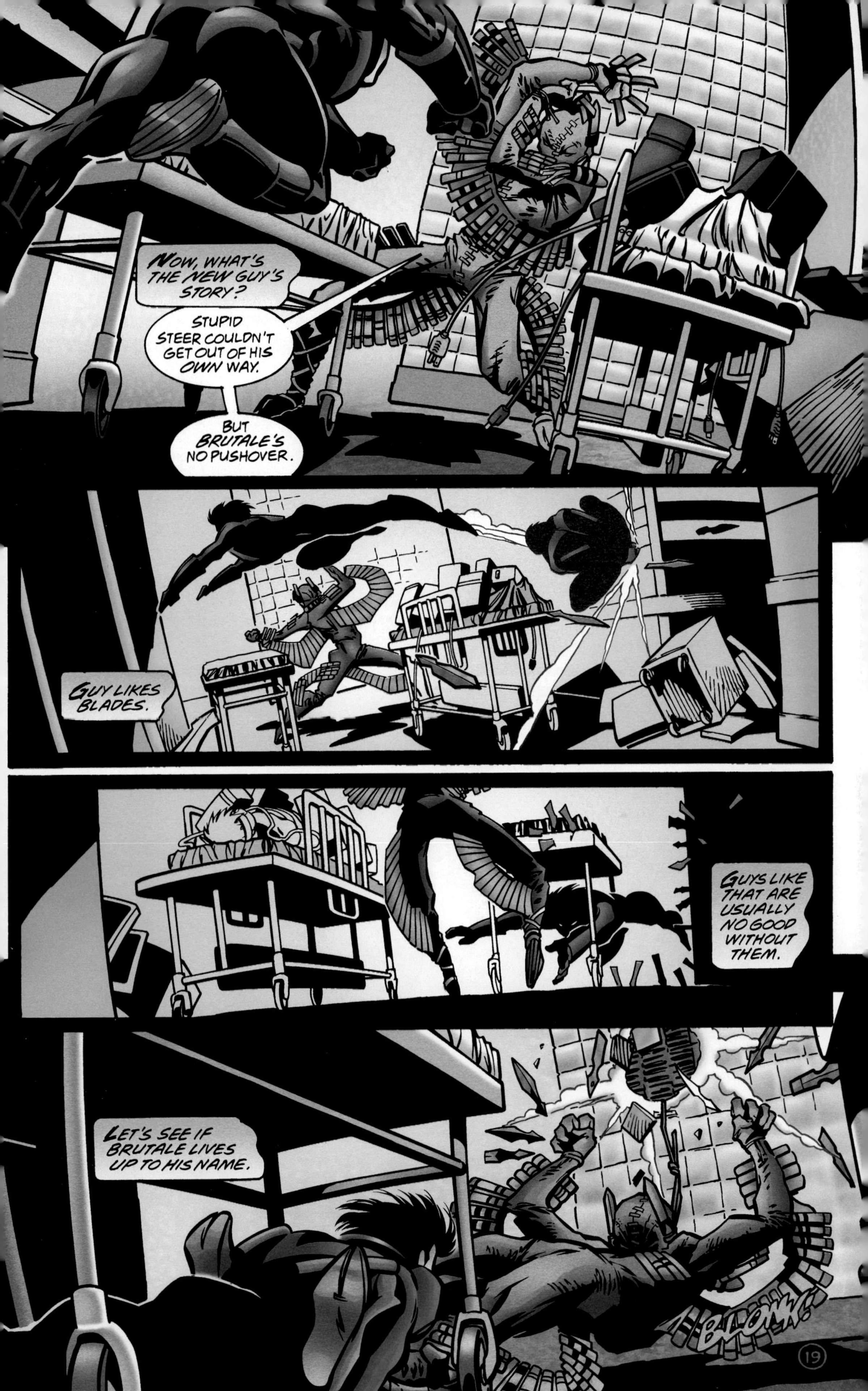
NOW, WHAT'S THE NEW GUY'S STORY?
STUPID STEER COULDN'T GET OUT OF HIS OWN WAY.
BUT BRUTALE'S NO PUSHOVER.
GUY LIKES BLADES.
GUYS LIKE THAT ARE USUALLY NO GOOD WITHOUT THEM.
LET'S SEE IF BRUTALE LIVES UP TO HIS NAME.
BALOOM!

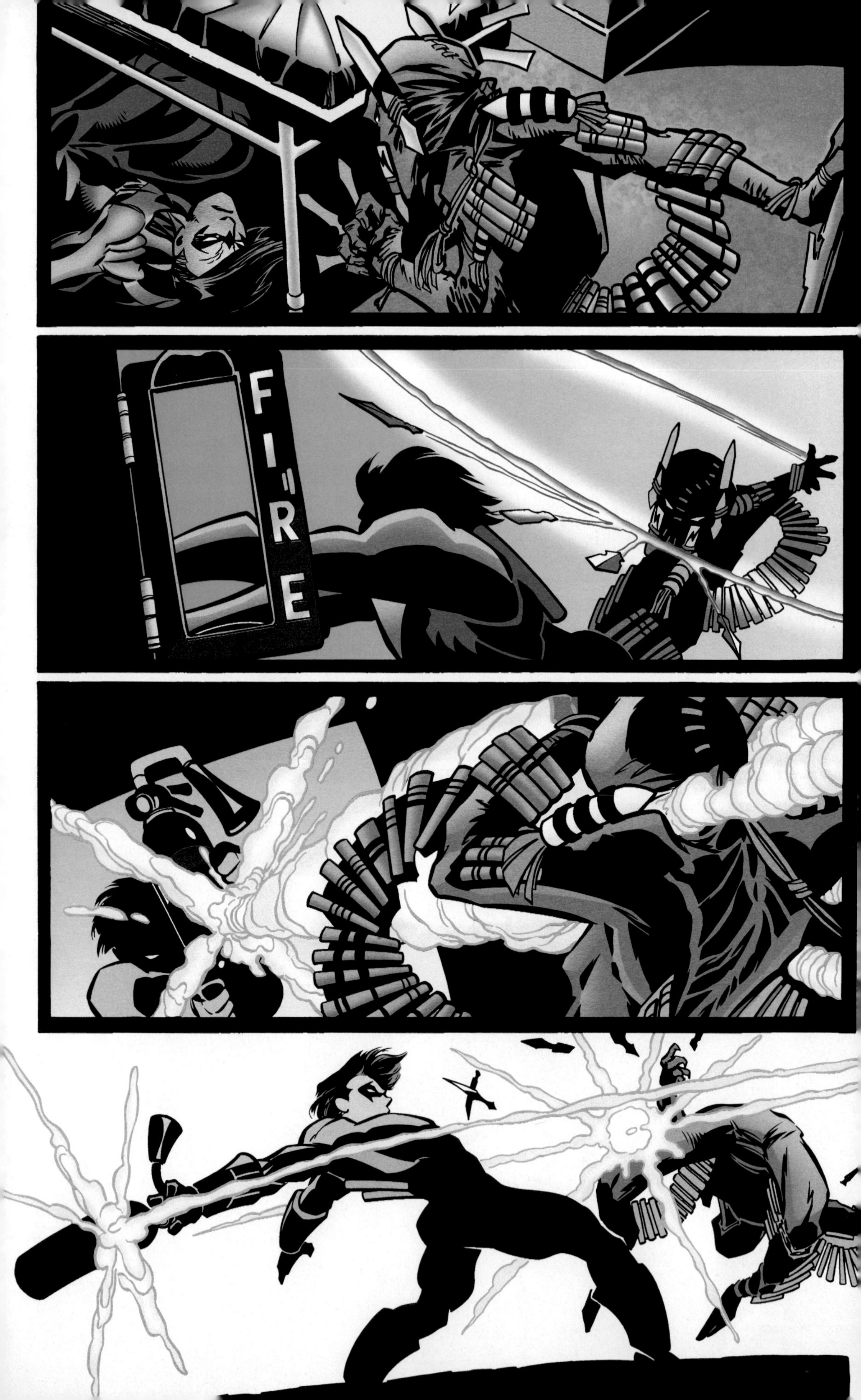
FIRE

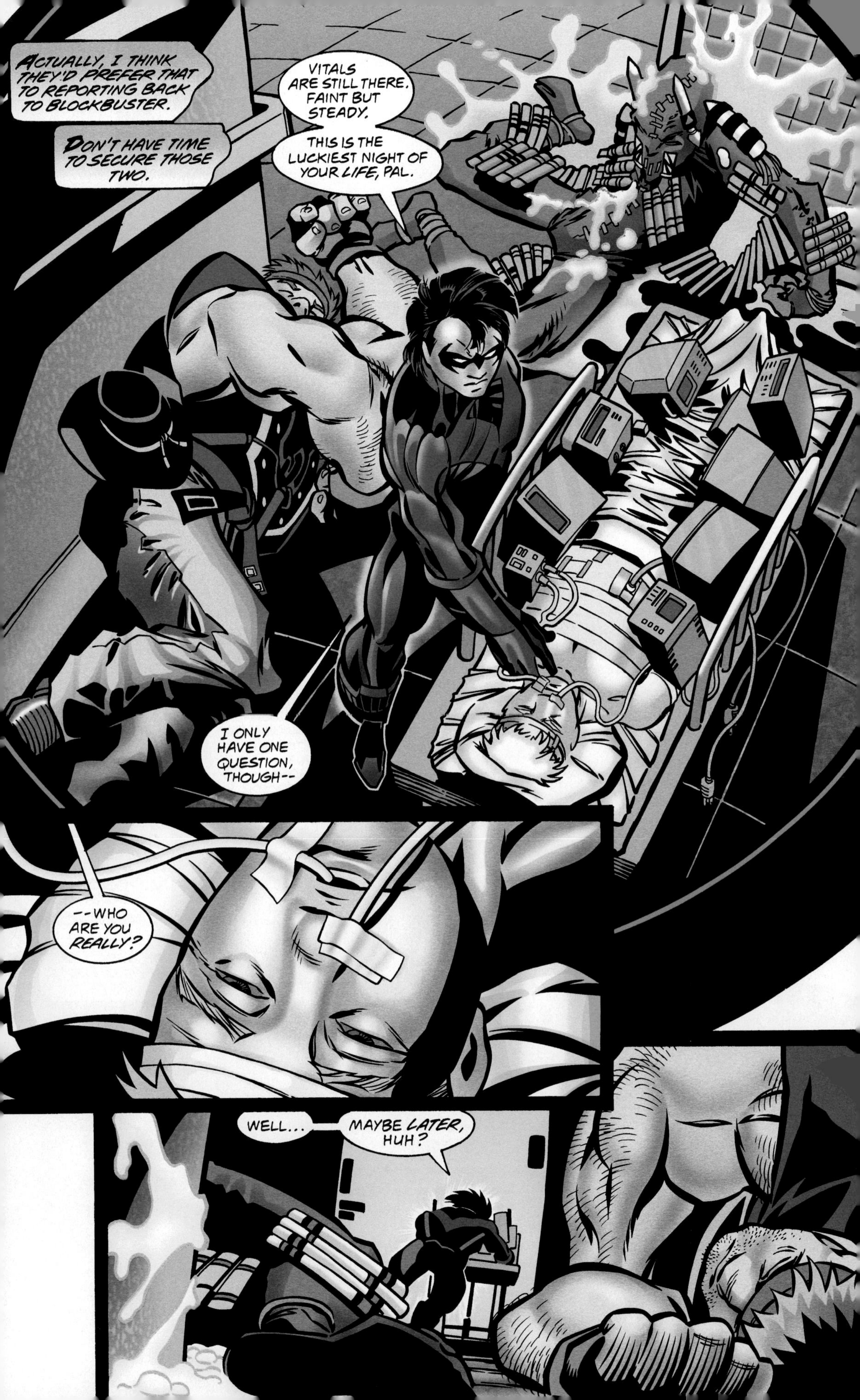
ACTUALLY, I THINK THEY'D PREFER THAT TO REPORTING BACK TO BLOCKBUSTER.
DON'T HAVE TIME TO SECURE THOSE TWO.
VITALS ARE STILL THERE. FAINT BUT STEADY.
THIS IS THE LUCKIEST NIGHT OF YOUR LIFE, PAL.
I ONLY HAVE ONE QUESTION, THOUGH--
--WHO ARE YOU REALLY?
WELL...
MAYBE LATER, HUH?

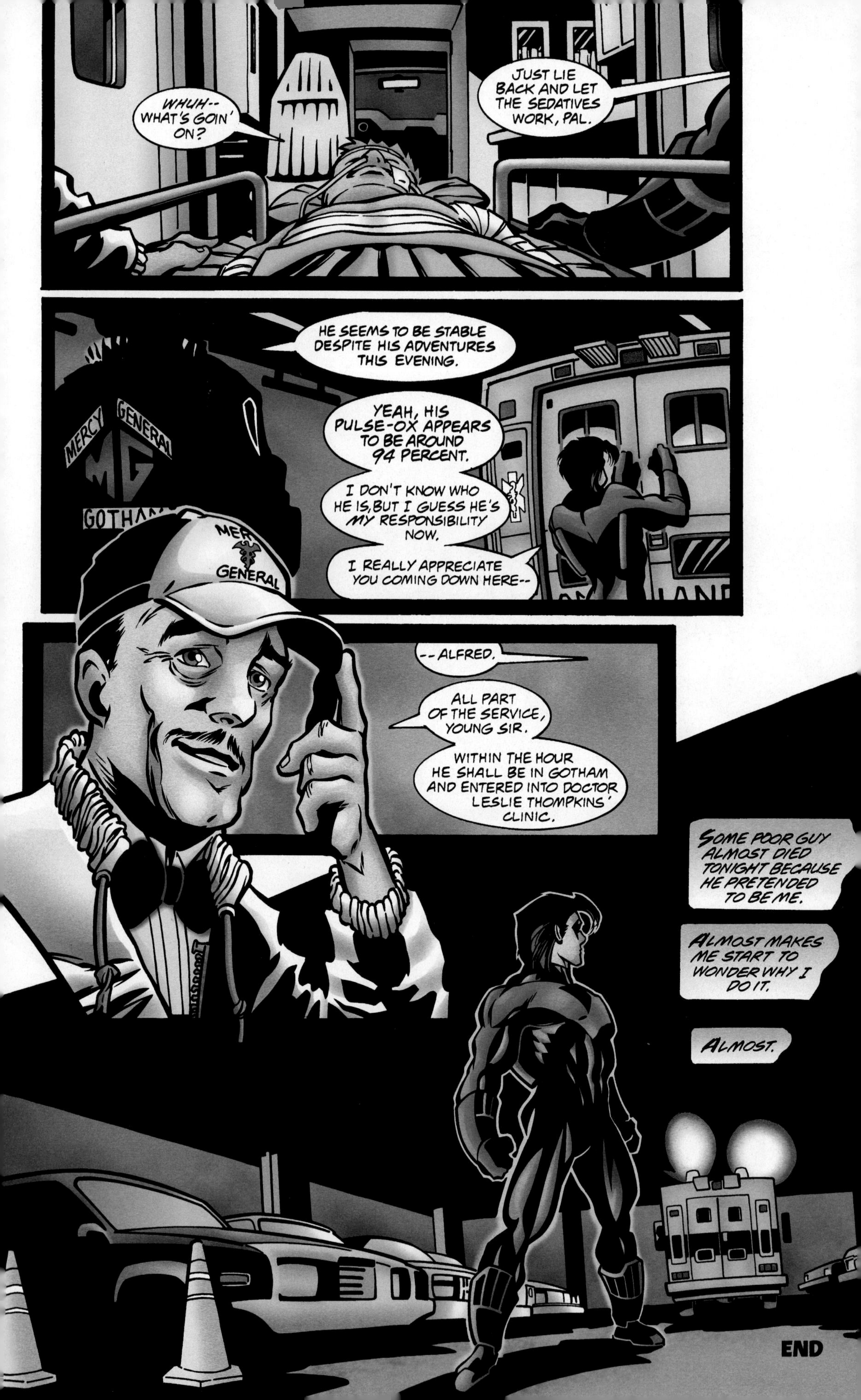
WHUH-- WHAT'S GOIN' ON?
JUST LIE BACK AND LET THE SEDATIVES WORK, PAL.
HE SEEMS TO BE STABLE DESPITE HIS ADVENTURES THIS EVENING.
MERCY GENERAL
MG
GOTHAM
YEAH, HIS PULSE-OX APPEARS TO BE AROUND 94 PERCENT.
I DON'T KNOW WHO HE IS, BUT I GUESS HE'S MY RESPONSIBILITY NOW.
I REALLY APPRECIATE YOU COMING DOWN HERE--
--ALFRED.
ALL PART OF THE SERVICE, YOUNG SIR.
WITHIN THE HOUR HE SHALL BE IN GOTHAM AND ENTERED INTO DOCTOR LESLIE THOMPKINS' CLINIC.
SOME POOR GUY ALMOST DIED TONIGHT BECAUSE HE PRETENDED TO BE ME.
ALMOST MAKES ME START TO WONDER WHY I DO IT.
ALMOST.
END

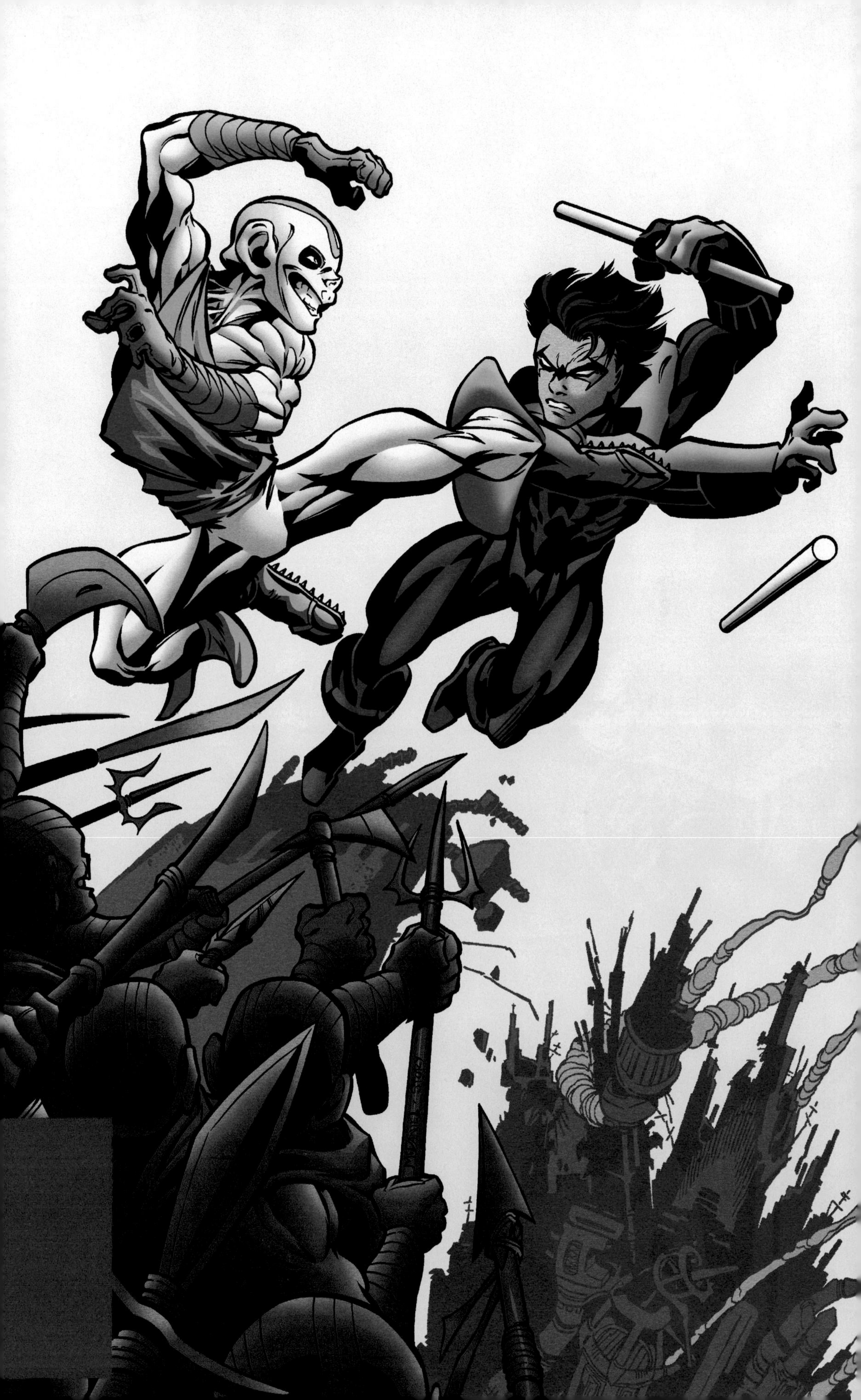

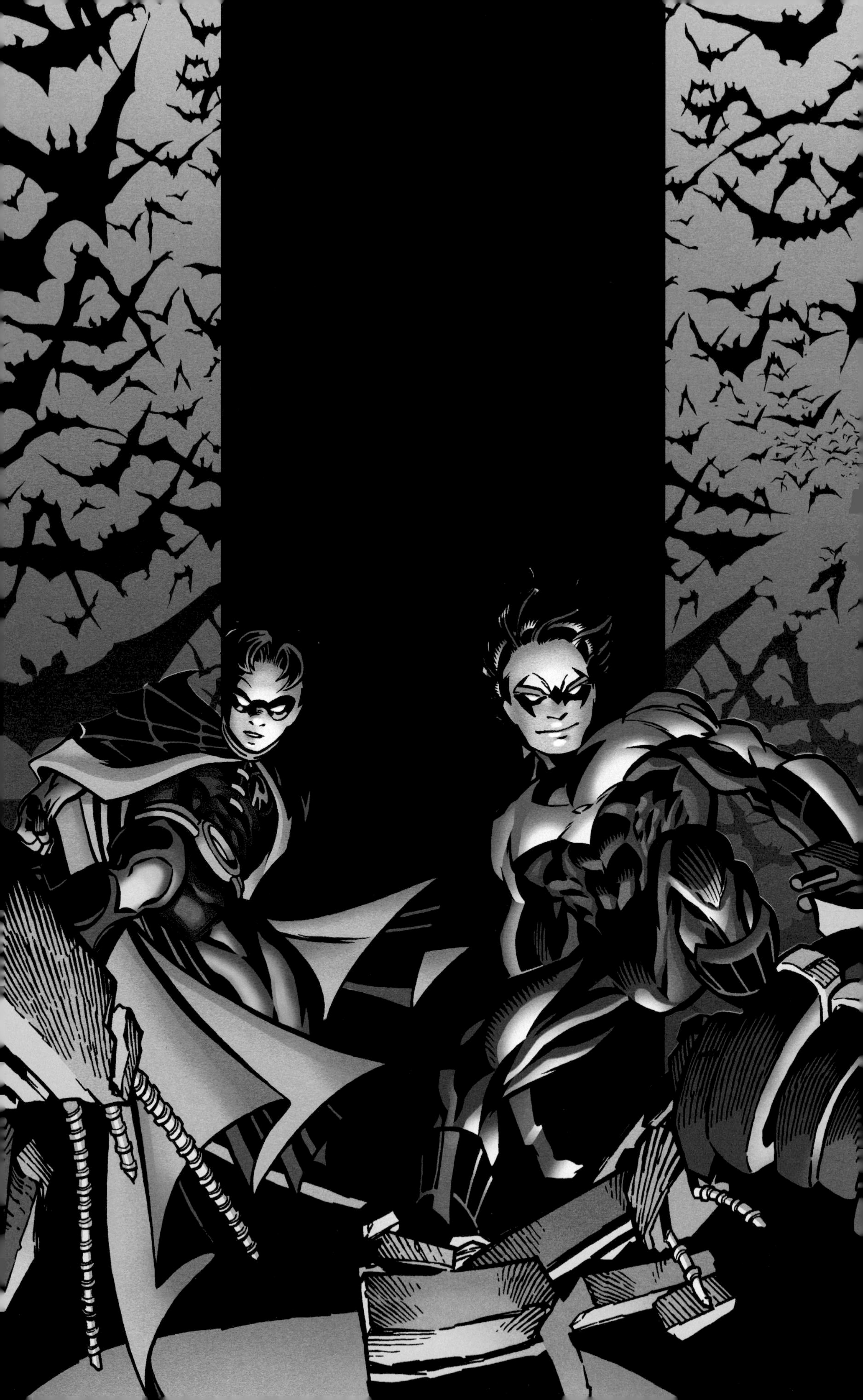

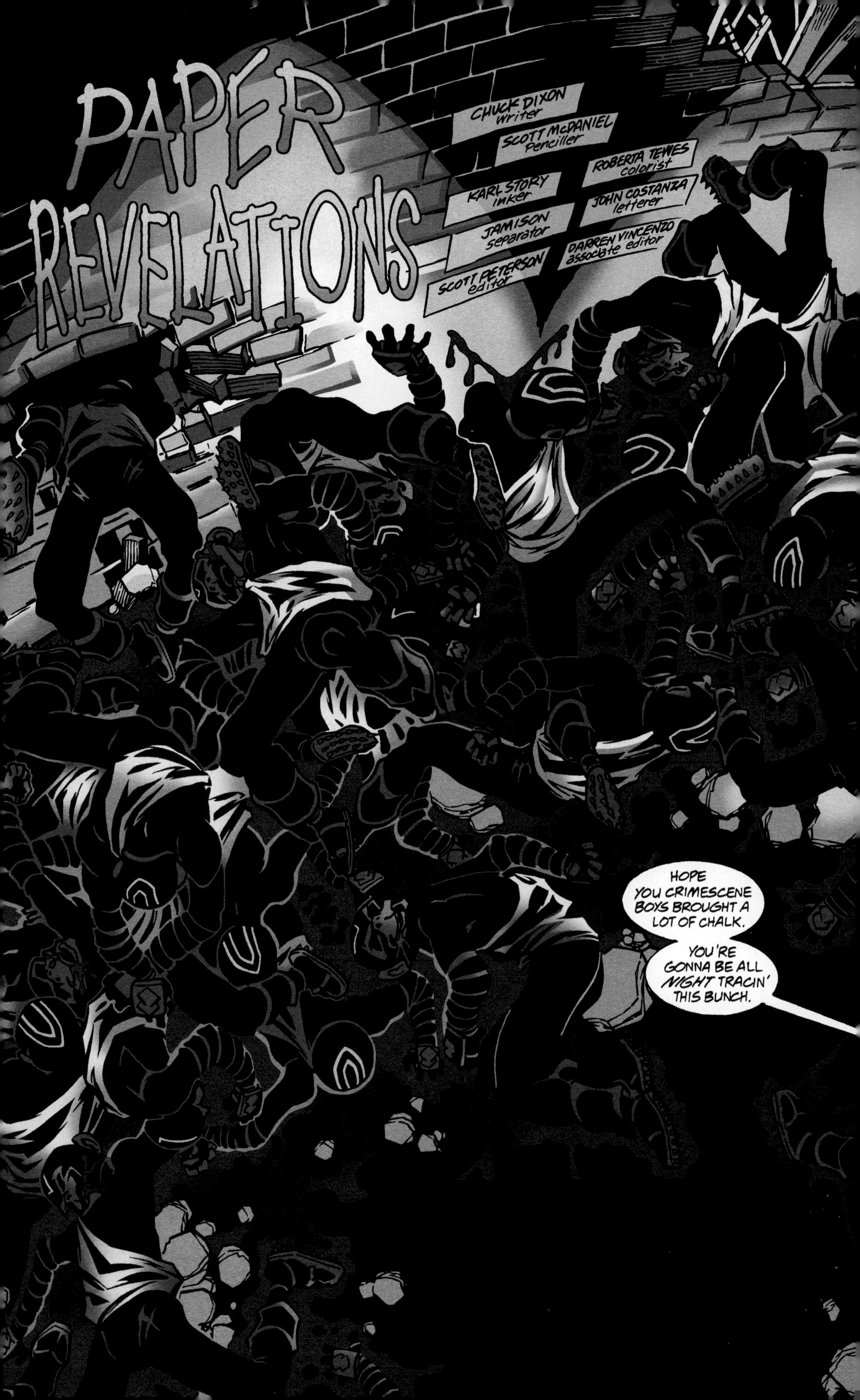
PAPER REVELATIONS
CHUCK DIXON writer
SCOTT McDANIEL penciller
KARL STORY inker
JAMISON separator
SCOTT PETERSON editor
ROBERTA TEWES colorist
JOHN COSTANZA letterer
DARREN VINCENZO associate editor
HOPE YOU CRIMESCENE BOYS BROUGHT A LOT OF CHALK.
YOU'RE GONNA BE ALL NIGHT TRACIN' THIS BUNCH.

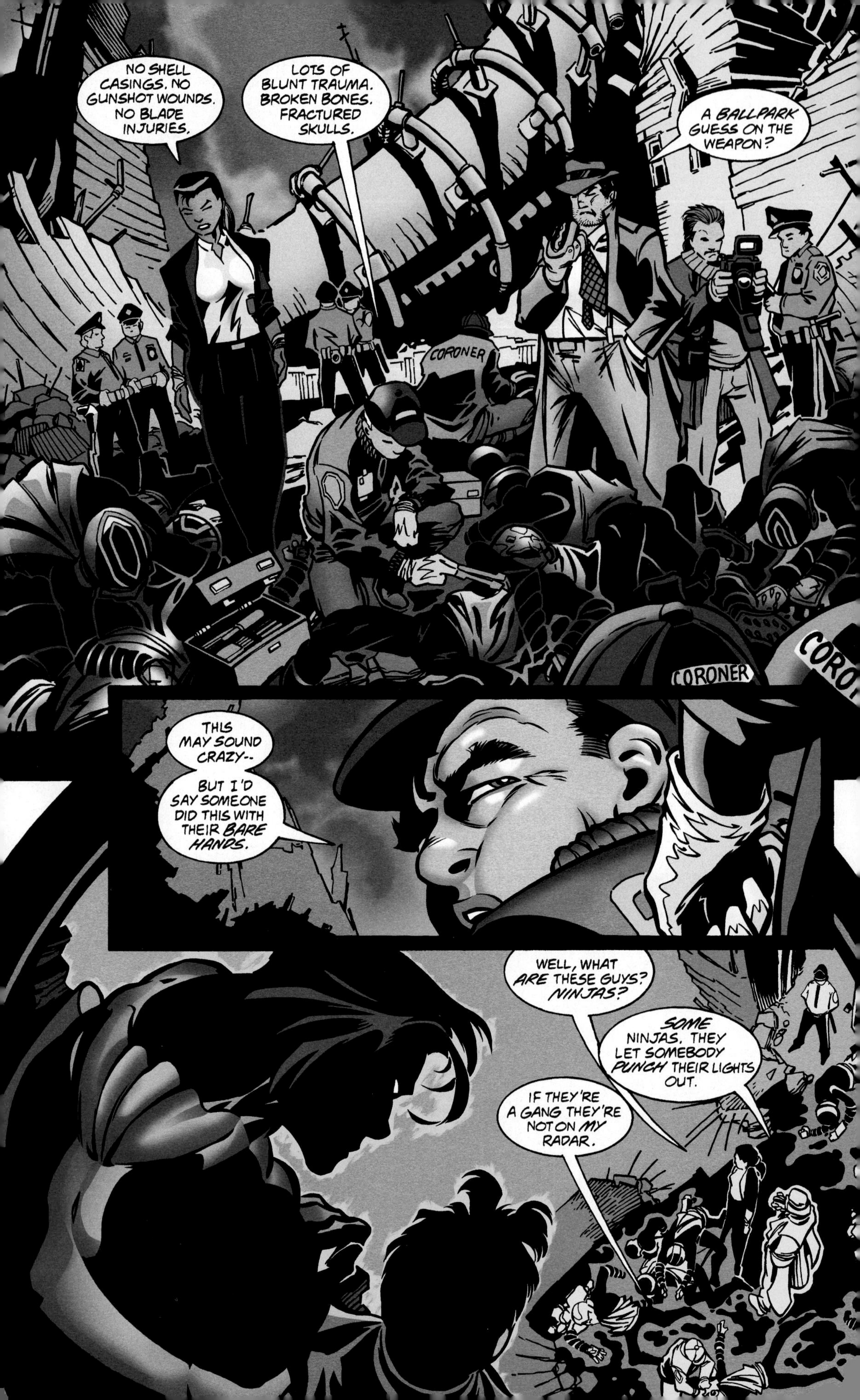
NO SHELL CASINGS. NO GUNSHOT WOUNDS. NO BLADE INJURIES.
LOTS OF BLUNT TRAUMA. BROKEN BONES. FRACTURED SKULLS.
A BALLPARK GUESS ON THE WEAPON?
CORONER
CORONER
CORO
THIS MAY SOUND CRAZY--
BUT I'D SAY SOMEONE DID THIS WITH THEIR BARE HANDS.
WELL, WHAT ARE THESE GUYS? NINJAS?
SOME NINJAS. THEY LET SOMEBODY PUNCH THEIR LIGHTS OUT.
IF THEY'RE A GANG THEY'RE NOT ON MY RADAR.

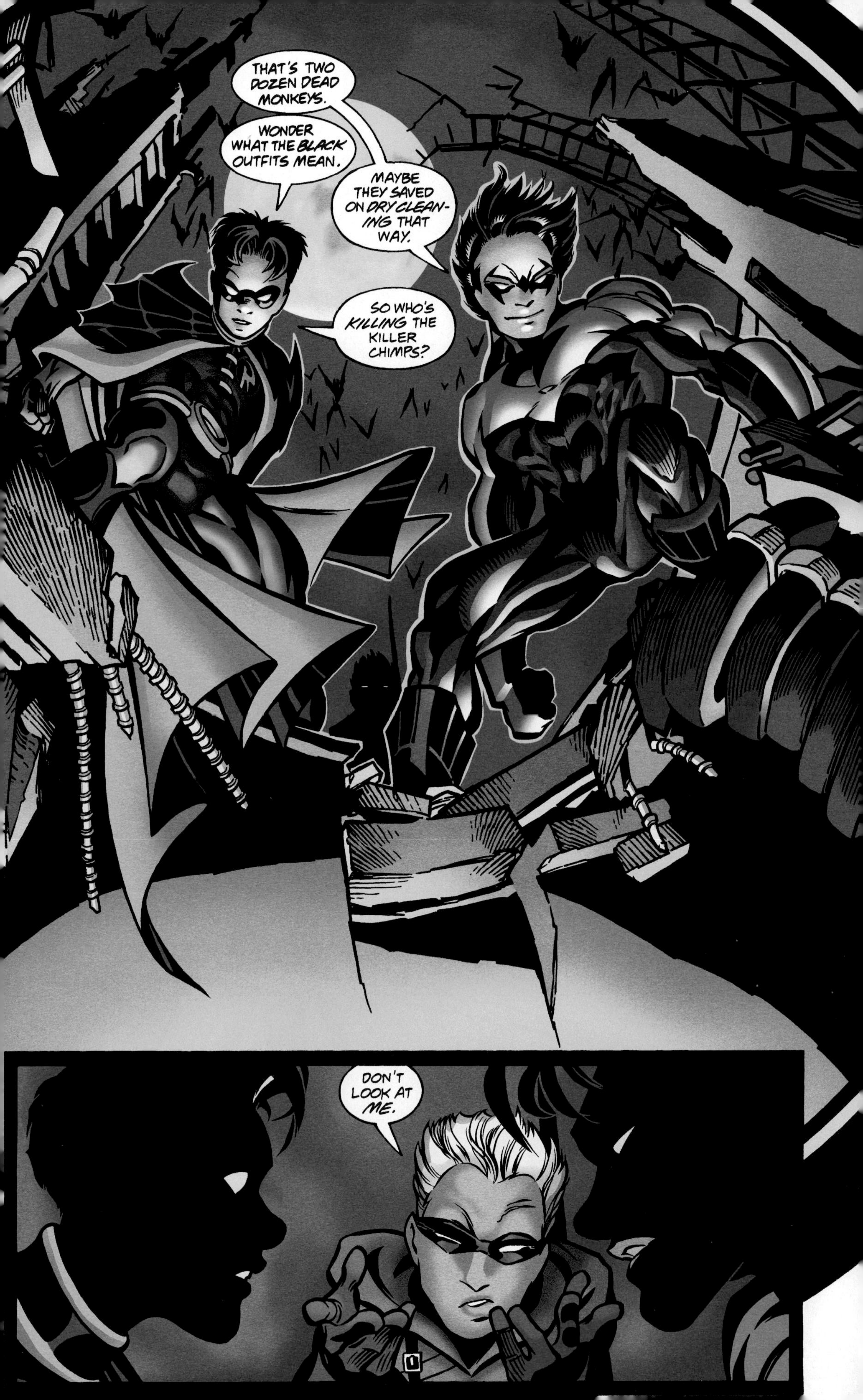

THAT'S TWO DOZEN DEAD MONKEYS.
WONDER WHAT THE BLACK OUTFITS MEAN.
MAYBE THEY SAVED ON DRY CLEANING THAT WAY.
SO WHO'S KILLING THE KILLER CHIMPS?
DON'T LOOK AT ME.

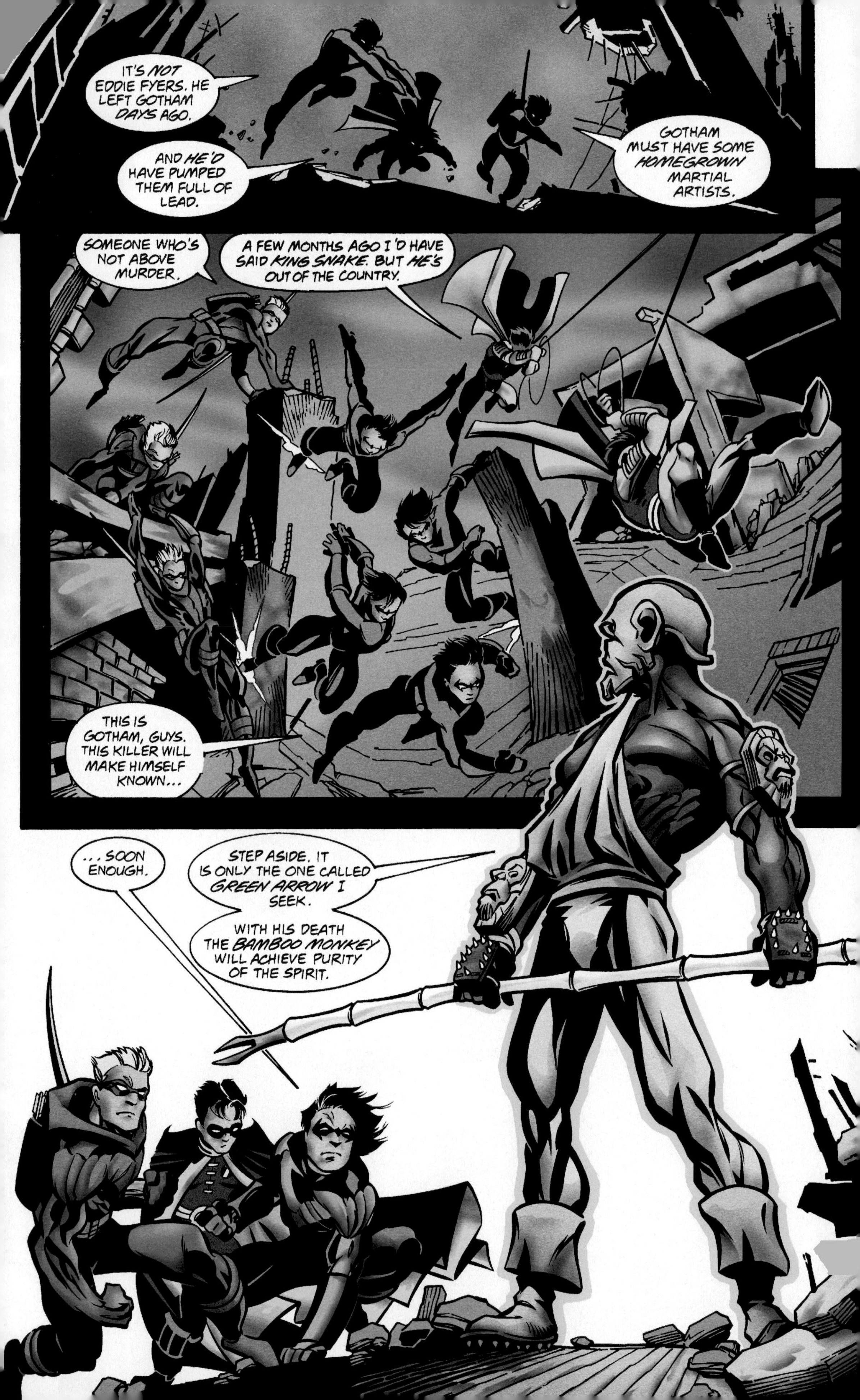
IT'S NOT EDDIE FYERS. HE LEFT GOTHAM DAYS AGO.
AND HE'D HAVE PUMPED THEM FULL OF LEAD.
GOTHAM MUST HAVE SOME HOMEGROWN MARTIAL ARTISTS.
SOMEONE WHO'S NOT ABOVE MURDER.
A FEW MONTHS AGO I'D HAVE SAID KING SNAKE. BUT HE'S OUT OF THE COUNTRY.
THIS IS GOTHAM, GUYS. THIS KILLER WILL MAKE HIMSELF KNOWN...
...SOON ENOUGH.
STEP ASIDE. IT IS ONLY THE ONE CALLED GREEN ARROW I SEEK.
WITH HIS DEATH THE BAMBOO MONKEY WILL ACHIEVE PURITY OF THE SPIRIT.

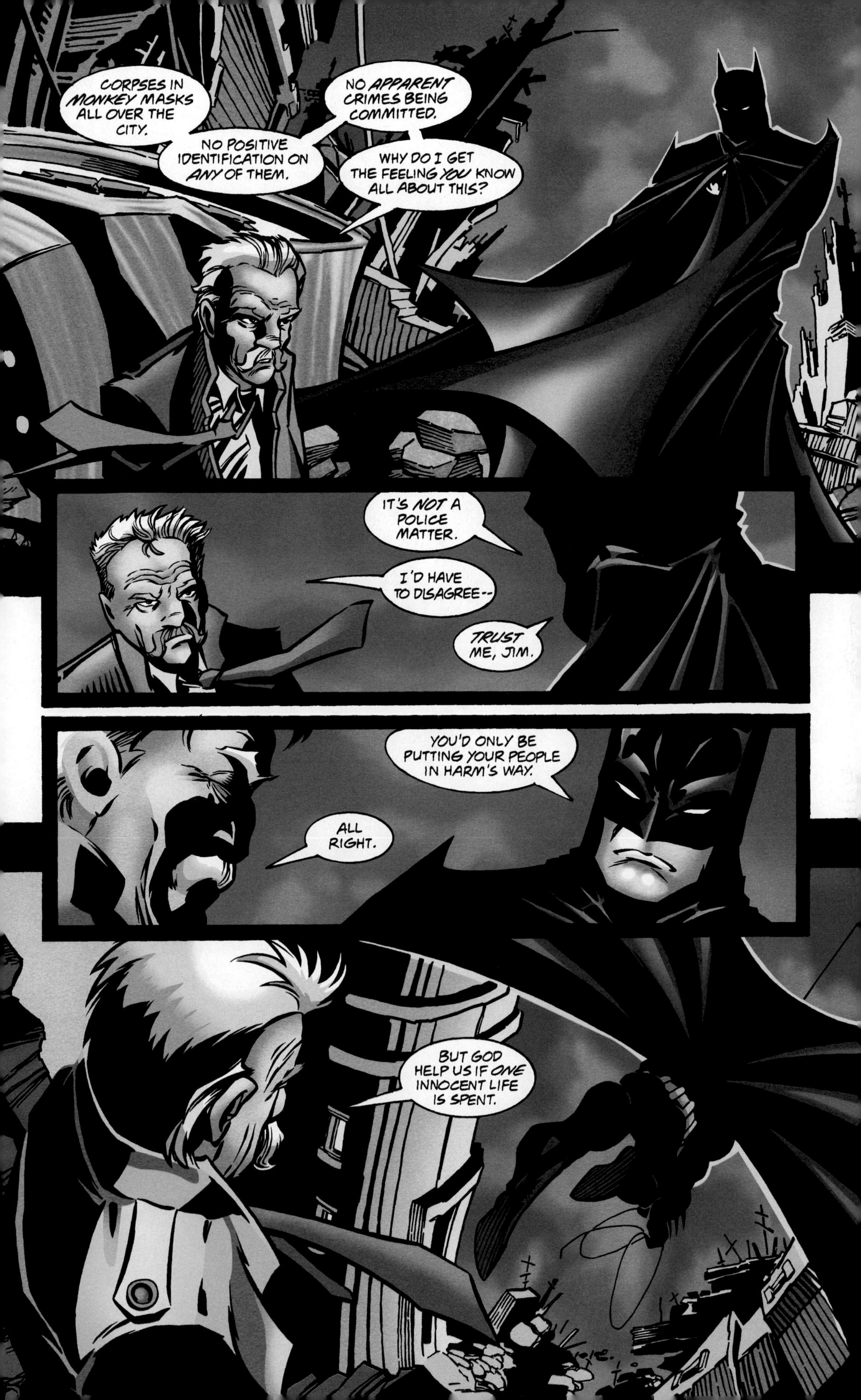
CORPSES IN MONKEY MASKS ALL OVER THE CITY.
NO POSITIVE IDENTIFICATION ON ANY OF THEM.
NO APPARENT CRIMES BEING COMMITTED.
WHY DO I GET THE FEELING YOU KNOW ALL ABOUT THIS?
IT'S NOT A POLICE MATTER.
I'D HAVE TO DISAGREE--
TRUST ME, JIM.
YOU'D ONLY BE PUTTING YOUR PEOPLE IN HARM'S WAY.
ALL RIGHT.
BUT GOD HELP US IF ONE INNOCENT LIFE IS SPENT.

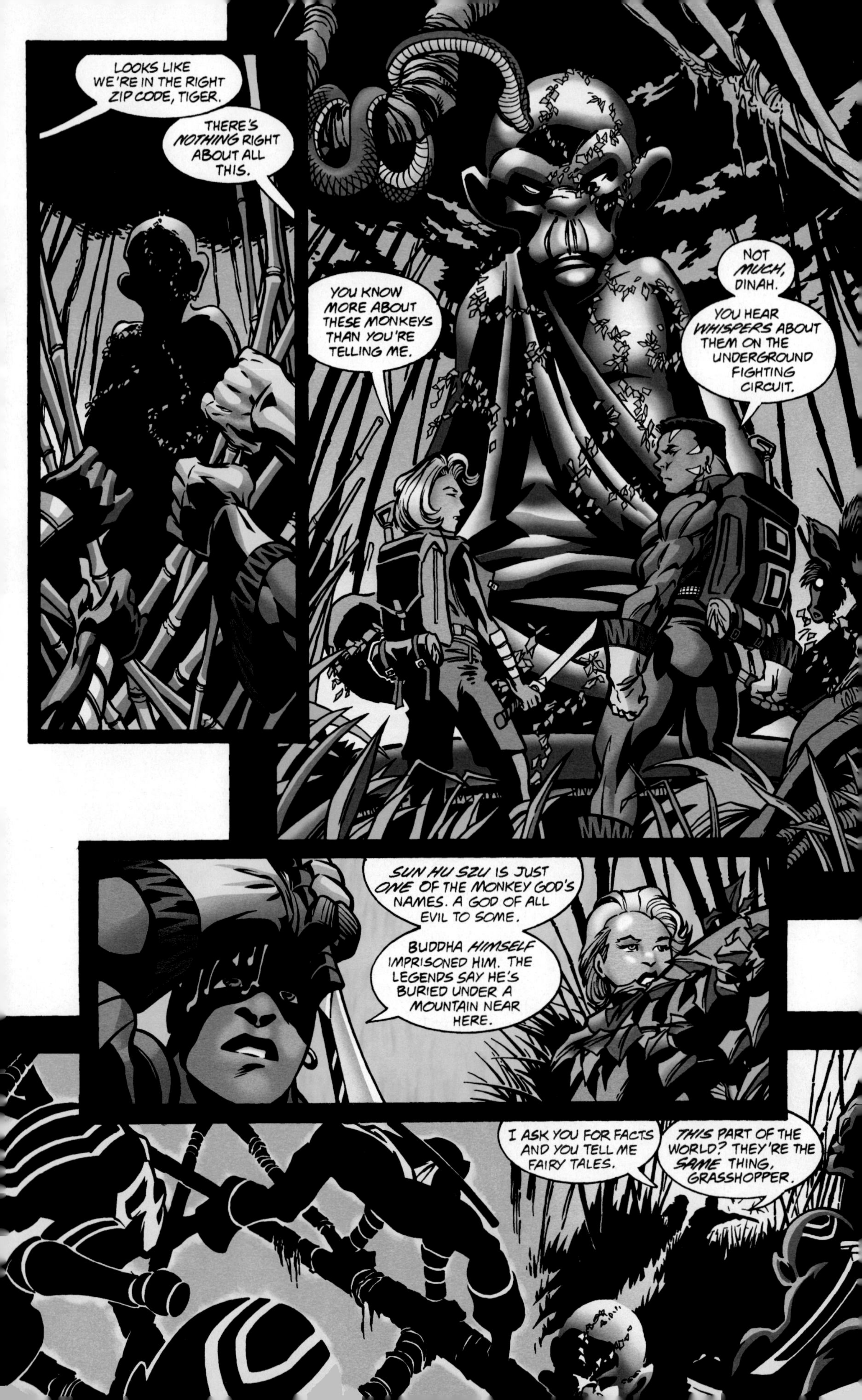
LOOKS LIKE WE'RE IN THE RIGHT ZIP CODE, TIGER.
THERE'S *NOTHING* RIGHT ABOUT ALL THIS.
YOU KNOW MORE ABOUT THESE MONKEYS THAN YOU'RE TELLING ME.
NOT *MUCH*, DINAH.
YOU HEAR *WHISPERS* ABOUT THEM ON THE UNDERGROUND FIGHTING CIRCUIT.
SUN HU SZU IS JUST *ONE* OF THE MONKEY GOD'S NAMES. A GOD OF ALL EVIL TO SOME.
BUDDHA *HIMSELF* IMPRISONED HIM. THE LEGENDS *SAY* HE'S BURIED UNDER A MOUNTAIN NEAR HERE.
I ASK YOU FOR FACTS AND YOU TELL ME FAIRY TALES.
THIS PART OF THE WORLD? THEY'RE THE *SAME* THING, GRASSHOPPER.

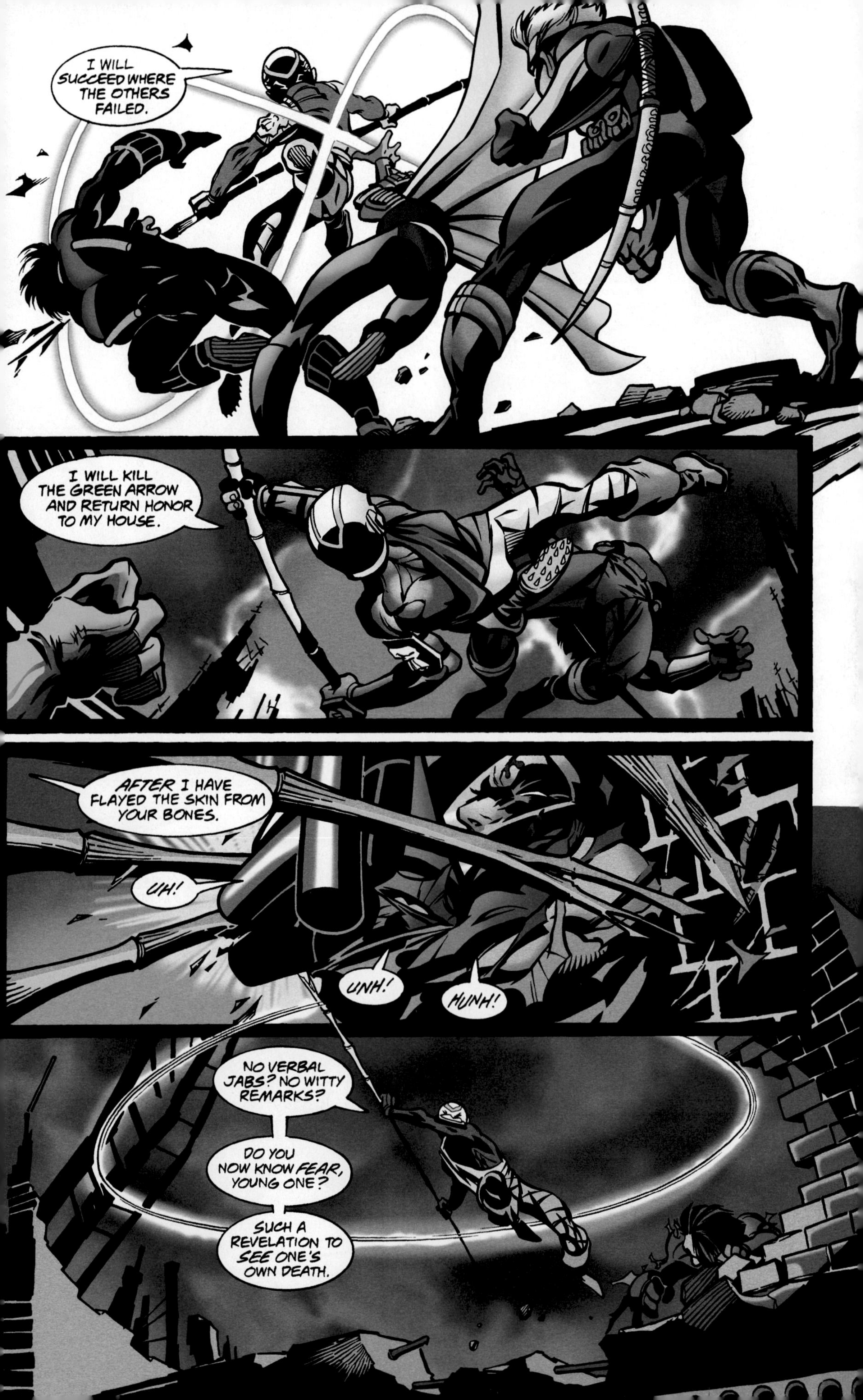
I WILL SUCCEED WHERE THE OTHERS FAILED.
I WILL KILL THE GREEN ARROW AND RETURN HONOR TO MY HOUSE.
AFTER I HAVE FLAYED THE SKIN FROM YOUR BONES.
UH!
UNH!
HUNH!
NO VERBAL JABS? NO WITTY REMARKS?
DO YOU NOW KNOW FEAR, YOUNG ONE?
SUCH A REVELATION TO SEE ONE'S OWN DEATH.

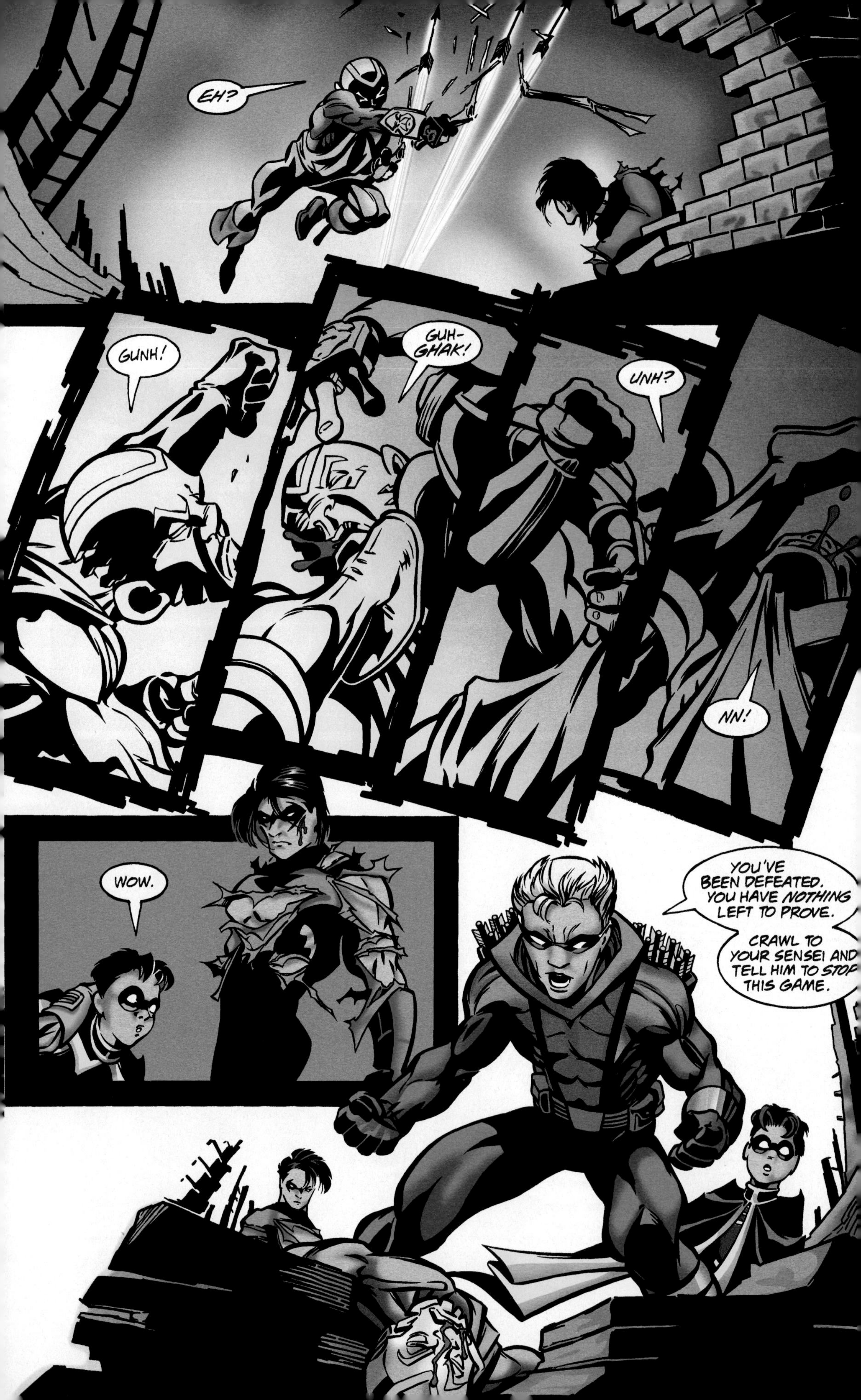
EH?
GUNH!
GUH-GHAK!
UNH?
NN!
WOW.
YOU'VE BEEN DEFEATED. YOU HAVE NOTHING LEFT TO PROVE.
CRAWL TO YOUR SENSEI AND TELL HIM TO STOP THIS GAME.

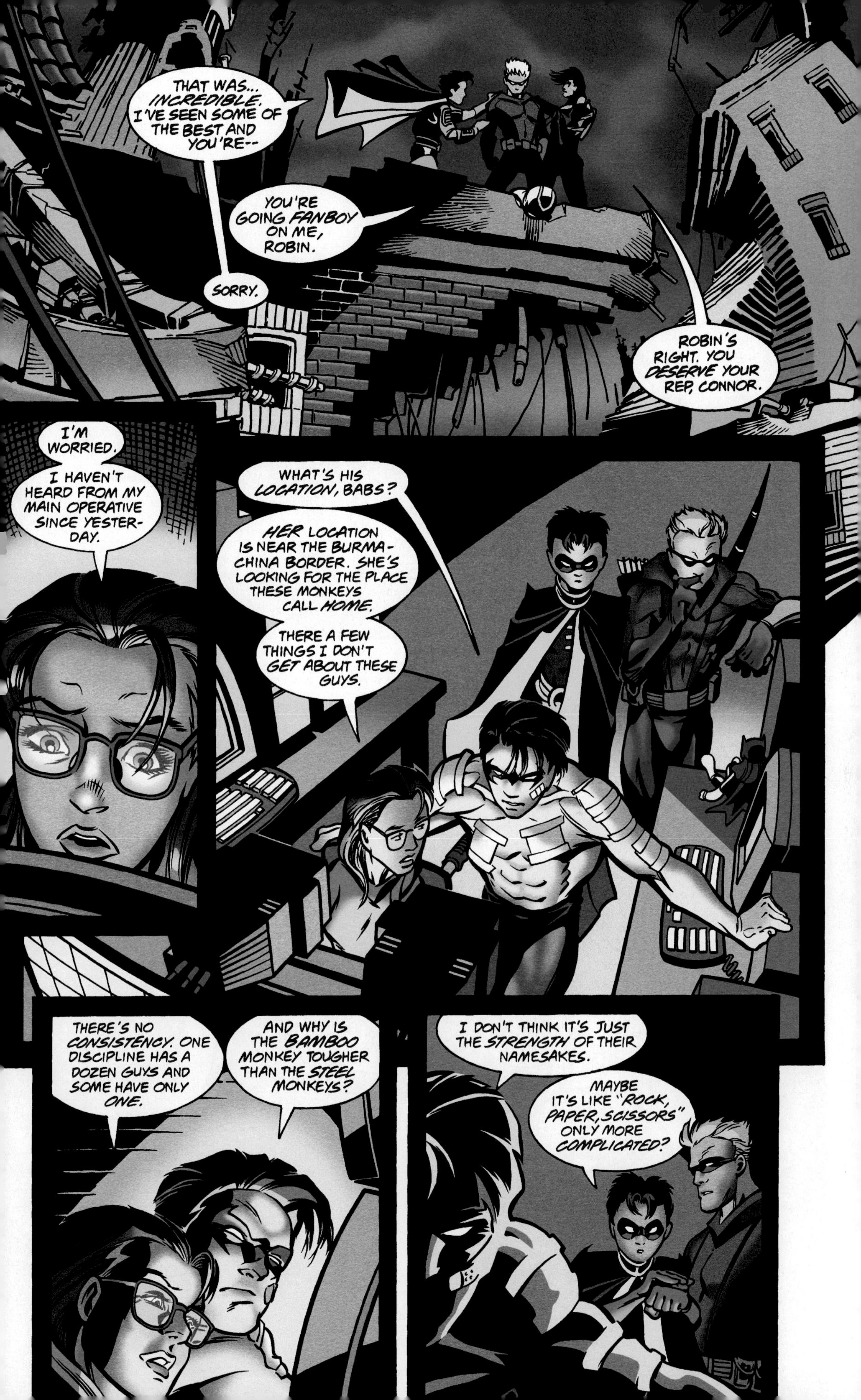
THAT WAS... INCREDIBLE. I'VE SEEN SOME OF THE BEST AND YOU'RE--
YOU'RE GOING FANBOY ON ME, ROBIN.
SORRY.
ROBIN'S RIGHT. YOU DESERVE YOUR REP, CONNOR.
I'M WORRIED.
I HAVEN'T HEARD FROM MY MAIN OPERATIVE SINCE YESTER-DAY.
WHAT'S HIS LOCATION, BABS?
HER LOCATION IS NEAR THE BURMA-CHINA BORDER. SHE'S LOOKING FOR THE PLACE THESE MONKEYS CALL HOME.
THERE A FEW THINGS I DON'T GET ABOUT THESE GUYS.
THERE'S NO CONSISTENCY. ONE DISCIPLINE HAS A DOZEN GUYS AND SOME HAVE ONLY ONE.
AND WHY IS THE BAMBOO MONKEY TOUGHER THAN THE STEEL MONKEYS?
I DON'T THINK IT'S JUST THE STRENGTH OF THEIR NAMESAKES.
MAYBE IT'S LIKE "ROCK, PAPER, SCISSORS" ONLY MORE COMPLICATED?

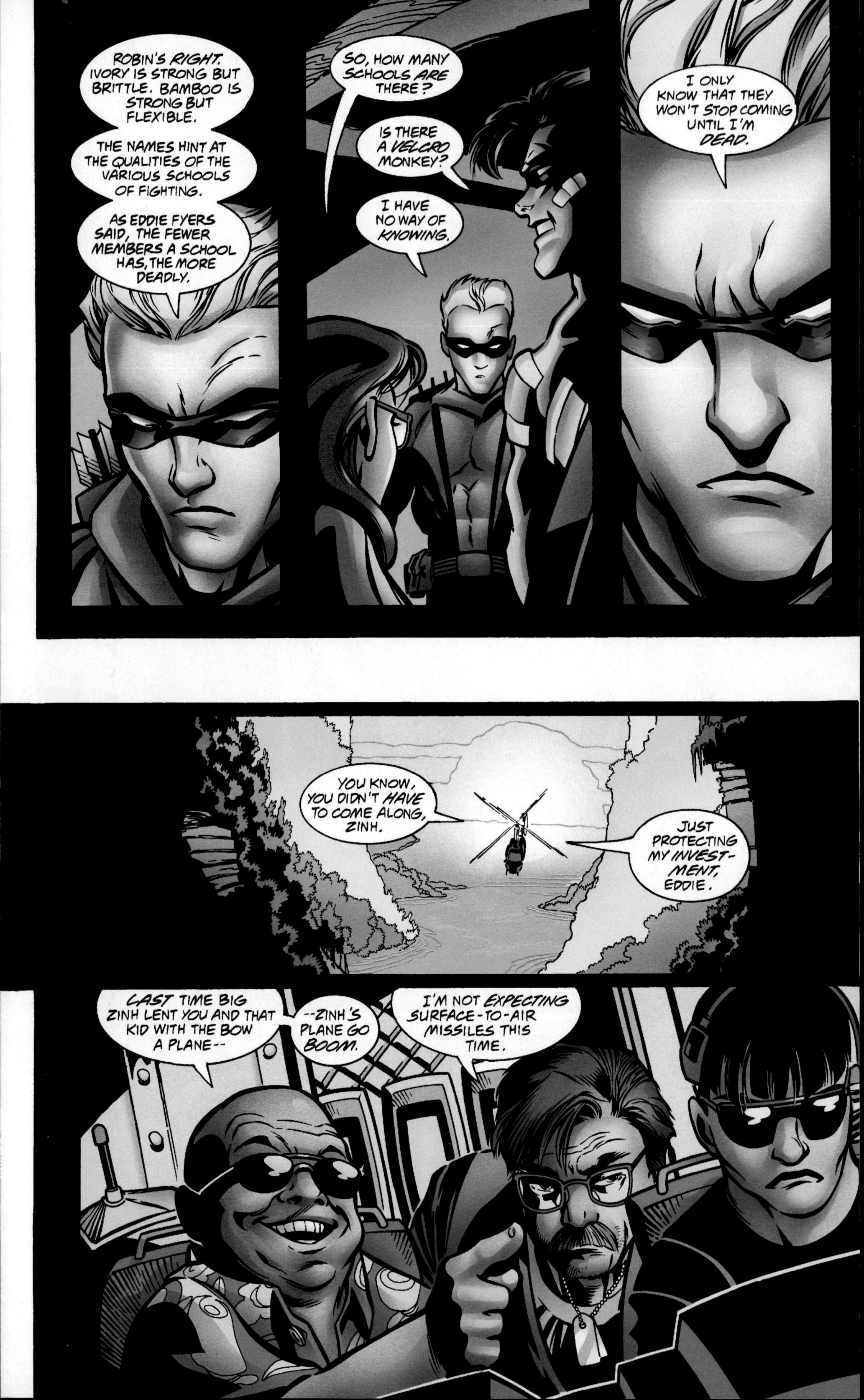
ROBIN'S *RIGHT.* IVORY IS STRONG BUT BRITTLE. BAMBOO IS STRONG BUT FLEXIBLE.
THE NAMES HINT AT THE QUALITIES OF THE VARIOUS SCHOOLS OF FIGHTING.
AS EDDIE FYERS SAID, THE FEWER MEMBERS A SCHOOL HAS, THE MORE DEADLY.
SO, HOW MANY SCHOOLS *ARE* THERE?
IS THERE A *VELCRO* MONKEY?
I HAVE NO WAY OF *KNOWING.*
I ONLY KNOW THAT THEY WON'T *STOP* COMING UNTIL I'M *DEAD.*
YOU KNOW, YOU DIDN'T *HAVE* TO COME ALONG, ZINH.
JUST PROTECTING MY *INVEST-MENT,* EDDIE.
LAST TIME BIG ZINH LENT *YOU* AND THAT KID WITH THE BOW A PLANE--
--ZINH'S PLANE GO *BOOM.*
I'M NOT *EXPECTING* SURFACE-TO-AIR MISSILES THIS TIME.

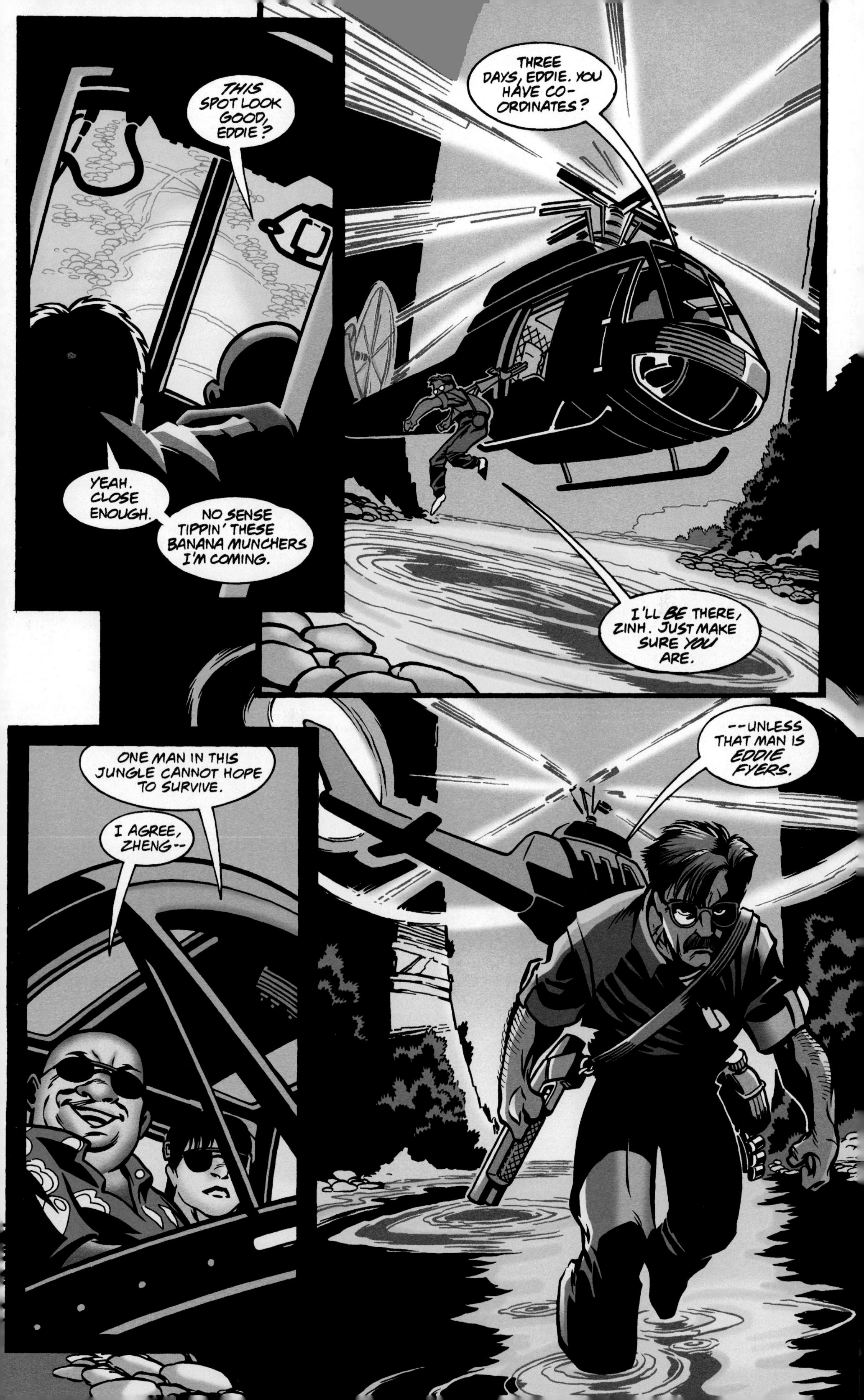
THIS SPOT LOOK GOOD, EDDIE?
YEAH. CLOSE ENOUGH.
NO SENSE TIPPIN' THESE BANANA MUNCHERS I'M COMING.
THREE DAYS, EDDIE. YOU HAVE CO-ORDINATES?
I'LL BE THERE, ZINH. JUST MAKE SURE YOU ARE.
ONE MAN IN THIS JUNGLE CANNOT HOPE TO SURVIVE.
I AGREE, ZHENG--
--UNLESS THAT MAN IS EDDIE FYERS.

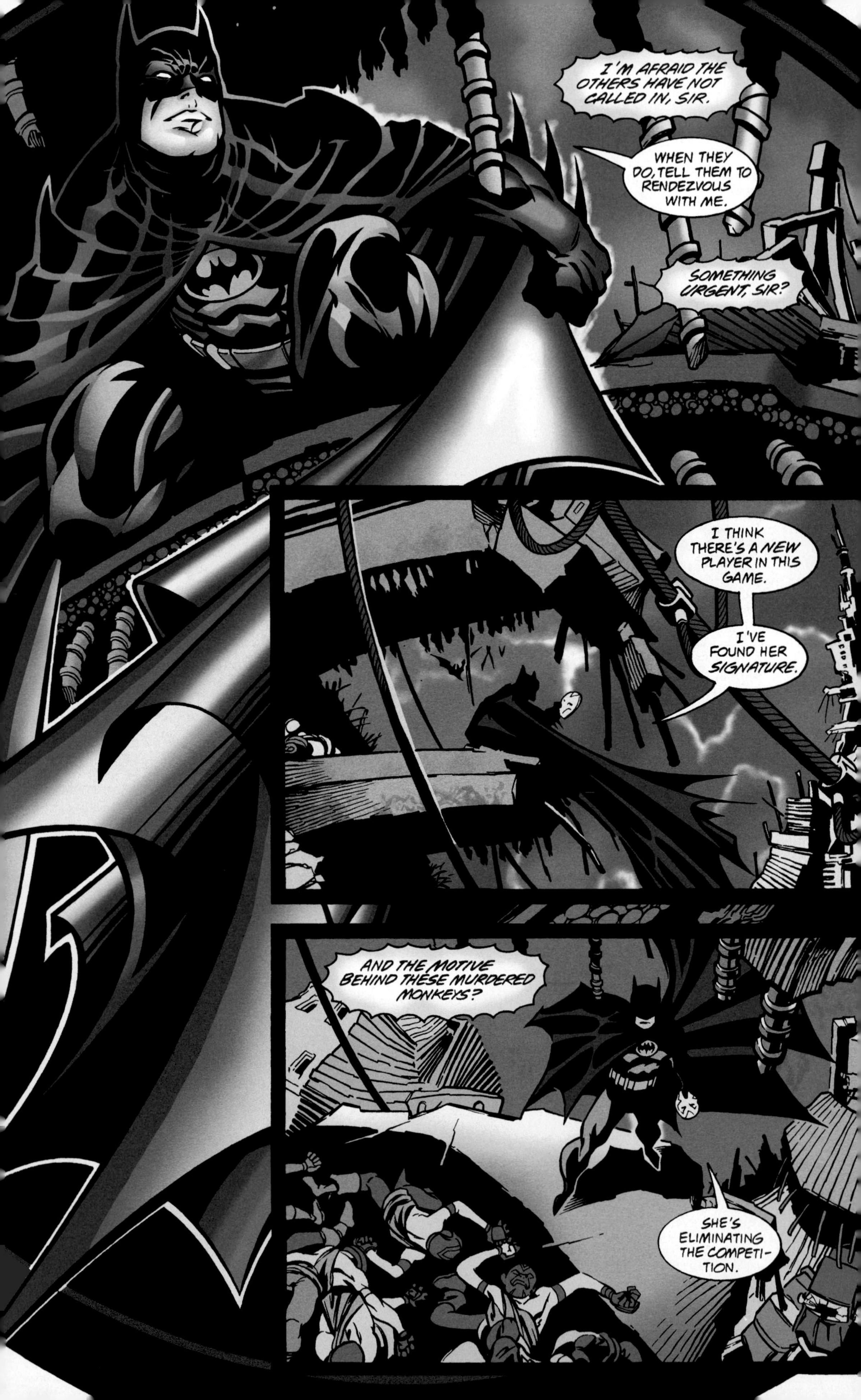
I'M AFRAID THE OTHERS HAVE NOT CALLED IN, SIR.
WHEN THEY DO, TELL THEM TO RENDEZVOUS WITH ME.
SOMETHING URGENT, SIR?
I THINK THERE'S A NEW PLAYER IN THIS GAME.
I'VE FOUND HER SIGNATURE.
AND THE MOTIVE BEHIND THESE MURDERED MONKEYS?
SHE'S ELIMINATING THE COMPETITION.

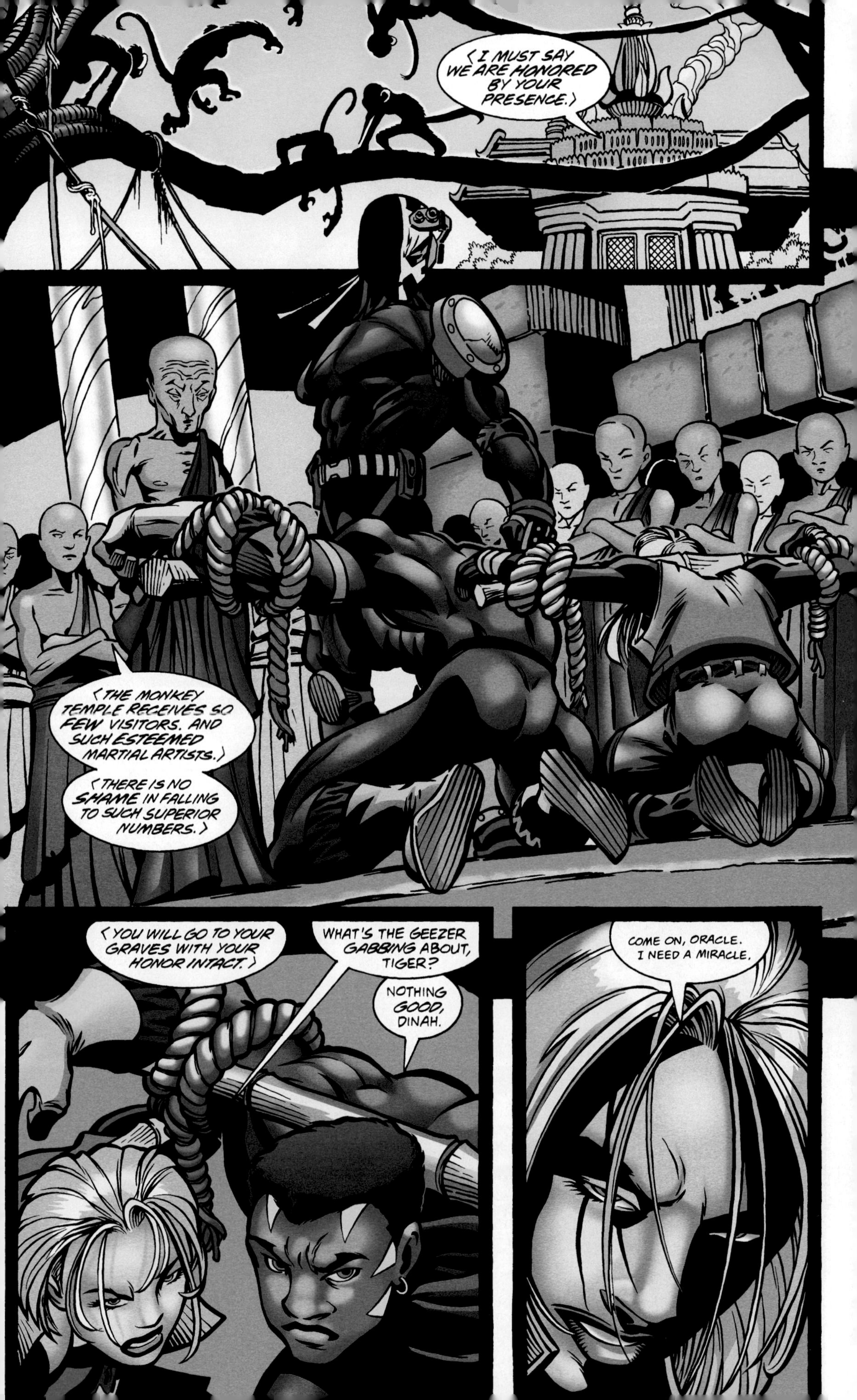

⟨I MUST SAY WE ARE HONORED BY YOUR PRESENCE.⟩
⟨THE MONKEY TEMPLE RECEIVES SO FEW VISITORS. AND SUCH ESTEEMED MARTIAL ARTISTS.⟩
⟨THERE IS NO SHAME IN FALLING TO SUCH SUPERIOR NUMBERS.⟩
⟨YOU WILL GO TO YOUR GRAVES WITH YOUR HONOR INTACT.⟩
WHAT'S THE GEEZER GABBING ABOUT, TIGER?
NOTHING GOOD, DINAH.
COME ON, ORACLE. I NEED A MIRACLE.

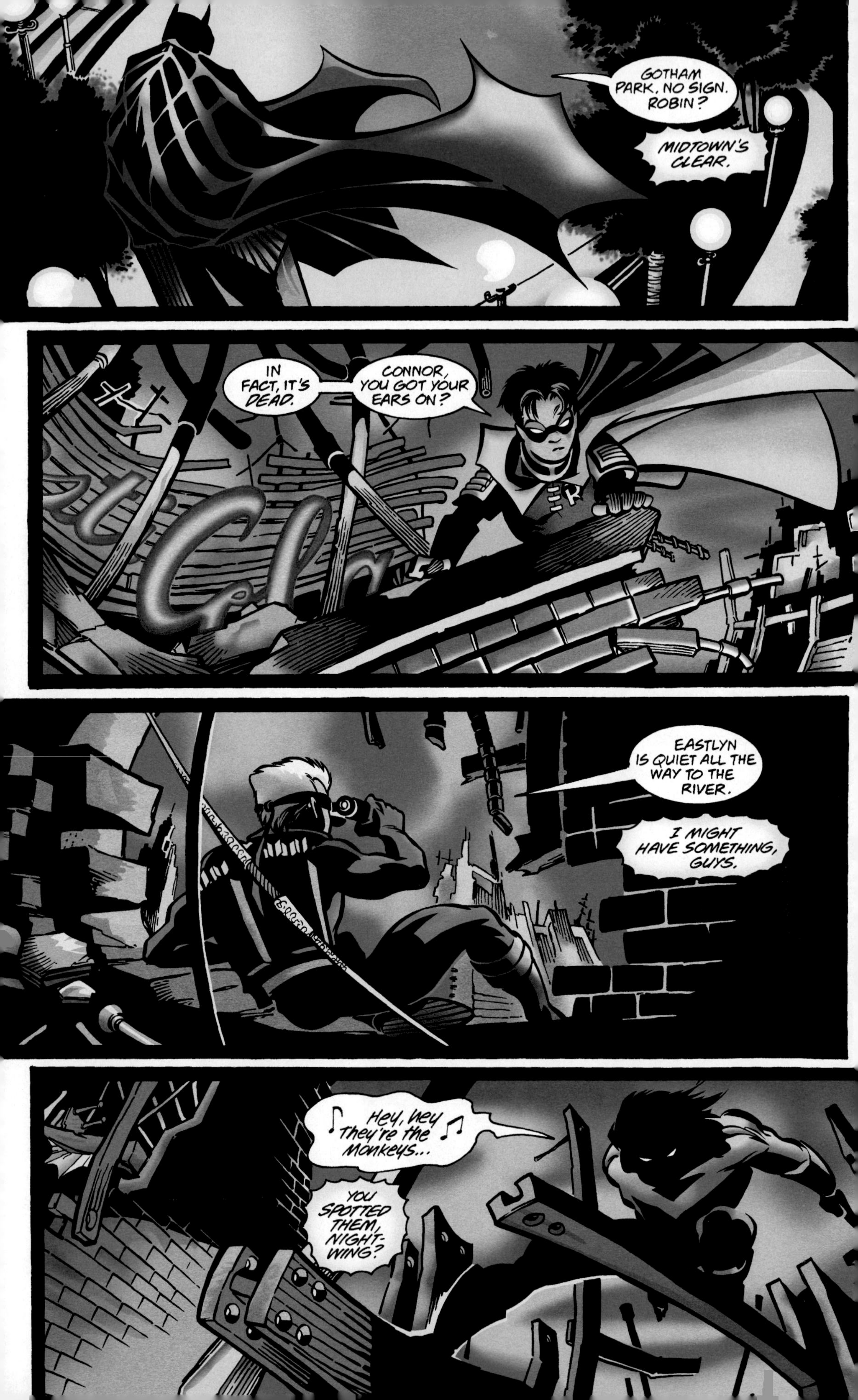
GOTHAM PARK, NO SIGN. ROBIN?
MIDTOWN'S CLEAR.
IN FACT, IT'S DEAD.
CONNOR, YOU GOT YOUR EARS ON?
EASTLYN IS QUIET ALL THE WAY TO THE RIVER.
I MIGHT HAVE SOMETHING, GUYS.
♪ Hey, hey they're the Monkeys... ♫
YOU SPOTTED THEM, NIGHTWING?

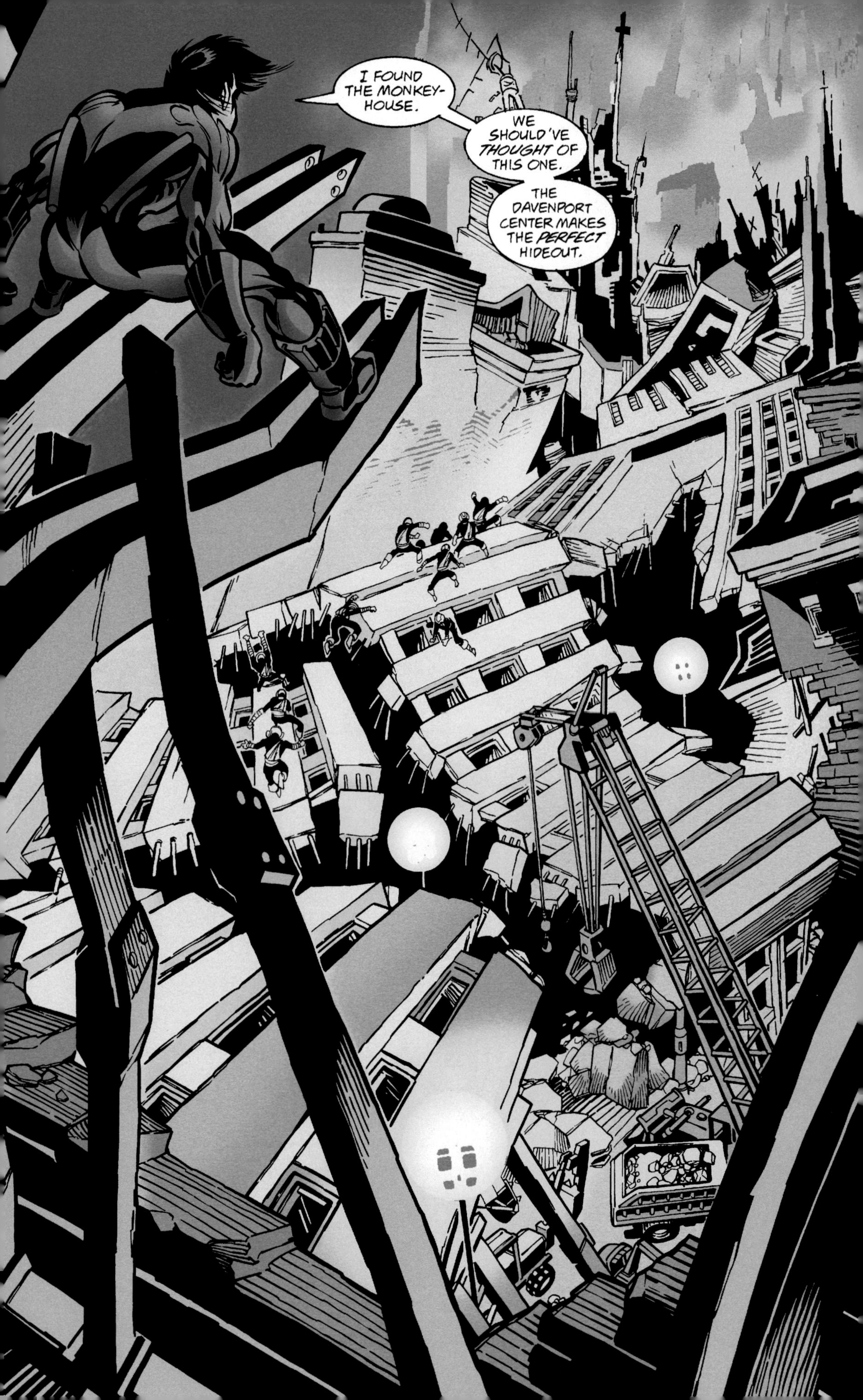
I FOUND THE MONKEY-HOUSE.
WE SHOULD'VE *THOUGHT* OF THIS ONE.
THE DAVENPORT CENTER MAKES THE *PERFECT* HIDEOUT.

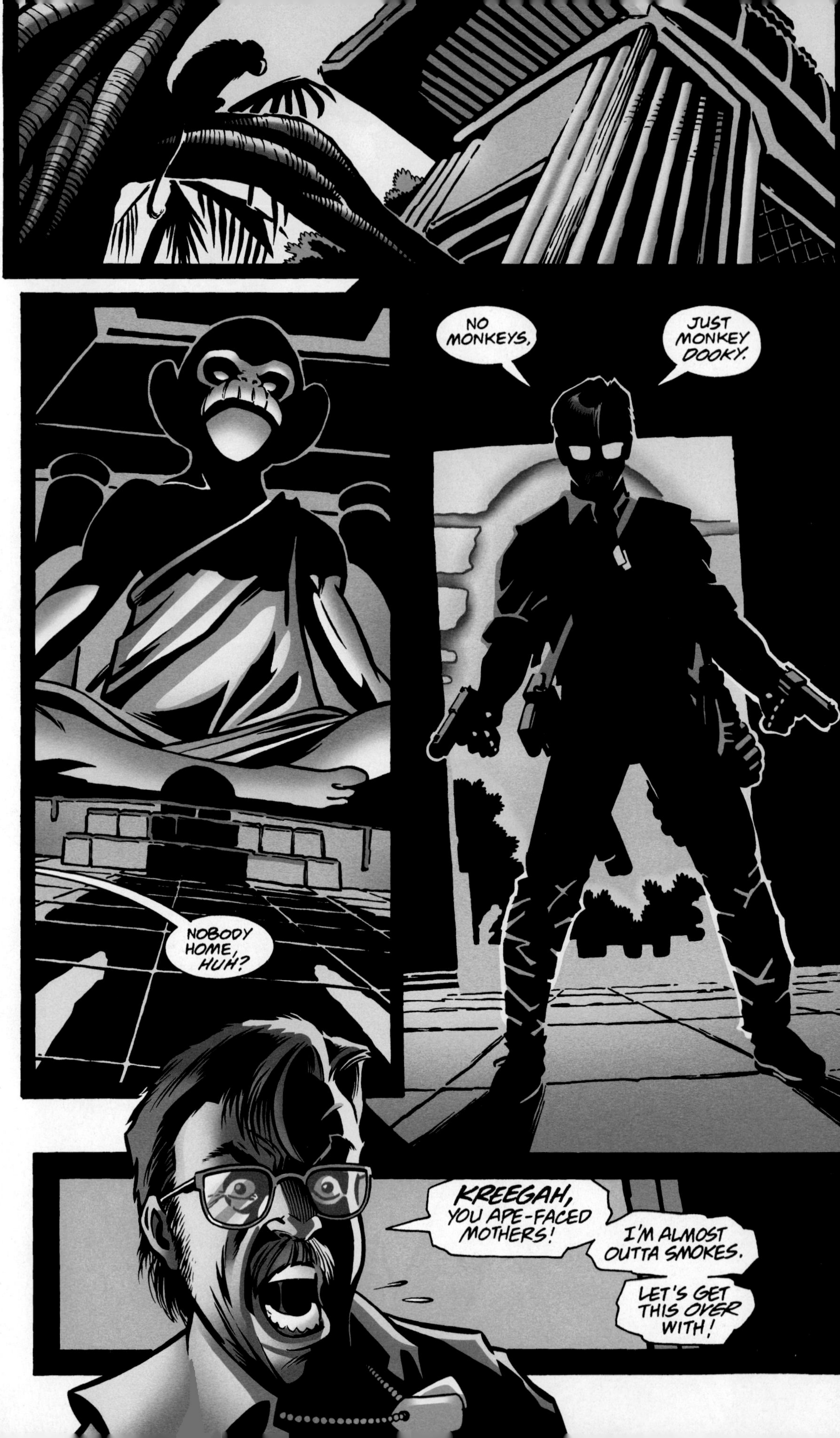
NO MONKEYS.
JUST MONKEY DOOKY.
NOBODY HOME, HUH?
KREEGAH, YOU APE-FACED MOTHERS!
I'M ALMOST OUTTA SMOKES.
LET'S GET THIS OVER WITH!

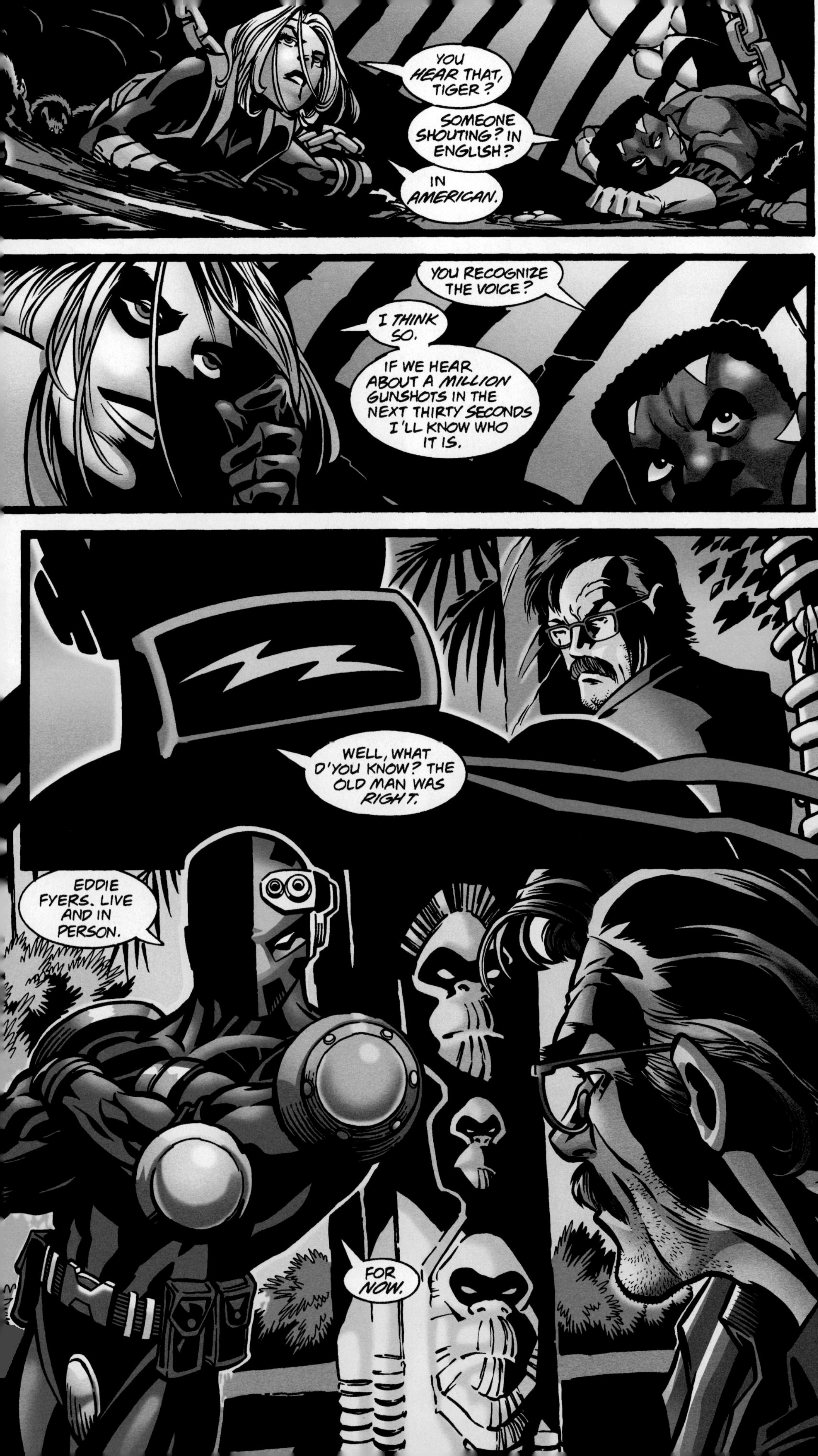
YOU HEAR THAT, TIGER?
SOMEONE SHOUTING? IN ENGLISH?
IN AMERICAN.
YOU RECOGNIZE THE VOICE?
I THINK SO.
IF WE HEAR ABOUT A MILLION GUNSHOTS IN THE NEXT THIRTY SECONDS I'LL KNOW WHO IT IS.
WELL, WHAT D'YOU KNOW? THE OLD MAN WAS RIGHT.
EDDIE FYERS. LIVE AND IN PERSON.
FOR NOW.

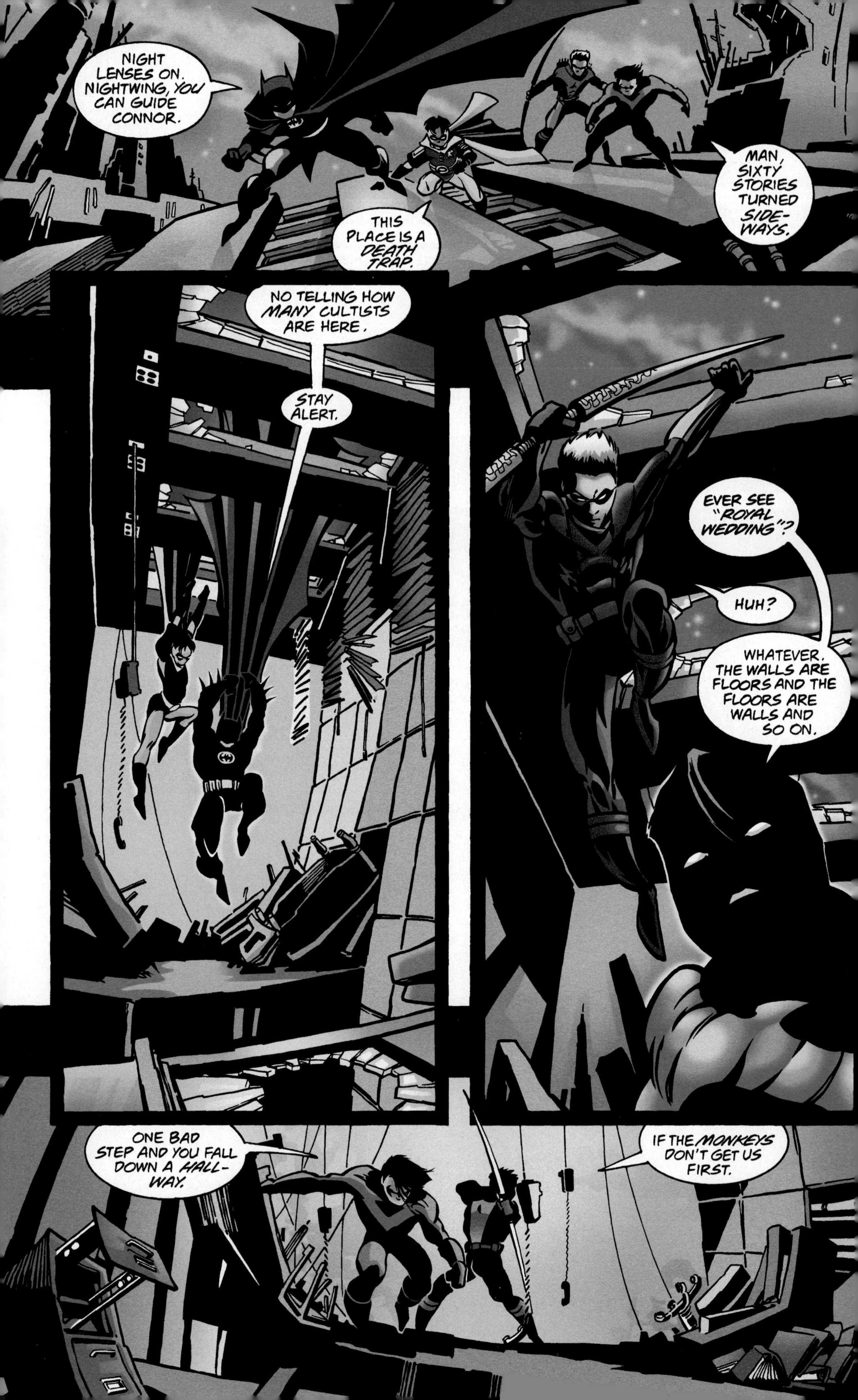
NIGHT LENSES ON. NIGHTWING, YOU CAN GUIDE CONNOR.
THIS PLACE IS A DEATH TRAP.
MAN, SIXTY STORIES TURNED SIDE-WAYS.
NO TELLING HOW MANY CULTISTS ARE HERE.
STAY ALERT.
EVER SEE "ROYAL WEDDING"?
HUH?
WHATEVER. THE WALLS ARE FLOORS AND THE FLOORS ARE WALLS AND SO ON.
ONE BAD STEP AND YOU FALL DOWN A HALL-WAY.
IF THE MONKEYS DON'T GET US FIRST.

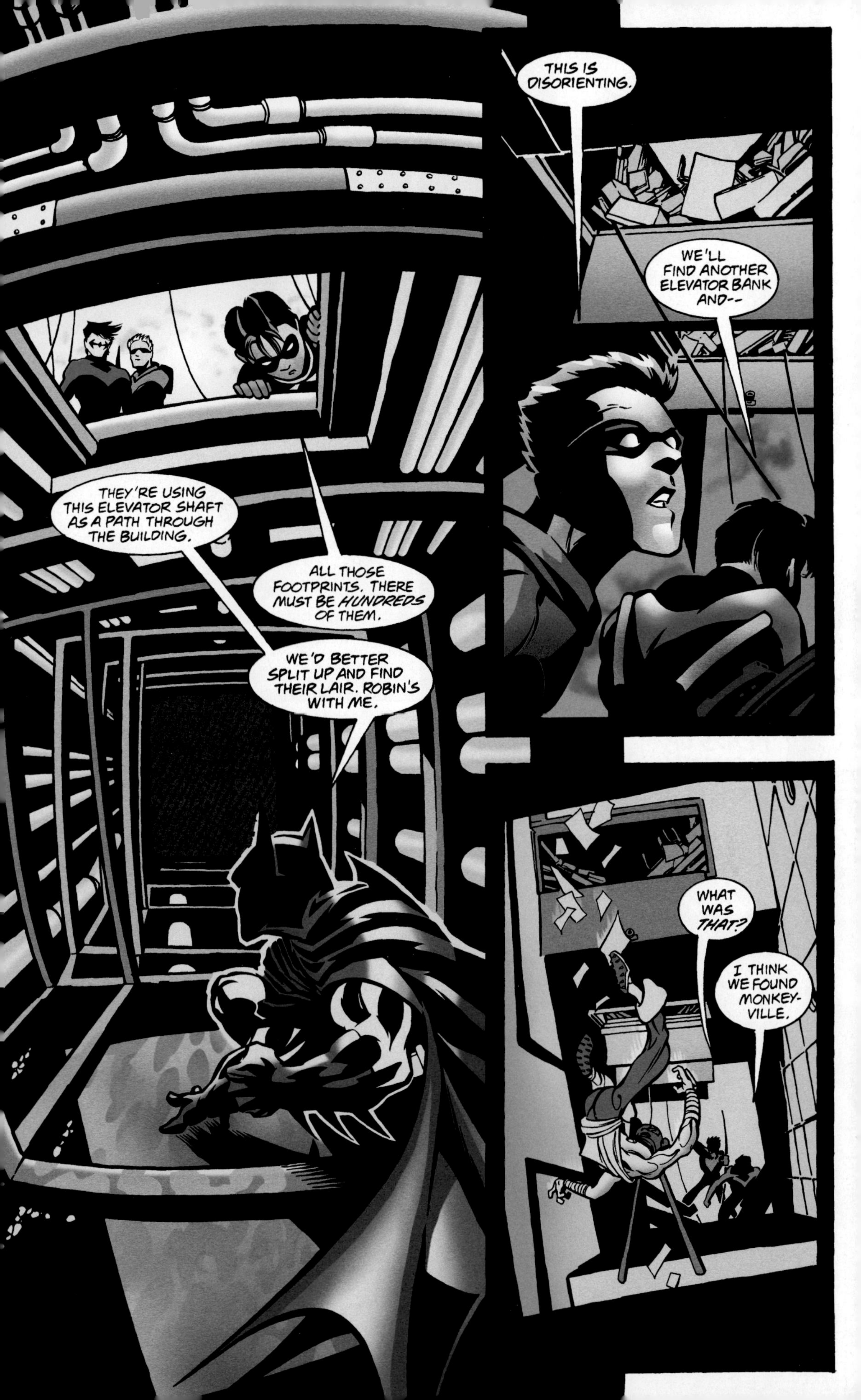
THEY'RE USING THIS ELEVATOR SHAFT AS A PATH THROUGH THE BUILDING.
ALL THOSE FOOTPRINTS. THERE MUST BE *HUNDREDS* OF THEM.
WE'D BETTER SPLIT UP AND FIND THEIR LAIR. ROBIN'S WITH ME.
THIS IS DISORIENTING.
WE'LL FIND ANOTHER ELEVATOR BANK AND--
WHAT WAS *THAT?*
I THINK WE FOUND MONKEY-VILLE.

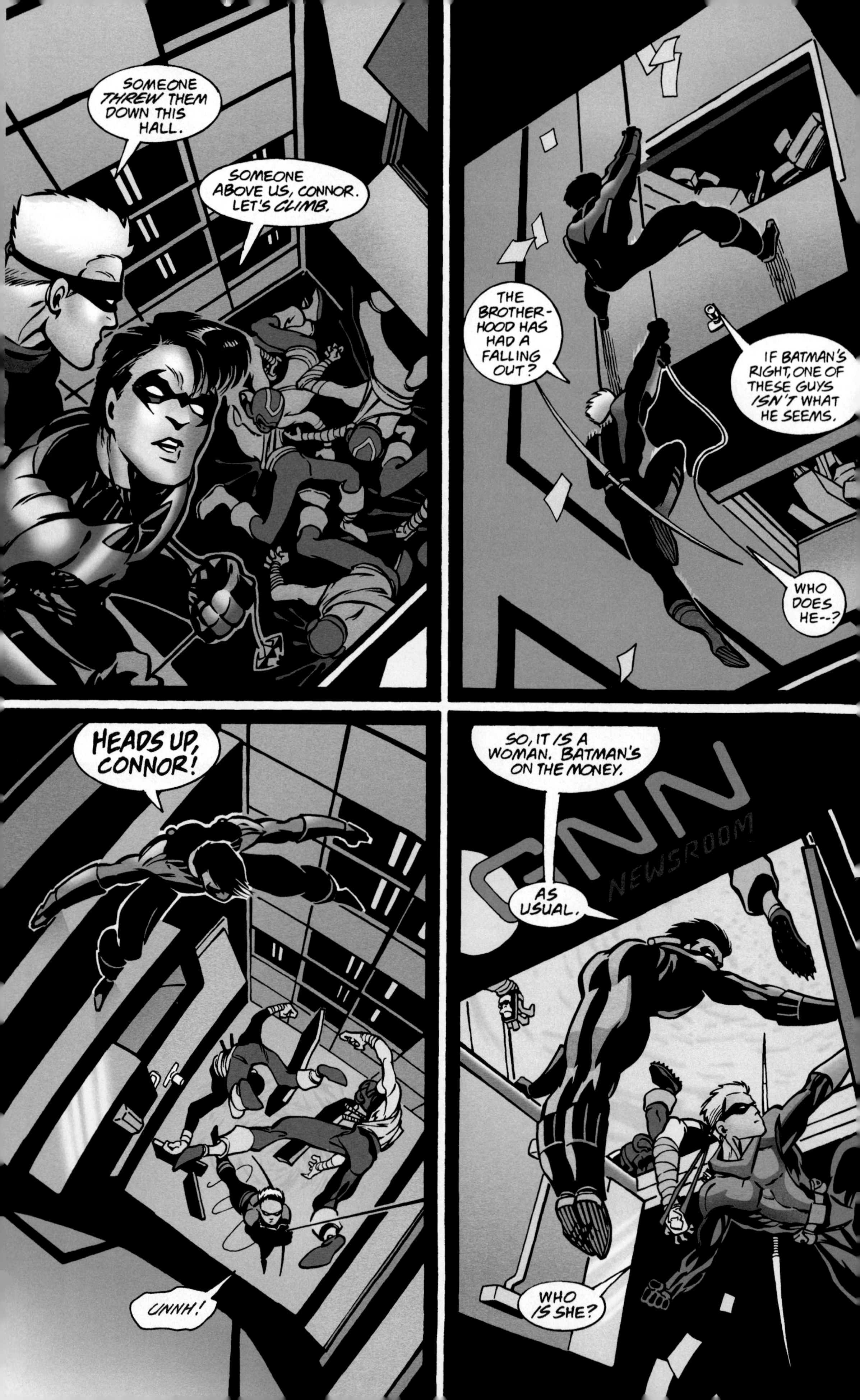
SOMEONE THREW THEM DOWN THIS HALL.
SOMEONE ABOVE US, CONNOR. LET'S CLIMB.
THE BROTHER-HOOD HAS HAD A FALLING OUT?
IF BATMAN'S RIGHT, ONE OF THESE GUYS ISN'T WHAT HE SEEMS.
WHO DOES HE--?
HEADS UP, CONNOR!
UNNH!
SO, IT IS A WOMAN. BATMAN'S ON THE MONEY.
AS USUAL.
WHO IS SHE?
GNN
NEWSROOM

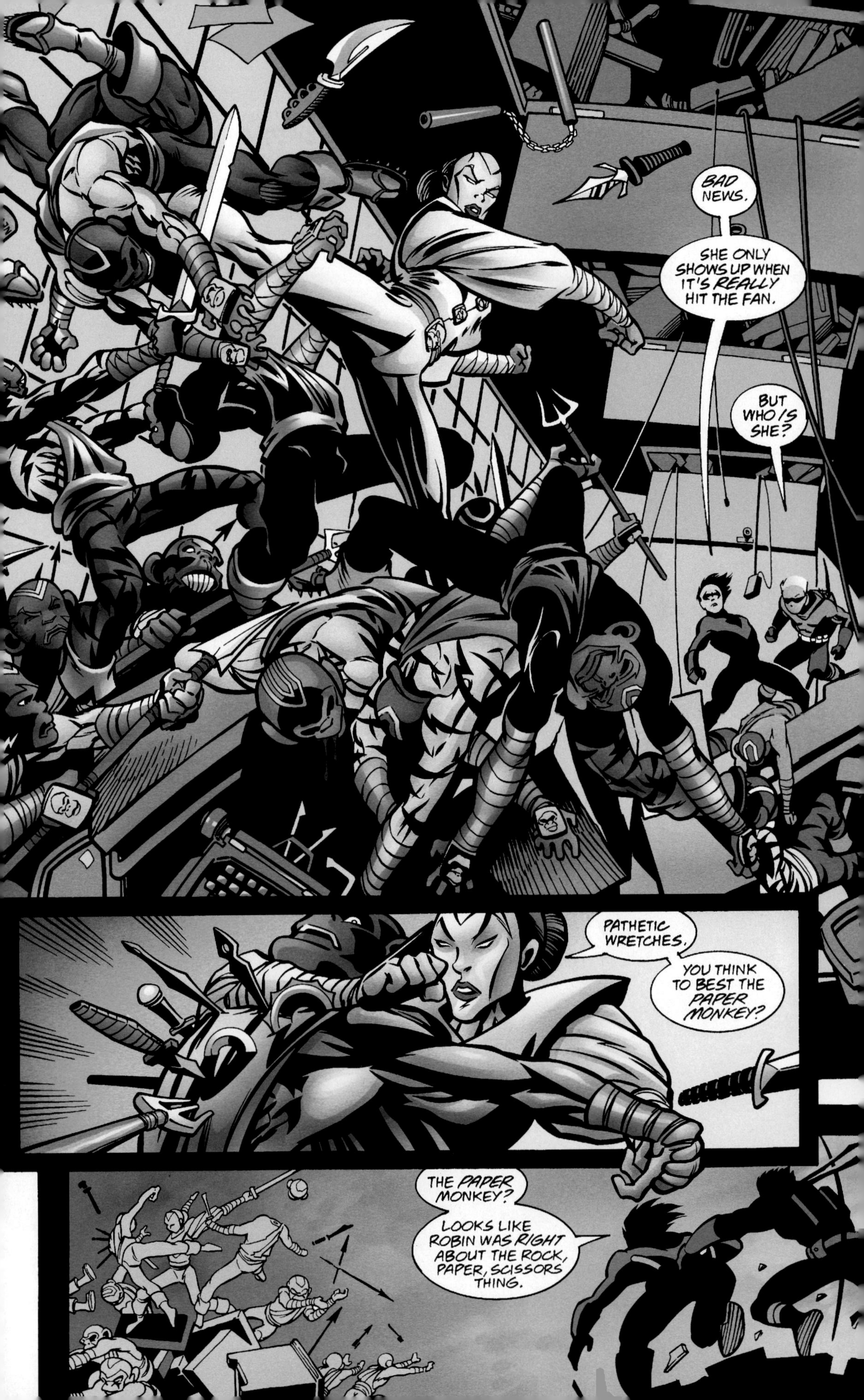
BAD NEWS.
SHE ONLY SHOWS UP WHEN IT'S *REALLY* HIT THE FAN.
BUT WHO *IS* SHE?
PATHETIC WRETCHES.
YOU THINK TO BEST THE *PAPER MONKEY*?
THE *PAPER* MONKEY?
LOOKS LIKE ROBIN WAS *RIGHT* ABOUT THE ROCK, PAPER, SCISSORS THING.

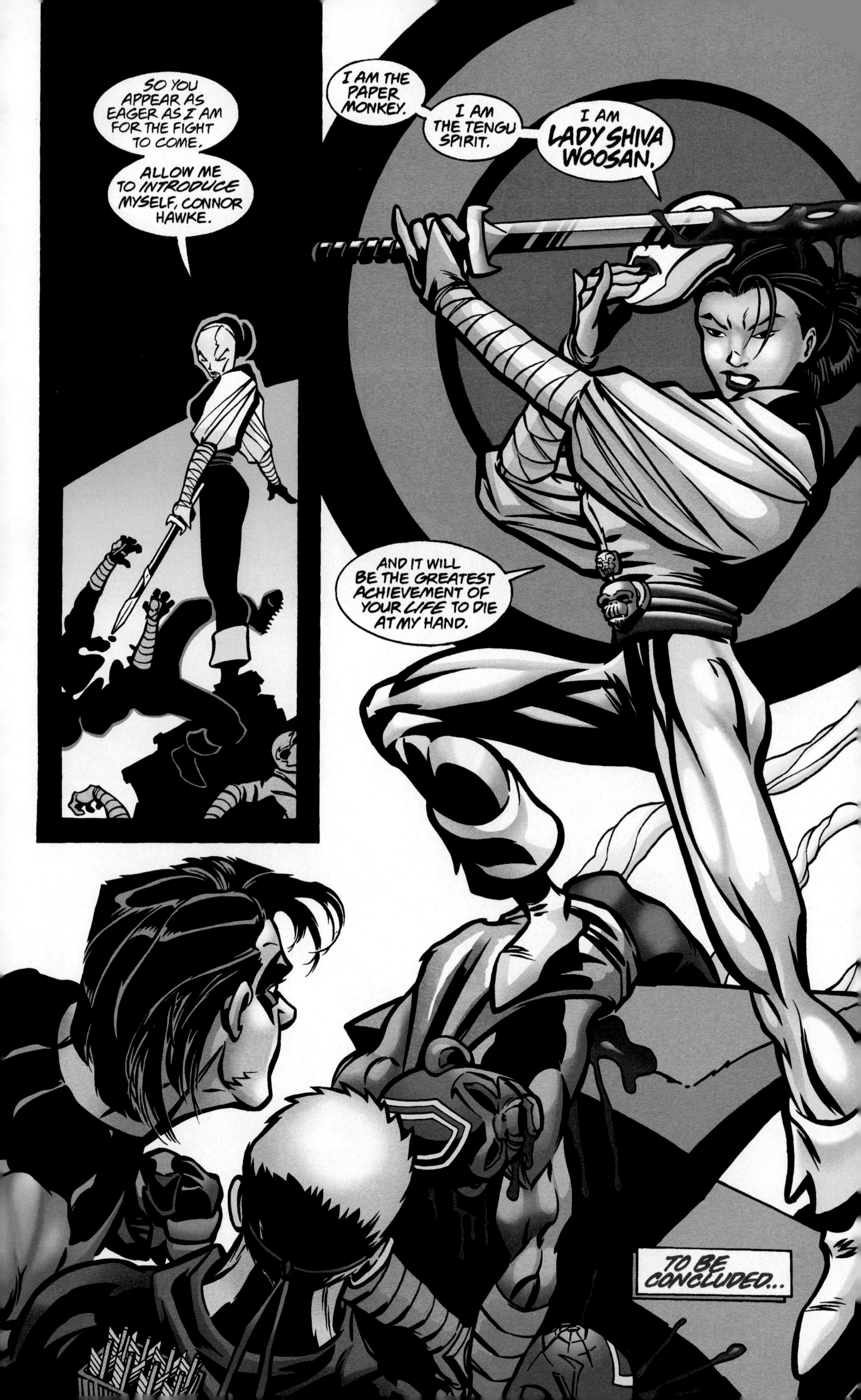
SO YOU APPEAR AS EAGER AS I AM FOR THE FIGHT TO COME.
ALLOW ME TO INTRODUCE MYSELF, CONNOR HAWKE.
I AM THE PAPER MONKEY.
I AM THE TENGU SPIRIT.
I AM LADY SHIVA WOOSAN.
AND IT WILL BE THE GREATEST ACHIEVEMENT OF YOUR LIFE TO DIE AT MY HAND.
TO BE CONCLUDED...

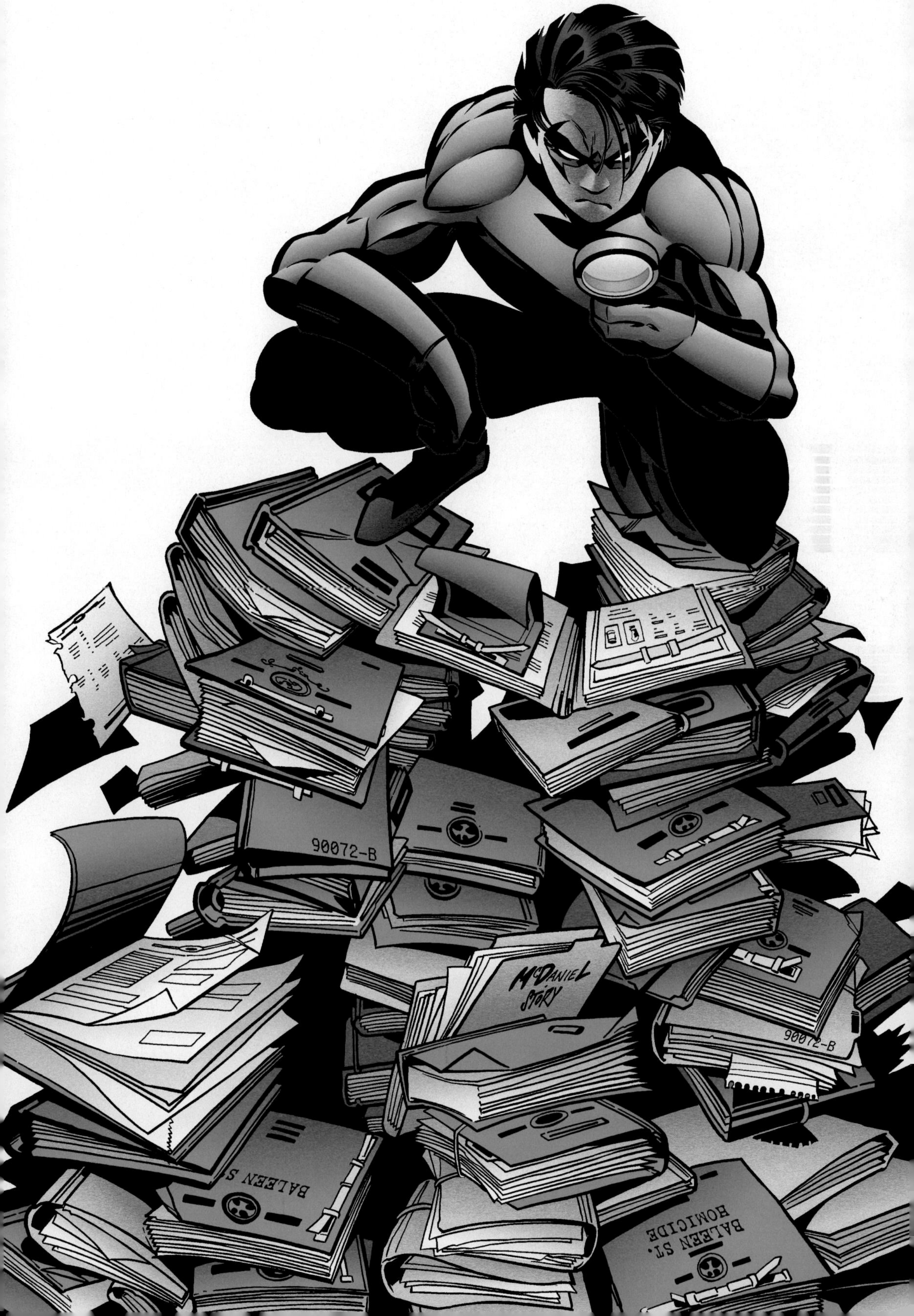

90072-B
McDANIEL STORY
90072-B
BALEEN S
BALEEN ST. HOMICIDE

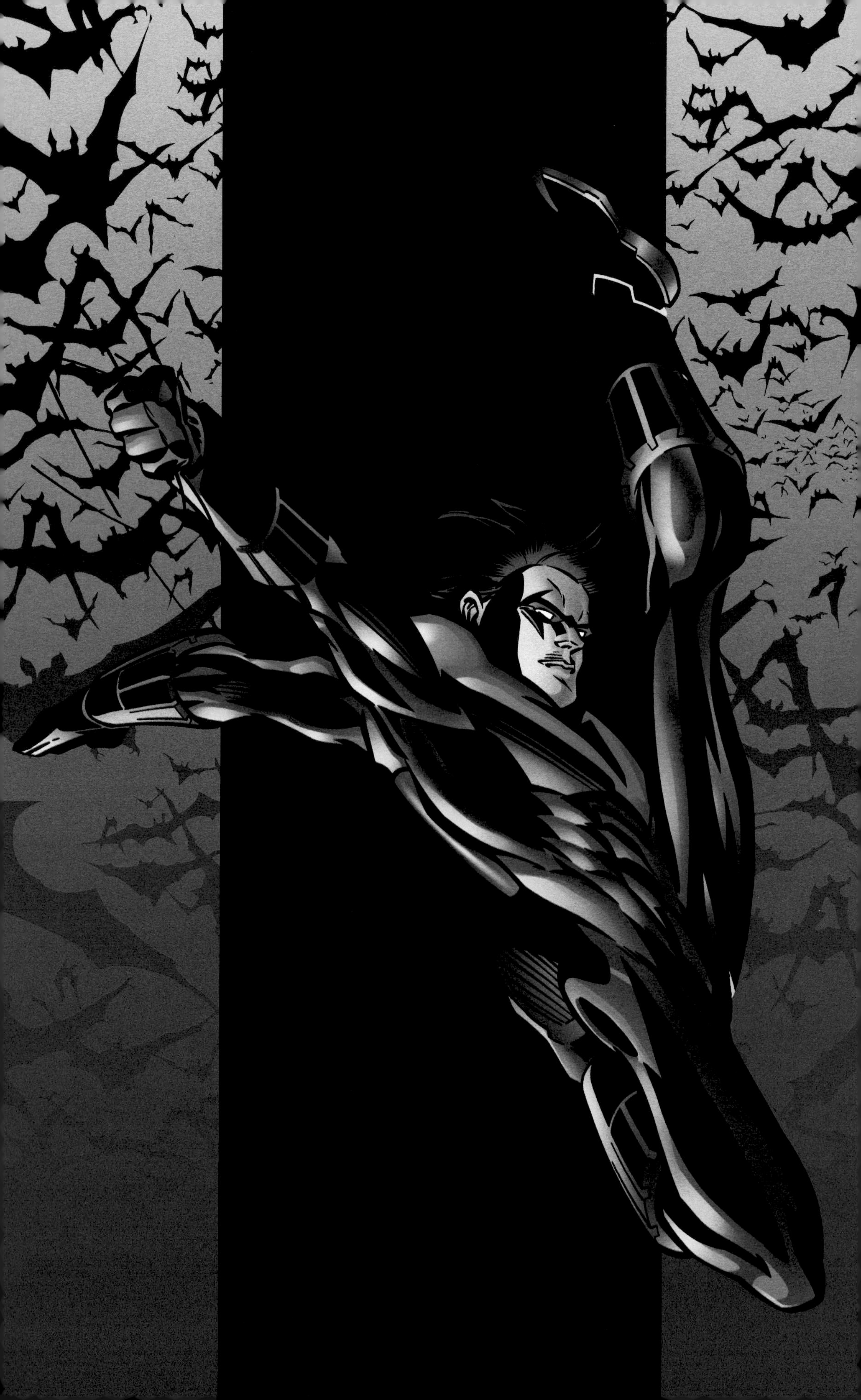

The FORGOTTEN DEAD

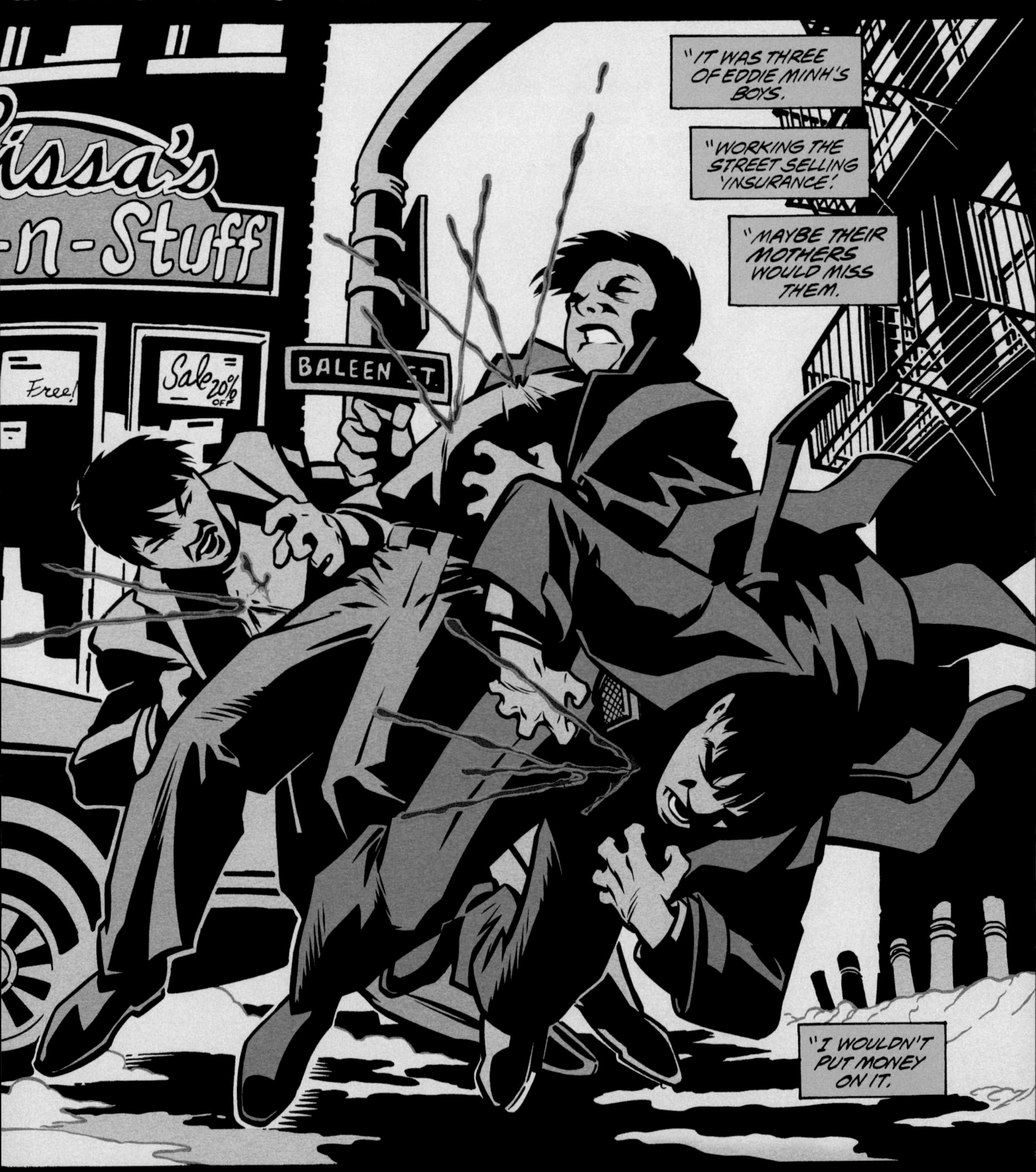
"IT WAS THREE OF EDDIE MINH'S BOYS.
"WORKING THE STREET SELLING 'INSURANCE.'
"MAYBE THEIR MOTHERS WOULD MISS THEM.
"I WOULDN'T PUT MONEY ON IT.
-n-Stuff
Free!
Sale 20% OFF
BALEEN ST.

CHUCK DIXON - writer SCOTT McDANIEL - penciller KARL STORY - inker ROBERTA TEWES - colorist JAMISON - separator
JOHN COSTANZA - letterer DARREN VINCENZO - associate editor SCOTT PETERSON - editor

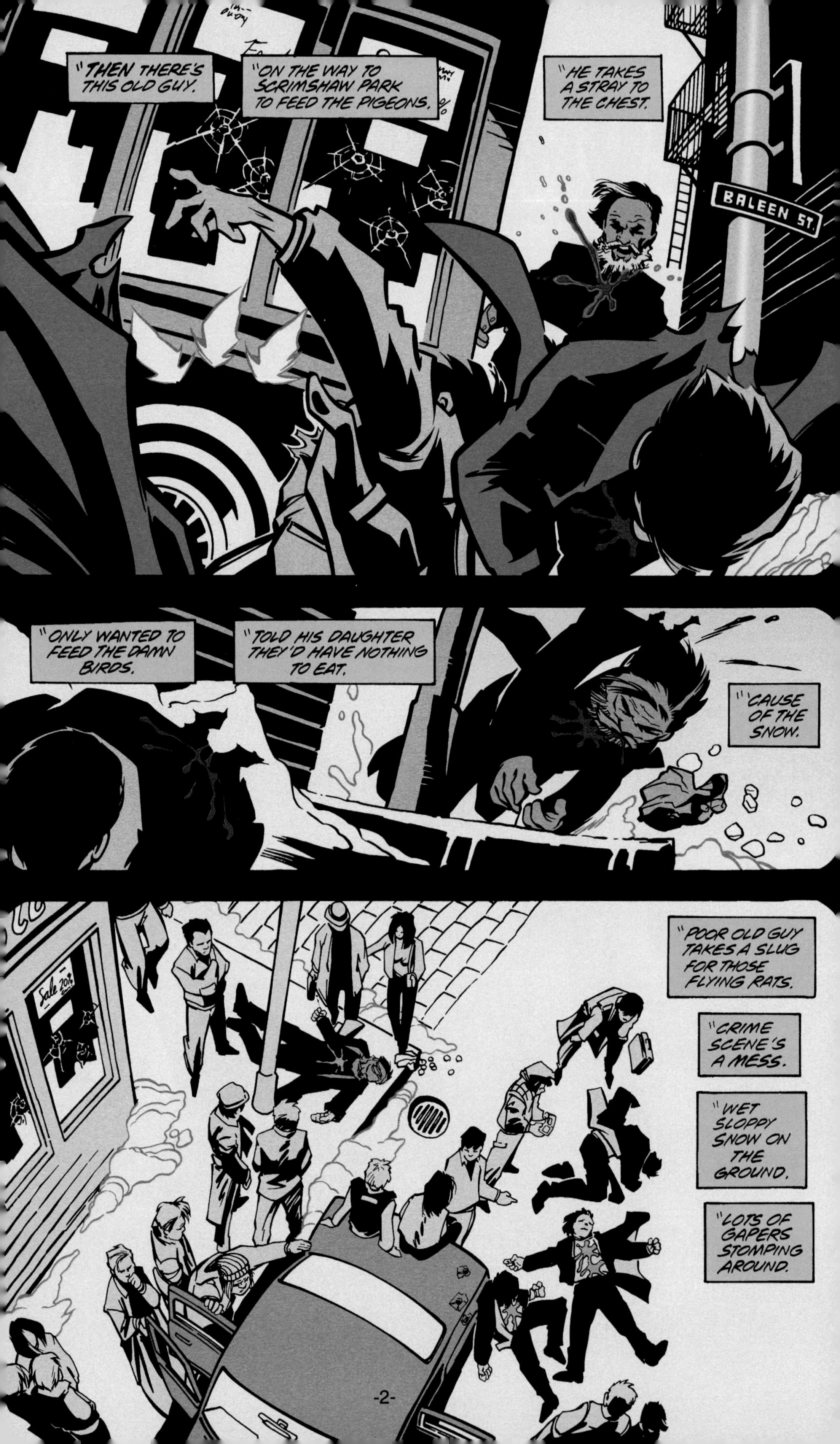

"THEN THERE'S THIS OLD GUY.
"ON THE WAY TO SCRIMSHAW PARK TO FEED THE PIGEONS.
"HE TAKES A STRAY TO THE CHEST.
BALEEN ST.
"ONLY WANTED TO FEED THE DAMN BIRDS.
"TOLD HIS DAUGHTER THEY'D HAVE NOTHING TO EAT.
"'CAUSE OF THE SNOW.
"POOR OLD GUY TAKES A SLUG FOR THOSE FLYING RATS.
"CRIME SCENE'S A MESS.
"WET SLOPPY SNOW ON THE GROUND.
"LOTS OF GAPERS STOMPING AROUND.

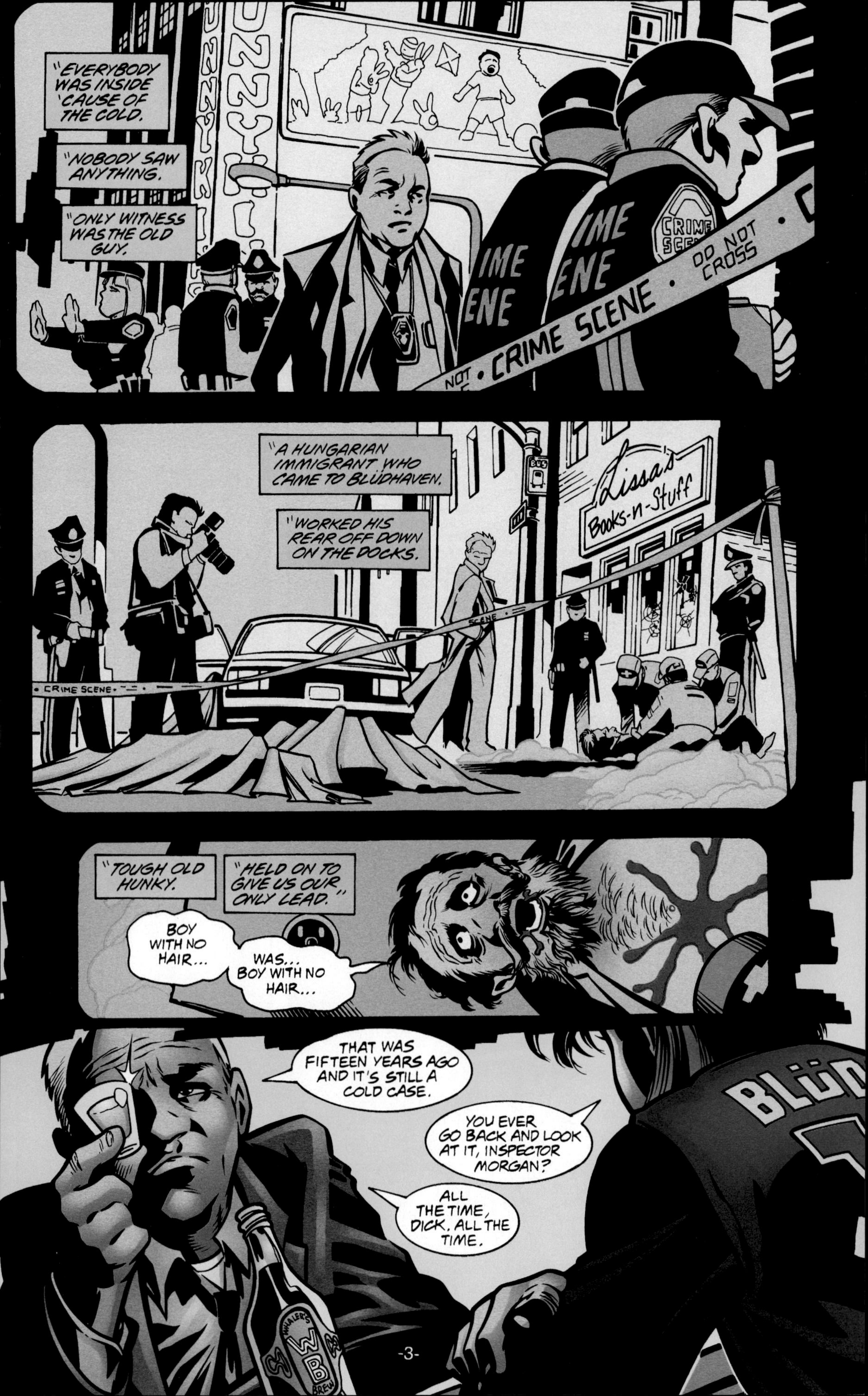
"EVERYBODY WAS INSIDE 'CAUSE OF THE COLD.
"NOBODY SAW ANYTHING.
"ONLY WITNESS WAS THE OLD GUY.
CRIME SCENE
DO NOT CROSS
"A HUNGARIAN IMMIGRANT WHO CAME TO BLÜDHAVEN.
"WORKED HIS REAR OFF DOWN ON THE DOCKS.
Lissa's Books-n-Stuff
CRIME SCENE
"TOUGH OLD HUNKY.
"HELD ON TO GIVE US OUR ONLY LEAD."
BOY WITH NO HAIR...
WAS... BOY WITH NO HAIR...
THAT WAS FIFTEEN YEARS AGO AND IT'S STILL A COLD CASE.
YOU EVER GO BACK AND LOOK AT IT, INSPECTOR MORGAN?
ALL THE TIME, DICK. ALL THE TIME.

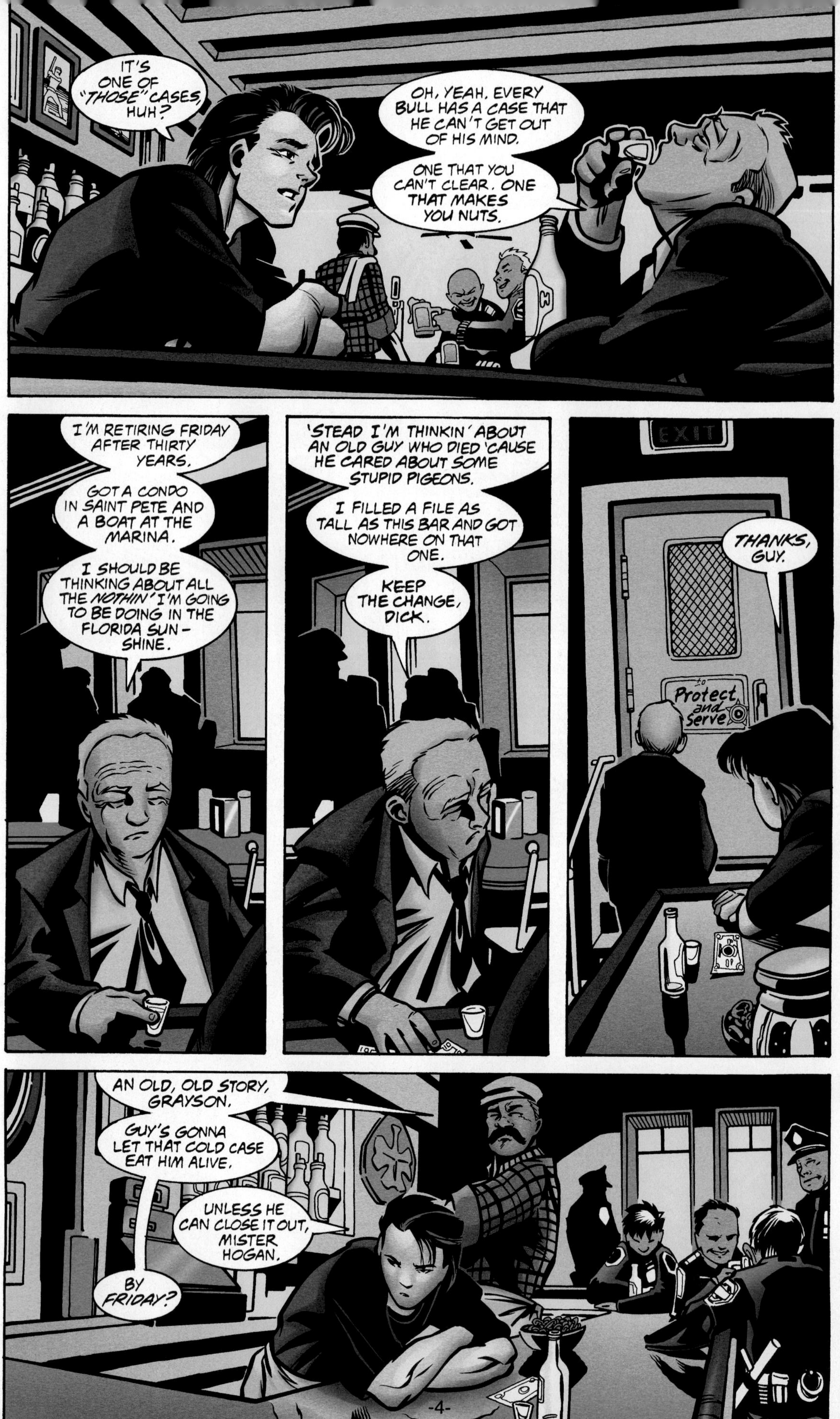
IT'S ONE OF "THOSE" CASES, HUH?
OH, YEAH. EVERY BULL HAS A CASE THAT HE CAN'T GET OUT OF HIS MIND.
ONE THAT YOU CAN'T CLEAR. ONE THAT MAKES YOU NUTS.
I'M RETIRING FRIDAY AFTER THIRTY YEARS.
GOT A CONDO IN SAINT PETE AND A BOAT AT THE MARINA.
I SHOULD BE THINKING ABOUT ALL THE NOTHIN' I'M GOING TO BE DOING IN THE FLORIDA SUN-SHINE.
'STEAD I'M THINKIN' ABOUT AN OLD GUY WHO DIED 'CAUSE HE CARED ABOUT SOME STUPID PIGEONS.
I FILLED A FILE AS TALL AS THIS BAR AND GOT NOWHERE ON THAT ONE.
KEEP THE CHANGE, DICK.
EXIT
THANKS, GUY.
to Protect and Serve
AN OLD, OLD STORY, GRAYSON.
GUY'S GONNA LET THAT COLD CASE EAT HIM ALIVE.
UNLESS HE CAN CLOSE IT OUT, MISTER HOGAN.
BY FRIDAY?

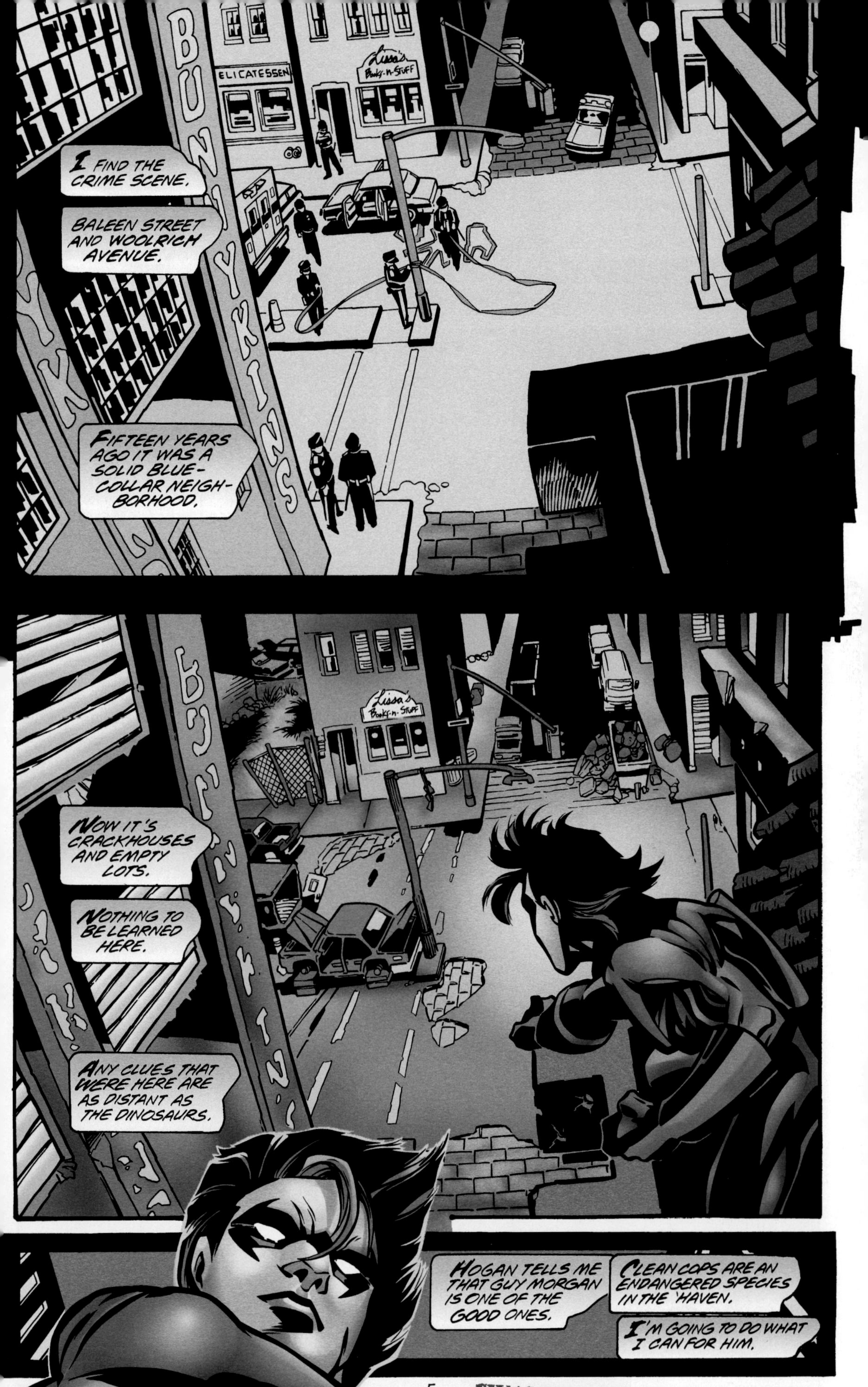
ELICATESSEN
Lissa's Books-n-Stuff
I FIND THE CRIME SCENE.
BALEEN STREET AND WOOLRICH AVENUE.
FIFTEEN YEARS AGO IT WAS A SOLID BLUE-COLLAR NEIGHBORHOOD.
Lissa's Books-n-Stuff
NOW IT'S CRACKHOUSES AND EMPTY LOTS.
NOTHING TO BE LEARNED HERE.
ANY CLUES THAT WERE HERE ARE AS DISTANT AS THE DINOSAURS.
HOGAN TELLS ME THAT GUY MORGAN IS ONE OF THE GOOD ONES.
CLEAN COPS ARE AN ENDANGERED SPECIES IN THE 'HAVEN.
I'M GOING TO DO WHAT I CAN FOR HIM.

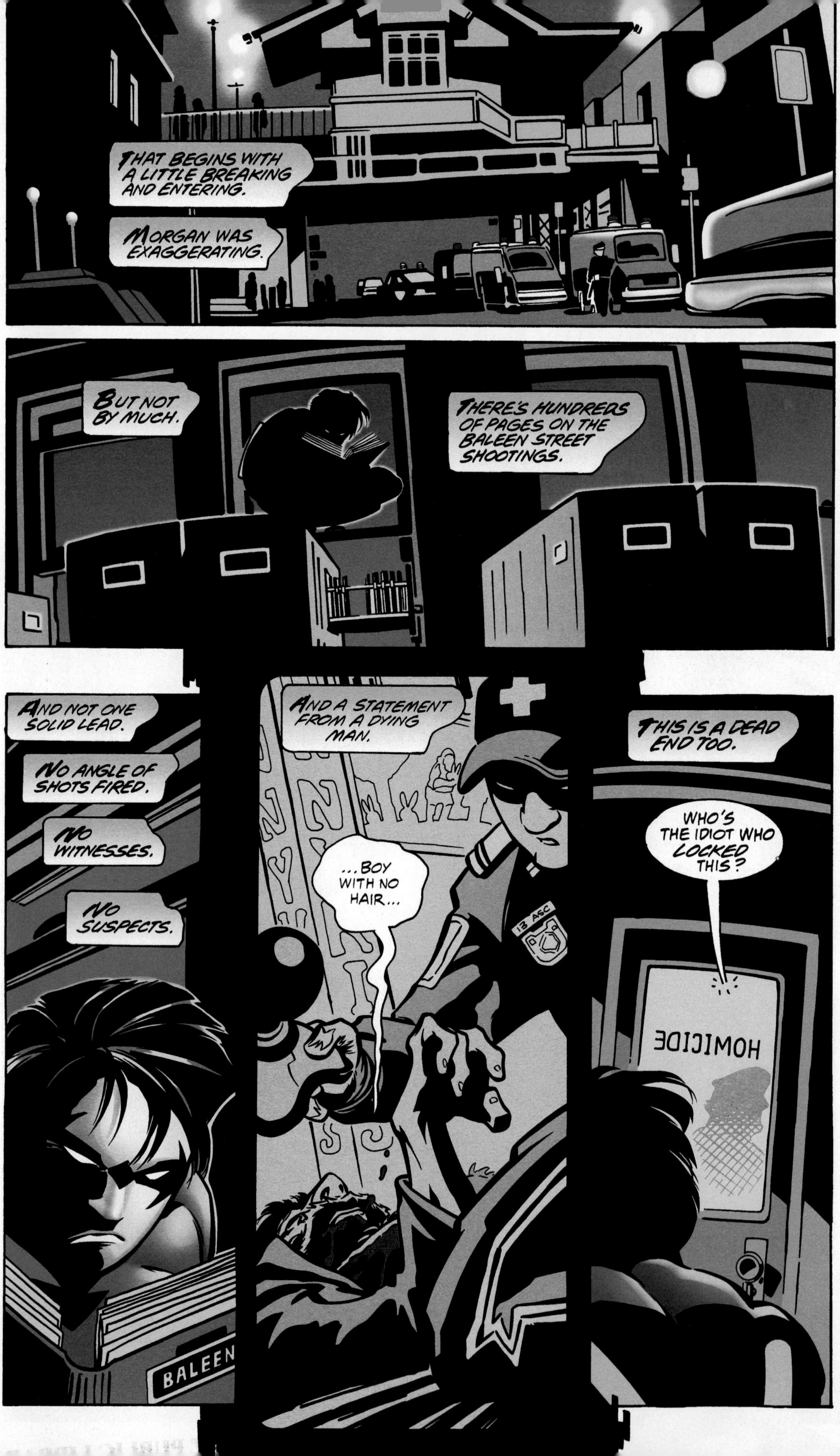
THAT BEGINS WITH A LITTLE BREAKING AND ENTERING.
MORGAN WAS EXAGGERATING.
BUT NOT BY MUCH.
THERE'S HUNDREDS OF PAGES ON THE BALEEN STREET SHOOTINGS.
AND NOT ONE SOLID LEAD.
NO ANGLE OF SHOTS FIRED.
NO WITNESSES.
NO SUSPECTS.
BALEEN
AND A STATEMENT FROM A DYING MAN.
...BOY WITH NO HAIR...
13 ASC
THIS IS A DEAD END TOO.
WHO'S THE IDIOT WHO LOCKED THIS?
HOMICIDE

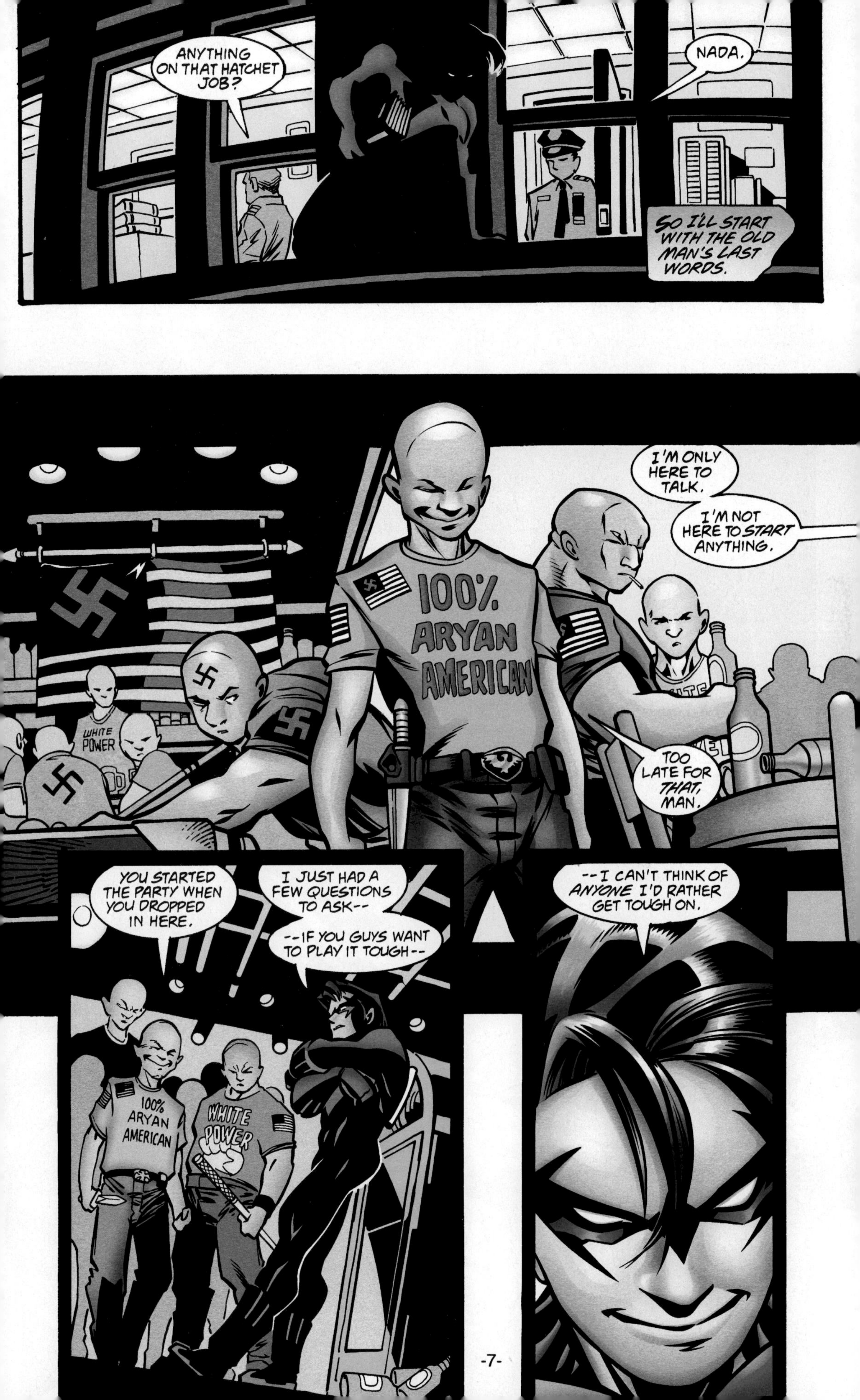
ANYTHING ON THAT HATCHET JOB?
NADA.
SO I'LL START WITH THE OLD MAN'S LAST WORDS.
I'M ONLY HERE TO TALK.
I'M NOT HERE TO START ANYTHING.
100% ARYAN AMERICAN
TOO LATE FOR THAT, MAN.
YOU STARTED THE PARTY WHEN YOU DROPPED IN HERE.
I JUST HAD A FEW QUESTIONS TO ASK--
--IF YOU GUYS WANT TO PLAY IT TOUGH--
--I CAN'T THINK OF ANYONE I'D RATHER GET TOUGH ON.
100% ARYAN AMERICAN
WHITE POWER

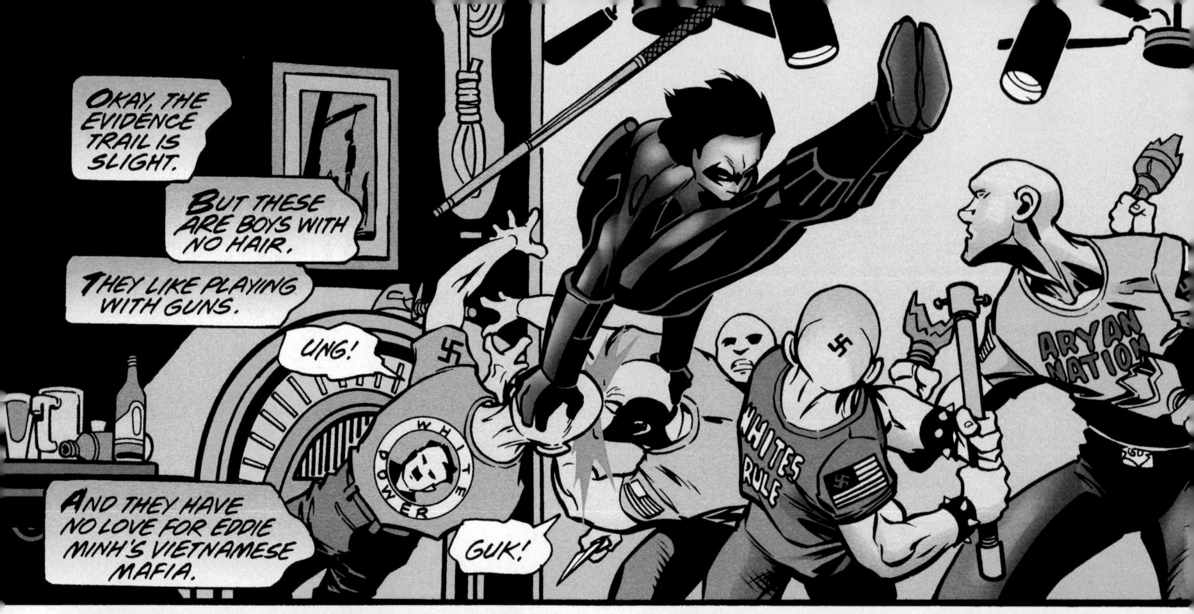
OKAY, THE EVIDENCE TRAIL IS SLIGHT.
BUT THESE ARE BOYS WITH NO HAIR.
THEY LIKE PLAYING WITH GUNS.
UNG!
ARYAN NATION
WHITE POWER
WHITES RULE
AND THEY HAVE NO LOVE FOR EDDIE MINH'S VIETNAMESE MAFIA.
GUK!

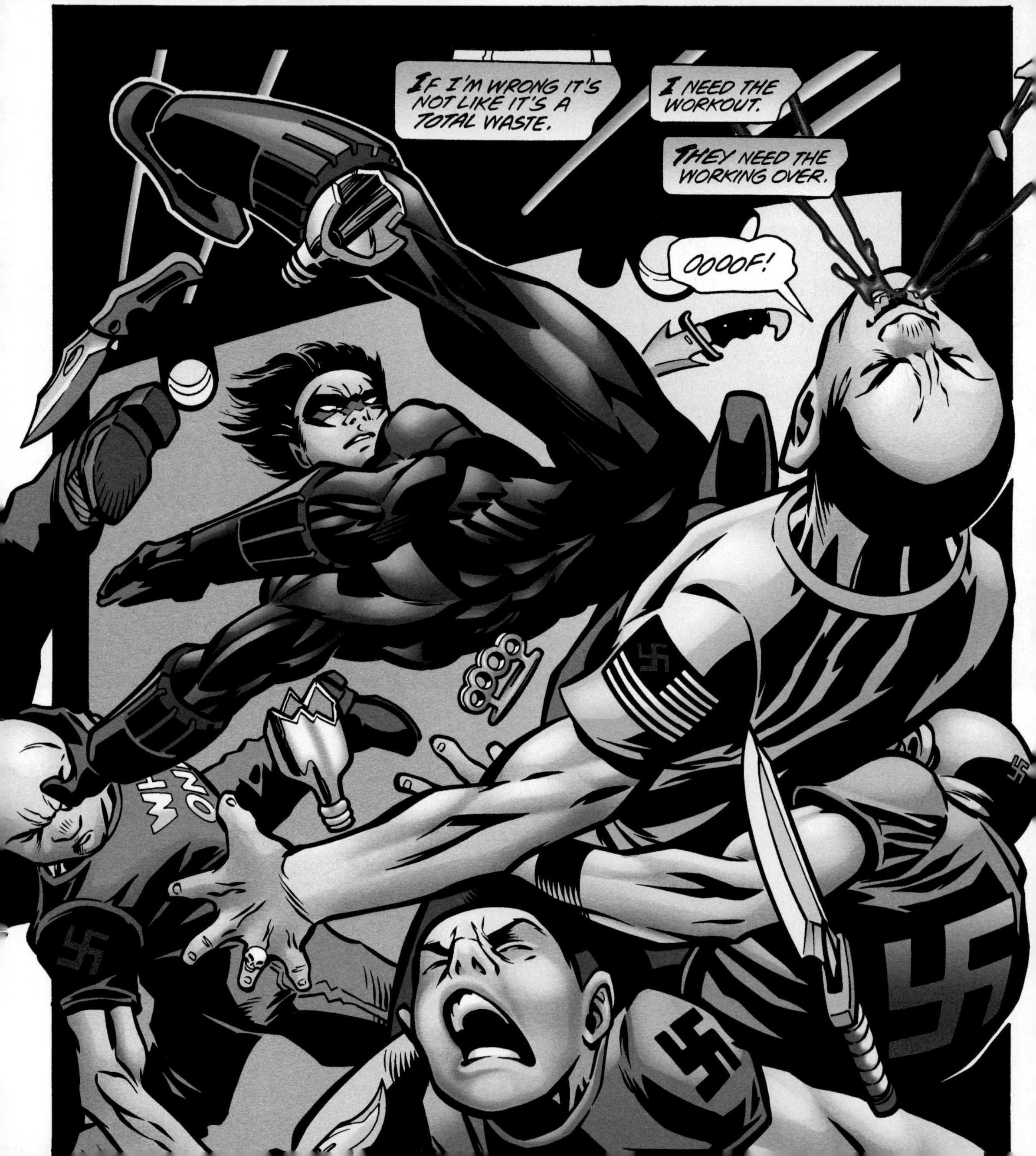
IF I'M WRONG IT'S NOT LIKE IT'S A TOTAL WASTE.
I NEED THE WORKOUT.
THEY NEED THE WORKING OVER.
OOOOF!

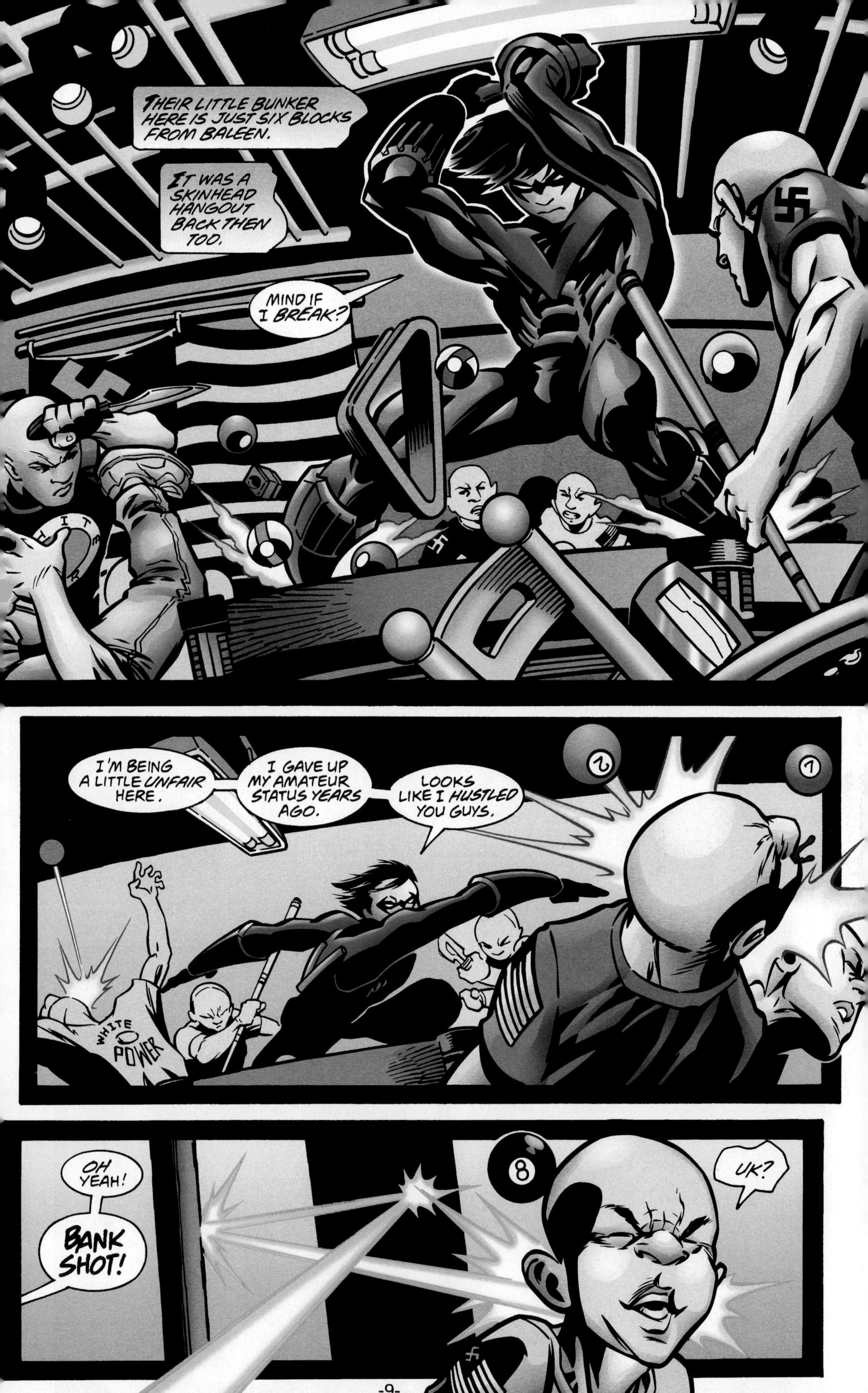
THEIR LITTLE BUNKER HERE IS JUST SIX BLOCKS FROM BALEEN.
IT WAS A SKINHEAD HANGOUT BACK THEN TOO.
MIND IF I BREAK?
I'M BEING A LITTLE UNFAIR HERE.
I GAVE UP MY AMATEUR STATUS YEARS AGO.
LOOKS LIKE I HUSTLED YOU GUYS.
WHITE POWER
OH YEAH!
BANK SHOT!
UK?

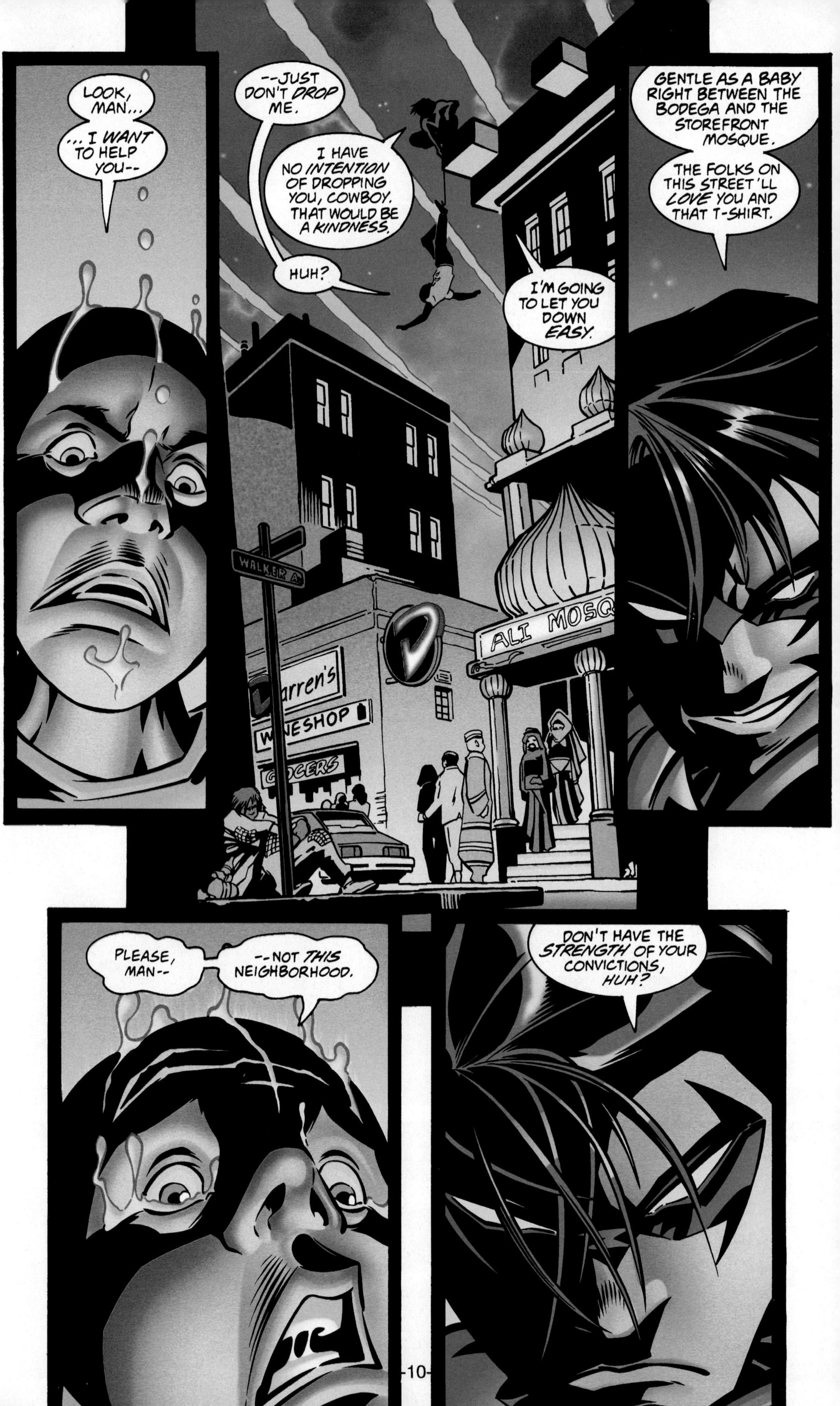
LOOK, MAN...
...I WANT TO HELP YOU--
--JUST DON'T DROP ME.
I HAVE NO INTENTION OF DROPPING YOU, COWBOY. THAT WOULD BE A KINDNESS.
HUH?
I'M GOING TO LET YOU DOWN EASY.
GENTLE AS A BABY RIGHT BETWEEN THE BODEGA AND THE STOREFRONT MOSQUE.
THE FOLKS ON THIS STREET'LL LOVE YOU AND THAT T-SHIRT.
WALKER A.
Darren's
WINESHOP
GROCERS
ALI MOSQ
PLEASE, MAN--
--NOT THIS NEIGHBORHOOD.
DON'T HAVE THE STRENGTH OF YOUR CONVICTIONS, HUH?

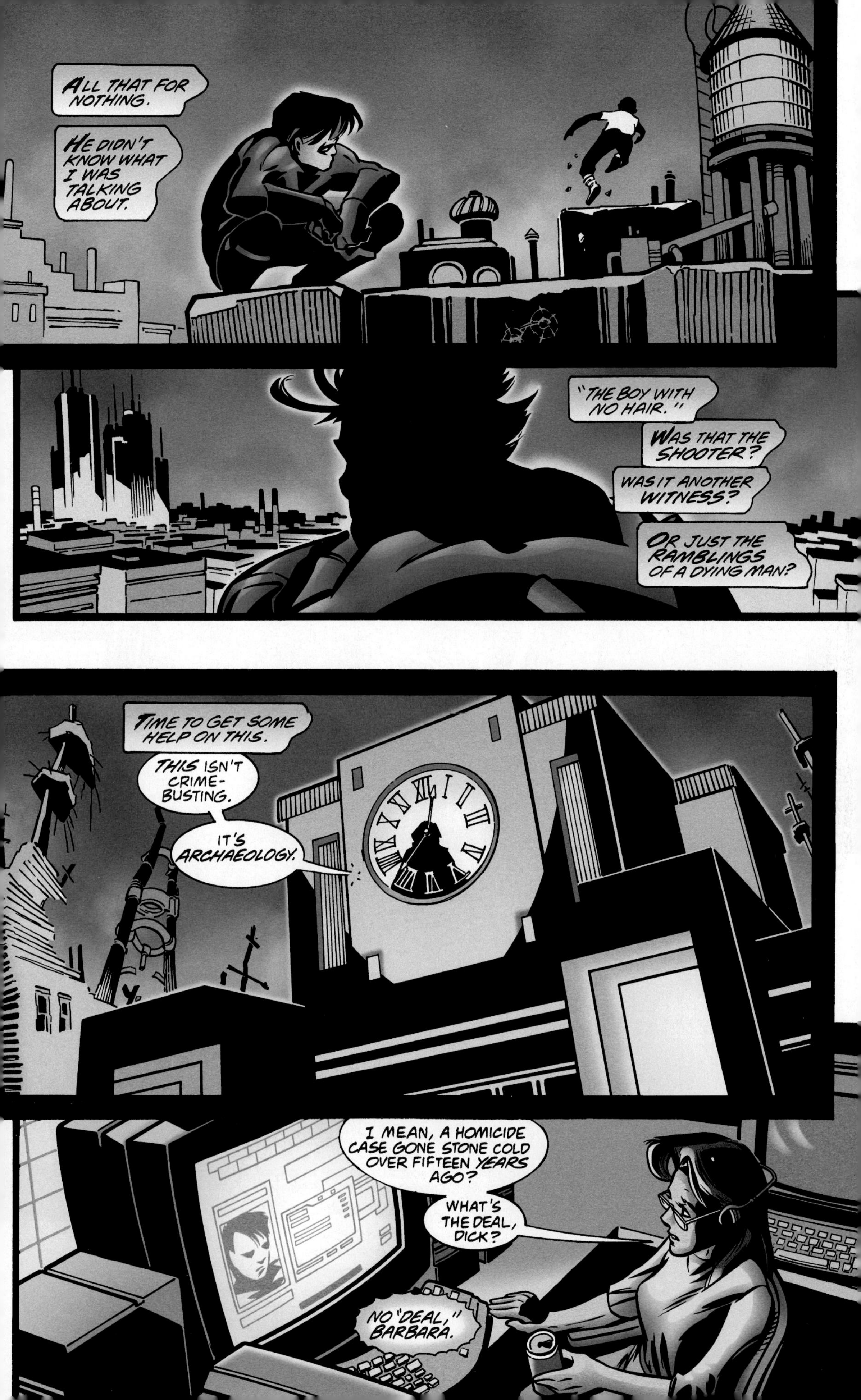
ALL THAT FOR NOTHING.
HE DIDN'T KNOW WHAT I WAS TALKING ABOUT.
"THE BOY WITH NO HAIR."
WAS THAT THE SHOOTER?
WAS IT ANOTHER WITNESS?
OR JUST THE RAMBLINGS OF A DYING MAN?
TIME TO GET SOME HELP ON THIS.
THIS ISN'T CRIME-BUSTING.
IT'S ARCHAEOLOGY.
I MEAN, A HOMICIDE CASE GONE STONE COLD OVER FIFTEEN YEARS AGO?
WHAT'S THE DEAL, DICK?
NO "DEAL," BARBARA.

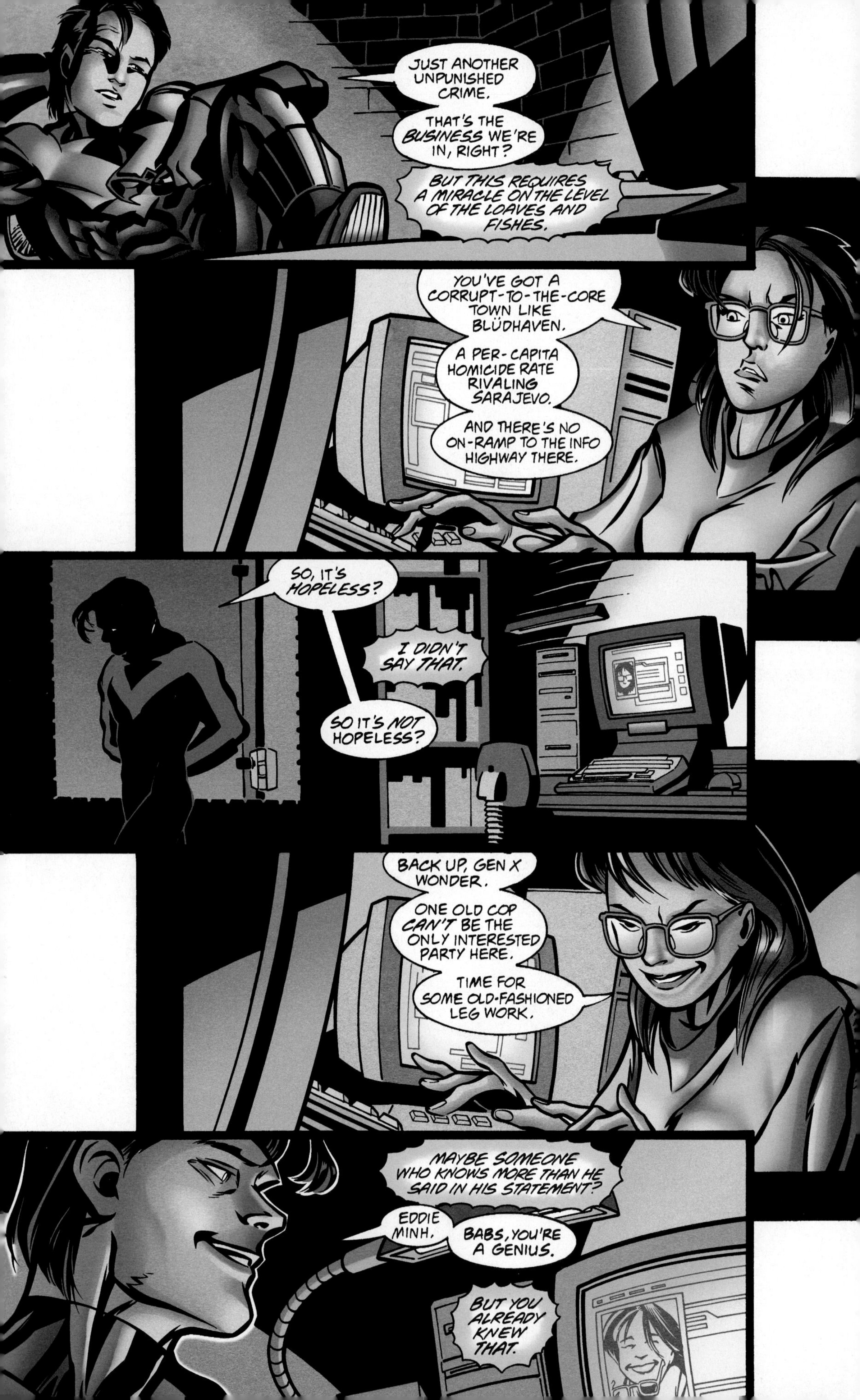
JUST ANOTHER UNPUNISHED CRIME.
THAT'S THE BUSINESS WE'RE IN, RIGHT?
BUT THIS REQUIRES A MIRACLE ON THE LEVEL OF THE LOAVES AND FISHES.
YOU'VE GOT A CORRUPT-TO-THE-CORE TOWN LIKE BLÜDHAVEN.
A PER-CAPITA HOMICIDE RATE RIVALING SARAJEVO.
AND THERE'S NO ON-RAMP TO THE INFO HIGHWAY THERE.
SO, IT'S HOPELESS?
I DIDN'T SAY THAT.
SO IT'S NOT HOPELESS?
BACK UP, GEN X WONDER.
ONE OLD COP CAN'T BE THE ONLY INTERESTED PARTY HERE.
TIME FOR SOME OLD-FASHIONED LEG WORK.
MAYBE SOMEONE WHO KNOWS MORE THAN HE SAID IN HIS STATEMENT?
EDDIE MINH.
BABS, YOU'RE A GENIUS.
BUT YOU ALREADY KNEW THAT.

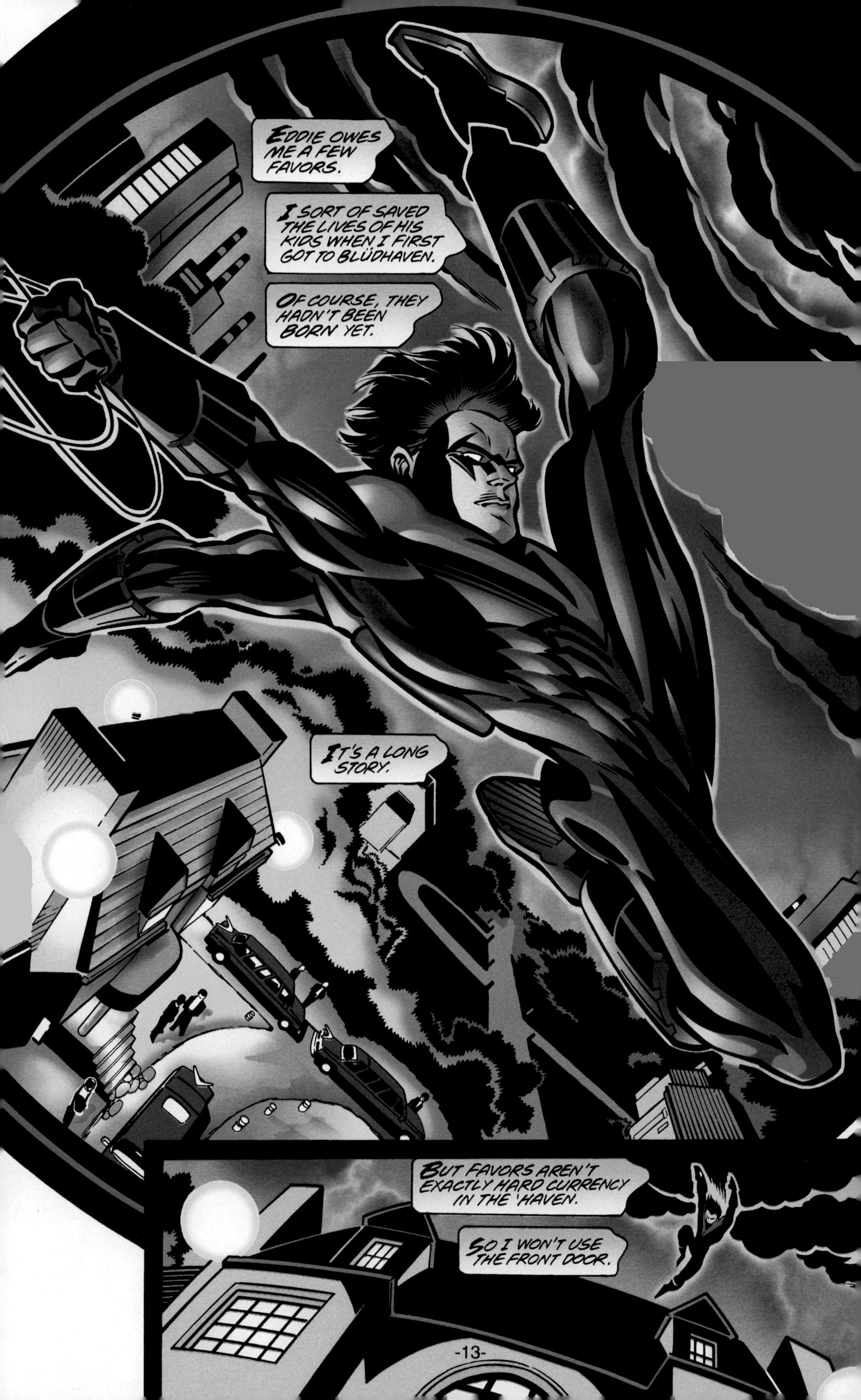
EDDIE OWES ME A FEW FAVORS.
I SORT OF SAVED THE LIVES OF HIS KIDS WHEN I FIRST GOT TO BLÜDHAVEN.
OF COURSE, THEY HADN'T BEEN BORN YET.
IT'S A LONG STORY.
BUT FAVORS AREN'T EXACTLY HARD CURRENCY IN THE 'HAVEN.
SO I WON'T USE THE FRONT DOOR.

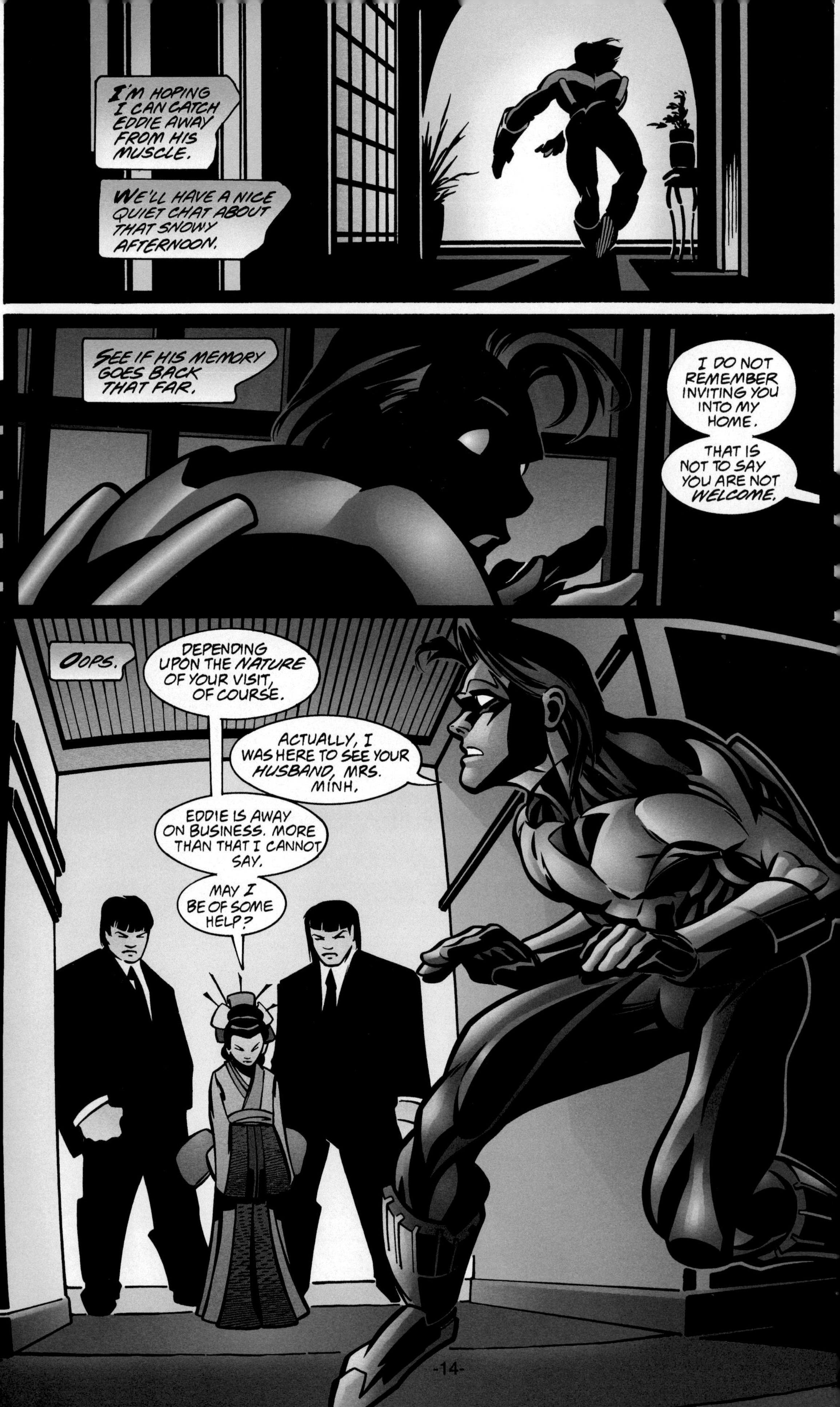
I'M HOPING I CAN CATCH EDDIE AWAY FROM HIS MUSCLE.
WE'LL HAVE A NICE QUIET CHAT ABOUT THAT SNOWY AFTERNOON.
SEE IF HIS MEMORY GOES BACK THAT FAR.
I DO NOT REMEMBER INVITING YOU INTO MY HOME.
THAT IS NOT TO SAY YOU ARE NOT WELCOME.
OOPS.
DEPENDING UPON THE NATURE OF YOUR VISIT, OF COURSE.
ACTUALLY, I WAS HERE TO SEE YOUR HUSBAND, MRS. MINH.
EDDIE IS AWAY ON BUSINESS. MORE THAN THAT I CANNOT SAY.
MAY I BE OF SOME HELP?

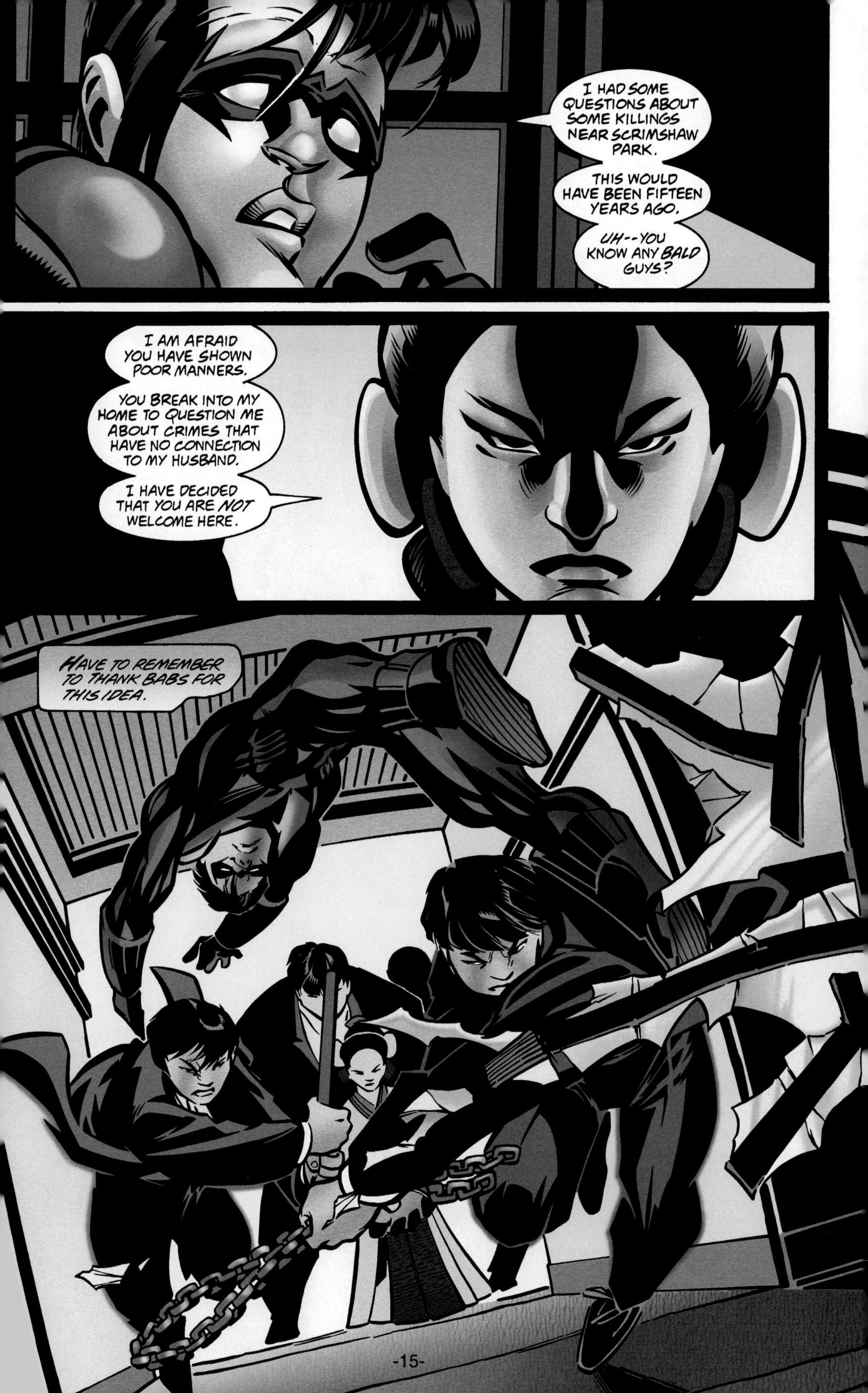
I HAD SOME QUESTIONS ABOUT SOME KILLINGS NEAR SCRIMSHAW PARK.
THIS WOULD HAVE BEEN FIFTEEN YEARS AGO.
UH--YOU KNOW ANY BALD GUYS?
I AM AFRAID YOU HAVE SHOWN POOR MANNERS.
YOU BREAK INTO MY HOME TO QUESTION ME ABOUT CRIMES THAT HAVE NO CONNECTION TO MY HUSBAND.
I HAVE DECIDED THAT YOU ARE NOT WELCOME HERE.
HAVE TO REMEMBER TO THANK BABS FOR THIS IDEA.

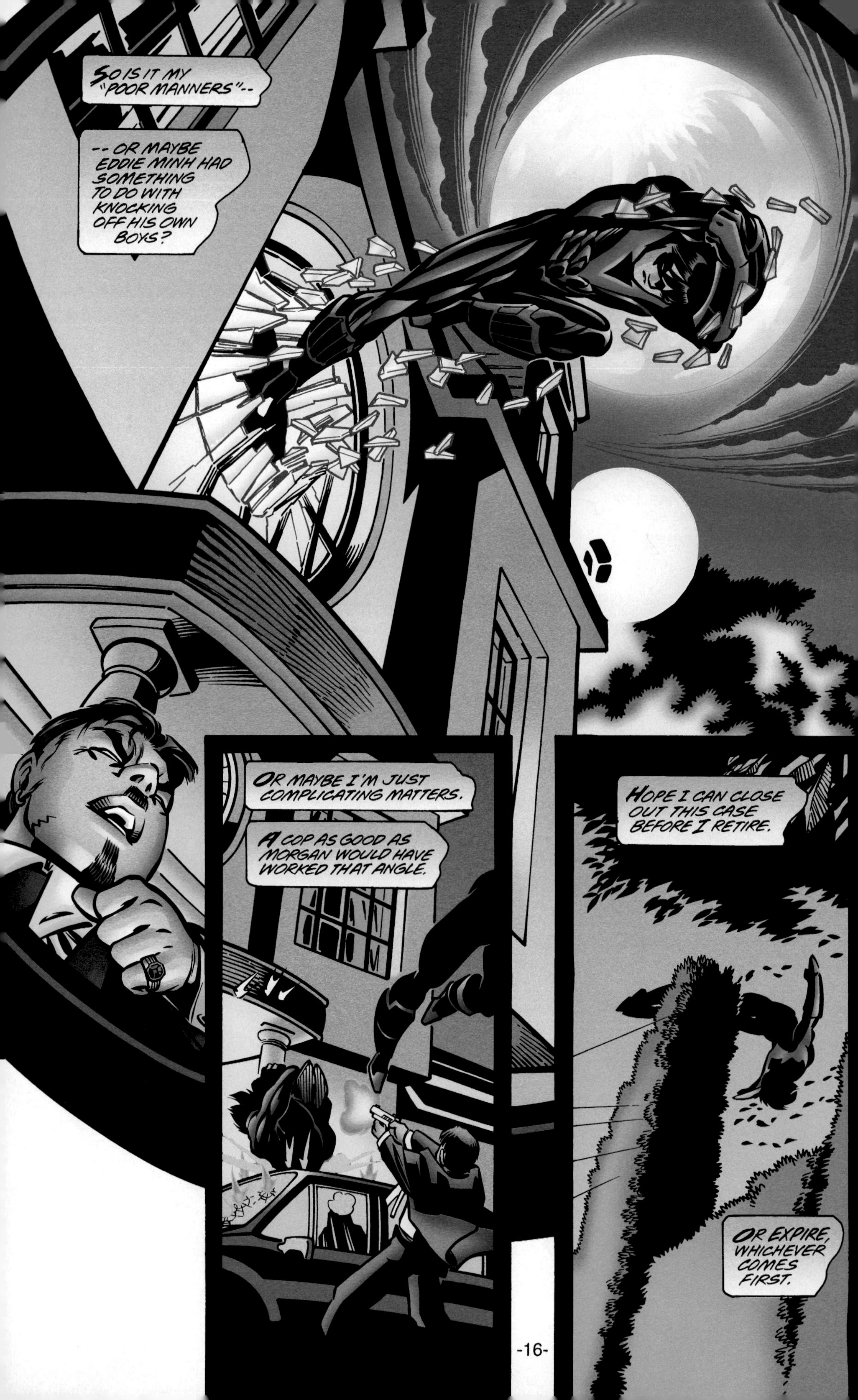
SO IS IT MY "POOR MANNERS"--
--OR MAYBE EDDIE MINH HAD SOMETHING TO DO WITH KNOCKING OFF HIS OWN BOYS?
OR MAYBE I'M JUST COMPLICATING MATTERS.
A COP AS GOOD AS MORGAN WOULD HAVE WORKED THAT ANGLE.
HOPE I CAN CLOSE OUT THIS CASE BEFORE I RETIRE.
OR EXPIRE, WHICHEVER COMES FIRST.

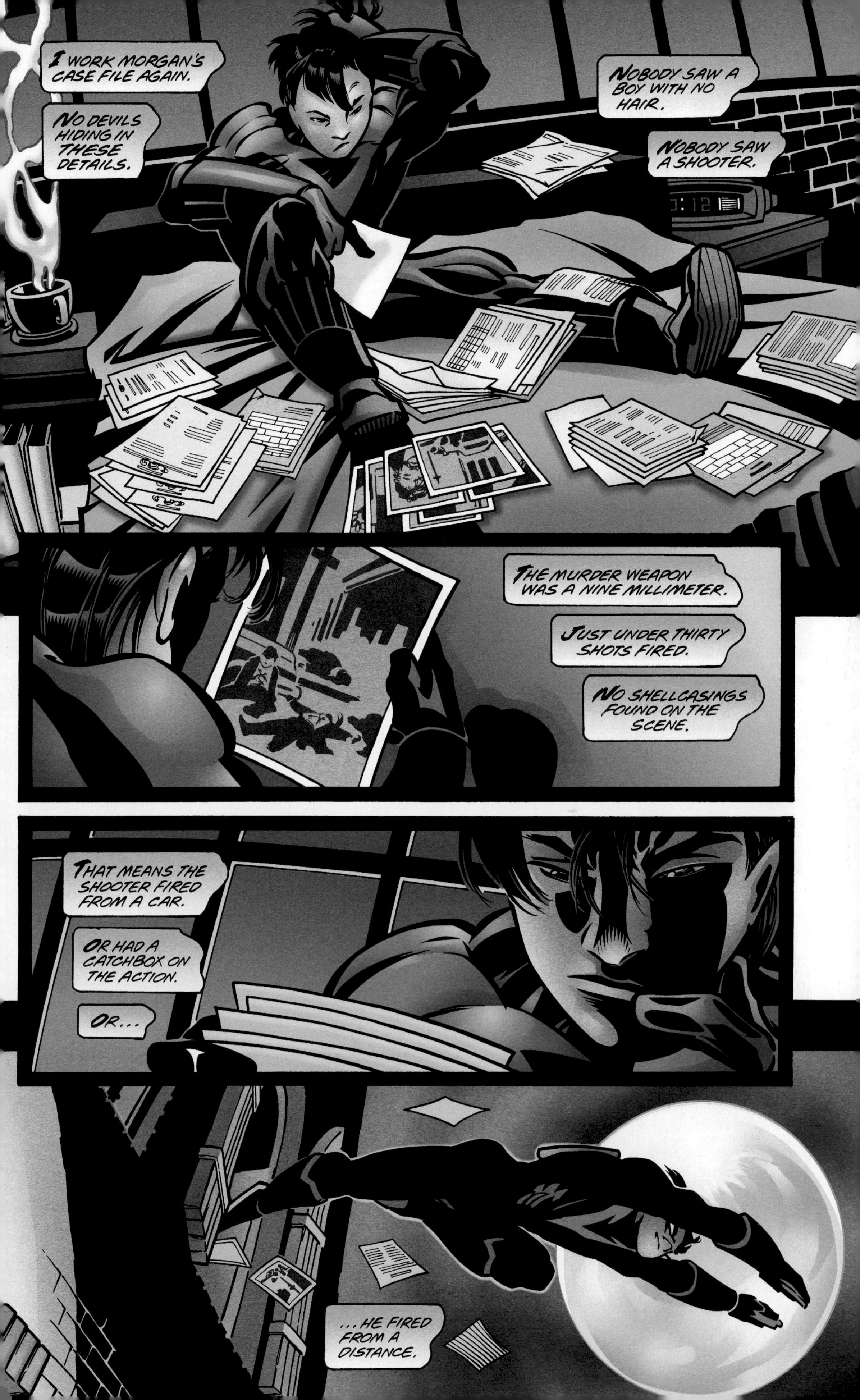
I WORK MORGAN'S CASE FILE AGAIN.
NO DEVILS HIDING IN THESE DETAILS.
NOBODY SAW A BOY WITH NO HAIR.
NOBODY SAW A SHOOTER.
THE MURDER WEAPON WAS A NINE MILLIMETER.
JUST UNDER THIRTY SHOTS FIRED.
NO SHELLCASINGS FOUND ON THE SCENE.
THAT MEANS THE SHOOTER FIRED FROM A CAR.
OR HAD A CATCHBOX ON THE ACTION.
OR...
...HE FIRED FROM A DISTANCE.

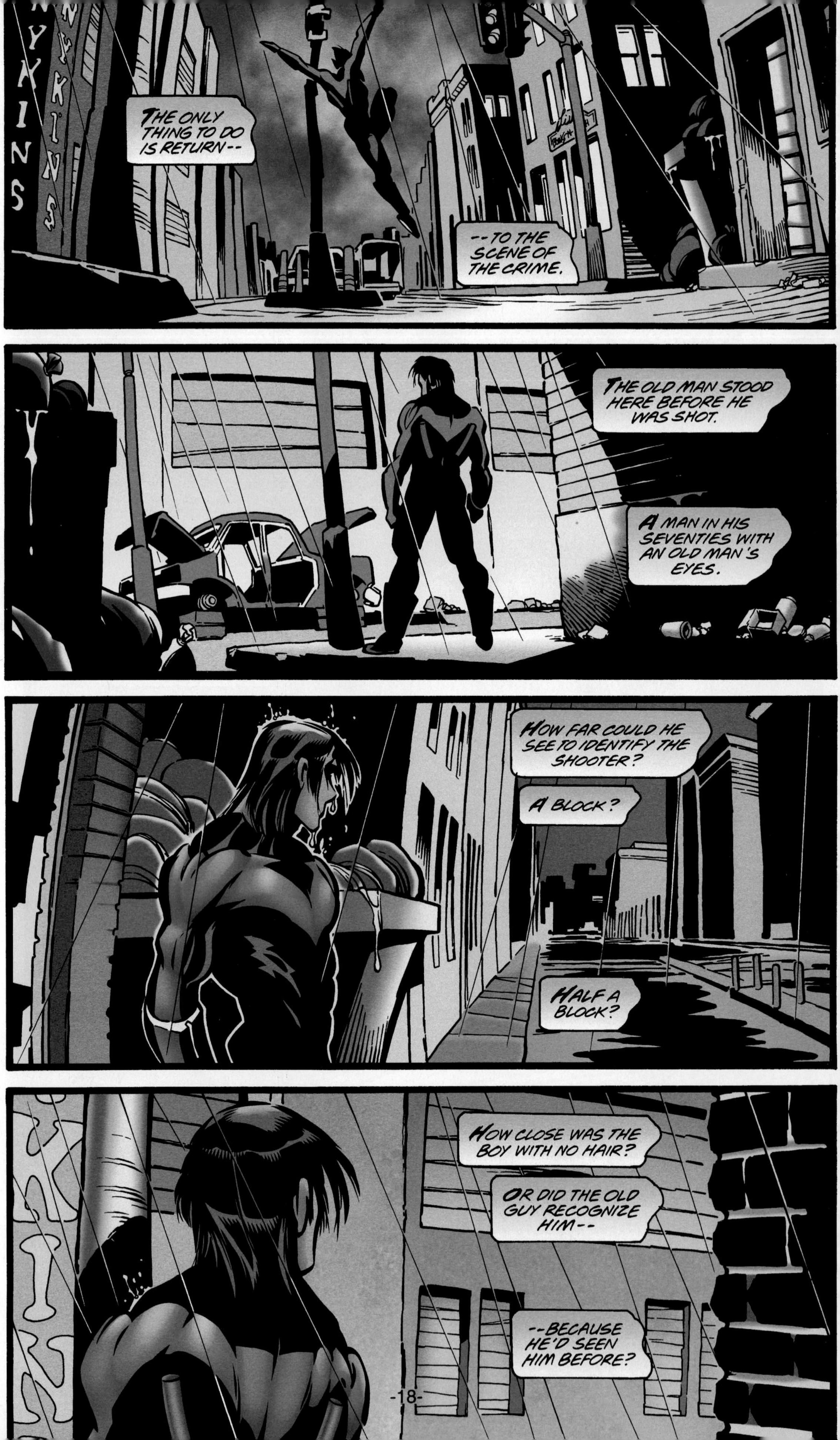
THE ONLY THING TO DO IS RETURN--
--TO THE SCENE OF THE CRIME.
THE OLD MAN STOOD HERE BEFORE HE WAS SHOT.
A MAN IN HIS SEVENTIES WITH AN OLD MAN'S EYES.
HOW FAR COULD HE SEE TO IDENTIFY THE SHOOTER?
A BLOCK?
HALF A BLOCK?
HOW CLOSE WAS THE BOY WITH NO HAIR?
OR DID THE OLD GUY RECOGNIZE HIM--
--BECAUSE HE'D SEEN HIM BEFORE?

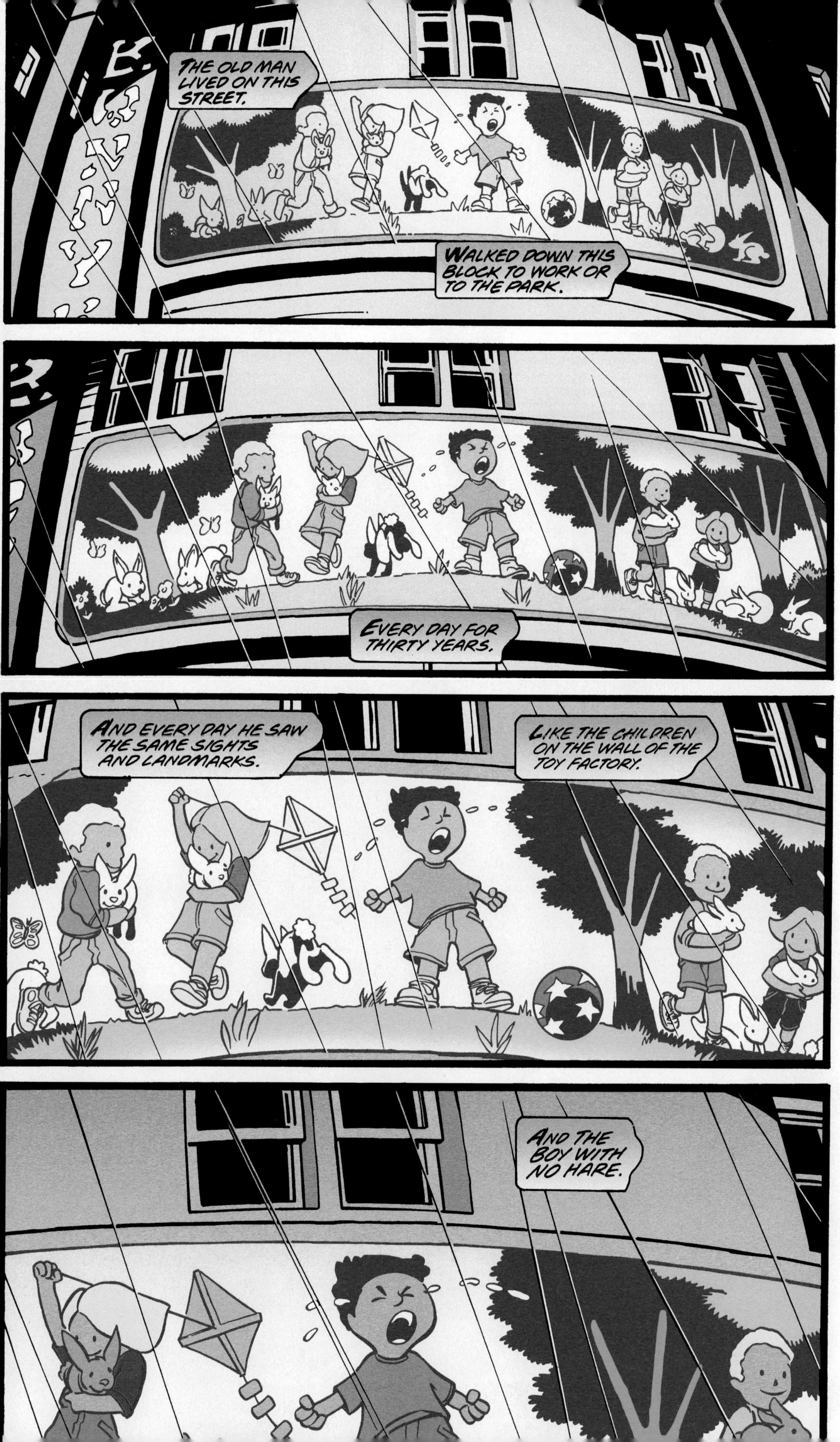
THE OLD MAN LIVED ON THIS STREET.
WALKED DOWN THIS BLOCK TO WORK OR TO THE PARK.
EVERY DAY FOR THIRTY YEARS.
AND EVERY DAY HE SAW THE SAME SIGHTS AND LANDMARKS.
LIKE THE CHILDREN ON THE WALL OF THE TOY FACTORY.
AND THE BOY WITH NO HARE.

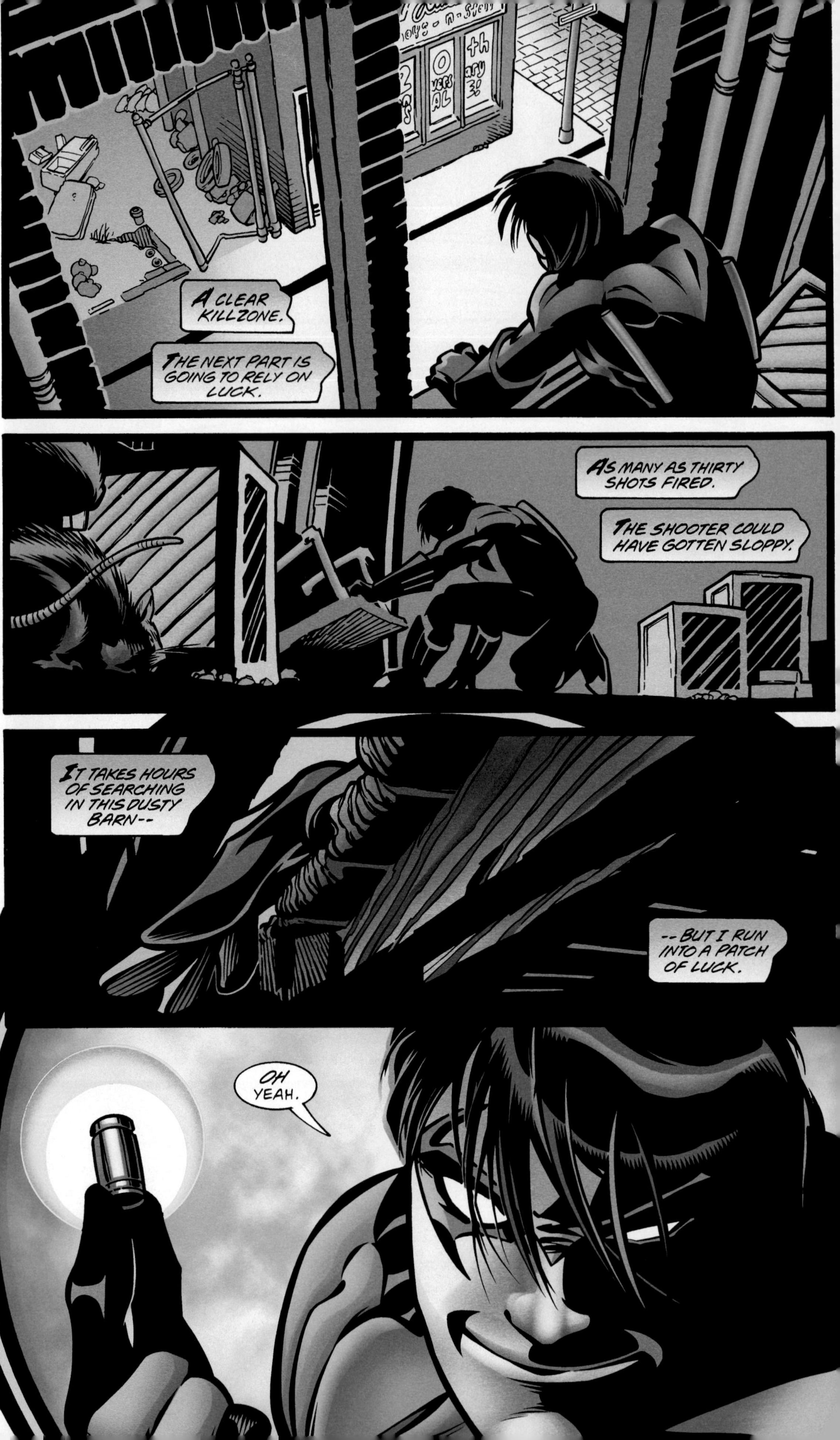
A CLEAR KILLZONE.
THE NEXT PART IS GOING TO RELY ON LUCK.
AS MANY AS THIRTY SHOTS FIRED.
THE SHOOTER COULD HAVE GOTTEN SLOPPY.
IT TAKES HOURS OF SEARCHING IN THIS DUSTY BARN--
--BUT I RUN INTO A PATCH OF LUCK.
OH YEAH.

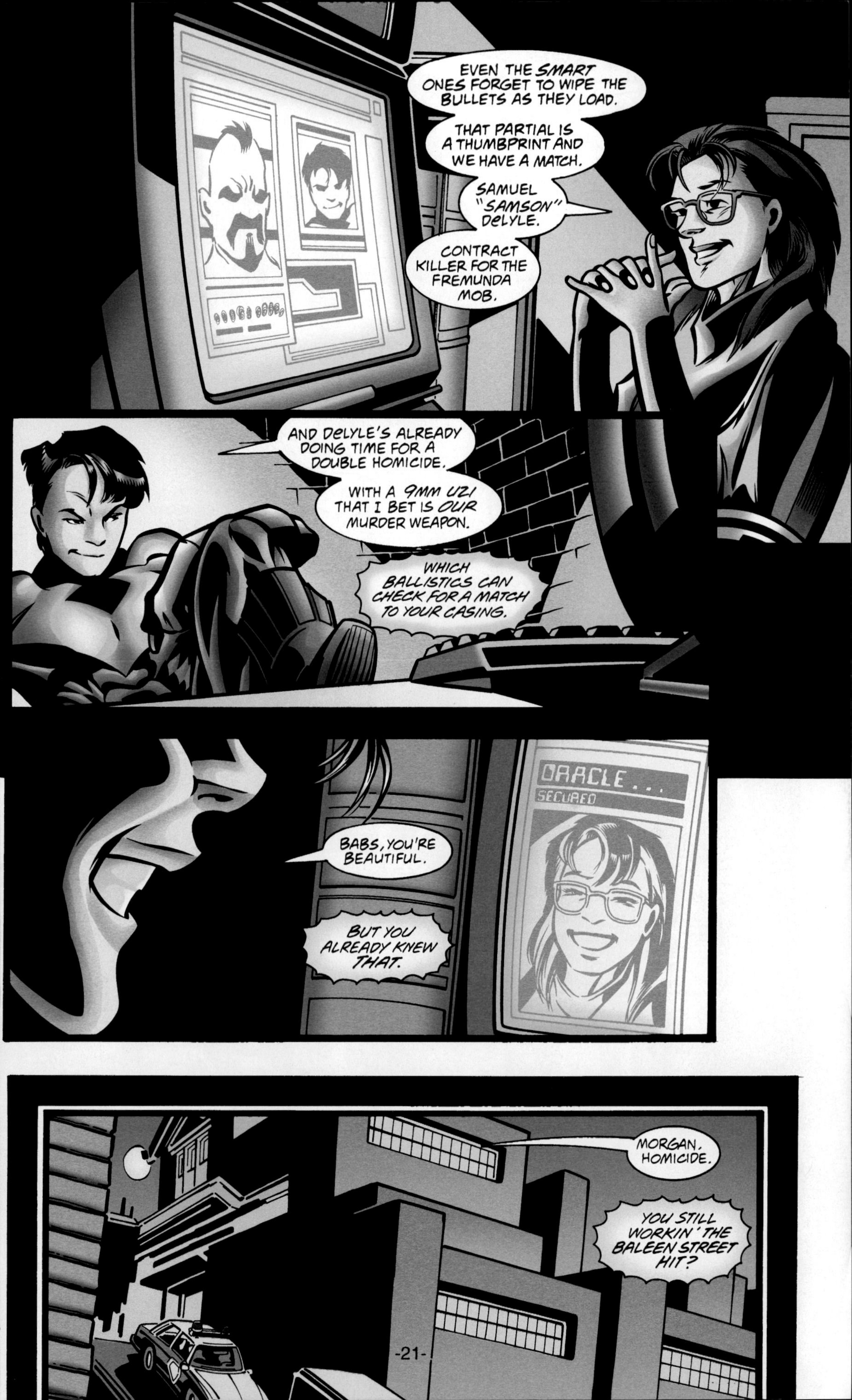
EVEN THE SMART ONES FORGET TO WIPE THE BULLETS AS THEY LOAD.
THAT PARTIAL IS A THUMBPRINT AND WE HAVE A MATCH.
SAMUEL "SAMSON" DeLYLE.
CONTRACT KILLER FOR THE FREMUNDA MOB.
AND DeLYLE'S ALREADY DOING TIME FOR A DOUBLE HOMICIDE.
WITH A 9MM UZI THAT I BET IS OUR MURDER WEAPON.
WHICH BALLISTICS CAN CHECK FOR A MATCH TO YOUR CASING.
ORACLE...
SECURED
BABS, YOU'RE BEAUTIFUL.
BUT YOU ALREADY KNEW THAT.
MORGAN, HOMICIDE.
YOU STILL WORKIN' THE BALEEN STREET HIT?

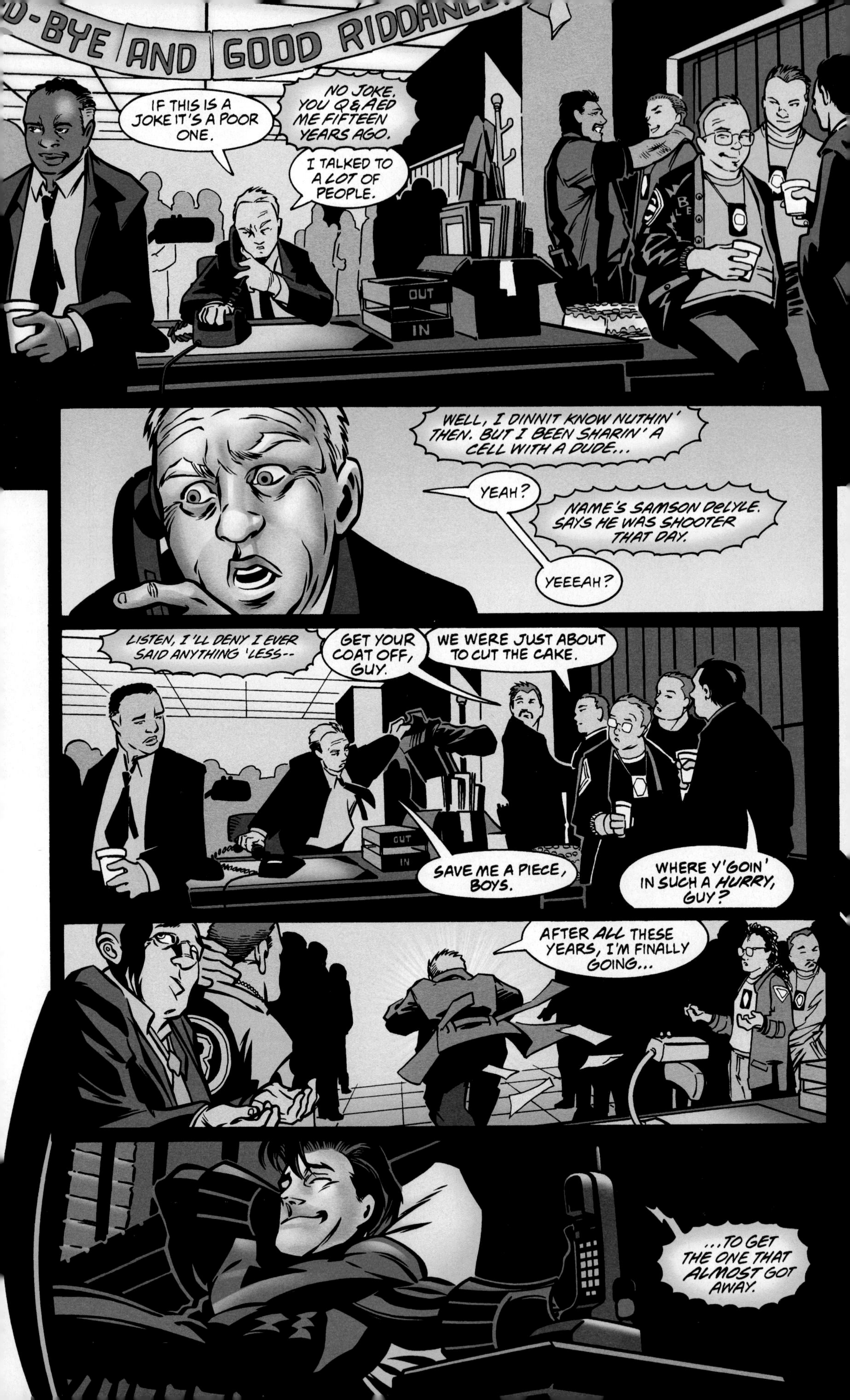
-BYE AND GOOD RIDDANCE
IF THIS IS A JOKE IT'S A POOR ONE.
NO JOKE. YOU Q & AED ME FIFTEEN YEARS AGO.
I TALKED TO A LOT OF PEOPLE.
OUT
IN
WELL, I DINNIT KNOW NUTHIN' THEN. BUT I BEEN SHARIN' A CELL WITH A DUDE...
YEAH?
NAME'S SAMSON DELYLE. SAYS HE WAS SHOOTER THAT DAY.
YEEEAH?
LISTEN, I'LL DENY I EVER SAID ANYTHING 'LESS--
GET YOUR COAT OFF, GUY.
WE WERE JUST ABOUT TO CUT THE CAKE.
OUT
IN
SAVE ME A PIECE, BOYS.
WHERE Y'GOIN' IN SUCH A *HURRY*, GUY?
AFTER *ALL* THESE YEARS, I'M FINALLY GOING...
...TO GET THE ONE THAT *ALMOST* GOT AWAY.

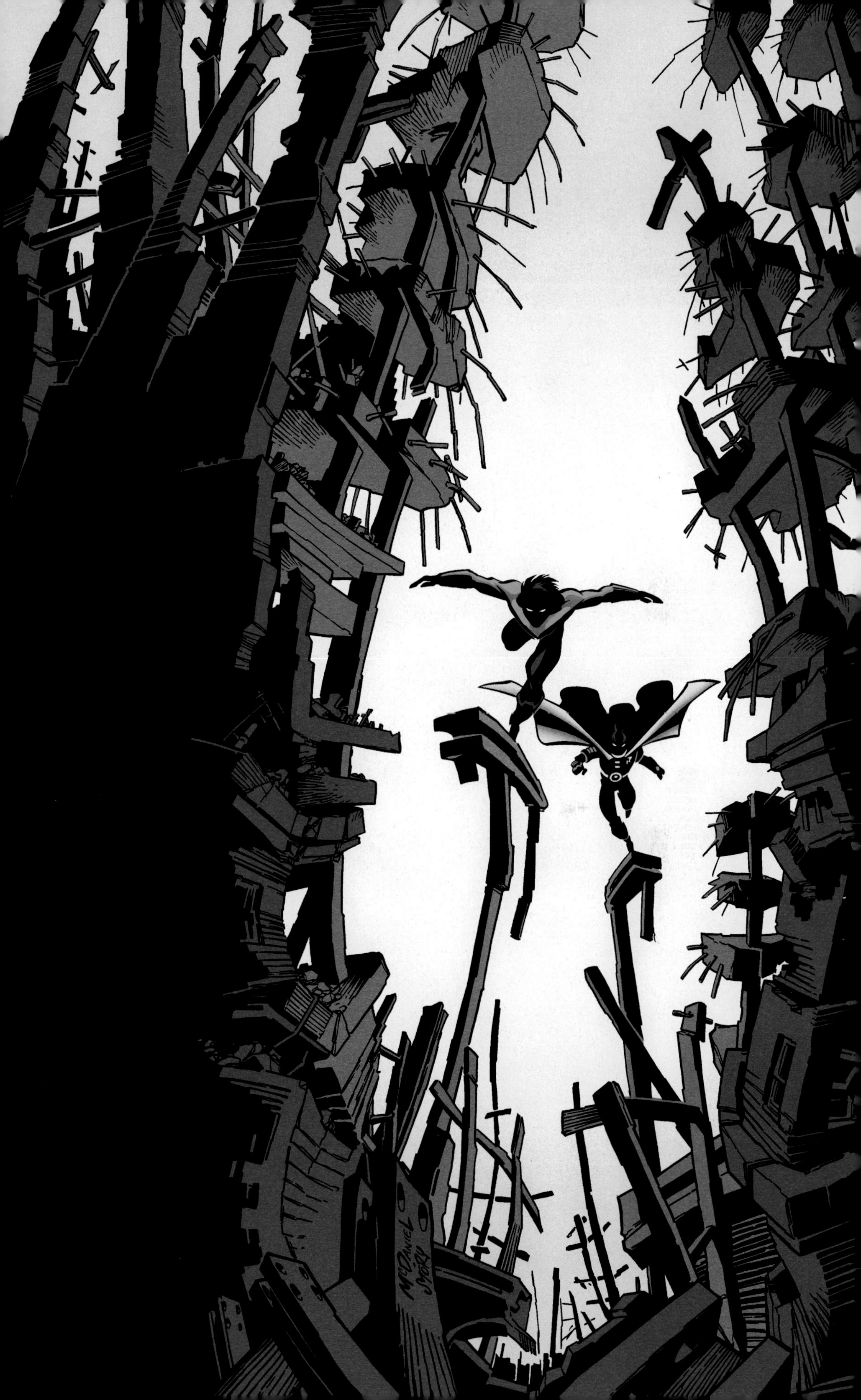
McDANIEL
STORY

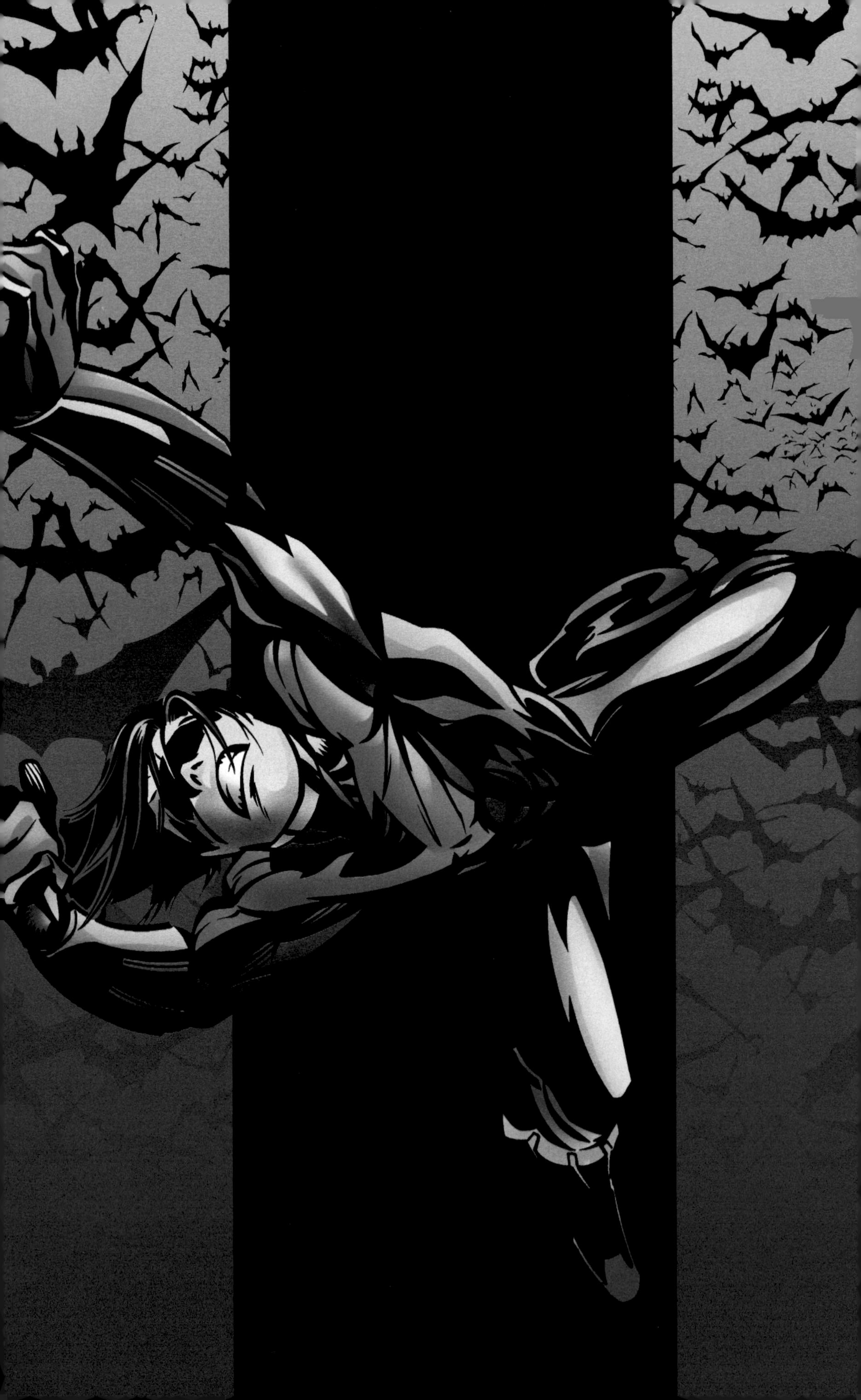

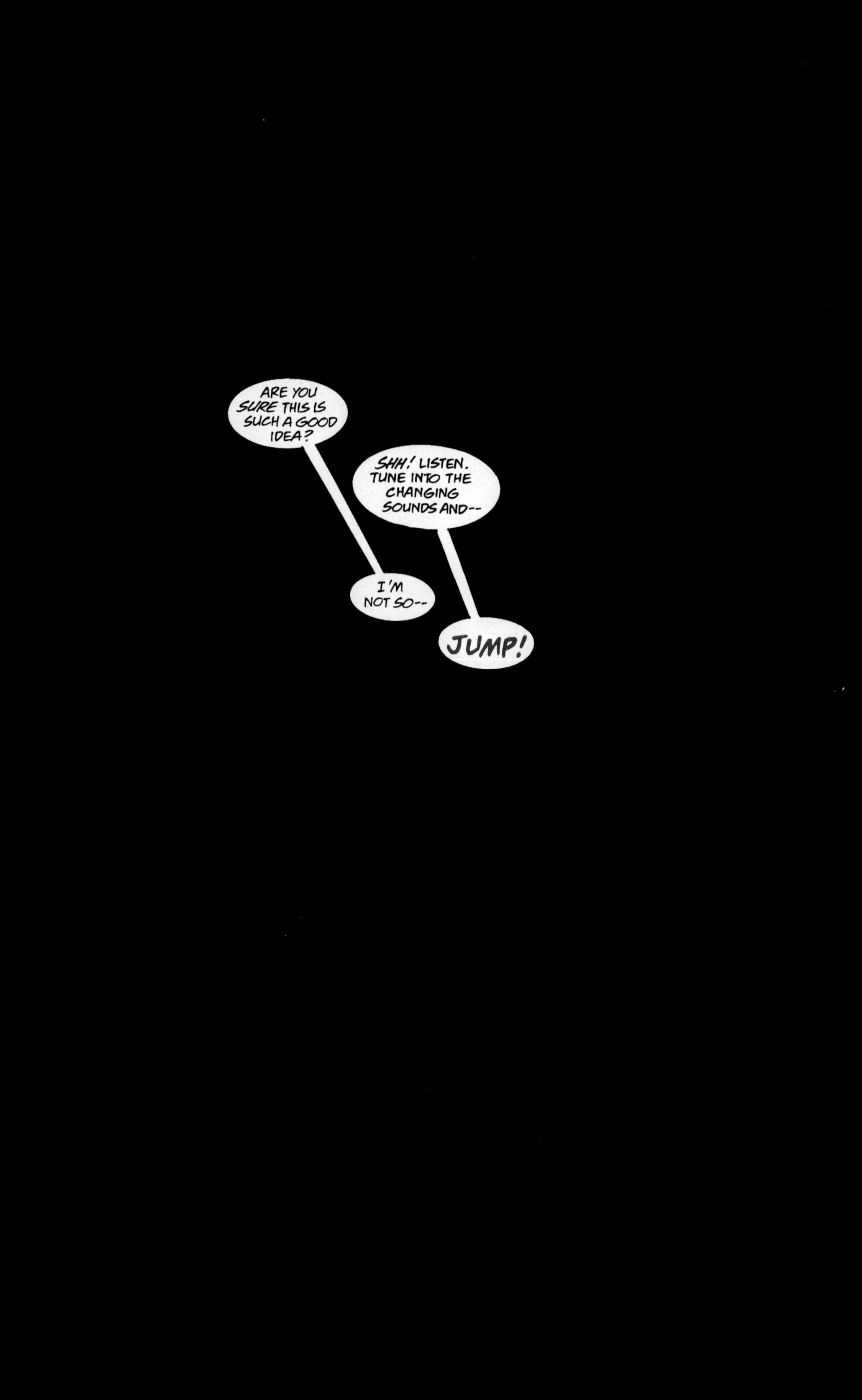
ARE YOU SURE THIS IS SUCH A GOOD IDEA?
SHH! LISTEN. TUNE INTO THE CHANGING SOUNDS AND--
I'M NOT SO--
JUMP!

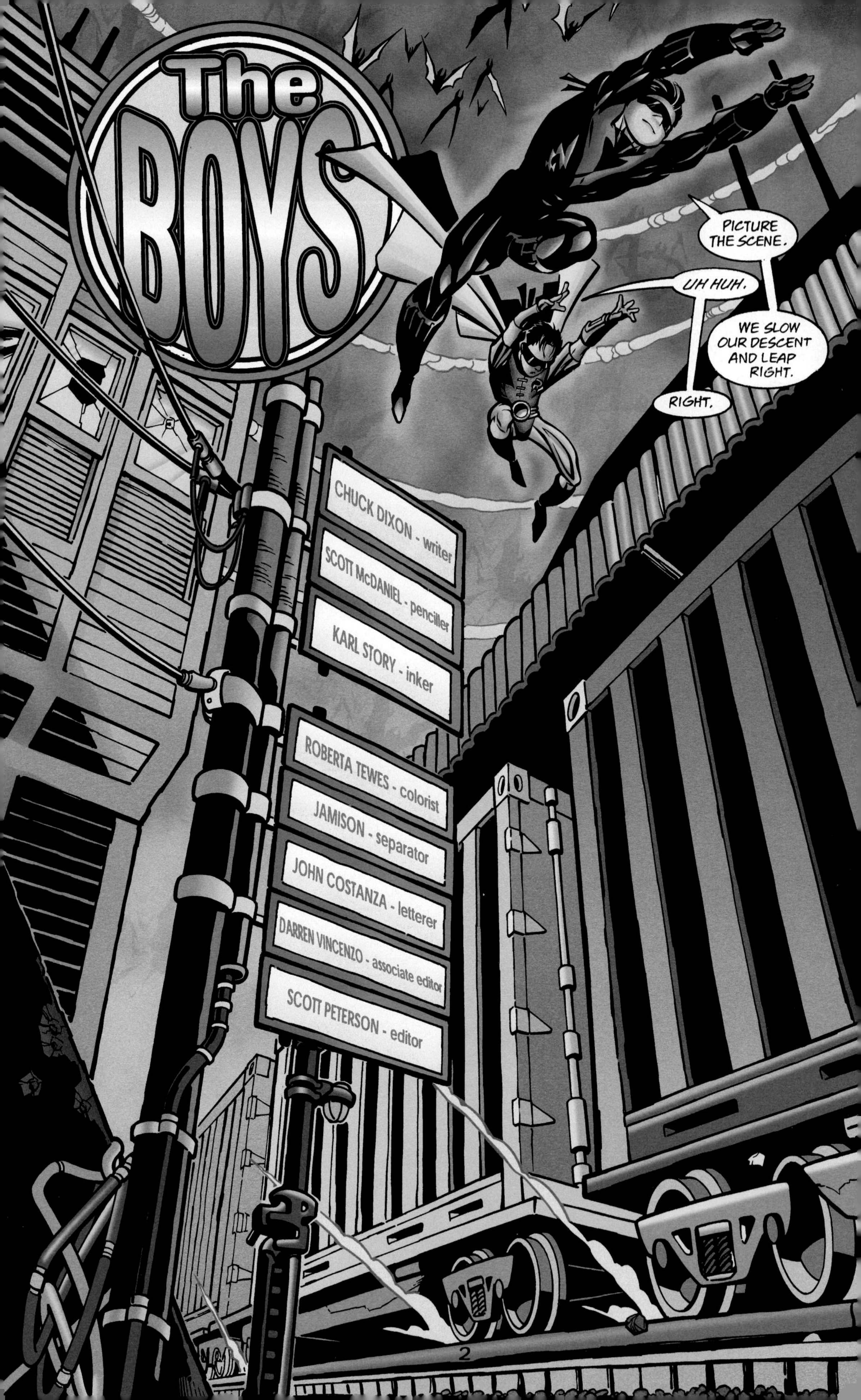
The BOYS
PICTURE THE SCENE.
UH HUH.
WE SLOW OUR DESCENT AND LEAP RIGHT.
RIGHT.
CHUCK DIXON - writer
SCOTT McDANIEL - penciller
KARL STORY - inker
ROBERTA TEWES - colorist
JAMISON - separator
JOHN COSTANZA - letterer
DARREN VINCENZO - associate editor
SCOTT PETERSON - editor

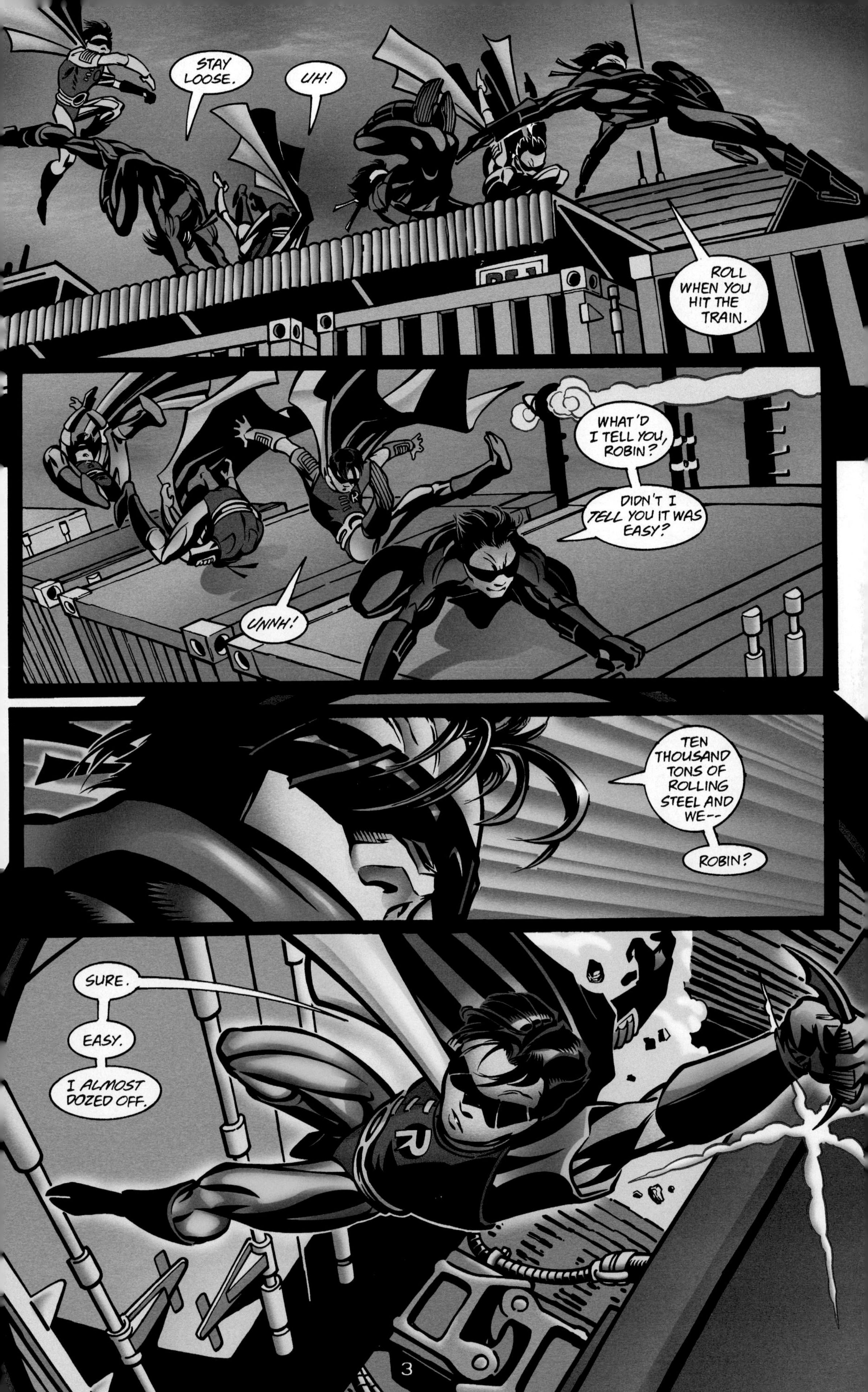
STAY LOOSE.
UH!
ROLL WHEN YOU HIT THE TRAIN.
WHAT'D I TELL YOU, ROBIN?
DIDN'T I TELL YOU IT WAS EASY?
UNNH!
TEN THOUSAND TONS OF ROLLING STEEL AND WE--
ROBIN?
SURE.
EASY.
I ALMOST DOZED OFF.

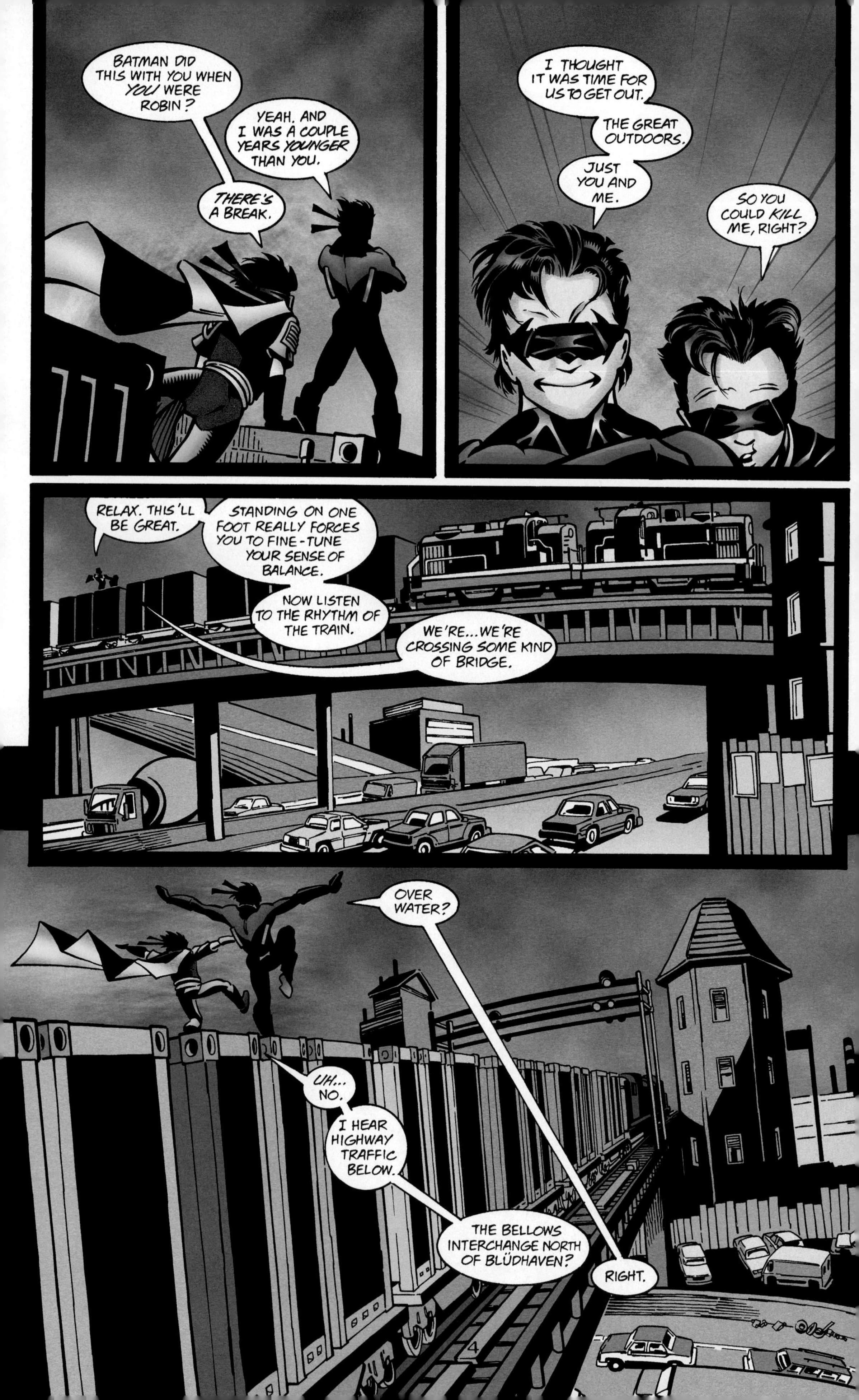
BATMAN DID THIS WITH YOU WHEN *YOU* WERE ROBIN?
YEAH. AND I WAS A COUPLE YEARS *YOUNGER* THAN YOU.
THERE'S A BREAK.
I THOUGHT IT WAS TIME FOR US TO GET OUT.
THE GREAT OUTDOORS.
JUST YOU AND ME.
SO YOU COULD *KILL* ME, RIGHT?
RELAX. THIS'LL BE GREAT.
STANDING ON ONE FOOT REALLY FORCES YOU TO FINE-TUNE YOUR SENSE OF BALANCE.
NOW LISTEN TO THE RHYTHM OF THE TRAIN.
WE'RE...WE'RE CROSSING SOME KIND OF BRIDGE.
OVER WATER?
UH... NO.
I HEAR HIGHWAY TRAFFIC BELOW.
THE BELLOWS INTERCHANGE NORTH OF BLÜDHAVEN?
RIGHT.

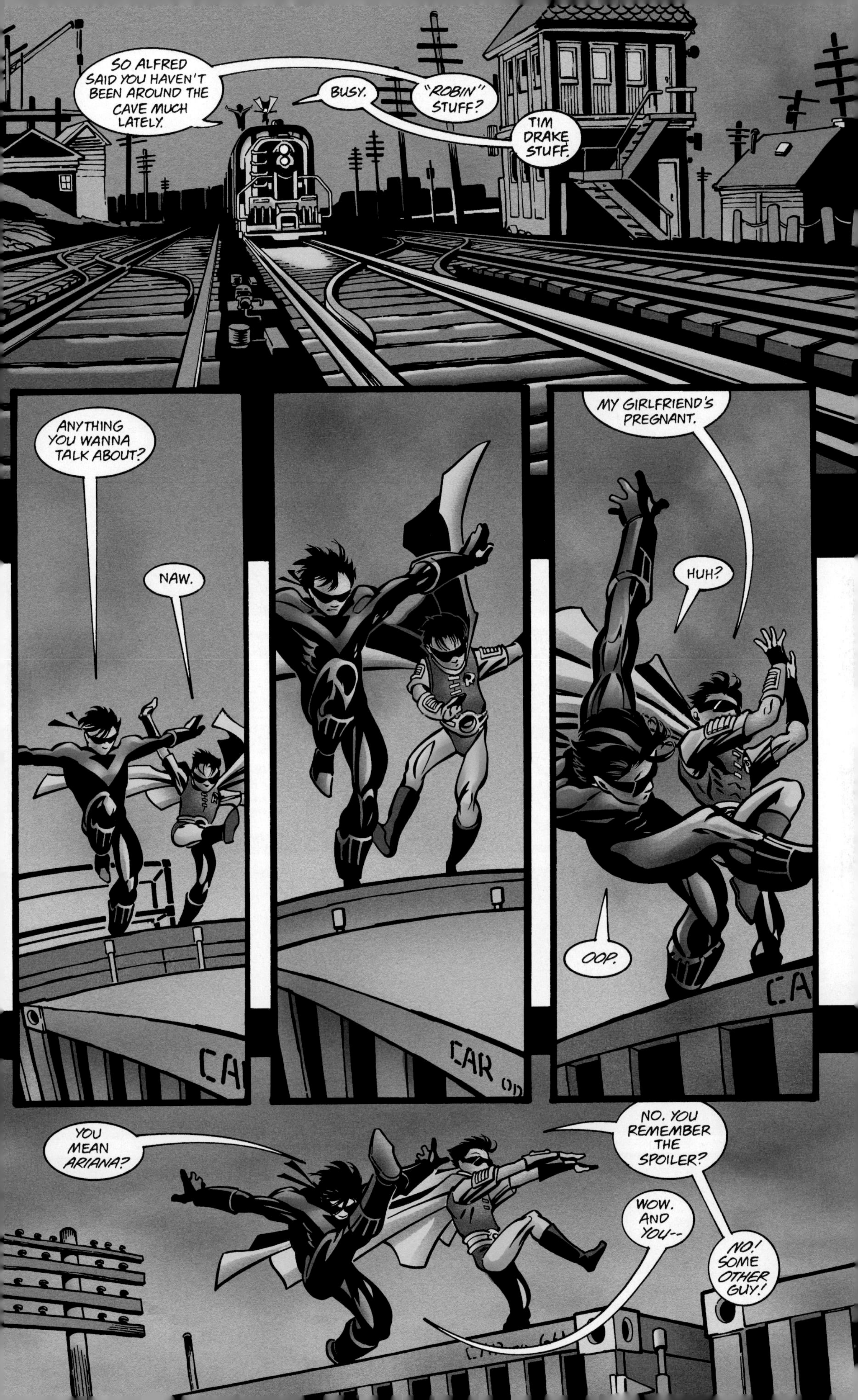
SO ALFRED SAID YOU HAVEN'T BEEN AROUND THE CAVE MUCH LATELY.
BUSY.
"ROBIN" STUFF?
TIM DRAKE STUFF.
ANYTHING YOU WANNA TALK ABOUT?
NAW.
MY GIRLFRIEND'S PREGNANT.
HUH?
OOP.
CAR
CAR
CA
YOU MEAN ARIANA?
NO. YOU REMEMBER THE SPOILER?
WOW. AND YOU--
NO! SOME OTHER GUY!

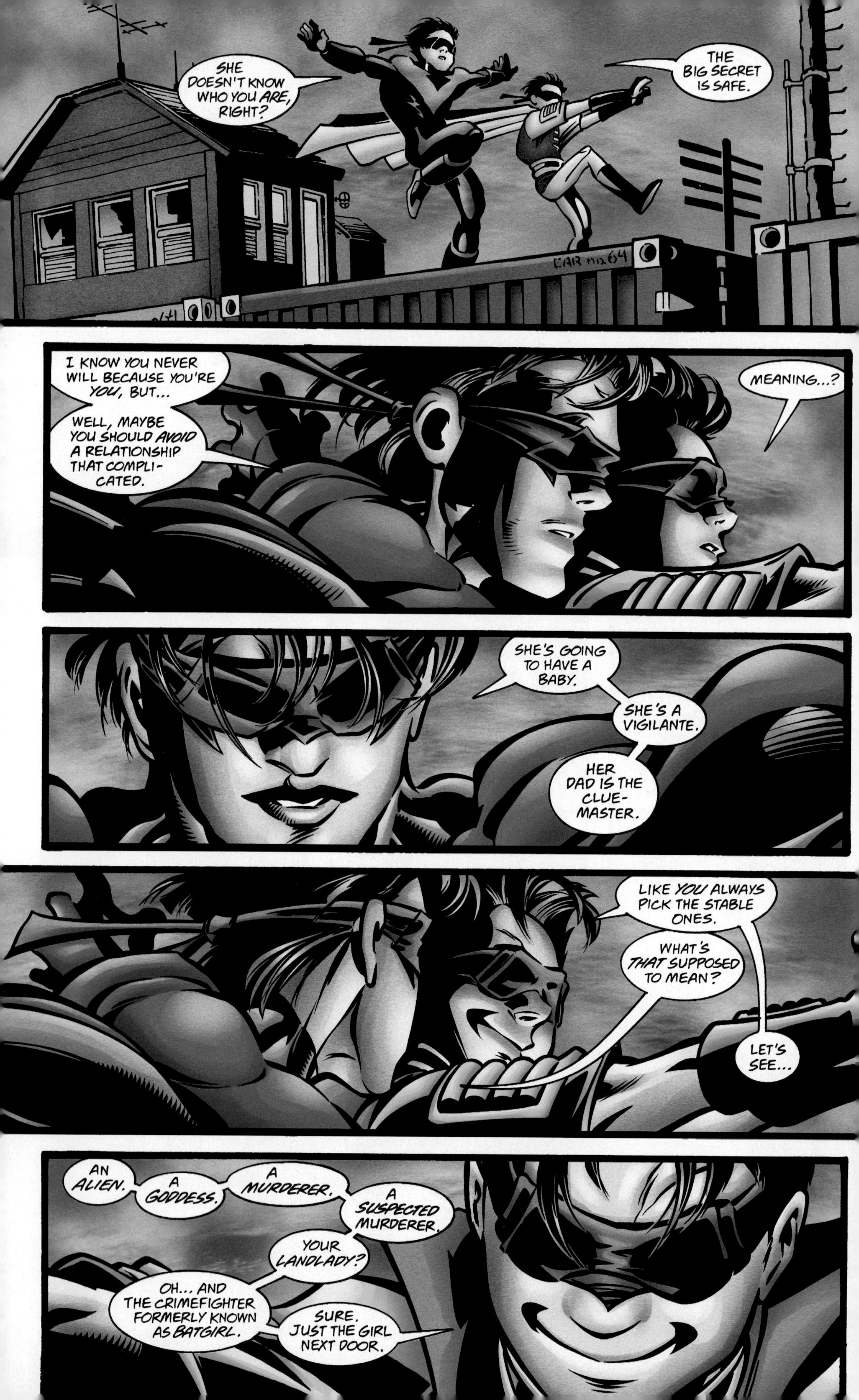
SHE DOESN'T KNOW WHO YOU ARE, RIGHT?
THE BIG SECRET IS SAFE.
CAR nix 64
I KNOW YOU NEVER WILL BECAUSE YOU'RE YOU, BUT...
WELL, MAYBE YOU SHOULD AVOID A RELATIONSHIP THAT COMPLI-CATED.
MEANING...?
SHE'S GOING TO HAVE A BABY.
SHE'S A VIGILANTE.
HER DAD IS THE CLUE-MASTER.
LIKE YOU ALWAYS PICK THE STABLE ONES.
WHAT'S THAT SUPPOSED TO MEAN?
LET'S SEE...
AN ALIEN.
A GODDESS.
A MURDERER.
A SUSPECTED MURDERER.
YOUR LANDLADY?
OH... AND THE CRIMEFIGHTER FORMERLY KNOWN AS BATGIRL.
SURE. JUST THE GIRL NEXT DOOR.

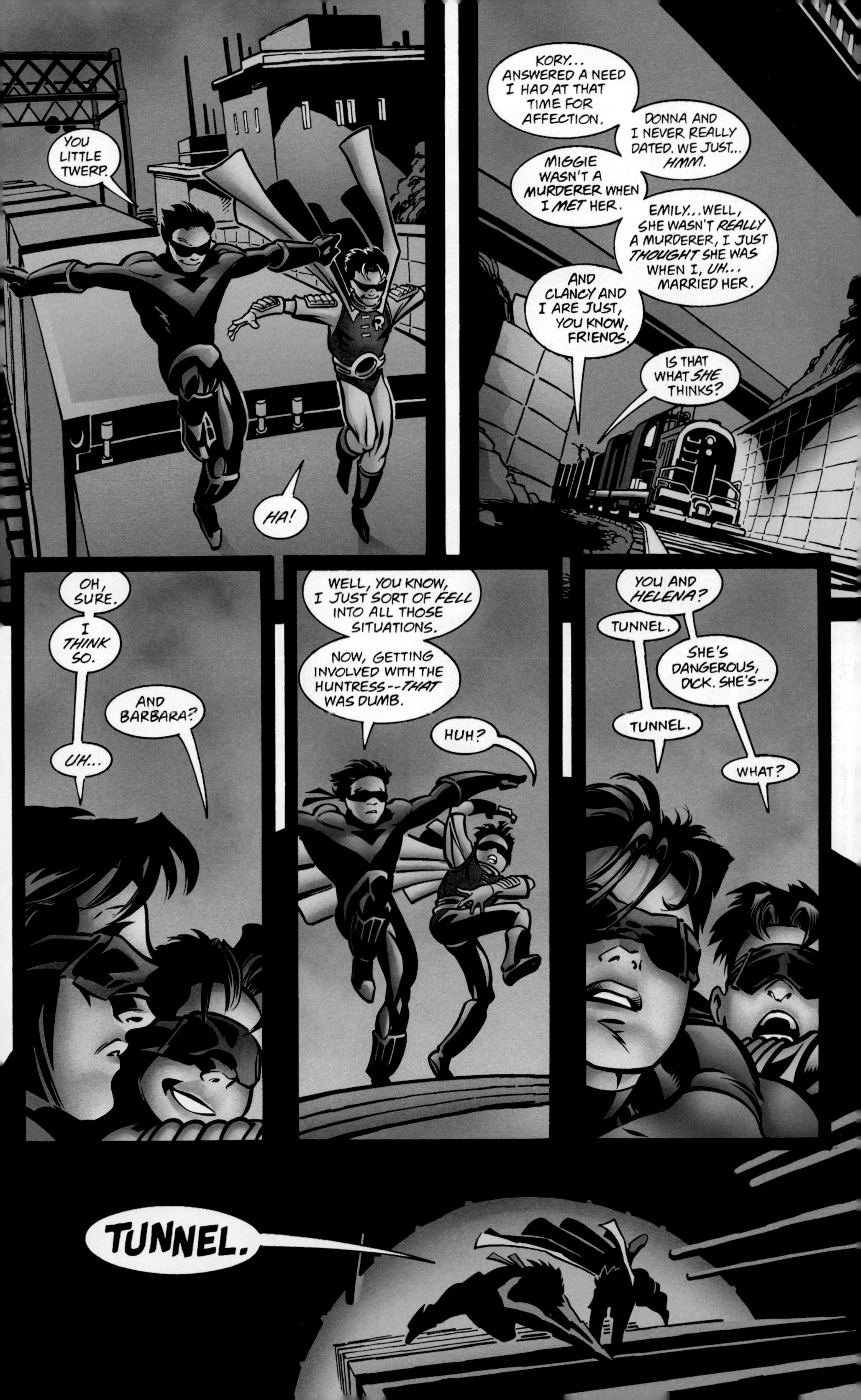
YOU LITTLE TWERP.
HA!
KORY... ANSWERED A NEED I HAD AT THAT TIME FOR AFFECTION.
DONNA AND I NEVER REALLY DATED. WE JUST... HMM.
MIGGIE WASN'T A MURDERER WHEN I MET HER.
EMILY...WELL, SHE WASN'T REALLY A MURDERER, I JUST THOUGHT SHE WAS WHEN I, UH... MARRIED HER.
AND CLANCY AND I ARE JUST, YOU KNOW, FRIENDS.
IS THAT WHAT SHE THINKS?
OH, SURE.
I THINK SO.
AND BARBARA?
UH...
WELL, YOU KNOW, I JUST SORT OF FELL INTO ALL THOSE SITUATIONS.
NOW, GETTING INVOLVED WITH THE HUNTRESS--THAT WAS DUMB.
HUH?
YOU AND HELENA?
TUNNEL.
SHE'S DANGEROUS, DICK. SHE'S--
TUNNEL.
WHAT?
TUNNEL.

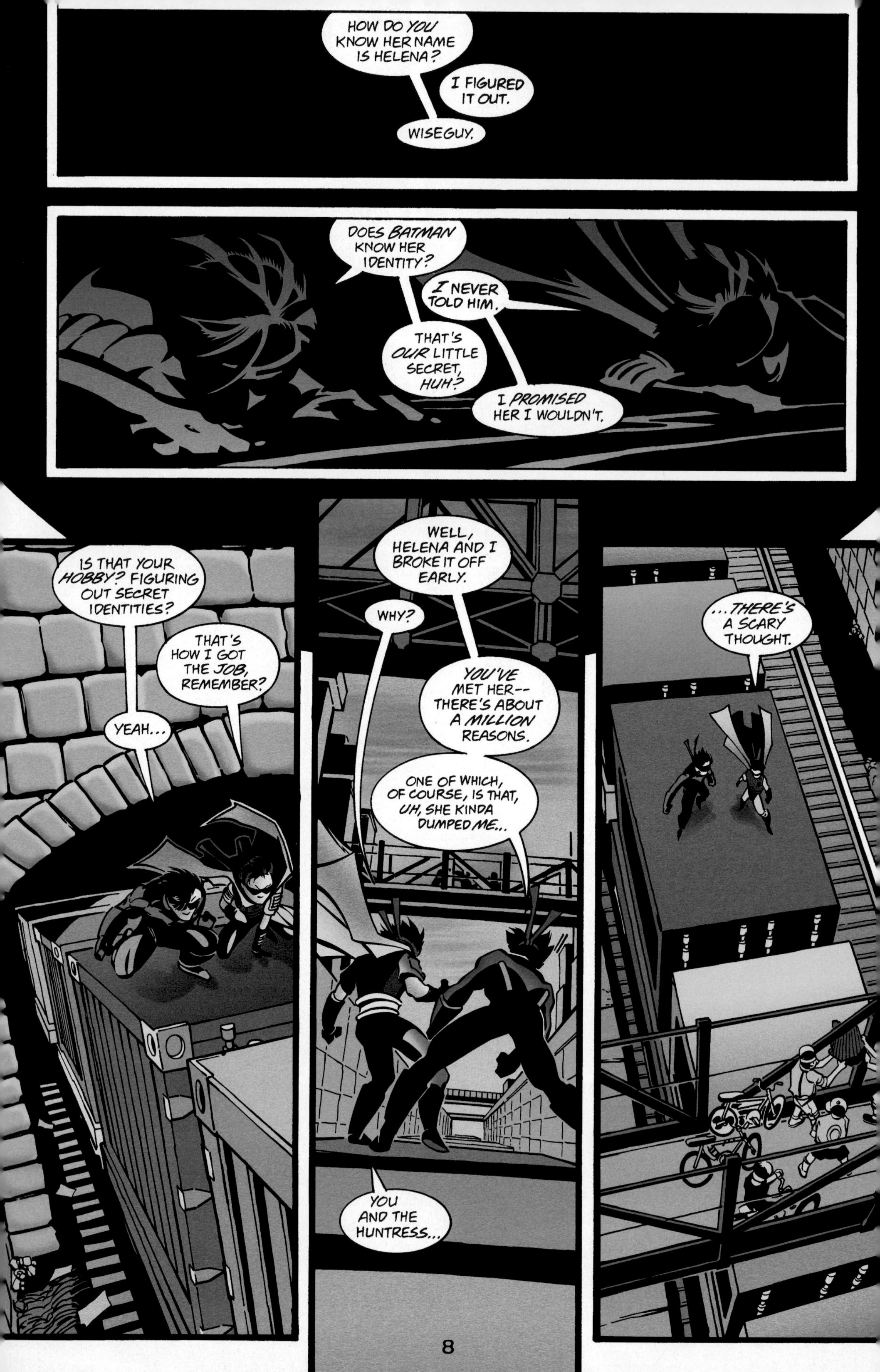
HOW DO YOU KNOW HER NAME IS HELENA?
I FIGURED IT OUT.
WISEGUY.
DOES BATMAN KNOW HER IDENTITY?
I NEVER TOLD HIM.
THAT'S OUR LITTLE SECRET, HUH?
I PROMISED HER I WOULDN'T.
IS THAT YOUR HOBBY? FIGURING OUT SECRET IDENTITIES?
THAT'S HOW I GOT THE JOB, REMEMBER?
YEAH...
YOU AND THE HUNTRESS...
WELL, HELENA AND I BROKE IT OFF EARLY.
WHY?
YOU'VE MET HER-- THERE'S ABOUT A MILLION REASONS.
ONE OF WHICH, OF COURSE, IS THAT, UH, SHE KINDA DUMPED ME...
...THERE'S A SCARY THOUGHT.

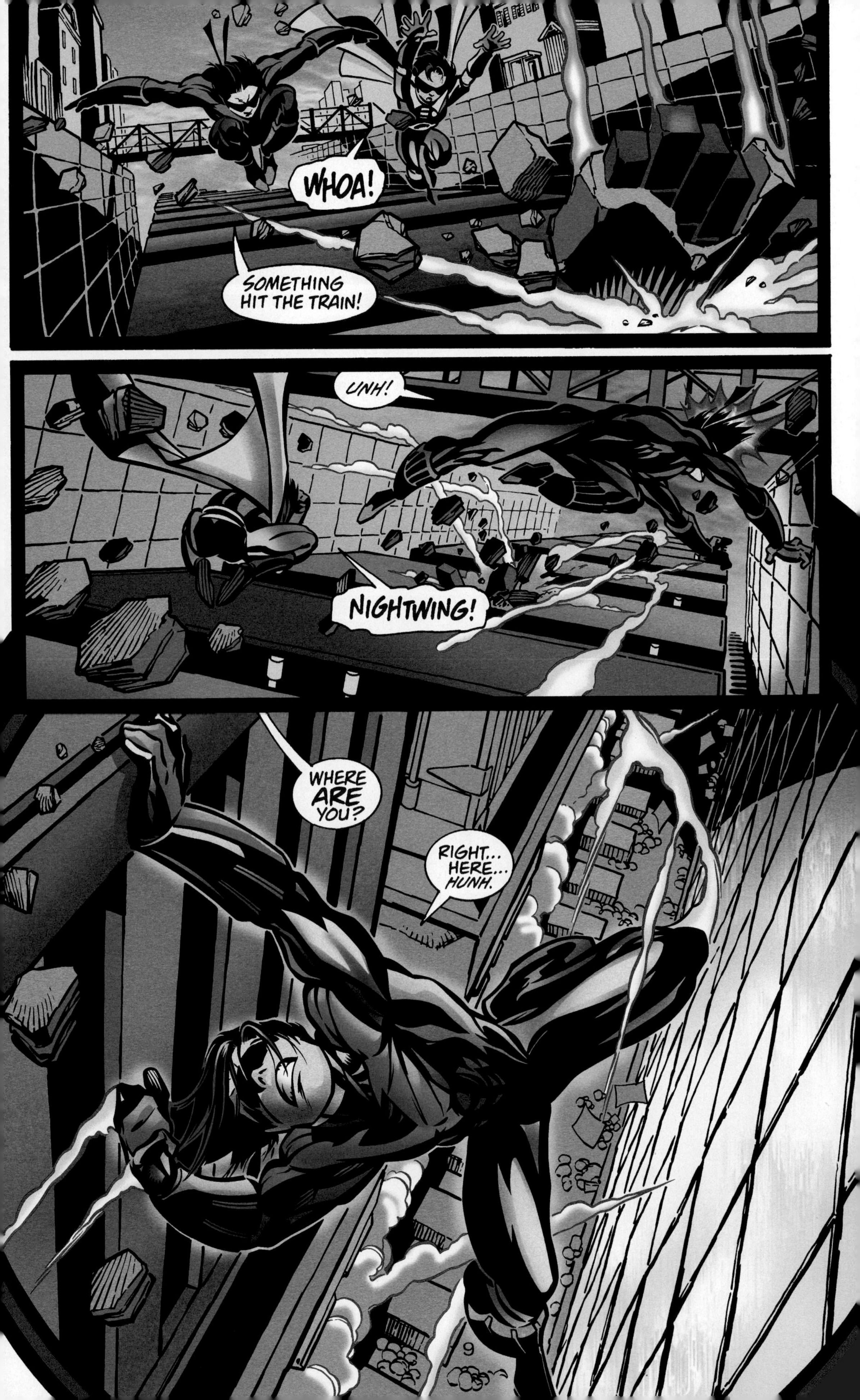
WHOA!
SOMETHING HIT THE TRAIN!
UNH!
NIGHTWING!
WHERE ARE YOU?
RIGHT... HERE... HUNH.

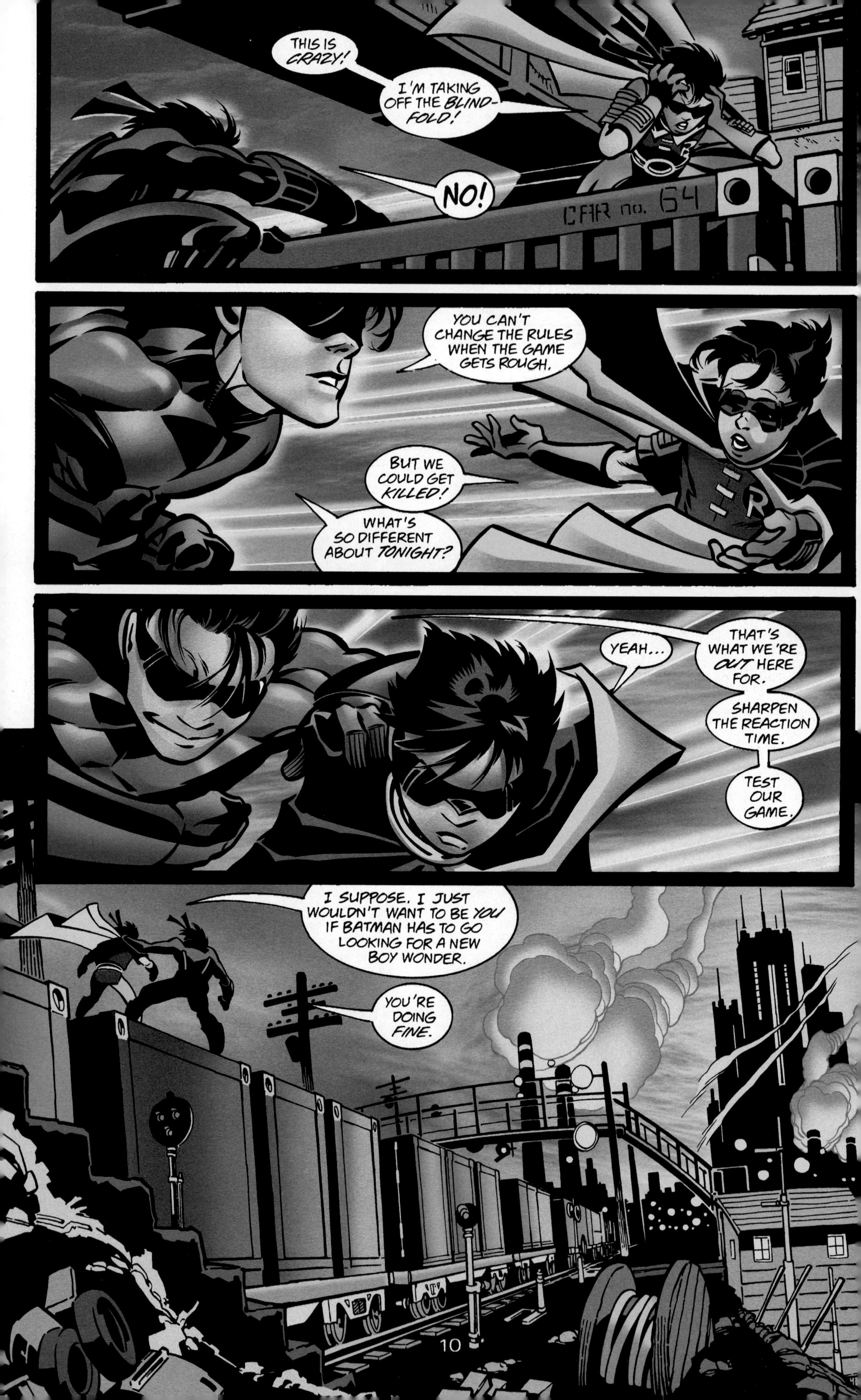
THIS IS CRAZY!
I'M TAKING OFF THE BLIND-FOLD!
NO!
CAR no. 64
YOU CAN'T CHANGE THE RULES WHEN THE GAME GETS ROUGH.
BUT WE COULD GET KILLED!
WHAT'S SO DIFFERENT ABOUT TONIGHT?
YEAH...
THAT'S WHAT WE'RE OUT HERE FOR.
SHARPEN THE REACTION TIME.
TEST OUR GAME.
I SUPPOSE. I JUST WOULDN'T WANT TO BE YOU IF BATMAN HAS TO GO LOOKING FOR A NEW BOY WONDER.
YOU'RE DOING FINE.

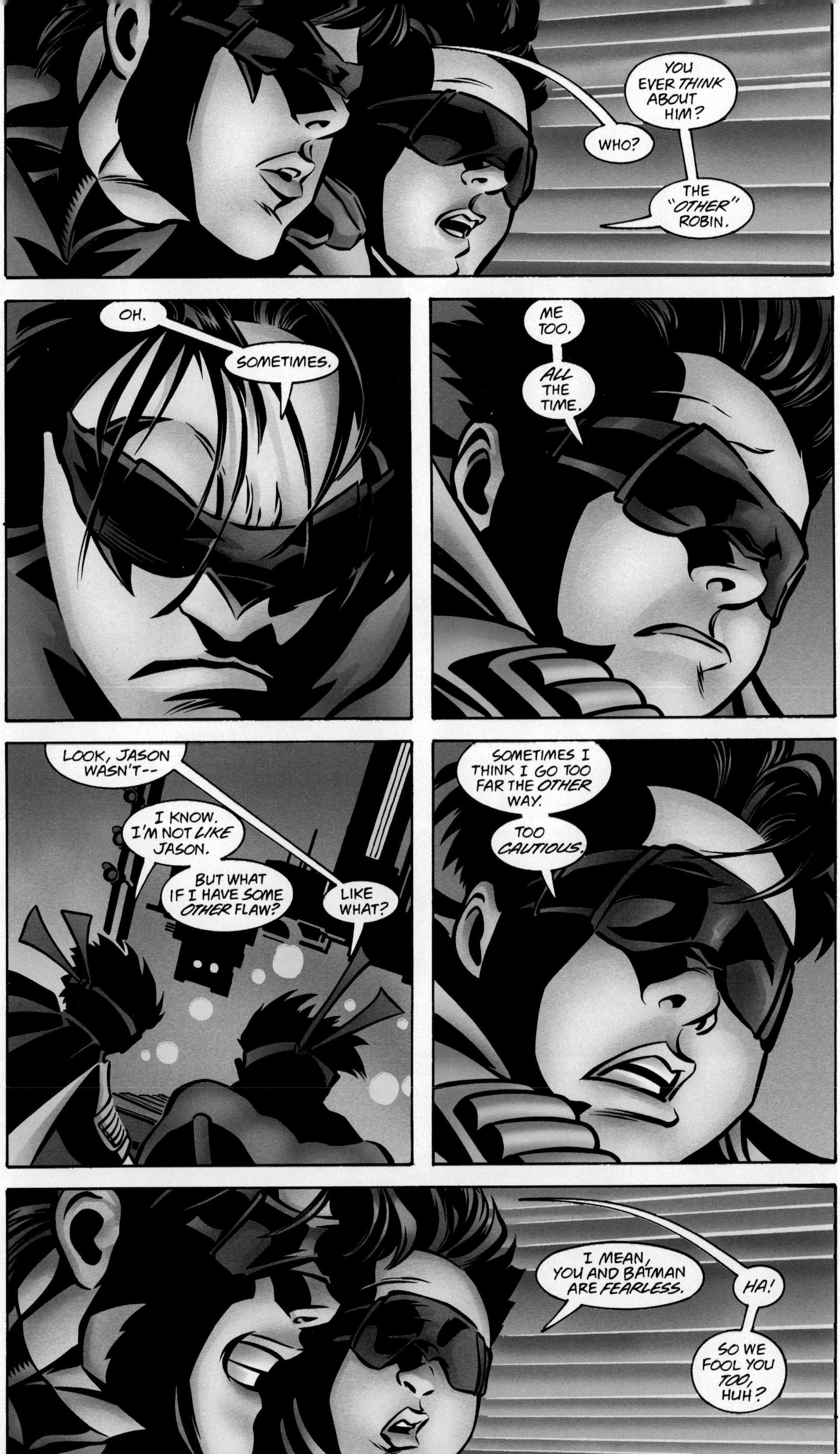
YOU EVER THINK ABOUT HIM?
WHO?
THE "OTHER" ROBIN.
OH.
SOMETIMES.
ME TOO.
ALL THE TIME.
LOOK, JASON WASN'T--
I KNOW. I'M NOT LIKE JASON.
BUT WHAT IF I HAVE SOME OTHER FLAW?
LIKE WHAT?
SOMETIMES I THINK I GO TOO FAR THE OTHER WAY.
TOO CAUTIOUS.
I MEAN, YOU AND BATMAN ARE FEARLESS.
HA!
SO WE FOOL YOU TOO, HUH?

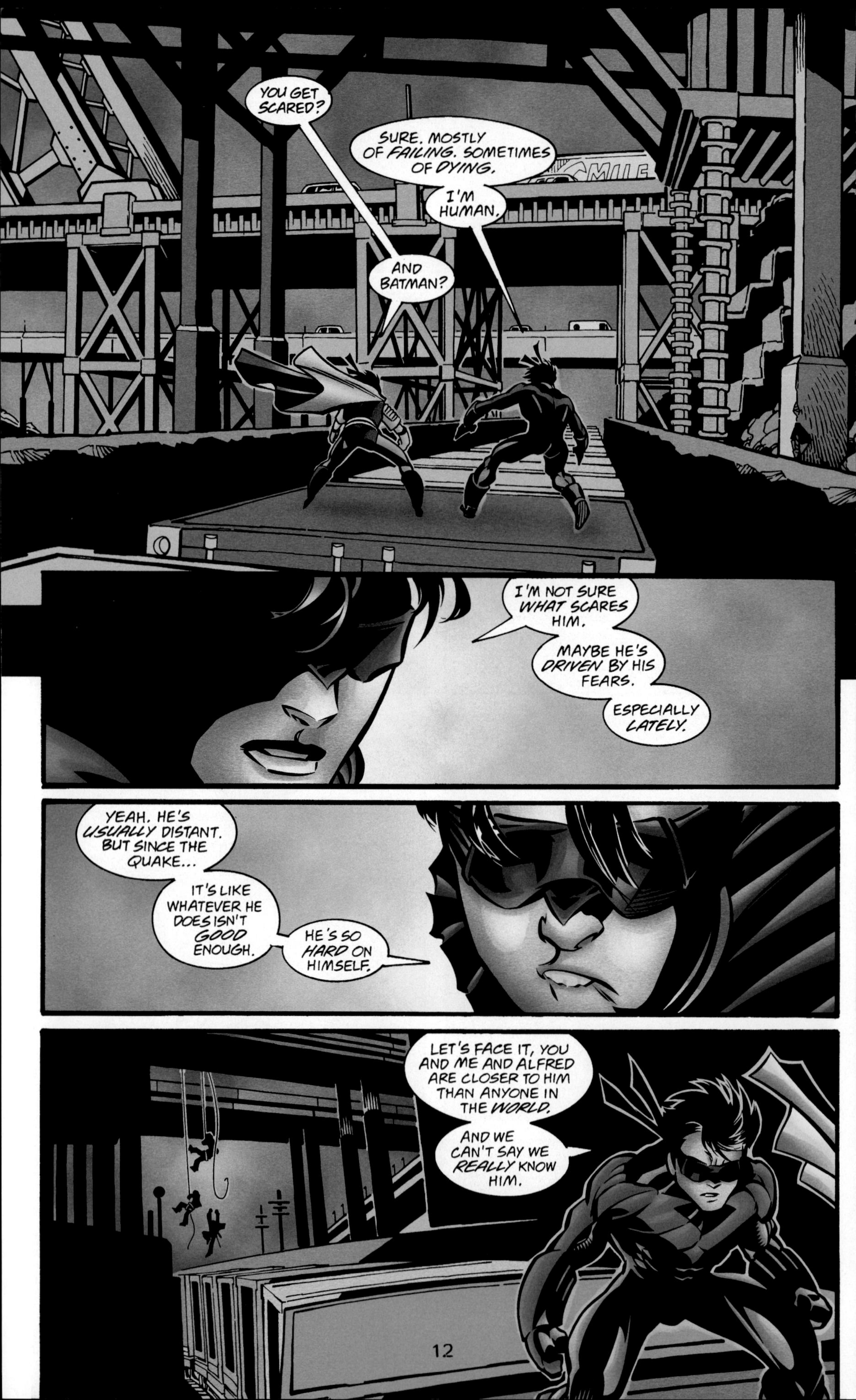
YOU GET SCARED?
SURE. MOSTLY OF FAILING. SOMETIMES OF DYING.
I'M HUMAN.
AND BATMAN?
MILE
I'M NOT SURE WHAT SCARES HIM.
MAYBE HE'S DRIVEN BY HIS FEARS.
ESPECIALLY LATELY.
YEAH. HE'S USUALLY DISTANT. BUT SINCE THE QUAKE...
IT'S LIKE WHATEVER HE DOES ISN'T GOOD ENOUGH.
HE'S SO HARD ON HIMSELF.
LET'S FACE IT, YOU AND ME AND ALFRED ARE CLOSER TO HIM THAN ANYONE IN THE WORLD.
AND WE CAN'T SAY WE REALLY KNOW HIM.

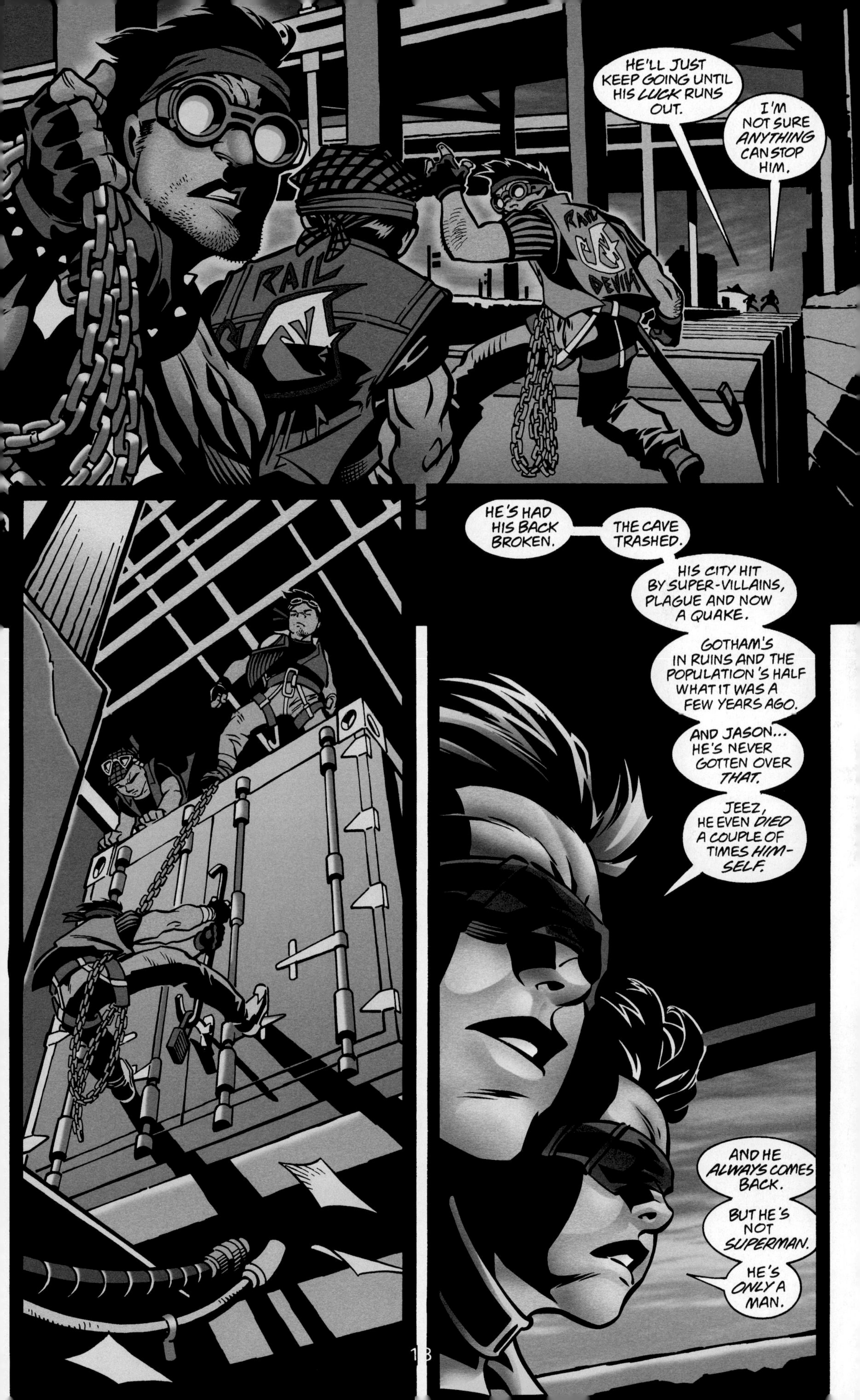
HE'LL JUST KEEP GOING UNTIL HIS LUCK RUNS OUT.
I'M NOT SURE ANYTHING CAN STOP HIM.
RAIL DEVILS
HE'S HAD HIS BACK BROKEN.
THE CAVE TRASHED.
HIS CITY HIT BY SUPER-VILLAINS, PLAGUE AND NOW A QUAKE.
GOTHAM'S IN RUINS AND THE POPULATION'S HALF WHAT IT WAS A FEW YEARS AGO.
AND JASON... HE'S NEVER GOTTEN OVER THAT.
JEEZ, HE EVEN DIED A COUPLE OF TIMES HIMSELF.
AND HE ALWAYS COMES BACK.
BUT HE'S NOT SUPERMAN.
HE'S ONLY A MAN.

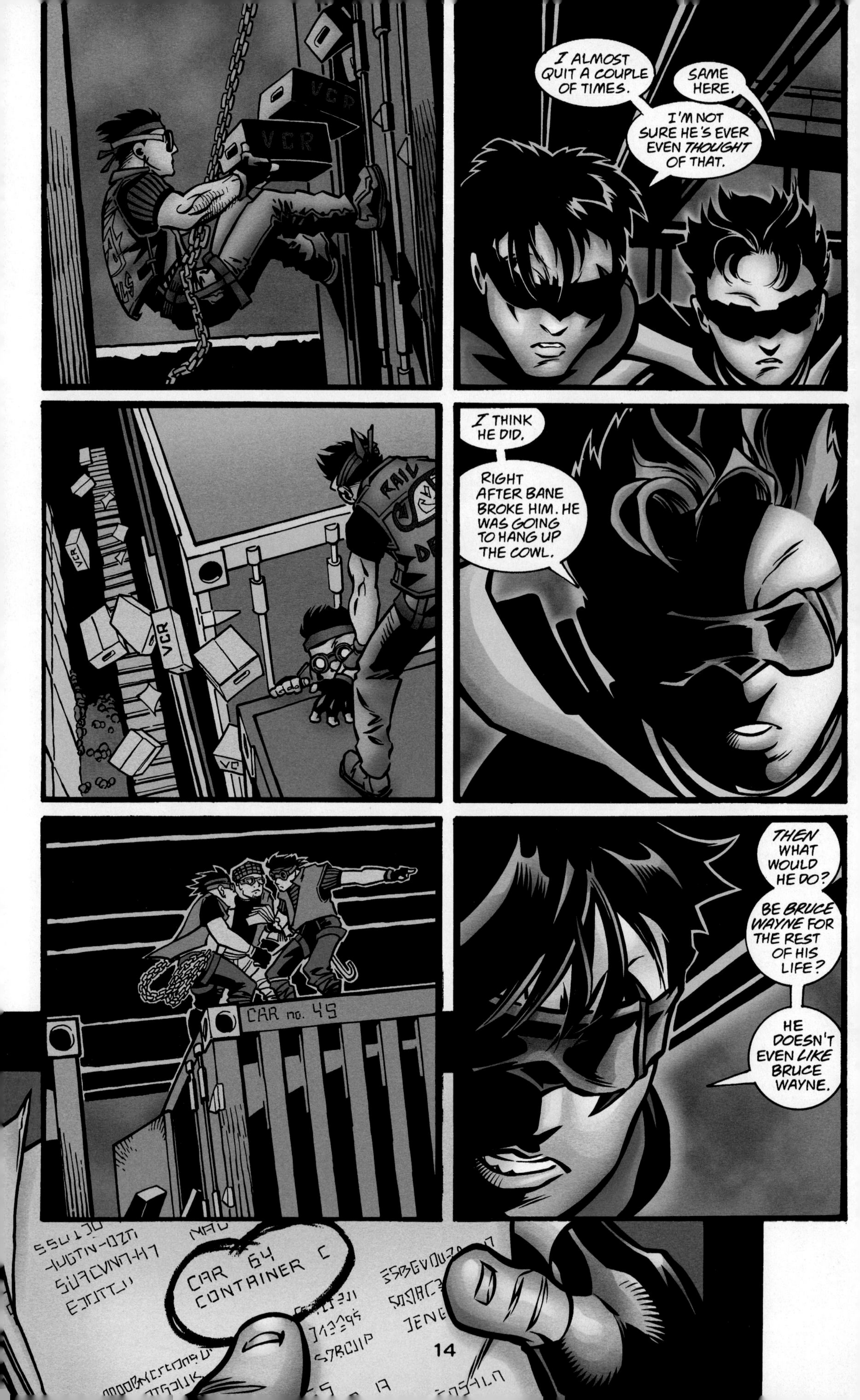
VCR
VCR
I ALMOST QUIT A COUPLE OF TIMES.
SAME HERE.
I'M NOT SURE HE'S EVER EVEN *THOUGHT* OF THAT.
RAIL
VCR
VCR
I THINK HE DID.
RIGHT AFTER BANE BROKE HIM. HE WAS GOING TO HANG UP THE COWL.
CAR no. 45
THEN WHAT WOULD HE DO?
BE *BRUCE WAYNE* FOR THE REST OF HIS LIFE?
HE DOESN'T EVEN *LIKE* BRUCE WAYNE.
CAR 64 CONTAINER C

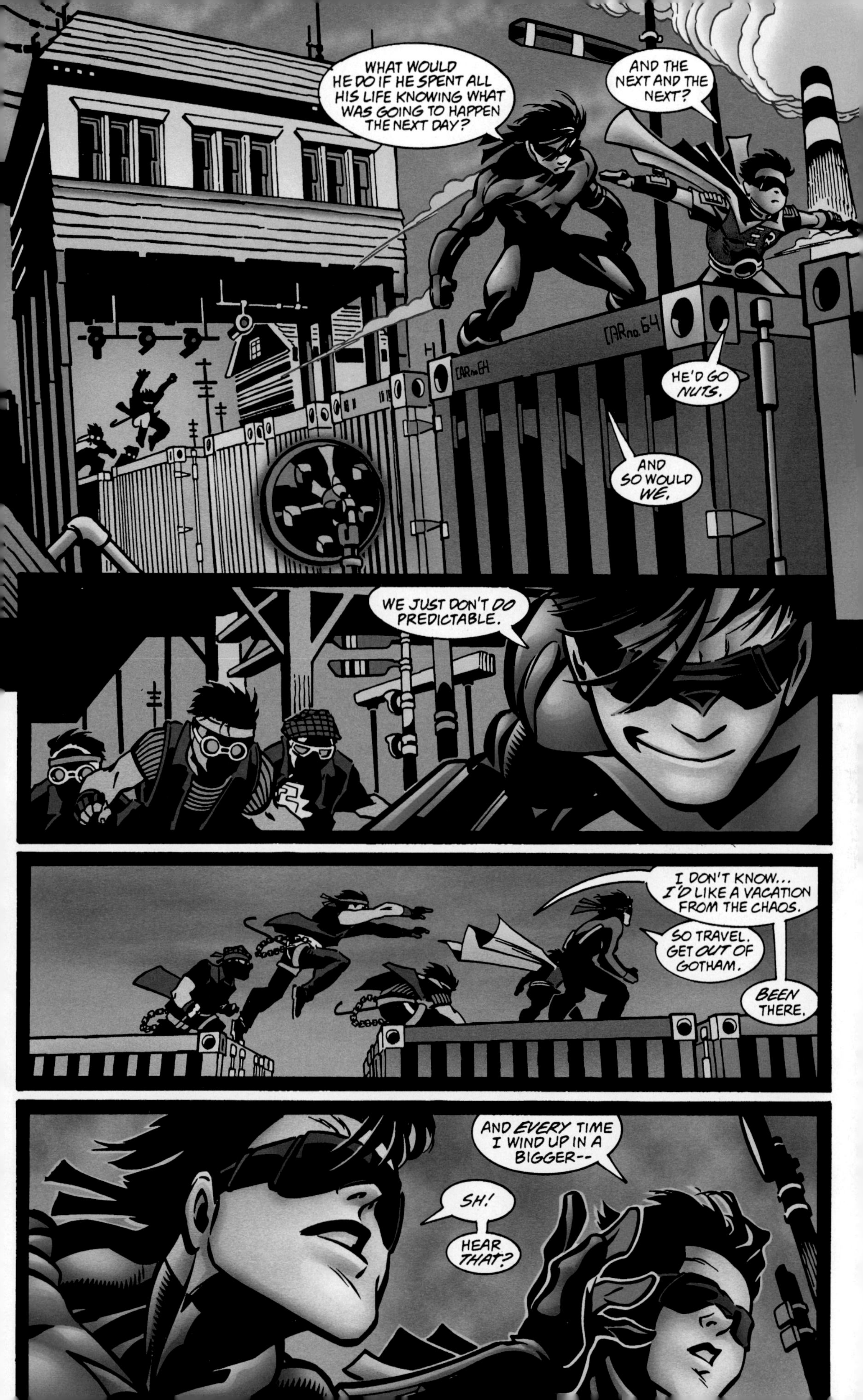
WHAT WOULD HE DO IF HE SPENT ALL HIS LIFE KNOWING WHAT WAS GOING TO HAPPEN THE NEXT DAY?
AND THE NEXT AND THE NEXT?
HE'D GO NUTS.
AND SO WOULD WE.
CAR no. 64
CAR no. 64
WE JUST DON'T DO PREDICTABLE.
I DON'T KNOW... I'D LIKE A VACATION FROM THE CHAOS.
SO TRAVEL. GET OUT OF GOTHAM.
BEEN THERE.
AND EVERY TIME I WIND UP IN A BIGGER--
SH!
HEAR THAT?

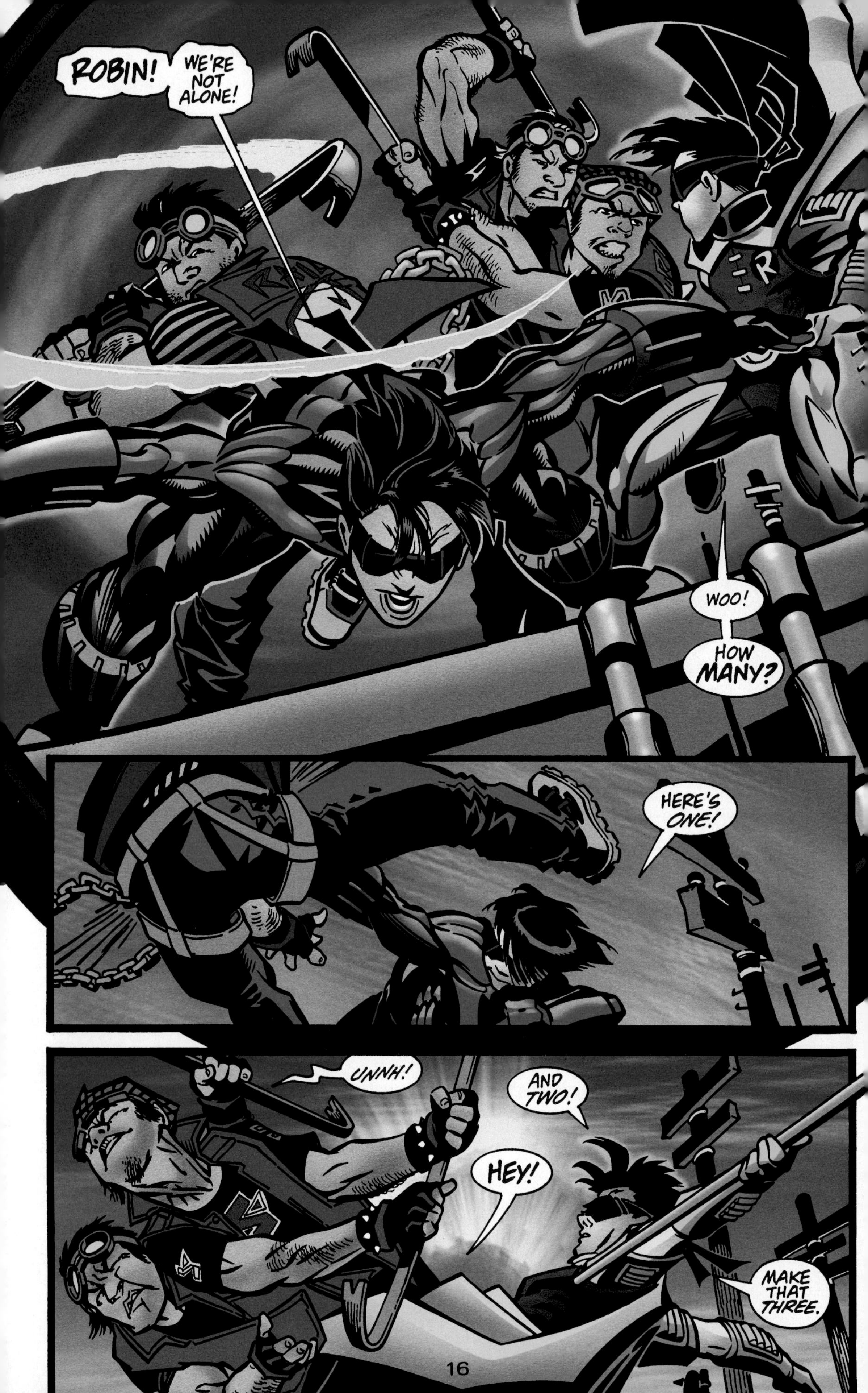
ROBIN!
WE'RE NOT ALONE!
WOO!
HOW MANY?
HERE'S ONE!
UNNH!
AND TWO!
HEY!
MAKE THAT THREE.

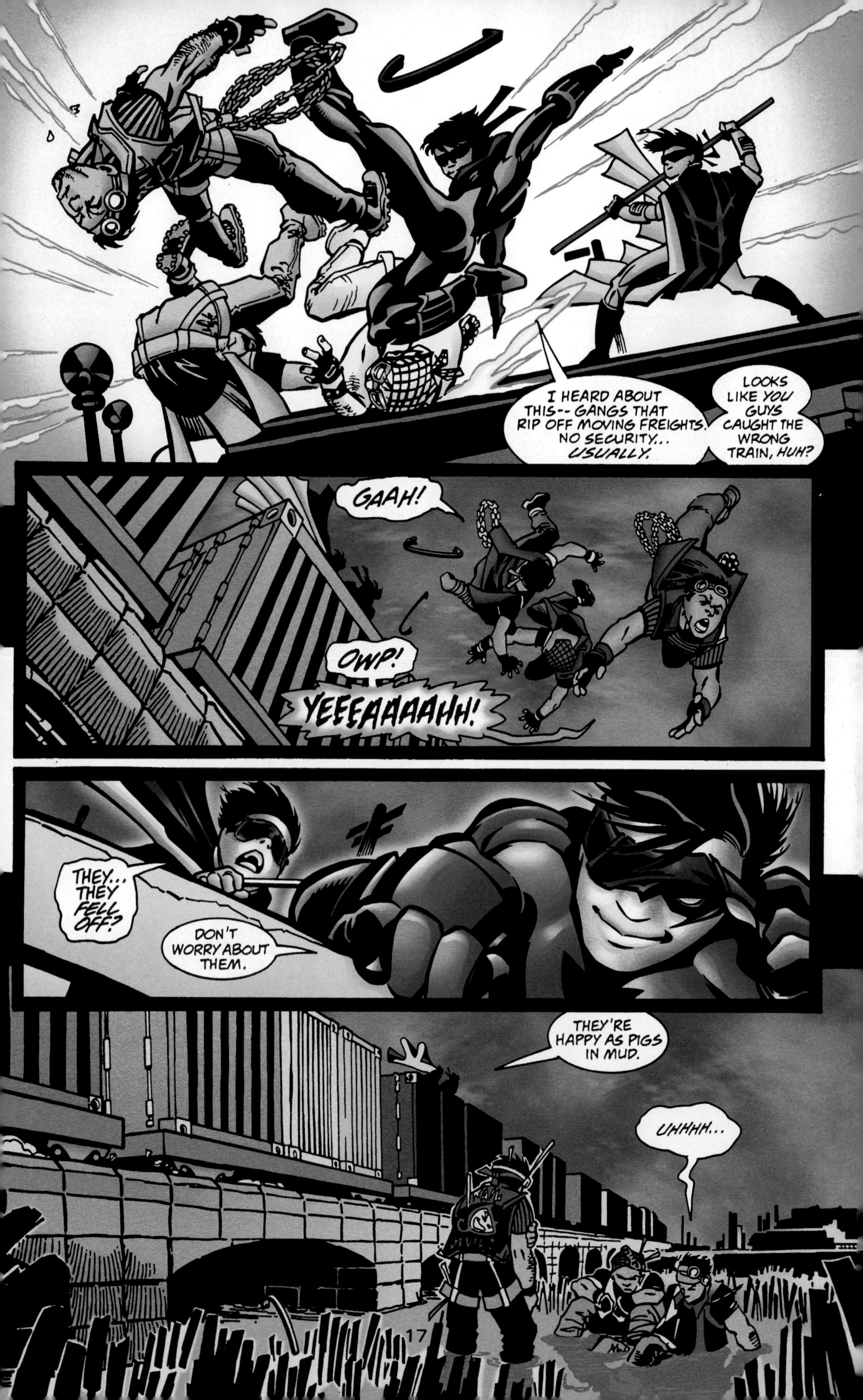
I HEARD ABOUT THIS-- GANGS THAT RIP OFF MOVING FREIGHTS. NO SECURITY... USUALLY.
LOOKS LIKE YOU GUYS CAUGHT THE WRONG TRAIN, HUH?
GAAH!
OWP!
YEEEAAAAAHH!
THEY... THEY FELL OFF?
DON'T WORRY ABOUT THEM.
THEY'RE HAPPY AS PIGS IN MUD.
UHHHH...

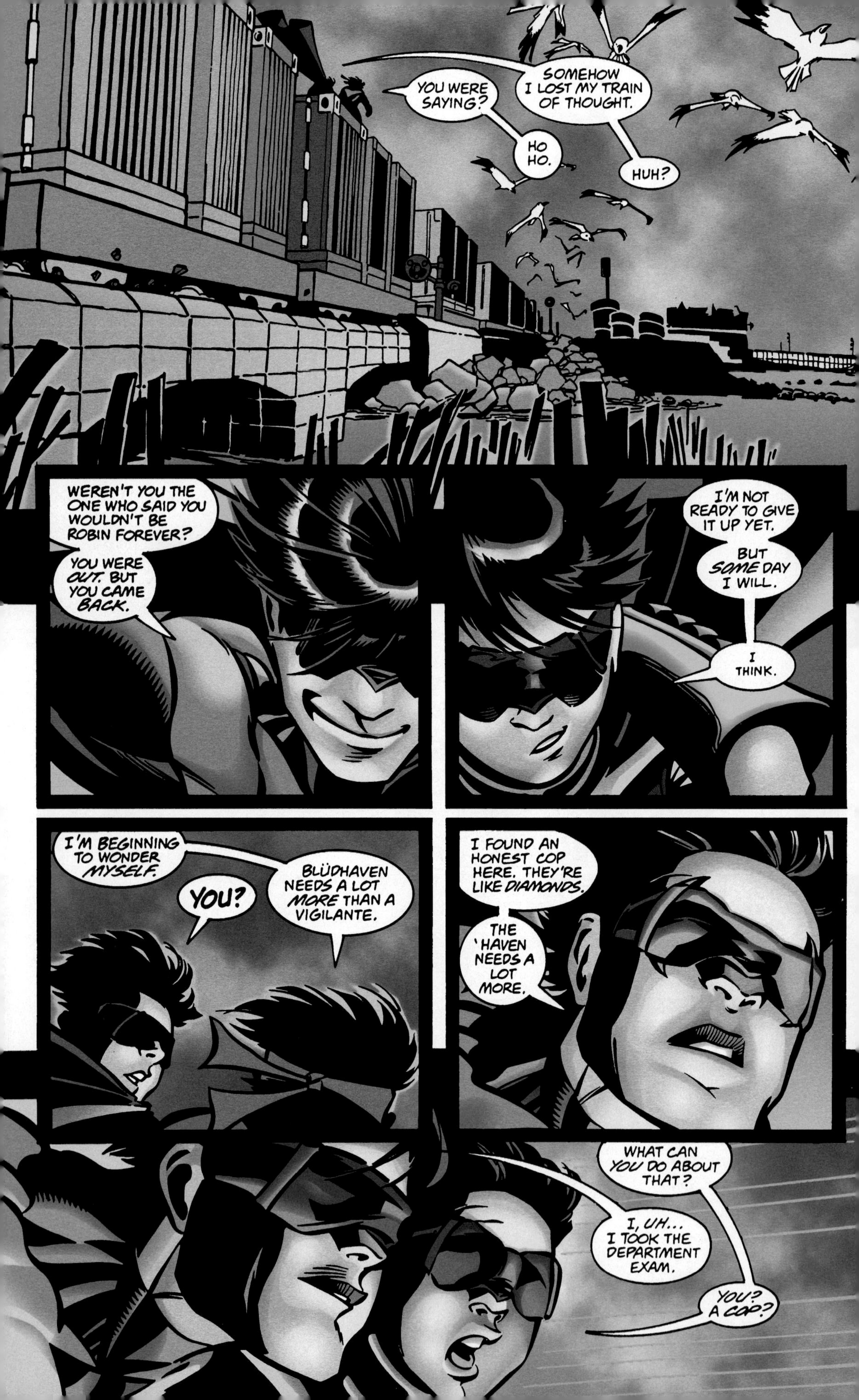
SOMEHOW I LOST MY TRAIN OF THOUGHT.
YOU WERE SAYING?
HO HO.
HUH?
WEREN'T YOU THE ONE WHO SAID YOU WOULDN'T BE ROBIN FOREVER?
YOU WERE OUT. BUT YOU CAME BACK.
I'M NOT READY TO GIVE IT UP YET.
BUT SOME DAY I WILL.
I THINK.
I'M BEGINNING TO WONDER MYSELF.
YOU?
BLÜDHAVEN NEEDS A LOT MORE THAN A VIGILANTE.
I FOUND AN HONEST COP HERE. THEY'RE LIKE DIAMONDS.
THE 'HAVEN NEEDS A LOT MORE.
WHAT CAN YOU DO ABOUT THAT?
I, UH... I TOOK THE DEPARTMENT EXAM.
YOU? A COP?

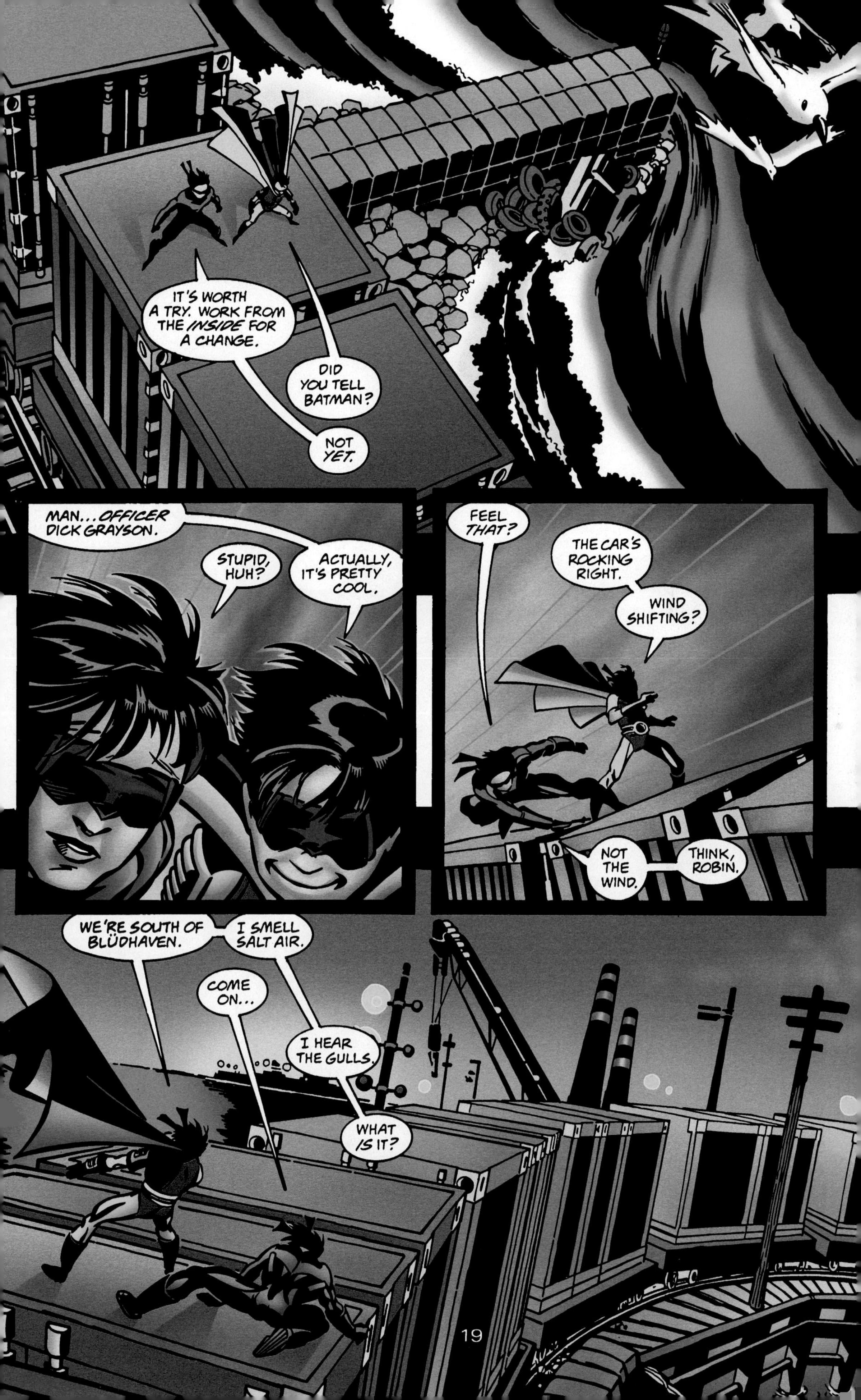
IT'S WORTH A TRY. WORK FROM THE *INSIDE* FOR A CHANGE.
DID YOU TELL BATMAN?
NOT *YET.*
MAN... *OFFICER* DICK GRAYSON.
STUPID, HUH?
ACTUALLY, IT'S PRETTY COOL.
FEEL *THAT?*
THE CAR'S ROCKING RIGHT.
WIND SHIFTING?
NOT THE WIND.
THINK, ROBIN.
WE'RE SOUTH OF BLÜDHAVEN.
I SMELL SALT AIR.
COME ON...
I HEAR THE GULLS.
WHAT *IS* IT?

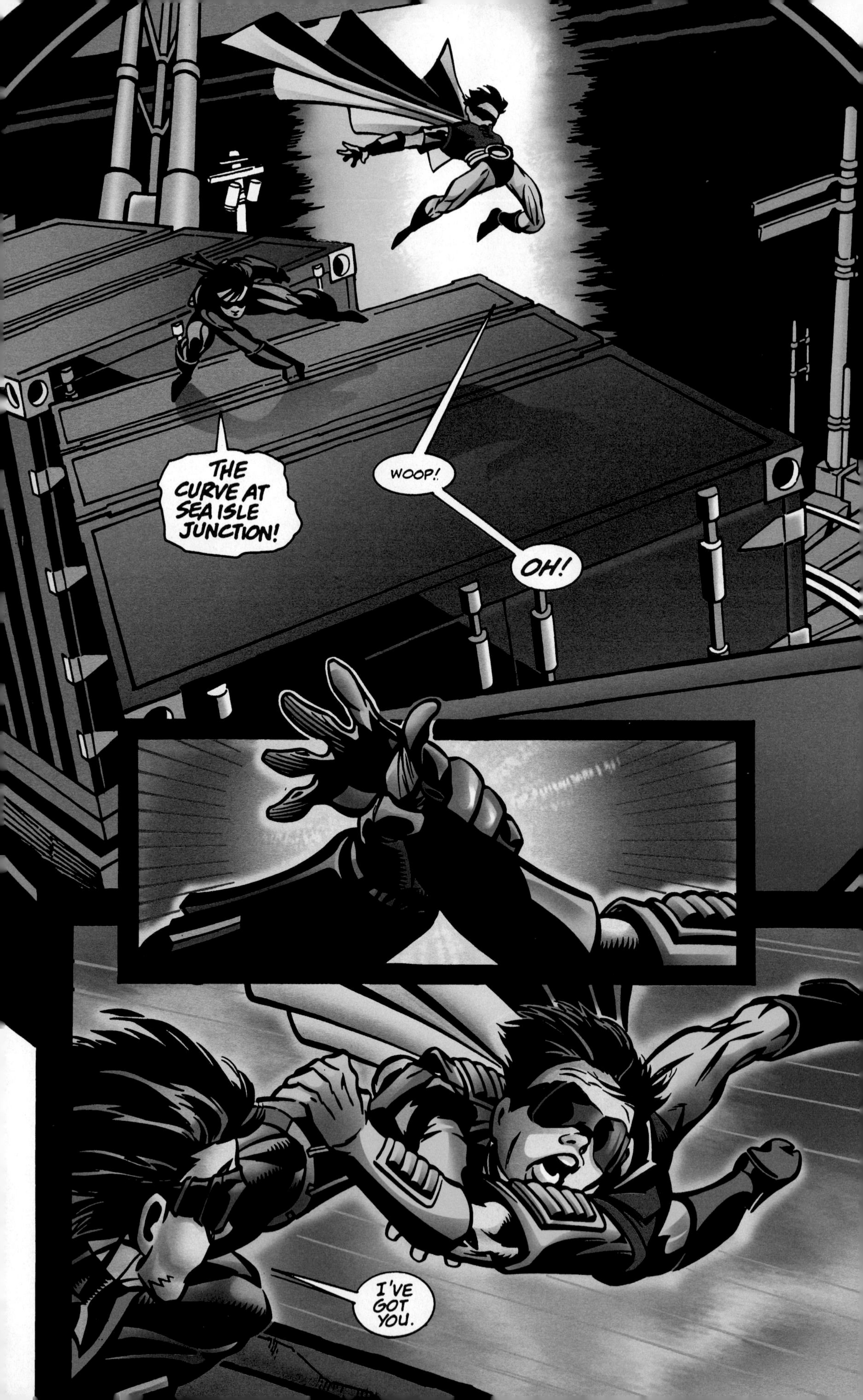
THE CURVE AT SEA ISLE JUNCTION!
WOOP!
OH!
I'VE GOT YOU.

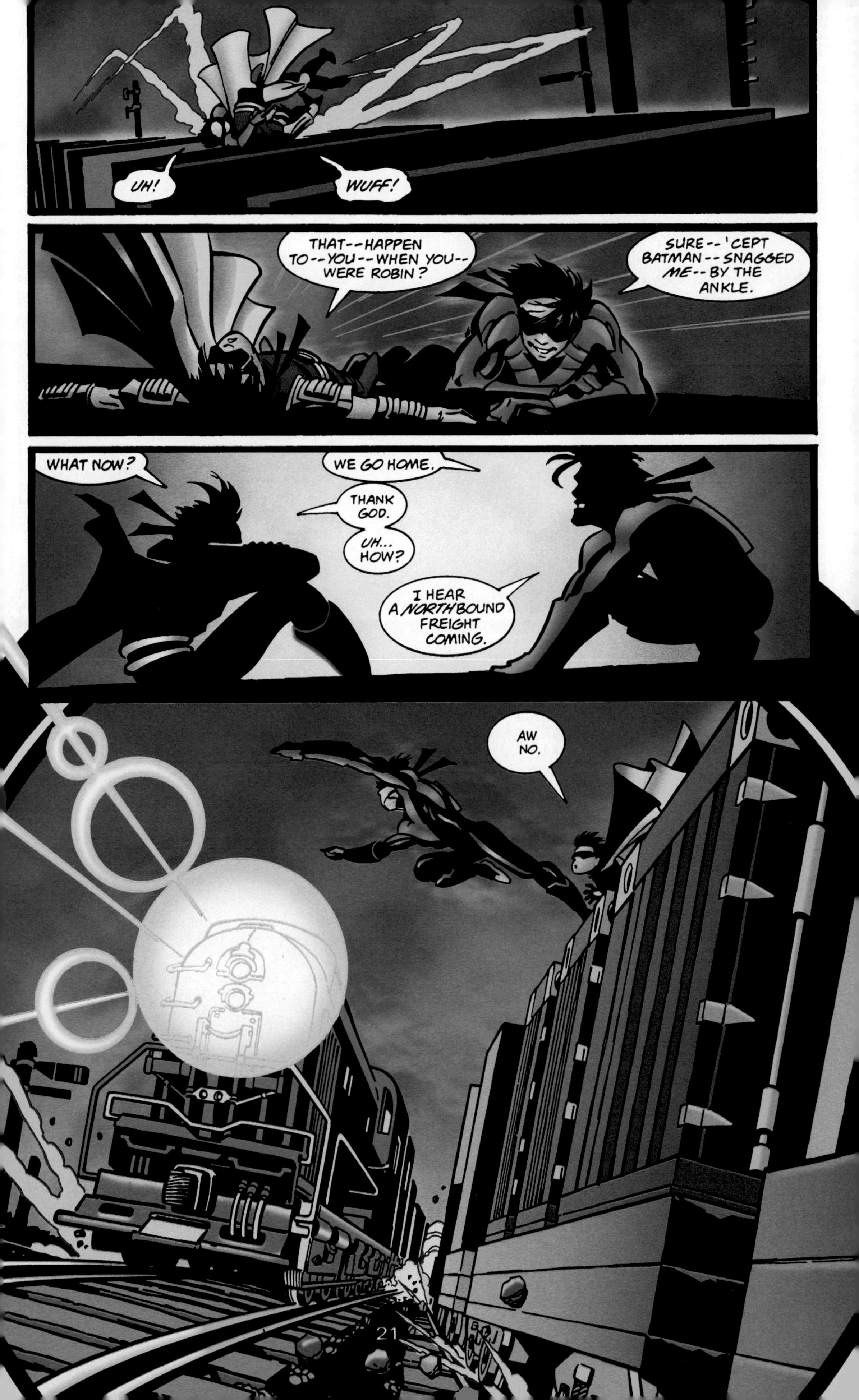
UH!
WUFF!
THAT--HAPPEN TO--YOU--WHEN YOU--WERE ROBIN?
SURE--'CEPT BATMAN--SNAGGED ME--BY THE ANKLE.
WHAT NOW?
WE GO HOME.
THANK GOD.
UH... HOW?
I HEAR A NORTHBOUND FREIGHT COMING.
AW NO.

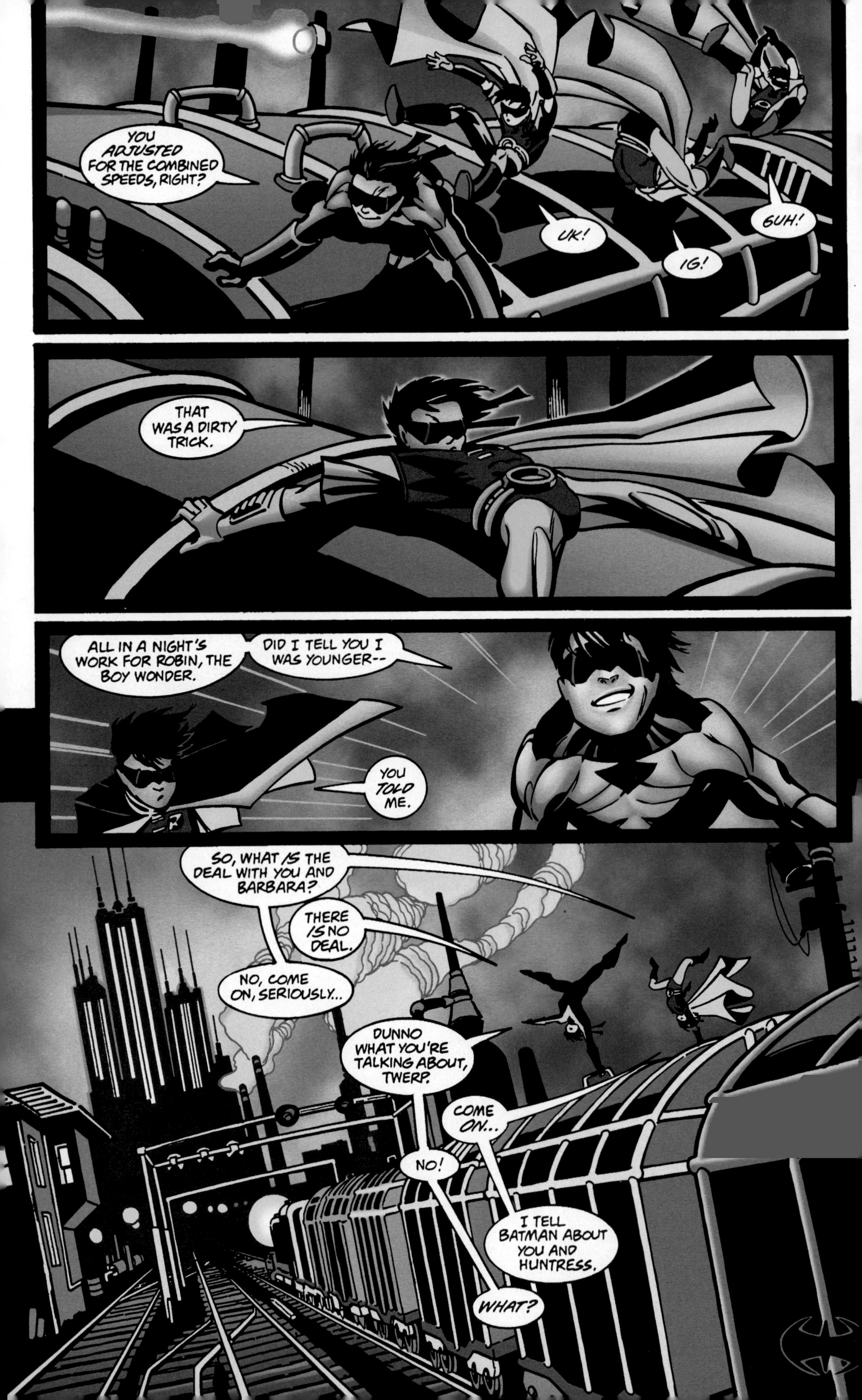
YOU ADJUSTED FOR THE COMBINED SPEEDS, RIGHT?
UK!
IG!
GUH!
THAT WAS A DIRTY TRICK.
ALL IN A NIGHT'S WORK FOR ROBIN, THE BOY WONDER.
DID I TELL YOU I WAS YOUNGER--
YOU TOLD ME.
SO, WHAT IS THE DEAL WITH YOU AND BARBARA?
THERE IS NO DEAL.
NO, COME ON, SERIOUSLY...
DUNNO WHAT YOU'RE TALKING ABOUT, TWERP.
COME ON...
NO!
I TELL BATMAN ABOUT YOU AND HUNTRESS.
WHAT?

sketchbook

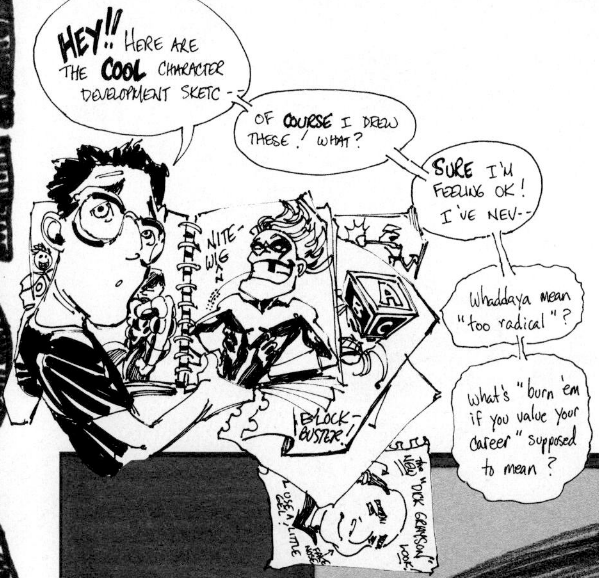
HEY!! HERE ARE THE COOL CHARACTER DEVELOPMENT SKETC--
OF COURSE I DREW THESE! WHAT?
SURE I'M FEELING OK! I'VE NEV--
Whaddaya mean "too radical"?
what's "burn 'em if you value your career" supposed to mean?
NITE-WIG
BLOCK-BUSTER!
the NEW "DICK GRAYSON" look!
USE A LITTLE GEL!
FAKE NOSE

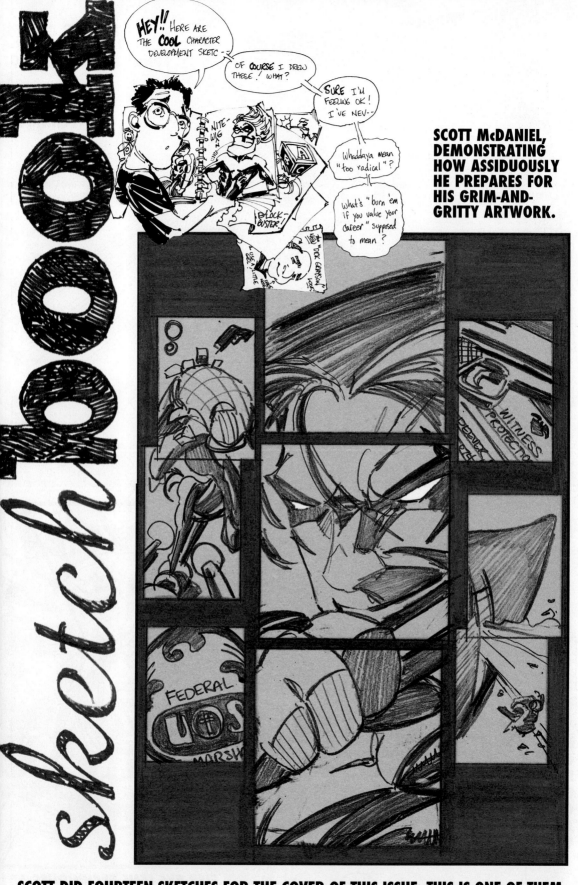

SCOTT McDANIEL, DEMONSTRATING HOW ASSIDUOUSLY HE PREPARES FOR HIS GRIM-AND-GRITTY ARTWORK.

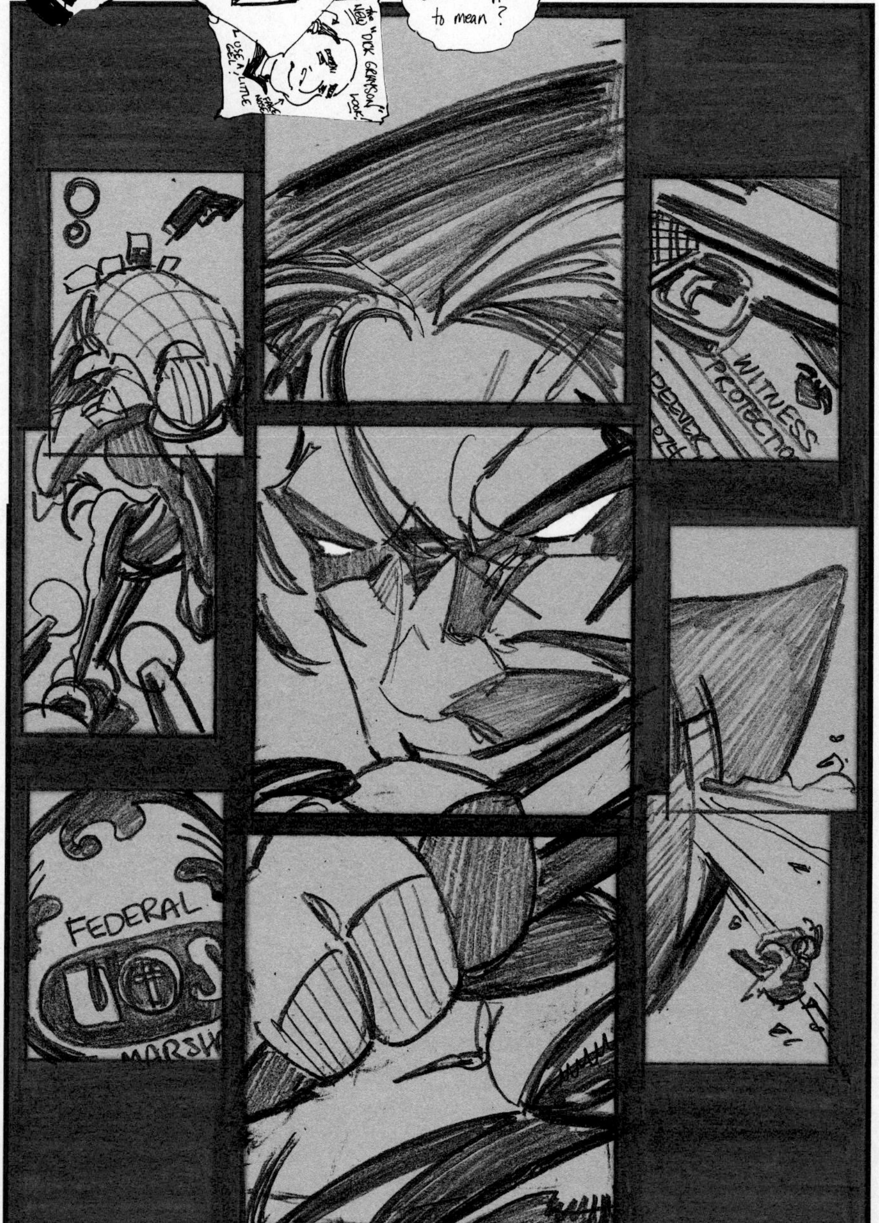
WITNESS
FEDERAL

SCOTT DID FOURTEEN SKETCHES FOR THE COVER OF THIS ISSUE: THIS IS ONE OF THEM. SINCE IT'S WAY TOO COOL TO JUST FORGET, AND WE BELIEVE RECYCLING IS GOOD FOR THE PLANET, DON'T BE SURPRISED IF A VARIATION TURNS UP ON THE MONTHLY SOMETIME IN THE FUTURE.

HOW TO DRAW A BUILDING FROM A FUNKY PERSPECTIVE 101.

NEXT SEMESTER: *FISH-EYE LENS TECHNIQUES*.

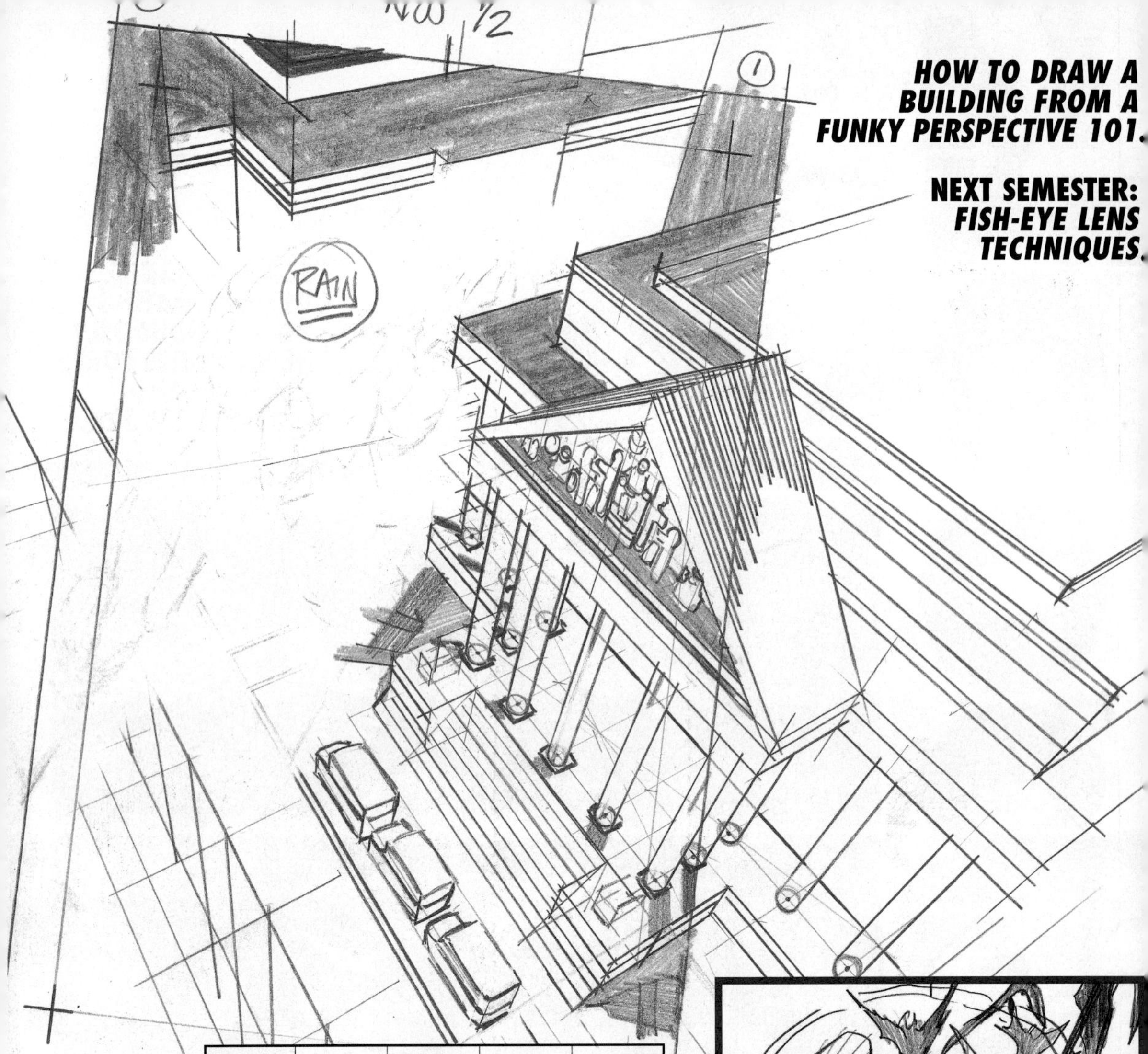
RAIN

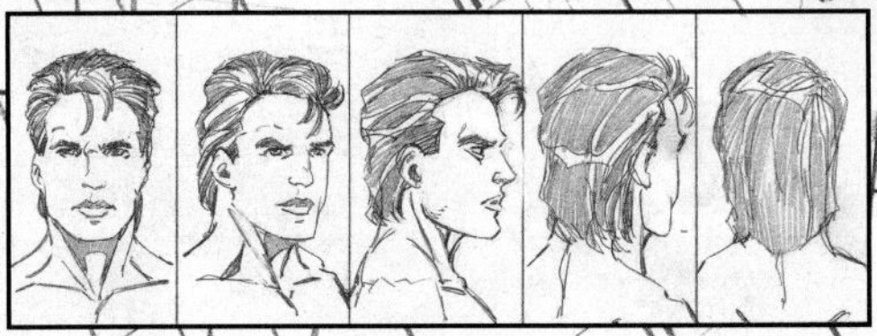

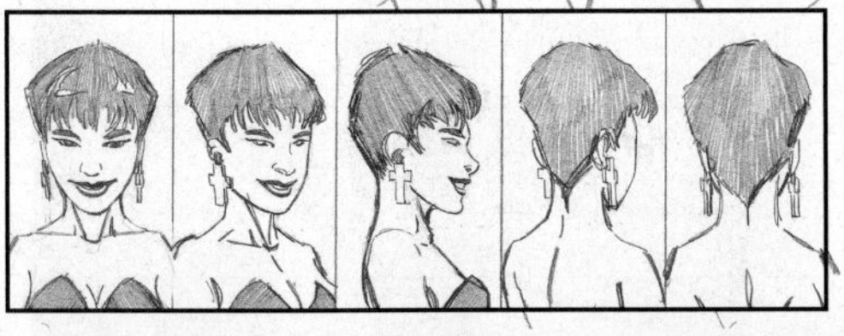

IN ORDER TO ENSURE HE CAN DRAW HIS CHARACTERS FROM ANY ANGLE, SCOTT PREPARES METICULOUS "TURN-AROUNDS" OF EACH BLÜDHAVEN DENIZEN. HE THEN CUTS THEM OUT, STAPLES THEM TOGETHER, AND CREATES A "FLIP BOOK." THIS MAKES HIM GIGGLE.

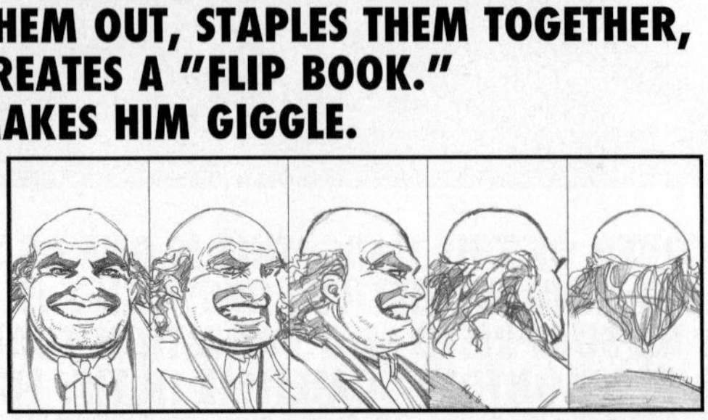

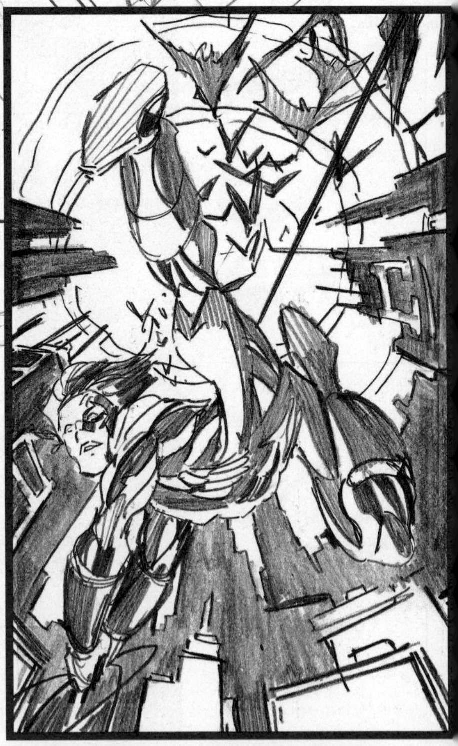

FISH-EYE LENS TECHNIQUES 101. **SCOTT MADE CHUCK DIXON HOLD THIS POSE FOR ALMOST TW HOURS, JUST TO MAKE SURE IT WAS PERFECT.**

"Stellar. A solid yarn that roots itself in Grayson's past, with gorgeous artwork by artist Eddy Barrows."—IGN

"Dynamic."—The New York Times

"A new generation is going to fall in love with Nightwing."
—MTV Geek

START AT THE BEGINNING!

NIGHTWING
VOLUME 1: TRAPS AND TRAPEZES

NIGHTWING VOL. 2:
NIGHT OF THE OWLS

NIGHTWING VOL. 3:
DEATH OF THE FAMILY

BATMAN:
NIGHT OF THE OWLS

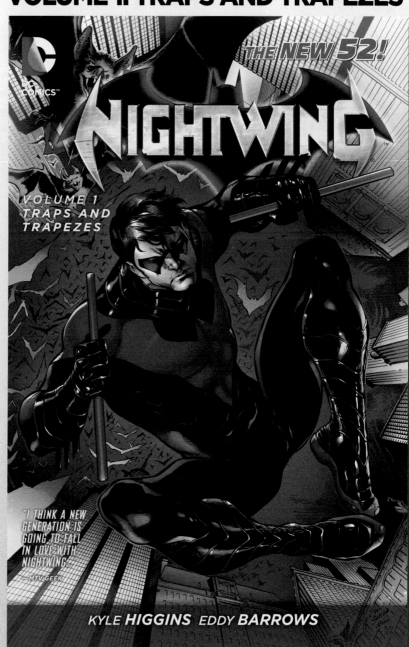

KYLE **HIGGINS** EDDY **BARROWS**

"Drips with energy."—IGN

"Grade A."—USA TODAY

START AT THE BEGINNING!

TEEN TITANS
VOLUME 1: IT'S OUR RIGHT TO FIGHT

TEEN TITANS
VOL. 2: THE CULLING

TEEN TITANS VOL. 3:
DEATH OF THE FAMILY

THE CULLING: RISE OF
THE RAVAGERS

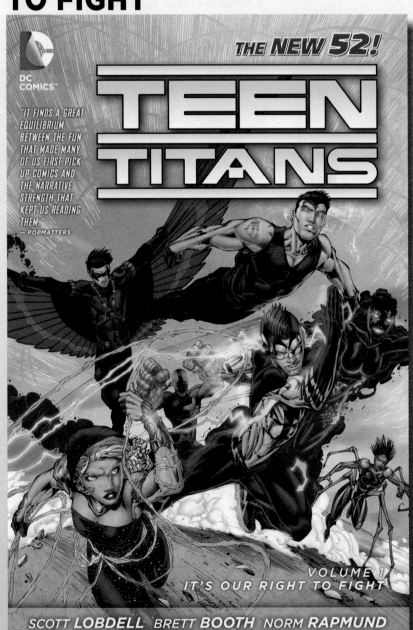

THE NEW 52!

"IT FINDS A GREAT
EQUILIBRIUM
BETWEEN THE FUN
THAT MADE MANY
OF US FIRST PICK
UP COMICS AND
THE NARRATIVE
STRENGTH THAT
KEPT US READING
THEM."
— POPMATTERS

DC COMICS™

TEEN TITANS

VOLUME 1
IT'S OUR RIGHT TO FIGHT

SCOTT **LOBDELL** BRETT **BOOTH** NORM **RAPMUND**